Data Structures
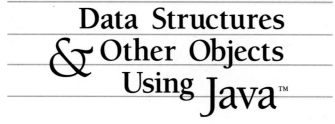
& Other Objects
Using Java™

Data Structures
& Other Objects
Using Java™

MICHAEL MAIN

University of Colorado at Boulder

Addison
Wesley
Longman

Addison-Wesley is an imprint
of Addison Wesley Longman, Inc.

Reading, Massachusetts   Harlow, England   Menlo Park, California
Berkeley, California   Don Mills, Ontario   Sydney   Bonn   Amsterdam
Tokyo   Mexico City

Acquisitions Editor: Susan Hartman
Assistant Editor: Julie Dunn
Production Editor: Patricia A. O. Unubun
Cover Design: Alwyn R. Velásquez

Access the latest supplements and source code for *Data Structures and Other Objects Using Java*™ at: http://www.cs.colorado.edu./~main/dsjava.html

The cover artwork *Web of Worlds* by Michael Main, copyright ©1999, was produced with the Persistence of Vision Ray Tracer (POV-Ray), and further edited with Fauve Matisse SE. The image is a single world set inside a triangle of three mirrors. The POV source code for the image is available at: http://www.cs.colorado.edu/~main/images/wow.pov

Library of Congress Cataloging-in-Publication Data
Main. M. (Michael), 1956-
    Data structures & other objects using java/Michael Main
      Includes index. p.   cm.
    ISBN 0-201-35744-5
    1. Java (Computer program language)   2. Data structures (Computer science)
QA76.73.J38D35   1999
005.13'3--dc21   98-36207
                                                    CIP

This book was typeset with FrameMaker. The fonts used were Arial, Helvetica, Lucida Handwriting, Lucida Sans-Typewriter, Script, and Times. It was printed on New Era Matte.

The programs and the applications presented in this book have been included for their instructional value. They have been tested with care but are not guaranteed for any particular purpose. Neither the publisher or the author offers any warranties or representations, nor do they accept any liabilities with respect to the programs or applications.

5 6 7 8 9 10–MA–0201

For Janet

Java provides programmers with an immediately attractive forum. With Java and the World Wide Web, a programmer's work can have quick global distribution with appealing graphics and a marvelous capability for feedback, modification, software reuse, and growth. Certainly Java's other qualities have also contributed to its rapid adoption—the ability to implement clean object-oriented designs, the familiarity of Java's syntactic constructs, the good collection of ready-to-use features in the Java Class Libraries. But its the winsome ways of the World Wide Web that have pulled Java to the front, for both experienced programmers and the newcomer entering a first-year computer science course.

With that said, it's satisfying to see that the core of the first-year courses—CS1 and CS2 in the ACM curricula—remain solid even as courses start using Java. The CS1 curriculum continues to emphasize the specification/design of algorithms, the use of basic control structures in an implementation, and fundamental testing/debugging techniques. The proven methods of representing and using data structures remain vital to beginning programmers in a CS2 course, even as the curriculum is shifting to accommodate an object-oriented approach and graphical programming via Java's applets.

This book is written for just such an evolving CS2 course, with the students' programming carried out in Java. The text's emphasis is on the specification, design, implementation, and use of the basic data types that are normally covered in a second-semester object-oriented course. There is wide coverage of important programming techniques in recursion, searching techniques, and sorting. The text also provides coverage of big-O time analysis of algorithms, writing an interactive applet to test an implementation of a data structure, and using Javadoc to specify precondition–postcondition contracts .

The text assumes that the student has already had an introductory computer science and programming class, but we do include coverage of those topics (such as the Java Object type and a precise description of parameter passing) that are not always covered completely in a first course. The running programs of the text are mostly Java applications, though there is also a self-contained introduction to how to write Java applets for specific purposes tied into the data structures material. In fact, I encourage the use of applets at some point in the CS1/CS2 curriculum. In many cases, its these graphical applications that have grabbed the student's attention in the first place, so let them run with it. I'll discuss some particular points where you might introduce applets at the end of this preface, but first I want to provide an overview of the text's other features.

The Five Steps for Each Data Type

The book's core consists of the well-known data types: sets, bags (or multisets), sequential lists, stacks, queues, tables, and graphs. There are also additional supplemental data types such as a priority queue. Some of the types are approached in multiple ways, such as the bag class that is first implemented by storing the elements in an array and later reimplemented using a binary search tree. Each of the data types is introduced following a pattern of five steps:

Step 1: Understand the Data Type Abstractly. At this level, a student gains an understanding of the data type and its operations at the level of concepts and pictures. For example, a student can visualize a stack and its operations of pushing and popping elements. Simple applications are understood and can be carried out by hand, such as using a stack to reverse the order of letters in a word.

Step 2: Write a Specification of the Data Type as a Java Class. In this step, the student sees and learns how to write a specification for a Java class that can implement the data type. The specification, written using the Javadoc tool, includes headings for the constructors, public methods, and sometimes other public features (such as restrictions tied to memory limitations). The heading of each method is presented along with a precondition–postcondition contract that completely specifies the behavior of the method. At this level, it's important for the students to realize that the specification is not tied to any particular choice of implementation techniques. In fact, this same specification may be used several times for several different implementations of the same data type.

Step 3: Use the Data Type. With the specification in place, students can write small applications or applets to show the data type in use. These applications are based solely on the data type's specification, as we still have not tied down the implementation.

Step 4: Select Appropriate Data Structures, and Proceed to Design and Implement the Data Type. With a good abstract understanding of the data type, we can select an appropriate data structure, such as an array, a linked list of nodes, or a binary tree of nodes. For many of our data types, a first design and implementation will select a simple approach, such as an array. Later, we will redesign and reimplement the same data type with a more complicated underlying structure.

Since we are using Java classes, an implementation of a data type will have the selected data structures (arrays, references to other objects, etc.) as private instance variables of the class. In my own teaching, I stress the necessity for a clear understanding of the rules that relate the private instance variables to the abstract notion of the data type. I require each student to write these rules in clear English sentences that is called the invariant of the abstract data type. Once the invariant is written, students can proceed to implementing various methods. The invariant helps in writing correct methods because of two facts: (a) Each method (except the constructors) knows that the invariant is true when the method begins its work; and (b) Each method is responsible for ensuring that the invariant is again true when the method finishes.

Step 5: Analyze the Implementation.   Each implementation can be analyzed for correctness, flexibility, and time analysis of the operations (using big-O notation). Students have a particularly strong opportunity for these analyses when the same data type has been implemented in several different ways.

Where Will the Students Be at the End of the Course?

At the end of our course, students understand the data types inside out. They know how to use the data types, they know how to implement them several ways, and they know the practical effects of the different implementation choices. The students can reason about efficiency with a big-O analysis and argue for the correctness of their implementations by referring to the invariant of the ADT.

One of the important lasting effects of the course is the specification, design, and implementation experience. The improved ability to reason about programs is also important. But perhaps most important of all is the exposure to classes that are easily used in many situations. The students no longer have to write everything from scratch. We tell our students that someday they will be thinking about a problem, and they will suddenly realize that a large chunk of the work can be done with a bag, or a stack, or a queue, or some such. And this large chunk of work is work that they won't have to do. Instead they will pull out the bag or stack or queue or some such that they wrote this semester—using it with no modifications. Or, more likely, they will use the familiar data type from a library of standard data types, such as the proposed Java Class Libraries. In fact, the behavior of some data types in this text is a cut-down version of the JCL, so when a student takes the step to the real JCL, they will be on familiar ground— from the standpoint of how to use the class and also a knowledge of the consid-

the data types in this book are cut-down versions of the Java Class Libraries erations that went into building the class. At that point of realization, knowing that a certain data type is the exact solution they need, the student graduates to being a real programmer.

Other Foundational Topics

Throughout the course, we also lay a foundation for other aspects of "real programming," with coverage of the following topics beyond the basic data structures material:

Object-Oriented Programming. The foundations of object-oriented programming are laid by giving students a strong understanding of Java classes. The important aspects of classes are covered early: the notion of a method, the separation into private and public members, the purpose of constructors, and a small exposure to cloning and testing for equality. This is primarily in Chapter 2, some of which can be skipped by students with a good exposure to Java classes in the CS1 course.

Further aspects of classes are introduced when the classes first use dynamic arrays (Chapter 3). At this point, the need for a more sophisticated clone method is explained. Teaching this OOP aspect with the first use of dynamic memory has the effect of giving the students a concrete picture of how an instance variable is used as a reference to a dynamic object such as an array.

Conceptually, the largest innovation of OOP is the software reuse that occurs via inheritance. And there are certainly opportunities for introducing inheritance right from the start of a data structures course (such as implementing a set class as a descendant of a bag class). However, an early introduction may also result in juggling too many new concepts at once, resulting in a weaker understanding of the fundamental data structures. Therefore, in my own course I introduce inheritance at the end, as a vision of things to come. But, the introduction to inheritance (Sections 13.1 and 13.2) could be covered as soon as classes are understood. With this in mind, some instructors may wish to cover Chapter 13 earlier, just before stacks and queues, so that stacks and queues can be derived from another class.

Another alternative is to identify students who already know the basics of classes. These students can carry out an inheritance project (such as the ecosystem of Section 13.2), while the rest of the students first learn about classes.

Java Objects. The Java Object type lies at the base of all the other Java types—or at least almost all the other types. The eight primitive types are not Java objects, and for many students the CS1 work has been primarily with the eight primitive types. Because of this, the first few data structures are collections of primitive values, such as a bag of integers or a sequence of double numbers.

Shortly after (in Chapter 5), the students are shown the Java Object type, and they realize that one implementation of a data structure (such as a bag of integers) can easily be changed to another (a bag of objects). The bag of objects is the most general type of bag, and by using the wrapper classes, even primitive values can be placed in a bag of objects. Most of the subsequent data structures are implemented with Java objects as the underlying type, though students are reminded that they could use a primitive underlying type if needed (such as the stack of double numbers used an application to evaluate arithmetic expressions).

Iterators. Iterators are an important part of Version 1.2 of the Java Class Libraries, allowing a programmer to easily step through the elements in a collection class. The Iterator interface is introduced in Chapter 5. Throughout the rest of the text, iterators are not directly used, although they provide a good opportunity for programming projects, such as using a stack to implement an iterator for a binary search tree (Chapter 9).

Recursion. First-semester courses often introduce students to recursion. But many of the first-semester examples are tail recursion, where the final act of the method is the recursive call. This may have given students a misleading impression that recursion is nothing more than a loop. Because of this, I prefer to avoid early use of tail recursion in a second-semester course. For example, list traversal and other operations on linked lists can be implemented with tail recursion, but the effect may reinforce wrong impressions about recursion (and the tail recursive list operations may need to be unlearned when the students work with real lists of thousands of items, running into potential execution stack overflow).

So, in our second-semester course, we emphasize recursive solutions that use more than tail recursion. The recursion chapter provides three examples along these lines. Two of the examples—generating random fractals and traversing a maze—are big hits with the students. The fractal example runs as a graphical applet, and although the maze example is text-based, an adventurous student can convert it to a graphical applet. These recursion examples (Chapter 8) appear just before trees (Chapter 9), since it is within recursive tree algorithms where recursion becomes vital. However, instructors who desire more emphasis on recursion can move that topic forward, even before Chapter 2.
In a course that has time for advanced tree projects (Chapter 10), we analyze the recursive tree algorithms, explaining the importance of keeping the trees balanced—both to improve worst-case performance, and to avoid potential execution stack overflow.

Searching and Sorting. Chapters 11 and 12 provide fundamental coverage of searching and sorting algorithms. The searching reviews binary search of an ordered array, which many students will have seen before. Hash tables also are introduced in the search chapter, by implementing a version of the JCL hash table and also a second hash table that uses chaining instead of open addressing. The sorting chapter reviews simple quadratic sorting methods, but the majority of the chapter focuses on faster algorithms: the recursive merge sort (with worst-case time of O(n log n)), Tony Hoare's recursive quicksort (with average-time O(n log n)), and the tree-based heap sort (with worst-case time of O(n log n)).

Advanced Projects

The text offers good opportunities for optional projects that can be undertaken by a more advanced class or by students with a stronger background in a large class. Particular advanced projects include the following:

- Interactive applet-based test programs for any of the data structures (out lined in Section 3.4)
- Implementing an Iterator for the sequence class (Chapter 5 Programming Projects)
- Writing a deep clone method for a collection class (Chapter 5 Programming Projects)
- Writing an applet version of an application program (such as the maze traversal in Section 8.1 or the ecosystem in Section 13.2)
- Using a stack to build an iterator for the binary search tree (Chapter 9 Programming Projects)
- A priority queue, implemented as an array of ordinary queues (Section 7.4), or implemented using a heap (Section 10.1)
- A set class, implemented with B-trees (Section 10.2). I have made a particular effort on this project to provide information that is sufficient for students to implement the class without need of another text. My advanced students have successfully completed this project as independent work.
- An inheritance project, such as an extension of the ecosystem of Section 13.2
- A graph class and associated graph algorithms from Chapter 14. This is another case where advanced students may do work on their own.

Java Language Versions

All the source code of the book has been tested to work correctly with Java Version 1.2. A few features, such as iterators, require Version 1.2 to work correctly, and these points are clearly marked in the source code. Information on all of the Java products from Sun Microsystems is available at:
`http://java.sun.com/products/index.html`

My latest notes on Java versions and Java-enabled browsers are available at:
`http://www.cs.colorado.edu/~main/java.html`

Flexibility of Topic Ordering

This book was written to allow instructors latitude in reordering the material to meet the specific background of students or to add early emphasis to selected topics. The dependencies among the chapters are shown on page xiv. A line joining two boxes indicates that the upper box should be covered before the lower box. Here are some suggested orderings of the material:

Typical Course. Start with Chapters 1–9, skipping parts of Chapter 2 if the students have a prior background in Java classes. Most chapters can be covered in a week, but you may want more time for Chapter 4 (linked lists), Chapter 8 (recursion), or Chapter 9 (trees). Typically, I cover the material in thirteen weeks, including time for exams and extra time for linked lists and trees. Remaining weeks can be spent on a tree project from Chapter 10, or on binary search (Section 11.1) and sorting (Chapter 12).

Heavy OOP emphasis. If students will cover sorting and searching elsewhere, then there is time for a heavier emphasis on object-oriented programming. The first three chapters are covered in detail, and then derived classes (Section 13.1) are introduced. At this point, students can do an interesting OOP project, perhaps based on the ecosystem of Section 13.2). The basic data structures (Chapters 4–7) are then covered, with the queue implemented as a derived class (Section 13.3). Finish up with recursion (Chapter 8) and trees (Chapter 9), placing special emphasis on recursive methods

Accelerated course. Assign the first three chapters as independent reading in the first week, and start with Chapter 4 (linked lists). This will leave two to three extra weeks at the end of the term, so that students may spend more time on searching, sorting, and the advanced topics (shaded on page xiv.)
We also have taught the course with further acceleration by spending no lecture time on stacks and queues (but assigning those chapters as reading).

Early Recursion / Early Sorting. One to three weeks may be spent at the start of class on recursive thinking. The first reading will then be Chapters 1 and 8, perhaps supplemented by additional recursive projects.
If the recursion is covered early, you may also proceed to cover binary search (Section 11.1) and most of the sorting algorithms (Chapter 12) before introducing collection classes.

Supplements Via Internet

The following support material is available via internet from the publishers:
- All Java source code
- An Instructor's Resource Guide, including sample assignments, exam questions, solutions, syllabi, Powerpoint lectures, and speaker's notes.
- A library of Java applets to demonstrate some data structures.

Chapter Dependencies

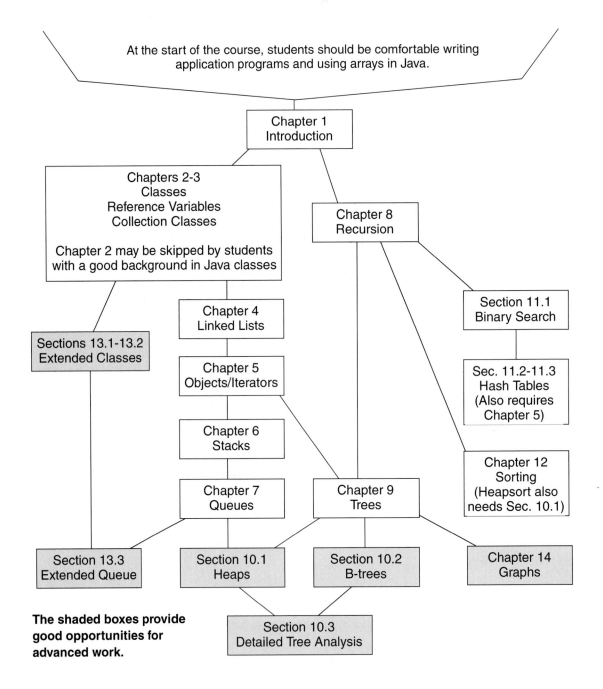

At the start of the course, students should be comfortable writing application programs and using arrays in Java.

Chapter 1
Introduction

Chapters 2-3
Classes
Reference Variables
Collection Classes

Chapter 2 may be skipped by students with a good background in Java classes

Chapter 8
Recursion

Section 11.1
Binary Search

Sections 13.1-13.2
Extended Classes

Chapter 4
Linked Lists

Chapter 5
Objects/Iterators

Sec. 11.2-11.3
Hash Tables
(Also requires
Chapter 5)

Chapter 6
Stacks

Chapter 12
Sorting
(Heapsort also
needs Sec. 10.1)

Chapter 7
Queues

Chapter 9
Trees

Section 13.3
Extended Queue

Section 10.1
Heaps

Section 10.2
B-trees

Chapter 14
Graphs

The shaded boxes provide good opportunities for advanced work.

Section 10.3
Detailed Tree Analysis

For information on obtaining the materials, please read the book's World Wide Web home page at:

`http://www.cs.colorado.edu/~main/dsjava.html`

or

`http://www.awl.com/cseng/titles/0-201-35744-5/`

Acknowledgments

This book grew from the joint work with Walter Savitch, who continues to be an ever present and enthusiastic supporter, colleague, and friend. My students from the University of Colorado at Boulder serve to provide inspiration and joy at every turn, particularly the Winter Park group of data structures mentors last fall. During this time, the book was also extensively reviewed by Arthur Crummer, Zoran Duric, Dan Grecu, Rod Howell, and Meiliu Lu. John Wegis provided an excellent technical review of all the code in the book. J.D. Baker provided continual input on the text topics plus help with the Java applets. I thank these colleagues for their excellent critique and their encouragement.

The editors and staff at Addison Wesley Longman have provided outstanding support. Susan Hartman and Julie Dunn provided daily advice, encouragement and support. Along with Susan and Julie, Pat Unubun incorporated new approaches to the production steps, resulting in a smooth process and much improved final book. I thank Alwyn Velasquez for the beautiful cover design incorporating the Web of Worlds artwork. I thank Brooke Albright and Jennifer Newburg for the friendly day-to-day interactions in the editing process and web page development.

Over the past two years, colleagues at the Computer Science Department and at Addison Wesley have provided daily support and encouragement. My thanks there go to David Benson, Ted Chen, Claire Collins, Pam Compo, Courtney Comstock, David DiLaura, Dirk Grunwald, Clayton Lewis, Michael Lightner, Jim H. Martin, Gary Nutt, Bobby Schnabel, Karl Winklmann, and Ben Zorn.

Michael Main
main@colorado.edu
Boulder, Colorado

CHAPTER
LIST

CONTENTS

Appendixes

The Phases of Software Development

Chapter the first which explains how, why, when, and
where there was ever any problem in the first place

NOEL LANGLEY
The Land of Green Ginger

This chapter illustrates the phases of software development. These phases occur in all software, including the small programs that you'll see in this first chapter. In subsequent chapters, you'll go beyond these small programs, applying the phases of software development to organized collections of data. These organized collections of data are called **data structures**, and the main topics of this book revolve around proven techniques for representing and manipulating such data structures.

Years from now you may be a software engineer writing large systems in a specialized area, perhaps computer graphics or artificial intelligence. Such futuristic applications will be exciting and stimulating, and within your work you will still see the phases of software development and fundamental data structures that you learn and practice now.

Here is a list of the phases of software development:

The Phases of Software Development

- Specification of the task
- Design of a solution
- Implementation (coding) of the solution
- Analysis of the solution
- Testing and debugging
- Maintenance and evolution of the system
- Obsolescence

---

the phases blur into each other

Do not memorize this list; throughout the book, your practice of these phases will achieve far better familiarity than mere memorization. Also, memorizing an "official list" is misleading because it suggests that there is a single sequence of discrete steps that always occur one after another. In practice, the phases blur into each other; for instance, the analysis of a solution's efficiency may occur hand in hand with the design, before any coding. Or low-level design decisions may be postponed until the implementation phase. Also, the phases might not occur one after another. Typically there is back and forth travel between the phases.

Most of the work in software development does not depend on any particular programming language. Specification, design, and analysis can all be carried out with little or no ties to a particular programming language. Nevertheless, when we get down to implementation details, we do need to decide on one particular programming language. The language we use in this book is Java.

What You Should Know about Java before Starting This Text

the origin of Java

The Java language was conceived by a group of programmers at Sun Microsystems in 1991. The group, led by James Gosling, had an initial design called Oak that was motivated by a desire for a single language where programs could be developed and easily moved from one machine to another. Over the next four years, many other Sun programmers contributed to the project and Gosling's Oak evolved to the Java language that is particularly suited to applications that can be moved from one machine to another over the Internet.

this book gives an introduction to OOP principles for information hiding and component reuse

Throughout the evolution of Java, the designers incorporated ideas from other modern programming languages. Most notably, Java supports **object-oriented programming (OOP)** in a manner that was partly taken from the C++ programming language. OOP is a programming approach that encourages strategies of information hiding and component reuse. In this book, you will be introduced to these important OOP principles to use in your designs and implementations.

There are many different Java development environments that you may successfully use with this text. You should be comfortable writing, compiling, and running short Java application programs in your environment. You should know how to use the Java primitive types (the number types, char, and boolean), and you should be able to use arrays.

you should already know how to write, compile, and run short Java programs

If you know how to use Java in these ways, then the rest of this chapter will prepare you to tackle the topic of data structures in Java. Section 1.1 focuses on a technique for specifying program behavior, and you'll also see some hints about design and implementation. Section 1.2 illustrates a particular kind of analysis: the running time analysis of a program. Section 1.3 provides some techniques for testing and debugging Java programs.

1.1 SPECIFICATION, DESIGN, IMPLEMENTATION

One begins with a list of difficult design decisions which are likely to change. Each module is then designed to hide such a decision from the others.

D. L. PARNAS
On the Criteria to Be Used in Decomposing Systems into Modules

As an example of software development in action, let's examine the specification, design, and implementation for a particular problem. The **specification** is a precise description of the problem; the **design** phase consists of formulating the steps to solve the problem; the **implementation** is the actual Java code to carry out the design.

The problem we have in mind is to display a table for converting Celsius temperatures to Fahrenheit, similar to the table shown in the margin. For a small problem, a sample of the desired output is a sufficient specification. Such a sample is a good specification because it is *precise,* leaving no doubt about what the program must accomplish. The next step is to design a solution.

An **algorithm** is a set of instructions for solving a problem. An algorithm for the temperature problem will print the conversion table. During the design of the algorithm, the details of a particular programming language can be distracting and obscure the simplicity of a solution. Therefore, during the design we generally write in English. We use a rather corrupted kind of English that mixes in Java when it's convenient. This mixture of English and a programming language is called **pseudocode.** When the Java code for a step is obvious, then the pseudocode may use Java. When a step is clearer in English, then we will use English. Keep in mind that the reason for pseudocode is to improve *clarity.*

```
TEMPERATURE CONVERSION
----------------------
Celsius        Fahrenheit
-50.00C
-40.00C        The equivalent
-30.00C        Fahrenheit
-20.00C        temperatures
-10.00C        will be
  0.00C        computed and
 10.00C        displayed on this
 20.00C        side of the table.
 30.00C
 40.00C
 50.00C
----------------------
```

We'll use pseudocode to design a solution for the temperature problem, and we'll also use the important design technique of decomposing the problem, which we discuss now.

Design Technique: Decomposing the Problem

A good technique for designing an algorithm is to break down the problem at hand into a few subtasks, then decompose each subtask into smaller subtasks, then replace the smaller subtasks with even smaller subtasks, and so forth. Eventually the subtasks become so small that they are trivial to implement in Java or whatever language you are using. When the algorithm is translated into Java code, each subtask is implemented as a separate Java method. In other programming languages, methods are called "functions" or "procedures," but it all boils down to the same thing: The large problem is decomposed into subtasks, and subtasks are implemented as separate pieces of your program.

For example, the temperature problem has at least two good subtasks: (1) converting a temperature from Celsius degrees to Fahrenheit, and (2) printing a number with a specified accuracy (such as rounding to the nearest hundredth). Using these two subproblems, the first draft of our pseudocode might look like this:

1. Display the labels at the top of the table.
2. For each line in the table (using variables `celsius` and `fahrenheit`):
   - 2a. Set `celsius` equal to the next Celsius temperature of the table.
   - **2b.** `fahrenheit` = the `celsius` temperature converted to Fahrenheit.
   - **2c.** Print `celsius`, rounding to the nearest hundredth.
   - 2d. Print the letter C and some spaces.
   - **2e.** Print `fahrenheit`, rounding to the nearest hundredth.
   - 2f. Print the letter F, and end the output line.
3. Print the line of dashes at the bottom of the table.

what makes a good decomposition?

The underlined steps (2b, 2c, and 2e) are the major subtasks that we have identified. But aren't there other ways to decompose the problem into subtasks? What are the aspects of a good decomposition? One primary guideline is that the subtasks should help you produce short pseudocode—no more than a page of succinct description to solve the entire problem, and ideally much less than a page. In your first designs, you can also keep in mind two considerations for selecting good subtasks: the potential for code reuse, and the possibility of future changes to the program. Let's see how our subtasks embody these considerations.

code reuse

Steps 2c and 2e both print a number with a specified accuracy, so we plan to write just a single Java method that "prints a number" and use this method for both steps. This is an example of **code reuse**, in which we use a single method for several related tasks. In fact, programmers often produce collections of related Java methods that are made available in packages to be reused over and over with many different application programs. Later we will write such a package of methods for producing nice output, including the "print a number" method. But for now, the nice package is unavailable, so we plan to write the printing method from scratch.

Decomposing problems also produces a good final program in the sense that the program is easy to understand, and subsequent maintenance and modifications are relatively easy. For example, our temperature program might later be modified to convert to Kelvin degrees instead of Fahrenheit. Since the conversion task is performed by a separate Java method, most of the modification will be confined to this one method. Easily modified code is vital since real-world studies show that a large proportion of programmers' time is spent maintaining and modifying existing programs.

easily modified code

In order for a problem decomposition to produce easily modified code, the Java methods that you write need to be genuinely separated from one another. An analogy can help explain the notion of "genuinely separated." Suppose you are moving a bag of gold coins to a safe hiding place. If the bag is too heavy to carry, you might divide the coins into three smaller bags and carry the bags one by one. Unless you are a character in a comedy, you would not try to carry all three bags at once. That would defeat the purpose of dividing the coins into three groups. This strategy works only if you carry the bags one at a time. Something similar happens in problem decomposition. If you divide your programming task into three subtasks and solve these subtasks by writing three Java methods, then you have traded one hard problem for three easier problems. Your total job has become easier—provided that you design the methods separately. When you are working on one method, you should not worry about how the other methods perform their jobs. But the methods do interact. So when you are designing one method, you need to know something about what the other methods do. The trick is to know *only as much as you need, but no more.* This is called **information hiding.** One technique for incorporating information hiding involves specifying your methods' behavior using *preconditions* and *postconditions*, which we discuss next.

How to Write a Specification for a Java Method

When you implement a method in Java, you give complete instructions for how the method performs its computation. However, when you are *using a method* in your pseudocode or writing other Java code, you only need to think about *what the method does.* You need not think about *how the method* does its work. For example, suppose you are writing the temperature conversion program and you are told that the following method is available for you to use:

```
// Convert a Celsius temperature c to Fahrenheit degrees
public static double celsiusToFahrenheit(double c)
```

In your program you might have a `double` variable called `celsius` that contains a Celsius temperature. Knowing this description, you can confidently write the following statement to convert the temperature to Fahrenheit degrees, storing the result in a `double` variable called `fahrenheit`:

```
fahrenheit = celsiusToFahrenheit(celsius);
```

When you use the `celsiusToFahrenheit` method, you do not need to know the details of how the method carries out its work. You need to know *what* the method does, but you do not need to know *how* the task is accomplished.

procedural abstraction

When we pretend that we do not know how a method is implemented, we are using a form of information hiding called **procedural abstraction**. This simplifies your reasoning by abstracting away irrelevant details, that is, by hiding the irrelevant details. When programming in Java, it might make more sense to call it "method abstraction," since you are abstracting away irrelevant details about how a method works. However, the term *procedure* is a more general term than *method*. Computer scientists use the term procedure for any sequence of instructions, and so they use the term *procedural abstraction*. Procedural abstraction can be a powerful tool. It simplifies your reasoning by allowing you to consider methods one at a time rather than all together.

To make procedural abstraction work for us, we need some techniques for documenting what a method does without indicating how the method works. Of course, we could just write a short comment as we did for `celsiusToFahrenheit`. However, the short comment is a bit incomplete, for instance the comment doesn't indicate what happens if the parameter `c` is smaller than the lowest Celsius temperature (−273.16°C, also called **absolute zero**). For better completeness and consistency, we will follow a fixed format that is guaranteed to provide the same kind of information about any method that you may write. The format has five parts, which are illustrated here for the `celsiusToFahrenheit` method:

- **celsiusToFahrenheit**
  `public static double celsiusToFahrenheit(double c)`
  Convert a temperature from Celsius degrees to Fahrenheit degrees.

  Parameters:
  `c` – a temperature in Celsius degrees

  Precondition:
  `c >= -273.16`.

  Returns:
  the temperature `c` converted to Fahrenheit degrees

  Throws: `IllegalArgumentException`
  Indicates that `c` is less than the smallest Celsius temperature (−273.16).

This documentation is called the method's **specification**. Let's look at the five parts of this specification.

1. Short introduction. The specification's first few lines are a brief introduction. The introduction includes the method's name, the complete heading (`public static double celsiusToFahrenheit(double c)`), and a short description of the action that the method performs.

2. Parameter description. The specification's second part is a list of the method's parameters. We have one parameter, `c`, which is a temperature in Celsius degrees.

3. Precondition. A **precondition** is a condition that is supposed to be true when a method is called. The method is not guaranteed to work correctly unless the precondition is true. Our method requires that the Celsius temperature `c` is no less than the smallest valid Celsius temperature ($-273.16°C$).

4. The returns condition or postcondition. A **returns** condition specifies the meaning of a method's return value. We used a returns condition for `celsiusToFahrenheit`, specifying that the method "returns the temperature `c` converted to Fahrenheit degrees." More complex methods may have additional effects beyond a single return value. For example, a method may print values or alter its parameters. To describe such effects, a general *postcondition* can be provided instead of just a returns condition. A **postcondition** is a complete statement describing what will be true when a method finishes. If the precondition was true when the method was called, then the method will complete and the postcondition will be true when the method completes. The connection between a precondition and a postcondition is given here:

A Method's Precondition and Postcondition

A **precondition** is a statement giving the condition that is supposed to be true when a method is called. The method is not guaranteed to perform as it should unless the precondition is true.

A **postcondition** is a statement describing what will be true when a method call is completed. If the method is correct and the precondition was true when the method was called, then the method will complete, and the postcondition will be true when the method's computation is completed.

For small methods that merely return a calculated value, the specification can provide a precondition and a returns condition. For more complex methods, the specfication can provide a precondition and a general postcondition.

5. The "throws" list. It is always the responsibility of the programmer who *uses* a method to ensure that the precondition is valid. Calling a method without ensuring a valid precondition is a programming error. Once the precondition fails, the method's behavior is unpredictable—the method *could* do anything at all. Nonetheless, the person who writes a method should make every effort to avoid the more unpleasant behaviors, even if the method is called incorrectly. As part of this effort, the first action of a method is often to check that its precondition has been satisfied. If the precondition fails, then the method *throws an exception.* You may have used exceptions in your previous programming, or maybe not. In either case, the next section describes the exact meaning of *throwing an exception* to indicate that a precondition has failed.

Throwing an Exception to Indicate a Failed Precondition

It is a programming error to call `celsiusToFahrenheit` with an argument that is below −273.16. Celsius temperatures below this level have no physical meaning, they cannot be converted to Fahrenheit, and the method cannot provide a meaningful return value. Despite this warning, some chilly programmer may try `celsiusToFahrenheit(-1000)` or `celsiusToFahrenheit(-273.17)`. In such a case, our `celsiusToFahrenheit` method will detect that the precondition has been violated, immediately halt its own work, and pass a "message" to the calling program to indicate that an illegal argument has occurred. Such messages for serious programming errors are called **exceptions.** The act of halting your own work and passing a message to the calling program is known as **throwing an exception.**

how to throw an exception

The Java syntax for throwing an exception is simple. For example, the implementation of `celsiusToFahrenheit` might have these statements:

```
if (c < -273.16)
    throw new IllegalArgumentException("Temperature too small.");
```

Simple exceptions such as this are easy to throw. You begin with the keyword "`throw`" and follow this pattern:

```
throw new _____ ("_____");
```

This is the type of the exception that we are throwing. To begin with, all of our exceptions will be the type IllegalArgumentException, which is provided as part of the Java language. This type of exception tells a programmer that one of the method's arguments violated a precondition.

This is an error message that will be passed as part of the exception. The message should describe the error in a way that will help the programmer fix the programming error.

When an exception is thrown within a method, the method immediately stops its computation. A new "exception object" is created, incorporating the indicated error message. The exception, along with its error message, is passed up to the method or program that made the illegal call in the first place. At that point, where the illegal call was made, there is a Java mechanism to "catch" the exception, try to fix the error, and continue with the program's computation. You can read about exception-catching in Appendix C. However, exceptions that arise from precondition violations should never be caught because they indicate programming errors that must be fixed. When an exception is not caught, the program halts, printing the error message along with a list of the method calls that led to the exception. This error message can help the programmer fix the programming error.

what happens when an exception is thrown?

Now you know the meaning of the specification's "throws list." It is a list of all the exceptions that the method can throw, along with a description of what causes each exception. Certain kinds of exceptions must also be listed in a method's implementation, after the parameter list, but an `IllegalArgument-Exception` is listed only in the method's specification.

With a method's specification in place, you can think more about the design. Perhaps the method needs to be broken into yet smaller tasks, or perhaps the task is now small enough to start the implementation—the actual writing of Java code. The `celsiusToFahrenheit` problem is small enough to implement, though during the implementation you may need to finish small design tasks such as finding the conversion formula (a celsius temperature C is converted to a Fahrenheit temperature F with the formula $F = \frac{9}{5}C + 32$). The complete implementation might be something like Figure 1.1 on page 10. The implementation illustrates two programming tips that we'll discuss now.

Programming Tip: How and When to Throw Exceptions

It is a programming error to call a method when the precondition is invalid. When a method detects an invalid precondition, then the method should throw an `IllegalArgumentException`. The exception usually includes a copy of the argument as part of its message. For example, the exception message in Figure 1.1 is:

```
"Argument " + c + " is too small."
```

The argument `c` is part of the message. If a programmer attempts to call `celsiusToFahrenheit(-300)`, the message will be "Argument −300 is too small."

FIGURE 1.1	Specification and Implementation of the `celsiusToFahrenheit` Method

Specification

◆ **celsiusToFahrenheit**

```
public static double celsiusToFahrenheit(double c)
```
Convert a temperature from Celsius degrees to Fahrenheit degrees.

Parameters:

c – a temperature in Celsius degrees

Precondition:

`c >= -273.16.`

Returns:

the temperature c converted to Fahrenheit degrees

Throws: `IllegalArgumentException`

Indicates that c is less than the smallest Celsius temperature (−273.16).

Implementation

```java
public static double celsiusToFahrenheit(double c)
{
    final double MINIMUM_CELSIUS = -273.16;

    if (c < MINIMUM_CELSIUS)
        throw new IllegalArgumentException("Argument " + c + " is too small.");
    return (9.0/5.0) * c + 32;
}
```

△ **TIP**

Programming Tip: Use Final Variables to Improve Clarity

The method implementation in Figure 1.1 has a local variable declared this way:

```java
final double MINIMUM_CELSIUS = -273.16;
```

This is a declaration of a `double` variable called `MINIMUM_CELSIUS`, which is given an initial value of −273.16. The keyword `final`, appearing before the declaration, makes `MINIMUM_CELSIUS` more than just an ordinary declaration. It is a **final variable**, which means that its value will never be changed while the program is running. A common programming style is to use all capital letters for the names of final variables. This makes it easy to determine which variables are final and which may have their values changed.

There are several advantages to defining `MINIMUM_CELSIUS` as a final variable, rather than using the constant −273.16 directly in the program. Using the name `MINIMUM_CELSIUS` makes the comparison (`c < MINIMUM_CELSIUS`) easy to understand; it's clear that we are testing whether c is below the minimum valid Celsius temperature. If we used the direct comparison (`c < -273.16`) instead, then a person reading our program would have to stop to remember that −273.16 is "absolute zero," the smallest Celsius temperature.

To increase clarity, some programmers declare *all* constants as final variables. As rules go, this is a reasonable rule, particularly if the same constant appears in several different places of the program or if you plan to compile the program some-time with a different value for the constant. However, there is another side to the issue. Well-known formulas may be more easily recognized in their original form (using constants rather than artificially introduced names). For example, the conversion from Celsius to Fahrenheit is recognizable as $F = \frac{9}{5}C + 32$. Thus, Fig-ure 1.1 uses the return statement shown here:

```
return (9.0/5.0) * c + 32;
```

This return statement is clearer and less error-prone than a version that uses final variables for the constants $\frac{9}{5}$ and 32.

Advice: Use final variables instead of constants. Make exceptions when con-stants are clearer or less error-prone. When in doubt, write both solutions and inter-view several colleagues to decide which is clearer.

The Method for Printing a Number

Our pseudocode for the temperature problem includes a step to print a number rounded to a specified accuracy. Here is a specification for a method that we can use to carry out this step:

- **printNumber**
    ```
    public static void printNumber(double d, int minimumWidth, int fractionDigits)
    ```
    Print a number to System.out, using a specified format.

    Parameters:
    d – the number to be printed
    minimumWidth – the minimum number of characters in the entire output
    fractionDigits – the number of digits to print on the right side of the
        decimal point

    Precondition:
    fractionDigits is not negative.

    Postcondition:
    The number d has been printed to System.out. This printed number is rounded to the specified number of digits on the right of the decimal. If fractionDigits is 0, then only the integer part of d is printed. If necessary, spaces appear at the front of the number to raise the total number of printed characters to the minimum. Additional formatting details are obtained from the current locale. For example, in the United States, a period is used for the decimal and commas are used to separate groups of integer digits.

    Throws: IllegalArgumentException
    Indicates that fractionDigits is negative.

    Example:
    ```
    printNumber(12345.27, 8, 1); // Prints 12,345.3 in the U.S.
    ```

Because printNumber is somewhat complex, we have added an example to the specification. An example helps a programmer quickly understand the intended use of a method.

With the specification in place, you can turn to the implementation—or if you are working in a programming team, you might ask another group member to implement the method. In fact, I asked several of my students to implement printNumber, using the specification shown earlier. The students researched how to round numbers and how to determine other formatting details. I decided to use one of the implementations, from a student named Judy Abbott. Her implementation of printNumber was interesting because it used several unfamiliar features of the Java language—unfamiliar to me anyway. Does this mean that I can't use the method? Of course not. The specification tells me how to use the method, even if I don't know the implementation details. In team situations, one programmer often does not know the implementation details of another programmer's work. In fact, sharing knowledge about how methods work can be counterproductive. Instead, the combination of the precondition and postcondition provide all the interaction that's needed. In effect, the precondition/postcondition pair forms a contract between the programmer who uses a method and the programmer who writes that method. If programmers were lawyers, the contract might look like the scroll shown in the margin. As a programmer, the contract tells me precisely what Judy's method does. It states that *if* I make sure that the precondition is met when the method is called, *then* Judy ensures that the method returns with the postcondition satisfied.

Whereas Judy Abbott has written printNumber (henceforth known as "the method") and Michael Main is going to use the method, we hereby agree that:

(i) Michael will never call the method unless he is certain that the precondition is true, and

(ii) Whenever the method is called and the precondition is true when the method is called, then Judy guarantees that:

    a. the method will eventually end (infinite loops are forbidden!), and

    b. when the method ends, the postcondition will be true.

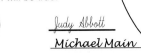

Judy Abbott
Michael Main

the precondition/ postcondition contract

If you are curious about the printNumber programming, you can read Appendix B, which provides some input/output ideas for Java programming. But even without the knowledge of how Judy writes printNumber, we can write a program that uses Judy's method. In particular, we can now implement the temperature program as a Java application program with three methods:

- a main method that follows the pseudocode from page 4: This main method prints the temperature conversion table using printNumber and celsiusToFahrenheit to carry out the work of its subtasks.

- the celsiusToFahrenheit method.

- the printNumber method.

The Java application program with these three methods appears in Figure 1.2 on page 14, together with the specifications that we already wrote.

The specification at the start of Figure 1.2 was produced in an interesting way. Most of it was automatically produced from the Java code by a tool called **Javadoc**. With a web browser, you can access this specification over the Internet at: `http://www.cs.colorado.edu/~main/docs/TemperatureConversion.html`.

the Javadoc tool automatically produces nicely formatted information about a class

To use Javadoc, the actual implementation needs special **Javadoc comments**. These necessary comments are not listed in Figure 1.2, but the techniques for writing these comments are described in Appendix H. You should consider using Javadoc to produce similar specifications for your programs.

Self-Test Exercises

Each section of this book finishes with a few self-test exercises. Answers to these exercises are given at the end of each chapter. The first exercise refers to a method that Judy has written for *you* to use. Here is the specification:

- **dateCheck**

  ```
  public static int dateCheck(int year, int month, int day)
  ```
  Compute how long until a given date will occur.

  Parameters:
  > year – the year for a given date
  > month – the month for a given date (using 1 for Jan, 2 for Feb, etc.)
  > day – the day of the month for the given date

  Precondition:
  > The three arguments are a legal year, month, and day of the month in the years 1900 to 2099.

  Returns:
  > If the given date has been reached on or before today, then the return value is zero. Otherwise the return value is the number of days until the given date returns.

  Throws: `IllegalArgumentException`
  > Indicates the arguments are not a legal date in the years 1900 to 2099.

1. Suppose you call the method `dateCheck(2003, 7, 29)`. What is the return value if today is July 22, 2003? What if today is July 30, 2003? What about February 1, 2004?

2. Can you use `dateCheck`, even if you don't know how it is implemented?

3. Suppose that `boodle` is a `double` variable. Write two statements that will print `boodle` to `System.out` in the following format: `$    42,567.19` The whole dollars part of the output can contain up to nine characters, so this example has three spaces before the six characters of `42,567`. The fractional part is rounded to the nearest hundredth. You may use the `printNumber` method from this section.

4. Consider a method with this heading:

   ```
   public static void printSqrt(double x)
   ```

   The method prints the square root of x to the standard output. Write a reasonable specification for this method, and compare your answer to the solution at the end of the chapter. The specification should forbid a negative argument.

5. Consider a method with this heading:

   ```
   public static double sphereVolume(double radius)
   ```

   The method computes and returns the volume of a sphere with the given radius. Write a reasonable specification for this method, and compare your answer to the solution at the end of the chapter. The specification should forbid a negative radius.

6. Write an if-statement to throw an IllegalArgumentException when x is less than zero. (Assume that x is a double variable.)

7. When can a final variable be used?

8. How was the specification produced at the start of Figure 1.2?

FIGURE 1.2	Specification and Implementation for the Temperature Conversion Application

Class TemperatureConversion

❖ **public class TemperatureConversion**

The TemperatureConversion Java application prints a table converting Celsius to Fahrenheit degrees.

Specification

◆ **main**

public static void main(String[ ] args)

The main method prints a Celsius to Fahrenheit conversion table. The String arguments (args) are not used in this implementation. The bounds of the table range from –50C to +50C in 10 degree increments.

(continued)

(FIGURE 1.2 continued)

- ### celsiusToFahrenheit

  ```
  public static double celsiusToFahrenheit(double c)
  ```
  Convert a temperature from Celsius degrees to Fahrenheit degrees.

  Parameters:
  c – a temperature in Celsius degrees

  Precondition:
  `c >= -273.16.`

  Returns:
  the temperature c converted to Fahrenheit degrees

  Throws: `IllegalArgumentException`
  Indicates that c is less than the smallest Celsius temperature (−273.16).

> Most of this information was automatically produced by the Javadoc tool. Appendix H describes how to use Javadoc to produce similar information for your programs.

- ### printNumber

  ```
  public static void printNumber(double d, int minimumWidth, int fractionDigits)
  ```
  Print a number to `System.out`, using a specified format.

  Parameters:
  d – the number to be printed
  `minimumWidth` – the minimum number of characters in the entire output
  `fractionDigits` – the number of digits to print on the right side of the decimal point

  Precondition:
  `fractionDigits` is not negative.

  Postcondition:
  The number d has been printed to `System.out`. This printed number is rounded to the specified number of digits on the right of the decimal. If `fractionDigits` is 0, then only the integer part of d is printed. If necessary, spaces appear at the front of the number to raise the total number of printed characters to the minimum. Additional formatting details are obtained from the current locale. For example, in the United States, a period is used for the decimal, and commas are used to separate groups of integer digits.

  Throws: `IllegalArgumentException`
  Indicates that `fractionDigits` is negative.

  Example:
  ```
  printNumber(12345.27, 8, 1); // Prints 12,345.3 in the U.S.
  ```

(continued)

(FIGURE 1.2 continued)

Java Application Program

The actual implementation includes Javadoc comments that are omitted here but are listed in Appendix H. The comments allow Javadoc to produce nicely formatted information automatically. See Appendix H to read about using Javadoc for your programs.

```java
// File: TemperatureConversion.java
// A Java application to print a
// temperature conversion table.
// Additional Javadoc information is available on pages 14-15 or at
//    http://www.cs.colorado.edu/~main/docs/TemperatureConversion.html

import java.text.NumberFormat;  // Used in the printNumber method.

public class TemperatureConversion
{
    public static void main(String[ ] args)
    {
        // Declare values that control the table's bounds.
        final double TABLE_BEGIN = -50.0;  // The table's first Celsius temperature
        final double TABLE_END   =  50.0;  // The table's final Celsius temperature
        final double TABLE_STEP  =  10.0;  // Increment between temperatures in table
        final int    WIDTH       =     6;  // Number of characters in output numbers
        final int    ACCURACY    =     2;  // Number of digits to right of decimal point

        double celsius;                    // A Celsius temperature
        double fahrenheit;                 // The equivalent Fahrenheit temperature

        System.out.println("TEMPERATURE CONVERSION");
        System.out.println("----------------------");
        System.out.println("Celsius      Fahrenheit");
        for (celsius = TABLE_BEGIN; celsius <= TABLE_END; celsius += TABLE_STEP)
        {   // The for-loop has set celsius equal to the next Celsius temperature of the table.
            fahrenheit = celsiusToFahrenheit(celsius);
            printNumber(celsius, WIDTH, ACCURACY);
            System.out.print("C       ");
            printNumber(fahrenheit, WIDTH, ACCURACY);
            System.out.println("F");
        }
        System.out.println("----------------------");
    }

    public static double celciusToFahrenheit(double c)
    {
        final double MINIMUM_CELSIUS = -273.16;
        if (c < MINIMUM_CELSIUS)
            throw new IllegalArgumentException("Argument " + c + " is too small.");
        return (9.0/5.0) * c + 32;
    }
```

(continued)

(FIGURE 1.2 continued)

```
public static void printNumber(double d, int minimumWidth, int fractionDigits)
{
    // Note: getNumberInstance( ) creates a NumberFormat object using local
    // information about the characters for a decimal point and separators.
    NumberFormat form = NumberFormat.getNumberInstance( );
    String output;
    int i;
    int length;

    // Set the number of digits to appear on the right of the decimal.
    if (fractionDigits < 0)
        throw new IllegalArgumentException("fractionDigits < 0:" + fractionDigits);
    form.setMinimumFractionDigits(fractionDigits);
    form.setMaximumFractionDigits(fractionDigits);

    // Round and format the number. I have added code to handle a Java bug that
    // occurs when fractionDigits is zero.
    output = form.format(d);
    length = output.length( );
    if (fractionDigits == 0 && length > 1 && output.charAt(length-2) == '.')
        output = "   " + output.substring(0,length-2);

    // Print any leading spaces and the number itself.
    for (i = output.length( ); i < minimumWidth; i++)
        System.out.print(' ');
    System.out.print(output);
}
}
```

Output of the Application

```
TEMPERATURE CONVERSION
----------------------
Celsius      Fahrenheit
-50.00C        -58.00F
-40.00C        -40.00F
-30.00C        -22.00F
-20.00C         -4.00F
-10.00C         14.00F
  0.00C         32.00F
 10.00C         50.00F
 20.00C         68.00F
 30.00C         86.00F
 40.00C        104.00F
 50.00C        122.00F
----------------------
```

1.2   RUNNING TIME ANALYSIS

Time analysis consists of reasoning about an algorithm's speed. *Does the algorithm work fast enough for my needs? How much longer does the algorithm take when the input gets larger? Which of several different algorithms is fastest?* We'll discuss these issues in this section. An example will start the discussion.

The Stair-Counting Problem

Suppose that you and your friend Judy are standing at the top of the Eiffel Tower. As you gaze out over the French landscape, Judy turns to you and says, "I wonder how many steps there are to the bottom?" You, of course, are the ever-accommodating host, so you reply, "I'm not sure, . . . but I'll find out." We'll look at three techniques that you could use and analyze the time requirements of each.

Technique 1: Walk down and keep a tally.   In the first technique, Judy gives you a pen and a sheet of paper. "I'll be back in a minute," you say as you dash down the stairs. Each time you take a step down, you make a mark on the sheet of paper. When you reach the bottom, you run back up, show Judy the piece of paper, and say, "There are this many steps."

Technique 2: Walk down, but let Judy keep the tally.   In the second technique, Judy is unwilling to let her pen or paper out of her sight. But you are undaunted. Once more you say, "I'll be back in a minute," and you set off down the stairs. But this time you stop after one step, lay your hat on the step, and run back to Judy. "Make a mark on the piece of paper!" you exclaim. Then you run back to your hat, pick it up, take one more step, and lay the hat down on the second step. Then back up to Judy: "Make another mark on the piece of paper!" you say. You run back down the two stairs, pick up your hat, move to the third step, and lay down the hat. Then back up the stairs to Judy: "Make another mark!" you tell her. This continues until your hat reaches the bottom, and you speed back up the steps one more time. "One more mark, please." At this point, you grab Judy's piece of paper and say, "There are this many steps."

Il y a 2689 marches dans cet escalier

(vraiment!)

Technique 3: Jervis to the rescue.   In the third technique, you don't walk down the stairs at all. Instead, you spot your friend Jervis by the staircase, holding the sign drawn here. The translation is *There are 2689 steps in this stairway (really!).* So, you take the paper and pen from Judy, write the number 2689, and hand the paper back to her, saying, "There are this many steps."

This is a silly example, but even so, it does illustrate the issues that arise when performing a time analysis for an algorithm or program. The first issue is deciding exactly how you will measure the time spent carrying out the work or executing the program. At first glance the answer seems easy: For each of the three stair-counting techniques, just measure the actual time it takes to carry out the work. You could do this with a stopwatch. But, there are some drawbacks to measuring actual time. Actual time can depend on various irrelevant details, such as whether you or somebody else carried out the work. The actual elapsed time may vary from person to person, depending on how fast each person can run the stairs. Even if we decide that *you* are the runner, the time may vary depending on other factors such as the weather, what you had for breakfast, and what other things are on your mind.

So, instead of measuring the actual elapsed time, we count certain operations that occur while carrying out the work. In this example, we will count two kinds of operations:

1. Each time you walk up or down one step, that is one operation.
2. Each time you or Judy marks a symbol on the paper, that is also one operation.

Of course, each of these operations takes a certain amount of time, and making a mark may take a different amount of time than taking a step. But this doesn't concern us because we won't measure the actual time taken by the operations. Instead, we will ask: *How many operations are needed for each of the three techniques?*

decide what operations to count

For the first technique, you take 2689 steps down, another 2689 steps up, and you also make 2689 marks on the paper, for a total of 3×2689 operations—that is 8067 total operations.

For the second technique, there are also 2689 marks made on Judy's paper, but the total number of operations is considerably more. You start by going down one step and back up one step. Then down two and up two. Then down three and up three, and so forth. The total number of operations taken is:

Downward steps	$= 3,616,705$ (which is $1 + 2 + \ldots + 2689$)
Upward steps	$= 3,616,705$
Marks made	$= 2689$
Total operations	$=$ Downward steps $+$ Upward steps $+$ Marks made $= 7,236,099$

The third technique is the quickest of all: Only four marks are made on the paper (that is, we're counting one "mark" for each digit of 2689), and there is no going up and down stairs. The number of operations used by each of the techniques is summarized here:

Technique 1	8067	operations
Technique 2	7,236,099	operations
Technique 3	4	operations

Doing a time analysis for a program is similar to the analysis of the stair-counting techniques. For a time analysis of a program, we do not usually measure the actual time taken to run the program because the number of seconds can depend on too many extraneous factors—such as the speed of the processor, and whether the processor is busy with other tasks. Instead, the analysis counts the number of operations required. There is no precise definition of what constitutes an **operation**, although an operation should satisfy your intuition of a "small step." An operation can be as simple as the execution of a single program statement. Or we could use a finer notion of operation that counts each arithmetic operation (addition, multiplication, etc.) and each assignment to a variable as a separate operation.

dependence on input size

For most programs, the number of operations depends on the program's input. For example, a program that sorts a list of numbers is quicker with a short list than with a long list. In the stairway example, we can view the Eiffel Tower as the input to the problem. In other words, the three different techniques all work on the Eiffel Tower, but the techniques also work on Toronto's CN Tower or on the stairway to the top of the Statue of Liberty or on any other stairway.

When a time analysis depends on the size of the input, then the time can be given as an expression, where part of the expression is the input's size. The time expressions for our three stair-counting techniques are:

Technique 1	$3n$
Technique 2	$n + 2\,(1 + 2 + \ldots + n)$
Technique 3	The number of digits in the number n

The expressions on the right give the number of operations performed by each technique when the stairway has n steps.

The expression for the second technique is not easy to interpret. It needs to be simplified in order to become a formula that we can easily compare to other formulas. So, let's simplify it. We start with the subexpression

$$(1 + 2 + \ldots + n)$$

simplification of the time analysis for Technique 2

There is a trick that will enable us to find a simplified form for this expression. The trick is to *compute twice the amount of the expression and then divide the result by 2.* Unless you've seen this trick before, it sounds crazy. But it works

FIGURE 1.3   Deriving a Handy Formula

$(1 + 2 + \ldots + n)$ can be computed by first computing the sum of twice $(1 + 2 + \ldots + n)$, as shown here:

$$
\begin{array}{ccccccccc}
1 & + & 2 & + \ldots + & (n-1) & + & n & \\
+ & n & + & (n-1) + \ldots + & 2 & + & 1 & \\
\hline
(n+1) & + & (n+1) & + \ldots + & (n+1) & + & (n+1) &
\end{array}
$$

The sum is $n(n + 1)$, so $(1 + 2 + \ldots + n)$ is half this amount:

$$(1 + 2 + \ldots + n) = \frac{n(n + 1)}{2}$$

---

fine. The trick is illustrated in Figure 1.3. Let's go through the computation of that figure step-by-step.

We write the expression $(1 + 2 + \ldots + n)$ twice and add the two expressions. But as you can see in Figure 1.3, we also use another trick: When we write the expression twice, *we write the second expression backwards*. After we write down the expression twice, we see the following:

$(1 + 2 + \ldots + n)$

$+(n + \ldots + 2 + 1)$

We want the sum of the numbers on these two lines. That will give us twice the value of $(1 + 2 + \ldots + n)$, and we can then divide by 2 to get the correct value of the subexpression $(1 + 2 + \ldots + n)$.

Now, rather than proceed in the most obvious way, we instead add pairs of numbers from the first and second lines. We add the 1 and the n to get $n + 1$. Then we add the 2 and the $n - 1$ to again get $n + 1$. We continue until we reach the last pair consisting of an n from the top line and a 1 from the bottom line. All the pairs add up to the same amount, namely $n + 1$. Now that is handy! We get n numbers, and all the numbers are the same, namely $n + 1$. So the total of all the numbers on the preceding two lines is

$n(n + 1)$

The value of twice the expression is n multiplied by $n + 1$. We are now essentially done. The number we computed is twice the quantity we want. So, to obtain our simplified formula, we only need to divide by 2. The final simplification is thus

$$(1 + 2 + \dots + n) = \frac{n(n + 1)}{2}$$

We will use this simplified formula to rewrite the Technique 2 time expression, but you'll also find that the formula occurs in many other situations. The simplification for the Technique 2 expression is as follows:

Number of operations for Technique 2

$$= n + 2(1 + 2 + \dots + n)$$

$$= n + 2\left(\frac{n(n + 1)}{2}\right) \qquad \textit{Plug in the formula for } (1 + 2 + \dots + n)$$

$$= n + n(n + 1) \qquad \textit{Cancel the 2s}$$

$$= n + n^2 + n \qquad \textit{Multiply out}$$

$$= n^2 + 2n \qquad \textit{Combine terms}$$

So, Technique 2 requires $n^2 + 2n$ operations.

simplification of time analysis for Technique 3

The number of operations for Technique 3 is just the number of digits in the integer n when written down in the usual way. The usual way of writing down numbers is called **base 10 notation**. As it turns out, the number of digits in a number n, when written in base 10 notation, is approximately equal to another mathematical quantity known as the **base 10 logarithm** of n. The notation for the base 10 logarithm of n is written:

$$\log_{10} n$$

base 10 notation and base 10 logarithms

The base 10 logarithm does not always give a whole number. For example, the actual base 10 logarithm of 2689 is about 3.43 rather than 4. If we want the actual number of digits in an integer n, we need to carry out some rounding. In particular, the exact number of digits in a positive integer n is obtained by rounding $\log_{10} n$ downward to the next whole number, and then adding 1. The notation for rounding down and adding 1 is obtained by adding some marks to the logarithm notation as follows:

$$\lfloor \log_{10} n \rfloor + 1$$

This is all fine if you already know about logarithms, but what if some of this is new to you? For now, you can simply define the notation to mean *the number of digits in the base 10 numeral for n.* You can do this because if others use any of the other accepted definitions for this formula, they will get the same answers that you do. You will be right! (And they will also be right.) In Section 10.3 of this book, we will show that the various definitions of the logarithm function are all equivalent. For now, we will not worry about all that detail. We have larger issues to discuss first. The table of the number of operations for each technique can now be expressed more concisely as shown here:

Technique 1	$3n$
Technique 2	$n^2 + 2n$
Technique 3	$\lfloor \log_{10} n \rfloor + 1$

Big-*O* Notation

The time analyses we gave for the three stair-counting techniques were very precise. They computed the exact number of operations for each technique. But such precision is sometimes not needed. Often it is enough to know in a rough manner how the number of operations is affected by the input size. In the stair example, we started by thinking about a particular tower, the Eiffel Tower, with a particular number of steps. We expressed our formulas for the operations in terms of n, which stood for the number of steps in the tower. Now suppose that we apply our various stair-counting techniques to a tower with ten times as many steps as the Eiffel Tower. If n is the number of steps in the Eiffel Tower, then this taller tower will have $10n$ steps. The number of operations needed for Technique 1 on the taller tower increases tenfold (from $3n$ to $3 \times (10n) = 30n$); the time for Technique 2 increases approximately 100-fold (from about n^2 to about $(10n)^2 = 100n^2$); and Technique 3 increases by only one operation (from the number of digits in n to the number of digits in $10n$, or to be very concrete, from the 4 digits in 2689 to the 5 digits in 26,890). We can express this kind of information in a format called **big-*O* notation**. The symbol O in this notation is the letter O, so big-*O* is pronounced "big Oh."

We will describe three common examples of the big-*O* notation. In these examples, we use the notion of "the largest term in a formula." Intuitively, this is the term with the largest exponent on n, or the term that grows the fastest as n itself becomes larger. For now, this intuitive notion of "largest term" is enough. Here are the examples:

Quadratic Time. If the largest term in a formula is no more than a constant times n^2, then the algorithm is said to be "**big-*O* of n^2**," written $O(n^2)$, and the algorithm is called **quadratic**. In a quadratic algorithm, doubling the input size makes the number of operations increase by approximately fourfold (or less). For a concrete example, consider Technique 2, requiring $n^2 + 2n$ operations. A 100-step tower requires 10,200 operations (that is, $100^2 + 2 \times 100$). Doubling the tower to 200 steps increases the time by approximately fourfold, to 40,400 operations (that is, $200^2 + 2 \times 200$).

quadratic time
$O(n^2)$

linear time O(n)   **Linear Time.**   If the largest term in the formula is a constant times n, then the algorithm is said to be "**big-O of n,**" written $O(n)$, and the algorithm is called **linear**. In a linear algorithm, doubling the input size makes the time increase by approximately twofold (or less). For example, a formula of $3n + 7$ is linear, so that $3 \times 200 + 7$ is about twice $3 \times 100 + 7$.

logarithmic time   **Logarithmic Time.**   If the largest term in the formula is a constant times a log-
O(log n)   arithm of n, then the algorithm is "**big-O of the logarithm of** n," written $O(\log n)$, and the algorithm is called **logarithmic**. (The base of the logarithm may be base 10, or possibly another base. We'll talk about the other bases in Section 10.3.) In a logarithmic algorithm, doubling the input size will make the time increase by no more than a fixed number of new operations, such as one more operation, or two more operations—or in general by c more operations, where c is a fixed constant. For example, Technique 3 for stair-counting has a logarithmic time formula. And doubling the size of a tower (perhaps from 500 stairs to 1000 stairs) never requires more than one extra operation.

Using big-O notation, we can express the time requirements of our three stair-counting techniques as follows:

Technique 1 $O(n)$
Technique 2 $O(n^2)$
Technique 3 $O(\log n)$

order of an   When a time analysis is expressed with big-O, the result is called the **order** of
algorithm   the algorithm. We want to reinforce one important point: Multiplicative con-
stants are ignored in the big-O notation. For example, both $2n$ and $42n$ are linear formulas, so both are expressed as $O(n)$, ignoring the multiplicative constants 2 and 42. As you can see, this means that a big-O analysis loses some information about relative times. Nevertheless, a big-O analysis does provide some useful information for comparing algorithms. The stair example illustrates the most important kind of information provided by the order of an algorithm.

The order of an algorithm generally is more important than the speed of the processor.

For example, using the quadratic technique (Technique 2) the fastest stair climber in the world is still unlikely to do better than a slowpoke—provided that the slowpoke uses one of the faster techniques. In an application such as sorting a list, a quadratic algorithm can be impractically slow on even moderately sized lists, regardless of the processor speed. To see this, notice the comparisons showing actual numbers for our three stair-counting techniques, which are shown in Figure 1.4.

FIGURE 1.4 Number of Operations for Three Techniques

Number of stairs (n)	Logarithmic $O(\log n)$ Technique 3, with $\lfloor \log_{10} n \rfloor + 1$ operations	Linear $O(n)$ Technique 1, with $3n$ operations	Quadratic $O(n^2)$ Technique 2, with $n^2 + 2n$ operations
10	2	30	120
100	3	300	10,200
1000	4	3000	1,002,000
10,000	5	30,000	100,020,000

Time Analysis of Java Methods

The principles of the stair-climbing example can be applied to counting the number of operations required by code written in a high-level language such as Java. As an example, consider the method implemented in Figure 1.5 on page 26. The method searches through an array of numbers to determine whether a particular number occurs.

As with the stair-climbing example, the first step of the time-analysis is to decide precisely what we will count as a single operation. For Java, a good choice is to count the total number of Java operations (such as an assignment, an arithmetic operation, or the < comparison). If a method calls other methods, then we would also need to count the operations that are carried out in the other methods.

With this in mind, let's do a first analysis of the search method for the case where the array's length is a non-negative integer *n,* and (just to be difficult) the number that we are searching for does not occur in the array. How many operations does the search method carry out in all? Our analysis has three parts:

for our first analysis, the number that we are searching for does not occur in the array

1. When the for-loop starts, there are two operations: an assignment to initialize the variable i to 0, and an execution of the test to determine whether i is less than data.length.

2. We then execute the body of the loop, and because the number that we are searching for does not occur, we will execute this body *n* times. How many operations occur during each execution of the loop body? We could count this number, but let's just say that each execution of the loop body requires *k* operations, where *k* is some number around 3 or 4 (including the work at the end of the loop where i is incremented and the termination test is executed). If necessary, we'll figure out *k* later, but for now it is enough to know that we execute the loop body *n* times, and each execution takes *k* operations, for a total of *kn* operations.

3. After the loop finishes, there is one more operation (a return statement).

The total number of operations is now $kn + 3$. The +3 is from the two operations before the loop and the one operation after the loop. Regardless of how big k is, this formula is always linear time. So, in the case where the sought-after number does not occur, the search method takes linear time. In fact, this is a frequent pattern that we summarize here:

Frequent Linear Pattern

A loop that does a fixed amount of operations n times requires $O(n)$ time.

FIGURE 1.5	Specification and Implementation of a `search` Method

Specification

- **search**

  ```
  public static boolean search(double[ ] data, double target)
  ```
  Search an array for a specified number.

  Notice that there is no precondition.

  Parameters:
  data − an array of double numbers
  target − a particular number that we are searching for

  Returns:
  true (to indicate that target occurs somewhere in the array),
  or false (to indicate that target does not occur in the array)

Implementation

```
public static boolean search(double[ ] data, double target)
{
    int i;

    for (i = 0; i < data.length; i++)
    {   // Check whether the target is at data[i].
        if (data[i] == target)
            return true;
    }

    // The loop finished without finding the target.
    return false;
}
```

Examples:

Suppose that the data array has the five numbers {2, 4, 6, 8, 10}. Then search(data, 10) *returns true, but* search(data, 42) *returns false.*

Later you will see additional patterns, resulting in quadratic, logarithmic, and other times. In fact, in Chapter 11 you will rewrite the `search` method in a way that uses an array that is sorted from smallest to largest, but requires only logarithmic time.

Worst-Case, Average-Case and Best-Case Analyses

The `search` method has another important feature: For any particular array size n, the number of required operations can differ depending on the exact parameter values. For example, with n equal to 100, the target could be 27 and the very first array element could also be 27—so the loop body executes just one time. On the other hand, maybe the number 27 doesn't occur until `data[99]` and the loop body executes the maximum number of times (n times). In other words, for any fixed n, different possible parameter values result in a different number of operations. When this occurs, we usually count the *maximum* number of required operations for inputs of a given size. Counting the maximum number of operations is called the **worst-case** analysis. In fact, the worst case for the `search` method occurs when the sought-after number is not in the array, which is the reason that we used the "not in array" situation in our previous analysis.

worst-case analysis

During a worst-case time analysis, you may sometimes find yourself unable to provide an exact count of the number of operations. If the analysis is a worst-case analysis, you may estimate the number of operations, always making sure that your estimate is on the high side. In other words, the actual number of operations must be guaranteed to be less than the estimate that you use in the analysis.

In Chapter 11, when we begin the study of searching and sorting, you'll see two other kinds of time-analysis: **average-case** analysis, which determines the average number of operations required for a given n, and **best-case** analysis, which determines the fewest number of operations required for a given n.

Self-Test Exercises

9. Each of the following is a formula for the number of operations in some algorithm. Express each formula in big-O notation.

   a. $n^2 + 5n$ 　　　　　　d. $100n + 5$

   b. $3n^2 + 5n$ 　　　　　　e. $5n + 3n^2$

   c. $(n + 7)(n - 2)$ 　　　f. the number of digits in $2n$

10. Write code for a method that computes the sum of all the numbers in an integer array. If the array's length is zero, then the sum should also be zero. Do a big-O time analysis of your method.

1.3   TESTING AND DEBUGGING

Always do right. This will gratify some people, and astonish the rest.

MARK TWAIN

To the Young People's Society, February 16, 1901

program testing   **Program testing** occurs when you run a program and observe its behavior. Each time you execute a program on some input, you are testing to see how the program works for that particular input, and you are also testing to see how long the program takes to complete. Part of the science of *software engineering* is the systematic construction of a set of test inputs that is likely to discover errors, and such test inputs are the topic of this section.

Choosing Test Data

To serve as good test data, your test inputs need two properties.

Properties of Good Test Data

1. You must know what output a correct program should produce for each test input.

2. The test inputs should include those inputs that are most likely to cause errors.

Do not take the first property lightly—you must choose test data for which you know the correct output. Just because a program compiles, runs, and produces output that looks about right does not mean the program is correct. If the correct answer is 3278 and the program outputs 3277, then something is wrong. How do you know the correct answer is 3278? The most obvious way to find the correct output value is to work it out with pencil and paper using some method other than that used by the program. To aid you in doing this, you might choose test data for which it is easy to calculate the correct answer, perhaps by using smaller input values or by using input values for which the answer is well known.

Boundary Values

We will focus on two approaches for finding test data that is most likely to cause errors. The first approach is based on identifying and testing inputs called *boundary values*, which are particularly apt to cause errors. A **boundary value** of a problem is an input that is one step away from a different kind of behavior.

For example, recall the `dateCheck` method from the first self-test exercise on page 13. It has the following precondition:

Precondition:
> The three arguments are a legal year, month, and day of the month in the years 1900 to 2099.

Two boundary values for `dateCheck` are January 1, 1900 (since one step below this date is illegal) and December 31, 2099 (since one step above this date is illegal). If we expect the method to behave differently for "leap days," then we should try days such as February 28, 2000 (just before a leap day), February 29, 2000 (a leap day), and March 1, 2000 (just after a leap day).

Frequently zero has special behavior, so it is a good idea to consider zero to be boundary values whenever it is a legal input. For example, consider the `search` method from Figure 1.5 on page 26. This method should be tested with a data array that contains no elements (`data.length` is 0). For example:

test zero as a boundary value

```
double[ ] EMPTY = new double[0]; // An array with no elements
```

```
// Searching the EMPTY array should always return false.
if (search(EMPTY, 0))
    System.out.println("Wrong answer for an empty array.");
else
    System.out.println("Right answer for an empty array.");
```

The numbers 1 and −1 also have special behavior in many situations, so they should be tested as boundary values whenever they are legal input. For example, the `search` method should be tested with an array that contains just one element (`data.length` is 1). In fact, it should be tested twice with a one-element array: once when the target is equal to the element, and once when the target is different from the element.

test 1 and −1 as boundary values

In general, there is no precise definition of a boundary value, but you should develop an intuitive feel for finding inputs that are "one step away from different behavior."

boundary values are "one step away from different behavior"

Test Boundary Values

If you cannot test all possible inputs, at least test the boundary values. For example, if legal inputs range from zero to one million, then be sure to test input 0 and input 1000000. It is a good idea also to consider 0, 1, and −1 to be boundary values whenever they are legal input.

Fully Exercising Code

The second widely used testing technique requires intimate knowledge of how a program has been implemented. The technique, called **fully exercising code**, is stated with two rules:

1. Make sure that each line of your code is executed at least once by some of your test data. For example, there might be a portion of your code that is only handling a rare situation. Make sure that this rare situation is included among your set of test data.

2. If there is some part of your code that is sometimes skipped altogether, then make sure that there is at least one test input that actually does skip this part of your code. For example, there might be a loop where the body is sometimes executed zero times. Make sure that there is a test input that causes the loop body to be executed zero times.

profiler

Some Java programming environments have a software tool called a **profiler** to help fully exercise code. A typical profiler will generate a listing indicating how many times each method was called, so you can easily check that each method has been executed at least once. Some profilers offer more complete information, telling how often each individual statement of your program was executed. This can help you spot parts of your program that were not tested.

Fully Exercising Code

1. Make sure that each line of your code is executed at least once by some of your test data.

2. If there is part of your code that is sometimes skipped altogether, then make sure that there is at least one test input that actually does skip this part of your code.

TIP

Programming Tip: **How to Debug**

Finding a test input that causes an error is only half the problem of testing and debugging. After an erroneous test input is found, you still must determine exactly why the "bug" occurs, and "debug the program." When you have found an error, there is an impulse to dive right in and start changing code. It is tempting to look for suspicious parts of your code and change these suspects to something "that might work better."

Avoid the temptation.

An impulsive change to suspicious code almost always makes matters worse. Instead, you must discover *exactly* why a test case is failing and limit your changes to *corrections of known errors.* Once you have corrected a known error, all test cases should be rerun.

Tracking down the exact reason why a test case is failing can be difficult. For large programs, tracking down errors is nearly impossible without the help of a software tool called a **debugger.** A debugger executes your code one line at a time, or it may execute your code until a certain condition arises. Using a debugger, you can specify what conditions should cause the program execution to pause. You can also keep a continuous watch on the location of the program execution and on the values of specified variables.

Debugging Tips

1. Never start changing suspicious code in the hope that the change "might work better."

2. Instead, discover *exactly* why a test case is failing and limit your changes to *corrections of known errors.*

3. Once you have corrected a known error, all test cases should be rerun.

Use a software tool called a *debugger* to help track down exactly why an error occurs.

Self-Test Exercises

11. Suppose you write a program that accepts as input any integer in the range –20 through 20, and outputs the number of digits in the input integer. What boundary values should you use as test inputs?

12. Suppose you write a program that accepts a single line as input, and outputs a message telling whether or not the line contains the letter A, and whether or not it contains more than three A's. What is a good set of test inputs?

13. What does it mean to "fully exercise" code?

CHAPTER SUMMARY

- The first step in producing a program is to write down a precise description of what the program is supposed to do.

- *Pseudocode* is a mixture of Java (or some other programming language) and English (or some other natural language). Pseudocode is used to express algorithms so that you are not distracted by details about Java syntax.

- One good method for specifying what a method is supposed to do is to provide a *precondition* and *postcondition* for the method. These form a contract between the programmer who uses the method and the program-mer who writes the method.

- *Time analysis* is an analysis of how many operations an algorithm requires. Often, it is sufficient to express a time analysis in big-*O* notation, which is the *order* of an algorithm. The order analysis is often enough to compare algorithms and estimate how running time is affected by chang-ing input size.

- Three important examples of big-*O* analyses are *linear* (i.e., $O(n)$), *quadratic* (i.e., $O(n^2)$), and *logarithmic* (i.e., $O(\log n)$).

- An important testing technique is to identify and test *boundary values*. These are values that lie on a boundary between different kinds of behav-ior for your program.

- A second important testing technique is to ensure that your test cases are *fully exercising* the code. A software tool called a *profiler* can aid in fully exercising code.

- During debugging, you should discover exactly why a test case is failing and limit your changes to corrections of known errors. Once you have cor-rected a known error, all test cases should be rerun. Use a software tool called a *debugger* to help track down exactly why an error occurs.

Solutions to Self-Test Exercises

1. The method returns 7 on July 22, 2003. On both July 30, 2003 and February 1, 2004 the method returns 0 (since July 29, 2003 has already passed).

2. Yes. In order to use a method, all you need to know is the specification.

3. ```
System.out.print("$");
printNumber(boodle, 12, 2);
```

4. **printSqrt**
    ```
    public static void
    printSqrt(double x)
    ```
    Prints the square root of a number.
    **Parameters:**
        x – any non-negative double number
    **Precondition:**
        x >= 0.
    **Postcondition:**
        The positive square root of x has been printed to standard output.
    **Throws:** `IllegalArgumentException`
        Indicates that x is negative.
    ```

5. **sphereVolume**
   ```
   public static double
   sphereVolume(double radius)
   ```
   Computes the volume of a sphere.
   Parameters:
   radius– any non-negative double number
   Precondition:
   radius >= 0.
   Returns:
   the volume of a sphere with the specified radius
   Throws: IllegalArgumentException
   Indicates that radius is negative.

6. ```
   if (x < 0)
      throw new IllegalArgumentException
      ("x is negative: " + x);
   ```

7. A final variable is given an initial value when it is declared, and this value will never change while the program is running.

8. Most of the specification was automatically produced using the Javadoc tool described in Appendix H.

9. Part d is linear (i.e., $O(n)$); part f is logarithmic (i.e., $O(\log n)$); all of the others are quadratic (i.e., $O(n^2)$).

10. Here is a specification for the method, along with an implementation:
    sum
    ```
    public static int sum(int[ ] a)
    ```
    Computes the sum of the numbers in an array.
    Parameters:
    a – an array whose numbers are to be summed
    Returns:
    the sum of the numbers in the array (which is zero if the array has no elements)

```
public static int sum(int[ ] a)
{
  int answer, i;

  answer = 0;
  for (i = 0; i < a.length; i++)
     answer += a[i];
  return answer;
}
```

Our solution uses answer += i, which causes the current value of i to be added to what's already in answer.

For a time analysis, let *n* be the array size. There are two assignment operations (i = 0 and answer = 0). The < test is executed *n* + 1 times (the first *n* times it is true, and the final time, with i equal to *n*, it is false). The ++ and += operations are each executed *n* times, and an array subscript (a[i]) is taken *n* times. The entire code is $O(n)$.

11. As always, 0, 1, and –1 are boundary values. In this problem, –20 (smallest value) and 20 (largest value) are also boundary values. Also 9 and 10 (since the number changes from a single digit to two digits) and –9 and –10. (By the way, this particular problem is small enough that it would be reasonable to test *all* legal inputs, rather than just testing the boundary values.)

12. You should include an empty line (with no characters before the carriage return) and lines with 0, 1, 2, 3 A's. Also include a line with 4 A's (the smallest case with more than three) and a line with more than 4 A's. For the lines with 1 or more A's, include lines that have only the A's, and also include lines that have A's together with other characters. Also test the case where all the A's appear at the front or the back of the line.

13. See the box "Fully Exercising Code" on page 30.
```

Abstract Data Types and Java Classes

*The happiest way to deal with a man is never to tell him
anything he does not need to know.*

ROBERT A. HEINLEIN
Time Enough for Love

Object-oriented programming (**OOP**) is an approach to programming where data occurs in tidy packages called *objects*. Manipulation of an object happens with functions called *methods,* which are part and parcel of their objects. The Java mechanism to create objects and methods is called a **class**. In fact, the keyword class at the start of each Java application program indicates that the program is itself a class with its own methods to carry out tasks.

This chapter moves you beyond small Java application programs. Your goal is to be able to write general purpose classes that can be used by many different programs. Each general purpose class will capture a certain functionality, and an application programmer can look through the available classes to select those that are useful for the job at hand.

For example, consider a programmer who is writing an application to simulate a Martian lander as it goes from orbit to the surface of Mars. This programmer could use classes to simulate the various mechanical components of the lander—the throttle that controls fuel flow, the rocket engine, and so on. If such classes are readily available in a package of "mechanical component classes," then the programmer could select and use the appropriate classes. Typically, one programming team designs and implements such classes, and other programmers use the classes. The programmers who use the classes must be provided with a *specification* of how the classes work, but they need no knowledge of how the classes are *implemented*.

The separation of specification from implementation is an example of *information hiding*, which was presented as a cornerstone of program design in Chapter 1. Such a strong emphasis on information hiding is partly motivated by mathematical research about how programmers can improve their reasoning about data types that are used in programs. These mathematical data types are called **abstract data types,** or ADTs—and therefore, programmers sometimes use the term **ADT** to refer to a class that is presented to other programmers with information hiding. This chapter presents two examples of such classes. The examples illustrate the features of Java classes, with emphasis on information hiding. By the end of the chapter you will be able to implement your own classes in Java. Other programmers could *use* one of your classes without knowing the details of *how* you implemented the class.

ADTs emphasize the specification rather than the implementation

2.1   CLASSES AND THEIR MEMBERS

A class is a new kind of data type. Each of your classes includes various *data*, such as integers, characters, and so on. In addition, a class has the ability to include two other items: *constructors* and *methods*. Constructors are designed to provide initial values to the class's data; methods are designed to manipulate the data. Taken together, the data, constructors, and methods of a class are called the class **members**.

But this abstract discussion does not really tell you what a class *is*. We need some examples. As you read the first example, concentrate on learning the techniques for implementing a class. Also notice how you use a class written by another programmer, without knowing details of the class's implementation.

PROGRAMMING EXAMPLE: **The Throttle Class**

Our first example of a class is a new data type to store and manipulate the status of a mechanical throttle. An object of this new class holds information about a throttle, as shown in the picture. The throttle is a lever that can be moved to control fuel flow. The throttle we have in mind has a single shutoff point (where there is no fuel flow) and a sequence of several on positions where the fuel is flowing at progressively higher rates. At the topmost position, the fuel flow is fully on. At intermediate positions, the fuel flow is proportional to the location of the lever. For example, with six possible positions, and the lever in the fourth position, the fuel flows at $\frac{4}{6}$ of its maximum rate.

A constructor is designed to provide initial values to a class's data. The throttle constructor permits a program to create a new throttle with a specified number of "on positions" above the shutoff position. For instance, a throttle for a lawn mower could specify six positions, whereas a throttle for a Martian lander could specify 1000 positions. The throttle's lever is initially placed in the shutoff position.

Once a throttle has been initialized, there two methods to shift the throttle's lever: One of the methods shifts the lever by a given amount, and the other method returns the lever to the shutoff position. We also have two methods to examine the status of a throttle. The first of these methods returns the amount of fuel currently flowing, expressed as a proportion of the maximum flow. For example, this method will return approximately 0.667 when a six-position throttle is in its fourth position. The other method returns a true-or-false value, telling whether the throttle is currently on (that is, whether the lever is above the shutoff position). Thus, the throttle has one constructor and four methods listed here:

- A constructor to create a new throttle with one shutoff position and a specified number of on positions (the lever starts in the shutoff position)

- A method that returns the fuel flow, expressed as a proportion of the maximum flow

- A method to tell us whether the throttle is currently on

- A method to shift a throttle's lever by a given amount

- A method to set the throttle's lever back to the shutoff position

one throttle constructor and four throttle methods

Defining a New Class

We're ready to define a new Java class called `Throttle`. The new class includes data (to store information about the throttle) plus the constructor and methods listed above. Once the `Throttle` class is defined, a programmer can create objects of type `Throttle` and manipulate those objects with the methods.

Here's an outline of the `Throttle` class definition:

```
public class Throttle
{
    private int top;       // The topmost position of the lever
    private int position;  // The current position of the lever
```

declaring the Throttle class

This part of the class definition provides the implementations of the constructor and methods.

```
}
```

This class definition defines a new data type called `Throttle`. The definition starts with the **class head,** which consists of the Java keywords `public class`, followed by the name of the new class. The keyword `public` is necessary before the `class` because we want to allow all other programmers (the "public") to use the new class. The name of the class may be any legal identifier. We chose the name `Throttle`. We always use a capital letter for the first character of names of new classes—this isn't required by Java, but it's a common programming style, making it easy to identify class names.

three varieties of class members appear in the class definition

The rest of the class definition, between the two brackets, lists all the components of the class. These components are called **members** of the class and they come in three varieties: instance variables, constructors, and methods.

Instance Variables

The first kind of member is a variable declaration. These variables are called **instance variables** (or sometimes "member variables"). The `Throttle` has two instance variables:

```
private int top;       // The topmost position of the lever
private int position;  // The current position of the lever
```

Each instance variable stores some piece of information about the status of an object. For example, consider a throttle with six possible positions and the lever in the fourth position. This throttle would have `top=6` and `position=4`.

The keyword `private` occurs in front of each of our instance variables. This keyword means that programmers who use the new class have no way to read or assign values directly to the private instance variables. It is possible to have public instance variables that can be accessed directly, but public instance variables tend to reveal too much information about how a class is implemented, violating the principle of information hiding. Therefore, our examples will use private instance variables. All access to private instance variables is carried out through the constructors and methods that are provided with the class.

Constructors

The second kind of member is a constructor. A constructor is a method that is responsible for initializing the instance variables. For example, our constructor creates a throttle with a specified number of on positions above the shutoff position. This constructor sets the instance variable `top` to a specified number, and sets `position` to zero (so that the throttle is initially shut off).

For the most part, implementing a constructor is no different than your past work (such as implementing a method for a Java application). The primary difference is that a constructor has access to the class's instance variables, and is responsible for initializing these variables. Thus, a throttle constructor must provide initial values to `top` and `position`. Before you implement the throttle constructor, you must know the several rules that make constructors special:

- Before any constructor begins its work, all instance variables are assigned Java "default values." For example, the Java default value for any number variable is zero.

- If an instance variable has an initialization value with its declaration, the initialization value replaces the default value. For example, suppose we have this instance variable:

    ```
    int jackie = 42;
    ```

    The instance variable `jackie` is first given its default value of zero; then the zero is replaced by the initialization value of 42.

- The name of a constructor must be the same as the name of the class. In our example, the name of the constructor is `Throttle`. This seems strange: Normally we *avoid* using the same name for two different things. But it is a requirement of Java that the constructor use the same name as the class.

- A constructor is not really a method, and therefore it does not have *any* return value. Because of this, you must *not* write `void` (or any other return type) at the front of the constructor's head. The compiler knows that every constructor has no return value, but a compiler error occurs if you actually write `void` at the front of the constructor's head.

With these rules, we can write the throttle's constructor as shown here (with its specification following the format from Section 1.1):

- **Constructor for the Throttle**
    ```
    public Throttle(int size)
    ```
    Construct a `Throttle` with a specified number of on positions.
    Parameters:
    　`size` – the number of on positions for this new `Throttle`
    Precondition:
    　`size > 0`.
    Postcondition:
    　This `Throttle` has been initialized with the specified number of on positions above the shutoff position, and it is currently shut off.
    Throws: `IllegalArgumentException`
    　Indicates that `size` is not positive.

```
public Throttle(int size)
{
    if (size <= 0)
        throw new IllegalArgumentException("Size <= 0: " + size);
    top = size;
    // No assignment needed for position -- it gets the default value of zero.
}
```

This constructor sets `top` according to the parameter, `size`. It does not explicitly set `position`, but the comment in the implementation indicates that we did not just forget about `position`—the default value of zero is its correct initial value. The implementation is preceded by the keyword `public` to make it available to all programmers.

a class may have many different constructors

The throttle has just one constructor, just one way of setting the initial values of the instance variables. Some classes may have many different constructors that set initial values in different ways. If there are several constructors, then each constructor must have a distinct sequence of parameters to distinguish it from the other constructors.

No-Arguments Constructors

Some classes have a constructor with no parameters, called a **no-arguments** constructor. In effect, a no-arguments constructor does not need any extra information to set the initial values of the instance variables.

If you write a class with no constructors at all, then Java automatically provides a no-arguments constructor that initializes each instance variable to its initialization value (if there is one) or to its default value (if there is no specified initialization value). There is one situation where Java does not provide an automatic no-arguments constructor, and you'll see this situation when you write subclasses in Chapter 13.

Methods

The third kind of class member is a method. A method does computations that access the class's instance variables. Classes tend to have two kinds of methods:

1. Accessor methods.   An **accessor method** gives information about an object without altering the object. In the case of the throttle, an accessor method can return information about the status of a throttle, but it must not change the position of the lever.

2. Modification methods.   A **modification method** may change the status of an object. For a throttle, a modification method may shift the lever up or down.

Each class method is designed for a specific manipulation of an object—in our case, the manipulation of a throttle. To carry out the manipulations, each of the throttle methods has access to the throttle's instance variables, `top` and `position`. The methods can examine `top` and `position` to determine the current status of the throttle, or `top` and `position` can be changed in order to alter the status of the throttle. Let's look at the details of the implementations of the throttle methods, beginning with the accessor methods.

Accessor Methods

Accessor methods provide information about an object without changing the object. Accessor methods are often short, just returning the value of an instance variable or performing a computation with a couple of instance variables. The first of the throttle accessor methods computes the current flow as a proportion of the maximum flow. The specification and implementation are shown here:

- **getFlow**

    ```
    public double getFlow( )
    ```
    Get the current flow of this `Throttle`.

    Returns:
    > the current flow rate (always in the range [0.0 ... 1.0]) as a proportion of the maximum flow

```
public double getFlow( )
{
    return (double) position / (double) top;
}
```

Accessor methods often have no parameters, no precondition, and only a simple return condition in the specification. How does an accessor method manage with no parameters? It needs no parameters because all of the necessary information is available in the instance variables.

accessor methods often have no parameters

Pitfall: Integer Division Throws Away the Fractional Part

PITFALL

The `getFlow` implementation computes and returns a fractional value. For example, if position is 4 and top is 6, then `getFlow` returns approximately 0.667. In order to get a fractional result in the answer, the integer numbers `position` and `top` cannot simply be divided with the expression `position/top`, since this would result in an integer division ($\frac{4}{6}$ results in the quotient 0, discarding any remainder). Instead, we must force Java to compute a fractional division by changing the integer values to double values. For example, expression `(double) position` is a "cast" that changes the integer value of position to a double value to use in the division.

The throttle's second accessor method returns a true-or-false value indicating whether the fuel flow is on. Here is this method with its specification:

- **isOn**

    ```
    public boolean isOn( )
    ```
    Check whether this `Throttle` is on.

    Returns:
    > If this `Throttle`'s flow is above zero, then the return value is `true`; otherwise the return value is `false`.

```
public boolean isOn( )
{
    return (position > 0);
}
```

Programming Tip: **Use the Boolean Type for True-or-False Values**

△ TIP

Java's basic boolean type may be relatively unfamiliar. You should use the boolean type for any true-or-false value such as the return value of the isOn method. The return statement for a boolean method can be any boolean expression, for example a comparison such as (position > 0). In this example, if position is greater than zero, then the comparison is true, and isOn returns true. On the other hand, if position is equal to zero, then the comparison is false, and isOn returns false.

By the way, the name "boolean" is derived from the name of George Boole, a 19th-century mathematician who developed the foundations of a formal calculus of logical values. Boole was a self-educated scholar with limited formal training. He began his teaching career at the age of 16 as an elementary school teacher and eventually took a position as professor at Queen's College in Cork. As a dedicated teacher, he died at the age of only 49—the result of pneumonia brought on by a two-mile trek through the rain to lecture to his students.

Modification Methods

There are two more throttle methods. These two are **modification methods**, which means that they are capable of changing the values of the instance variables. Here is the first modification method:

- **shutOff**
  ```
  public void shutOff( )
  ```
  Turn off this Throttle.

  Postcondition:
  This Throttle's flow has been shut off.

```
public void shutOff( )
{
    position = 0;
}
```

modification methods are usually void

Modification methods are usually void, meaning that there is no return value. In the specification of a modification method, the method's work is fully described in the postcondition.

The throttle's shutOff method has no parameters—it doesn't need parameters because it just moves the throttle's position down to zero, shutting off the flow. However, most modification methods do have parameters, such as a throttle method to shift the throttle's lever by a specified amount. This shift method has one integer parameter called amount. If amount is positive, then the throttle's lever is moved up by that amount (but never beyond the topmost position). A negative amount causes the lever to move down (but never below zero). The specification and implementation appear at the top of the next page.

♦ **shift**

```
public void shift(int amount)
```
Move this Throttle's position up or down.

Parameters:

amount – the amount to move the position up or down (a positive amount moves the position up, a negative amount moves it down)

Postcondition:

This Throttle's position has been moved by the specified amount. If the result is more than the topmost position, then the position stays at the topmost position. If the result is less than the zero position, then the position stays at the zero position.

```
public void shift(int amount)
{
    if (amount > top - position)
        // Adding amount would put the position above the top.
        position = top;
    else if (position + amount < 0)
        // Adding amount would put the position below zero.
        position = 0;
    else
        // Adding amount puts position in the range [0...top].
        position += amount;
}
```

This might be the first time you've seen the += operator. Its effect is to take the value on the right side (such as amount) and add it to what's already in the variable on the left (such as position). This sum is then stored back in the variable on the left side of +=.

The shift method requires care to ensure that the position does not go above the topmost position nor below zero. For example, the first test in the method checks whether (amount > top - position). If so, then adding amount to position would push the position over top. In this case, we simply set position to top.

It is tempting to write the test (amount > top - position) in a slightly different way, like this:

```
if (position + amount > top)
    // Adding amount would put the position above the top.
    position = top;
```

This seems okay at first glance, but there is a potential problem: What happens if both position and amount are large integers such as 2,000,000,000? The subexpression position + amount should be 4,000,000,000, but Java tries to temporarily store the subexpression as a Java integer, which is limited to the range −2,147,483,648 to 2,147,483,647. The result is an **arithmetic overflow**, which is defined as trying to compute or store a number that is beyond the legal range of the data type. When an arithmetic overflow occurs, the program might stop with an error message or it might continue computing with wrong data.

We avoided the arithmetic overflow by rearranging the first test to avoid the troublesome subexpression. The test we use is:

```
if (amount > top - position)
    // Adding amount would put the position above the top.
    position = top;
```

This test uses the subexpression `top - position`. Since `top` is never negative, and `position` is in the range [0...top], the subexpression `top - position` is always a valid integer in the range [0...top].

What about the second test in the method? In the second test, we use the subexpression `position + amount`, but at this point, `position + amount` can no longer cause an arithmetic overflow. Do you see why? If `position + amount` is bigger than `top`, then the first test would have been `true` and the second test is never reached. Therefore, by the time we reach the second test, the subexpression `position + amount` is guaranteed to be in the range [amount...top], and arithmetic overflow cannot occur.

PITFALL

Pitfall: Potential Arithmetic Overflows

Check all arithmetic expressions for potential arithmetic overflow. The limitations for Java variables and subexpressions are given in Appendix A. Often you can rewrite an expression to avoid overflow, or you can use `long` variables (with a range from –9,223,372,036,854,775,808 to 9,223,372,036,854,775,807). If overflow cannot be avoided altogether, then include a note in the documentation to describe the situation that causes overflow.

---

the name of the java file must match the name of the class

We have completed the `Throttle` class implementation and can now put the complete definition in a file called `Throttle.java`, as shown in Figure 2.1. The name of the file must be `Throttle.java` since the class is `Throttle`.

| **FIGURE 2.1** | Specification and Implementation for the `Throttle` Class |

Class Throttle

❖ **public class Throttle**
    A `Throttle` object simulates a throttle that is controlling fuel flow.

(continued)

(FIGURE 2.1 continued)

Specification

- **Constructor for the Throttle**
    ```
    public Throttle(int size)
    ```
    Construct a `Throttle` with a specified number of on positions.
    Parameters:
    `size` – the number of on positions for this new `Throttle`
    Precondition:
    `size > 0`.
    Postcondition:
    This `Throttle` has been initialized with the specified number of on positions above the shutoff position, and it is currently shut off.
    Throws: `IllegalArgumentException`
    Indicates that `size` is not positive.

- **getFlow**
    ```
    public double getFlow( )
    ```
    Get the current flow of this `Throttle`.
    Returns:
    the current flow rate (always in the range [0.0 ... 1.0]) as a proportion of the maximum flow

- **isOn**
    ```
    public boolean isOn( )
    ```
    Check whether this `Throttle` is on.
    Returns:
    If this `Throttle`'s flow is above zero, then the return value is `true`; otherwise the return value is `false`.

- **shift**
    ```
    public void shift(int amount)
    ```
    Move this `Throttle`'s position up or down.
    Parameters:
    `amount` – the amount to move the position up or down (a positive amount moves the position up, a negative amount moves it down)
    Postcondition:
    This `Throttle`'s position has been moved by the specified amount. If the result is more than the topmost position, then the position stays at the topmost position. If the result is less than the zero position, then the position stays at the zero position.

- **shutOff**
    ```
    public void shutOff( )
    ```
    Turn off this `Throttle`.
    Postcondition:
    This Throttle has been shut off.

(continued)

(FIGURE 2.1 continued)

Implementation

```java
// File: Throttle.java

public class Throttle
{
    private int top;        // The topmost position of the throttle
    private int position;   // The current position of the throttle

    public Throttle(int size)
    {
        if (size <= 0)
            throw new IllegalArgumentException("Size <= 0: " + size);
        top = size;
        // No assignment needed for position -- it gets the default value of zero.
    }

    public double getFlow( )
    {
        return (double) position / (double) top;
    }

    public boolean isOn( )
    {
        return (getFlow( ) > 0);
    }

    public void shift(int amount)
    {
        if (amount > top - position)
            // Adding amount would put the position above the top.
            position = top;
        else if (position + amount < 0)
            // Adding amount would put the position below zero.
            position = 0;
        else
            // Adding amount puts position in the range [0...top].
            position += amount;
    }

    public void shutOff( )
    {
        position = 0;
    }

}
```

Methods May Activate Other Methods

The throttle's isOn method in Figure 2.1 has one change from the original implementation. The change is highlighted here:

```
public boolean isOn( )
{
    return (getFlow( ) > 0);
}
```

In this implementation, we have checked whether the flow is on by calling the getFlow method rather than looking directly at the position instance variable. Both implementations work: Using position directly probably executes quicker, but you could argue that using getFlow makes the method's intent clearer. Anyway, the real purpose of this change is just to illustrate that one method can call another to carry out a subtask. In this example, the isOn method calls getFlow. An OOP programmer usually would use slightly different terminology, saying that the isOn method **activated** the flow method. **Activating a method** is nothing more than OOP jargon for "calling a method."

Programming Tip: Private Versus Public

TIP

Our Throttle class follows a common pattern: The data about a throttle is stored in private instance variables, indicated by the keyword private before each declaration of an instance variable. A throttle is manipulated through public methods, indicated by the keyword public before each implementation of a method.

The pattern of "private data, public methods" is a good idea. It forbids other programmers from using our instance variables in unintended ways. Later you will see examples that include private methods (i.e., methods that can be activated within other methods of the class, but may not be used by other programmers). For now, though, the common pattern will serve you well.

Self-Test Exercises

1. Name and describe the three kinds of class members we have used. In this section, which kinds of members were public and which were private?

2. Write a new throttle constructor with no arguments. The constructor sets the top position to 1 and sets the current position off.

3. Write another throttle constructor with two arguments: the total number of positions for the throttle, and its initial position.

4. Add a new throttle method that will return true if the current flow is more than half. The body of your implementation should activate get-Flow.

5. Design and implement a class called Clock. A Clock object holds one instance of a time value such as 9:48 P.M. Have at least these public methods:

- A no-arguments constructor that initializes the time to midnight—see page 40 for the discussion of a no-arguments constructor

- A method to explicitly assign a given time—you will have to give some thought to appropriate arguments for this method

- Methods to retrieve information: the current hour, the current minute, and a boolean method to determine whether the time is at or before noon

- A method to advance the time forward by a given number of minutes (which could be negative to move the clock backward or positive to move the clock forward)

2.2   USING A CLASS

programs can create new objects of a class

How do you use a new class such as Throttle? Within any program, you may create new throttles, and refer to these throttles by names that you define. We can illustrate the general syntax for creating and using these objects by an example.

Creating and Using Objects

Suppose a program needs a new throttle with 100 positions above the shutoff. Within the program, we want to refer to the throttle by the name control. The Java syntax has these parts:

```
Throttle control = new Throttle(100);
```

The first part of this statement—Throttle control—declares a new variable called control. The control variable is capable of refering to a throttle. The second part of the statement—new Throttle(100)—creates a new throttle and initializes control to refer to this new throttle. A new throttle that is created in this way is called a Throttle **object**.

There are a few points to notice about the syntax for creating a new Throttle object: new is a keyword to create a new object; Throttle is the data type of the new object; and (100) is the list of parameters for the constructor of the new object. So, we are creating a new throttle and 100 is the argument for the constructor, so the new throttle will have 100 positions above the shutoff.

Once the throttle is created, we can refer to the throttle by the name that we selected: `control`. For example, suppose we want to shift the lever up to its third notch. We do this by calling the `shift` method, as shown here:

```
control.shift(3);
```

Calling a method always involves these four pieces:

1. Start with a reference to the object that you are manipulating. In this example, we want to manipulate `control`, so we begin with "`control`". Remember that you cannot just call a method—you must always indicate which object is being manipulated.

2. Next, place a single period.

3. Next, write the name of the method. In our example, we call the `shift` method, so we write "`control.shift`"—which you can pronounce "control *dot* shift."

4. Finally, list the parameters for the method call. In our example, `shift` requires one parameter, which is the amount (3) that we are shifting the throttle. Thus, the entire statement is `control.shift(3);`

how to use a method

Our example called the `shift` method. As you've seen before, OOP programmers like their own terminology and they would say that we **activated** the `shift` method. In the rest of the text, we'll try to use "activate" rather than "call." (This will keep us on the good side of OOP programmers.)

As another example, here is a sequence of several statements to set a throttle to a certain point, and then print the throttle's flow:

```
final int SIZE = 8;   // The size of the Throttle
final int SPOT = 3;   // Where to move the Throttle's lever

Throttle small = new Throttle(SIZE);

small.shift(SPOT);
System.out.print("My small throttle is now at position ");
System.out.println(SPOT + " out of " + SIZE + ".");
System.out.println("The flow is now: " + small.getFlow( ));
```

Notice how the return value of `small.getFlow` is used directly in the output statement. As with any other method, the return value of an accessor method can be used as part of an output statement or other expression. The output from this code is:

```
My small throttle is now at position 3 out of 8.
The flow is now: 0.375
```

A Program with Several Throttle Objects

A single program may have many throttle objects. For example, this code will declare two throttle objects, shifting each throttle to a different point:

```
Throttle tiny = new Throttle(4);
Throttle huge = new Throttle(10000);

tiny.shift(2);
huge.shift(2500);
```

Here's an important concept to keep in mind:

> When a program has several objects of the same type, each object has its own copies of the instance variables.

In the example above, `tiny` has its own instance variables (`top` will be 4 and `position` will be 2); `huge` also has its own instance variables (`top` will be 10000 and `position` will be 2500). When we activate a method such as `tiny.shift`, the method uses the instance variables from `tiny`; when we activate `huge.shift`, the method uses the instance variables from `huge`.

The variables in our examples—`control`, `small`, `tiny`, `huge`—are called **reference variables** because they are used to *refer* to objects (in our case, throttles). There are several differences between a reference variable (used by Java for all classes) and an ordinary variable (used by Java for the primitive data types of `int`, `char`, and so on). Let's look at these differences, beginning with a special value called `null` that is used only with reference variables.

Null References

The creation of a new object can be separated from the declaration of a variable. For example, the following two statements can occur far apart in a program:

```
Throttle control;
...
control = new Throttle(100);
```

Once both statements finish, `control` refers to a newly created throttle with 100 positions. But what is the status of `control` between the statements? At this point, `control` does not yet refer to any throttle, because we haven't yet created a throttle. In this situation, we can assign a special value to control, indicating that control does not yet refer to anything. The value is called the **null reference**, written with the keyword `null` in Java. So we could change the above example to this:

```
Throttle control = null;
...                          ← In this area, control
control = new Throttle(100);    does not refer to
                                anything.
```

Null Reference

Sometimes a reference variable does not refer to anything. This is a **null reference**, and the value of the variable is called **null**.

Sometimes a program finishes using an object. In this case, the program may explicitly set a reference variable to null, as shown here:

```
Throttle control = new Throttle(100);

// Various statements that use the Throttle appear next...
...

// Now we are done with the control Throttle, so we can set
// the reference to null.
control = null;
```

Once a reference variable is no longer needed, it's a good idea to set it to null, allowing Java to economize on certain resources (such as the memory used by a throttle).

Pitfall: Null Pointer Exception

PITFALL

When a variable such as control becomes null, it no longer refers to any throttle. If control is null, then it is a programming error to activate a method such as control.shift. The result is an exception called NullPointer-Exception.

Assignment Statements with Reference Variables

The usual assignment statement may be used with reference variables. For example, we might have two Throttle variables t1 and t2, and an assignment such as t2 = t1 is permitted. But what is the effect of the assignment? For starters, if t1 is null, then the assignment t2 = t1 also makes t2 null. Here is a more complicated case where t1 is not null:

```
Throttle t1;
Throttle t2;

t1 = new Throttle(100);
t1.shift(25);
t2 = t1;
```

The effect of the assignment t2 = t1 is somewhat different than assignments for integers or other primitive data types. The effect of t2 = t1 is to "make t2 refer to the same object that t1 is already refering to." In other words, we have two reference variables (t1 and t2), but we created only one throttle (with one new statement). This one throttle has 100 positions, and is currently in the 25th position. After the assignment statement, both t1 and t2 refer to this one throttle.

As an example, let's start with the two declarations:

```
Throttle t1;
Throttle t2;
```

We now have two variables, t1 and t2. If these variables are declared in a method, then they don't yet have an initial value (not even null). We can draw this situation with a question mark for each value, as shown here:

The next two statements are:

```
t1 = new Throttle(100);
t1.shift(25);
```

These statements create a new throttle for t1 to refer to, and shift the throttle's position to 25. We will draw a separate box for the throttle and indicate its instance variables (top at 100 and position at 25). To show that t1 refers to this throttle, we draw an arrow from the t1 box to the throttle, like this:

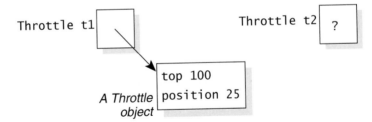

At this point, we can execute the assignment:

```
t2 = t1;
```

After the assignment, t2 will refer to the same object that t1 refers to, as shown here:

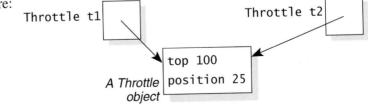

There are now two references to the same throttle, which can cause some surprising results. For example, suppose we shift t2 down five notches and then print the flow of t1, like this:

```
t2.shift(-5);
System.out.println("Flow of t1 is: " + t1.getFlow( ));
```

What flow rate is printed? The t1 throttle was set to position 25 out of 100, and we never directly altered its position. But t2.shift(-5) moves the throttle's position down to 20. Since t1 refers to this same throttle, t1.getFlow now returns 20/100, and the output statement prints "Flow of t1 is: 0.2". Here's the entire code that we executed and the final situation drawn as a picture:

```
Throttle t1;
Throttle t2;

t1 = new Throttle(100);
t1.shift(25);
t2 = t1;
t2.shift(-5);
```

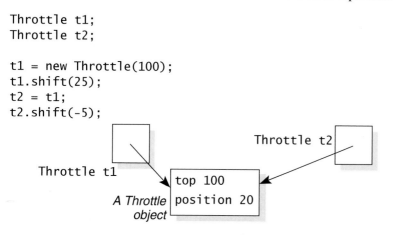

Throttle t2

Throttle t1

A Throttle object | top 100 / position 20

Assignment Statements with Reference Variables

If t1 and t2 are reference variables, then the assignment t2 = t1 is allowed.

If t1 is null, then the assignment also makes t2 null.

If t1 is not null, then the assignment changes t2 so that it refers to the same object that t1 already refers to. At this point, changes can be made to that one object through either t1 or t2.

The situation of an assignment statement contrasts with a program that actually creates two separate throttles for t1 and t2. For example, two separate throttles can be created with each throttle in the 25th position out of 100, as shown in the code at the top of the next page.

```
Throttle t1;
Throttle t2;

t1 = new Throttle(100);
t1.shift(25);
t2 = new Throttle(100);
t2.shift(25);
```

With this code, we have two separate throttles:

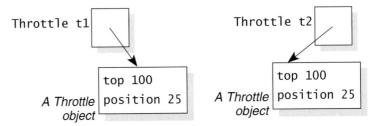

Changes that are now made to one throttle will not effect the other, because there are two completely separate throttles.

Clones

A programmer sometimes needs to make an exact copy of an existing object. The copy must be just like the existing object, but separate. Subsequent changes to the copy should not alter the original, nor should subsequent changes to the original alter the copy. A separate copy such as this is called a **clone**.

An assignment operation `t2 = t1` does not create a clone, and in fact the `Throttle` class does not permit the easy creation of clones. But many other classes have a special method called `clone` for just this purpose. Writing a useful `clone` method has some requirements that may not be evident just now, so we will postpone a complete discussion until Section 2.4.

Testing for Equality

A test for equality (`t1 == t2`) can be carried out with reference variables. The equality test (`t1 == t2`) is `true` if both `t1` and `t2` are null, or if they both refer to the exact same object (not two different objects that happen to have the same values for their instance variables). An inequality test (`t1 != t2`) can also be carried out. The result of an inequality test is always the opposite of an equality test. Let's look at two examples.

The first example creates just one throttle; t1 and t2 both refer to this throttle as shown in the following picture:

```
Throttle t1;
Throttle t2;

t1 = new Throttle(100);
t1.shift(25);
t2 = t1;
```

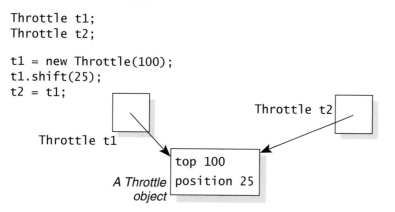

At this point in the computation, (t1 == t2) is true. Both reference variables refer to the same object.

On the other hand, consider this code, which creates two separate throttles:

```
Throttle t1;
Throttle t2;

t1 = new Throttle(100);
t1.shift(25);
t2 = new Throttle(100);
t2.shift(25);
```

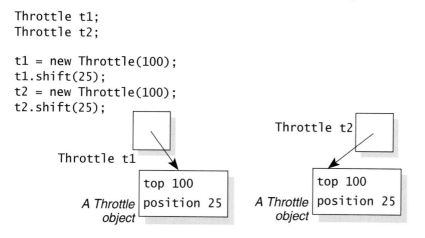

After this computation, (t1 == t2) is false. The two throttles have the same value (with top at 100 and position at 25), but the equality test returns false because they are two separate throttles.

Test for Equality with Reference Variables

For reference variables t1 and t2, the test (t1 == t2) is true if both references are null, or if t1 and t2 refer to the exact same object (not two different objects that happen to have the same values for their instance variables).

Terminology Controversy: "The Throttle That t Refers To"

A declaration such as `Throttle t = new Throttle(42)` declares a reference variable t, and makes it refer to a newly created throttle. We can then talk about "the throttle that t refers to." This is the correct terminology, but sometimes a programmer's thinking is clarified by shortening the terminology and saying things like "the throttle t is on" rather than "the throttle that t refers to is on."

Which is right? In general, use the longer terminology when there may be several different variables referring to the same throttle. Otherwise use the shorter phrase "the throttle t is on," but somewhere, deep in your mind, remember that you are shortening things for convenience and that the longer phrase is right.

Self-Test Exercises

6. Write some Java code that creates a new throttle with six positions, shifts the throttle halfway up (to the third position), and prints the current flow.

7. A method declares a `Throttle` variable called `control`, but there is not yet a throttle. What value should be assigned to `control`?

8. Suppose that `control` is a null reference. What happens if a program tries to activate `control.shift`?

9. What is the output of this code:
   ```
   Throttle t1;
   Throttle t2;
   t1 = new Throttle(100);
   t2 = t1;
   t1.shift(40);
   t2.shift(2);
   System.out.println(t1.getFlow( ));
   ```

10. Consider the code from the previous question. At the end of the computation, is (`t1 == t2`) `true` or `false`?

11. Write some code that will make `t1` and `t2` refer to two different throttles with 100 positions each. Both throttles are shifted up to position 42. At the end of your code, is (`t1 == t2`) `true` or `false`?

2.3   PACKAGES

You now know enough to write a Java application program that uses a throttle. The `Throttle` class would be in one file (`Throttle.java` from Figure 2.1 on page 46) and the program that uses the `Throttle` class would be in a separate file. However, there's one more level of organization that will make it easier for other programmers to use your classes. The organization, called a Java **package**, is a group of related classes put together in a way that makes it easy for programs to use the classes.

Declaring a Package

The first step in declaring a package of related classes is to decide on a name for the package. For example, perhaps we are declaring a bunch of Java classes to simulate various real-world devices such as a throttle. A good short name for the package is the `simulations` package. But there's a problem with good short names: Other programmers might decide to use the same good short name for their packages, resulting in the same name for two different packages.

The solution is to include your Internet domain name as part of the package name. For example, at the University of Colorado the Internet domain name is `colorado.edu` (my e-mail address is `main@colorado.edu`). Therefore, instead of using the package name `simulations`, I will use the longer package name `edu.colorado.simulations` (package names may include a "dot" as part of the name). Many programmers follow this convention, using the Internet domain name in reverse. The only likely conflicts are with other programmers at your own Internet domain, and those conflicts can be prevented by internal cooperation. *use your Internet domain name*

Once you have decided on a package name, a *package declaration* must be made at the top of each source file of the package. The **package declaration** consists of the keyword `package` followed by the full package name and a semicolon. The declaration appears at the start of each source file, before any class declarations. For example, the start of `Throttle.java` is changed to include the package declaration shown here:

```
package edu.colorado.simulations;
```

The revised `Throttle.java`, with a package declaration, is shown in Figure 2.2. Some Java development environments require you to create a directory structure for your classes to match the structure of package names. For example, suppose that you are doing your code development in your own directory called `classes`, and you want to use the `edu.colorado.simulations` package. Then you would follow these steps:

- Make sure that your Java development environment can find and run any classes in your `classes` directory. The exact method of setting this up varies from one environment to another, but a typical approach is to define a system CLASSPATH variable to include your own `classes` directory.
- Underneath the `classes` directory, create a subdirectory called `edu`.
- Underneath `edu`, create a subdirectory called `colorado`.
- Underneath `colorado`, create a subdirectory called `simulations`.
- All the `.java` and `.classes` files for the package must be placed in the `simulations` subdirectory.

If the `edu.colorado.simulations` package has other classes, then their files are also placed in the `simulations` subdirectory, and the package declaration is placed at the start of each `.java` file.

| FIGURE 2.2 | Defining `Throttle.java` as Part of the `edu.colorado.simulations` Package |

Implementation

```
// File: Throttle.java from the package edu.colorado.simulations
// Documentation is in Figure 2.1 on page 44 or from the Throttle link in
//    http://www.cs.colorado.edu/~main/docs/

package edu.colorado.simulations;          ◄───────  the package
                                                     declaration
public class Throttle
{
    private int top;        // The topmost position of the throttle
    private int position;  // The current position of the throttle

    public Throttle(int size)
    {
        if (size <= 0)
            throw new IllegalArgumentException("Size <= 0: " + size);
        top = size;
        // No assignment needed for position -- it gets the default value of zero.
    }

    public double getFlow( )
    {
        return (double) position / (double) top;
    }

    public boolean isOn( )
    {
        return (getFlow( ) > 0);
    }

    public void shift(int amount)
    {
        if (amount > top - position)
            // Adding amount would put the position above the top.
            position = top;
        else if (position + amount < 0)
            // Adding amount would put the position below zero.
            position = 0;
        else
            // Adding amount puts position in the range [0...top].
            position += amount;
    }
```

(continued)

FIGURE 2.5	Specification and Implementation for the Location Class

Class Location

❖ **public class Location from the package edu.colorado.geometry**
A Location object keeps track of a location on a two-dimensional plane.

Specification

◆ **Constructor for the Location**
```
public Location(double xInitial, double yInitial)
```
Construct a Location with specified coordinates.

Parameters:
xInitial – the initial x coordinate of this Location
yInitial – the initial y coordinate of this Location

Postcondition:
This Location has been initialized at the given coordinates.

◆ **clone**
```
public Object clone( )
```
Generate a copy of this Location.

Returns:
The return value is a copy of this Location. Subsequent changes to the copy will not affect the original, nor vice versa. Note that the return value must be typecast to a Location before it can be used.

◆ **distance**
```
public static double distance(Location p1, Location p2)
```
Compute the distance between two Locations.

Parameters:
p1 – the first Location
p2 – the second Location

Returns:
the distance between p1 and p2

Note:
The answer is Double.POSITIVE_INFINITY if the distance calculation overflows. The answer is Double.NaN if either Location is null.

(continued)

(FIGURE 2.5 continued)

- **equals**

  ```
  public boolean equals(Object obj)
  ```
  Compare this `Location` to another object for equality.

  Parameters:
  `obj` – an object with which this `Location` is compared

  Returns:
  A return value of `true` indicates that `obj` refers to a `Location` object with the same value as this `Location`. Otherwise the return value is `false`.

  Note:
  If `obj` is null or it is not a `Location` object, then the answer is `false`.

- **getX** and **GetY**

  ```
  public double getX( )      –and–      public double getY( )
  ```
  Get the x or y coordinate of this `Location`.

  Returns:
  the x or y coordinate of this `Location`

- **midpoint**

  ```
  public static Location midpoint(Location p1, Location p2)
  ```
  Generates and returns a `Location` halfway between two others.

  Parameters:
  `p1` – the first `Location`
  `p2` – the second `Location`

  Returns:
  a `Location` that is halfway between p1 and p2

  Note:
  The answer is null if either p1 or p2 is null.

- **rotate90**

  ```
  public void rotate90( )
  ```
  Rotate the `Location` 90° in a clockwise direction.

  Postcondition:
  This `Location` has been rotated clockwise 90° around the origin.

- **shift**

  ```
  public void shift(double xAmount, double yAmount)
  ```
  Move this `Location` by given amounts along the x and y axes.

  Postcondition:
  This `Location` has been moved by the given amounts along the two axes.

  Note:
  The shift may cause a coordinate to go above `Double.MAX_VALUE` or below `-Double.MAX_VALUE`. In these cases, subsequent calls of `getX` or `getY` will return `Double.POSITIVE_INFINITY` or `Double.NEGATIVE_INFINITY`.

(continued)

(FIGURE 2.5 continued)

* **toString**
  ```
  public String toString( )
  ```
  Generate a string representation of this Location.
  Returns:
    a string representation of this Location

Implementation

```
// File: Location.java from the package edu.colorado.geometry
// Documentation is available on pages 63-64 or from the Location link in
//    http://www.cs.colorado.edu/~main/docs/

package edu.colorado.geometry;

public class Location implements Cloneable
{
    private double x; // The x coordinate of the Location
    private double y; // The y coordinate of the Location

    public Location(double xInitial, double yInitial)
    {
        x = xInitial;
        y = yInitial;
    }

    public Object clone( )
    {  // Clone a Location object.
        Location answer;

        try
        {
            answer = (Location) super.clone( );
        }
        catch (CloneNotSupportedException e)
        {  // This exception should not occur. But if it does, it would indicate a programming
           // error that made super.clone unavailable. The most common cause would be
           // forgetting the "implements Cloneable" clause at the start of the class.
            throw new RuntimeException
            ("This class does not implement Cloneable.");
        }

        return answer;
    }
```

the meaning of "implements Cloneable" and the clone method are discussed on page 76

(continued)

(FIGURE 2.5 continued)

```java
public static double distance(Location p1, Location p2)
{
    double a, b, c_squared;

    // Check whether one of the Locations is null.
    if ((p1 == null) || (p2 == null))
        return Double.NaN;

    // Calculate differences in x and y coordinates.
    a = p1.x - p2.x;
    b = p1.y - p2.y;

    // Use Pythagorean Theorem to calculate the square of the distance
    // between the Locations.
    c_squared = a*a + b*b;

    return Math.sqrt(c_squared);
}
```

the meaning of a static method is discussed on page 68

the Java constant, double.NaN, is discussed on page 70

```java
public boolean equals(Object obj)
{
    if (obj instanceof Location)
    {
        Location candidate = (Location) obj;
        return (candidate.x == x) && (candidate.y == y);
    }
    else
        return false;
}
```

the equals method is discussed on page 73

```java
public double getX( )
{
    return x;
}
```

```java
public double getY( )
{
    return y
}
```

(continued)

(FIGURE 2.5 continued)

```
public static Location midpoint(Location p1, Location p2)
{
    double xMid, yMid;

    // Check whether one of the Locations is null.
    if ((p1 == null)  ||  (p2 == null))
        return null;

    // Compute the x and y midpoints.
    xMid = (p1.x/2) + (p2.x/2);
    yMid = (p1.y/2) + (p2.y/2);

    // Create a new Location and return it.
    Location answer = new Location(xMid, yMid);
    return answer;
}

public void rotate90( )
{
    double xNew;
    double yNew;

    // For a 90 degree clockwise rotation, the new x is the original y
    // and the new y is -1 times the original x.
    xNew = y;
    yNew = -x;
    x = xNew;
    y = yNew;
}

public void shift(double xAmount, double yAmount)
{
    x += xAmount;
    y += yAmount;
}

public String toString( )
{
    return "(x=" + x + "  y=" + y + ")";
}

}
```

Static Methods

The implementation of the `Location` class has several features that may be new to you. Some of the features are in a method called `distance`, with this specification:

- **distance**

    ```
    public static double distance(Location p1, Location p2)
    ```
    Compute the distance between two `Locations`.

    Parameters:
    p1 – the first `Location`
    p2 – the second `Location`

    Returns:
    the distance between p1 and p2

FIGURE 2.6   The Distance between Locations

The distance between p and s can be computed with the Pythagorean Theorem.

Horizontal distance: $a = 2.7$

Vertical distance: $b = 2.0$

Distance between the locations =

$$\sqrt{a^2 + b^2} = \sqrt{2.7^2 + 2.0^2} = \text{about } 3.36$$

For example, consider the locations p and s in Figure 2.6. Along a straight line, the distance between these two locations is about 3.36. Using the `distance` method, we can create these two locations and print the distance between them as follows:

```
Location p = new Location(-1, 0.8);
Location s = new Location(1.7, -1.2);

double d = Location.distance(p, s);
System.out.println(d);
```

This code prints the distance between the two locations—a little bit more than 3.36.

The `distance` method is modified by an extra keyword: `static`. The `static` keyword means that the method is not activated by any one object. In other words, we do not write `p.distance` or `s.distance`. Instead we write `Location.distance`.

Because the `distance` method is not activated by any one object, the method does not have direct access to the instance variables of a location that activates the method. Within the `distance` implementation, we cannot write simply x or y (the instance variables). Instead, the implementation must carry out its computation based on the arguments that it's given. For example, if we activate `Location.distance(p, s)`, then the `distance` method works with its two arguments p and s. These two arguments are both `Location` objects. Let's examine exactly what happens when an argument is an object rather than a primitive value such as an integer.

Parameters That Are Objects

What happens when `Location.distance(p, s)` is activated? For example, suppose we have the two declarations shown previously for p and s. After these declarations, we have these two separate locations:

Now we can activate the method `Location.distance(p, s)`, which has an implementation that starts like this:

```
public static distance(Location p1, Location p2)
{
    ...
```

The names used within the method (p1 and p2) are usually called **parameters** to distinguish them from the values that are passsed in (p and s). On the other hand, the values that are passed in (p and s) are called the **arguments**. Anyway, the first step of any method activation is to use the *arguments* to provide initial values for the *parameters*. Here's the important fact you need to know about objects:

"parameters"
versus
"arguments"

> When a parameter is an object, such as a `Location`, then the parameter is initialized so that it refers to the same object that the actual argument refers to.

In our example, `Location.distance(p, s)`, the parameters p1 and p2 are initialized to refer to the two locations that we created, like this:

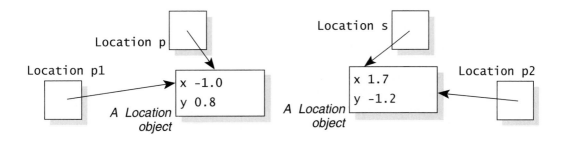

Within the body of the `distance` method we can access `p1` and `p2`. For example, we can access `p1.x` to obtain the `x` coordinate of the first parameter. This kind of access is okay in a static method. The only forbidden expression is a direct `x` or `y` (without a qualifier such as `p1`).

be careful about changing the value of a parameter

Some care is needed in accessing a parameter that is an object. For instance, any change to `p1.x` will affect the actual argument `p.x`. We don't want the `distance` method to make changes to its arguments; it should just compute the distance between the two locations and return the answer. This computation occurs in the implementation of `distance` on page 66.

The implementation also handles a couple of special cases. One special case is when an argument is null. In this case, the corresponding parameter will be initialized as null, and the distance method executes this code:

```
// Check whether one of the Locations is null.
if ((p1 == null)  ||  (p2 == null))
    return Double.NaN;
```

the "not-a-number" constant

If either parameter is null, then the method returns a Java constant named `Double.NaN`. This is a constant that a program uses to indicate that a double value is "not a number."

Another special case for the `distance` method is the possibility of a numerical overflow. The numbers obtained during a computation may go above the largest `double` number or below the smallest `double` number. These numbers are pretty large, but the possibility of overflow still exists. When an arithmetic expression with double numbers goes beyond the legal range, Java assigns a special constant

the "infinity" constant

to the answer. The constant is named `Double.POSITIVE_INFINITY` if it is too large (above about 1.7^{308}), and it is named `Double.NEGATIVE_INFINITY` if it is too small (below about -1.7^{308}). Of course, these constants are not really "infinity." They are merely indications to the programmer that a computation has overflowed. In the distance method, we indicate the possibility of overflow with the following comment:

Note:
The answer is `Double.POSITIVE_INFINITY` if the distance calculation overflows. The answer is `Double.NaN` if either `Location` is null.

The Return Value of a Method May Be an Object

The return value of a method may also be an object, such as a `Location` object. For example, the `Location` class has this static method that creates and returns a new location that is halfway between two other locations. The method's specification and implementation are shown at the top of the next page.

◆ **midpoint**

```
public static Location midpoint(Location p1, Location p2)
```
Generates and returns a Location halfway between two others.

Parameters:

p1 – the first Location

p2 – the second Location

Returns:

a Location that is halfway between p1 and p2

Note:

The answer is null if either Location is null.

```
public static Location midpoint(Location p1, Location p2)
{
    double xMid, yMid;

    // Check whether one of the Locations is null.
    if ((p1 == null) || (p2 == null))
        return null;

    // Compute the x and y midpoints.
    xMid = (p1.x/2) + (p2.x/2);
    yMid = (p1.y/2) + (p2.y/2);

    // Create a new Location and return it.
    Location answer = new Location(xMid, yMid);
    return answer;
}
```

The method creates a new location using the local variable answer, and then returns this location. Often the return value is stored in a local variable such as answer, but not always. For example, we could have eliminated answer by combining the last two statements in our implementation to a single statement:

```
return new Location(xMid, yMid);
```

Either way—with or without the local variable—is fine.

Here's an example to show how the static midpoint method is used. The method creates two locations and then computes their midpoint:

```
Location low = new Location(0, 0);
Location high = new Location(1000, 5280);
Location medium = Location.midpoint(low, high);
```

In this example, the answer from the midpoint method is stored in a variable called medium. After the three statements, we have three locations, drawn at the top of the next page.

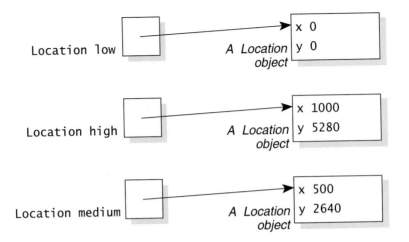

Programming Tip: How to Choose the Names of Methods

Accessor methods: The name of a boolean accessor method will usually begin with "is" followed by an adjective (such as "isOn"). Methods that convert to another kind of data start with "to" (such as "toString"). Other accessor methods start with "get" or some other verb followed by a noun that describes the return value (such as "getFlow").

Modification methods: A modification method can be named by a descriptive verb (such as "shift") or or a short verb phrase (such as "shutOff").

Static methods that return a value: Try to use a noun that describes the return object (such as "distance" or "midpoint").

Rules like these make it easier to determine the purpose of a method.

Java's Object Type

One of the `Location` methods is an accessor method called `equals` with this heading:

```
public boolean equals(Object obj)
```

An accessor method with this name has a special meaning in Java. Before we discuss that meaning, you need to know a bit about the parameter type "Object." In Java, `Object` is a kind of "super data type" that encompasses all data except the eight primitive types. So a primitive variable (`byte`, `short`, `int`, `long`, `char`, `float`, `double`, or `boolean`) is *not* an `Object`, but everything else is. A `String` is an `Object`, a `Location` is an `Object`, even an array is an `Object`.

Using and Implementing an Equals Method

As your programming progresses, you'll learn a lot about Java's Object type, but to start you need just a few common patterns that use Object. For example, many classes implement an equals method with the heading that we have seen. An equals method has one argument: an Object called obj. The method should return true if obj has the same value as the object that activated the method. Otherwise, the method returns false. Here is an example to show how the equals method works for the Location class:

```
Location p = new Location(10, 2); // Declare p at coordinates (10,2)
Location s = new Location(10, 0); // Declare s at coordinates (10,0)
```

After these two declarations, we have two separate locations:

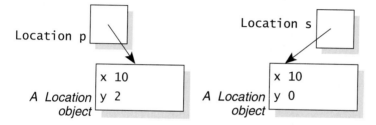

In this example, p and s refer to two separate objects with different values (their y coordinates are different), so both p.equals(s) and s.equals(p) are false.

Here's a slightly different example:

```
Location p = new Location(10, 2); // Declare p at coordinates (10,2)
Location s = new Location(10, 0); // Declare s at coordinates (10,0)
s.shift(0, 2);                    // Move s to (10,2)
```

We have the same two declarations, but afterward we shift the y coordinate of s so that the two separate locations have identical values, like this:

Now p and s refer to identical locations, so both p.equals(s) and s.equals(p) are true. However, the test (p == s) is still false. Remember that (p == s) returns true only if p and s refer to the exact same location (as opposed to two separate locations that happen to contain identical values).

a location can be compared to any object

The argument to the `equals` method can be any object, not just a location. For example, we can try to compare a location with a string, like this:

```
Location p = new Location(10, 2);
System.out.println(p.equals("10, 2"); // Prints false.
```

This example prints `false`; a `Location` object is not equal to the string `"10, 2"` even if they are similar. You can also test to see whether a location is equal to null, like this:

```
Location p = new Location(10, 2);
System.out.println(p.equals(null)); // Prints false.
```

The location is not null, so the result of `p.equals(null)` is `false`. Be careful with the last example: The argument to `p.equals` may be null and the answer will be `false`. However, when p itself is null, it is a programming error to activate any method of p. Trying to activate `p.equals` when p is null results in a `NullPointerException` (see page 51).

implementing an equals method

Now you know how to use an `equals` method. How do you write an `equals` method so that it returns `true` when its argument has the same value as the object that activates the method? A typical implementation follows an outline that is used for the `equals` method of the `Location` class, as shown here:

```
public boolean equals(Object obj)
{
    if ( obj is actually a Location )
    {
            Figure out whether the location that obj refers to has the same
            value as the location that activated this method. Return true if
            they are the same, otherwise return false.
    }
    else
        return false;
}
```

the instanceof operator

The method starts by determining whether `obj` actually refers to a `Location` object. In pseudocode we wrote this as "obj is actually a `Location`". In Java, this is accomplished with the test `(obj instanceof Location)`. This test uses the keyword `instanceof`, which is a boolean operator. On the left of the operator is a variable, such as `obj`. On the right of the operator is a class name, such as `Location`. The test returns `true` if it is valid to convert the object (`obj`) to the given data type (`Location`). In our example, suppose that `obj` does not refer to a valid `Location`. It might be some other type of object, or perhaps it is simply null. In either case, we go to the else-statement and return `false`.

On the other hand, suppose that `(obj instanceof Location)` is `true`, so the code enters the first part of the if-statement. Then `obj` does refer to a `Location` object. We need to determine whether the x and y coordinates of obj are the same as the location that activated the method. Unfortunately, we can't just look at obj.x and obj.y because the compiler thinks of obj as a bare object with no x and y instance variables. The solution is an expression (Location) obj. This expression is called a *typecast*, as if we were pouring obj into a casting mold that creates a Location object. The expression can be used to initialize a Location reference variable, like this:

```
Location candidate = (Location) obj;
```

The **typecast**, on the right side of the declaration, consists of the new data type (Location) in parentheses, followed by the reference variable that is being cast. After this declaration, candidate is a reference variable that refers to the same object that obj refers to. However, the compiler *does* know that candidate refers to a Location object, so we can look at candidate.x and candidate.y to see if they are the same as the x and y coordinates of the object that activated the equals method. The complete implementation looks like this:

```
public boolean equals(Object obj)
{
    if (obj instanceof Location)
    {
        Location candidate = (Location) obj;
        return (candidate.x == x) && (candidate.y == y);
    }
    else
        return false;
}
```

The implementation has the return statement:

```
return (candidate.x == x) && (candidate.y == y);
```

The boolean expression in this return statement is true if candidate.x and candidate.y are the same as the instance variables x and y. As with any method, these instance variables come from the object that activated the method. For future reference, the details of using a typecast are given in Figure 2.7.

Pitfall: Class Cast Exception

Suppose that you have a variable such as obj, which is an Object. You can try a typecast to use the object as if it were another type. For example, we used the typecast Location candidate = (Location) obj.
   What happens if obj doesn't actually refer to a Location object? The result is a runtime exception called ClassCastException. To avoid this, you must ensure that a typecast is valid before trying to execute the cast. For example, the instanceof operator can validate the actual type of an object before a typecast.

PITFALL

FIGURE 2.7 Typecasts

A Simple Pattern for Typecasting an Object

A common situation in Java programming is a variable or other expression that is an `Object`, but the program needs to treat the `Object` as a specific data type such as `Location`. The problem is that when a variable is declared as an `Object`, that variable cannot immediately be used as if it were a `Location` (or some other type). For example, consider the parameter `obj` in the equals method of the `Location` class:

```
public boolean equals(Object obj)
```

Within the implementation of the `equals` method, we need to treat `obj` as a `Location` rather than a mere `Object`. The solution has two parts: (1) Check that `obj` does indeed refer to a valid `Location`, and (2) Declare a new variable of type `Location`, and initialize this new variable to refer to the same object that `obj` refers to, like this:

```
public boolean equals(Object obj)          The parameter, obj, is an Object
{
    if (obj instanceof Location)           Use the instanceof operator to check that
    {                                      obj is a valid Location
        Location candidate = (Location) obj;
        ...                                After this declaration, candidate refers to
                                           the Location object that obj also refers to.
```

The expression `(Location) obj`, used in the declaration of `candidate`, is a typecast to tell the compiler that `obj` may be used as a `Location`.

Every Class Has an Equals Method

You may write a class without an `equals` method, but Java automatically provides an `equals` method anyway. The `equals` method that Java provides is actually taken from the `Object` class, and it works exactly like the `==` operator. In other words, it returns `true` only when the two objects are the exact same object—but it returns `false` for two separate objects that happen to have the same values for their instance variables.

Using and Implementing a Clone Method

Another feature of our `Location` class is a method with this heading:

```
public Object clone( )
```

The purpose of a `clone` method is to create a copy of an object. The copy is separate from the original, so that subsequent changes to the copy won't change the original, nor will subsequent changes to the original change the copy. Here's an example showing how the clone method is used for the Location class:

```
Location p = new Location(10, 2);    // Declare p at (10,2)
Location s = (Location) p.clone( );  // Initialize as a copy of p
```

The expression p.clone( ) activates the clone method for p. The method creates and returns an exact copy of p, which we use to initialize the new location s. After these two declarations, we have two separate locations, as shown in this picture:

As you can see, s and p have the same values for their instance variables, but the two objects are separate. Changes to p will not affect s, nor will changes to s affect p.

Pitfall: A Typecast Is Needed to Use the Clone Return Value

The data type of the return value of the clone method is actually an Object and not a Location. This is a requirement of Java. Because of this requirement, we usually cannot use the clone return value directly. For example, we cannot write a declaration:

```
Location s = p.clone( );  ◄─────── this has a compile-time error
```

Instead, we must apply a typecast to the clone return value, converting it to a Location before we use it to initialize the new variable s, like this:

```
Location s = (Location) p.clone( );
```

Cloning is considerably different than using an assignment statement. For example, consider this code that does not make a clone:

```
Location p = new Location(10, 2); // Declare p at coordinates (10,2)
Location s = p;                   // Declare s and make it refer
                                  // to the same object that p
                                  // refers to
```

PITFALL

After these two declarations, we have just one location, and both variables refer to this location:

This is the situation with an ordinary assignment. Subsequent changes to the object that p refers to will affect the object that s refers to, because there is only one object.

*implementing a
clone method*

You now know how to use a `clone` method. How do you implement such a method? You should follow a three-step pattern outlined here:

1. Modify the class head. You must add the words "`implements Cloneable`" in the class head, as shown here for the `Location` class:

```
public class Location implements Cloneable
```

The modification informs the Java compiler that you plan to implement certain features that are specified elsewhere in a format called an *interface*. The full meaning of interfaces will be discussed in Chapter 5. At the moment, it is enough to know that `implements Cloneable` is necessary when you implement a `clone` method.

By the way, "Cloneable" is a misspelling of "Clonable." Some future version of Java may correct the spelling, but for now it's nice to know that spell checkers haven't completely taken over the world.

2. Use `super.clone` to make a copy. The implementation of a `clone` method should begin by making a copy of the object that activated the method. The best way to make the copy is to follow this pattern from the `Location` class:

```
public Object clone( )
{ // Clone a Location object.
   Location answer;

   try
   {
      answer = (Location) super.clone( );
   }
   catch (CloneNotSupportedException e)
   {
      throw new RuntimeException
      ("This class does not implement Cloneable.");
   }
   ...
```

In an actual implementation, you would use the name of your own class (rather than `Location`), but otherwise you should follow this pattern exactly.

It's useful to know what's happening in this pattern. The pattern starts by declaring a local `Location` variable called `answer`. We then have this block:

```
try
{
    answer = (Location) super.clone( );
}
```

This is an example of a *try block*. If you plan extensive use of Java exceptions, then you should read all about try blocks in Appendix C. But for your first try block, all you need to know is that the code in the try block is executed, and the try block will be able to handle some of the possible exceptions that may arise in the code. In this example, the try block has just one assignment statement: `answer = (Location) super.clone( )`. The right side of the assignment activates a method called `super.clone( )`. This is actually the `clone` method from Java's `Object` type. It checks that the `Location` class specifies that it "implements `Cloneable`," and then correctly makes a copy of the location, assigning the result to the local variable `answer`.

After the try block is a sequence of one or more *catch blocks*. Each catch block can catch and handle an exception that may arise in the try block. Our example has one catch block:

```
catch (CloneNotSupportedException e)
{
    throw new RuntimeException
    ("This class does not implement Cloneable.");
}
```

This catch block will handle a `CloneNotSupportedException`. This exception is thrown by the `clone` method from Java's `Object` type when a programmer tries to call `super.clone( )`, without including the `implements Cloneable` clause as part of the class definition. The best solution is to throw a new `RuntimeException`, which is the general exception used to indicate a programmer error.

Anyway, after the try and catch blocks, the local variable `answer` refers to an exact copy of the location that activated the `clone` method, and we can move to the third part of the `clone` implementation.

3. Make necessary modifications and return. The answer is present, and it refers to an exact copy of the object that activated the `clone` method. Sometimes, further modifications must be made to the copy before returning. You'll see the reasons for such modifications in Chapter 3. However, the `Location` clone needs no modifications, so the end of the `clone` method consists of just the return statement: `return answer`.

The complete `clone` implementation for the `Location` class looks like this, including an indication of the likely cause of the `CloneNotSupportedException`:

```
public Object clone( )
{   // Clone a Location object.
    Location answer;

    try
    {
        answer = (Location) super.clone( );
    }
    catch (CloneNotSupportedException e)
    {   // This exception should not occur. But if it does, it would indicate a
        // programming error that made super.clone unavailable. The
        // most common cause would be forgetting the
        // "implements Cloneable" clause at the start of the class.
        throw new RuntimeException
        ("This class does not implement Cloneable.");
    }

    return answer;
}
```

The method returns the local variable, `answer`, which is a `Location` object. This is allowed, even though the return type of the `clone` method is `Object`. A Java `Object` may be anything except the eight primitive types. It might be better if the actual return type of the `clone` method was `Location` rather than `Object`. Using `Location` for the return type would be more accurate and would make the `clone` method easier to use (without having to put a typecast with every usage). Unfortunately, the improvement is not allowed: The return type of the `clone` method must be `Object`.

Programming Tip: Always Use super.clone for Your Clone Methods

△ TIP

Perhaps you thought of a simpler way to create a clone. Instead of using `super.clone` and the try/catch blocks, could you write this code:

```
Location answer = new Location(x, y);
return answer;
```

You could combine these into one statement: `return new Location(x, y)`. This creates and returns a new location, using the instance variables x and y to initialize the new location. These instance variables come from the location that activated the `clone` method, so `answer` will indeed be a copy of that location. This is a nice direct approach, but the direct approach will encounter problems when we start building new classes that are based on existing classes (See page 655). Therefore, it is better to stick with the pattern that uses `super.clone` and a try/catch block.

Programming Tip: When to Throw a Runtime Exception

A `RuntimeException` is thrown to indicate a programming error. For example, the `clone` method from Java's `Object` type is not supposed to be called by an object unless that object's class has implemented the `Cloneable` interface. If we detect that the exception has been thrown by the `Object clone` method, then the programmer probably forgot to include the "`implements Cloneable`" clause.

When you throw a `RuntimeException`, include a message with your best guess about the programming error.

A Demonstration Program for the Location Class

As one last example, let's look at a program that creates two locations called `still` and `mobile`. Both are initially placed at $x = -2$ and $y = -1.5$, as shown in Figure 2.8(a). To be more precise, the `still` location is placed at this spot, and then `mobile` is initialized as a clone of the `still` location. Because the `mobile` location is a clone, later changes to one location will not affect the other.

FIGURE 2.8

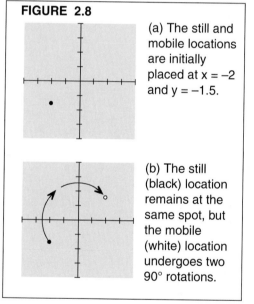

(a) The still and mobile locations are initially placed at x = −2 and y = −1.5.

(b) The still (black) location remains at the same spot, but the mobile (white) location undergoes two 90° rotations.

The program prints some information about both locations, and then the `mobile` location undergoes two 90° rotations as shown in Figure 2.8(b). The information about the locations is then printed a second time.

The complete program is shown in Figure 2.9 on page 82. Pay particular attention to the `specifiedRotation` method, which illustrates some important principles about what happens when a parameter is changed within a method. We'll look at those principles in a moment, but first let's take a look at the complete output from the program, as shown here:

```
The still location is at:  (x=-2.0 y=-1.5)
The mobile location is at: (x=-2.0 y=-1.5)
Distance between them:  0.0
These two locations have equal coordinates.

I will rotate one location by two 90 degree turns.
The still location is at:  (x=-2.0 y=-1.5)
The mobile location is at: (x=2.0 y=1.5)
Distance between them:  5.0
These two locations have different coordinates.
```

FIGURE 2.9	A Demonstration Program for the Location Class

Java Application Program

```java
// FILE: LocationDemonstration.java
// This small demonstration program shows how to use the Location class
// from the edu.colorado.geometry package.

import edu.colorado.geometry.Location;

class LocationDemonstration
{
    public static void main(String[ ] args)
    {
        final double STILL_X = -2.0;
        final double STILL_Y = -1.5;
        final int ROTATIONS = 2;

        Location still = new Location(STILL_X, STILL_Y);
        Location mobile = (Location) still.clone( );
        printData(still, mobile);

        System.out.println("I will rotate one location by two 90 degree turns.");
        specifiedRotation(mobile, ROTATIONS);
        printData(still, mobile);
    }

    // Rotate a Location p by a specified number of 90 degree clockwise rotations.
    public static void specifiedRotation(Location p, int n)
    {
        while (n > 0)
        {
            p.rotate90( );
            n--;
        }
    }

    // Print some information about two locations: s (a "still" location) and m (a "mobile" location).
    public static void printData(Location s, Location m)
    {
        System.out.println("The still location is at:  " + s.toString( ));
        System.out.println("The mobile location is at: " + m.toString( ));
        System.out.println("Distance between them:  " + Location.distance(s, m));
        if (s.equals(m))
            System.out.println("These two locations have equal coordinates.");
        else
            System.out.println("These two locations have different coordinates.");
        System.out.println( );
    }
}
```

What Happens When a Parameter Is Changed within a Method?

Let's examine the program's `specifiedRotation` method to see exactly what happens when a parameter is changed within a method. Here is the method's implementation:

```
// Rotate a Location p by a number of 90 degree clockwise rotations.
public static void specifiedRotation(Location p, int n)
{
   while (n > 0)
   {
      p.rotate90( );
      n--;
   }
}
```

The method rotates the location p by n 90° clockwise rotations.

In Java, a parameter that is a reference variable (such as the `Location p`) has different behavior than a parameter that is one of the eight primitive types (such as `int n`). Here is the difference:

- When a parameter is one of the eight primitive types, the actual argument provides an initial value for that parameter. To be more precise, the parameter is implemented as a local variable of the method and the argument is used to initialize this variable. Changes that are made to the parameter do not affect the actual argument.

- When a parameter is a reference variable, the parameter is initialized so that it refers to the same object as the actual argument. Subsequent changes to this object do affect the actual argument's object.

For example, suppose that we have initialized a location called `mobile` at the coordinates $x = -2$ and $y = -1.5$. Suppose that we also have an integer variable called `rotations`, with a value of 2, as shown here:

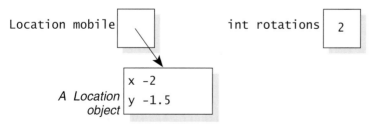

Now, suppose the program activates `specifiedRotation(mobile, rotations)`. The method's first parameter, p, is initialized to refer to the same location that `mobile` refers to. And the method's second parameter, n, is initialized with the value 2 (from the `rotations` argument). So, when the method begins its work, the situation looks like the picture at the top of the next page.

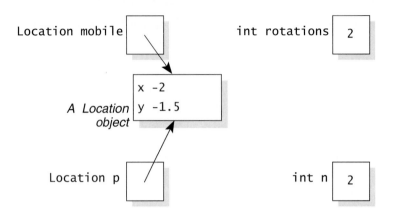

The method now executes its loop:

```
while (n > 0)
{
    p.rotate90( );
    n--;
}
```

The first iteration of the loop rotates the location by 90° and decreases n to 1. The second iteration does another rotation of the location and decreases n to 0. Now the loop ends, with these values for the variables:

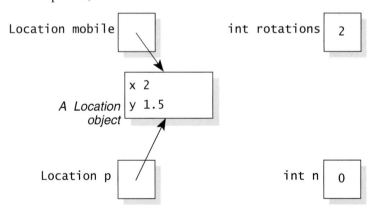

Notice the difference between the two kinds of parameters. The integer parameter n has changed to zero without affecting the actual argument rotations. On the other hand, rotating the location p has changed the object that mobile refers to. When the method returns, the parameters p and n disappear, leaving the situation shown at the top of the next page.

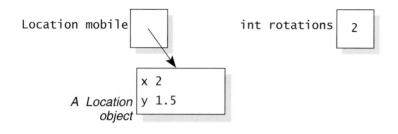

Java Parameters

The eight primitive types (byte, short, int, long, char, float, double, or boolean): The parameter is initialized with the value of the argument. Subsequent changes to the parameter do not affect the argument.

Reference variables: When a parameter is a reference variable, the parameter is initialized so that it refers to the same object as the actual argument. Subsequent changes to this object do affect the actual argument's object.

Self-Test Exercises

17. Write some code that declares two locations: one at the origin and the other at the coordinates $x = 1$ and $y = 1$. Print the distance between the two locations, then create a third location that is at the midpoint between the first two locations.

18. The location's distance method is a static method. What effect does this have on how the method is used? What effect does this have on how the method is implemented?

19. What is the purpose of the Java constant Double.NaN?

20. What is the result when you add two double numbers and the answer is larger than the largest possible double number?

21. In the midpoint method we used the expression (p1.x/2) + (p2.x/2). Can you think of a reason why this expression is better than (p1.x + p2.x)/2?

22. Implement an equals method for the Throttle class from Section 2.1.

23. If you don't implement an equals method for a class, then Java automatically provides one. What does the automatic equals method do?

24. Implement a clone method for the Throttle class from Section 2.1.

25. When should a program throw a RuntimeException?

26. Suppose that a method has an `int` parameter called x, and the body of the method changes x to zero. When the method is activated, what happens to the argument that corresponds to x?

27. Suppose that a method has a `Location` parameter called x, and the body of the method activates `x.rotate90( )`. When the method is activated, what happens to the argument that corresponds to x?

CHAPTER SUMMARY

- In Java, object-oriented programming (OOP) is supported by implementing *classes*. Each class defines a collection of data, called its *instance variables*. In addition, a class has the ability to include two other items: *constructors* and *methods*. Constructors are designed to provide initial values to the class's data; methods are designed to manipulate the data. Taken together, the instance variables, constructors, and methods of a class are called the class *members*.

- We generally use *private instance variables* and *public methods*. This approach supports information hiding by forbidding data components of a class to be directly accessed outside of the class.

- A new class can be implemented in a Java package that is provided to other programmers to use. The package includes documentation to tell programmers what the new class does without revealing the details of how the new class is implemented.

- A program uses a class by creating new objects of that class, and activating these objects' methods through *reference variables*.

- When a method is activated, each of its parameters is initialized. If a parameter is one of the eight primitive types, then the parameter is initialized by the value of the argument, and subsequent changes to the parameter do not affect the actual argument. On the other hand, when a parameter is a reference variable, the parameter is initialized so that it refers to the same object as the actual argument. Subsequent changes to this object do affect the actual argument's object.

- Java programmers must understand how these items work for classes:
  — the assignment operator (x = y)
  — the equality test (x == y)
  — a `clone` method to create a copy of an object
  — an `equals` method to test whether two separate objects are equal to each other

1. We have used *private* instance variables, *public* constructors, and *public* methods.

2. In this solution, the assignment to `position` is not really needed since `position` will be given its default value of zero before the constructor executes. However, including the assignment makes it clear that we intended for `position` to start at zero:
```
public Throttle( )
{
    top = 1;
    position = 0;
}
```

3. Notice that our solution has the precondition that `size` is positive, and `initial` lies in the range from zero to `size`.
```
public Throttle(int size, int initial)
{
    if (size <= 0)
        throw new
        IllegalArgumentException
        ("Size <= 0:" + size);
    if (initial < 0)
        throw new
        IllegalArgumentException
        ("Initial < 0:" + initial);
    if (initial > size)
        throw new
        IllegalArgumentException
        ("Initial too big:" + initial);
    top = size;
    position = initial;
}
```

4. The method implementation is:
```
public boolean isAboveHalf( )
{
    return (getFlow( ) > 0.5);
}
```

5. You'll find part of a solution in Figure 13.1 on page 618.

6. The program should include the following statements:
```
Throttle exercise = new Throttle(6);
exercise.shift(3);
System.out.println(exercise.flow( ));
```

7. The `control` should be assigned the value of null. By the way, if it is an instance variable of a class, then it is initialized to null.

8. A `NullPointerException` is thrown.

9. Both `t1` and `t2` refer to the same throttle, which has been shifted up 42 positions. So the output is 0.42.

10. At the end of the code (`t1 == t2`) is `true` since there is only one throttle that both variables refer to.

11. Here is the code (and at the end `t1==t2` is `false` since there are two separate throttles):
```
Throttle t1;
Throttle t2;
t1 = new Throttle(100);
t2 = new Throttle(100);
t1.shift(42);
t2.shift(42);
```

12. `com.knafn.statistics`

13. Underneath your `classes` directory, create a subdirectory `com`. Underneath `com` create a subdirectory `knafn`. Underneath `knafn` create a subdirectory `statistics`. Your package is placed in the `statistics` subdirectory.

14. `import com.knafn.statistics.*;`

15. Java automatically imports `java.lang`; no explicit import statement is needed.

16. Public access is obtained with the keyword `public`, and it allows access by any program. Private access is obtained with the keyword `private`, and it allows access only by the methods of the class. Package access is obtained with no keyword, and it allows access within the package but not elsewhere.

17. Here is the code:
```
Location p1 = new Location(0, 0);
Location p2 = new Location(1, 1);
System.out.println
   (Location.distance(p1, p2));
Location p3 =
   Location.midpoint(p1, p2);
```

18. A static method is not activated by any one object. Instead, the class name is placed in front of the method to activate it. For example, the distance between two locations p1 and p2 is computed by:
```
Location.distance(p1, p2);
```
Within the implementation of a static method, we cannot directly refer to the instance variables.

19. The constant `Double.NaN` is used when there is no valid number to store in a double variable ("not a number").

20. The result is the constant `Double.POSITIVE_INFINITY`.

21. The alternative (p1.x + p2.x)/2 has a subexpression p1.x + p2.x which could result in an overflow.

22. Here is the implementation for the throttle:
```
public boolean equals(Object obj)
{
   if (obj instanceof Throttle)
   {
     Throttle candidate = (Throttle) obj;
     return
        (candidate.top==top)
        &&
        (candidate.position==position);
   }
   else
     return false;
}
```

23. The automatic `equals` method returns `true` only when the two objects are the exact same object (as opposed to two separate objects that have the same value).

24. The solution is the same as the `Location` clone on page 65, but change the `Location` type to `Throttle`.

25. A `runtimeException` indicates a programming error. When you throw a `RuntimeException`, you should provide an indication of the most likely cause of the error.

26. The argument remains unchanged.

27. The object that the argument refers to has been rotated 90°.

 PROGRAMMING PROJECTS

1 Specify, design, and implement a class that can be used in a program that simulates a combination lock. The lock has a circular knob, with the numbers 0 through 39 marked on the edge, and it has a three-number combination, which we'll call *x, y, z*. To open the lock, you must turn the knob clockwise at least one entire revolution, stopping with *x* at the top; then turn the knob counterclockwise, stopping the *second* time that *y* appears at the top; finally turn the knob clockwise again, stopping the next time that *z* appears at the top. At this point, you may open the lock.

Your `Lock` class should have a constructor that initializes the three-number combination. Also provide methods:

(a) To alter the lock's combination to a new three-number combination

(b) To turn the knob in a given direction until a specified number appears at the top

(c) To close the lock

(d) To attempt to open the lock

(e) To inquire the status of the lock (open or shut)

(f) To tell what number is currently at the top

2 Specify, design, and implement a class called `Statistician`. After a statistician is initialized, it can be given a sequence of double numbers. Each number in the sequence is given to the statistician by activating a method called `nextNumber`. For example, we can declare a statistician called `s`, and then give it the sequence of numbers 1.1, −2.4, 0.8 as shown here:

```
Statistician s = new Statistician;
s.nextNumber(1.1);
s.nextNumber(-2.4);
s.nextNumber(0.8);
```

After a sequence has been given to a statistician, there are various methods to obtain information about the sequence. Include methods that will provide the length of the sequence, the last number of the sequence, the sum of all the numbers in the sequence, the arithmetic mean of the numbers (i.e., the sum of the numbers divided by the length of the sequence), the smallest number in the sequence, and the largest number in the sequence. Notice that the length and sum methods can be called at any time, even if there are no numbers in the sequence. In this case of an "empty" sequence, both length and sum will be zero. The other methods should return `Double.NaN` if they are called for an empty sequence.

Notes: Do not try to store the entire sequence (because you don't know how long this sequence will be). Instead, just store the necessary information about the sequence: What is the sequence length, what is the sum of the numbers in the sequence, what are the last, smallest, and largest numbers? Each of these pieces of information can be stored in a private instance variable that is updated whenever `nextNumber` is activated.

3 Write a new static method to allow you to "add" two statisticians from the previous project. If `s1` and `s2` are two statisticians, then the result of adding them should be a new statistician that behaves as if it had all of the numbers of `s1` followed by all of the numbers of `s2`.

4 Specify, design, and implement a class that can be used to keep track of the position of a location in three-dimensional space. For example, consider the location drawn here:

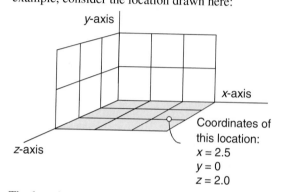

The location shown in the picture has three coordinates: $x = 2.5$, $y = 0$, and $z = 2.0$. Include methods to set a location to a specified point, to shift a location a given amount along one of the axes, and to retrieve the coordinates of a location. Also provide methods that will rotate the location by a specified angle around a specified axis.

To compute these rotations, you will need a bit of trigonometry. Suppose you have a location with coordinates x, y, and z. After rotating this location by an angle θ, the location will have new coordinates, which we'll call x', y', and z'. The equations for the new coordinates use the `java.lang` methods `Math.sin` and `Math.cos`, as shown here:

After a θ rotation around the x-axis:
$$x' = x$$
$$y' = y\,\cos(\theta) - z\,\sin(\theta)$$
$$z' = y\,\sin(\theta) + z\,\cos(\theta)$$

After a θ rotation around the y-axis:
$$x' = x\,\cos(\theta) + z\,\sin(\theta)$$
$$y' = y$$
$$z' = -x\,\sin(\theta) + z\,\cos(\theta)$$

After a θ rotation around the z-axis:
$$x' = x\,\cos(\theta) - y\,\sin(\theta)$$
$$y' = x\,\sin(\theta) + y\,\cos(\theta)$$
$$z' = z$$

In three-dimensional space, a line segment is defined by its two endpoints. Specify, design, and implement a class for a line segment. The class should have two private instance variables that are 3D locations from the previous project.

 Specify, design, and implement a class for a card in a deck of playing cards. The class should contain methods for setting and retrieving the suit and rank of a card.

 Specify, design, and implement a class that can be used to hold information about a musical note. A programmer should be able to set and retrieve the length of the note and the value of the note. The length of a note may be a sixteenth note, eighth note, quarter note, half note, or whole note. A value is specified by indicating how far the note lies above or below the A note that orchestras use in tuning. In counting "how far," you should include both the white and black notes on a piano. For example, the note numbers for the octave beginning at middle C are shown here:

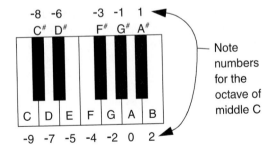

The constructor should set a note to a middle C quarter note. Include methods to set a note to a specified length and value. Write methods to retrieve information about a note, including methods to tell you the letter of the note (A, B, C, etc.), whether the note is natural or sharp (i.e., white or black on the piano), and the frequency of a note in hertz. To calculate the frequency, use the formula $440 \times 2^{n/12}$, where n is the note number. Feel free to include other useful methods.

8 A one-variable **quadratic expression** is an arithmetic expression of the form $ax^2 + bx + c$, where a, b, and c are some fixed numbers (called the **coefficients**) and x is a variable that can take on different values. Specify, design, and implement a class that can store information about a quadratic expression. The constructor should set all three coefficients to zero, and another method should allow you to change these coefficients. There should be accessor methods to retrieve the current values of the coefficients. There should also be a method to allow you to "evaluate" the quadratic expression at a particular value of x (i.e., the method has one parameter x, and returns the value of the expression $ax^2 + bx + c$).

Also write the following static methods to perform these indicated operations:

```
public static Quadratic sum(
    Quadratic q1,
    Quadratic q2
)
// Postcondition: The return value is the
// quadratic expression obtained by adding
// q1 and q2. For example, the c coefficient
// of the return value is the sum of q1's c
// coefficient and q2's c coefficient.

public static Quadratic scale(
    double r,
    Quadratic q
)
// Postcondition: The return value is the
// quadratic expression obtained by
// multiplying each of q's
// coefficients by the number r.
```

Notice that the first argument of the `scale` method is a double number (rather than a quadratic expression). For example, this allows the method activation `Quadratic.scale(3.14, q)` where `q` is a quadratic expression.

9 This project is a continuation of the previous project. For a quadratic expression such as $ax^2 + bx + c$, a **real root** is any double number x such that $ax^2 + bx + c = 0$. For example, the quadratic expression $2x^2 + 8x + 6$ has one of its real roots at $x = -3$, because substituting $x = -3$ in the formula $2x^2 + 8x + 6$ yields the value:

$$2 \times (-3^2) + 8 \times (-3) + 6 = 0$$

There are six rules for finding the real roots of a quadratic expression:

(1) If a, b, and c are all zero, then every value of x is a real root.

(2) If a and b are zero, but c is nonzero, then there are no real roots.

(3) If a is zero, and b is nonzero, then the only real root is $x = -c/b$.

(4) If a is nonzero and $b^2 < 4ac$, then there are no real roots.

(5) If a is nonzero and $b^2 = 4ac$, then there is one real root $x = -b/2a$.

(6) If a is nonzero, and $b^2 > 4ac$, then there are two real roots:

$$x = \frac{-b - \sqrt{b^2 - 4ac}}{2a}$$

$$x = \frac{-b + \sqrt{b^2 - 4ac}}{2a}$$

Write a new method that returns the number of real roots of a quadratic expression. This answer could be 0, or 1, or 2, or infinity. In the case of an infinite number of real roots, have the method return 3. (Yes, we know that 3 is not infinity, but for this purpose it is close enough!) Write two other methods that calculate and return the real roots of a quadratic expression. The precondition for both methods is that the expression has at least one real root. If there are two real roots, then one of the methods returns the smaller of the two roots, and the other method returns the larger of the two roots. If every value of x is a real root, then both methods should return zero.

10 Specify, design, and implement a class that can be used to simulate a lunar lander, which is a small spaceship that transports astronauts from lunar orbit to the surface of the moon. When a lunar lander is constructed, the following items should be initialized as follows:

(1) Current fuel flow rate as a fraction of the maximum fuel flow (initially zero)

(2) Vertical speed of the lander (initially zero meters/sec)

(3) Altitude of the lander (specified as a parameter of the constructor)

(4) Amount of fuel (specified as a parameter of the constructor)

(5) Mass of the lander when it has no fuel (specified as a parameter of the constructor)

(6) Maximum fuel consumption rate (specified as a parameter of the constructor)

(7) Maximum thrust of the lander's engine (specified as a parameter of the constructor)

Don't worry about other properties (such as horizontal speed).

The lander has accessor methods that allow a program to retrieve the current values of any of the preceding seven items. There are only two modification methods, described below.

The first modification method changes the current fuel flow rate to a new value ranging from 0.0 to 1.0. This value is expressed as a fraction of the maximum fuel flow.

The second modification method simulates the passage of a small amount of time. This time, called t, is expressed in seconds and will typically be a small value such as 0.1 seconds. The method will update the first four values in the preceding list, to reflect the passage of t seconds. To implement this method, you will require a few physics formulas listed below. These formulas are only approximate, because some of the lander's values are changing during the simulated time period. But if the time span is kept short, these formulas will suffice.

Fuel flow rate: Normally, the fuel flow rate does not change during the passage of a small amount of time. But there is one exception: If the fuel flow rate is greater than zero, and the amount of fuel left is zero, then you should reset the fuel flow rate to zero (because there is no fuel to flow).

Velocity change: During t seconds, the velocity of the lander changes by approximately this amount (measured in meters/sec):

$$t \times \left(\frac{f}{m} - 1.62 \right)$$

Collection Classes

(I am large. I contain multitudes.)

WALT WHITMAN
Song of Myself

CHAPTER

3

The Throttle and Location classes in Chapter 2 are good examples of abstract data types. But their applicability is limited to a few specialized programs. This chapter begins the presentation of several ADTs with broad applicability to programs large and small. The ADTs in this chapter—bags and sequences—are small, but they provide the basis for more complex ADTs. The chapter also includes information about how to write a test program for a class.

All of the ADTs in this chapter are examples of **collection classes**. Intuitively, a collection class is a class where each object contains a collection of elements. For example, one program might keep track of a collection of integers, perhaps the collection of test scores for a group of students. Another program, perhaps a cryptography program, can use a collection of characters.

an ADT in which each object contains a collection of elements

There are many different ways to implement a collection class; the simplest approach utilizes an array, so this chapter begins with a quick review of Java arrays before approaching actual collection classes.

95

3.1 A REVIEW OF JAVA ARRAYS

An array is a sequence with a certain number of components. We draw arrays with each component in a separate box. For example, here's an array of the four integers 7, 22, 19, and 56:

7	22	19	56

Each component of an array can be accessed through an index. In Java, the indexes are written with square brackets, beginning with [0], [1],.... The array shown has four components, so the indexes are [0] through [3], as shown here:

7	22	19	56

[0]   [1]   [2]   [3]

In these examples, each component is an integer, but arrays can be built for any fixed data type: arrays of double numbers, arrays of boolean values, even arrays where the components are objects from a new class that you write yourself.

An array is declared like any other variable, except that a pair of square brackets is placed after the name of the data type. For example, a program can declare an array of integers like this:

```
int[ ] scores;
```

The name of this array is `scores`. The components of this array are integers, but as we have mentioned, the components may be any fixed type. For example, an array of double numbers would use `double[ ]` instead of `int[ ]`.

An array variable, such as `scores`, is capable of referring to an array of any size. In fact, an array variable is a reference variable, just like the reference variables we have used for other objects, and arrays are created with the same `new` operator that allocates other objects. For example, we can write these statements:

```
int[ ] scores;
scores = new int[4];
```

The number [4], occurring with the `new` operator, indicates that we want a new array with four components. Once both statements finish, `scores` refers to an array with four integer components, as shown here:

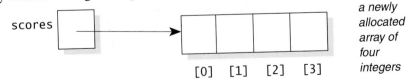

scores

[0]   [1]   [2]   [3]

a newly allocated array of four integers

This is an accurate picture, showing how `scores` refers to a new array of four integers, but the picture has some clutter that we can usually omit. Here is a simpler picture that we'll usually use to show that `scores` refers to an array of four integers:

Both pictures mean the same thing. The first picture is a more accurate depiction of what Java actually does; the second is a kind of shorthand which is typical of what programmers draw to illustrate an array.

Once an array has been allocated, individual components can be selected using the square bracket notation with an index. For example, with scores allocated as shown, we can set its [2] component to 42 with the assignment `scores[2] = 42`. The result is shown here:

Pitfall: Exceptions That Arise from Arrays

Two kinds of exceptions commonly arise from programming errors with arrays. One problem is to try to use an array variable before the array has been allocated. For example, suppose we declare `int[ ] scores`, but we forget to use the new operator to create an array for `scores` to refer to. At this point, `scores` is actually a reference variable, just like the reference variables that we discussed for other kinds of objects on page 50. But merely declaring a reference variable does not allocate an array, and it is a programming error to try to access a component such as `scores[2]`. A program that tries to access a component of a nonexistent array may throw a `NullPointerException` (if the reference is null) or there may be a compile-time error (if the variable is an uninitialized local variable).

A second common programming error is trying to access an array outside of its bounds. For example, suppose that `scores` refers to an array with four components. The indexes are [0] through [3], so it is an error to use an index that is too small (such as `scores[-1]`) or too large (such as `scores[4]`). A program that tries to use these indexes will throw an `ArrayIndexOutOfBoundsException`.

The Length of an Array

Every array has an instance variable called `length`, which tells the number of components in the array. For example, consider `scores = new int[4]`. After this allocation, `scores.length` is 4. Notice that `length` is not a method, so the syntax is merely `scores.length` (with no argument list). By the way, if an array variable is the null reference, then you cannot ask for its length (trying to do so results in a `NullPointerException`).

Assignment Statements with Arrays

A program can use an assignment statement to make two array variables refer to the same array. Here's some example code:

```
int[ ] scores;
int[ ] exams;

scores = new int[4];
scores[0] = 7;
scores[1] = 22;
scores[2] = 19;
scores[4] = 56;
exams = scores;
```

After these statements, scores refers to an array containing the four integers 7, 22, 19, and 56. The assignment statement, exams = scores, causes exams to refer to the exact same array. Here is an accurate drawing of the situation:

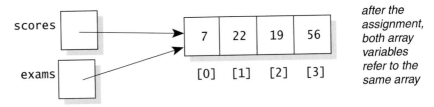

Here's a shorthand drawing of the same situation to show that scores and exams refer to the same array:

In this example, there is only one array, and both array variables refer to this one array. Any change to the array will affect both scores and exams. For example, after the above statements we might assign exams[2] = 42. The situation after the assignment to exams[2] is shown here:

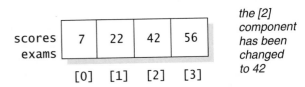

At this point, both exams[2] and scores[2] are 42.

Clones of Arrays

In Chapter 2 you saw how to use a `clone` method to create a completely separate copy of an object. Every Java array comes equipped with a `clone` method to
create a copy of the array. Just like the other clones that you've seen, changes to
the original array don't affect the clone, and changes to the clone don't affect the
original array. Here's an example:

```
int[ ] scores;
int[ ] exams;

scores = new int[4];
scores[0] = 7;
scores[1] = 22;
scores[2] = 19;
scores[3] = 56;
exams = (int[ ]) scores.clone( );
```

The final statement in this example uses `scores.clone( )` to create a copy of
the `scores` array. The data type of the return value of any `clone` method is
Java's `Object` data type and not an array. Because of this, we usually cannot use
the `clone` return value directly. For example, we cannot write an assignment:

```
exams = scores.clone( );   ◄──────── this has a compile-time error
```

Instead, we must apply a typecast to the `clone` return value, converting it to an
integer array before we assign it to exams, like this:

```
exams = (int[ ]) scores.clone( );
```

The expression `(int[ ])` tells the compiler to treat the return value of the
clone method as an integer array.

After the assignment statement, exams refers to a new array which is an exact
copy of the `scores` array, as shown here:

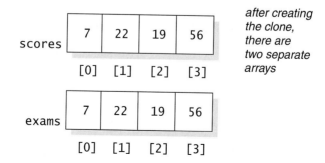

There are now two separate arrays. Changes to one array do not affect the other.
For example, after the above statements we might assign `exams[2] = 42`.

The situation after the assignment to `exams[2]` is shown here:

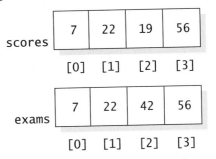

exams[2] has changed to 42, but scores[2] is unchanged

At this point, `exams[2]` is 42, but `scores[2]` is unchanged.

Array Parameters

An array can be a parameter to a method. Here's an example method with an array as a parameter:

- **put42s**

      public static void put42s(int[ ] data)
  Put 42 in every component of an array.

  Parameters:
     data – an array of integers

  Postcondition:
     All components of data have been set to 42.

```
public static void put42s(int[ ] data)
{
    int i;
    for (i = 0; i < data.length; i++)
        data[i] = 42;
}
```

Perhaps this is a silly example (when was the last time you really wanted to put 42 in *every* component of an array?), but the example is a good way to show how an array works as a parameter. Notice how the array parameter is indicated by placing array brackets after the parameter name. In the `put42s` example, the array is called `data`, so the parameter list is `(int[ ] data)`.

When a method is activated with an array parameter, the parameter is initialized to refer to the same array that the actual argument refers to. Therefore, if the method changes the components of the array, the changes do affect the actual argument. For example, this code activates the `put42s` method:

```
int[ ] example = new int[7];
put42s(example);
```

After these statements, all seven components of the `example` array contain 42.

Array Parameters

When a parameter is an array, then the parameter is initialized to refer to the same array that the actual argument refers to. Therefore, if the method changes the components of the array, the changes do affect the actual argument.

Self-Test Exercises

1. Write code that follows these steps: (1) Declare an integer array variable called b; (2) Allocate a new array of 1000 integers for b to refer to; and (3) Place the numbers 1 through 1000 in the array.

2. Write a Java expression that will indicate how many elements are in the array b (from the previous exercise).

3. What is the output from this code:
    ```
    int[ ] a, b;
    a = new int[10];
    a[5] = 0;
    b = a;
    a[5] = 42;
    System.out(b[5]);
    ```

4. What is the output from this code:
    ```
    int[ ] a, b;
    a = new int[10];
    a[5] = 0;
    b = (int [ ]) a.clone( );
    a[5] = 42;
    System.out(b[5]);
    ```

5. Suppose that an array is passed as a parameter to a method, and the method changes the first component of the array to 42. What effect does this have on the actual argument back in the calling program?

6. Write a method that copies *n* elements from the front of one integer array to the front of another. The two arrays and the number *n* are all arguments to the method. Include a precondition/postcondition contract as part of your implementation.

3.2 AN ADT FOR A BAG OF INTEGERS

This section provides an example of a collection class. In this first example, the collection class will use an array to store its collection of elements (but later we will see other ways to store collections).

The example collection class is called a *bag of integers*. To describe the bag data type, think about an actual bag—a grocery bag or a garbage bag—and imagine writing integers on slips of paper and putting them in the bag. A **bag of integers** is similar to this imaginary bag: a container that holds a collection of integers that we place into it. A bag of integers can be used by any program that needs to store a collection of integers for its own use. For example, later we will write a program that keeps track of the ages of your family's members. If you have a large family with ten people, the program keeps track of ten ages—and these ages are kept in a bag of integers.

The Bag ADT—Specification

We've given an intuitive description of a bag of integers. We will implement this bag as a class called `IntArrayBag`, in which the integers are stored in an array. In general, we'll use a three-part name for a collection: "`Int`" specifies the type of the elements in the bag; "`Array`" indicates the mechanism for storing the elements; and "`Bag`" indicates the kind of collection. For a precise specification of the `IntArrayBag` class, we must describe each of the public methods to manipulate an `IntArrayBag` object. These descriptions will later become our specifications, including a precondition/postcondition contract for each method. Let's look at the methods one at a time.

The Constructors.   The `IntArrayBag` class has two constructors to initialize a new, empty bag. One constructor has a parameter, as shown in this heading:

```
public IntArrayBag(initialCapacity)
```

The parameter, `initialCapacity`, is the initial capacity of the bag—the number of elements that the bag can hold. Once this capacity is reached, more elements can still be added and the capacity will automatically increase in a manner that you'll see in a moment.

The other constructor has no parameters, and it constructs a bag with an initial capacity of ten.

The add Method.   This is a modification method that places a new integer, called `element`, into a bag. Here is the heading:

```
public void add(int element)
```

As an example, here are some statements for a bag called `firstBag`:

```
IntArrayBag firstBag = new IntArrayBag( );
firstBag.add(8);
firstBag.add(4);          After these statements, firstBag
firstBag.add(8);          contains two 8s and a 4.
```

After these statements are executed, `firstBag` contains three integers: the number 4 and two copies of the number 8. It is important to realize that a bag can contain many copies of the same integer, such as this example, which has two copies of 8.

The remove Method. This modification method removes a particular number from a bag. The heading is shown here:

```
public boolean remove(int target)
```

Provided that `target` is actually in the bag, the method removes one copy of `target` and returns `true` to indicate that something has been removed. If `target` is not in the bag, then the method returns `false` without changing the bag.

The size Method. This accessor method returns the count of how many integers are in a bag. The heading for the `size` method is:

```
public int size( )
```

For example, suppose `firstBag` contains one copy of the number 4 and two copies of the number 8. Then `firstBag.size( )` returns 3.

The countOccurrences Method. This is an accessor method that determines how many copies of a *particular* number are in a bag. The heading is:

```
public int countOccurrences(int target)
```

The activation of `countOccurrences(n)` returns the number of occurrences of n in a bag. For example, if `firstBag` contains the number 4 and two copies of the number 8, then we will have these values:

```
System.out.println(firstBag.countOccurrences(1));   ← Prints 0
System.out.println(firstBag.countOccurrences(4));   ← Prints 1
Systme.out.println(firstBag.countOccurrences(8));   ← Prints 2
```

The addAll Method. The addAll method allows us to add the contents of one bag to the existing contents of another bag. The method has this heading:

```
public void addAll(IntArrayBag addend)
```

This is an interesting method for the `IntArrayBag` class because the parameter is also an `IntArrayBag` object. We use the name `addend` for the parameter, meaning "something to be added." As an example, suppose we create two bags called `helter` and `skelter`, and we then want to add all the contents of `skelter` to `helter`. This is done with `helter.addAll(skelter)`, as shown here:

```
IntArrayBag helter= new IntArrayBag( );
IntArrayBag skelter = new IntArrayBag( );
helter.add(8);          This adds the contents of
skelter.add(4);         skelter to what's
skelter.add(8);         already in helter.
helter.addAll(skelter);
```

After these statements, `helter` contains one 4 and two 8s.

The union Method. The **union** of two bags is a new larger bag that contains all the numbers in the first bag and all the numbers in the second bag, as shown here:

The union of and is

We will implement union with a static method that has the two parameters shown here:

```
public static IntArrayBag union(IntArrayBag b1, IntArrayBag b2)
```

The union method computes the union of b1 and b2. For example:

```
IntArrayBag part1 = new IntArrayBag( );
IntArrayBag part2 = new IntArrayBag( );

part1.add(8);
part1.add(9);
part2.add(4);
part2.add(8);
```

This computes the union of the two bags, putting the result in a third bag.

```
IntArrayBag total = IntArrayBag.union(part1, part2);
```

After these statements, total contains one 4, two 8s, and one 9.

The union method is similar to addAll, but the usage is different. The addAll method is an ordinary method that is activated by a bag, for example helter.addAll(skelter), which adds the contents of skelter to helter. On the other hand, union is a static method with two arguments. As a static method, union is not activated by any one bag. Instead, the activation of IntArrayBag.union(part1, part2) creates and returns a new bag that includes the contents of both part1 and part2.

The clone Method. As part of our specification, we require that bag objects can be copied with a clone method. For example:

b now contains a 42.

```
IntArrayBag b = new IntArrayBag( );
b.add(42);
IntArrayBag c = (IntArrayBag) b.clone( );
```

c is initialized as a clone of b.

At this point, because we are only specifying which operations can manipulate a bag, we don't need to say anything more about the clone method.

Three Methods That Deal with Capacity. Each bag has a current **capacity**, which is the number of elements the bag can hold without having to request more memory. Once the capacity is reached, more elements can still be added by the add method. In this case, the add method itself will increase the capacity as needed. In fact, our implementation of add will double the capacity whenever the bag becomes full.

With this in mind, you might wonder why a programmer needs to worry about the capacity at all. For example, why does the constructor require the programmer to specify an initial capacity? Couldn't we always use the constructor that has an initial capacity of ten and have the add method increase capacity as more and more elements are added? Yes, this approach will always work correctly. But if there are many elements, then many of the activations of add would need to increase the capacity. This could be inefficient—in fact, increasing the capacity will be the least efficient operation of the entire bag. To avoid repeatedly increasing the capacity, a programmer provides an initial guess at the needed capacity for the constructor.

For example, suppose a programmer expects no more than 1000 elements for a bag named kilosack. The bag is declared this way, with an initial capacity of 1000:

```
IntArrayBag kilosack = new IntArrayBag(1000);
```

After this declaration, the programmer can place 1000 elements in the bag without worrying about the capacity. Later, the programmer can add more elements to the bag, maybe even more than 1000. If there are more than 1000 elements, then add increases the capacity as needed.

There are three methods that allow a programmer to manipulate a bag's capacity after the bag is in use. The methods have these headers:

```
public int getCapacity( )
public void ensureCapacity(int minimumCapacity)
public void trimToSize( )
```

The first method, getCapacity, just returns the current capacity of the bag. The second method, ensureCapacity, increases the capacity to a specified minimum amount. For example, in order to ensure that a bag called bigboy has a capacity of at least 10,000, we would activate bigboy.ensureCapacity(10000).

The third method, trimToSize, reduces the capacity of a bag to its current size. For example, suppose that bigboy has a current capacity of 10,000, but it contains only 42 elements and we are not planning to add any more. Then we can reduce the current capacity to 42 with the activation bigboy.trimToSize( ). Trimming the capacity is never required, but doing so can reduce the memory used by a program.

That's all the methods, and we're almost ready to write the methods' specifications. But first, there are some limitations that we'd like to discuss.

`OutOfMemoryError` and Other Limitations for Collection Classes

Our plan is to store a bag's elements in an array, and to increase the capacity of the array as needed. The memory for any array comes from a location called the program's **heap** (also called the **free store**). In fact, the memory for all Java objects comes from the heap. Some computers provide huge heaps—Java implementations running on a machine with a "64-bit address space" have the potential for more than 10^{18} integers. But even the largest heap can be exhausted by creating large arrays or other objects.

what happens when the heap runs out of memory?

If a heap has insufficient memory for a new object or array, then the result is a Java exception called `OutOfMemoryError`. This exception is thrown automatically by an unsuccessful "new" operation. For example, if there is insufficient memory for a new `Throttle` object, then `Throttle t = new Throttle( )` throws an `OutOfMemoryError`. Experienced programmers may monitor the size of the heap and the amount that is still unused. Our programs won't attempt such monitoring, but our specification for any collection class will always mention that the maximum capacity is limited by the amount of free memory. To aid more experienced programmers, the specification will also indicate precisely which methods have the possibility of throwing an `OutOfMemoryError`. (Any method that uses the "new" operation could throw this exception.)

collection classes may be limited by the maximum value of an integer

Many collection classes have another limitation that is tied to the maximum value of an integer. In particular, our bag stores the elements in an array, and every array has integers for its indexes. Java integers are limited to no more than 2,147,483,647, which is also written as `Integer.MAX_VALUE`. An attempt to create an array with a size beyond `Integer.MAX_VALUE` results in an arithmetic overflow during the calculation of the size of the array. Such an overflow usually produces an array size that Java's runtime system sees as negative. This is because Java represents integers so that the "next" number after `Integer.MAX_VALUE` is actually the smallest negative number.

Programmers often ignore the array-size overflow problem (since today's machines generally have an `OutOfMemoryError` before `Integer.MAX_VALUE` is approached). We won't provide special code to handle this problem, but we won't totally ignore the problem either. Instead, our documentation will indicate precisely which methods have the potential for an array-size overflow. We'll also add a note to advise that large bags should probably use a different implementation method anyway, because many of the array-based algorithms are slow for large bags ($O(n)$, where n is the number of elements in the bag).

The `IntArrayBag` Class—Specification

We now know enough about the bag to write a specification, as shown in Figure 3.1. We've used the name `IntArrayBag` for this class, and it is the first class of a package named `edu.colorado.collections`.

The specification also states the bag's limitations: the possibility of an `OutOfMemoryError` (when the heap is exhausted), a note about the limitation of the capacity, and a note indicating that large bags will have poor performance.

FIGURE 3.1	Specification for the `IntArrayBag` Class

Class IntArrayBag

❖ **public class IntArrayBag from the package edu.colorado.collections**
An `IntArrayBag` is a collection of `int` numbers.

Limitations:

(1) The capacity of one of these bags can change after it's created, but the maximum capacity is limited by the amount of free memory on the machine. The constructor, `add`, `clone`, and `union` will result in an `OutOfMemoryError` when free memory is exhausted.

(2) A bag's capacity cannot exceed the largest integer 2,147,483,647 (`Integer.MAX_VALUE`). Any attempt to create a larger capacity results in failure due to an arithmetic overflow.

(3) Because of the slow linear algorithms of this class, large bags will have poor performance.

Specification

◆ **Constructor for the IntArrayBag**
`public IntArrayBag( )`
Initialize an empty bag with an initial capacity of 10. Note that the `add` method works efficiently (without needing more memory) until this capacity is reached.

Postcondition:
This bag is empty and has an initial capacity of 10.

Throws: `OutOfMemoryError`
Indicates insufficient memory for: `new int[10]`.

◆ **Second Constructor for the IntArrayBag**
`public IntArrayBag(int initialCapacity)`
Initialize an empty bag with a specified initial capacity. Note that the `add` method works efficiently (without needing more memory) until this capacity is reached.

Parameters:
`initialCapacity` – the initial capacity of this bag

Precondition:
`initialCapacity` is non-negative.

Postcondition:
This bag is empty and has the given initial capacity.

Throws: `IllegalArgumentException`
Indicates that `initialCapacity` is negative.

Throws: `OutOfMemoryError`
Indicates insufficient memory for: `new int[initialCapacity]`.

(continued)

(FIGURE 3.1 continued)

◆ **add**
```
public void add(int element)
```
Add a new element to this bag. If this new element would take this bag beyond its current capacity, then the capacity is increased before adding the new element.

Parameters:
  `element` – the new element that is being added

Postcondition:
  A new copy of the element has been added to this bag.

Throws: `OutOfMemoryError`
  Indicates insufficient memory for increasing the capacity.

Note:
  An attempt to increase the capacity beyond `Integer.MAX_VALUE` will cause this bag to fail with an arithmetic overflow.

◆ **addAll**
```
public void addAll(IntArrayBag addend)
```
Add the contents of another bag to this bag.

Parameters:
  `addend` – a bag whose contents will be added to this bag

Precondition:
  The parameter, addend, is not null.

Postcondition:
  The elements from addend have been added to this bag.

Throws: `NullPointerException`
  Indicates that addend is null.

Throws: `OutOfMemoryError`
  Indicates insufficient memory to increase the size of this bag.

Note:
  An attempt to increase the capacity beyond `Integer.MAX_VALUE` will cause this bag to fail with an arithmetic overflow.

◆ **clone**
```
public Object clone( )
```
Generate a copy of this bag.

Returns:
  The return value is a copy of this bag. Subsequent changes to the copy will not affect the original, nor vice versa. The return value must be typecast to an `IntArrayBag` before it is used.

Throws: `OutOfMemoryError`
  Indicates insufficient memory for creating the clone.

(continued)

(FIGURE 3.1 continued)

◆ **countOccurrences**

```
public int countOccurrences(int target)
```

Accessor method to count the number of occurrences of a particular element in this bag.

Parameters:

target – the element that needs to be counted

Returns:

the number of times that target occurs in this bag

◆ **ensureCapacity**

```
public void ensureCapacity(int minimumCapacity)
```

Change the current capacity of this bag.

Parameters:

minimumCapacity – the new capacity for this bag

Postcondition:

This bag's capacity has been changed to at least minimumCapacity. If the capacity was already at or greater than minimumCapacity, then the capacity is left unchanged.

Throws: OutOfMemoryError

Indicates insufficient memory for: new int[minimumCapacity].

◆ **getCapacity**

```
public int getCapacity( )
```

Accessor method to determine the current capacity of this bag. The add method works efficiently (without needing more memory) until this capacity is reached.

Returns:

the current capacity of this bag

◆ **remove**

```
public boolean remove(int target)
```

Remove one copy of a specified element from this bag.

Parameters:

target – the element to remove from this bag

Postcondition:

If target was found in this bag, then one copy of target has been removed and the method returns true. Otherwise this bag remains unchanged and the method returns false.

◆ **size**

```
public int size( )
```

Accessor method to determine the number of elements in this bag.

Returns:

the number of elements in this bag

(continued)

(FIGURE 3.1 continued)

- **trimToSize**

  `public void trimToSize( )`

  Reduce the current capacity of this bag to its actual size (i.e., the number of elements it contains).

  Postcondition:
  This bag's capacity has been changed to its current size.

  Throws: `OutOfMemoryError`
  Indicates insufficient memory for altering the capacity.

- **union**

  `public static IntArrayBag union(IntArrayBag b1, IntArrayBag b2)`

  Create a new bag that contains all the elements from two other bags.

  Parameters:
  b1 – the first of two bags
  b2 – the second of two bags

  Precondition:
  Neither b1 nor b2 is null.

  Returns:
  a new bag that is the union of b1 and b2

  Throws: `NullPointerException`
  Indicates that one of the arguments is null.

  Throws: `OutOfMemoryError`
  Indicates insufficient memory for the new bag.

  Note:
  An attempt to create a bag with capacity beyond `Integer.MAX_VALUE` will cause the bag to fail with an arithmetic overflow.

The `IntArrayBag` Class—Demonstration Program

With the specification in hand, we can write a program that uses a bag. We don't need to know what the instance variables of a bag are, and we don't need to know how the methods are implemented. As an example, a demonstration program appears in Figure 3.2. The program asks a user about the ages of family members. The user enters the ages followed by a negative number to indicate the end of the input. (Using a special value to end a list is a common technique called a **sentinel value**.) A typical dialogue with the program looks like this:

```
Type the ages of your family members.
Type a negative number at the end and press return.
5   19    47    -1
Type those ages again. Press return after each age.
Age: 19
Yes, I've got that age and will remove it.
```

```
Age: 36
No, that age does not occur!
Age: 5
Yes, I've got that age and will remove it.
Age: 47
Yes, I've got that age and will remove it.
May your family live long and prosper.
```

The program puts the ages in a bag and then asks the user to type the ages again. The program's interaction with the user is handled through a class called EasyReader, which contains various simple input methods. The class is fully described in Appendix B, but for this program all that's needed is a single EasyReader called stdin, which is attached to standard input (System.in).

the EasyReader class from Appendix B allows simple kinds of input

Once stdin is set up, an integer can be read with either of two methods: (1) stdin.intInput (which simply reads an integer input), or (2) stdin.intQuery (which prints a prompt and then reads an integer input). You may find the Easy-Reader class useful for your own demonstration programs.

As for the IntArrayBag class itself, we still don't know how the implementation will work, but we're getting there.

FIGURE 3.2 | Demonstration Program for the Bag Class

Java Application Program

```java
// FILE: BagDemonstration.java
// This small demonstration program shows how to use the IntArrayBag class
// from the edu.colorado.collections package.

import edu.colorado.collections.IntArrayBag;
import edu.colorado.io.EasyReader;

class BagDemonstration
{
    private static EasyReader stdin = new EasyReader(System.in);

    public static void main(String[ ] args)
    {
        IntArrayBag ages = new IntArrayBag( );
        getAges(ages);
        checkAges(ages);
        System.out.println("May your family live long and prosper.");
    }
```

the EasyReader class is described in Appendix B

(continued)

(FIGURE 3.2 continued)

```
public static void getAges(IntArrayBag ages)
// The getAges method prompts the user to type in the ages of family members. These
// ages are read and placed in the ages bag, stopping when the user types a negative
// number. This demonstration does not worry about the possibility of running out
// of memory (therefore, an OutOfMemoryError is possible).
{
    int userInput; // An age from the user's family

    System.out.println("Type the ages of your family members.");
    System.out.println("Type a negative number at the end and press return.");
    userInput = stdin.intInput( );
    while (userInput >= 0)
    {
        ages.add(userInput);
        userInput = stdin.intInput( );
    }
}


public static void checkAges(IntArrayBag ages)
// The checkAges method prompts the user to type in the ages of family members once
// again. Each age is removed from the ages bag when it is typed, stopping when the bag
// is empty.
public static void checkAges(IntArrayBag ages)
{
    int userInput; // An age from the user's family

    System.out.print("Type those ages again. ");
    System.out.println("Press return after each age.");
    while (ages.size( ) > 0)
    {
        userInput = stdin.intQuery("Next age:   ");
        if (ages.countOccurrences(userInput) == 0)
            System.out.println("No, that age does not occur!");
        else
        {
            System.out.println("Yes, I've got that age and will remove it.");
            ages.remove(userInput);
        }

    }
}

}
```

The `IntArrayBag` Class—Design

There are several ways to design the `IntArrayBag` class. For now, we'll keep things simple and design a somewhat inefficient data structure using an array. The data structure will be redesigned several times to obtain more efficiency.

We start the design by thinking about the data structure—the actual configuration of private instance variables used to implement the class. The primary structure for our design is an array that stores the elements of a bag. Or, to be more precise, we use the *beginning* part of a large array. Such an array is called a **partially filled array**. For example, if the bag contains the integer 4 and two copies of 8, then the first part of the array could look this way:

use the beginning part of an array

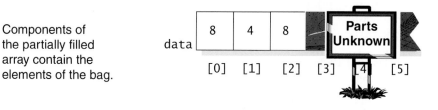

Components of
the partially filled
array contain the
elements of the bag.

This array, called `data`, will be one of the private instance variables of the `IntArrayBag` class. The length of the array will be determined by the current capacity, but as the picture indicates, when we are using the array to store a bag with just three elements, we don't care what appears beyond the first three components. Starting at index 3, the array might contain all zeros, or it might contain garbage, or our favorite number—it really doesn't matter.

Because part of the array can contain garbage, the `IntArrayBag` class must keep track of one other item: *How much of the array is currently being used?* For example, in the previous picture, we are using only the first three components of the array because the bag contains three elements. The amount of the array being used can be as small as zero (an empty bag) or as large as the current capacity. The amount increases as elements are added to the bag, and it decreases as elements are removed. In any case, we will keep track of the amount in a private instance variable called `manyItems`. With this approach, there are two instance variables for a bag:

the bag's instance variables

```
public class IntArrayBag implements Cloneable
{
    private int[ ] data;     // An array to store elements
    private int manyItems;   // How much of the array is used

    │ The public methods will be given in a moment.
}
```

Notice that we are planning to implement a `clone` method, therefore we indicate "`implements Cloneable`" at the start of the class definition.

The Invariant of an ADT

We've defined the bag data structure, and we have a good intuitive idea of how the structure will be used to represent a bag of elements. But as an aid in implementing the class we should also write down an explicit statement of how the data structure is used to represent a bag. In the case of the bag, we need to state how the instance variables of the class are used to represent a bag of elements. There are two rules for our bag implementation:

rules that dictate how the instance variables are used to represent a value

1. The number of elements in the bag is stored in the instance variable `manyItems`.
2. For an empty bag, we do not care what is stored in any of `data`; for a nonempty bag, the elements of the bag are stored in `data[0]` through `data[manyItems-1]`, and we don't care what is stored in the rest of `data`.

The rules that dictate how the instance variables of a class represent a value (such as a bag of elements) are called the **invariant of the ADT**. The knowledge of these rules is essential to the correct implementation of the ADT's methods. With the exception of the constructors, each method depends on the invariant being valid when the method is activated. And each method, including the constructors, has a responsibility of ensuring that the invariant is valid when the method finishes. In some sense, the invariant of an ADT is a condition that is an *implicit* part of every method's postcondition. And (except for the constructors) it is also an implicit part of every method's precondition. The invariant is not usually written as an *explicit* part of the precondition and postcondition because the programmer who uses the ADT does not need to know about these conditions. But to the implementor of the ADT, the invariant is indispensable. In other words, the invariant is a critical part of the implementation of an ADT, but it has no effect on the way the ADT is used.

> **Key Design Concept**
>
> *The invariant is a critical part of an ADT's implementation.*

The Invariant of an ADT

When you design a new class, always make an explicit statement of the rules that dictate how the instance variables are used. These rules are called the **invariant of the ADT**. All of the methods (except the constructors) can count on the invariant being valid when the method is called. Each method also has the responsibility of ensuring that the invariant is valid when the method finishes.

Once the invariant of an ADT is stated, the implementation of the methods is relatively simple because there is no interaction between the methods—except for their cooperation at keeping the invariant valid. We'll look at these implementations one at a time, starting with the constructors.

The `IntArrayBag` ADT—Implementation

The Constructor. Every constructor has one primary job: to set up the instance variables correctly. In the case of the bag, the constructor must set up the instance variables so that they represent an empty bag with a current capacity given by the parameter `initialCapacity`. The bag has two instance variables, so its constructor will include two assignment statements shown in this implementation of one of the constructors:

```
public IntArrayBag(int initialCapacity)
{
   if (initialCapacity < 0)
      throw new IllegalArgumentException
      ("initialCapacity is negative: " + initialCapacity);
   manyItems = 0;
   data = new int[initialCapacity];
}
```

The if-statement at the start checks the constructor's precondition. The first assignment statement, `manyItems = 0`, simply sets manyItems to zero, indicating that the bag does not yet have any elements. The second assignment statement, `data = new int[initialCapacity]`, is more interesting. This statement allocates an array of the right capacity (initialCapacity), and makes data refer to the new array. For example, suppose that initialCapacity is 6. After the two assignment statements, the instance variables look like this:

implementing the constructor

The private instance variables of this bag include an array of six integers. The bag does not yet contain any elements, so none of the array is being used.

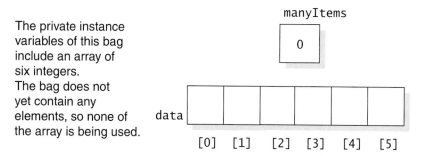

Later, the program could add many elements to this bag, maybe even more than six. If there are more than six elements, then the bag's methods will increase the array's capacity as needed.

The other constructor is similar, except it always provides an initial capacity of ten.

The add Method. The add method checks that there is room to add a new element. If not, then the array capacity is increased before proceeding. (The new capacity is twice the old capacity plus 1. The extra +1 deals with the case where the original size was zero.) The attempt to increase the array capacity may lead to an OutOfMemoryError or an arithmetic overflow as discussed on page 106. But usually these errors do not occur, and we can place the new element in the next available location of the array. What is the index of the next available location? For example, if manyItems is 3, then data[0], data[1], and data[2] are already occupied, and the next location is data[3]. In general, the next available location will be data[manyItems]. We can place the new element in data[manyItems], as shown in this implementation:

implementing add

```
public void add(int element)
{
    if (manyItems == data.length)
    {
        // Double the capacity and add 1; this works even if manyItems is 0.
        // However, in the case that manyItems*2 + 1 is beyond
        // Integer.MAX_VALUE, there will be an arithmetic overflow and
        // the bag will fail.
        ensureCapacity(manyItems*2 + 1);
    }

    data[manyItems] = element;    ←──  See Self-Test Exercise 11
    manyItems++;                        for an alternative approach
}                                       to these steps.
```

Within a method we can activate other methods, such as the way that the add implementation activates ensureCapacity to increase the capacity of the array.

The remove Method. The remove method takes several steps to remove an element named target from a bag. In the first step, we find the index of target in the bag's array, and store this index in a local variable named index. For example, suppose that target is the number 6 in the bag drawn here:

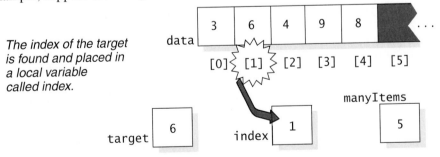

The index of the target is found and placed in a local variable called index.

In this example, target is a parameter to the remove method, index is a local variable in the remove method, and manyItems is the bag instance variable. As you can see in the drawing, the first step of remove is to locate the target (6) and place the index of the target in the local variable called index.

Once the index of the target is found, the second step is to take the *final* element in the bag and copy it to `data[index]`. The reason for this copying is so that all the bag's elements stay together at the front of the partially filled array, with no "holes." In our example, the number 8 is copied to `data[index]` as shown here:

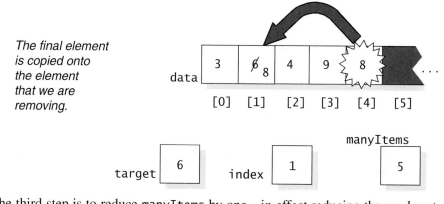

The final element is copied onto the element that we are removing.

The third step is to reduce `manyItems` by one—in effect reducing the used part of the array by one. In our example, `manyItems` is reduced from 5 to 4:

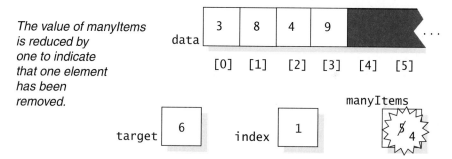

The value of manyItems is reduced by one to indicate that one element has been removed.

The code for the `remove` method, shown in Figure 3.3, follows these three steps. There is also a check that the target is actually in the bag. If we discover that the target is not in the bag, then we do not need to remove anything. Also note that our method works correctly for the boundary values of removing the first or last element in the array.

Before we continue, we want to point out some programming techniques. Look at the following for-loop from Figure 3.3:

implementing remove

```
for (index = 0; (index < manyItems) && (target != data[index]); index++)
    // No work is needed in the body of this for-loop.
    ;
```

Instead of the usual loop body, there is merely a semicolon, which means that the body of this loop has no statements; all of the work is accomplished by the loop's three clauses. The first clause initializes `index` to zero. The second clause indicates that the loop continues as long as `index` is still a location in the used part of the array (i.e., `index < manyItems`) and we have not yet found the target (i.e., `target != data[index]`). Each time through the loop, the third clause increments `index` by one (`index++`). No other work is needed in the loop, so the body of the loop has no statements.

A second programming technique concerns the boolean expression used to control the loop:

```
for (index = 0; (index < manyItems) && (target != data[index]); index++)
    // No work is needed in the body of this for-loop.
    ;
```

Look at the expression `data[index]` in the second part of the test. The valid indexes for `data` range from 0 to `manyItems-1`. But, if the target is not in the array, then `index` will eventually reach `manyItems`, which could be an invalid index. At that point, with `index` equal to `manyItems`, we must not evaluate the expression `data[index]`. Trying to evaluate `data[index]` with an invalid index will cause an `ArrayIndexOutOfBoundsException`.

The general rule: *Never use an invalid index with an array.*

FIGURE 3.3 | Implementation of the Bag's Method to Remove an Element

---

Implementation

```
public boolean remove(int target)
{
    int index; // The location of target in the data array

    // First, set index to the location of target in the data array,
    // which could be as small as 0 or as large as manyItems-1.
    // If target is not in the array, then index will be set equal to manyItems.
    for (index = 0; (index < manyItems) && (target != data[index]); index++)
        // No work is needed in the body of this for-loop.
        ;

    if (index == manyItems)
        // The target was not found, so nothing is removed.
        return false;
    else
    {   // The target was found at data[index].
        manyItems--;
        data[index] = data[manyItems];    See Self-Test Exercise 11 for an
        return true;                      alternative approach to this step.
    }
}
```

Avoiding the invalid index is the reason for the first part of the boolean test (i.e., `index < manyItems`). Moreover, the test for (`index < manyItems`) must appear *before* the other part of the test. Placing (`index < manyItems`) first ensures that only valid indexes are used. The insurance comes from a technique called *short-circuit evaluation,* which Java uses to evaluate boolean expressions. In **short-circuit evaluation** a boolean expression is evaluated from left to right, and the evaluation stops as soon as there is enough information to determine the value of the expression. In our example, if `index` equals `manyItems`, then the first part of the boolean expression (`index < manyItems`) is `false`, so the entire `&&` expression *must* be `false`. It doesn't matter whether the second part of the `&&` expression is `true` or `false`. Therefore, Java doesn't bother to evaluate the second part of the expression, and the potential error of an invalid index is avoided.

short-circuit evaluation of boolean expressions

The `countOccurrences` Method. To count the number of occurrences of a particular element in a bag, we step through the used portion of the partially filled array. Remember that we are using locations `data[0]` through `data[manyItems-1]`, so the correct loop is shown in this implementation:

```
public int countOccurrences(int target)
{
    int answer;
    int index;

    answer = 0;
    for (index = 0; index < manyItems; index++)
        if (target == data[index])
            answer++;
    return answer;
}
```

implementing the countOccurrences method

The `addAll` Method. The `addAll` method has this heading:

```
public void addAll(IntArrayBag addend)
```

implementing the addAll method

The bag that activates `addAll` is increased by adding all the elements from `addend`. Our implementation follows these steps:

1. Ensure that the capacity of the bag is large enough to contain its current elements plus the extra elements that will come from `addend`, as shown here:

    ```
    ensureCapacity(manyItems + addend.manyItems);
    ```

    By the way, what happens in this statement if `addend` is null? Of course, a null value violates the precondition of `addAll`, but a programmer could mistakenly provide null. In that case, a `NullPointerException` will be thrown, and this possibility is documented in the specification of `addAll` on page 108.

2. Copy the elements from addend.data to the next available positions in our own data array. In other words, we will copy addend.manyItems elements from the front of addend.data. These elements go into our own data array beginning at the next available spot, data[manyItems]. We could write a loop to copy these elements, but a quicker approach is to use Java's System.arraycopy method, which has these five arguments:

```
System.arraycopy(source, si, destination, di, n);
```

the arraycopy method

The arguments source and destination are two arrays, and the other arguments are integers. The method copies n elements from source (starting at source[si]) to the destination array (with the elements being placed at destination[di] through destination[di+n-1]). For our purposes, we call the arraycopy method as shown here:

```
System.arraycopy
    (addend.data, 0, data, manyItems, addend.manyItems);
```

3. Increase our own manyItems by addend.manyItems, as shown here:

```
manyItems += addend.manyItems;
```

These three steps are shown in the addAll implementation of Figure 3.4.

FIGURE 3.4   Implementation of the Bag's addAll Method

Implementation

```
public void addAll(IntArrayBag addend)
{
    // If addend is null, then a NullPointerException is thrown.
    // In the case that the total number of items is beyond Integer.MAX_VALUE, there will be
    // arithmetic overflow and the bag will fail.
    ensureCapacity(manyItems + addend.manyItems);

    System.arraycopy(addend.data, 0, data, manyItems, addend.manyItems);
    manyItems += addend.manyItems;
}
```

The union Method. The `union` method is different from our other methods. It is a *static* method, which means that it is not activated by any one bag object. Instead, the method must take its two parameters (bags `b1` and `b2`), combine these two bags together into a third bag, and return this third bag. The third bag is declared as a local variable called `answer` in the implementation of Figure 3.5. The capacity of the answer bag must be the sum of the capacities of `b1` and `b2`, so the actual answer bag is allocated by the statement:

implementing the union method

```
answer = new IntArrayBag(b1.getCapacity( ) + b2.getCapacity( ));
```

This calls the `IntArrayBag` constructor to create a new bag with an initial capacity of `b1.getCapacity( ) + b2.getCapacity( )`.

The `union` implementation also makes use of the `System.arraycopy` method to copy elements from `b1.data` and `b2.data` into `answer.data`.

FIGURE 3.5	Implementation of the Bag's `union` Method

Implementation

```java
public static IntArrayBag union(IntArrayBag b1, IntArrayBag b2)
{
    // If either b1 or b2 is null, then a NullPointerException is thrown.
    // In the case that the total number of items is beyond Integer.MAX_VALUE,
    // there will be an arithmetic overflow and the bag will fail.
    IntArrayBag answer =
        new IntArrayBag(b1.getCapacity( ) + b2.getCapacity( ));

    System.arraycopy(b1.data, 0, answer.data, 0, b1.manyItems);
    System.arraycopy(b2.data, 0, answer.data, b1.manyItems, b2.manyItems);
    answer.manyItems = b1.manyItems + b2.manyItems;

    return answer;
}
```

The clone Method. The clone method of a class allows a programmer to make a copy of an object. For example, the IntArrayBag class has a clone method to allow a programmer to make a copy of an existing bag. The copy is separate from the original, so that subsequent changes to the copy won't change the original, nor will subsequent changes to the original change the copy.

The IntArrayBag clone method will follow the pattern introduced in Chapter 2 on page 78. Therefore, the start of the clone method is:

```
public Object clone( )
{ // Clone an IntArrayBag object.
   IntArrayBag answer;

   try
   {
      answer = (IntArrayBag) super.clone( );
   }
   catch (CloneNotSupportedException e)
   {
      throw new RuntimeException
      ("This class does not implement Cloneable.");
   }
   ...
```

As explained in Chapter 2, this code uses the super.clone method to make answer be an exact copy of the bag that activated the clone method. But for the bag class, an exact copy is not quite correct. The problem occurs because super.clone copies each instance variable of the class without concern for whether the instance variable is a primitive type (such as an int) or a more complicated type (such as an array or some other kind of reference to an object).

To see why this causes a problem, suppose we have a bag that contains three elements, as shown here:

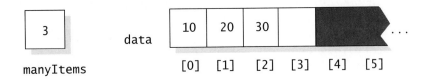

This drawing uses the "array shorthand" that we've been using—just putting the name of the array right next to it. But in fact, as with every array, the instance variable data is actually a reference to the array, so a more accurate picture looks like the drawing at the top of the next page.

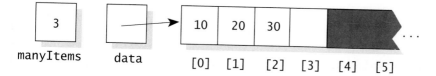

Now, suppose we activate clone( ) to create a copy of this bag. The clone method executes the statement answer = (IntArrayBag) super.clone( ). What does super.clone( ) do? It creates a new IntArrayBag object and answer will refer to this new IntArrayBag. But the new IntArrayBag has instance variables (answer.manyItems and answer.data) that are merely copied from the original. So, after the statement answer = (IntArrayBag) super.clone( ) the situation looks like this (where manyItems and data are the instance variables from the original bag that activated the clone method):

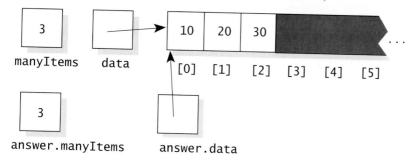

As you can see, answer.manyItems has a copy of the number 3, and that is fine. But answer.data merely refers to the original's array. Subsequent changes to answer.data will affect the original and vice versa. This is incorrect behavior for a clone. To fix the problem, we need an additional statement before the return of the clone method. The purpose of the statement is to create a new array for the clone's data instance variable to refer to. Here's the statement:

```
answer.data = (int [ ]) data.clone( );
```

After this statement, answer.data refers to a separate array, as shown here:

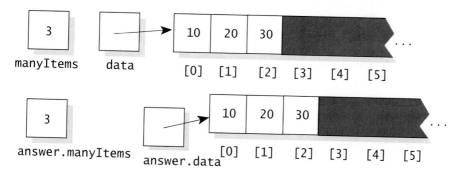

The new `answer.data` array was created by creating a clone of the original array (as described on page 99). Subsequent changes to `answer` will not affect the original, nor will changes to the original affect `answer`. The complete `clone` method, including the extra statement at the end, is shown in Figure 3.6.

   TIP

Programming Tip: **Cloning a Class That Contains an Array**

If a class has an instance variable that is an array, then the clone method needs extra work before it returns. The extra work creates a new array for the clone's instance variable to refer to.

The class may have other instance variables that are references to objects. In such a case, the clone method also carries out extra work. The extra work creates a new object for each such instances variable to refer to.

FIGURE 3.6   Implementation of the Bag's `clone` Method

Implementation

```
public Object clone( )
{
    { // Clone an IntArrayBag object.
    IntArrayBag answer;

    try
    {
        answer = (IntArrayBag) super.clone( );
    }
    catch (CloneNotSupportedException e)
    {
        // This exception should not occur. But if it does, it would probably indicate a
        // programming error that made super.clone unavailable. The most common
        // error would be forgetting the "Implements Cloneable"
        // clause at the start of this class.
        throw new RuntimeException
            ("This class does not implement Cloneable.");
    }

    answer.data = (int [ ]) data.clone( );

    return answer;
}
```

This step creates a new array for answer.data to refer to. The new array is separate from the original array so that subsequent changes to one will not affect the other.

FIGURE 3.7   Implementation of the Bag's `ensureCapacity` Method

Implementation

```
public void ensureCapacity(int minimumCapacity)
{
    int biggerArray[ ];

    if (data.length < minimumCapacity)
    {
        biggerArray = new int[minimumCapacity];
        System.arraycopy(data, 0, biggerArray, 0, manyItems);
        data = biggerArray;
    }
}
```

The `ensureCapacity` Method.   This method ensures that a bag's array has at least a certain minimum length. Here is the method's heading:

```
public void ensureCapacity(int minimumCapacity)
```

The method checks whether the bag's array has a length below `minimum-Capacity`. If so, then the method allocates a new larger array with a length of `minimumCapacity`. The elements are copied into the larger array, and the `data` instance variable is then made to refer to the larger array. Figure 3.7 shows our implementation, which follows the steps we have outlined.

The Bag ADT—Putting the Pieces Together

Three bag methods remain to be implemented: `size` (which returns the number of elements currently in the bag), `getCapacity` (which returns the current length of the bag's array, including the part that's not currently being used), and `trimToSize` (which reduces the capacity of the bag's array to equal exactly the current number of elements in the bag).

The `size` and `getCapacity` methods are implemented in one line each, and `trimToSize` is similar to `ensureCapacity`, so we won't discuss these methods. But you should examine these methods in the complete implementation file of Figure 3.8 on page 126. Also notice that the `IntArrayBag` class is placed in a package called `edu.colorado.collections`. Throughout the rest of this book, we will add other collection classes to this package.

FIGURE 3.8   Implementation File for the `IntArrayBag` Class

Implementation

```
// File: IntArrayBag.java from the package edu.colorado.collections
// Complete documentation is in Figure 3.1 on page 107 or from the IntArrayBag link in
//    http://www.cs.colorado.edu/~main/docs/

package edu.colorado.collections;

public class IntArrayBag implements Cloneable
{
   // Invariant of the IntArrayBag class:
   //    1. The number of elements in the Bag is in the instance variable manyItems.
   //    2. For an empty Bag, we do not care what is stored in any of data;
   //       for a nonempty Bag, the elements in the Bag are stored in data[0]
   //       through data[manyItems-1], and we don't care what's in the rest of data.
   private int[ ] data;
   private int manyItems;

   public IntArrayBag( )
   {
      final int INITIAL_CAPACITY = 10;
      manyItems = 0;
      data = new int[INITIAL_CAPACITY];
   }

   public IntArrayBag(int initialCapacity)
   {
      if (initialCapacity < 0)
         throw new IllegalArgumentException
         ("initialCapacity is negative: " + initialCapacity);
      manyItems = 0;
      data = new int[initialCapacity];
   }

   public void add(int element)
   {
      if (manyItems == data.length)
      {
         // Double the capacity and add 1; this works even if manyItems is 0. However, in
         // case that manyItems*2 + 1 is beyond Integer.MAX_VALUE, there will be an
         // arithmetic overflow and the bag will fail.
         ensureCapacity(manyItems*2 + 1);
      }
      data[manyItems] = element;
      manyItems++;
   }
```

(continued)

(FIGURE 3.8 continued)

```java
public void addAll(IntArrayBag addend)
{
    // If addend is null, then a NullPointerException is thrown.
    // In the case that the total number of items is beyond Integer.MAX_VALUE, there will
    // be an arithmetic overflow and the bag will fail.
    ensureCapacity(manyItems + addend.manyItems);

    System.arraycopy(addend.data, 0, data, manyItems, addend.manyItems);
    manyItems += addend.manyItems;
}


public Object clone( )
{   // Clone an IntArrayBag object.
    IntArrayBag answer;

    try
    {
        answer = (IntArrayBag) super.clone( );
    }
    catch (CloneNotSupportedException e)
    {
        // This exception should not occur. But if it does, it would probably indicate a
        // programming error that made super.clone unavailable. The most common
        // error would be forgetting the "Implements Cloneable"
        // clause at the start of this class.
        throw new RuntimeException
        ("This class does not implement Cloneable.");
    }

    answer.data = (int [ ]) data.clone( );

    return answer;
}


public int countOccurrences(int target)
{
    int answer;
    int index;

    answer = 0;
    for (index = 0; index < manyItems; index++)
        if (target == data[index])
            answer++;
    return answer;
}
```

(continued)

(FIGURE 3.8 continued)

```java
public void ensureCapacity(int minimumCapacity)
{
   int biggerArray[ ];

   if (data.length < minimumCapacity)
   {
      biggerArray = new int[minimumCapacity];
      System.arraycopy(data, 0, biggerArray, 0, manyItems);
      data = biggerArray;
   }
}


public int getCapacity( )
{
   return data.length;
}


public boolean remove(int target)
{
   int index; // The location of target in the data array

   // First, set index to the location of target in the data array,
   // which could be as small as 0 or as large as manyItems-1.
   // If target is not in the array, then index will be set equal to manyItems.
   for (index = 0; (index < manyItems) && (target != data[index]); index++)
      // No work is needed in the body of this for-loop.
      ;

   if (index == manyItems)
      // The target was not found, so nothing is removed.
      return false;
   else
   {  // The target was found at data[index].
      manyItems--;
      data[index] = data[manyItems];   // See Self-Test Exercise 11 for an
      return true;                     // alternative approach to this step.
   }
}


public int size( )
{
   return manyItems;
}
```

(continued)

(FIGURE 3.8 continued)

```java
public void trimToSize( )
{
    int trimmedArray[ ];

    if (data.length != manyItems)
    {
        trimmedArray = new int[manyItems];
        System.arraycopy(data, 0, trimmedArray, 0, manyItems);
        data = trimmedArray;
    }
}


public static IntArrayBag union(IntArrayBag b1, IntArrayBag b2)
{
    // If either b1 or b2 is null, then a NullPointerException is thrown.
    // In the case that the total number of items is beyond Integer.MAX_VALUE, there will
    // be an arithmetic overflow and the bag will fail.
    IntArrayBag answer = new IntArrayBag(b1.getCapacity( ) + b2.getCapacity( ));

    System.arraycopy(b1.data, 0, answer.data, 0, b1.manyItems);
    System.arraycopy(b2.data, 0, answer.data, b1.manyItems, b2.manyItems);
    answer.manyItems = b1.manyItems + b2.manyItems;
    return answer;
}

}
```

Programming Tip: Document the ADT Invariant in the Implementation File

TIP

The invariant of an ADT describes the rules that dictate how the instance variables are used. This information is important to the programmer who implements the class. Therefore, you should write this information in the implementation file, just before the declarations of the private instance variables. For example, the invariant for the `IntArrayBag` class appears before the declarations of `manyItems` and `data` in the implementation file of Figure 3.8 on page 126.

This is the best place to document the ADT's invariant. In particular, do not write the invariant as part of the class's specification, because a programmer who uses the ADT does not need to know about private instance variables. But the programmer who implements the ADT does need to know about the invariant.

The Bag ADT—Testing

Thus far, we have focused on the design and implementation of new classes and their methods. But it's also important to continue practicing the other aspects of software development, particularly testing. Each of the bag's new methods must be tested. As shown in Chapter 1, it is important to concentrate the testing on boundary values. At this point, we will alert you to only one potential pitfall, leaving the complete testing to Programming Project 2 on page 168.

PITFALL

Pitfall: An Object Can Be an Argument to Its Own Method

A class can have a method with a parameter that is the same data type as the class itself. For example, one of the `IntArrayBag` methods, addAll, has a parameter that is an `IntArrayBag` itself, as shown in this heading:

```
public void addAll(IntArrayBag addend)
```

An `IntArrayBag` can be created and activate its addAll method using itself as the argument. For example:

```
IntArrayBag b = new IntArrayBag( );
b.add(5);                    ──── b now contains a 5 and a 2.
b.add(2);  ◄────
b.addAll(b);  ◄────          ──── Now b contains two 5s and two 2s.
```

The highlighted statement takes all the elements in b (the 5 and the 2) and adds them to what's already in b, so b ends up with two copies of each number.

In the highlighted statement, the bag b is activating the addAll method, but this same bag b is the actual argument to the method. This is a situation that must be carefully tested. As an example of the danger, consider the incorrect implementation of addAll in Figure 3.9. Do you see what goes wrong with `b.addAll(b)`? (See the answer to Self-Test Exercise 12.)

FIGURE 3.9 | Wrong Implementation of the Bag's addAll Method

A Wrong Implementation

WARNING!

There is a bug in this implementation. See Self-Test Exercise 12.

```
public void addAll(IntArrayBag addend)
{
    int i; // An array index

    ensureCapacity(manyItems + addend.manyItems);
    for (i = 0; i < addend.manyItems; i++)
        add(addend.data[i]);
}
```

The Bag ADT—Analysis

We finish this section with a time analysis of the bag's methods. Generally, we'll use the number of elements in a bag as the input size. For example, if b is a bag containing n integers, then the number of operations required by b.count-Occurrences is a formula involving n. To determine the operations, we'll see how many statements are executed by the method, although we won't need an exact determination since our answer will use big-O notation. Except for two declarations and two statements, all of the work in countOccurrences happens in this loop:

```
for (index = 0; index < manyItems; index++)
    if (target == data[index])
        answer++;
```

We can see that the body of the loop will be executed exactly n times—once for each element in the bag. The body of the loop also has another important property: The body contains no other loops or calls to methods that contain loops. This is enough to conclude that the total number of statements executed by countOccurrences is no more than:

$$n \times \text{(number of statements in the loop)} + 4$$

The extra +4 at the end is for the two declarations and two statements outside the loop. Regardless of how many statements are actually in the loop, the time expression is *always* $O(n)$—so the countOccurrences method is linear.

A similar analysis shows that remove is also linear, although remove's loop sometimes executes fewer than n times. However, the fact that remove *sometimes* requires less than $n \times$ (number of statements in the loop) does not change the fact that the method is $O(n)$. In the worst case, the loop does execute a full n iterations, therefore the correct time analysis is no better than $O(n)$.

The analysis of the constructor is a special case. The constructor allocates an array of initialCapacity integers, and in Java all array components are initialized (integers are set to zero). The initialization time is proportional to the capacity of the array, so an accurate time analysis is $O(\text{initialCapacity})$.

Several of the other bag methods do not contain any loops or array allocations. This is a pleasant situation because the time required for any of these methods does not depend on the number of elements in the bag. For example, when an element is added to a bag that does not need to grow, the new element is placed at the end of the array, and the add method never looks at the elements that were already in the bag. When the time required by a method does not depend on the size of the input, the procedure is called **constant time**, which is written $O(1)$.

The add method has two distinct cases. If the current capacity is adequate for a new element, then the time is $O(1)$. But if the capacity needs to be increased, then the time increases to $O(n)$ because of the array allocation and copying of elements from the old array to the new array.

constant time
O(1)

The time analyses of all methods are summarized here for our `IntArrayBag`:

Operation	Time Analysis	
Constructor	$O(c)$	c is the initial capacity
add without capacity increase	$O(1)$	Constant time
add with capacity increase	$O(n)$	Linear time
b1.addAll(b2) without capacity increase	$O(n_2)$	Linear in the size of the added bag
b1.addAll(b2) with capacity increase	$O(n_1 + n_2)$	n_1 and n_2 are the sizes of the bags
clone	$O(c)$	c is the bag's capacity

Operation	Time Analysis	
countOccurrences	$O(n)$	linear time
ensureCapacity	$O(c)$	c is the specified minimum capacity
getCapacity	$O(1)$	Constant time
remove	$O(n)$	Linear time
size	$O(1)$	Constant time
trimToSize	$O(n)$	Linear time
union of b1 and b2	$O(c_1 + c_2)$	c_1 and c_2 are the bags' capacities

Self-Test Exercises

7. Draw a picture of `mybag.data` after these statements:
   ```
   IntArrayBag mybag = new IntArrayBag(10);
   mybag.add(1);
   mybag.add(2);
   mybag.add(3);
   mybag.remove(1);
   ```

8. The bag in the previous question has a capacity of 10. What happens if you try to add more than ten elements to the bag?

9. Write the invariant of the bag ADT.

10. What is the meaning of a *static* method? How is the activation different than an ordinary method?

11. Use the expression `--manyItems` (with the `--` *before* `manyItems`) to rewrite the last two statements of `remove` (Figure 3.3 on page 118) as a single statement. If you are unsure of the difference between `many-Items--` and `--manyItems`, then go ahead and peek at our answer at the back of the chapter. Use `manyItems++` to make a similar alteration to the add method.

12. Suppose we implement `addAll` as shown in Figure 3.9 on page 130. What goes wrong with `b.addAll(b)`?

13. Describe the extra work that must be done at the end of the `clone` method. Draw pictures to show what goes wrong if this step is omitted.

14. Suppose x and y are arrays with 100 elements each. Use the `arraycopy` method to copy x[10]...x[25] to y[33]...y[48].

3.3 PROGRAMMING PROJECT: THE SEQUENCE ADT

You are ready to tackle a collection class implementation on your own. The data type is called a **sequence**. A sequence is similar to a bag—both contain a bunch of elements. But unlike a bag, the elements in a sequence are arranged one after another.

How does this differ from a bag? After all, aren't the bag elements arranged one after another in the partially filled array that implements the bag? Yes, but that's a quirk of our particular bag implementation, and the order is just happenstance. Moreover, there is no way that a program using the bag can refer to the bag elements by their position in the array. *how a sequence differs from a bag*

In contrast, the elements of a sequence are kept one after another, and the sequence's methods allow a program to step through the sequence one element at a time, using the order in which the elements are stored. Methods also permit a program to control precisely where elements are inserted and removed within the sequence.

The Sequence ADT—Specification

Our bag happened to be a bag of *integers*. We could have had a different underlying element type such as a bag of *double* numbers or a bag of *characters*. In fact, in Chapter 5, we'll see how to construct a collection that can simultaneously handle many different types of elements, rather than being restricted to one type of element. But for now, our collection classes will have just one kind of element for each collection. In particular, for our sequence class each element will be a *double* number, and the class itself is called `DoubleArraySeq`. We could have chosen some other type for the elements, but double numbers are as good as anything for your first implementation of a collection class.

As with the bag, each sequence will have a current capacity, which is the number of elements the sequence can hold without having to request more memory. The initial capacity will be set by the constructor. The capacity can be increased in several different manners, which we'll see as we specify the various methods of the new class.

Constructor. The `DoubleArraySeq` has two constructors—a constructor that constructs an empty sequence with an initial capacity of 10, and another constructor that constructs an empty sequence with some specified initial capacity.

The size Method. The size method returns the number of elements in the sequence. Here is the heading:

```
public int size( )
```

For example, if scores is a sequence containing the values 10.1, 40.2, and 1.1, then scores.size( ) returns 3. Throughout our examples, we will draw sequences vertically, with the first element on top, as shown in the picture in the margin (where the first element is 10.1).

```
┌──────────┐
│  10.1    │
│  40.2    │
│   1.1    │
└──────────┘
```

Methods to Examine a Sequence. We will have methods to build a sequence, but it will be easier to explain first the methods to examine a sequence that has already been built. The elements of a sequence can be examined one after another, but the examination must be in order, from the first to the last. Three methods work together to enforce the in-order retrieval rule. The methods' headings are:

```
public void start( )
public double getCurrent( )
public void advance( )
```

When we want to retrieve the elements of a sequence, we begin by activating start. After activating start, the getCurrent method returns the first element of the sequence. Each time we call advance, the getCurrent method changes so that it returns the next element of the sequence. For example, if a sequence called numbers contains the four numbers 37, 10, 83, and 42, then we can write the following code to print the first three numbers of the sequence:

*start,
getCurrent,
advance*

```
numbers.start( );
System.out.println(numbers.getCurrent( ));        ← Prints 37
numbers.advance( );
System.out.println(numbers.getCurrent( ));        ← Prints 10
numbers.advance( );
System.out.println(numbers.getCurrent( ));        ← Prints 83
```

isCurrent

One other method cooperates with getCurrent. The isCurrent method returns a boolean value to indicate whether there actually is a current element for getCurrent to provide, or whether we have advanced right off the end of the sequence.

Using all four of the methods with a for-loop, we can print an entire sequence, as shown here for the numbers sequence:

```
for (numbers.start( ); numbers.isCurrent( ); numbers.advance( ))
    System.out.println(numbers.getCurrent( ));
```

The `addBefore` and `addAfter` Methods. There are two methods to add a new element to a sequence, with these headers:

```
public void addBefore(double element)
public void addAfter(double element)
```

The first method, `addBefore`, places a new element before the current element. For example, suppose that we have created the sequence shown in the margin, and that the current element is 8.8. In this example, we want to add 10.0 to our sequence, immediately before the current element. When 10.0 is added before the current element, other elements in the sequence—such as 8.8 and 99.0— will move down the sequence to make room for the new element. After the addition, the sequence has the four elements shown in the lower box.

If there is no current element, then `addBefore` places the new element at the front of the sequence. In any case, after the `addBefore` method returns, the new element will be the current element. In the example shown in the margin, the 10.0 becomes the new current element.

A second method, called `addAfter`, also adds a new element to a sequence— but the new element is added *after* the current element. If there is no current element, then the `addAfter` method places the new element at the end of the sequence (rather than the front). In all cases, when the method finishes, the new element will be the current element.

Either `addBefore` or `addAfter` can be used on an empty sequence to add the first element.

The `removeCurrent` Method. The current element can be removed from a sequence. The method for a removal has no parameters, but the precondition requires that there is a current element; it is this current element that is removed, as specified here:

- **removeCurrent**
  ```
  public boolean removeCurrent( )
  ```
  Removes the current element from this sequence.
  Precondition:
  `isCurrent( )` returns true.
  Postcondition:
  The current element has been removed from this sequence. If this was the final element of the sequence (with nothing after it), then after the removal there is no longer a current element; otherwise the new current element is the one that used to be after the removed element.

For example, suppose `scores` is the four-element sequence shown at the top of the box in the margin, and the highlighted 8.3 is the current element. After activating `scores.removeCurrent( )`, the 8.3 has been deleted, and the 4.1 is now the current element.

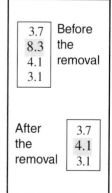

| 42.1 |
| 8.8 |
| 99.0 |

The sequence grows by adding 10.0 before the current element.

| 42.1 |
| 10.0 |
| 8.8 |
| 99.0 |

3.7	Before
8.3	the
4.1	removal
3.1	

After the removal

| 3.7 |
| 4.1 |
| 3.1 |

The addAll Method. The addAll method is similar to the bag's addAll method. It allows us to place the contents of one sequence at the end of what we already have. The method has this heading:

```
public void addAll(DoubleArraySeq addend)
```

As an example, suppose we create two sequences called helter and skelter. The sequences contain the elements shown in the box in the margin (helter has four elements and skelter has three). We can then activate the method:

```
helter.addAll(skelter);
```

After the addAll activation, the helter sequence will have seven elements: 3.7, 8.3, 4.1, 3.1, 4.9, 9.3, 2.5 (its original four elements followed by the three elements of skelter). The current element of the helter sequence remains where it was (at the number 8.3), and the skelter sequence still has its original three elements.

The concatenation Method. The **concatenation** of two sequences is a new sequence obtained by placing one sequence after the other. We will implement concatenation with a static method that has the following two parameters:

```
public static DoubleArraySeq concatenation
(DoubleArraySeq s1, DoubleArraySeq s2)
```

A concatenation is somewhat similar to the union of two bags. For example:

```
DoubleArraySeq part1 = new DoubleArraySeq( );
DoubleArraySeq part2 = new DoubleArraySeq( );

part1.addAfter(3.7);
part1.addAfter(9.5);
part2.addAfter(4.0);
part2.addAfter(8.6);
```

This computes the concatenation of the two sequences, putting the result in a third sequence.

```
DoubleArraySeq total = DoubleArraySeq.concatenation(part1, part2)
```

After these statements, total is the sequence consisting of 3.7, 9.5, 4.0, 8.6. The new sequence computed by concatenation has no current element. The original sequences, part1 and part2, are unchanged.

Notice the effect of having a *static* method: concatenation is not activated by any one sequence. Instead, the activation of

```
DoubleArraySeq.concatenation(part1, part2)
```

creates and returns a new sequence that includes the contents of part1 followed by the contents of part2.

The clone Method. As part of our specification, we require that a sequence can be copied with a clone method. The clone contains the same elements as the original. If the original had a current element, then the clone has a current element in the corresponding place. For example:

```
DoubleArraySeq s = new DoubleArraySeq( );
s.addAfter(4.2);
s.addAfter(1.5);
s.start( );
IntArrayBag t = (DoubleArraySeq) s.clone( );
```

At the point when the clone is made, the sequence s has two elements (4.2 and 1.5) and the current element is the 4.2. Therefore, t will end up with the same two elements (4.2 and 1.5) and its current element will be the number 4.2. Subsequent changes to s will not affect t, nor vice versa.

Three Methods That Deal with Capacity. The sequence class has three methods for dealing with capacity—the same three methods that the bag has:

```
public int getCapacity( )
public void ensureCapacity(int minimumCapacity)
public void trimToSize( )
```

As with the bag, the purpose of these methods is to allow a programmer to explicitly set the capacity of the collection. If a programmer does not explicitly set the capacity, then the class will still work correctly, but some operations will be less efficient because the capacity might be repeatedly increased.

The Sequence ADT—Documentation

The complete specification for this first version of our sequence class is shown in Figure 3.10 on page 138. This specification is also available from the DoubleArraySeq link at the web address

```
http://www.cs.colorado.edu/~main/docs/
```

When you read the specification, you'll see that the package name is edu.colorado.collections. So, you should create a subdirectory called edu/colorado/collections for your implementation.

The specification also indicates some limitations—the same limitations that we saw for the bag class. For example, an OutOfMemoryError can occur in any method that increases the capacity. Several of the methods throw an IllegalStateException to indicate that they have been illegally activated (with no current element). Also, an attempt to move the capacity beyond the maximum integer causes the class to fail by an arithmetic overflow.

After you've looked through the specifications, we'll suggest a design that uses three private instance variables.

FIGURE 3.10	Specification for the `DoubleArraySeq` Class

Class DoubleArraySeq

❖ **public class DoubleArraySeq from the package edu.colorado.collections**

A `DoubleArraySeq` keeps track of a sequence of double numbers. The sequence can have a special "current element," which is specified and accessed through four methods that are not available in the bag class (`start`, `getCurrent`, `advance` and `isCurrent`).

Limitations:

(1) The capacity of a sequence can change after it's created, but the maximum capacity is limited by the amount of free memory on the machine. The constructor, `addAfter`, `addBefore`, `clone`, and `concatenation` will result in an `OutOfMemoryError` when free memory is exhausted.

(2) A sequence's capacity cannot exceed the largest integer 2,147,483,647 (`Integer.MAX_VALUE`). Any attempt to create a larger capacity results in failure due to an arithmetic overflow.

Specification

◆ **Constructor for the DoubleArraySeq**

`public DoubleArraySeq(int initialCapacity)`

Initialize an empty sequence with a specified initial capacity. Note that the `addAfter` and `addBefore` methods work efficiently (without needing more memory) until this capacity is reached.

Postcondition:

This sequence is empty and has an initial capacity of 10.

Throws: `OutOfMemoryError`

Indicates insufficient memory for: `new double[10]`.

◆ **Second Constructor for the DoubleArraySeq**

`public DoubleArraySeq(int initialCapacity)`

Initialize an empty sequence with a specified initial capacity. Note that the `addAfter` and `addBefore` methods work efficiently (without needing more memory) until this capacity is reached.

Parameters:

`initialCapacity` – the initial capacity of this sequence

Precondition:

`initialCapacity` is non-negative.

Postcondition:

This sequence is empty and has the given initial capacity.

Throws: `IllegalArgumentException`

Indicates that `initialCapacity` is negative.

Throws: `OutOfMemoryError`

Indicates insufficient memory for: `new double[initialCapacity]`.

(continued)

(FIGURE 3.10 continued)

◆ addAfter and addBefore

```
public void addAfter(double element)
public void addBefore(double element)
```

Adds a new element to this sequence, either before or after the current element. If this new element would take this sequence beyond its current capacity, then the capacity is increased before adding the new element.

Parameters:
element – the new element that is being added

Postcondition:
A new copy of the element has been added to this sequence. If there was a current element, then addAfter places the new element after the current element and addBefore places the new element before the current element. If there was no current element, then addAfter places the new element at the end of this sequence and addBefore places the new element at the front of this sequence. In all cases, the new element becomes the new current element of this sequence.

Throws: OutOfMemoryError
Indicates insufficient memory to increase the size of this sequence.

Note:
An attempt to increase the capacity beyond Integer.MAX_VALUE will cause this sequence to fail with an arithmetic overflow.

◆ addAll

```
public void addAll(DoubleArraySeq addend)
```
Place the contents of another sequence at the end of this sequence.

Parameters:
addend – a sequence whose contents will be placed at the end of this sequence

Precondition:
The parameter, addend, is not null.

Postcondition:
The elements from addend have been placed at the end of this sequence. The current element of this sequence remains where it was, and the addend is also unchanged.

Throws: NullPointerException
Indicates that addend is null.

Throws: OutOfMemoryError
Indicates insufficient memory to increase the capacity of this sequence.

Note:
An attempt to increase the capacity beyond Integer.MAX_VALUE will cause this sequence to fail with an arithmetic overflow.

(continued)

(FIGURE 3.10 continued)

- **advance**
    ```
    public void advance( )
    ```
    Move forward, so that the current element is now the next element in this sequence.

    Precondition:
    isCurrent( ) returns true.

    Postcondition:
    If the current element was already the end element of this sequence (with nothing after it), then there is no longer any current element. Otherwise, the new element is the element immediately after the original current element.

    Throws: IllegalStateException
    Indicates that there is no current element, so advance may not be called.

- **clone**
    ```
    public Object clone( )
    ```
    Generate a copy of this sequence.

    Returns:
    The return value is a copy of this sequence. Subsequent changes to the copy will not affect the original, nor vice versa. The return value must be typecast to a DoubleArraySeq before it is used.

    Throws: OutOfMemoryError
    Indicates insufficient memory for creating the clone.

- **concatenation**
    ```
    public static DoubleArraySeq concatenation
    (DoubleArraySeq s1, DoubleArraySeq s2)
    ```
    Create a new sequence that contains all the elements from one sequence followed by another.

    Parameters:
    s1 – the first of two sequences
    s2 – the second of two sequences

    Precondition:
    Neither s1 nor s2 is null.

    Returns:
    a new sequence that has the elements of s1 followed by the elements of s2 (with no current element)

    Throws: NullPointerException
    Indicates that one of the arguments is null.

    Throws: OutOfMemoryError
    Indicates insufficient memory for the new sequence.

    Note:
    An attempt to increase the capacity beyond Integer.MAX_VALUE will cause this sequence to fail with an arithmetic overflow.

(continued)

(FIGURE 3.10 continued)

◆ ensureCapacity

```
public void ensureCapacity(int minimumCapacity)
```

Change the current capacity of this sequence.

Parameters:

    `minimumCapacity` – the new capacity for this sequence

Postcondition:

    This sequence's capacity has been changed to at least `minimumCapacity`.

Throws: `OutOfMemoryError`

    Indicates insufficient memory for: `new double[minimumCapacity]`.

◆ getCapacity

```
public int getCapacity( )
```

Accessor method to determine the current capacity of this sequence. The `addBefore` and `addAfter` methods works efficiently (without needing more memory) until this capacity is reached.

Returns:

    the current capacity of this sequence

◆ getCurrent

```
public double getCurrent( )
```

Accessor method to determine the current element of this sequence.

Precondition:

    `isCurrent( )` returns `true`.

Returns:

    the current element of this sequence

Throws: `IllegalStateException`

    Indicates that there is no current element.

◆ isCurrent

```
public boolean isCurrent( )
```

Accessor method to determine whether this sequence has a specified current element that can be retrieved with the `getCurrent` method.

Returns:

    `true` (there is a current element) or `false` (there is no current element at the moment)

◆ removeCurrent

```
public void removeCurrent( )
```

Remove the current element from this sequence.

Precondition:

    `isCurrent( )` returns `true`.

Postcondition:

    The current element has been removed from this sequence, and the following element (if there is one) is now the new current element. If there was no following element, then there is now no current element.

Throws: `IllegalStateException`

    Indicates that there is no current element, so `removeCurrent` may not be called. *(continued)*

(FIGURE 3.10 continued)

◆ **size**
```
public int size( )
```
Accessor method to determine the number of elements in this sequence.

Returns:
the number of elements in this sequence

◆ **start**
```
public void start( )
```
Set the current element at the front of this sequence.

Postcondition:
The front element of this sequence is now the current element (but if this sequence has no elements at all, then there is no current element).

◆ **trimToSize**
```
public void trimToSize( )
```
Reduce the current capacity of this sequence to its actual size (i.e., the number of elements it contains).

Postcondition:
This sequence's capacity has been changed to its current size.

Throws: `OutOfMemoryError`
Indicates insufficient memory for altering the capacity.

The Sequence ADT—Design

Our suggested design for the sequence ADT has three private instance variables. The first variable, `data`, is an array that stores the elements of the sequence. Just like the bag, `data` is a partially filled array, and a second instance variable, called `manyItems`, keeps track of how much of the `data` array is currently being used. Therefore, the used part of the array extends from `data[0]` to `data[manyItems-1]`. The third instance variable, `currentIndex`, gives the index of the current element in the array (if there is one). Sometimes a sequence has no current element, in which case `currentIndex` will be set to the same number as `manyItems` (since this is larger than any valid index). The complete invariant of our ADT is stated as three rules:

1. The number of elements in the sequence is stored in the instance variable `manyItems`.

2. For an empty sequence (with no elements), we do not care what is stored in any of `data`; for a nonempty sequence, the elements of the sequence are stored from the front to the end in `data[0]` to `data[manyItems-1]`, and we don't care what is stored in the rest of `data`.

3. If there is a current element, then it lies in `data[currentIndex]`; if there is no current element, then `currentIndex` equals `manyItems`.

As an example, suppose that a sequence contains four numbers, with the current element at data[2]. The instance variables of the object might appear as shown here:

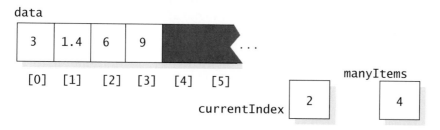

In this example, the current element is at data[2], so the getCurrent( ) method would return the number 6. At this point, if we called advance( ), then currentIndex would increase to 3, and getCurrent( ) would then return the 9.

Normally, a sequence has a current element, and the instance variable currentIndex contains the location of that current element. But if there is no current element, then currentIndex contains the same value as manyItems. In the above example, if currentIndex was 4, then that would indicate that there is no current element. Notice that this value (4) is beyond the used part of the array (which stretches from data[0] to data[3]).

The stated requirements for the instance variables form the invariant of the sequence ADT. You should place this invariant at the top of your implementation file (DoubleArraySeq.java). We will leave most of this implementation file up to you, but we will offer some hints and a bit of pseudocode.

invariant of the ADT

The Sequence ADT—Pseudocode for the Implementation

The removeCurrent Method.   This method removes the current element from the sequence. First check that the precondition is valid (use isCurrent( )). Then remove the current element by shifting each of the subsequent elements leftward one position. For example, suppose we are removing the current element from the sequence drawn here:

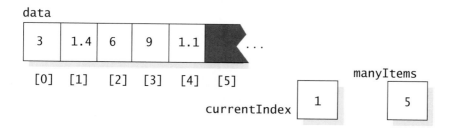

What is the current element in this picture? It is the 1.4, since currentIndex is 1 and data[1] contains 1.4.

In the case of the bag, we could remove an element such as 1.4 by copying the final element (1.1) onto the 1.4. But this approach won't work for the *sequence* because the elements would lose their sequence order. Instead, each element after the 1.4 must be moved leftward one position. The 6 moves from data[2] to data[1]; the 9 moves from data[3] to data[2]; the 1.1 moves from data[4] to data[3]. This is a lot of movement, but a small for-loop suffices to carry out all the work. This is the pseudocode:

```
for (i = the index after the current element; i < manyItems; i++)
    Move an element from data[i] back to data[i-1];
```

When the loop completes, you should reduce manyItems by one. The final result for our example is:

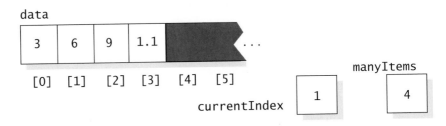

After the removal, the value in currentIndex is unchanged. In effect, this means that the element that was just after the removed element is now the current element. You must check that the method works correctly for boundary values—removing the first element and removing the end element. In fact, both these cases work fine. When the end element is removed, currentIndex will end up with the same value as manyItems, indicating that there is no longer a current element.

The addBefore Method. If there is a current element, then addBefore must take care to put the new element just before the current position. Elements that are already at or after the current position must be shifted rightward to make room for the new element. We suggest that you start by shifting elements at the end of the array rightward one position each until you reach the position for the new element.

For example, suppose you are putting 1.4 at the location data[1] in the following sequence:

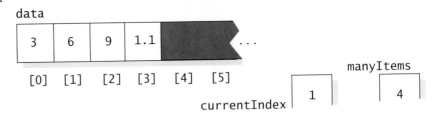

You would begin by shifting the 1.1 rightward from `data[3]` to `data[4]`; then move the 9 from `data[2]` to `data[3]`; then the 6 moves from `data[1]` rightward to `data[2]`. At this point, the array looks like this:

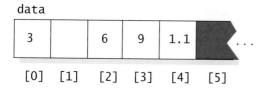

Of course, `data[1]` actually still contains a 6 since we just copied the 6 from `data[1]` to `data[2]`. But we have drawn `data[1]` as an empty box to indicate that `data[1]` is now available to hold the new element (the 1.4 that we are putting in the sequence). At this point we can place the 1.4 in `data[1]` and add one to `manyItems`, as shown here:

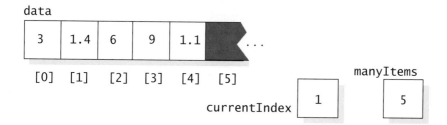

The pseudocode for shifting the elements rightward uses a for-loop. Each iteration of the loop shifts one element, as shown here:

```
for (i = manyItems;  data[i] is the wrong spot for element ;  i--)
    data[i] = data[i-1];
```

The key to the loop is the test `data[i] is the wrong spot for element`. How do we test whether a position is the wrong spot for the new element? A position is wrong if (`i > currentIndex`). Can you now write the entire method in Java? (See the solution to Self-Test Exercise 15, and don't forget to handle the special case when there is no current element.)

Other Methods. The other sequence methods are straightforward; for example, the `addAfter` method is similar to `addBefore`. Some additional useful methods are described in Programming Project 4 on page 168. You'll also need to be careful that you don't mindlessly copy the implementation of a bag method. For example, the `concatenation` method is similar to the bag's `union` method, but there is one extra step that concatenation must take (it sets `currentIndex` to `manyItems`).

Self-Test Exercises

15. Write the sequence's `addBefore` method.

16. Suppose that a sequence has 24 elements, and there is no current element. According to the invariant of the ADT, what is `currentIndex`?

17. Suppose g is a sequence with 10 elements and you activate `g.start( )` and then activate `g.advance( )` three times. What value is then in `g.currentIndex`?

18. What are good boundary values to test the `removeCurrent` method?

19. Write a demonstration program that asks the user for a list of family member ages, then prints the list in the same order that it was given.

20. Write a new method to remove a specified element from a sequence. The method has one parameter (the element to remove).

21. For a sequence of numbers, suppose that you insert 1, then 2, then 3, and so on up to *n*. What is the big-*O* time analysis for the combined time of inserting all *n* numbers with `addAfter`? How does the analysis change if you insert *n* first, then *n*–1, and so on down to 1—always using `add-Before` instead of `addAfter`?

22. Which of the ADTs—the bag or the sequence—*must* be implemented by storing the elements in an array? (Hint: We are not beyond asking a trick question.)

3.4 APPLETS FOR INTERACTIVE TESTING

When you implement a new class, it's useful to have a small interactive test program to help you test the class methods. Such a program can be written as a Java **applet**, which is a Java program written in a special format to have a graphical user interface. The graphical user interface is also called a GUI (pronounced "gooey"), and it allows a user to interact with a program by clicking the mouse, typing information into boxes, and performing other familiar actions. With a Java applet, GUIs are easy to create even if you've never run into such goo before.

This section shows a pattern for developing such applets. To illustrate the pattern, we'll implement an applet that lets you test three of the bag's methods (`size`, `add`, and `countOccurrences`). When the bag applet starts, a GUI is created, similar to the drawing in Figure 3.11(a).

By the way, the word "applet" means a particular kind of Java program, so you might show Figure 3.11 to your boss and say, "My applet created this nice GUI." But you can also use the word "applet" to talk about the GUI itself, such as "The applet in Figure 3.11(a) has three buttons in its middle section." And in fact, there are three buttons in that applet—the rectangles labeled `size( )`, `add( )`, and `countOccurrences( )`.

| **FIGURE 3.11** | Two Views of the Applet to Test the `IntArrayBag` Class |

(a) When the applet first opens, the applet has the components shown here.

(b) The user interacts with the applet by typing information and clicking on the buttons with the mouse. In this example, the user has typed 42 into the add text field, and then clicked the add button. The applet responds with a message "42 has been added to the bag," written in the text area at the bottom of the applet.

The applet in Figure 3.11 is intended to be used by the programmer who wrote the `IntArrayBag` class, to check interactively that the class is working correctly. When the applet starts, two sentences appear at the top: "`This test program has created a bag. Press buttons to activate the bag's methods.`" Above these sentences are some extra items, shown here:

The display above our sentences is created automatically by the applet display mechanism. The exact form of this display varies from one system to another, but the dark bar across the top generally contains controls such as the ☒ in the top right corner. Clicking on that ☒ with the mouse closes the applet on this particular system.

A series of buttons appears in the middle part of the applet, like this:

To test the bag, the user clicks on the various buttons. For example, the user can click on `size()` and a new message will appear in the large text area at the bottom of the applet. The message will tell the current size of the bag, as obtained by activating the `size()` method. If you click on this button right at the start, you'll get the message "`The bag's size is 0.`"

The user can also activate `add` or `countOccurrences`, but these methods each need an argument. For example, to add the number 42 to the bag, the user types the number 42 in the white box next to the `add` button, then clicks `add()`. The result of adding 42 is shown in Figure 3.11(b). After elements have been added, the user can test `countOccurrences`. For example, to count the occurrences of the number 10, the user types 10 in the box by the `countOccurrences` button and then clicks `countOccurrences()`. The applet activates `countOccurrences(10)` and prints the method's return value in the large text area at the bottom.

Anyway, that's the behavior that we want. Let's look at an outline of the Java programming techniques to produce such behavior, as shown in Figure 3.12.

FIGURE 3.12	Outline for the Interactive Applet to Test the `IntArrayBag` class

Java Applet Outline

```
//  FILE: BagApplet.java
```

1. Import statements. These statements import the class that is being tested and also the Java classes that are needed by the applet. For this applet, we must import the `IntArrayBag` class:

```
import edu.colorado.collections.IntArrayBag;
```

Most applets will also have these three import statements:

```
import java.applet.Applet;   // Provides the Applet class.
import java.awt.*;           // Provides Button class, etc.
import java.awt.event.*;     // Provides ActionEvent, ActionListener.
```

```
public class BagApplet extends Applet
{
```

2. The class definition.

```
    // Declare an IntArrayBag object for the Applet to manipulate:
    IntArrayBag b = new IntArrayBag( );
```

3. Declarations of the applet's components. These are the declarations of buttons, text areas, and other GUI components that appear in the applet.

```
    public void init( )
    {
       ...
    }
```

4. The `init` method.

5. Implementations of the action listeners. This code tells the applet what to do when each of the buttons is pressed.

6. Implementations of other methods. These are methods that are activated from within `init` to carry out various subtasks.

```
}
```

Six Parts of a Simple Interactive Applet

Figure 3.12 on page 149 shows an outline for the Java code of the applet that tests the `IntArrayBag`. The same outline can be used for an applet that interactively tests any class. The code has six parts, which we'll discuss now.

1. Import statements.   As with any Java program, we begin with a collection of import statements to tell the compiler about the other classes that we'll be using. In the case of the bag applet, we import the `IntArrayBag` class (using the statement `import edu.colorado.collections.IntArrayBag;`). Most applets also have these three import statements:

```
import java.applet.Applet;
import java.awt.*;
import java.awt.event.*;
```

abstract windowing toolkit

The first import statement provides a class called `Applet`, which we'll use in a moment. The other two import statements provide items from the **abstract windowing toolkit** (the "AWT"), which is a collection of classes for drawing buttons and other GUI items.

2. The class definition.   After the import statements, we define a class, much like any other Java class. This class definition begins with the line:

```
public class IntArrayBag Applet extends Applet
```

inheritance: the BagApplet gets a bunch of methods from the Applet class

The definition continues down to the last closing bracket of the file. The class for the bag applet is called `BagApplet`, which is certainly a good name, but what does "extends Applet" mean? It means that the `BagApplet` class will not be written entirely by us. Instead, the class begins by already having all the non-private methods of another class called `Applet`. We imported the `Applet` class from `java.applet.Applet`, and it is provided as part of the Java language so that a class such as `BagApplet` does not have to start from scratch. The act of obtaining methods from another class is called **inheritance**. The class that provides these methods (such as the `Applet` class) is called the **superclass**, and the new class (such as `BagApplet`) is called the **extended class**. Chapter 13 studies inheritance in detail, but for now all you need to know is that the `BagApplet` obtains a bunch of methods from the `Applet` class without having to do anything more than "extends Applet."

At the top of the class we define an `IntArrayBag` instance variable:

```
IntArrayBag b = new IntArrayBag( );
```

This bag, b, will be manipulated when the user clicks on the applet's buttons. In general, an interactive test applet will have one or more objects declared here, and these objects are manipulated by clicking the applet's buttons.

3. Declarations of the applet's components. An applet's components are the buttons and other items that are displayed when the applet runs. These components are declared as instance variables of the class. Our bag applet has several kinds of components: buttons (such as size()), text fields (which are the white rectangles next to some of the buttons), and a text area (which is the large rectangle in the bottom third of the applet). In all, there are six important components in the bag applet, represented by these six instance variables:

```
Button     sizeButton             = new Button("size( )");
Button     addButton              = new Button("add( )");
TextField  elementText            = new TextField(10);
Button     countOccurrencesButton = new Button("countOccurrences( )");
TextField  targetText             = new TextField(10);
TextArea   feedback               = new TextArea(7, 60);
```

All the instance variables are declared near the top of the class definition, before any of the method definitions. They cannot have the usual private access because they'll be accessed from other classes that we'll see shortly. But before that, let's look at the three kinds of components: button, text field, and text area.

A **button** is a grey rectangle with a label. When a button is created, the con-   *button*
structor is given a string that is printed in the middle of the button. For example, this declaration creates a button called sizeButton, and the label on the button is the string "size( )":

```
Button sizeButton = new Button("size( )");
```

The bag applet has three Button objects: sizeButton, addButton, and count-OccurrencesButton.

A **text field** is a white rectangle that can display one line of text. A text field   *text field*
is set up so that the program's user can click on the field and type information, and the applet can then read that information. Our applet has two text fields, one next to the add button and one next to the countOccurrences button. The TextField class has a constructor with one argument—an integer that specifies approximately how many characters can fit in the text field. For example, one of our text fields is declared as:

```
TextField elementText = new TextField(10);
```

The elementText text field can hold about 10 characters. The user can actually type beyond 10 characters, but only 10 characters of a long string will be displayed. We plan to display elementText right beside the add button, like this:

To test the add method, the user will type a number in the text field and click on the add button.

text area

A **text area** is like a text field with more than one line. Its constructor has two arguments that specify the number of rows and columns of text to display. Our bag applet has one text area, declared like this:

```
TextArea feedback = new TextArea(7, 60);
```

This large text area appears at the bottom of the applet. The intention is to use the text area to display messages to the user.

The declarations we have seen created the three kinds of components: `Button`, `TextField`, and `TextArea`. All three classes are part of the `java.awt` package that is imported by our applet. When we declare a button (or other component) and create it with the constructor, it does not immediately appear in the GUI. How do the objects get placed in the GUI? Also, how does the applet know what to do when the user clicks on a button or takes some other action? The answers to these two questions lie in a special applet method called `init`, which we'll discuss next.

4. The init method. A Java application program has a special static method called `main`. A Java applet does not have `main`. Instead, an applet has a special nonstatic method called `init`. When an applet runs, the runtime system creates an object of the applet class, and activates `init()` for that object. There are several other applet methods that the runtime system also activates at various times, but an interactive test program needs only `init`.

Our `init` method carries out four kinds of actions:

> **A. The add method.** We can add one of the interactive components to the GUI. This is done with an applet method called add. The method has one argument, which is the component that is being added to the GUI. For example, one of our buttons is `sizeButton`, so we can write the statement:

the applet's add method

```
        add(sizeButton);
```

> As components are added, the GUI fills up from left to right. If there is no room for a component on the current line, then the GUI moves down and starts a new row of components. Later you can learn more sophisticated ways of laying out the components of a GUI, but the simple left-to-right method used by an applet is a good starting point.

> **B. Displaying messages.** We can display messages in the GUI. Each message is a fixed string that provides some information to the user. Each of these messages is a `Label` object (from the package `java.awt`). To create and display a message, we activate add, with a newly created `Label` as the argument. For example:

```
        add(new Label("This test program has created a bag"));
```

printing a message in the GUI

> The `Label` constructor has one argument, which is the string that you want to display. The add method will put the message in the next available spot of the GUI.

C. New lines and horizontal lines. If our applet class has other methods (besides `init`), then we can activate these other methods. For example, we plan to have two other methods in the `IntArrayBag` class:

```
void addNewLine( );
void addHorizontalLine(Color c);
```

addNewLine
addHorizontalLine

The `addNewLine` method forces the GUI to start a new line, even if there's room for more components on the current line. The second method, `addHorizontalLine`, draws a horizontal line in the specified color. We'll have to define these two methods as part of `BagApplet.Java`, but they won't be difficult. (The data type `Color` is part of `java.lang`. It includes `Color.blue` and twelve other colors plus the ability to define your own colors.)

D. Activate methods of the components. The buttons and other components have methods that can be activated. For example, one of the methods of a `TextArea` is called `append`. The method has one argument, which is a string, and this string is appended to the end of what's already in the text field. One of the statements in our `init` method will activate `append` in this way:

```
feedback.append("I am ready for your first action.\n");
```

append

This causes the message "`I am ready for your first action.`" to be written in the `feedback` text field (with a newline character `\n` at the end of the message).

The most important method for buttons involves a new kind of object called an action listener. An action listener is object that an applet programmer creates to describe the action that should be taken when certain events occur. Our bag applet will have a different kind of action listener for each of the three buttons:

action listener
objects

Kind of Action Listener	Purpose
`SizeListener`	Describes the actions to be taken when `sizeButton` is clicked.
`AddListener`	Describes the actions to be taken when `addButton` is clicked.
`CountOccurrencesListener`	Describes the actions to be taken when `countOccurrencesButton` is clicked.

Each kind of action listener is actually a new class that we'll define in a moment. But the only thing you need to know for the `init` method is how to connect an action listener to a `Button`. The solution is to activate a method called addActionListener for each Button. For example, to connect sizeButton to its action listener, we place this statement in the init method:

```
sizeButton.addActionListener(new SizeListener( ));
```

Notice that addActionListener is a method of the Button class, and its one argument is a new SizeListener object. Of course, we still need to implement the SizeListener class, as well as the other two action listener classes. But first, let's summarize all the pieces that are part of the init method for the BagApplet. Within init, we expect to activate these methods to carry our work:

- add—an Applet method to add the buttons and other components to the display
- addNewLine and addHorizontalLine—two methods that we will write for the BagApplet
- feedback.append—a method of the TextField to place the message "I am ready for your first action" in feedback (a TextField object)
- addActionListener—a method that will be called once for each of the three buttons

The complete init implementation is shown in Figure 3.13 on page 156. We've used just one method that we haven't yet mentioned. That one method (setEditable) is summarized in Figure 3.14 on page 157 along with the other applet-oriented methods that we have used or plan to use.

5. Implementations of the action listeners. The next step of the applet implementation is to design and implement three action listener classes—one for each of our three buttons. The purpose of an action listener is to describe the actions that are carried out when a button is pushed.

Here's the Java syntax for defining an action listener class—the blank line is filled in with your choice of a name for the action listener class.

```
class _____ implements ActionListener
{
    void actionPerformed(ActionEvent event)
    {
        ...
    }
}
```

The phrase "implements ActionListener" informs the Java compiler that the class will have a certain method that is specified in the ActionListener interface that is part of java.awt.*. The method, called actionPerformed, is shown with "..." to indicate its body. The actionPerformed method will be executed when an action occurs in the action listener's component, such as clicking a button. For example, here is the complete definition of the action listener that handles the clicking of the size() button of our test applet:

```
class SizeListener implements ActionListener
{
    void actionPerformed(ActionEvent event)
    {
        feedback.append("The bag has size " + b.size( ) + ".\n");
    }
}
```

*an action
listener for
sizeButton*

This declares a class called SizeListener, which includes its own actionPerformed method. For most classes, the class definition would go in a separate file called SizeListener.java. But a separate file is undesirable here because the actionPerformed method needs access to two instance variables: the bag b and the text area feedback. The necessary access can be provided by placing the entire SizeListener definition within the BagApplet. This is an example of an **inner class,** where the definition of one class is placed inside of another. An inner class has two key properties:

- The larger class that encloses an inner class may use the inner class; but the inner class may not be used elsewhere.

- The inner class may access nonprivate instance variables and methods of the larger class. Some Java implementations also permit an inner class to access private instance variables of the larger class. But other implementations forbid private access from an inner class. (Java implementations that are built into web browsers are particularly apt to forbid the private access.)

So, by making SizeListener an inner class, the actionPerformed method can activate feedback.append to print a message in the feedback component of the applet. The message itself includes an activation of b.size( ), so an entire message is something like "The bag has size 42."

The actionPerformed Method

The SizeListener class is an inner class, declared within BagApplet. Therefore, its actionPerformed method has access to the instance variables of the BagApplet.

By the way, the actionPerformed method has a parameter called event. For more complex actions, the event can provide more information about exactly which kind of action triggered the actionPerformed method.

(Text continues on page 158)

FIGURE 3.13	Implementation of the BagApplet's `init` Method

Implementation

```
public void init( )
{
    // Some messages for the top of the Applet:
    add(new Label("This test program has created a bag."));
    add(new Label("Press buttons to activate the bag's methods."));
    addHorizontalLine(Color.blue);

    // The Button for testing the size method:
    add(sizeButton);
    addNewLine( );

    // The Button and TextField for testing the add method:
    add(addButton);
    add(elementText);
    addNewLine( );

    // The Button and TextField for testing the countOccurrences method:
    add(countOccurrencesButton);
    add(targetText);
    addNewLine( );

    // A TextArea at the bottom to write messages:
    addHorizontalLine(Color.blue);
    addNewLine( );
    feedback.setEditable(false);
    feedback.append("I am ready for your first action.\n");
    add(feedback);

    // Tell the Buttons what they should do when they are clicked:
    sizeButton.addActionListener(new SizeListener( ));
    addButton.addActionListener(new AddListener( ));
    countOccurrencesButton.addActionListener(new CountOccurrencesListener( ));

}
```

FIGURE 3.14	Guide to Building an Applet for Interactive Testing

Methods to Call from an Applet or from a Class That Extends an Applet	
`add(component)`	*The component may be any of Java's AWT components such as Button, TextArea, or Text-Field. As components are added, the applet fills up from left to right. If there is no room for a component on the current line, then the applet moves down and starts a new row of components.*
`addNewLine( )` `addHorizontalLine(Color c)`	*These are not actually Applet methods—you'll need to define them if you want to use them (see page 160).*

Constructors for Three Useful Applet Components	
`Button(String label)`	*Creates a button with a given label.*
`TextField(int size)`	*Creates a white box for the user to type information. The size is the number of characters.*
`TextArea(int rows, int columns)`	*Creates a box with the given number of rows and columns—often for displaying information to the user.*

Six Useful Methods for a Component	
`b.setActionListener` `  (ActionListener act)`	*We use b.setActionListener for a Button b. The ActionListener, act, describes the actions to take when the Button b is pressed. See page 154 for information on how to create an ActionListener.*
`t.append(String message)`	*We use t.append for a TextArea t. The specified message is added to the end of the TextArea.*
`t.getText( )`	*We use t.getText for a TextField t. The method returns a copy of the String that the user has typed in the field.*
`t.setEditable(boolean editable)`	*The component t can be a TextArea or a Text-Field. The boolean parameter tells whether you want the user to be able to type text into the component.*
`t.requestFocus( )` `t.selectAll( )`	*We use these methods with a TextField. The requestFocus method causes the mouse to go to the field, and selectAll causes all text to be highlighted.*
`c.setSize(int width, int height)`	*This method may be used with any component c. The component's width and height are set to the given values in pixels.*

registering an
ActionListener
Once an action listener is created, it must be registered with its particular button. The registration is made in the init method. Our applet had these three
statements to register the three ActionListener objects:

```
sizeButton.addActionListener(new SizeListener( ));
addButton.addActionListener(new AddListener( ));
countOccurrencesButton.addActionListener
    (new CountOccurrencesListener( ));
```

For example, the first of these statements creates a new SizeListener and reg-
isters it with the button sizeButton.

Let's look at the second action listener class for our applet: AddListener.
This action listener handles the actions of addButton, which is shown here along
with the TextField that's right beside it in the applet:

What actions should occur when the user clicks the addButton? The text should
be read from the TextField. This text is a String, such as "42", but it can
be converted to its value as an integer by using the Java method
Integer.parseInt. The method Integer.parseInt has one argument (a
String which should contain an integer value), and the return value is the int
value of the String. Once we know the value of the integer provided by the
user, we can add it to the bag b and print an appropriate message in the applet's
feedback area. Following these ideas, we have this first try at implementing
AddListener:

```
class AddListener implements ActionListener
{
   void actionPerformed(ActionEvent event)
   {
      String userInput = elementText.getText( );
      int element = Integer.parseInt(userInput);
      b.add(element);
      feedback.append(element + " has been added to the bag.\n");
   }
}
```

The actionPerformed method defined here uses three of the applet's instance
variables: (1) elementText, which is the TextField where the user typed a
number; (2) the bag b, where the new element is added; and (3) the TextArea
feedback, where a message is printed providing feedback to the user.

The method works fine, though a problem arises if the user forgets to type a
number in the TextField before clicking the button. In this case, a Number-
FormatException will occur when Integer.parseInt tries to convert the
user's string to an integer.

The best solution to this problem is to "catch" the exception when it occurs, rather than allowing the exception to stop the applet. The syntax for catching a NumberFormatException looks like this:

catching the possible exception

```
try
{
    ...code that might throw a NumberFormatException...
}
catch (NumberFormatException e)
{
    ...code to execute if the NumberFormatException happens...
}
```

The words `try` and `catch` are Java keywords for handling exceptions. The full power of `try` and `catch` are described in Appendix C. For our purposes, we'll follow the preceding pattern to write a better version of AddListener:

```
class AddListener = implements ActionListener
{
    void actionPerformed(ActionEvent event)
    {
        try
        {
            String userInput = elementText.getText( );
            int element = Integer.parseInt(userInput);
            b.add(element);
            feedback.append
                (element + " has been added to the bag.\n");
        }
        catch (NumberFormatException e)
        {
            feedback.append
                ("Type an integer before clicking button.\n");
            elementText.requestFocus( );
            elementText.selectAll( );
        }
    }
}
```

an action listener for addButton

If a NumberFormatException occurs, then the code in the `catch` block is executed. This code prints a message in the feedback area of the applet, then activates two methods for `elementText` (which is the `TextField` where the user was supposed to type a number):

```
elementText.requestFocus( );
elementText.selectAll( );
```

requestFocus and selectAll

The requestFocus method causes the mouse cursor to jump into the Text-Field, and the selectAll method causes any text in the field to be highlighted. So now, if the user forgets to type a number, the applet will print a nice error message and provide a second chance.

Our applet needs one more action listener for the countOccurrences button. That implementation is part of Figure 3.2 on page 112.

6. Implementations of other methods. Our applet has two other methods that we've mentioned: (1) addHorizontalLine, which draws a horizontal line in a specified color; and (2) addNewLine, which causes a new line to start in the GUI, even if there's room for more components on the current line.

Our addHorizontalLine doesn't really draw a line. Instead, it adds a component called a Canvas to the applet. A Canvas is another applet component, like a Button, primarily used for drawing graphical images. The size of the Canvas can be set in **pixels**, which are the individual dots on a computer screen. Today's typical screens have about 100 pixels per inch, so a Canvas that is only one pixel high looks like a horizontal line. Here's our implementation:

implementation of addHorizontalLine

```
private void addHorizontalLine(Color c)
{
    // Add a Canvas 10000 pixels wide but
    // only 1 pixel high, which acts as
    // a horizontal line.
    Canvas line = new Canvas( );
    line.setSize(10000, 1);
    line.setBackground(c);
    add(line);
}
```

Notice that the Canvas is 10,000 pixels wide, which is wide enough to span even the largest applet—at least on today's computer screens.

implementation of addNewLine

Our last method, addNewLine, works by calling addHorizontalLine with the color set to the background color of the applet. In effect, we are drawing a horizontal line, but it is invisible since it's the same color as the applet's background.

The implementation of addNewLine is given in Figure 3.15 as part of the complete applet. Look through the implementation with an eye toward how it can be expanded to test all of the bag's methods or to test a different class such as the DoubleArraySeq class.

FIGURE 3.15	Complete Implementation of the `BagApplet`

Java Applet Implementation

```
//  File: BagApplet.java
//  This applet is a small example to illustrate how to write an interactive applet that
//  tests the methods of another class. This first version tests three of the IntArrayBag methods.

import edu.colorado.collections.IntArrayBag;
import java.applet.Applet;
import java.awt.*;           // Imports Button, Canvas, TextArea, TextField
import java.awt.event.*;     // Imports ActionEvent, ActionListener

public class BagApplet extends Applet
{
    //  An IntArrayBag for this applet to manipulate:
    IntArrayBag b = new IntArrayBag( );

    //  These are the interactive components that will appear in the applet.
    //  We declare one Button for each IntArrayBag method that we want to be able to
    //  test. If the method has an argument, then there is also a TextField
    //  where the user can enter the value of the argument.
    //  At the bottom, there is a TextArea to write messages.
    Button    sizeButton              = new Button("size( )");
    Button    addButton               = new Button("add( )");
    TextField elementText             = new TextField(10);
    Button    countOccurrencesButton  = new Button("countOccurrences( )");
    TextField targetText              = new TextField(10);
    TextArea  feedback                = new TextArea(7, 60);

    public void init( )
    {
        See the implementation in Figure 3.13 on page 156.
    }

    class SizeListener implements ActionListener
    {
        public void actionPerformed(ActionEvent event)
        {
            feedback.append("The bag has size " + b.size( ) + ".\n");
        }
    }
```

(continued)

(FIGURE 3.15 continued)

```java
class AddListener implements ActionListener
{
   public void actionPerformed(ActionEvent event)
   {
      try
      {
         String userInput = elementText.getText( );
         int element = Integer.parseInt(userInput);
         b.add(element);
         feedback.append(element + " has been added to the bag.\n");
      }
      catch (NumberFormatException e)
      {
         feedback.append("Type an integer before clicking button.\n");
         elementText.requestFocus( );
         elementText.selectAll( );
      }
   }
}

class CountOccurrencesListener implements ActionListener
{
   public void actionPerformed(ActionEvent event)
   {
      try
      {
         String userInput = targetText.getText( );
         int target = Integer.parseInt(userInput);
         feedback.append(target + " occurs ");
         feedback.append(b.countOccurrences(target) + "times.\n");
      }
      catch (NumberFormatException e)
      {
         feedback.append("Type a target before clicking button.\n");
         targetText.requestFocus( );
         targetText.selectAll( );
      }
   }
}
```

(continued)

(FIGURE 3.15 continued)

```
private void addHorizontalLine(Color c)
{
    // Add a Canvas 10000 pixels wide but only 1 pixel high, which acts as
    // a horizontal line to separate one group of components from the next.
    Canvas line = new Canvas( );
    line.setSize(10000,1);
    line.setBackground(c);
    add(line);
}

private void addNewLine( )
{
    // Add a horizontal line in the background color. The line itself is
    // invisible, but it serves to force the next component onto a new line.
    addHorizontalLine(getBackground( ));
}

}
```

How to Compile and Run an Applet

An applet can be compiled just like any other Java program. For example, using the Java Development Kit we can compile `BagApplet.java` with the command line:

```
javac BagApplet.java
```

You may have some other way of compiling Java programs in your development environment, but the result will be the same. The act of compiling produces the file `BagApplet.class`. The compilation will probably produce three other files with names such as `BagApplet$SizeListener.class`. These are the compiled versions of the inner classes.

applets were created to be viewed over the Internet

Applets were actually created to run as part of a page that you view over the Internet with a web browser. These pages are called **html pages**, which stands for "hyper-text markup language." So, to run the `BagApplet`, we need a small html file. The file, called `BagApplet.html`, should be created by you in the same directory as `BagApplet.class`, and it should contain the two lines of html code shown at the top of the next page.

```
<applet code="BagApplet.class" width=480 height=340>
</applet>
```

The first line, containing `<applet...>` tells the web browser that you are going to start an applet. Usually, you will have at least three pieces of information about the applet:

`code = "BagApplet.class"`	*Tells the browser where to find the compiled class.*

`width = 480`
 	
`height = 340`
	Sets the applet's size in pixels. Today's typical screens have about 100 pixels per inch, so a size of 480 x 340 is about 4.8 inches by 3.4 inches.

Many Java development environments have a feature to automatically create a small html file such as this.

Once the html file is in place, you can run the applet in one of two ways. One approach is to run an **appletviewer,** which is a tool that reads an html file and runs any applets that it finds. The Java Development Kit has an appletviewer that is executed from the command line. For example, to run the JDK appletviewer you change to the directory that contains `BagApplet.html` and type the command:

```
appletviewer BagApplet.html
```

This command runs the applet, resulting in the display shown in Figure 3.11 on page 147.

The applet can also be displayed by putting it in a location that's available to your web browser. My latest information about this approach is available at `http://www.cs.colorado.edu/~main/java.html`.

Beyond the `init` Method

Our test applet needed to define only the `init` method. More complex applets can also be created, involving graphical images plus interaction. Graphical applets will generally provide other methods called `start`, `paint`, `update`, `stop`, and `destroy`. A good resource is *Graphic Java Mastering the AWT* by David M. Geary.

Self-Test Exercises

23. Write three declarations of instance variables that might appear in an applet. Include a constructor activation in each declaration. The first declaration is a button with the label "Mmm, good." The second declaration is for a text

field of 15 characters. The third declaration is for a text area with 12 rows and 60 columns.

24. Write three statements that could appear in the `init` method of an applet. The statements should take the three components from the previous exercise and add them to the applet's GUI.

25. Write a statement that could appear in the `init` method of an applet to display the message "FREE Consultation!"

26. Describe the technique used in the implementation of `addHorizontalLine`.

27. Write a new action listener that can be registered to a button of the `BagApplet`. The `actionPerformed` method should print feedback to indicate how many copies of the numbers 1 through 10 appear in the applet's bag.

28. Suppose that `b` is a button in the `BagApplet`. Write a statement that could appear in the `init` method to create an action listener of the previous exercise and register it to the button `b`.

29. Suppose that `s` is a `String` that may or may not contain a sequence of digits representing a valid integer. Write a `try-catch` statement that will try to convert the `String` to an integer and print two times this integer. If the `String` does not represent a valid integer, then an error message should be printed.

CHAPTER SUMMARY

- A *collection class* is an ADT where each object contains a collection of elements. Bags and sequences are two examples of collection classes.

- The simplest implementations of collection classes use a *partially filled array*. Using a partially filled array requires each object to have at least two instance variables: the array itself and an `int` variable to keep track of how much of the array is being used.

- When a collection class is implemented with a partially filled array, the capacity of the array should grow as elements are added to the collection. The class should also provide explicit methods to allow a programmer to control the capacity of the array.

- In a collection class, some methods allocate additional memory (such as changing the capacity of an array). These methods have the possibility of throwing an `OutOfMemoryError` (when the machine runs out of memory).

- A class may have other instance variables that are references to objects or arrays. In such a case, the `clone` method must carry out extra work. The extra work creates a new object or array for each such instance variable to refer to.

- When you design an ADT, always make an explicit statement of the rules that dictate how the instance variables are used. These rules are called the *invariant of the ADT*, and should be written at the top of the implementation file for easy reference.
- Small ADTs can be tested effectively with an *interactive test applet* that follows the standard format of the BagApplet in Section 3.4.

? Solutions to Self-Test Exercises

1. ```
   int i;
   int[ ] b;
   b = new int[1000];
   for (i = 1; i <= 1000; i++)
       b[i-1] = i;
   ```

2. b.length

3. 42 (since a and b refer to the same array)

4. 0 (since b is a clone of a)

5. The array referred to by the parameter in the method is the same as the array referred to by the actual argument. So, the actual argument will have its first component changed to 42.

6. ```
   void copyFront(int[] a, int[] b, int n)
   // Precondition: a.length and b.length are
   // both greater than or equal to n.
   // Postcondition: n integers have been cop-
   // ied from the front of a to the front of b.
   {
       int i;
       for (i = 0; i < n; i++)
           b[i] = a[i];
   }
   ```

7.
3	2
[0]	[1]

   We don't care what appears beyond data[1].

8. When the 11th element is added, the add method will increase the capacity.

9. See the two rules on page 114.

10. A static method is not activated by any one particular object. It is activated by writing the class name, a dot, the method name, and the argument list. For example:

    IntArrayBag.union(b1, b2)

11. The two statements can be replaced by one: data[index] = data[--manyItems]; When --manyItems appears as an expression, the variable manyItems is decremented by one, and the resulting value is the value of the expression. (On the other hand, if many-Items-- appears as an expression, the value of the expression is the value of manyItems prior to subtracting one.) Similarly, the last two statements of add can be combined to data[manyItems++] = element;

12. For the incorrect implementation of addAll, suppose we have a bag b and we activate b.addAll(b). Then the private instance variable manyItems is the same variable as addend.manyItems. Each iteration of the loop adds 1 to manyItems, and hence addend.manyItems is also increasing, and the loop never ends.

    One warning: Some collection classes in the Java libraries have an addAll method that fails for the statement b.addAll(b). The reason is improved efficiency. So, before you use an addAll method, check the specification for restrictions.

13. At the end of the clone implementation we need an additional statement to make a separate copy of the data array for the clone to use. If we don't make this copy, then our own data array and the clone's data array will be one and the same (see the pictures on page 123).

14. System.arrayCopy(x, 10, y, 33, 16);

15.
```
void addBefore(double element)
{
    int i;

    if (manyItems == data.length)
    {  // Try to double the capacity
        ensureCapacity(manyItems*2 + 1);
    }

    if (!isCurrent( ))
        currentIndex = 0;
    for
    (i=manyItems; i>currentIndex; i--)
        data[i] = data[i-1];
    data[currentIndex] = element;
    manyItems++;
}
```

16. 24

17. g.currentIndex will be 3 (since the 4th element occurs at data[3]).

18. The removeCurrent method should be tested when the sequence's size is just 1, and when the sequence is at its full capacity. At full capacity you should try removing the first element, and the last element of the sequence.

19. Your program can be similar to Figure 3.2 on page 111.

20. Here is our method's heading, with a postcondition:
```
void remove(int target);
// Postcondition: If target was in the
// sequence, then the first copy of target
// has been removed, and the element after
// the removed element (if there is one)
// becomes the new current element; other-
// wise the sequence remains unchanged.
```
The easiest implementation searches for the index of the target. If this index is found, then set currentIndex to this index, and activate the ordinary removeCurrent method.

21. The total time to add 1, 2, ... , *n* with add-After is $O(n)$. The total time to add *n*, *n*–1, ..., 1 with addBefore is $O(n^2)$. The larger time for the second approach is because an addition at the front of the sequence requires all of the existing elements to be shifted right to make room for the new element. Hence, on the second addition, one element is shifted. On the third addition, two elements are shifted. And so on to the nth element which needs n–1 shifts. The total number of shifts is 1+2+...+(n–1), which is $O(n^2)$. (To show that this sum is $O(n^2)$, use a technique similar to Figure 1.3 on page 21.)

22. Neither of the classes *must* use an array. In later chapters we will see both classes implemented without arrays.

23.
```
Button b = new Button("Mmm, good");
TextField f = new TextField(15);
TextArea a = new TextArea(12, 60);
```

24. add(b); add(f); add(a);

25.
```
add
(new Label("FREE Consultation!"));
```

26. The "horizontal line" is actually a Canvas that is one pixel high and very wide.

27.
```
class InfoListener
implements ActionListener
{
    public void
    actionPerformed(ActionEvent event)
    {
        int i;
        int count;

        for (i = 1; i <= 10; i++)
        {
            count = b.countOccurrences(i);
            feedback.append
            (i + " occurs " + count + ".\n");
        }
    }
}
```

28.
```
b.addActionListener
(new InfoListener( ));
```

29.
```
try
{
    int value = Integer.parseInt(s);
    System.out.println(2 * value);
}
catch (NumberFormatException e)
{
    System.out.println("Not number");
}
```

PROGRAMMING PROJECTS

1 For the `IntArrayBag` class, implement a new method called `equals` with a boolean return value and one parameter. The parameter, called b, is another `IntArrayBag`. The method returns `true` if b and the bag that activates the method have exactly the same number of every element. Otherwise the method returns `false`. Notice that the locations of the elements in the data arrays are not necessarily the same. It is only the number of occurrences of each element that must be the same.

The worst-case time for the method should be $O(mn)$, where m is the size of the bag that activates the method and n is the size of b.

2 A **black box** test of a class is a program that tests the correctness of a class without directly examining the private instance variables of the class. You can imagine that the private instance variables are inside an opaque black box where they cannot be seen, so all testing must occur only through activating the public methods.

Write a noninteractive black box test program for the `IntArrayBag` class. Make sure that you test the boundary values, such as an empty bag, a bag with just one element, and a full bag.

3 Expand the `BagApplet` from Figure 3.15 on page 161. The expanded version should have three bags and buttons to activate any method of any bag. Also include a button that will carry out an action such as:
```
b1 = IntArrayBag.union(b2, b3).
```

4 Implement the sequence class from Section 3.3. You may wish to provide some additional useful methods, such as: (1) a method to add a new element at the front of the sequence; (2) a method to remove the element at the front of the sequence; (3) a method to add a new element at the end of the sequence; (4) a method that makes the last element of the sequence become the current element; (5) a method that returns the ith element of the sequence (starting with the 0th at the front); (6) a method that makes the ith element become the current element.

5 Implement an applet for interactive testing of the sequence class from the previous project.

6 A bag can contain more than one copy of an element. For example, the chapter describes a bag that contains the number 4 and two copies of the number 8. This bag behavior is different from a **set**, which can contain only a single copy of any given element. Write a new collection class called `SetOfInt`, which is similar to a bag, except that a set can contain only one copy of any given element. You'll need to change the specification a bit. For example, instead of the bag's `countOccurrences` method, you'll want a method such as this:

```
boolean contains(int target)
// Postcondition: The return value is true if
// target is in the set; otherwise the return
// value is false.
```

Make an explicit statement of the invariant of the set ADT. Do a time analysis for each operation. At this point, an efficient implementation is not needed. For example, just adding a new element to a set will take linear time because you'll need to check that the new element isn't already present. Later we'll explore more efficient implementations.

You may also want to add additional methods to your set ADT, such as a method for subtracting one set from another.

- **setLink**

    `public void setLink(IntNode newLink)`

    Modification method to set the reference to the next node after this node.

    Parameters:

    `newLink` – a reference to the node that should appear after this node in the linked list (or the null reference if there should be no node after this node)

    Postcondition:

    The link to the node after this node has been set to `newLink`. Any other node (that used to be in this link) is no longer connected to this node.

The implementations of the four methods are each short. For example:

```
public void setLink(IntNode newLink)
{
    link = newLink;
}
```

Public versus Private Instance Variables

In addition to `setLink`, there are the three other short methods that we'll leave for you to implement. You may wonder why bother having these short methods at all. Wouldn't it be simpler and more efficient to just make `data` and `link` public, and do away with the short methods altogether? Yes, public instance variables probably are simpler, and in Java the direct access of an instance variable is considerably more efficient than calling a method. On the other hand, debugging can be easier with access and modification methods in place because we can set breakpoints to see whenever an instance variable is accessed or modified. Also, private instance variables provide good information hiding so that later changes to the class won't affect programs that use the class.

Anyway, the public-versus-private question should be addressed for many of your classes, with the answer based on the intended use and required efficiency together with software engineering principles such as information hiding. For the classes in this text, we'll lean toward information hiding and avoid public instance variables.

Adding a New Node at the Head of a Linked List

New nodes can be added at the head of a linked list. To accomplish this, the program needs a reference to the head node of a list as shown here:

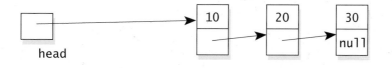

In this example, suppose that we want to add a new node to the front of this list, with 5 as the data. Using the node constructor, we can write

```
head = new IntNode(5, head);
```

how to add a new node at the head of a linked list

Let's step through the execution of this statement to see how the new node is added at the front of the list. When the constructor is executed, a new node is created with 5 as the data and with the link refering to the same node that head refers to. Here's what the picture looks like, with the link of the new node shaded:

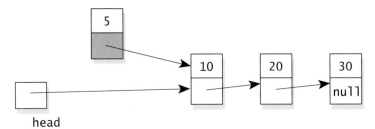

The constructor returns a reference to the newly created node, and in the statement we wrote `head = new IntNode(5, head)` . You can read this statement as saying "make head refer to the newly created node." Therefore, we end up with this situation:

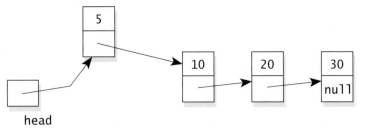

By the way, the technique works correctly even if we start with an empty list (in which the head reference is null). In this case, the statement `head = new IntNode(5, head)` creates the first node of the list. To see this, suppose we start with a null head and execute the statement. The constructor creates a new node with 5 as the data and with head as the link. Since the head reference is null, the new node looks like this (with the link of the new node shaded):

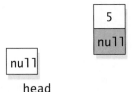

After the constructor returns, head is assigned to refer to the new node, so the final situation looks like this:

As you can see, the statement head = new IntNode(5, head) has correctly added the first node to a list. If we are maintaining a reference to the tail node, then we would also set the tail to refer to this one node.

Adding a New Node at the Head of a Linked List

Suppose that head is the head reference of a linked list. Then this statement adds a new node at the front of the list with the specified new data:

```
head = new IntNode(newData, head);
```

This statement works correctly even if we start with an empty list (in which case the head reference is null).

Removing a Node from the Head of a Linked List

Nodes can be removed from the head of the linked list. To accomplish this, we need a reference to the head node of a list as shown here:

To remove the first node, we simply move the head, so that it refers to the next node. This is accomplished with one statement:

```
head = head.getLink( );
```

The right side of the assignment, head.getLink( ), is a reference to the second node of the list. So, after the assignment, head refers to the second node, as shown at the top of the next page.

how to remove a node from the head of a linked list

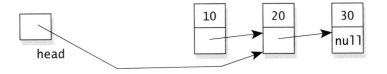

This picture is peculiar. It looks like we've still got a linked list with three nodes containing 10, 20, and 30. But if we start at the head, there are only the two nodes with 20 and 30. The node with 10 can no longer be accessed starting at the head, so it is not really part of the linked list any more. In fact, if a situation arises where a node can no longer be accessed from anywhere in a program, then the Java runtime system recognizes that the node has strayed, and the memory used by that node will be reused for other things. This technique of rounding up stray memory is called **garbage collection**, and it happens automatically for Java programs. In other programming languages, the programmer is responsible for identifying memory that is no longer used, and explicitly returning that memory to the runtime system.

automatic garbage collection has some inefficiency, but it's less prone to programming errors

What are the tradeoffs between automatic garbage collection and programmer-controlled memory handling? Automatic garbage collection is slower when a program is executing, but the automatic approach is less prone to errors and it frees the programmer to concentrate on more important issues.

Anyway, we'll remove a node from the front of a list with the statement `head = head.getLink( )`. This statement also works when the list has only one node, and we want to remove this one node. For example, consider this list:

In this situation, we can execute `head = head.getLink( )`. The `getLink( )` method returns the link of the head node—in other words, it returns null. So, the null reference is assigned to the head, ending up with this situation:

Now, the head is null, which indicates that the list is empty. If we are maintaining a reference to the tail, then we would also have to set the tail reference to null. The automatic garbage collection will take care of reusing the memory occupied by the one node.

> ### Removing a Node from the Head of a Linked List
>
> Suppose that head is the head reference of a linked list. Then this statement removes a node from the front of the list:
>
>   head = head.getLink( );
>
> This statement works correctly even when the list has just one node (in which case the head reference becomes null).

Adding a New Node That Is Not at the Head

New nodes are not always placed at the head of a linked list. They may be added in the middle or at the tail of a list. For example, suppose you want to add the number 42 after the 20 in this list:

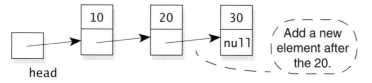

After the addition, the new, longer list has these four nodes:

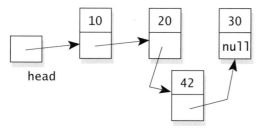

Whenever a new node is not at the head, the process requires a reference to the node that is just *before* the intended location of the new node. In our example, we would require a reference to the node that contains 20, since we want to place the new node after this node. This special node is called the "selected node"— the new node will go just after the selected node. We'll use the name selection for a reference to the selected node. So to add an element after the 20, we would first have to set up selection as shown here:

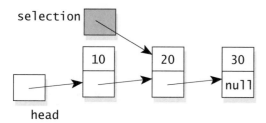

Once a program has calculated `selection`, the new node with data of 42 can be added with a method of the `IntNode` class, specified here:

addNodeAfter

◆ **addNodeAfter**
   `public void addNodeAfter(int element)`
   Modification method to add a new node after this node.

   Parameters:
   `element` – the data to be placed in the new node

   Postcondition:
   A new node has been created and placed after this node. The data for the new node is `element`. Any other nodes that used to be after this node are now after the new node.

   Throws: `OutOfMemoryError`
   Indicates that there is insufficient memory for a new `IntNode`.

For example, to add a new node with data 42 after the selected node, we can activate `selection.addNodeAfter(42)`.

The implementation of `addNodeAfter` requires just one line, shown here:

```
public void addNodeAfter(int element)
{
    link = new IntNode(element, link);
}
```

Let's see exactly what happens when we set up `selection` as shown earlier and then execute `selection.addNodeAfter(42)`. The value of element is 42, so we have the situation shown here:

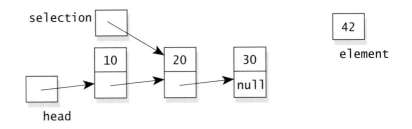

The method executes `link = new IntNode(element, link)`, where element is 42 and `link` is from the selected node—in other words, `link` is `selection.link`. On the right side of the statement, the `IntNode` constructor is executed, and a new node is created with 42 as the `data` and with the `link` of the new node being the same as `selection.link`. The situation is shown at the top of the next page, with the new node shaded.

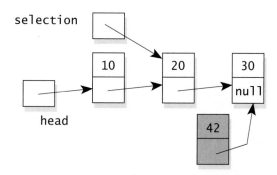

The constructor returns a reference to the newly created node, and in the assignment statement we wrote `link = new IntNode(element, link)`. You can read this statement as saying "change the link part of the selected node so that it refers to the newly created node." This change is made in the following drawing, which highlights the link part of the selected node:

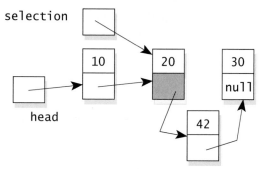

After adding the new node with 42, you can step through the complete linked list, starting at the head node 10, then 20, then 42, and finally 30.

The approach we have used works correctly even if the selected node is the tail of a list. In this case, the new node is added after the tail. If we were maintaining a reference to the tail node, then we would have to update this reference to refer to the newly added tail.

Adding a New Node That is Not at the Head

Suppose that `selection` is a reference to a node of a linked list. Activating the following method adds a new node after the cursor node with `element` as the new data:

```
selection.addNodeAfter(element);
```

The implementation of `addNodeAfter` needs only one statement to accomplish its work:

```
link = new IntNode(element, link);
```

Removing a Node That Is Not at the Head

It is also possible to remove a node that is not at the head of a linked list. The approach is similar to adding a node in the middle of a linked list. To remove a midlist node, we must set up a reference to the node that is just *before* the node that we are removing. For example, in order to remove the 42 from the following list, we would need to set up `selection` as shown here:

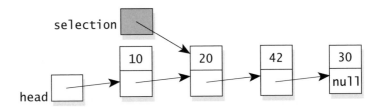

As you can see, `selection` does not actually refer to the node that we are deleting (the 42); instead it refers to the node that is just before the condemned node. This is because the link of the *previous* node must be reassigned, hence we need a reference to this previous node. The removal method's specification is shown here:

removeNodeAfter
- **removeNodeAfter**
    `public void removeNodeAfter( )`
    Modification method to remove the node after this node.

    Precondition:
    This node must not be the tail node of the list.

    Postcondition:
    The node after this node has been removed from the linked list. If there were further nodes after that one, they are still present on the list.

For example, to remove the 42 from the list drawn above, we would activate `selection.removeNodeAfter( )`. After the removal, the new list will look like this (with the changed link highlighted):

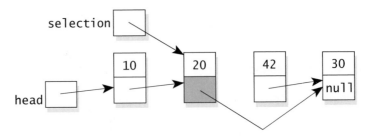

At this point, the node containing 42 is no longer part of the linked list. The list's first node contains 10, the next node has 20, and following the links we arrive at the third and last node containing 30. Java's automatic garbage collection will reuse the memory of the removed node.

As you can see from the example, the implementation of removeNodeAfter must alter the link of the node that activated the method. How is the alteration carried out? Let's go back to our starting position, but we'll put a bit more information in the picture:

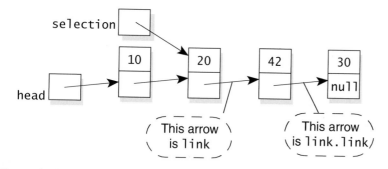

To work through this example, you need some patterns that can be used within the method to refer to the various data and link parts of the nodes. Remember that we activated selection.removeNodeAfter( ). So the node that activated the method has 20 for its data, and its link is indicated by the caption "This arrow is link." So we can certainly use these two names within the method:

data   This is the data of the node that activated the method (20).

link   This is the link of the node that activated the method. This link refers to the node that we are removing.

Because the name link refers to a node, we can also use the names link.data and link.link:

link.data   This notation means "go to the node that link refers to and use the data instance variable." In our example, link.data is 42.

link.link   This notation means "go to the node that link refers to and use the link instance variable." In our example, link.link is the reference to the node that contains 30.

In the implementation of removeNodeAfter, we need to make link refer to the node that contains 30. So, using the notation just shown, we need to assign link = link.link . The complete implementation is at the top of the next page.

```
public void removeNodeAfter( )
{
    link = link.link;
}
```

The notation link.link does look strange, but just read it from left to right so that it means "go to the node that link refers to and use the link instance variable." In our example, the final situation after assigning link = link.link is just what we want, as shown here:

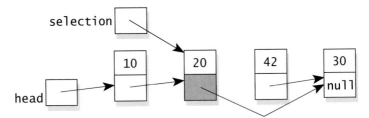

The removeNodeAfter implementation works fine, even if we want to remove the tail node. Here's an example where we have set selection to refer to the node that's just before the tail of a small list:

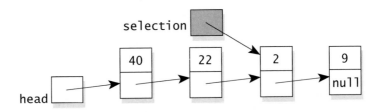

When we activate selection.removeNodeAfter( ), the link of the selected node will be assigned the value null (which is obtained from the link of the next node). The result is this picture:

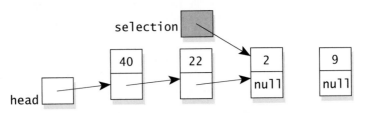

The tail node has been removed from the list. If the program maintains a reference to the tail node, then that reference must be updated to refer to the new tail.

In all cases, Java's automatic garbage collection takes care of reusing the memory of the removed node.

Removing a Node That is Not at the Head

Suppose that `selection` is a reference to a node of a linked list. Activating the following method removes the node after the selected node:

```
selection.removeNodeAfter( );
```

The implementation of `removeNodeAfter` needs only one statement to accomplish its work:

```
link = link.link;
```

Pitfall: Null Pointer Exceptions with `removeNodeAfter`

The `removeNodeAfter` method has a potential problem. What happens if the tail node activates `removeNodeAfter`? This is a programming error because `removeNodeAfter` would try to remove the node after the tail node, and there is no such node. The precondition of `removeNodeAfter` explicitly states that it must not be activated by the tail node. Still, what will happen in this case? For the tail node, `link` is the null reference, so trying to access the instance variable `link.link` will result in a `NullPointerException`.

When we write the complete specification of the node methods, we will include a note indicating the possibility of a `NullPointerException` in this method.

PITFALL

Self-Test Exercises

5. Suppose that `head` is a head reference for a linked list of integers. Write a few lines of code that will add a new node with the number 42 as the second element of the list. (If the list was originally empty, then 42 should be added as the first node instead of the second.)

6. Suppose that `head` is a head reference for a linked list of integers. Write a few lines of code that will remove the second node of the list. (If the list originally had only one node, then remove that node instead; if it had no nodes, then leave the list empty.)

7. Examine the techniques for adding and removing a node at the head. Why are these techniques implemented as static methods rather than ordinary `IntNode` methods?

8. Write some code that could appear in a main program. The code should declare head and tail references for a linked list of integers, then add nodes with the numbers 1 through 100 (in that order). Throughout the program, `head` and `tail` should remain valid references to the head and tail nodes.

4.3 MANIPULATING AN ENTIRE LINKED LIST

We can now write programs that use linked lists. Such a program declares some references to nodes, such as a head and tail reference. The nodes are manipulated with the methods and other techniques that we have already seen. But all these methods and techniques deal with just one or two nodes at an isolated part of the linked list. Many programs also need techniques for carrying out computations on an entire list, such as computing the number of nodes on a list. This suggests that we should write a few more methods for the IntNode class—methods that carry out some computation on an entire linked list. For example, we can provide a method with this heading:

```
public static int listLength(IntNode head)
```

The listLength method computes the number of nodes in a linked list. The one parameter, head, is a reference to the head node of the list. For example, the last line of this code prints the length of a short list:

```
IntNode small; // Head reference for a small list
small = new IntNode(42, null);
small.addNodeAfter(17);
System.out.println( IntNode.listLength(small) ); // Prints 2
```

By the way, the listLength return value is int, so that the method can be used only if a list has fewer than Integer.MAX_VALUE nodes. Beyond this length, the listLength method will return a wrong answer because of arithmetic overflow. We'll make a note of the potential problem in the listLength specification.

Notice that listLength is a static method. It is not activated by any one node; instead we activate IntNode.listLength . But why is it a *static* method—wouldn't it be easier to write an ordinary method that is activated by the head node of the list? Yes, an ordinary method might be easier, but a static method is better because a static method can be used even for an empty list. For example, these two statements create an empty list and print the length of that list:

```
IntNode empty = null; // empty is null, representing an empty list
System.out.println( IntNode.listLength(empty) ); // Prints 0
```

An ordinary method could not be used to compute the length of the empty list, because the head reference is null.

Manipulating an Entire Linked List

To carry out computations on an entire linked list, we will write static methods in the IntNode class. Each such method has one or more parameters that are references to nodes in the list. Most of the methods will work correctly even if the references are null (indicating an empty list).

Computing the Length of a Linked List

Here is the complete specification of the `listLength` method that we've been discussing:

> ◆ **listLength**   *listLength*
> ```
> public static int listLength(IntNode head)
> ```
> Compute the number of nodes in a linked list.
>
> **Parameters:**
> > head – the head reference for a linked list (which may be an empty list with a null head)
>
> **Returns:**
> > the number of nodes in the list with the given head
>
> **Note:**
> > A wrong answer occurs for lists longer than `Int.MAX_VALUE`, because of arithmetic overflow.

The precondition indicates that the parameter, `head`, is the head reference for a linked list. If the list is not empty, then `head` refers to the first node of the list. If the list is empty, then `head` is the null reference (and the method returns zero, since there are no nodes).

Our implementation uses a reference variable to step through the list, counting the nodes one at a time. Here are the three steps of the pseudocode, using a reference variable named `cursor` to step through the nodes of the list one at a time. (We often use the name `cursor` for such a variable, since "cursor" means "something that runs through a structure.")

1. Initialize a variable named `answer` to zero (this variable will keep track of how many nodes we have seen so far).

2. Make `cursor` refer to each node of the list, starting at the head node. Each time `cursor` moves, add one to `answer`.

3. `return answer`.

Both `cursor` and `answer` are local variables in the method.

The first step initializes `answer` to zero, because we have not yet seen any nodes. The implementation of Step 2 is a for-loop, following a pattern that you should use whenever *all of the nodes of a linked list must be traversed*. The general pattern looks like this:

```
for (cursor = head; cursor != null; cursor = cursor.link)
{

        ...    Inside the body of the loop, you may
               carry out whatever computation is
               needed for a node in the list.

}
```
how to traverse all the nodes of a linked list

For the `listLength` method, the "computation" inside the loop is simple because we are just counting the nodes. Therefore, in our body we will just add one to `answer`, as shown here:

```
for (cursor = head; cursor != null; cursor = cursor.link)
    answer++;
```

Let's examine the loop on an example. Suppose that the linked list has three nodes containing the numbers 10, 20, and 30. After the loop initializes (with `cursor = head`), we have this situation:

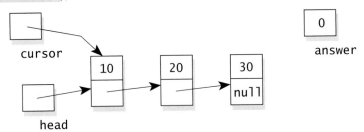

Notice that `cursor` refers to the same node that `head` refers to.

Since `cursor` is not `null`, we enter the body of the loop. Each iteration increments `answer` and then executes `cursor = cursor.link`. The effect of `cursor = cursor.link` is to copy the `link` part of the first node into `cursor` itself, so that `cursor` ends up refering to the second node. In general, the statement `cursor = cursor.link` moves `cursor` to the next node. So, at the completion of the loop's first iteration, the situation is this:

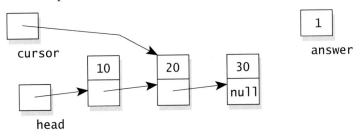

The loop continues. After the second iteration, `answer` is 2, and `cursor` refers to the third node of the list, as shown here:

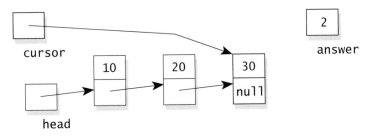

Each time we complete an iteration of the loop, `cursor` refers to some location in the list, and `answer` is the number of nodes *before* this location. In our example, we are about to enter the loop's body for the third and last time. During the last iteration, `answer` is incremented to 3, and `cursor` becomes `null`, as shown here:

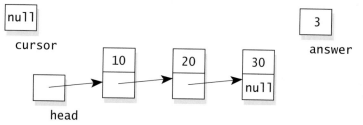

The variable `cursor` has become `null` because the loop control statement `cursor = cursor.link` copied the `link` part of the third node into `cursor`. Since this `link` part is `null`, the value in `cursor` is now `null`.

At this point, the loop's control test `cursor != null` is false. The loop ends, and the method returns the answer 3. The complete implementation of the `listLength` method is shown in Figure 4.4.

FIGURE 4.4   A Static Method to Compute the Length of a Linked List

Implementation

```
public static int listLength(IntNode head)
{
    IntNode cursor;
    int answer;

    answer = 0;
    for (cursor = head; cursor != null; cursor = cursor.link)
        answer++;

    return answer;
}
```

Step 2 of the pseudocode

TIP

Programming Tip: How to Traverse a Linked List

You should learn the important pattern for traversing a linked list, as used in the `listLength` method (Figure 4.4). The same pattern can be used whenever you need to step through the nodes of a linked list one at a time.

The first part of the pattern concerns moving from one node to another. Whenever we have a variable that refers to some node, and we want the variable to refer to the next node, we must use the `link` part of the node. Here is the reasoning that we follow:

1. Suppose `cursor` refers to some node;
2. Then `cursor.link` refers to the next node (if there is one), as shown here:

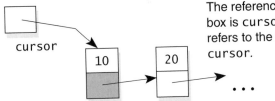

The reference in the shaded box is `cursor.link`, and it refers to the next node after `cursor`.

3. To move `cursor` to the next node, we use one of these assignment statements:

$$cursor = cursor.link;$$

or

$$cursor = cursor.getLink( );$$

Use the first version, `cursor = cursor.link`, if you have access to the `link` instance variable (inside one of the `IntNode` methods). Otherwise, use the second version, `cursor = cursor.getLink( )`. In both cases, if there is no next node, then `cursor.link` will be `null`, and therefore our assignment statement will set `cursor` to `null`.

The key is to know that the assignment statement `cursor = cursor.link` moves `cursor` so that it refers to the next node. If there is no next node, then the assignment statement sets `cursor` to `null`.

The second part of the pattern shows how to traverse all of the nodes of a linked list, starting at the head node. The pattern of the loop looks like this:

```
for (cursor = head; cursor != null; cursor = cursor.link)
{
    . . .        Inside the body of the loop, you may
                 carry out whatever computation is
                 needed for a node in the list.
}
```

You'll find yourself using this pattern continually in methods that manipulate linked lists.

Pitfall: Forgetting to Test the Empty List

Methods that manipulate linked lists should always be tested to ensure that they have the right behavior for the empty list. When `head` is `null` (indicating the empty list), our `listLength` method should return 0. Testing this case shows that `listLength` does correctly return 0 for the empty list.

PITFALL

Searching for an Element in a Linked List

In Java, a method may return a reference to a node. Hence, when the job of a subtask is to find a single node, it makes sense to implement the subtask as a method that returns a reference to that node. Our next method follows this pattern, returning a reference to a node that contains a specified element. The specification is given here:

- **listSearch**

  listSearch

  ```
  public static IntNode listSearch(IntNode head, int target)
  ```
  Search for a particular piece of data in a linked list.

  Parameters:

  head – the head reference for a linked list (which may be an empty list with a null head)

  target – a piece of data to search for

  Returns:

  The return value is a reference to the first node that contains the specified target. If there is no such node, the null reference is returned.

As indicated by the return type of `IntNode`, the method returns a reference to a node in a linked list. The node is specified by a parameter named `target`, which is the integer that appears in the sought-after node. For example, the activation `IntNode.listSearch(head, -4)` in Figure 4.5 will return a reference to the shaded node.

Sometimes, the specified target does not appear in the list. In this case, the method returns the null reference.

The implementation of `listSearch` is shown in Figure 4.6. Most of the work is carried out with the usual traversal pattern, using a local variable called `cursor` to step through the nodes one at a time:

```
for (cursor = head; cursor != null; cursor = cursor.link)
{
    if (target == the data in the node that cursor refers to)
        return cursor;
}
```

As the loop executes, `cursor` refers to the nodes of the list, one after another. The test inside the loop determines whether we have found the sought-after node, and if so, then a reference to the node is immediately returned with the

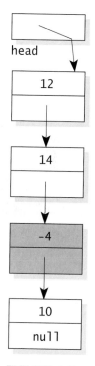

FIGURE 4.5
Example for
`listSearch`

FIGURE 4.6 A Static Method to Search for a Target in a Linked List

Implementation

```
public static IntNode listSearch(IntNode head, int target)
{
    IntNode cursor;

    for (cursor = head; cursor != null; cursor = cursor.link)
        if (target == cursor.data)
            return cursor;

    return null;
}
```

return statement `return cursor`. When a return statement occurs like this, inside a loop, the method returns without ado—the loop is not run to completion.

On the other hand, should the loop actually complete by eventually setting cursor to `null`, then the sought-after node is not on the list. According to the method's postcondition, the method returns `null` when the node is not on the list. This is accomplished with one more return statement—`return null`—at the end of the method's implementation.

Finding a Node by Its Position in a Linked List

Here's another method that returns a reference to a node in a linked list:

listPosition

+ **listPosition**
    ```
    public static IntNode listPosition(IntNode head, int position)
    ```
    Find a node at a specified position in a linked list.

    Parameters:
    head – the head reference for a linked list (which may be an empty list with a null head)
    position – a node number

    Precondition:
    position > 0

    Returns:
    The return value is a reference to the node at the specified position in the list. (The head node is position 1, the next node is position 2, and so on.) If there is no such position (because the list is too short), then the null reference is returned.

    Throws: IllegalArgumentException
    Indicates that position is not positive.

In this method, a node is specified by giving its position in the list, with the head node at position 1, the next node at position 2, and so on. For example, with the linked list from Figure 4.7, `IntNode.listPosition(head, 3)` will return a reference to the shaded node. Notice that the first node is number 1, not number 0 as in an array. The specified position might also be larger than the length of the list, in which case, the method returns the null reference.

The implementation of `listPosition` is shown in Figure 4.8. It uses a variation of the list traversal technique that we have already seen. The variation is useful when we want to move to a particular node in a linked list and we know the ordinal position of the node (such as position number 1, position number 2, and so on). We start by setting a reference variable, `cursor`, to the head node of the list. A loop then moves the `cursor` forward the correct number of spots, as shown here:

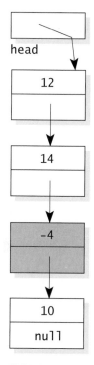

head

```
cursor = head;
for (i = 1; (i < position) && (cursor != null); i++)
    cursor = cursor.link;
```

Each iteration of the loop executes `cursor = cursor.link` to move the cursor forward one node. Normally, the loop stops when i reaches `position`, and cursor refers to the correct node. The loop can also stop if cursor becomes `null`, indicating that `position` was larger than the number of nodes on the list.

FIGURE 4.7
Example for
`listPosition`

| **FIGURE 4.8** | A Static Method to Find a Particular Position in a Linked List |

Implementation

```
public static IntNode listPosition(IntNode head, int position)
{
    IntNode cursor;
    int i;

    if (position <= 0)
        throw new IllegalArgumentException("position is not positive.");

    cursor = head;
    for (i = 0; (i < position) && (cursor != null); i++)
        cursor = cursor.link;

    return cursor;
}
```

Copying a Linked List

Our next static method makes a copy of a linked list, returning a head reference for the newly created copy. Here is the specification:

listCopy

♦ **listCopy**

```
public static IntNode listCopy(IntNode source)
```
Copy a list.

Parameters:
source–the head reference for a linked list that will be copied (which may be an empty list where source is null)

Returns:
The method has made a copy of the linked list starting at source. The return value is the head reference for the copy.

Throws: OutOfMemoryError
Indicates that there is insufficient memory for the new list.

For example, suppose that source refers to the following list:

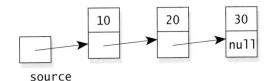

source

The listCopy method creates a completely separate copy of the three-node list. The copy of the list has its own three nodes, which also contain the numbers 10, 20, and 30. The return value is a head reference for the new list, and the original list remains intact.

The pseudocode begins by handling one special case—the case where the original list is the empty list (so that source is null). In this case the method simply returns null, indicating that its answer is the empty list. So, the first step of the pseudocode is:

1. if (source == null), then return null.

After dealing with the special case, the method uses two local variables called copyHead and copyTail, which will be maintained as the head and tail references for the new list. The pseudocode for creating this new list is given in the next three steps:

2. Create a new node for the head node of the new list that we are creating. Make both copyHead and copyTail refer to this new node, which contains the same data as the head node of the source list.

3. Make `source` refer to the second node of the original list, then the third node, then the fourth node, and so on until we have traversed all of the original list. At each node that `source` refers to, add one new node to the tail of the new list, and move `copyTail` forward to the newly added node, as follows:

```
copyTail.addNodeAfter(source.data);
copyTail = copyTail.link;
```

4. After Step 3 completes, return `copyHead` (a reference to the head node of the list that we created).

Step 3 of the pseudocode is completely implemented by this loop:

```
while (source.link != null)
{  // There are more nodes, so copy the next one.
   source = source.link;
   copyTail.addNodeAfter(source.data);
   copyTail = copyTail.link;
}
```

The while-loop starts by checking `source.link != null` to determine whether there is another node to copy. If there is another node, then we enter the body of the loop and move `source` forward with the assignment statement `source = source.link`. The second and third statements in the loop add a node at the tail end of the newly created list and move `copyTail` forward.

As an example, consider again the three-node list with data 10, 20, and 30. The first two steps of the pseudocode are carried out and then we enter the body of the while-loop. We execute the first statement of the loop: `source = source.link`. At this point, the variables look like this:

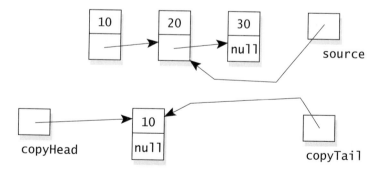

Notice that we have already copied the first node of the linked list. During the first iteration of the while-loop, we will copy the second node of the linked list—the node that is now referred to by source. The first part of copying the node works by activating one of our other methods, addNodeAfter, as shown here:

```
copyTail.addNodeAfter(source.data);
```

This activation adds a new node to the end of the list that we are creating (i.e., *after* the node referred to by copyTail), and the data in the new node is the number 20 (i.e., the data from source.data). Immediately after adding the new node, the variables look like this:

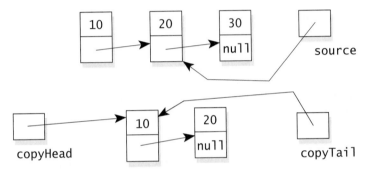

The last statement in the while-loop body moves copyTail forward to the new tail of the new list, as shown here:

```
copyTail = copyTail.link;
```

This is the usual way that we make a node reference "move to the next node," as we have seen in other methods such as listSearch. After moving copyTail, the variables look like this:

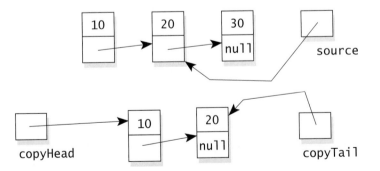

In this example, the body of the while-loop will execute one more time to copy the third node to the new list. Then the loop will end, and the method returns the new head reference, copyHead.

The complete implementation of listCopy is shown in Figure 4.9.

FIGURE 4.9   A Static Method to Copy a Linked List

Implementation

```java
public static IntNode listCopy(IntNode source)
{
    IntNode copyHead;
    IntNode copyTail;

    // Handle the special case of an empty list.
    if (source == null)
        return null;

    // Make the first node for the newly created list.
    copyHead = new IntNode(source.data, null);
    copyTail = copyHead;

    // Make the rest of the nodes for the newly created list.
    while (source.link != null)
    {
        source = source.link;
        copyTail.addNodeAfter(source.data);
        copyTail = copyTail.link;
    }

    // Return the head reference for the new list.
    return copyHead;
}
```

Here's an example of how the `listCopy` method might be used in a program:

```java
IntNode shortList;
IntNode copy;

shortList = new IntNode(10, null);
shortList.addNodeAfter(20);
shortList.addNodeAfter(20);
```

At this point, `shortList` is the head of a small list shown here:

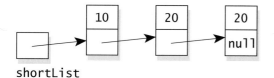

shortList

We could now use `listCopy` to make a second copy of this list:

```
copy = IntNode.listCopy(shortList);
```

At this point, we have two separate lists:

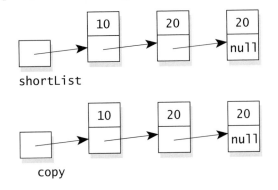

listCopyWithTail

why is listCopy a static method?

Keep in mind that `listCopy` is a static method, so we must write the expression `IntNode.listCopy(shortList)` rather than `shortList.listCopy( )`. This may seem strange—why not make `listCopy` an ordinary method? The answer is that an ordinary method could not copy the empty list (because the empty list is represented by the null reference).

A Second Copy Method, Returning Both Head and Tail References

We're going to have a second way to copy a list, with a slightly different specification, shown here:

listCopyWithTail

◆ **listCopyWithTail**
  `public static IntNode[ ] listCopyWithTail(IntNode source)`
  Copy a list, returning both a head and tail reference for the copy.

  Parameters:
    `source` – the head reference for a linked list that will be copied (which may be an empty list where `source` is null)

  Returns:
    The method has made a copy of the linked list starting at `source`. The return value is an array where the `[0]` element is a head reference for the copy and the `[1]` element is a tail reference for the copy.

  Throws: `OutOfMemoryError`
    Indicates that there is insufficient memory for the new list.

The listCopyWithTail makes a copy of a list, but the return value is more than a head reference for the copy. Instead, the return value is an array with two components. The [0] component of the array contains the head reference for the new list, and the [1] component contains the tail reference for the new list. The listCopyWithTail method is important because many algorithms must copy a list and obtain access to both the head and tail nodes of the copy.

As an example, a program can create a small list, then create a copy with both a head and tail reference for the copy:

```
IntNode shortList;
IntNode copyInfo[ ];

shortList = new IntNode(10, null);
shortList.addNodeAfter(20);
shortList.addNodeAfter(20);
copyInfo = IntNode.listCopyWithTail(source);
```

At this point, copyInfo[0] is the head reference for a copy of the short list, and copyInfo[1] is the tail reference for the same list, as shown here:

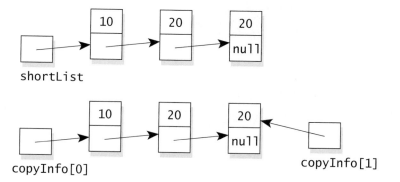

The implementation of listCopyWithTail is shown in the first part of Figure 4.10. It's nearly the same as listCopy, except there is an extra local variable called answer, which is an array of two IntNode components. These two components are set to the head and tail of the new list, and the method finishes with the return statement: `return answer`.

Programming Tip: A Method Can Return an Array

The return value from a method can be an array. This is useful if the method returns more than one piece of information. For example, listCopyWithTail returns an array with two components containing the head and tail references for a new list.

FIGURE 4.10	A Second Static Method to Copy a Linked List

Implementation

```
public static IntNode[ ] listCopyWithTail(IntNode source)
{
    // Notice that the return value is an array of two IntNode components.
    // The [0] component is the head reference for the new list and
    // the [1] component is the tail reference for the new list.
    // Also notice that the answer array is automatically initialized to contain
    // two null values. Arrays with components that are references are always
    // initialized this way.
    IntNode copyHead;
    IntNode copyTail;
    IntNode[ ] answer = new IntNode[2];

    // Handle the special case of an empty list.
    if (source == null)
        return answer; // The answer has two null references.

    // Make the first node for the newly created list.
    copyHead = new IntNode(source.data, null);
    copyTail = copyHead;

    // Make the rest of the nodes for the newly created list.
    while (source.link != null)
    {
        source = source.link;
        copyTail.addNodeAfter(source.data);
        copyTail = copyTail.link;
    }

    // Return the head and tail reference for the new list.
    answer[0] = copyHead;
    answer[1] = copyTail;
    return answer;
}
```

Copying Part of a Linked List

Sometimes a program needs to copy only part of a linked list rather than the entire list. The task can be done by a static method, listPart, which copies part of a list, as specified next.

- **listPart**

  ```
  public static IntNode[ ] listPart
    (IntNode start, IntNode end)
  ```
  Copy part of a list, providing a head and tail reference for the new copy.

  Parameters:
  start and end – references to two nodes of a linked list

  Precondition:
  start and end are non-null references to nodes on the same linked list, with the start node at or before the end node.

  Returns:
  The method has made a copy of part of a linked list, from the specified start node to the specified end node. The return value is an array where the [0] component is a head reference for the copy and the [1] component is a tail reference for the copy.

  Throws: IllegalArgumentException
  Indicates that start and end do not satisfy the precondition.

  Throws: OutOfMemoryError
  Indicates that there is insufficient memory for the new list.

The listPart implementation is given as part of the complete IntNode class in Figure 4.11 on page 204. In all, there is one constructor, five ordinary methods, and six static methods. The class is placed in a package called edu.colorado.nodes.

Using Linked Lists

Any program can use linked lists created from our nodes. Such a program must have this import statement:

```
import edu.colorado.nodes.IntNode;
```

The program can then use the various methods to build and manipulate linked lists. In fact, the edu.colorado.nodes package includes many different kinds of nodes: IntNode, DoubleNode, CharNode, etc. You can get these classes from http://www.cs.colorado.edu/~main/edu/colorado/nodes. (There is also a special kind of node that can handle many different kinds of data, but you'll have to wait until Chapter 5 for that.)

nodes with different kinds of data

For a programmer to use our nodes, the programmer must have some understanding of linked lists and our specific nodes. It might be better if we use the node classes ourselves to build various collection classes. The different collection classes that we build can be used by any programmer, with no knowledge of nodes and linked lists. This is what we will do in the rest of the chapter, providing two ADTs that use the linked lists.

FIGURE 4.11 Specification and Implementation of the `IntNode` Class

Class IntNode

❖ **public class IntNode from the package edu.colorado.nodes**

An `IntNode` provides a node for a linked list with integer data in each node. Lists can be of any length, limited only by the amount of free memory on the heap. But beyond `Integer.MAX_VALUE`, the answer from `listLength` is incorrect because of arithmetic overflow.

Specification

• **Constructor for the IntNode**

`public IntNode(int initialData, IntNode initialLink)`

Initialize a node with a specified initial data and link to the next node. Note that the `initialLink` may be the null reference, which indicates that the new node has nothing after it.

Parameters:

`initialData` – the initial data of this new node

`initialLink` – a reference to the node after this new node—this reference may be null to indicate that there is no node after this new node.

Postcondition:

This new node contains the specified data and link to the next node.

• **addNodeAfter**

`public void addNodeAfter(int element)`

Modification method to add a new node after this node.

Parameters:

`element` – the data to be placed in the new node

Postcondition:

A new node has been created and placed after this node. The data for the new node is `element`. Any other nodes that used to be after this node are now after the new node.

Throws: `OutOfMemoryError`

Indicates that there is insufficient memory for a new `IntNode`.

• **getData**

`public int getData( )`

Accessor method to get the data from this node.

Returns:

the data from this node

• **getLink**

`public IntNode getLink( )`

Accessor method to get a reference to the next node after this node.

Returns:

a reference to the node after this node (or the null reference if there is nothing after this node)

(continued)

(FIGURE 4.11 continued)

- **listCopy**

    ```
    public static IntNode listCopy(IntNode source)
    ```
    Copy a list.

    Parameters:

    source – the head reference for a linked list that will be copied (which may be an empty list where source is null)

    Returns:

    The method has made a copy of the linked list starting at source. The return value is the head reference for the copy.

    Throws: OutOfMemoryError

    Indicates that there is insufficient memory for the new list.

- **listCopyWithTail**

    ```
    public static IntNode[ ] listCopyWithTail(IntNode source)
    ```
    Copy a list, returning both a head and tail reference for the copy.

    Parameters:

    source – the head reference for a linked list that will be copied (which may be an empty list where source is null)

    Returns:

    The method has made a copy of the linked list starting at source. The return value is an array where the [0] element is a head reference for the copy and the [1] element is a tail reference for the copy.

    Throws: OutOfMemoryError

    Indicates that there is insufficient memory for the new list.

- **listLength**

    ```
    public static int listLength(IntNode head)
    ```
    Compute the number of nodes in a linked list.

    Parameters:

    head – the head reference for a linked list (which may be an empty list with a null head)

    Returns:

    the number of nodes in the list with the given head

    Note:

    A wrong answer occurs for lists longer than Int.MAX_VALUE, because of arithmetic overflow.

(continued)

(FIGURE 4.11 continued)

- **listPart**
    ```
    public static IntNode[ ] listPart(IntNode start, IntNode end)
    ```
    Copy part of a list, providing a head and tail reference for the new copy.

    Parameters:
    start and end – references to two nodes of a linked list

    Precondition:
    start and end are non-null references to nodes on the same linked list, with the start node at or before the end node.

    Returns:
    The method has made a copy of part of a linked list, from the specified start node to the specified end node. The return value is an array where the [0] component is a head reference for the copy and the [1] component is a tail reference for the copy.

    Throws: IllegalArgumentException
    Indicates that start and end do not satisfy the precondition.

    Throws: OutOfMemoryError
    Indicates that there is insufficient memory for the new list.

- **listPosition**
    ```
    public static IntNode listPosition(IntNode head, int position)
    ```
    Find a node at a specified position in a linked list.

    Parameters:
    head – the head reference for a linked list (which may be an empty list with a null head)
    position – a node number

    Precondition:
    position > 0

    Returns:
    The return value is a reference to the node at the specified position in the list. (The head node is position 1, the next node is position 2, and so on.) If there is no such position (because the list is too short), then the null reference is returned.

    Throws: IllegalArgumentException
    Indicates that position is zero.

- **listSearch**
    ```
    public static IntNode listSearch(IntNode head, int target)
    ```
    Search for a particular piece of data in a linked list.

    Parameters:
    head – the head reference for a linked list (which may be an empty list with a null head)
    target – a piece of data to search for

    Returns:
    The return value is a reference to the first node that contains the specified target. If there is no such node, the null reference is returned.

    (continued)

(FIGURE 4.11 continued)

♦ **removeNodeAfter**
```
public void removeNodeAfter( )
```
Modification method to remove the node after this node.

Precondition:
This node must not be the tail node of the list.

Postcondition:
The node after this node has been removed from the linked list. If there were further nodes after that one, they are still present on the list.

Throws: `NullPointerException`
Indicates that this was the tail node of the list, so there is nothing after it to remove.

♦ **setData**
```
public void setData(int newdata)
```
Modification method to set the data in this node.

Parameters:
`newData` – the new data to place in this node

Postcondition:
The data of this node has been set to `newData`.

♦ **setLink**
```
public void setLink(IntNode newLink)
```
Modification method to set a reference to the next node after this node.

Parameters:
`newLink` – a reference to the node that should appear after this node in the linked list (or the null reference if there should be no node after this node)

Postcondition:
The link to the node after this node has been set to `newLink`. Any other node (that used to be in this link) is no longer connected to this node.

Implementation

```
// File: IntNode.java from the package edu.colorado.nodes
// Documentation is available from pages 204-207 or from the IntNode link in
//    http://www.cs.colorado.edu/~main/docs/

package edu.colorado.nodes;
```

(continued)

(FIGURE 4.11 continued)

```
public class IntNode
{
    // Invariant of the IntNode class:
    //   1. The node's integer data is in the instance variable data.
    //   2. For the final node of a list the link part is null.
    //      Otherwise, the link part is a reference to the next node of the list.
    private int data;
    private IntNode link;

    public IntNode(int initialData, IntNode initialLink)
    {
        data = initialData;
        link = initialLink;
    }

    public void addNodeAfter(int element)
    {
        link = new IntNode(element, link);
    }

    public int getData( )
    {
        return data;
    }

    public IntNode getLink( )
    {
        return link;
    }

    public static IntNode listCopy(IntNode source)
    || See the implementation in Figure 4.9 on page 199.

    public static IntNode[ ] listCopyWithTail(IntNode source)
    || See the implementation in Figure 4.10 on page 202.

    public static int listLength(IntNode head)
    || See the implementation in Figure 4.4 on page 191.
```

(continued)

(FIGURE 4.11 continued)

```
public static IntNode[ ] listPart(IntNode start, IntNode end)
{
    // Notice that the return value is an array of two IntNode components.
    // The [0] component is the head reference for the new list and
    // the [1] component is the tail reference for the new list.
    IntNode copyHead;
    IntNode copyTail;
    IntNode[ ] answer = new IntNode[2];

    // Check for illegal null at start or end.
    if (start == null)
        throw new IllegalArgumentException("start is null");
    if (end == null)
        throw new IllegalArgumentException("end is null");

    // Make the first node for the newly created list.
    copyHead = new IntNode(start.data, null);
    copyTail = copyHead;

    // Make the rest of the nodes for the newly created list.
    while (start != end)
    {
        start = start.link;
        if (start == null)
            throw new IllegalArgumentException
            ("end node was not found on the list");
        copyTail.addNodeAfter(start.data);
        copyTail = copyTail.link;
    }

    // Return the head and tail reference for the new list.
    answer[0] = copyHead;
    answer[1] = copyTail;
    return answer;
}
```

```
public static IntNode listPosition(IntNode head, int position)
```
See the implementation in Figure 4.8 on page 195.

```
public static IntNode listSearch(IntNode head, int target)
```
See the implementation in Figure 4.6 on page 194.

(continued)

(FIGURE 4.11 continued)

```
public void removeNodeAfter( )
{
   link = link.link;
}

public void setData(int newData)
{
   data = newData;
}

public void setLink(IntNode newLink)
{
   link = newLink;
}
}
```

Self-Test Exercises

9. Look at `http://www.cs.colorado.edu/~main/edu/colorado/nodes`. How many different kinds of nodes are there? If you implemented one of these nodes, what extra work would be required to implement another?

10. Suppose that `locate` is a reference to a node in a linked list (and it is not the null reference). Write an assignment statement that will make `locate` move to the next node in the list. You should write two versions of the assignment—one that can appear in the `IntNode` class itself, and another that can appear outside of the class. What do your assignment statements do if `locate` was already refering to the last node in the list?

11. Which of the node methods use `new` to allocate at least one new node? Check your answer by looking at the documentation in Figure 4.11 on page 204 (to see which methods can throw an `OutOfMemoryError`).

12. Suppose that `head` is a head reference for a linked list with just one node. What will `head` be after `head = head.getLink( )`?

13. What technique would you use if a method needs to return more than one `IntNode`, such as a method that returns both a head and tail reference for a list.

14. Suppose that `head` is a head reference for a linked list. Also suppose that `douglass` and `adams` are two other `IntNode` variables. Write one assignment statement that will make `douglass` refer to the first node in the list that contains the number 42. Write a second assignment statement that will make `adams` refer to the 42nd node of the list. If these nodes don't exist, then the assignments should set the variables to null.

4.4   THE BAG ADT WITH A LINKED LIST

We're ready to write an ADT that is implemented with a linked list. We'll start with the familiar bag ADT, which we have previously implemented with an array (Section 3.2). At the end of this chapter we'll compare the advantages and disadvantages of these different implementations. But first, let's see how a linked list is used in our second bag implementation.

Our Second Bag—Specification

The advantage of using a familiar ADT is that you already know most of the specification. The specification, given in Figure 4.12, is nearly identical to our previous bag. The major difference is that our new bag has no worries about capacity: There is no initial capacity and no need for an `ensureCapacity` method. This is because our planned implementation—storing the bag's elements on a linked list—can easily grow and shrink by adding and removing nodes from the linked list.

The new bag class will be called `IntLinkedBag`, meaning that the underlying elements are integers, the implementation will use a linked list, and the collection itself is a bag. The `IntLinkedBag` will be placed in the same package that we used in Chapter 3—`edu.colorado.collections`, as shown in the specification of Figure 4.12.

the new bag class is called IntLinkedBag

FIGURE 4.12 | Specification and Implementation of the `IntLinkedBag` Class

Class IntLinkedBag

❖ **public class IntLinkedBag from the package edu.colorado.collections**
An `IntLinkedBag` is a collection of `int` numbers.
Limitations:
(1) Beyond `Int.MAX_VALUE` elements, `countOccurrences`, `size` and `grab` are wrong.
(2) Because of the slow linear algorithms of this class, large bags have poor performance.

Specification

◆ **Constructor for the IntLinkedBag**
`public IntLinkedBag( )`
Initialize an empty bag.
Postcondition:
This bag is empty.

(continued)

(FIGURE 4.12 continued)

♦ **add**
```
public void add(int element)
```
Add a new element to this bag.

Parameters:
element – the new element that is being added

Postcondition:
A new copy of the element has been added to this bag.

Throws: `OutOfMemoryError`
Indicates insufficient memory for adding a new element.

♦ **addAll**
```
public void addAll(IntLinkedBag addend)
```
Add the contents of another bag to this bag.

Parameters:
addend – a bag whose contents will be added to this bag

Precondition:
The parameter, addend, is not null.

Postcondition:
The elements from addend have been added to this bag.

Throws: `NullPointerException`
Indicates that addend is null.

Throws: `OutOfMemoryError`
Indicates insufficient memory to increase the size of this bag.

♦ **clone**
```
public Object clone( )
```
Generate a copy of this bag.

Returns:
The return value is a copy of this bag. Subsequent changes to the copy will not affect the original, nor vice versa. The return value must be typecast to an `IntLinkedBag` before it is used.

Throws: `OutOfMemoryError`
Indicates insufficient memory for creating the clone.

♦ **countOccurrences**
```
public int countOccurrences(int target)
```
Accessor method to count the number of occurrences of a particular element in this bag.

Parameters:
target – the element that needs to be counted

Returns:
the number of times that target occurs in this bag

(continued)

(FIGURE 4.12 continued)

- **grab**
    ```
    public int grab( )
    ```
    Accessor method to retrieve a random element from this bag.

    Precondition:
    This bag is not empty.

    Returns:
    a randomly selected element from this bag

    Throws: `IllegalStateException`
    Indicates that the bag is empty.

- **remove**
    ```
    public boolean remove(int target)
    ```
    Remove one copy of a specified element from this bag.

    Parameters:
    `target` – the element to remove from the bag

    Postcondition:
    If `target` was found in this bag, then one copy of `target` has been removed and the method returns `true`. Otherwise this bag remains unchanged and the method returns `false`.

- **size**
    ```
    public int size( )
    ```
    Accessor method to determine the number of elements in this bag.

    Returns:
    the number of elements in this bag

- **union**
    ```
    public static IntLinkedBag union(IntLinkedBag b1, IntLinkedBag b2)
    ```
    Create a new bag that contains all the elements from two other bags.

    Parameters:
    `b1` – the first of two bags
    `b2` – the second of two bags

    Precondition:
    Neither `b1` nor `b2` is null.

    Returns:
    a new bag that is the union of `b1` and `b2`

    Throws: `NullPointerException`
    Indicates that one of the arguments is null.

    Throws: `OutOfMemoryError`
    Indicates insufficient memory for the new bag.

The grab Method

The new bag has one other minor change, which is specified as part of Figure 4.12. Just for fun, we've included a new method called grab, which returns a randomly selected element from a bag. Later we'll use the grab method in some game-playing programs.

Our Second Bag—Class Declaration

Our plan has been laid. We will implement the new bag by storing the elements on a linked list. The class will have two private instance variables: (1) a reference to the head of a linked list that contains the elements of the bag; and (2) an int variable that keeps track of the length of the list. The second instance variable isn't really needed since we could use listLength to determine the length of the list. But by keeping the length in an instance variable, the length can be quickly determined by accessing the variable (a constant time operation). This is in contrast to actually counting the length by traversing the list (a linear time operation).

In any case, we can now write an outline for our implementation. The class goes in the package edu.colorado.collections, and we import the node class from edu.colorado.nodes.IntNode. Then we declare our new bag class with two instance variables as shown here:

```
package edu.colorado.collections;
import edu.colorado.nodes.IntNode;

class IntLinkedBag
{
    private IntNode head;        // Head reference for the list
    private int manyNodes;       // Number of nodes on the list

    Method implementations will be placed here later.
}
```

To avoid confusion over how we are using our linked list, we now make an explicit statement of the invariant for our second design of the bag ADT.

Invariant for the Second Bag ADT

1. The elements in the bag are stored on a linked list.

2. The head reference of the list is stored in the instance variable head.

3. The total number of elements in the list is stored in the instance variable manyNodes.

The Second Bag—Implementation

With our invariant in mind, we can implement each of the methods, starting with the constructor. The key to simple implementations is to use the node methods whenever possible.

Constructor. The constructor sets head to be the null reference (indicating the empty list) and sets manyNodes to zero. Actually, these two values (null and zero) are the default values for the instance variables, so one possibility is to not implement the constructor at all. When we implement no constructor, Java provides an automatic no-arguments constructor that initializes all instance variables to their default values. If we take this approach, then our implementation should include a comment to indicate that we are using Java's automatic no-arguments constructor.

However, we will actually implement the constructor, as shown here:

```
public IntLinkedBag( )
{
    head = null;
    manyNodes = 0;
}
```

constructor

Having an actual implementation makes it easier to make future changes. Also, without the implementation, we could not include a Javadoc comment to specify exactly what the constructor does.

The clone Method. The clone method needs to create a copy of a bag. The IntLinkedBag clone method will follow the pattern introduced in Chapter 2 on page 78. Therefore, the start of the clone method is the code shown here:

```
public Object clone( )
{   // Clone an IntLinkedBag.
    IntLinkedBag answer;

    try
    {
        answer = (IntLinkedBag) super.clone( );
    }
    catch (CloneNotSupportedException e)
    {   // This exception should not occur. But if it does, it would
        // probably indicate a programming error that made
        // super.clone unavailable. The most common error would be
        // forgetting the "Implements Cloneable" clause.
        throw new RuntimeException
        ("This class does not implement Cloneable.");
    }
    . . .
```

clone method

This is the same as the start of the `clone` method for our Chapter 3 bag. As with the Chapter 3 bag, this code uses the `super.clone` method to make `answer` be an exact copy of the bag that activated the `clone` method. With the Chapter 3 bag, we needed some extra statements at the end of the `clone` method—otherwise the original bag and the clone would share the same array.

Our new bag, using a linked list, runs into a similar problem. To see this problem, consider a bag that contains three elements, as shown here:

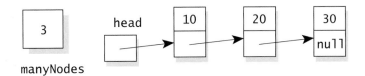

Now, suppose we activate `clone( )` to create a copy of this bag. The clone method executes the statement `answer = (IntLinkedBag) super.clone( )`. What does `super.clone( )` do? It creates a new `IntLinkedBag` object and `answer` will refer to this new `IntLinkedBag`. But the new `IntLinkedBag` has instance variables (`answer.manyNodes` and `answer.head`) that are merely copied from the original. So, after `answer = (IntLinkedBag) super.clone( )`, the situation looks like this (where `manyNodes` and `head` are the instance variables from the original bag that activated the `clone` method):

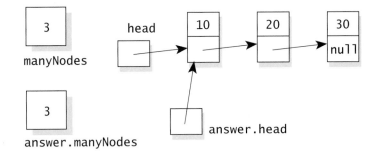

As you can see, `answer.head` refers to the original's head node. Subsequent changes to the linked list will affect both the original and the clone. This is incorrect behavior for a clone. To fix the problem, we need an additional statement before the return of the `clone` method. The purpose of the statement is to create a new linked list for the clone's `head` instance variable to refer to. Here's the statement:

```
answer.head = IntNode.listCopy(head);
```

This statement activates the `listCopy` method. The argument, `head`, is the head reference from the linked list of the bag that we are copying. When the assignment statement finishes, answer.head will refer to the head node of the new list. Here's the situation after the copying:

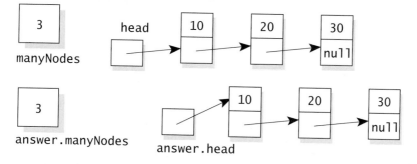

The new linked list for answer was created by copying the original linked list. Subsequent changes to answer will not affect the original, nor will changes to the original affect answer. The complete clone method, including the extra statement at the end, is shown in Figure 4.13.

| **FIGURE 4.13** | Implementation of the Second Bag's clone Method |

Implementation

```
public Object clone( )
{
    { // Clone an IntLinkedBag.
    IntLinkedBag answer;

    try
    {
        answer = (IntLinkedBag) super.clone( );
    }
    catch (CloneNotSupportedException e)
    {   // This exception should not occur. But if it does, it would probably indicate a
        // programming error that made super.clone unavailable. The most common
        // error would be forgetting the "Implements Cloneable"
        // clause at the start of this class.
        throw new RuntimeException
        ("This class does not implement Cloneable.");
    }

    answer.head = IntNode.listCopy(head);

    return answer;
}
```

This step creates a new linked list for answer. The new linked list is separate from the original array so that subsequent changes to one will not affect the other.

TIP

Programming Tip: Cloning a Class That Contains a Linked List

If the instance variables of a class contain a linked list, then the clone method needs extra work before it returns. The extra work creates a new linked list for the clone's instance variable to refer to.

The remove Method. There are two approaches to implementing the remove method. The first approach uses the nodes removal methods—changing the head if the removed element is at the head of the list, and using the ordinary removeNodeAfter to remove an element that is farther down the line. This first approach is fine, although it does require a bit of thought because removeNodeAfter requires a reference to the node that is just *before* the element that you want to remove. We could certainly find this "before" node, but not by using the node's listSearch method.

The second approach actually uses listSearch to obtain a reference to the node that contains the element to be deleted. For example, suppose our target is the number 42 in the bag shown here:

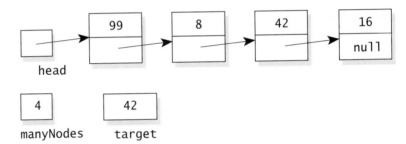

Our approach begins by setting a local variable named targetNode to refer to the node that contains our target. This is accomplished with the assignment targetNode = listSearch(head, target). After the assignment, the targetNode is set this way:

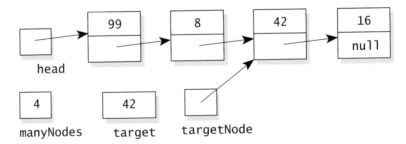

Now we can remove the target from the list with two more steps. First, copy the data from the head node to the target node, as shown at the top of the next page.

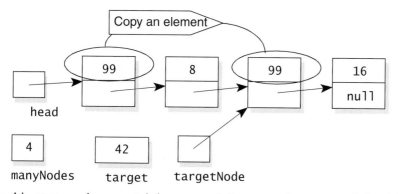

After this step, we have certainly removed the target, but we are left with two 99s. So, we proceed to a second step: Remove the head node (that is, one of the copies of 99). These steps are all implemented in the remove method shown in Figure 4.14. The only other steps in the implementation are a test to ensure that the target is actually in the bag and subtracting one from manyNodes.

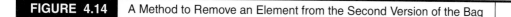

FIGURE 4.14   A Method to Remove an Element from the Second Version of the Bag

Implementation

```
public boolean remove(int target)
{
    IntNode targetNode; // The node that contains the target

    targetNode = IntNode.listSearch(head, target);
    if (targetNode == null)
        // The target was not found, so nothing is removed.
        return false;
    else
    {   // The target was found at targetNode. So copy the head data to targetNode
        // and then remove the extra copy of the head data.
        targetNode.setData(head.getData( ));
        head = head.getLink( );
        manyNodes--;
        return true;
    }
}
```

Programming Tip: How to Choose between Different Approaches

We had two possible approaches for the remove method. How do we select the better approach? Normally, when two different approaches have equal efficiency, we will choose the approach that makes better use of the node's methods. This saves us work and also reduces the chance of new errors from writing new code to do an old job. In the case of remove we choose the second approach because it made better use of listSearch.

The countOccurrences Method. Two possible approaches come to mind for the countOccurrences method. One of the approaches simply steps through the linked list one node at a time, checking each piece of data to see whether it is the sought-after target. We count the occurrences of the target and return the answer. The second approach uses listSearch to find the first occurrence of the target, then uses listSearch again to find the next occurrence, and so on until we have found all occurrences of the target. The second approach makes better use of the node's methods, so that is the approach we will take.

As an example of the second approach to the countOccurrences method, suppose we want to count the number of occurrences of 42 in the bag shown here:

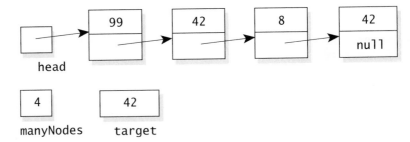

We'll use two local variables: answer, which keeps track of the number of occurrences that we have seen so far, and cursor, which is a reference to a node in the list. We initialize answer to zero, and we use listSearch to make cursor refer to the first occurrence of the target (or to be null if there are no occurrences). After this initialization, we have this situation:

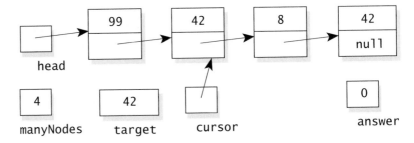

Next, we enter a loop. The loop stops when `cursor` becomes `null`, indicating that there are no more occurrences of the target. Each time through the loop we do two steps: (1) Add one to `answer`, and (2) Move `cursor` to refer to the next occurrence of the target (or to be `null` if there are no more occurrences). Can we use a node method to execute Step 2? At first, it might seem that the node methods are of no use, since `listSearch` finds the *first* occurrence of a given target. But there is an approach that will use `listSearch` together with the `cursor` to find the *next* occurrence of the target. The approach begins by moving cursor to the next node in the list, using the statement `cursor = cursor.getLink( )`. In our example, this results in the following:

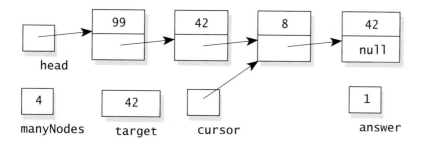

As you can see, `cursor` now refers to a node in the middle of a linked list. But, any time that a variable refers to a node in the middle of a linked list, we can pretend that the node is the head of a smaller linked list. In our example, `cursor` refers to the head of a two-element list containing the numbers 8 and 42. Therefore, we can use `cursor` as an argument to `listSearch` in the assignment statement `cursor = IntNode.listSearch(cursor, target)`. This statement moves `cursor` to the next occurrence of the target. This occurrence could be at the cursor's current spot, or it could be farther down the line. In our example, the next occurrence of 42 is farther down the line, so `cursor` is moved as shown here:

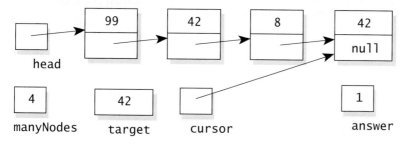

Eventually there will be no more occurrences of the target and `cursor` becomes `null`, ending the loop. At that point the method returns `answer`. The complete implementation of `countOccurrences` is shown in Figure 4.15.

FIGURE 4.15	Implementation of countOccurrences for the Second Version of the Bag

Implementation

```
public int countOccurrences(int target)
{
    int answer;
    IntNode cursor;

    answer = 0;
    cursor = IntNode.listSearch(head, target);
    while (cursor != null)
    {   // Each time that cursor is not null, we have another occurrence of target, so we
        // add one to answer and then move cursor to the next occurrence of the target.
        answer++;
        cursor = cursor.getLink( );
        cursor = IntNode.listSearch(cursor, target);
    }
    return answer;
}
```

Finding the Next Occurrence of an Element

The situation: A variable named cursor refers to a node in a linked list that contains a particular element called target.

The task: Make cursor refer to the next occurrence of target (or null if there are no more occurrences).

The solution:
```
    cursor = cursor.getLink( );
    cursor = IntNode.listSearch(cursor, target);
```

The grab Method. The bag has a new `grab` method, specified here:

- **grab**

  `public int grab( )`

  Accessor method to retrieve a random element from this bag.

  Precondition:

  This bag is not empty.

  Returns:

  a randomly selected element from this bag

  Throws: `IllegalStateException`

  Indicates that the bag is empty.

The implementation will start by generating a random `int` value between 1 and the size of the bag. The random value can then be used to select a node from the bag, and we'll return the data from the selected node. So, the body of the method will look something like this:

```
i = some random int value between 1 and the size of the bag;
cursor = listPosition(head, i);
return cursor.getData( );
```

Of course the trick is to generate "some random `int` value between 1 and the size of the bag." The Java class libraries can help. Within `java.lang.math` is a method that (sort of) generates random numbers, with this specification:

- **Math.random**

  `public static double random( )`

  Generates a pseudorandom number in the range 0.0 to 1.0.

  Returns:

  a pseudorandom number in the range 0.0 and 1.0 (this return value may be zero, but it's always less than 1.0)

The values returned by `Math.random` are not truly random. They are generated by a simple rule. But the numbers *appear* random and so the method is referred to as a **pseudorandom number generator**. For most applications, a pseudorandom number generator is a close enough approximation to a true random number generator. In fact, a pseudorandom number generator has one advantage over a true random number generator: The sequence of numbers it produces is repeatable. If run twice with the same initial conditions, a pseudorandom number generator will produce exactly the same sequence of numbers. This is handy when you are debugging programs that use these sequences. When an error is discovered, the corrected program can be tested with the *same* sequence of pseudorandom numbers that produced the original error.

But at this point we don't need a complete memoir on pseudorandom numbers. All we need is a way to use the `Math.random` to generate a number between

Math.random

1 and the size of the bag. The following assignment statement does the trick:

```
// Set i to a random number from 1 to the size of the bag:
i = (int) (Math.random( ) * manyNodes) + 1;
```

Let's look at how the expression works. The method `Math.random` gives us a number that's in the range 0.0 to 1.0. The value is actually in the "half-open range" of [0 .. 1), which means that the number could be from zero up to, but not including, 1. Therefore, the expression `Math.random( ) * manyNodes` is in the range zero to manyNodes—or to be more precise, from zero up to, but not including, manyNodes.

The operation `(int)` is an operation that truncates a double number, keeping only the integer part. Therefore, `(int) (Math.random( ) * manyNodes)` is an `int` value that could be from zero to manyNodes-1. The expression cannot actually be manyNodes. Since we want a number from 1 to manyNodes, we add one, resulting in `i = (int) (Math.random( ) * manyNodes) + 1`. This assignment statement is used in the complete grab implementation shown in Figure 4.16.

The Second Bag—Putting the Pieces Together

The remaining methods are straightforward. For example, the `size` method just returns manyNodes. All these methods are given in the complete implementation of Figure 4.17. Take particular notice of how the bag's addAll method is implemented. The implementation makes a copy of the linked list for the bag that's being added. This copy is then attached at the front of the linked list for the bag that's being added to. The bag's `union` method is implemented by using the addAll method.

| FIGURE 4.16 | Implementation of a Method to Grab a Random Element |

Implementation

```
public int grab( )
{
    int i; // A random value between 1 and the size of the bag
    IntNode cursor;

    if (manyNodes == 0)
        throw new IllegalStateException("Bag size is zero.");

    i =  (int) (Math.random( ) * manyNodes) + 1;
    cursor = IntNode.listPosition(head, i);
    return cursor.getData( );
}
```

FIGURE 4.17	Implementation of Our Second Bag Class

Implementation

```
// FILE: IntLinkedBag.java from the package edu.colorado.collections
// Documentation is available in Figure 4.12 on page 211 or from the IntLinkedBag link in
//    http://www.cs.colorado.edu/~main/docs/

package edu.colorado.collections;
import edu.colorado.nodes.IntNode;

public class IntLinkedBag implements Cloneable
{
    // INVARIANT for the Bag ADT:
    //    1. The elements in the Bag are stored on a linked list.
    //    2. The head reference of the list is in the instance variable head.
    //    3. The total number of elements in the list is in the instance variable manyNodes.
    private IntNode head;
    private int manyNodes;

    public IntLinkedBag( )
    {
        head = null;
        manyNodes = 0;
    }

    public void add(int element)
    {
        head = new IntNode(element, head);
        manyNodes++;
    }

    public void addAll(IntLinkedBag addend)
    {
        IntNode[ ] copyInfo;

        if (addend == null)
            throw new IllegalArgumentException("addend is null.");
        if (addend.manyNodes > 0)
        {
            copyInfo = IntNode.listCopyWithTail(addend.head);
            copyInfo[1].setLink(head); // Link the tail of the copy to my own head...
            head = copyInfo[0];        // and set my own head to the head of the copy.
            manyNodes += addend.manyNodes;
        }
    }
}
```

(continued)

(FIGURE 4.17 continued)

```
public Object clone( )
|| See the implementation in Figure 4.13 on page 217.


public int countOccurrences(int target)
|| See the implementation in Figure 4.15 on page 222.


public int grab( )
|| See the implementation in Figure 4.16 on page 224.


public boolean remove(int target)
|| See the implementation in Figure 4.14 on page 219.


public int size( )
{
    return manyNodes;
}


public static IntLinkedBag union(IntLinkedBag b1, IntLinkedBag b2)
{
    if (b1 == null)
        throw new IllegalArgumentException("b1 is null.");
    if (b2 == null)
        throw new IllegalArgumentException("b2 is null.");

    IntLinkedBag answer = new IntLinkedBag( );

    answer.addAll(b1);
    answer.addAll(b2);
    return answer;
}
}
```

Self-Test Exercises

15. Suppose you want to use a bag where the elements are double numbers instead of integers. How would you do this?

16. Write a few lines of code to declare a bag of integers and place the integers 42 and 8 in the bag. Then grab a random integer from the bag, printing it. Finally print the size of the bag.

17. In general, which is preferable: an implementation that uses the node methods, or an implementation that manipulates a linked list directly?

18. Suppose that p is a reference to a node in a linked list of integers and that p.getData( ) has a copy of an integer called d. Write two lines of code that will move p to the next node that contains a copy of d (or set p to null if there is no such node). How can you combine your two statements into just one?

19. Describe the steps taken by countOccurrences if the target is not in the bag.

20. Describe one of the boundary values for testing remove.

21. Write an expression that will give a random integer between –10 and 10.

22. Do big-*O* time analyses of the bag's methods.

4.5 PROGRAMMING PROJECT: THE SEQUENCE ADT WITH A LINKED LIST

In Section 3.3 on page 133 we gave a specification for a sequence ADT that was implemented using an array. Now you can reimplement this ADT using a *linked list* as the data structure rather than an array. Start by rereading the ADT's specification on page 138, then return here for some implementation suggestions.

The Revised Sequence ADT—Design Suggestions

Using a linked list to implement the sequence ADT seems natural. We'll keep the elements stored on a linked list, in their sequence order. The "current" element on the list can be maintained by an instance variable that refers to the node that contains the current element. When the start method is activated, we set this cursor to refer to the first node of the linked list. When advance is activated, we move the cursor to the next node on the linked list.

With this in mind, we propose five private instance variables for the new sequence class:

- The first variable, `manyNodes`, keeps track of the number of nodes in the list.

- `head` and `tail`—these are references to the head and tail nodes of the linked list. If the list has no elements, then these references are both `null`. The reason for the tail reference is the `addAfter` method. Normally this method adds a new element immediately after the current element. But if there is no current element, then `addAfter` places its new element at the tail of the list, so it makes sense to maintain a connection with the list's tail.

- `cursor`—refers to the node with the current element (or `null` if there is no current element).

- `precursor`—refers to the node before current element (or `null` if there is no current element, or the current element is the first node). Can you figure out why we propose a *pre*cursor? The answer is the `addBefore` method, which normally adds a new element immediately *before* the current element. But there is no node method to add a new node before a specified node. We can only add new nodes after a specified node. Therefore, the `addBefore` method will work by adding the new element *after* the precursor node—which is also just *before* the cursor node.

The sequence class that you implement could have integer elements, or double number elements, or several other possibilities. The choice of element type will determine which kind of node you use for the linked list. If you choose integer elements, then you will use `edu.colorado.nodes.IntNode`. All the node classes, including `IntNode`, are available for you to view at `http://www.cs.colorado.edu/~main/edu/colorado/nodes`.

For this programming project, you should use double numbers for the elements and follow these guidelines:

- The name of the class is `DoubleLinkedSeq`;

- You'll use `DoubleNode` for your node class;

- Put your class in a package `edu.colorado.collections`;

- Follow the specification from Figure 4.18 on page 230. This specification is also available at the `DoubleLinkedSeq` link in
  `http//www.cs.colorado.edu/~main/docs/`

Notice that the specification states a limitation that beyond `Int.MAX_VALUE` elements the `size` method does not work (though all other methods should be okay).

Here's an example of the five instance variables for a sequence with four elements and the current element at the third location:

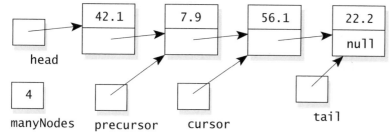

Notice that `cursor` and `precursor` are *references* to two nodes—one right after the other.

Start your implementation by writing the invariant for the new sequence ADT. You might even write the invariant in large letters on a sheet of paper and pin it up in front of you as you work. Each of the methods counts on that invariant being true when the method begins. And each method is responsible for ensuring that the invariant is true when the method finishes.

what is the invariant of the new list ADT?

As you implement each modification method, you might use the following matrix to increase your confidence that the method works correctly.

	manyNodes	head	tail	cursor	precursor
An empty list					
A nonempty list with no current element					
Current element at the head					
Current element at the tail					
Current element not at head or tail					

Here's how to use the matrix: Suppose you have just implemented one of the modification methods such as `addAfter`. Go through the matrix one row at a time, executing your method with pencil and paper. For example, with the first row of the matrix you would try `addAfter` to see its behavior for an empty list. As you execute each method by hand, keep track of the five instance variables, and put five check marks in the row to indicate that the final values correctly satisfy the invariant.

The Revised Sequence ADT—Clone Method

The sequence class has a `clone` method to make a new copy of a sequence. The sequence that you are copying activates the `clone` method, and we'll call it the "original sequence." As with all `clone` methods, you should start with the pattern from page 78. After activating `super.clone`, the extra work must make a separate copy of the linked list for the clone, and correctly set the clone's head, tail, cursor, and precursor. We suggest that you handle the work with the following three cases:

- If the original sequence has no current element, then simply copy the original's linked list with `listCopy`. Then set both `precursor` and `cursor` to null.

- If the current element of the original sequence is its first element, then copy the original's linked list with `listCopy`. Then set `precursor` to null, and set `cursor` to refer to the head node of the newly created linked list.

- If the current element of the original sequence is after its first element, then copy the original's linked list in two pieces using `listPart`: The first piece goes from the head node to the precursor; the second piece goes from the cursor to the tail. Put these two pieces together by making the link part of the precursor node refer to the cursor node. The reason for copying in two separate pieces is to easily set the precursor and cursor of the newly created list.

FIGURE 4.18 | Specification for the Second Version of the `DoubleLinkedSeq` Class

---

Class DoubleLinkedSeq

❖ **public class DoubleLinkedSeq from the package edu.colorado.collections**
A `DoubleLinkedSeq` is a sequence of double numbers. The sequence can have a special "current element," which is specified and accessed through four methods that are not available in the bag class (`start`, `getCurrent`, `advance`, and `isCurrent`).

Limitations:
Beyond `Int.MAX_VALUE` elements, the `size` method does not work.

Specification

♦ **Constructor for the DoubleLinkedSeq**
`public DoubleLinkedSeq( )`
Initialize an empty sequence.

Postcondition:
This sequence is empty.

(continued)

(FIGURE 4.18 continued)

◆ addAfter and addBefore

```
public void addAfter(double element)
public void addBefore(double element)
```

Adds a new element to this sequence, either before or after the current element.

Parameters:
element – the new element that is being added

Postcondition:
A new copy of the element has been added to this sequence. If there was a current element, addAfter places the new element after the current element and addBefore places the new element before the current element. If there was no current element, addAfter places the new element at the end of the sequence and addBefore places the new element at the front of the sequence. The new element always becomes the new current element of the sequence.

Throws: OutOfMemoryError
Indicates insufficient memory for a new node.

◆ addAll

```
public void addAll(DoubleLinkedSeq addend)
```
Place the contents of another sequence at the end of this sequence.

Parameters:
addend – a sequence whose contents will be placed at the end of this sequence

Precondition:
The parameter, addend, is not null.

Postcondition:
The elements from addend have been placed at the end of this sequence. The current element of this sequence remains where it was, and the addend is also unchanged.

Throws: NullPointerException
Indicates that addend is null.

Throws: OutOfMemoryError
Indicates insufficient memory to increase the size of the sequence.

◆ advance

```
public void advance( )
```
Move forward, so that the current element is now the next element in the sequence.

Precondition:
isCurrent( ) returns true.

Postcondition:
If the current element was already the end element of the sequence (with nothing after it), then there is no longer any current element. Otherwise, the new element is the element immediately after the original current element.

Throws: IllegalStateException
Indicates that there is no current element, so advance may not be called.

(continued)

(FIGURE 4.18 continued)

◆ **clone**

> `public Object clone( )`
>
> Generate a copy of this sequence.
>
> **Returns:**
>> The return value is a copy of this sequence. Subsequent changes to the copy will not affect the original, nor vice versa. The return value must be typecast to a `DoubleLinkedSeq` before it is used.
>
> **Throws:** `OutOfMemoryError`
>> Indicates insufficient memory for creating the clone.

◆ **concatenation**

> `public static DoubleLinkedSeq concatenation`
> `(DoubleLinkedSeq s1, DoubleLinkedSeq s2)`
>
> Create a new sequence that contains all the elements from one sequence followed by another.
>
> **Parameters:**
>> `s1` – the first of two sequences
>> `s2` – the second of two sequences
>
> **Precondition:**
>> Neither `s1` nor `s2` is null.
>
> **Returns:**
>> a new sequence that has the elements of `s1` followed by `s2` (with no current element)
>
> **Throws:** `IllegalArgumentException`
>> Indicates that one of the arguments is null.
>
> **Throws:** `OutOfMemoryError`
>> Indicates insufficient memory for the new sequence.

◆ **getCurrent**

> `public double getCurrent( )`
>
> Accessor method to determine the current element of the sequence.
>
> **Precondition:**
>> `isCurrent( )` returns `true`.
>
> **Returns:**
>> the current element of the sequence
>
> **Throws:** `IllegalStateException`
>> Indicates that there is no current element.

◆ **isCurrent**

> `public boolean isCurrent( )`
>
> Accessor method to determine whether this sequence has a specified current element that can be retrieved with the `getCurrent` method.
>
> **Returns:**
>> `true` (there is a current element) or `false` (there is no current element at the moment)

(continued)

(FIGURE 4.18 continued)

- ◆ **removeCurrent**
    ```
    public void removeCurrent( )
    ```
    Remove the current element from this sequence.

    Precondition:
    `isCurrent( )` returns `true`.

    Postcondition:
    The current element has been removed from the sequence, and the following element (if there is one) is now the new current element. If there was no following element, then there is now no current element.

    Throws: `IllegalStateException`
    Indicates that there is no current element, so `removeCurrent` may not be called.

- ◆ **size**
    ```
    public int size( )
    ```
    Accessor method to determine the number of elements in this sequence.

    Returns:
    the number of elements in this sequence

- ◆ **start**
    ```
    public void start( )
    ```
    Set the current element at the front of the sequence.

    Postcondition:
    The front element of this sequence is now the current element (but if the sequence has no elements at all, then there is no current element).

Self-Test Exercises

23. Suppose a sequence contains your three favorite numbers, and the current element is the first element. Draw the instance variables of this sequence using our implementation.

24. Write a new method to remove a specified element from a sequence of double numbers. The method has one parameter (the element to remove). After the removal, the current element should be the element after the removed element (if there is one).

25. Which of the sequence methods use the `new` operator to allocate at least one new node?

26. Which of the sequence methods use `DoubleNode.listPart`?

4.6 ARRAYS VS. LINKED LISTS VS. DOUBLY LINKED LISTS

Many ADTs can be implemented with either arrays or linked lists. Certainly the bag and the sequence ADT could each be implemented with either approach.

Which approach is better? There is no absolute answer. But there are certain operations that are better performed by arrays and others where linked lists are preferable. This section provides some guidelines.

Arrays Are Better at Random Access. The term **random access** refers to examining or changing an arbitrary element that is specified by its position in a list. For example: *What is the 42ⁿᵈ element in the list?* Or another example: *Change the element at position 1066 to a 7.* These are constant time operations for an array. But, in a linked list, a search for the ith element must begin at the head and will take $O(i)$ time. Sometimes there are ways to speed up the process, but even improvements remain linear time in the worst case.

If an ADT makes significant use of random access operations, then an array is better than a linked list.

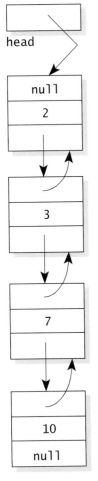

Linked Lists Are Better at Additions/Removals at a Cursor. Our sequence ADT maintains a *cursor* that refers to a "current element." Typically, a cursor moves through a list one element at a time without jumping around to random locations. If all operations occur at the cursor, then a linked list is preferable to an array. In particular, additions and removals at a cursor generally are linear time for an array (since elements that are after the cursor must *all* be shifted up or back to a new index in the array). But these operations are constant time operations for a linked list. Also remember that effective additions and removals in a linked list generally require maintaining both a cursor and a *precursor* (which refers to the node before the cursor).

If an ADT's operations take place at a cursor, then a linked list is better than an array.

Doubly Linked Lists Are Better for a Two-way Cursor. Sometimes list operations require a cursor that can move forward and backward through a list—a kind of **two-way cursor**. This situation calls for a **doubly linked list**, which is like an ordinary linked list, except that each node contains two references: one linking to the next node and one linking to the previous node. An example of a doubly linked list of integers is shown in Figure 4.19 (in the margin). A possible start of a declaration for a doubly linked list of elements is the following:

```
public class DIntNode
{
    private int data;
    private DIntNode backlink;
    private DIntNode forelink;
    ...
```

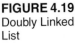

FIGURE 4.19
Doubly Linked List

The `backlink` refers to the previous node, and the `forelink` refers to the next node in the list.

If an ADT's operations take place at a two-way cursor, then a doubly linked list is the best implementation.

Resizing Can Be Inefficient for an Array. A collection class that uses an array generally provides a method to allow a programmer to adjust the capacity as needed. But changing the capacity of an array can be inefficient. The new memory must be allocated and initialized, and the elements are then copied from the old memory to the new memory. If a program can predict the necessary capacity ahead of time, then capacity is not a big problem, since the object can be given sufficient capacity from the outset. But sometimes the eventual capacity is unknown and a program must continually adjust the capacity. In this situation, a linked list has advantages. When a linked list grows, it grows one node at a time, and there is no need to copy elements from old memory to new memory.

If an ADT is frequently adjusting its capacity, then a linked list may be better than an array.

Making the Decision

Your decision on what kind of implementation to use is based on your knowledge of which operations occur in the ADT, which operations you expect to be performed most often, and whether you expect your arrays to require frequent capacity changes. Figure 4.20 summarizes these considerations.

Self-Test Exercises

27. What underlying data structure is quickest for random access?
28. What underlying data structure is quickest for additions/removals at a cursor?
29. What underlying data structure is best if a cursor must move both forward and backward?
30. What is the typical worst-case time analysis for changing the capacity of a collection class that is implemented with an array?

FIGURE 4.20 Guidelines for Choosing between an Array and a Linked List

Frequent random access operations	Use an array
Operations occur at a cursor	Use a linked list
Operations occur at a two-way cursor	Use a doubly linked list
Frequent capacity changes	A linked list avoids resizing inefficiency

CHAPTER SUMMARY

- A *linked list* consists of nodes; each *node* contains some data and a link to the next node in the list. The link part of the final node contains the null reference.

- Typically, a linked list is accessed through a *head reference* that refers to the *head node* (i.e., the first node). Sometimes a linked list is accessed elsewhere, such as through the *tail reference* that refers to the last node.

- You should be familiar with the methods of our node class, which provides fundamental operations to manipulate linked lists. These operations follow basic patterns that every programmer uses.

- Our linked lists can be used to implement ADTs. Such an ADT will have one or more private instance variables that are references to nodes in a linked list. The methods of the ADT will use the node methods to manipulate the linked list.

- You have seen two ADTs implemented with linked lists: a bag and a sequence. You will see more in the chapters that follow.

- ADTs often can be implemented in many different ways, such as by using an array or using a linked list. In general, arrays are better at *random access*; linked lists are better at additions/removals at a *cursor*.

- A *doubly linked list* has nodes with two references: one to the next node and one to the previous node. Doubly linked lists are a good choice for supporting a cursor that moves forward and backward.

? Solutions to Self-Test Exercises

1. ```
public class DoubleNode
{
    double data;
    DoubleNode link;
    ...
```

2. The head node and the tail node.

3. The null reference is used for the link part of the final node of a linked list; it is also used for the head and tail references of a list that doesn't yet have any nodes.

4. A `NullPointerException` is thrown.

5. Using techniques from Section 4.2:
```
if (head == null)
    head = new IntNode(42, null);
else
    head.addNodeAfter(42);
```

6. Using techniques from Section 4.2:
```
if (head != null)
{
    if (head.getLink( ) == null)
        head = null;
    else
        head.removeNodeAfter( );
}
```
```

7. They cannot be implemented as ordinary methods of the `IntNode` class because they must change the head reference (making it refer to a new node).

8.
```
IntNode head;
IntNode tail;
int i;
head = new IntNode(1, null);
tail = head;
for (i = 2; i <= 100; i++)
{
    tail.addNodeAfter(i);
    tail = tail.getLink( );
}
```

9. There are eight different nodes for the eight primitive data types (boolean, int, long, byte, short, double, float, and char). These are called `BooleanNode`, `IntNode`, and so on. There is one more class simply called `Node`, which will be discussed in Chapter 5. The data type in the `Node` class is Java's `Object` type. So there are nine different nodes in all.

   If you implement one of these nine node types, implementing another one takes little work—just change the type of the data and the type of any method parameters that refer to the data.

10. Within the `IntNode` class you may write:
```
locate = locate.link;
```
Elsewhere you must write:
```
locate = locate.getLink( );
```
If `locate` is already referring to the last node before the assignment statement, then the assignment will set `locate` to null.

11. The new operator is used in the methods: add-NodeAfter, listCopy, `listCopyWithTail`, and `listPart`.

12. It will be the null reference.

13. The `listCopyWithTail` method does exactly this by returning an array with two `IntNode` components.

14.
```
douglass =
    IntNode.listSearch(head, 42);
adams =
    IntNode.listPosition(head, 42);
```

15. Use `DoubleNode` instead of `IntNode`. There are a few other changes, such as changing some parameters from `int` to `double`.

16. We could write this code:
```
IntLinkedBag exercise =
    new IntLinkedBag( );
exercise.add(42);
exercise.add(8);
System.out.println
    (exercise.grab( ));
System.out.println
    (exercise.size( ));
```

17. Generally we will choose the approach that makes the best use of the node methods. This saves us work and also reduces the chance of new errors from writing new code to do an old job. The preference would change if the other approach offered better efficiency.

18. The two lines of code that we have in mind:
```
p = p.getLink( );
p = listSearch(p, d);
```
These two lines are the same as the single line:
```
p = listSearch(p.getLink( ), d);
```

19. When the target is not in the bag, the first assignment statement to `cursor` will set it to null. This means that the body of the loop will not execute at all, and the method returns the answer zero.

20. Test the case where you are removing the last element from the bag.

21. `(int) (Math.random( ) * 21) - 10`

22. All the methods are constant time except for `remove`, `grab`, `countOccurrences`, and `clone` (all of which are linear); the `addAll` method (which is $O(n)$, where n is the size of the addend); and the `union` method (which is $O(m+n)$, where m and n are the sizes of the two bags).

23. `manyNodes` is 3, and these are the other instance variables:

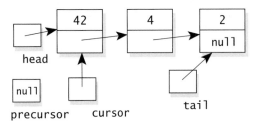

24. First check that the element occurs somewhere in the sequence. If it doesn't, then return with no work. If the element is in the sequence, then set the current element to be equal to this element, and activate the ordinary remove method.

25. The two `add` methods both allocate dynamic memory, as do `addAll`, `clone`, and `concatenation`.

26. The `clone` method should use `listPart`, as described on page 230.

27. Arrays are quickest for random access.

28. Linked lists are quickest for additions/removals at a cursor.

29. A doubly linked list.

30. At least $O(n)$, where n is the size of the array prior to changing the size. If the new array is initialized, then there is also $O(m)$ work, where m is the size of the new array.

PROGRAMMING PROJECTS

1 For this project, you will use the bag of integers from Section 4.4. The bag includes the `grab` method from Figure 4.16 on page 224. Use this class in an applet that has three components:

1. A button

2. A small text field

3. A large text area

Each time the button is clicked, the applet should read an integer from the text field, and put this integer in a bag. Then a random integer is grabbed from the bag and a message is printed in the text area—something like "My favorite number is now...."

2 Write a new static method for the node class. The method has one parameter which is a head node for a linked list of integers. The method computes a new linked list, which is the same as the original list, but in which all repetitions are removed. The method's return value is a head reference for the new list.

3 Write a method with three parameters. The first parameter is a head reference for a linked list of integers, and the next two parameters are integers x and y. The method should write a line to `System.out`, containing all integers in the list that are between the first occurrence of x and the first occurrence of y.

4 Write a method with one parameter that is a head reference for a linked list of integers. The method creates a new list that has the same elements as the original list, but in the reverse order. The method returns a head reference for the new list.

5 Write a method that has two linked list head references as parameters. Assume that linked lists contain integer data, and on each list, every element is less than the next element on the same list. The method should create a new linked list that contains all the elements on both lists, and the new linked list should also be ordered (so that every element is less than the next element on the list). The new linked list should not eliminate duplicate elements (i.e., if the same element appears on both input lists, then two copies are placed in the newly constructed linked list). The method should return a head reference for the newly constructed linked list.

6 Write a method that starts with a single linked list of integers and a special value called the splitting value. The elements of the list are in no particular order. The method divides the nodes into two linked lists: one containing all the nodes that contain an element less than the splitting value and one that contains all the other nodes. If the original linked list had any repeated integers (i.e., any two or more nodes with the same element in them), then the new linked list that has this element should have the same number of nodes that repeat this element. It does not matter whether you preserve the original linked list or destroy it in the process of building the two new lists, but your comments should document what happens to the original linked list. The method returns two head references—one for each of the linked lists that were created.

7 Write a method that takes a linked list of integers and rearranges the nodes so that the integers stored are sorted into the order smallest to largest, with the smallest integer in the node at the head of the list. Your method should preserve repetitions of integers. If the original list had any integers occurring more than once, then the changed list will have the same number of each integer. For concreteness you will use lists of integers, but your method should still work if you replace the integer type with any other type for which the less-than operation is defined. Use the following specification:

```
IntNode listSort(IntNode head)
// Postcondition: The return value is a head
// reference of a linked list with exactly the
// same entries as the original list (including
// repetitions if any), but the entries
// in this list are sorted from smallest to
// largest. The original linked list is no longer
// available.
```

Your method will implement the following algorithm (which is often called **selection sort**): The algorithm removes nodes one at a time from the original list and adds the nodes to a second list until all the nodes have been moved to the second list. The second list will then be sorted.

```
// Pseudocode for selection sort
while (the first list still has some nodes)
{
    1. Find the node with the largest element
       of all the nodes in the first list.
    2. Remove this node from the first list.
    3. Add this node at the head of the second
       list.
}
```

Note that your method will move entire nodes, not just elements, to the second list. Thus, the first list will get shorter and shorter until it is an empty list. Your method should not need to use the new operator since it is just moving nodes from one list to another (not creating new nodes).

8 Implement a new method for the bag class from Section 4.4. The new method allows you to subtract the contents of one bag from another. For example, suppose that x has seven copies of the number 3 and y has two copies of the number 3. Then after activating x.subtract(y), the bag x will have five remaining copies of the number 3.

9 Implement the Sequence class from Section 4.5. You may wish to provide some additional useful methods, such as: (1) a method to add a new element at the front of the sequence; (2) a method to remove the element at the front of the sequence; (3) a method to add a new element at the end of the sequence; (4) a method that makes the last element of the sequence become the current element; (5) a method that returns the ith element of the sequence (starting with the 0th at the front); (6) a method that makes the ith element become the current element.

10 You can represent an integer with any number of digits by storing the integer as a linked list of digits. A more efficient representation will store a larger integer in each node. Design and implement an ADT for unbounded whole numbers in which a number is implemented as a linked list of integers. Each node will hold an integer less than or equal to 999. The number represented is the concatenation of the numbers in the nodes. For example, if there are four nodes with the four integers 23, 7, 999, and 0, then this represents the number 23,007,999,000. Note that the number in a node is always considered to be three digits long. If it is not three digits long, then leading zeros are added to make it three digits long. Include methods for the usual integer operators to work with your new class.

11 Revise one of the collection classes from Chapter 3, so that it uses a linked list. Some choices are: (a) the set (Project 6 on page 168); (b) the sorted sequence (Project 7 on page 169).

12 Revise the Chapter 3 polynomial class from Project 8 on page 169, so that the coefficients are stored in a linked list and there is no maximum degree. Include an operation to allow you to multiply two polynomials in the usual way. For example:

$$(3x^2 + 7) \ * \ (2x + 4) = (6x^3 + 12x^2 + 14x + 28)$$

Java Objects and Iterators

I never knew just what it was, and I guess I never will.

TOM PAXTON
Marvelous Toy

CHAPTER

5

Professional programmers try to write classes that have general applicability in many settings. To some extent, our classes do this already. Certainly, the bag and sequence classes can be used in many different settings. However, both our bag and our sequence suffer from the fact that they require the underlying element type to be fixed. We started with a bag of integers (`IntArrayBag`). If we later need a bag of double numbers, then a second implementation (`DoubleArrayBag`) is required. We can end up with eight different bags—one for each of Java's eight primitive types. But even then we're not done; we could use a bag of locations (with the `Location` class in Figure 2.5 on page 63) or a bag of strings (using Java's built-in `String` class, which is not one of the primitive types). It seems as if the onslaught of different bags will never stop.

The framework of Java's data types provides a solution. In Java, there are the eight primitive data types, and everything else is a reference to an object.

241

This chapter uses Java's built-in Object type to create collection classes that can contain references to objects of any type. A single bag can hold references to a String or a Location or any other kind of object that may be invented in the future. In fact, as the programmer who writes these collection classes, we don't need to know exactly what the underlying objects are—"and perhaps we'll never know." All we know is that we're implementing collections to contain references to Java objects. To implement these collections effectively, we'll start with a discussion of Java's Object type.

5.1   JAVA'S OBJECT TYPE

Eight Primitive Types	
byte	
short	
int	
long	
float	*...and everything*
double	*else is a*
char	*reference to an*
boolean	*object*

A Java variable can be one of the eight primitive data types. Anything that's not one of the eight primitive types is a reference to an object. For example, if you declare a Location variable, that variable is capable of holding a reference to a Location object; if you declare a String variable, that variable is capable of holding a reference to a String object.

Java has an important built-in data type called Object. An Object variable is capable of holding a reference to any kind of object. To see how this is useful, let's look at how assignment statements can go back and forth between an Object variable and other data types.

Widening Conversions

Here's some code to show how an assignment can be made to an Object variable. The code declares a String with the value "Objection overruled!" A second Object variable is then declared and made to refer to the same string.

```
String s = new String("Objection overruled!");
Object obj;

obj = s;
```

At this point, there is only one string—"Objection overruled!"—with both s and obj referring to this one string, as shown here:

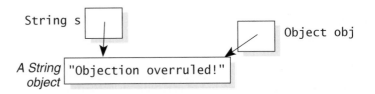

String s

Object obj

A String object "Objection overruled!"

Assigning a specific kind of object to an `Object` variable is an example of a **widening conversion**. The term "widening" means that the `obj` variable has a "wide" ability to refer to different things; in fact, `obj` is very "wide" because it *could* refer to anything. On the other hand, the variable `s` is relatively narrow with regard to the things that it can refer to—`s` can refer to only a `String`.

Widening Conversions with Reference Variables

Suppose `x` and `y` are reference variables. An assignment `x = y` is a **widening conversion** if the data type of `x` is capable of referring to a wider variety of things than the type of `y`.

Example:
```
String s = new String("Objection overruled!");
Object obj;
obj = s;
```

Java permits all widening conversions.

Narrowing Conversions

After the widening conversion `obj = s`, our program can continue to do other things, perhaps even making `s` refer to a new string, as shown here:

```
String s = new String("Objection overruled!");
Object obj;

obj = s;
s = new String("Make it so.");
```

At this point, `s` refers to a new string, and `obj` still refers to the original string, as shown here:

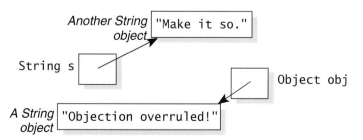

At a later point in the program, we can make `s` refer to the original string once again with an assignment statement, but the assignment needs more than merely `s = obj`. In fact, the Java compiler forbids the assignment `s = obj`. As far as the compiler knows, `obj` could refer to anything—it does not have to refer to a `String`, so the compiler forbids `s = obj`. The way around the restriction is to use the extra expression shown here:

```
s = (String) obj;
```

The expression `(String) obj` tells the compiler that the reference variable `obj` is really referring to a `String` object. This is a typecast, as discussed in Chapter 2. With the typecast, the compiler allows the assignment statement, though you must still be certain that `obj` actually does refer to a `String` object. Otherwise, when the program runs there will be a `ClassCastException` (see "Pitfall: Class Cast Exception" on page 75).

The complete assignment `s = (String) obj` is an example of a **narrowing conversion**. The term "narrowing" means that the left side of the assignment has a smaller ability to refer to different things than the right side.

Narrowing Conversion with Reference Variables

Suppose x and y are reference variables, and that x has a smaller ability to refer to things than y. A narrowing conversion using a typecast can be made to assign x from y.

Example:
```
String s = new String("Objection overruled!");
Object obj;
obj = s;
...
s = (String) obj;
```

By using a typecast, Java permits all narrowing conversions, though a `ClassCastException` may be thrown at run time if the object does not satisfy the typecast.

Narrowing conversions also occur when a method returns an `Object`, and the program assigns that `Object` to a variable of a particular type. For example, the `IntLinkedBag` class from Chapter 4 has a `clone` method:

- **clone**
  ```
  public Object clone( )
  ```
  Generate a copy of this bag.

  Returns:
  The return value is a copy of this bag. Subsequent changes to the copy will not affect the original, nor vice versa. The return value must be typecast to a `IntLinkedBag` before it is used.

The clone method returns an Object. Of course, *we* know that this Object is really an IntLinkedBag, but *the compiler* doesn't know that. Therefore, to use the clone method, we need a typecast, as shown here:

```
IntLinkedBag c;
IntLinkedBag b = new IntLinkedBag( );
b.add(42);
c = (IntLinkedBag) b.clone( );        ← c is assigned with a
                                         narrowing conversion.
```

The highlighted assignment statement is a narrowing, using a typecast to convert from the Object type (returned by b.clone) to the IntLinkedBag type.

Methods That Return Objects

If a method returns an Object, then a narrowing conversion is usually needed to actually use the return value.

Wrapper Classes

As a programmer, it's annoying that *almost* everything is a Java object. It's those eight darn primitive types that cause the problem. For example, in Section 5.2 we'll create a bag that can hold any Java object. It's a powerful bag, but it can't hold int values or any of the other primitive types.

Java's *wrapper classes* offer a partial solution to this annoyance. A **wrapper class** is a class in which each object holds a primitive value. For example, a wrapper class called Integer is designed so that each Integer object holds one int value. The two most important Integer methods are the constructor (which creates an Integer object from an int value) and the intValue method (which accesses the int value stored in an Integer object). Here are the specifications for these two Integer methods:

- **Constructor for the Integer class**
  ```
  public Integer(int value)
  ```
  Construct an Integer object from an int value.

  Parameters:
  value – the int value for this Integer to hold

  Postcondition:
  This Integer has been initialized with the specified int value.

- **intValue**
  ```
  public int intValue( )
  ```
  Accessor method to retrieve the int value of this object.

  Returns:
  the int value of this object

Here's an example to show how an integer is placed into an `Integer` object and taken back out:

```
int i = 42;
int j;
Integer example(i);      // The example has value 42
j = example.intValue( ); // j is now 42 too.
```

advantages and disadvantages of wrapper objects

The advantage of putting a value in a wrapper object is that the wrapper object is a full-blown Java object. For example, it can be put into a bag of `Objects`. The disadvantage is that the ordinary primitive operations are no longer available. For example, suppose that x and y are `Integer` objects. The expression `x + y` is not valid because the "+" operation is defined for `int` but not for `Integer`. In this case, we could calculate the sum x+y, but only by pulling the `int` values out of the wrapper objects and adding the resulting `int` values.

Here's a table of eight Java wrapper classes, along with their constructors and an accessor method to retrieve the stored value:

Wrapper Class	Constructor	Accessor Method
Byte	`public Byte(byte value)`	`public byte byteValue( )`
Short	`public Short(short value)`	`public short shortValue( )`
Integer	`public Integer(int value)`	`public int intValue( )`
Long	`public Long(long value)`	`public long longValue( )`
Float	`public Float(float value)`	`public float floatValue( )`
Double	`public Double(double value)`	`public double doubleValue( )`
Character	`public Character(char value)`	`public char charValue( )`
Boolean	`public Boolean(boolean value)`	`public boolean booleanValue( )`

Self-Test Exercises

1. Can an `Object` variable refer to a `String`? To a `Location`? To an `Int-ArrayBag`?

2. Write some code that includes both a widening conversion and a narrowing conversion. Draw a black circle by the widening and a white triangle by the narrowing.

3. Write an example of a narrowing conversion that will cause a `Class-CastException` at run time.

4. Write some code that creates a `Character` wrapper object called `example`, initializing with the char `'w'`.

5. Describe an advantage and a disadvantage of wrapper objects.

5.2   A BAG OF OBJECTS

In this section, we'll convert our bag class so that it handles Java objects. The new bag is called `ArrayBag`, and it will be based on the `IntArrayBag` in Chapter 3, storing the objects in an array with a certain capacity. But instead of `int` values, we are now storing Java objects, and this change effects the parameters for several of the methods. For example, here is the specification for the new add method:

- **add**

  ```
  public void add(Object element)
  ```
  Put a reference to an object into this bag. If the addition would take this bag beyond its current capacity, then the capacity is increased before adding the new element. The new element may be the null reference.

  Parameters:
  `element` – the element to be added to this bag

  Postcondition:
  A reference to the specified object has been added to this bag.

  Throws: `OutOfMemoryError`
  Indicates insufficient memory for increasing the capacity.

  Note:
  An attempt to increase the capacity beyond `Integer.MAX_VALUE` will cause this bag to fail with an arithmetic overflow.

Here's a small sample to show how `String` objects can be placed in a bag:

```
ArrayBag nouns = new ArrayBag( );

// Add two copies of the String "animal" and one copy of "vegetable" :
nouns.add("animal");
nouns.add("animal");
nouns.add("vegetable");

// Print the number of occurrences of "animal":
System.out.println(nouns.countOccurrences("animal"));
```

The sample prints the number 2 because `"animal"` occurs twice in the bag.

Counting the Occurrences of an Object

Counting the occurrences of an object in a bag requires some thought. Here's an example to get you thinking. Suppose you construct a bag with an initial capacity of 10, and create two identical `Location` objects with coordinates of x=2, y=4 (using the `Location` class from Section 2.4). The locations are then added to the bag as shown at the top of the next page.

```
ArrayBag spots = new ArrayBag( );
Location p1 = new Location(2, 4);  // x=2 and y=4
Location p2 = new Location(2, 4);  // Also at x=2 and y=4

spots.add(p1);
spots.add(p2);
```

The two locations are identical but separate objects, as shown in this drawing:

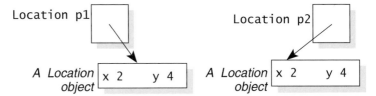

Keep in mind that the boolean expression (p1 == p2) is false because "=="
returns true only if p1 and p2 refer to the exact same object (as opposed to two
separate objects that happen to contain identical values). On the other hand, the
Location class has an equals method with the specification:

> ◆ **equals (from the Location class)**
>    ```
>    public boolean equals(Object obj)
>    ```
>   Compare this Location to another object for equality.
>   **Parameters:**
>   obj – an object with which this Location is compared
>   **Returns:**
>   A return value of true indicates that obj refers to a Location object with
>   the same value as this Location. Otherwise the return value is false.

Both p1.equals(p2) and p2.equals(p1) are true.

So here's the question to get you thinking: With both locations in the bag,
what is the value of spots.countOccurrences(p1)? In other words, how many
times does the target p1 appear in the bag? The answer depends on exactly how
we implement countOccurrences, with these two possibilities:

1. countOccurrences could step through the elements of the bag, using the
   "==" operator to look for the target. In this case, we find one occurrence
   of the target p1, and spots.countOccurrences(p1) is 1.

2. countOccurrences could step through the elements of the bag, using
   equals to look for the target. In this case, both locations are equal to the
   target, and spots.countOccurrences(p1) is 2.

Every class has an equals method. For example, the equals method of the
String class returns true if the two strings have the same sequence of charac-
ters. The equals method of the Integer wrapper class returns true if the two
Integer objects hold the same int value. Anyway, because the equals method

is always available, we'll use the second approach toward counting occurrences—and `spots.countOccurrences(p1)` is 2. Our bag documentation will make it clear that we count the occurrences of a non-null element by using its `equals` method.

> **Collections of Objects Should Use the `equals` Method**
>
> When a collection of objects tests for the presence of a non-null element, you should generally use the `equals` method rather than the "==" operator.

The Collection Is Really a Collection of References to Objects

There is one more critical aspect that you must understand before using a collection of objects. Although we use the phrase "bag of objects," what we really have is a collection of *references* to objects. In other words, the bag does not contain separate copies of each object. Instead, the bag contains only references to each object that is added to the bag.

Let's draw some pictures to see what this means. Once again, we'll create two identical locations and put them in a bag:

```
ArrayBag spots = new ArrayBag( );
Location p1 = new Location(2, 4);   // x=2 and y=4
Location p2 = new Location(2, 4);   // Another at x=2 and y=4
spots.add(p1);
spots.add(p2);
```

Here's a picture of the two locations and the bag after the five statements:

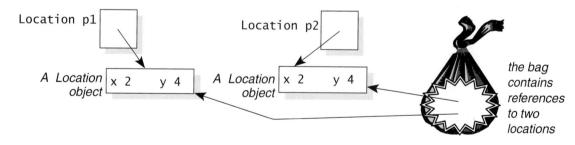

The references to the two locations are now in the bag. As we have already discussed, `spots.countOccurrences(p1)` is 2 because there are two locations with the coordinates x=2, y=4. What happens if we change p1 or p2? For example, after putting the two locations in the bag, we could execute the statement:

```
p1.shift(40, 0);
```

This shifts p1 by 40 units along the x axis, and leaves y alone, so p1 is now at x=42, y=4, as shown here:

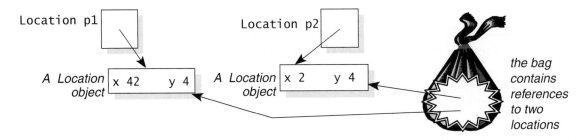

The bag still has two locations, but one of those locations has shifted to x=42, y=2. Therefore, spots.countOccurrences(p1) is now just 1 (there is one location in the bag with the coordinates of p1).

Five Steps for Converting a Collection Class to Hold Objects

We're now ready to implement the bag of objects. We'll use the original IntArrayBag from Section 3.2, and make these changes:

1. The name of the class. Every occurrence of the old class name, IntArray-Bag, is changed to the new name, ArrayBag. The name "ArrayBag" indicates that we have an array implemention of a bag, but we do not have any single underlying data type (such as Int) because the new bag can hold any type of Java object.

2. The type of the underlying element. Find all the spots where the old class used int to refer to an element in the bag. Change these spots to Object. For example, the old bag had an array of integers as one of its instance variables. The new bag has an array of objects, as shown in these declarations of the new bag's instance variables:

```
public class ArrayBag implements Cloneable
{
    public Object [ ] data;   // An array to store elements
    private int manyItems;    // How much of the array is used
    ...
```

Be careful because some int values must stay int (such as the manyItems instance variable).

3. Equality tests. Find all the spots where the old class used "==" or "!=" to compare two elements. Change these spots so that they use the equals method instead. For example, instead of target != data[index] we will write !target.equals(data[index]).

4. Decide on how to treat the null reference. The new bag stores references to objects. You must decide whether to allow the null reference to be placed in the bag. For our bag, we'll allow the null reference to be placed in the bag, and we'll indicate this in the documentation. Some of the bag's methods will need special cases to deal with null references. For example, `countOccurrences` will search for a null target using "==" to count the number of times that null is in the bag, but a non-null target is counted by using its `equals` method.

5. Update all documentation. All documentation must be updated to show that the bag is a collection of references to objects.

Any collection class can be converted to a collection of objects by following these five steps. For example, Programming Project 1 on page 277 asks you to convert the `Sequence` class from Section 3.3.

As for the new `ArrayBag` class, its specification and implementation are given in Figure 5.1. The five changes are marked in the figure, and you'll also find one other improvement: We have included a `grab` method to allow a program to grab a randomly selected object from the bag. The implementation of the new `grab` method is similar to the `grab` method in the linked list version of the bag (see page 223 in Chapter 4).

Deep Clones for Collection Classes

The `clone` method creates a copy of an `ArrayBag`. As with other `clone` methods, adding or removing elements from the original will not affect the copy, nor vice versa. However, these elements are now references to objects; both the original and the copy contain references to the same underlying objects. Changing these underlying objects will affect both the original and the copy. An alternative cloning method, called **deep cloning**, can avoid the problem, as discussed in Programming Project 5 on page 277.

| FIGURE 5.1 | Specification and Implementation for the `ArrayBag` |

Class ArrayBag

❖ **public class ArrayBag from the package edu.colorado.collections**
An `ArrayBag` is a collection of references to Objects.
Limitations:

(1) The capacity of one of these bags can change after it's created, but the maximum capacity is limited by the amount of free memory on the machine. The constructors, `add`, `clone`, and `union` will result in an `OutOfMemoryError` when free memory is exhausted.

(2) A bag's capacity cannot exceed the largest integer 2,147,483,647 (`Integer.MAX_VALUE`). Any attempt to create a larger capacity results in failure due to an arithmetic overflow.

(3) Because of the slow linear algorithms of this class, large bags will have poor performance. *(continued)*

(FIGURE 5.1 continued)

Specification

- ◆ **Constructor for the ArrayBag**
  ```
  public ArrayBag( )
  ```
  Initialize an empty bag with an initial capacity of 10. Note that the add method works efficiently (without needing more memory) until this capacity is reached.

  Postcondition:
    This bag is empty and has an initial capacity of 10.

  Throws: OutOfMemoryError
    Indicates insufficient memory for: new Object[10].

- ◆ **Second Constructor for the ArrayBag**
  ```
  public ArrayBag(int initialCapacity)
  ```
  Initialize an empty bag with a specified initial capacity. Note that the add method works efficiently (without needing more memory) until this capacity is reached.

  Parameters:
    initialCapacity – the initial capacity of this bag

  Precondition:
    initialCapacity is non-negative.

  Postcondition:
    This bag is empty and has the given initial capacity.

  Throws: IllegalArgumentException
    Indicates that initialCapacity is negative.

  Throws: OutOfMemoryError
    Indicates insufficient memory for
    new Object[initialCapacity].

  > All documentation has been updated to indicate that we now have a bag of references to objects.

- ◆ **add**
  ```
  public void add(Object element)
  ```
  Put a reference to an object into this bag. If the addition would take this bag beyond its current capacity, then the capacity is increased before adding the new element. The new element may be the null reference.

  Parameters:
    element – the element to be added to this bag

  Postcondition:
    A reference to the specified object has been added to this bag.

  Throws: OutOfMemoryError
    Indicates insufficient memory for increasing the capacity.

  Note:
    An attempt to increase the capacity beyond Integer.MAX_VALUE will cause this bag to fail with an arithmetic overflow.

(continued)

(FIGURE 5.1 continued)

♦ addAll
```
public void addAll(ArrayBag addend)
```
Add the contents of another bag to this bag.

Parameters:
addend – a bag whose contents will be added to this bag

Precondition:
The parameter, addend, is not null.

Postcondition:
The elements from addend have been added to this bag.

Throws: `NullPointerException`
Indicates that addend is null.

Throws: `OutOfMemoryError`
Indicates insufficient memory to increase the size of this bag.

Note:
An attempt to increase the capacity beyond `Integer.MAX_VALUE` will cause this bag to fail with an arithmetic overflow.

♦ clone
```
public Object clone( )
```
Generate a copy of this bag.

Returns:
The return value is a copy of this bag. Subsequent changes to the copy will not affect the original, nor vice versa. The return value must be typecast to an `ArrayBag` before it is used.

Throws: `OutOfMemoryError`
Indicates insufficient memory for creating the clone.

♦ countOccurrences
```
public int countOccurrences(Object target)
```
Accessor method to count the number of occurrences of a particular element in this bag.

Parameters:
target – the reference to an `Object` to be counted

Returns:
The return value is the number of times that `target` occurs in this bag. If `target` is non-null, then the occurrences are found using the `target.equals` method.

(continued)

(FIGURE 5.1 continued)

- **ensureCapacity**

    ```
    public void ensureCapacity(int minimumCapacity)
    ```
    Change the current capacity of this bag.

    Parameters:
    minimumCapacity – the new capacity for this bag

    Postcondition:
    This bag's capacity has been changed to at least minimumCapacity. If the capacity was already at or greater than minimumCapacity, then the capacity is left unchanged.

    Throws: OutOfMemoryError
    Indicates insufficient memory for: new Object[minimumCapacity].

- **getCapacity**

    ```
    public int getCapacity( )
    ```
    Accessor method to determine the current capacity of this bag. The add method works efficiently (without needing more memory) until this capacity is reached.

    Returns:
    the current capacity of this bag

- **grab**

    ```
    public Object grab( )
    ```
    Accessor method to retrieve a random element from this bag.

    Precondition:
    This bag is not empty.

    Returns:
    a randomly selected element from this bag

    Throws: IllegalStateException
    Indicates that the bag is empty.

- **remove**

    ```
    public boolean remove(Object target)
    ```
    Remove one copy of a specified element from this bag.

    Parameters:
    target – an element to remove from this bag

    Postcondition:
    If target was found in the bag, then one copy of target has been removed and the method returns true. Otherwise the bag remains unchanged and the method returns false. Note that if target is non-null, then target.equals is used to find target in the bag.

- **size**

    ```
    public int size( )
    ```
    Accessor method to determine the number of elements in this bag.

    Returns:
    the number of elements in this bag

(continued)

(FIGURE 5.1 continued)

- **trimToSize**
  ```
  public void trimToSize( )
  ```
  Reduce the current capacity of this bag to its size (i.e., the number of elements it contains).
  Postcondition:
  This bag's capacity has been changed to its current size.
  Throws: `OutOfMemoryError`
  Indicates insufficient memory for altering the capacity.

- **union**
  ```
  public static ArrayBag union(ArrayBag b1, ArrayBag b2)
  ```
  Create a new bag that contains all the elements from two other bags.
  Parameters:
  b1 and b2 – two bags
  Precondition:
  Neither b1 nor b2 is null.
  Returns:
  a new bag that is the union of b1 and b2
  Throws: `NullPointerException`
  Indicates that one of the arguments is null.
  Throws: `OutOfMemoryError`
  Indicates insufficient memory for the new bag.
  Note:
  An attempt to create a bag with capacity beyond `Integer.MAX_VALUE` will cause the bag to fail with an arithmetic overflow.

Implementation

```
// File: ArrayBag.java from the package edu.colorado.collections
// Complete documentation is on pages 251–255 or from the ArrayBag link in:
//     http://www.cs.colorado.edu/~main/docs/

package edu.colorado.collections;

public class ArrayBag implements Cloneable
{
    // Invariant of the ArrayBag class:
    //    1. The number of elements in the bag is in the instance variable manyItems.
    //    2. For an empty bag, we do not care what is stored in any of data;
    //       for a nonempty bag, the elements in the bag are stored in data[0]
    //       through data[manyItems-1], and we don't care what's in the rest of data.
    private Object[ ] data;
    private int manyItems;
```

The name of the new class is ArrayBag rather than IntArrayBag.

The new bag stores an array of objects rather than an array of int values.

(continued)

(FIGURE 5.1 continued)

```java
public ArrayBag( )
{
    final int INITIAL_CAPACITY = 10;
    manyItems = 0;
    data = new Object[INITIAL_CAPACITY];
}


public ArrayBag(int initialCapacity)
{
    if (initialCapacity < 0)
        throw new IllegalArgumentException
        ("initialCapacity is negative: " + initialCapacity);
    manyItems = 0;
    data = new Object[initialCapacity];
}


public void add(Object element)
{
    if (manyItems == data.length)
    {
        // Double the capacity and add 1; this works even if manyItems is 0. However, in
        // case that manyItems*2 + 1 is beyond Integer.MAX_VALUE, there will be an
        // arithmetic overflow and the bag will fail.
        ensureCapacity(manyItems*2 + 1);
    }
    data[manyItems] = element;
    manyItems++;
}


public void addAll(ArrayBag addend)
{
    // If addend is null, then a NullPointerException is thrown.
    // In the case that the total number of items is beyond Integer.MAX_VALUE, there will
    // be an arithmetic overflow and the bag will fail.
    ensureCapacity(manyItems + addend.manyItems);

    System.arraycopy(addend.data, 0, data, manyItems, addend.manyItems);
    manyItems += addend.manyItems;
}
```

(continued)

(FIGURE 5.1 continued)

```java
public Object clone( )
{  // Clone an ArrayBag.
   ArrayBag answer;

   try
   {
      answer = (ArrayBag) super.clone( );
   }
   catch (CloneNotSupportedException e)
   {
      // This exception should not occur. But if it does, it would probably indicate a
      // programming error that made super.clone unavailable.
      // The most common error would be forgetting the "Implements Cloneable"
      // clause at the start of this class.
      throw new RuntimeException
      ("This class does not implement Cloneable");
   }

   answer.data = (Object[ ]) data.clone( );

   return answer;
}


public int countOccurrences(Object target)
{
   int answer;
   int index;

   answer = 0;

   if (target == null)
   {  // Count how many times null appears in the bag.
      for (index = 0; index < manyItems; index++)
         if (data[index] == null)
            answer++;
   }
   else
   {  // Use target.equals to determine how many times the target appears.
      for (index = 0; index < manyItems; index++)
         if (target.equals(data[index]))
            answer++;
   }

   return answer;
}
```

Special code is needed to handle the case where the target is null.

For a non-null target, we use target.equals instead of the "==" operator.

(continued)

(FIGURE 5.1 continued)

```
public void ensureCapacity(int minimumCapacity)
```
The implementation is unchanged from the original in Figure 3.8 on page 128.

```
public int getCapacity( )
```
The implementation is unchanged from the original in Figure 3.8 on page 128.

```
public Object grab( )
{
   int i;

   if (manyNodes == 0)
      throw new IllegalStateException("Bag size is zero.");

   i =  (int) (Math.random( ) * manyNodes); // From 0 to manyItems-1
   return data[i];
}


public boolean remove(Object target)
{
   int index; // The location of target in the data array

   // First, set index to the location of target in the data array,
   // which could be as small as 0 or as large as manyItems-1.
   // If target is not in the array, then index will be set equal to manyItems.
   if (target == null)
   {  // Find the first occurrence of the null reference in the bag.
      for (index = 0; (index < manyItems) && (data[index] != null); index++)
      // No work is needed in the body of this for-loop.
      ;
   }
   else
   {  // Use target.equals to find the first occurrence of the target.
      for (index = 0; (index < manyItems) && (!target.equals(data[index])); index++)
      // No work is needed in the body of this for-loop.
      ;
   }

   if (index == manyItems)
      // The target was not found, so nothing is removed.
      return false;
   else
   {  // The target was found at data[index].
      manyItems--;
      data[index] = data[manyItems];
      return true;
   }
}
```

(continued)

(FIGURE 5.1 continued)

```java
public int size( )
   The implementation is unchanged from the original in Figure 3.8 on page 128.

public void trimToSize( )
   The implementation is unchanged from the original in Figure 3.8 on page 129.

public static ArrayBag union(ArrayBag b1, ArrayBag b2)
{
    // If either b1 or b2 is null, then a NullPointerException is thrown.
    // In the case that the total number of items is beyond Integer.MAX_VALUE, there will
    // be an arithmetic overflow and the bag will fail.
    ArrayBag answer = new ArrayBag(b1.getCapacity( ) + b2.getCapacity( ));

    System.arraycopy(b1.data, 0, answer.data, 0, b1.manyItems);
    System.arraycopy(b2.data, 0, answer.data, b1.manyItems, b2.manyItems);
    answer.manyItems = b1.manyItems + b2.manyItems;
    return answer;
}

}
```

Using the Bag of Objects

Using the bag of objects is easy. The program imports `edu.colorado.collec-tions.ArrayBag`, and then a bag of objects can be declared. The same program may have several different bags for different purposes, or it may even have some of the original bags such as an `IntArrayBag`.

Figure 5.2 on page 260 shows a demonstration program that uses three bags of objects, which hold various strings. The program asks the user to type several adjectives and names. These words are placed in the bags, and then words are grabbed out of the bags in order for the program to write a silly story called "Life."

The bags are declared in the demonstration program as you would expect:

```java
ArrayBag good   = new ArrayBag(WORDS_PER_BAG);
ArrayBag bad;   = new ArrayBag(WORDS_PER_BAG);
ArrayBag names; = new ArrayBag(WORDS_PER_BAG);
```

The number, `WORDS_PER_BAG`, is 4 in the story program, so each of these bags has an initial capacity of 4.

FIGURE 5.2   Demonstration Program for the `ArrayBag` Class

Java Application Program

```
// FILE: Author.java
// This program reads some words into bags. Then a silly story is written using these words.

import edu.colorado.collections.ArrayBag;
import edu.colorado.io.EasyReader;          the EasyReader class is
                                            described in Appendix B
public class Author
{
    private static EasyReader stdin = new EasyReader(System.in);

    public static void main(String[ ] args)
    {
        final int WORDS_PER_BAG = 4;   // Number of words per bag
        final int MANY_SENTENCES = 3;  // Number of sentences in story

        ArrayBag good  = new ArrayBag(WORDS_PER_BAG);
        ArrayBag bad   = new ArrayBag(WORDS_PER_BAG);
        ArrayBag names = new ArrayBag(WORDS_PER_BAG);
        int line;

        // Fill the three bags with words typed by the program's user.
        System.out.println("Help me write a story.\n");
        getWords(good,  WORDS_PER_BAG, "adjectives that describe a good mood");
        getWords(bad,   WORDS_PER_BAG, "adjectives that describe a bad mood");
        getWords(names, WORDS_PER_BAG, "first names");
        System.out.println("Thank you for your kind assistance.\n");

        // Use the words to write a silly story.
        System.out.println("LIFE");
        System.out.println("by A. Computer\n");
        for (line = 1; line <= MANY_SENTENCES; line++)
        {
            System.out.print((String) names.grab( ));
            System.out.print(" was feeling ");
            System.out.print((String) bad.grab( ));
            System.out.print(", yet he/she was also ");
            System.out.print((String) good.grab( ));
            System.out.println(".");
        }
        System.out.println("Life is " + (String) bad.grab( ) + ".\n");
        System.out.println("The " + (String) good.grab( ) + " end.");
    }
```

(continued)

(FIGURE 5.2 continued)

```
public static void getWords(ArrayBag b, int n, String description)
// Postcondition: The parameter, description, has been written as a prompt
// to System.out. Then n strings have been read using stdin.inputString,
// and these strings have been placed in the bag.
{
    String userInput;
    int i;

    System.out.print("Please type " + n + " " + description);
    System.out.println(", separated by spaces.");
    System.out.println("Press the <return> key after the final entry:");
    for (i = 1; i <= n; i++)
    {
        userInput = stdin.stringInput( );
        b.add(userInput);
    }
    System.out.println( );
}
```

A Sample Dialogue

```
Help me write a story.

Please type 4 adjectives that describe a good mood, separated by spaces.
Press the <return> key after the final entry:
joyous  happy  lighthearted  glad

Please type 4 adjectives that describe a bad mood, separated by spaces.
Press the <return> key after the final entry:
sad  glum  melancholy  blue

Please type 4 first names, separated by spaces.
Press the <return> key after the final entry:
Michael  Janet  Tim  Hannah

Thank you for your kind assistance.

LIFE
by A. Computer

Tim was feeling glum, yet he/she was also glad.
Michael was feeling melancholy, yet he/she was also joyous.
Hannah was feeling blue, yet he/she was also joyous.
Life is blue.

The lighthearted end.
```

Details of the Story-Writing Program

The story-writing program uses a method, getWords, with this specification:

- **getWords**
  ```
  public static void getWords
     (ArrayBag collection, int n, String description)
  ```
  Read n strings and place them in a bag.

  Parameters:
  collection – a bag which will have strings added to it
  n – the number of strings to read and add to the bag
  description – a prompt that will be displayed to the user

  Postcondition:
  The parameter, description, has been written as a prompt to
  System.out. Then n strings have been read using stdin.inputString,
  and these strings have been placed in the bag.

The method uses the third parameter, description, as part of a prompt that asks the user to type n words. For example, if description is the string constant "first names" and n is 4, then the getWords method writes this prompt:

```
Please type 4 first names, separated by spaces.
Press the <return> key after the final entry:
```

The method then reads n strings. Each string is read by using the EasyReader class, which we first used for various input operations in Chapter 3. The Easy-Reader is fully described in Appendix B. The story program has a single EasyReader called stdin, which is attached to standard input (System.in). Once stdin is set up, a string is read with the method stdin.stringInput. This method reads one word at a time, stopping when it finds a *whitespace* character. **Whitespace characters** include the ordinary space character plus some special characters such as the return key and the tab key.

As the strings are read, the getWords method places them in the bag by activating collection.add. In all, the main program activates getWords three times to get three different kinds of strings. The literary merit of the program's story is debatable, but the ability to use bags of objects is clearly important.

Self-Test Exercises

6. We converted an IntArrayBag to an ArrayBag. During the conversion, does every occurrence of int get changed to Object?

7. Our bag is a bag of references to objects. Can the null reference be placed into our bag?

8. Write some code that declares a bag of objects and then puts the numbers 1 through 10 into the bag. The numbers are objects of the wrapper class, `Integer`, not the primitive class `int`.

9. The original `countOccurrences` method tested for the occurrence of a target with the boolean expression `target == data[index]`. What different boolean expression is used in the `countOccurrences` method of the bag of objects?

10. What technique did the story-writing program use to read strings from the keyboard?

5.3 JCL COLLECTIONS AND NODES OF OBJECTS

Vectors and Other JCL Collections

The Java Class Libraries provide several other collection classes for storing Java objects. The simplest JCL collection class is called `Vector`, which is similar to an array because you can place an object at a particular index. But unlike an array, a vector automatically grows if you place an object at a location beyond its current capacity. Other JCL collections, first introduced in Java Version 1.2, include sets, lists, and maps.

Nodes That Contain Object Data

Our nodes from Chapter 4 can also be converted to handle objects. In the conversion, the new class, called `Node`, allows us to build linked lists of nodes, and each node contains a Java object rather than an integer. Here is a comparison of the original `IntNode` declaration with our new class:

Original IntNode:
```
public class IntNode
{
    private int data;
    IntNode link;

    The methods use
    the int data.

}
```

New Node Class:
```
public class Node
{
    private Object data;
    Node link;

    The methods use
    the Object data.

}
```

With the new `Node` class, each node contains a piece of data that is a reference to an `Object`. The implementation of the methods is based on the `IntNode` methods, following the same five steps that we used before on page 250. The resulting `Node` class is given in Appendix E, where it will be easy for you to find for applications in future chapters. You may find yourself using it beyond this book too.

Pitfall: **Misuse of the equals Method**

When you convert a collection class to contain objects, it is tempting to blindly change every occurrence of the "==" operator to use the equals method instead. There are two pitfalls to beware.

First, beware of null references. You cannot activate the equals method of a null reference. For example, here is the implementation of the new listSearch method from the Node. The method searches the linked list for an occurrence of a particular target, and returns a reference to the node that contains the target. If no such node is found, then the null reference is returned:

```
public static Node listSearch(Node head, Object target)
{
    Node cursor;

    if (target == null)
    {   // Search for a node in which the data is the null reference.
        for (cursor = head; cursor != null; cursor = cursor.link)
            if (cursor.data == null)
                return cursor;
    }
    else
    {   // Search for a node that contains the non-null target.
        for (cursor = head; cursor != null; cursor = cursor.link)
            if (target.equals(cursor.data))
                return cursor;
    }

    return null;
}
```

The target may be the null reference—in that case, we're searching for a node in which the data is null. This search is carried out in the first part of the large if-statement. We test whether a particular node contains null data with the boolean expression cursor.data == null. On the other hand, for a non-null target, the search is carried out in the else-part of the large if-statement. We test whether a particular node contains a non-null target with the boolean expression target.equals(cursor.data).

In general, the equals *method may be used only when you know that the target is non-null.*

The second thing to beware: An eqality test "==" is changed to the equals method only at points where the program is comparing data. Don't change other comparisons. For example, here is the listPart method of the new Node class of Appendix E:

```
public static Node[ ] listPart(Node start, Node end)
{
    Node copyHead;
    Node copyTail;
    Node cursor;
    Node[ ] answer = new Node[2];

    // Check for illegal null at start or end.
    if (start == null)
        throw new IllegalArgumentException("start is null.");

    if (end == null)
        throw new IllegalArgumentException("end is null.");

    // Make the first node for the newly created list.
    copyHead = new Node(start.data, null);
    copyTail = copyHead;
    cursor = start;

    // Make the rest of the nodes for the newly created list.
    while (cursor != end)
    {
        cursor = start.link;
        if (cursor == null)
            throw new IllegalArgumentException
                ("end node was not found on the list.");
        copyTail.addNodeAfter(cursor.data);
        copyTail = copyTail.link;
    }

    // Return the head and tail references
    answer[0] = copyHead;
    answer[1] = copyTail;
    return answer;
}
```

The method copies part of a linked list, extending from the specified start node to the specified end node. The large while-loop does most of the work, and this loop continues while cursor != end . This boolean expression is checking whether cursor refers to a different node than end. The expression becomes false when cursor refers to the exact same node that end refers to, and at that point the loop ends. Do not change this expression to use the equals method.

When the purpose of a boolean expression is to test whether or not two references refer to the exact same object, then use the "==" or "!=" operator. Do not use the equals method.

Other Collections That Use Linked Lists

Using the new Node class from Appendix E, we can implement other collections that use linked lists. For example, we can implement another bag of objects, which stores its objects on a linked list. In fact, we'll do exactly this, but first you need to see a Java feature called *iterators*, which will be used as part of the new bag. Iterators and the new bag are both covered in the next section.

Self-Test Exercises

11. What class from the Java Class Library is a collection of objects?

12. Why was extra code added to the new node's listSearch method?

13. Suppose that x and y are non-null references to two nodes. The data in each node is a non-null Object. Write two boolean expressions: (1) an expression that is true if x and y refer to exactly the same node; and (2) an expression that is true if the data from the x node is equal to the data from the y node. Use the equals method where appropriate.

5.4   ITERATORS

Interfaces

A Java **interface** is usually a list of methods that a class may implement. For example, Java's AudioClip interface indicates that a class that implements the AudioClip interface will have three methods with these headings:

```
public void loop( )
public void play( )
public void stop( )
```

Any class that implements the AudioClip interface must implement these three methods.

The AudioClip interface is intended for classes where each object can produce a sound on a computer with sound capabilities. For example, the play method is supposed to play the sound one time. If you're writing a class with these kinds of audio capabilities, then following the headers of a known interface will help other programmers understand your intentions.

When you write a class that implements a Java interface, you should tell the compiler that you are doing so. The syntax uses the keyword implements in the class head. For example, you may write a class called ThemeSong that implements the AudioClip interface. The start of the ThemeSong implementation would be:

```
public class ThemeSong implements AudioClip
```

If a class implements several different interfaces, then the names of the interfaces appear one after another, separated by commas. This example shows the beginning of a class that implements both the `Cloneable` and `AudioClip` interfaces:

```
public class Example implements Cloneable, AudioClip
```

A programmer can test whether a given object actually does implement a specified interface. For example, suppose you are writing a method with one object as a parameter. The method needs to test whether the object implements the `AudioClip` interface, and if so then the play method is activated. Otherwise, some other technique is used to display some information about the object. The method could begin like this:

```
public static show(Object information)
{
   if ((information instanceof AudioClip)
      information.play( );
   else
      ...
```

The test is carried out with the `instanceof` operator, with the general form:

```
variable instanceof interface-or-class-name
```

The test is `true` if the variable on the left is a reference to an object of the specified type. Notice that the type name can be an ordinary class name (such as `(information instanceof String)`), or it may be the name of an interface (such as `(information instanceof AudioClip)`).

The first version of Java included 40 interfaces; later versions have expanded on this, and programmers can define their own interfaces too. So far, in this book we've used two interfaces: `Cloneable` and `ActionListener`. The `Cloneable` interface has a special meaning that we look at next.

The Meaning of the Cloneable Interface

All of our collection classes have implemented the `Cloneable` interface, which has a somewhat peculiar meaning. You might think that the `Cloneable` interface specifies that the class must implement a `clone` method, but this is wrong; there are no methods specified in the `Cloneable` interface. So what's the purpose of the `Cloneable` interface? The purpose comes from the behavior of the `clone( )` method of Java's `Object` class. The `Object clone` method carries out the two steps shown at the top of the next page.

Steps of the `clone` method of Java's `Object` type:

1. Check to see whether the class has implemented the `Cloneable` interface. If not, then a `CloneNotSupportedException` is thrown.

2. Otherwise, the clone is made by copying each of the instance variables of the original.

As you can see, the `Object clone` method checks to see whether the object has implemented the `Cloneable` interface. It does this by using the boolean test `(obj instanceof Cloneable)` and in fact, the only real purpose of implementing the `Cloneable` interface is so that the `Object clone` method can test `(obj instanceof Cloneable)`. Therefore, if you write a clone method of your own, and that `clone` method activates `super.clone` from Java's `Object` type, then your class must implement `Cloneable` to avoid a `CloneNotSupportedException`.

The Iterator Interface

A class that implements Java's `Iterator` interface must provide three methods:

```
public boolean hasNext( )
public Object next( )
public void remove( )
```

Intuitively, an `Iterator` is able to step through a series of elements. Usually the elements come from a collection such as a bag. A program activates `hasNext( )` to determine whether there are any more elements in the series. If there are more elements, then a program can activate `next( )` to obtain the next element in the series.

An `Iterator` also has a `remove` method. This method removes the element that was given by the most recent call to `next( )`. Sometimes an `Iterator` does not allow elements to be removed. In this case, activating the remove method results in an `UnsupportedOperationException`.

We could write many interesting classes that implement the `Iterator` interface. We're going to write one particular class called `Lister`. When a `Lister` is constructed, it is given a specific linked list of objects. It sets up a reference to the first element in the linked list. Each subsequent activation of `next` returns one element from the list, and moves on to the next element. When the last element has been returned, `hasNext` will return `false`. The `Lister` does not allow removal of elements, so any attempt to activate `remove` results in an exception.

The specification and implementation of the `Lister` class is shown in Figure 5.3 on page 270. We discuss the `Lister` class next.

The Lister Class

The Lister class is part of the package edu.colorado.nodes. The Iterator interface is actually part of java.util, so the implementation imports java.util.Iterator. Also, the next method throws a NoSuchElement-Exception to indicate that it has run out of elements, so we also import java.util.NoSuchElementException. The remove method also throws an exception—UnsupportedOperationException—but no import statement is needed because UnsupportedOperationException is part of java.lang (which is automatically imported for any program).

Any program that creates linked lists can use the Lister class. For example, here's some code that creates a list of strings, then uses a Lister to step through those strings one at a time:

```
import edu.colorado.nodes.Node;
import edu.colorado.nodes.Lister;

 . . .

Node head;      // Head node of a small linked list
Node middle;    // Second node of the same list
Node tail;      // Tail node of the same list
Lister print;   // Used to print the small linked list

// Create a small linked list.
tail   = new Node("Larry", null);
middle = new Node("Curly", tail);
head   = new Node("Moe", middle);

// The list now has "Moe", "Curly", and "Larry". We'll print these strings.
print = new Lister(head);
while (print.hasNext( ))
   System.out.println(print.next( ));
```

The while-loop steps through the three elements of the list, printing the three strings:

```
Moe
Curly
Larry
```

The Lister contains one warning in the constructor documentation: If the linked list changes in any way before all the elements have been returned, then the subsequent behavior of the Lister is unspecified. In other words, while the Lister is being used, the underlying linked list must not be altered.

FIGURE 5.3	Specification and Implementation for the Lister Class

Class Lister

❖ **public class Lister from the package edu.colorado.nodes**

A Lister implements Java's Iterator interface for a linked list of Objects. Note that this implementation of an Iterator does not support the remove method. Any activation of remove results in an UnsupportedOperationException.

Specification

◆ **Constructor for the Lister**

public Lister(Node head)

Initialize a Lister with a particular linked list of objects.

Parameters:

head – a head reference for a linked list of objects

Postcondition:

Subsequent activations of next will return the elements from this linked list, one after another. If the linked list changes in any way before all the elements have been returned, then the subsequent behavior of this Lister is unspecified.

◆ **hasNext**

public boolean hasNext( )

Determine whether there are any more elements in this Lister.

Returns:

true if there are more elements in this Lister; false otherwise.

◆ **next**

public Object next( )

Retrieve the next element of this Lister.

Precondition:

hasNext( ).

Returns:

The return value is the next element of this Lister. Note that each element is returned only once, and then the Lister automatically advances to the next element.

Throws: NoSuchElementException:

Indicates that hasNext( ) is false.

Implementation

```
// File: Lister.java from the package edu.colorado.nodes
// Documentation is available at the top of this page or from the Lister link in
//   http://www.cs.colorado.edu/~main/docs/
```

(continued)

(FIGURE 5.3 continued)

```java
package edu.colorado.nodes;

import java.util.Iterator;
import java.util.NoSuchElementException;
import edu.colorado.nodes.Node;

public class Lister implements Iterator
{
    // Invariant of the Lister class:
    //    The instance variable list is the head reference for the linked list that contains
    //    the elements that have not yet been provided by the next method. If there
    //    are no more elements to provide, then list is the null reference.
    private Node list;

    public Lister(Node head)
    {
        list = head;
    }

    public boolean hasNext( )
    {
        return (list != null);
    }

    public Object next( )
    {
        Object answer;

        if (!hasNext( ))
            throw new NoSuchElementException("The Lister is empty.");

        answer = list.getData( );
        list = list.getLink( );

        return answer;
    }

    public void remove( )
    {
        throw new UnsupportedOperationException("Lister has no remove method.");
    }

}
```

A Collection Can Provide an Iterator for Its Own Elements

Normally, when a program needs to keep track of some elements, it puts the elements into a bag or some other collection, rather than building a linked list in a haphazard manner. Then, if the program needs to step through the elements, it will ask the bag to provide a `Lister` that contains all of the elements.

With this in mind, we'll implement one more bag class. The bag will be called `LinkedBag` in the package `edu.colorado.collections`, with these features:

- The elements in the bag are Java `Objects`

- The elements are stored on a linked list

- The bag has a new method with the heading:
    ```
    public Lister iterator( )
    ```
    This new method returns a `Lister` that contains all the elements that are currently in the bag.

Here's part of a program that uses the new `iterator` method:

```
import edu.colorado.collections.LinkedBag;
import edu.colorado.nodes.Lister;


...


LinkedBag stooges = new LinkedBag( );
Lister print;       // Used to print the strings from the bag

// Put a few strings in the bag
stooges.add("Larry");
stooges.add("Curly");
stooges.add("Moe");

// The bag now has "Moe", "Curly", and "Larry". We'll print these strings.
print = stooges.iterator( );
while (print.hasNext( ))
    System.out.println(print.next( ));
```

The while-loop will print the strings "Moe", "Curly", and "Larry"—although the order of printing depends on exactly how the bag stores the elements on the linked list.

Implementing the Bag of Objects Using a Linked List and an `iterator` Method

For the most part, the implementation of the new bag is the same as the Chapter 4 class, `IntLinkedBag`, which stored its elements on a linked list. To convert to a bag of Java Objects, we'll follow the five steps listed on page 250. We'll also implement the new iterator method, which needs only one line to construct a Lister that contains all the elements. Here's the implementation:

```
public Lister iterator( )
// Method of the LinkedBag class to return a Lister that
// contains all the elements that are currently in the bag.
{
    return new Lister(head);
}
```

In this implementation, head is the bag's instance variable that is a reference to the head node of the linked list where the bag keeps its elements. There's little new in the rest of the implementation of edu.colorado.collections.LinkedBag, so we've stuck it in Appendix F. If you find that you need a collection class in the future, and none of the built-in Java classes suits the bill, turn to Appendix F to see if that bag will do.

Programming Tip: External Iterators versus Internal Iterators

TIP △

The iterator method of the bag class provides an iterator for all the elements in the bag. This kind of iterator is called an **external iterator** because it is an object separate from the bag. This is different than our original bags (which had only a countOccurrences method to examine elements). The iterator method also differs from the sequence class of Section 3.3. With a sequence, a program can step through the elements, but only by accessing the sequence's current element. This kind of access, directly through a method of the class, is called an **internal iterator**.

Internal iterators are a simple solution to the problem of stepping through the elements of a collection class. But internal iterators also have a problem. Suppose that your program needs to step through the elements of a bag in two different ways. With an internal iterator, the two traversals of the collection elements must occur sequentially—stepping through all the elements for the first time, then restarting the iterator, and finally stepping through all the elements for the second time. However, sometimes you would like to have the two different traversals occurring simultaneously. The first traversal could start, stepping through part of the elements, but before the first traversal is finished, the second traversal starts its work. Simultaneous traversals are not easily handled with internal iterators.

The problem is solved by having a method that provides an external iterator. The bag's iterator method does just this. If we need to step through the elements of a bag two different times, then we can create two separate external iterators for the bag.

In general, a method that provides an external iterator is better than providing just an internal iterator.

Summary of the Four Bag Implementations

If nothing else, you should now know how to program your way out of a paper bag, using one of the four bag classes of Figure 5.4. The bag class is a good example to show all these different approaches to implementing a collection class, but keep in mind that the same approaches can be used for other collection classes.

Self-Test Exercises

14. What is the primary difference between the `LinkedBag` suggested in this section, and the `IntLinkedBag` from Section 4.4?

15. What is the primary difference between the `LinkedBag` suggested in this section, and the `ArrayBag` from Section 5.2?

16. Write a class, `ArrayIterator`, which implements the `Iterator` interface. The constructor has one argument, which is an array of objects. The `ArrayIterator` returns the components of the array one at a time through its `next` method.

17. Write some code that allows the user to type in ten strings. Each string is put in a bag (using the `LinkedBag` from Appendix F). When the user is finished, the ten strings are printed.

18. Compare the benefits of an internal iterator to a method that provides an external iterator.

FIGURE 5.4 Our Four Bag Classes

Approach	Class	Where to find it
Store integer elements in an array.	`edu.colorado.` `collections.IntArrayBag`	Figure 3.1 on page 107 and Figure 3.8 on page 126
Store integer elements in a linked list.	`edu.colorado.` `collections.IntLinkedBag`	Figure 4.12 on page 211 and Figure 4.17 on page 225
Store Java Objects in an array.	`edu.colorado.` `collections.ArrayBag`	Figure 5.1 on page 251
Store Java Objects in a linked list. This version also has a method to provide an Iterator.	`edu.colorado.` `collections.LinkedBag`	Appendix F

CHAPTER SUMMARY

- A Java variable can be one of the eight primitive data types. Anything that's not one of the eight primitive types is a reference to a Java `Object`.

- An assignment `x = y` is a **widening conversion** if the data type of x is capable of referring to a wider variety of things than the type of y. It is a **narrowing conversion** if the data type of x is capable of referring to a smaller variety of things than the type of y. Java always permits widening conversions, but narrowing conversions require a typecast.

- A **wrapper class** is a class in which each object holds a primitive value. Java provides wrapper classes for each of the eight primitive types.

- Converting a collection so that it holds objects is usually a small task. For example, we converted the `IntArrayBag` to an `ArrayBag` by following the five steps on page 250.

- A class that implements Java's `Iterator` interface must provide two methods:
  ```
  public boolean hasNext( )
  public Object next( )
  ```
  An `Iterator` must also have a `remove` method, although if removal is not supported, then the `remove` method can simply throw an exception.

- Two of the classes in this chapter have wide applicability, and you may find them useful in the future: (1) the `Node` class from Appendix E, which is a node from a linked list of objects; and (2) the `LinkedBag` class from Appendix F, which includes a method to generate an `Iterator` for its elements.

Solutions to Self-Test Exercises **?**

1. Yes, yes, yes.

2. This code has both widening conversion (marked with the circle) and a narrowing conversion (marked with a triangle):
   ```
   String s = new String("Liberty!");
   Object obj;
   obj = s; ●
   s = (String) obj; △
   ```

3. Here is one example that causes a class cast exception at run time:
   ```
   String s = new String("Liberty!");
   Integer i;
   Object obj;
   obj = s;
   i = (Integer) obj;
   ```

4. `Character example = new Character('w');`

5. Advantage: When a primitive value is placed in a wrapper object, then it can be treated just like any other Java `Object`. Disadvantage: A wrapper object can no longer use the primitive operations, such as the arithmetic operations.

6. No. The only conversions from `int` to `Object` are the places where the data type refers to an element in the bag. For example, the return value from `size` remains an `int`.

7. Yes, we allow `add(null)`, but we also need special code in `countOccurrences` and `remove` to handle the null reference.

8. Here is the code:
```
ArrayBag numbers;
int i;
numbers = new ArrayBag( );
for (i = 1; i <= 10; i++)
    numbers.add(new Integer(i));
```

9. In the new `countOccurrences` we use this for non-null targets:
```
target.equals(data[index])
```

10. It used `stdin.stringInput`, where `stdin` is an `EasyReader` from Appendix B.

11. `Vector`.

12. To handle searching for a null target.

13. The expression `(x == y)` is `true` if x and y refer to exactly the same node. The expression `(x.data.equals(y.data))` is `true` if the data in the two nodes is the same.

14. The elements in the new bag are Java objects rather than integers. Also, the new bag has an `iterator` method to return a `Lister`.

15. The bag from this section stores its elements on a linked list rather than in an array. Also, the new bag has an `iterator` method to return a `Lister`.

16. `import java.util.Iterator;`
```
public class ArrayIterator
implements Iterator
{
    private Object[ ] array;
    private int index;

    public ArrayIterator
    (Object[ ] things)
    {
        array = things;
        index = 0;
    }
```

```
    public boolean hasNext( )
    {
        return (index < array.length);
    }

    public Object next( )
    {
        return array[index++];
    }

    ...See page 271 for remove...
}
```

17. This uses three import statements:
```
import edu.colorado.io.EasyReader;
import
 edu.colorado.collections.LinkedBag;
import edu.colorado.nodes.Lister;
```

The code is:
```
EasyReader stdin =
  new EasyReader(System.in);
LinkedBag b = new LinkedBag( );
Lister list;
String s;
int i;
for (i = 1; i <= 10; i++)
{
    System.out.print("Next: ");
    s = stdin.stringInput( );
    b.add(s);
}

list = b.iterator( );
while (list.hasNext( ))
{
    s = (String) list.next( );
    System.out.println(s);
}
```

18. An internal iterator is quick to implement and use, but an external iterator provides more flexibility such as the ability to have two or more iterators active at once.

PROGRAMMING PROJECTS

1 Implement a class for a sequence of Java objects. You may store the objects in an array (as in Section 3.3) or in a linked list (as in Section 4.5). The class should include a method that returns an `Iterator` for all the objects in the sequence.

2 Write a program that uses a bag of strings to keep track of a list of chores that you have to accomplish today. The user of the program can request several services: (1) Add an item to the list of chores; (2) Ask how many chores are in the list; (3) Print the list of chores to the screen; (4) Delete an item from the list; (5) Exit the program.

If you know how to read and write strings from a file, then have the program obtain its initial list of chores from a file. When the program ends, it should write all unfinished chores back to this file.

3 For this project, you will use the bag ADT from Appendix F, including the grab method that returns a randomly selected element. Use this ADT in a program that does the following:

1. Asks the user for a list of ten nouns.
2. Asks the user for a list of ten verbs.
3. Prints some random sentences using the provided nouns and verbs.

For example, if two of the nouns were "monkey" and "piano," and two of the verbs were "eats" and "plays," then we can expect any of these sentences:

```
The monkey eats the piano.
The monkey plays the piano.
The piano eats the monkey.
The piano plays the monkey.
```

Needless to say, the sentences are not entirely sensible. Your program will need to declare two bags: one to store the nouns and one to store the verbs. Use an appropriate top-down design.

4 Write a program for keeping a course list for each student in a college. The information about each student should be kept in an object that contains the student's name and a list of courses completed by the student. The courses taken by a student are stored as a linked list in which each node contains the name of a course, the number of units for the course, and the course grade. The program gives a menu with choices that include adding a student's record, deleting a student's record, adding a single course record to a student's record, deleting a single course record from a student's record, and printing a student's record to the screen. The program input should accept the student's name in any combination of upper- and lowercase letters. A student's record should include the student's GPA (grade point average) when displayed on the screen. When the user is through with the program, the program should store the records in a file. The next time the program is run, the records should be read back out of the file and the list should be reconstructed. (Ask your instructor if there are any rules about what type of file you should use.)

5 The bag's `clone` method creates a copy of an `ArrayBag`. As with other `clone` methods, adding or removing elements from the original bag will not affect the copy, nor vice versa. However, these elements are now references to objects, both the original and the copy contain references to the same underlying objects. Changing these underlying objects can affect both the original and the copy.

An alternative cloning method, called **deep cloning**, can avoid the problem. A deep cloning method has one extra step: Each reference to an object in the bag is examined to see whether that object itself can be cloned. If so, then the object is cloned and the new bag is given a reference to the clone of the object rather than a reference to the same object that the original bag contains.

Rewrite the bag's clone method to perform a deep cloning.

Stacks

The pushdown store is a "first in-last out" list. That is, symbols may be entered or removed only at the top of the list.

JOHN E. HOPCROFT AND JEFFREY D. ULLMAN
Formal Languages and Their Relation to Automata

CHAPTER

6

This chapter introduces a data structure known as a *stack*, or as it is sometimes called, a *pushdown store*. It is a simple structure, even simpler than a linked list. Yet it turns out to be one of the most useful data structures known to computer science.

6.1   INTRODUCTION TO STACKS

The drawings to the right depict some stacks. There is a stack of pancakes, some stacks of coins, and a stack of books. A *stack* is an ordered collection of items that can be accessed only at one end. That may not sound like what you see in these drawings, but think for a moment. Each of the stacks is ordered from top to bottom; you can identify any item in a stack by saying it is the top item, second from the top, third from the top, and so on. Unless you mess up one of the neat stacks, you can access only the top item. To remove the bottom book from the stack, you must first remove the two books that are on top of it. The abstract definition of a stack reflects this intuition.

Stack Definition

A **stack** is a data structure of ordered items such that items can be inserted and removed only at one end (called the **top**).

When we say that the items in a stack are *ordered,* all we mean is that there is one that can be accessed first (the one on top), one that can be accessed second (just below the top), a third one, and so forth. We do *not* require that the items can be compared using the < operator. The items may be of any type.

Stack items must be removed in the reverse order to that in which they are placed on the stack. For example, you can create a stack of books by first placing a dictionary, placing a thesaurus on top of the dictionary, and placing a novel on top of those, so the stack has the novel on top. When the books are removed, the novel must come off first (since it is on top), and then the thesaurus, and finally the dictionary. Because of this property, a stack is called a "Last-In/First-Out" data structure (abbreviated **LIFO**).

LIFO

A stack is a Last-In/First-Out data structure. Items are taken out of the stack in the reverse order of their insertion.

Of course, a stack that is used in a program stores information rather than physical items, such as books or pancakes. Therefore, it may help to visualize a stack as a pile of papers on which information is written. To place some information on the stack, you write the information on a new sheet of paper and place this sheet of paper on top of the stack. Getting information out of the stack is also accomplished by a simple operation, since the top sheet of paper can be removed and read. There is just one restriction: Only the top sheet of paper is accessible. To read the third sheet from the top, for example, the top two sheets must be removed from the stack.

A stack is analogous to a mechanism that is used in a popular candy holder called a *Pez®* *dispenser*, shown in the margin. The dispenser stores candy in a slot underneath an animal head figurine. Candy is loaded into the dispenser by pushing each piece into the hole. There is a spring under the candy with the tension adjusted so that when the animal head is tipped backward, one piece of candy pops out. If this sort of mechanism were used as a stack data structure, then the data would be written on the candy (which may violate some health laws, but it still makes a good analogy). Using this analogy, you can understand why adding an item to a stack is called a **push** operation, and removing an item from a stack is called a **pop** operation.

Pushing

The Stack ADT—Specification

The key methods of a stack class are specified in Figure 6.1. Our specification lists a stack constructor and five methods. The most important methods are push (to add an item at the top of the stack) and pop (to remove the top item). Another method, called peek, allows a programmer to examine the top item without actually removing it. There are no methods that allow a program to access items other than the top. To access any item other than the top one, the program must remove items one at a time from the top until the desired item is reached.

Popping

If a program attempts to pop an item off an empty stack, then it is asking for the impossible; this error is called **stack underflow**. The pop method indicates a stack underflow by throwing an EmptyStackException. This exception is defined in java.util.EmptyStackException. To help you avoid a stack underflow, the class provides a method to determine whether a stack is empty. There is also a method to obtain the stack's current size.

FIGURE 6.1 | Specification of the Key Methods of a Stack Class

Specification

These are the key methods of a stack class, which we will implement in several different ways. The first part of the class name, Object Stack, is drawn in a box throughout the specification to indicate that the underlying type of items in the stack can be implemented as Java's Object type or as any of the primitive data types. For example, we can implement an Int Stack, Double Stack, etc. The Java Class Libraries also provide a stack class called java.util.Stack, which has these same key methods.

- ◆ **Constructor for the Object Stack**
  public Object Stack( )
  Initialize an empty stack.
  Postcondition:
  This stack is empty.

(continued)

(FIGURE 6.1 continued)

- **isEmpty**

  `public boolean isEmpty( )`

  Determine whether this stack is empty.

  Returns:
  `true` if this stack is empty; otherwise `false`.

- **peek**

  `public` `Object` `peek( )`

  Get the top item of this stack, without removing the item.

  Precondition:
  This stack is not empty.

  Returns:
  the top item of the stack

  Throws: `EmptyStackException`
  Indicates that this stack is empty.

- **pop**

  `public` `Object` `pop( )`

  Get the top item, removing it from this stack.

  Precondition:
  This stack is not empty.

  Postcondition:
  The return value is the top item of this stack, and the item has been removed.

  Throws: `EmptyStackException`
  Indicates that this stack is empty.

- **push**

  `public void push(`Object` item)`

  Push a new item onto this stack. The new item may be the null reference.

  Parameters:
  `item` – the item to be pushed onto this stack

  Postcondition:
  The item has been pushed onto this stack.

  Throws: `OutOfMemoryException`
  Indicates insufficient memory for pushing a new item onto this stack.

- **size**

  `public int size( )`

  Accessor method to determine the number of items in this stack.

  Returns:
  the number of items in this stack

Writing Nine Stack Classes at Once

Later we will implement the stack in several different ways. Some of our implementations will have extra methods beyond the five given in the figure. Also, each of our implementations will be a stack of objects; in other words, each item we push or pop is a Java Object. We'll call the class Object Stack, but we'll put the word Object in a box. When you see the box, think to yourself, "This is a Java Object, but it could be changed to any of Java's primitive data types with no trouble." For example, in an implementation we could change Object to int and we would then have an Int Stack. In effect, each time we implement an Object Stack, we're really implementing nine different classes at once.

The Java Class Libraries also provide a stack of objects called java.util.Stack, with the same five methods from Figure 6.1.

> *In an implementation of* Object Stack, *we can change* Object *to any of the primitive types, so we're really doing these nine implementations at once:*
>   ObjectStack
>   BooleanStack
>   ByteStack
>   CharStack
>   DoubleStack
>   FloatStack
>   IntStack
>   LongStack
>   ShortStack

PROGRAMMING EXAMPLE: Reversing a Word

Stacks are very intuitive—even cute—but are they good for anything? Surprisingly, they have many applications. Most compilers use stacks to analyze the syntax of a program. Stacks are used to keep track of local variables when a program is run. Stacks can be used to search a maze or a family tree or other types of branching structures. In this book, we will discuss examples related to each of these applications. But before we present any complicated applications of the stack ADT, let us first practice with a simple problem, so that we can see how a stack is used.

uses for stacks

Suppose you want a program to read in a word and then write it out backwards. If the program reads in NAT, then it will output TAN. If it reads in TAPS it will output SPAT. The author Roald Dahl wrote a book called ESIOTROT, which our program converts to TORTOISE. One way to accomplish this task is to read the input one letter at a time and place each letter in a stack of characters. After the word is read, the letters in the stack are written out, but because of the way a stack works, they are written out in reverse order. The outline is shown here:

```
// Reversing the spelling of a word
Declare a stack of characters;

while (there are more characters of the word to read)
    Read a character, and push the character onto the stack.
while (the stack is not empty)
    Pop a character off the stack, and write that character to the screen.
```

FIGURE 6.2 Using a Stack to Reverse Spelling

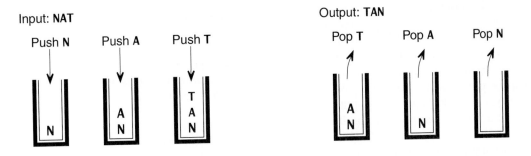

This computation is illustrated in Figure 6.2. At all times in the computation, the only available item is on "top." Figure 6.2 suggests another intuition for thinking about a stack. You can view a stack as a hole in the ground and view the items as being placed in the hole one on top of the other. To retrieve an item, you must first remove the items on top of it.

Self-Test Exercises

1. Suppose a program uses a stack of characters to read in a word and then write the word out backwards, as described in this section. Now suppose the input word is DAHL. List all the activations of the push and pop methods. List them in the order in which they will be executed and indicate the character that is pushed or popped. What is the output?

2. Consider the stack class given in Figure 6.1 on page 281. The peek method lets you look at the top item in the stack without changing the stack. Describe how you can define a new method that returns the second item from the top of the stack without changing the stack. Your description will be in terms of peek, pop, and push. Give your solution in pseudocode, not in Java.

6.2 STACK APPLICATIONS

To write programs that use the stack class, we will assume that the specification of Figure 6.1 on page 281 has been implemented in nine ways:

edu.colorado.collections.ObjectStack	— a stack of Java objects
edu.colorado.collections.BooleanStack	— a stack of boolean values
edu.colorado.collections.ByteStack	— a stack of byte values
edu.colorado.collections.CharStack	— a stack of char values
edu.colorado.collections.DoubleStack	— a stack of double values
edu.colorado.collections.FloatStack	— a stack of float values
edu.colorado.collections.IntStack	— a stack of int values
edu.colorado.collections.LongStack	— a stack of long values
edu.colorado.collections.ShortStack	— a stack of short values

We'll implement these classes later. For now, we'll just use the classes as we need them, such as the next example, which uses CharStack.

PROGRAMMING EXAMPLE: Balanced Parentheses

Later in this chapter we will describe how stacks can be used to evaluate arithmetic expressions. At the moment, we will describe a simpler method called isBalanced that does a closely related task. The algorithm checks an expression to see if the parentheses match correctly. It allows three kinds of parentheses: ( ), [ ], or { }. Any symbol other than one of these parentheses is ignored.

For example, consider the string "{[X + Y*(Z + 7)]*(A + B)}". Each of the left parentheses has a corresponding right parenthesis. Also, as the string is read from left to right, there is never an occurrence of a right parenthesis that cannot be matched with a corresponding left parenthesis. Therefore the activation of isBalanced("{[X + Y*(Z + 7)]*(A + B)}") returns true.

On the other hand, consider the string "((X + Y*{Z + 7}*[A + B])". The parentheses around the subexpression Z + 7 match each other, as do the parentheses around A + B. And the second left parenthesis in the expression matches the final right parenthesis. But the first left parenthesis has no matching right parenthesis. Hence, isBalanced("((X + Y*{Z + 7}*[A + B])") returns false.

The technique used is simple: The algorithm scans the characters of the string from left to right. Every time a left parenthesis occurs, it is pushed onto the stack. Every time a right parenthesis occurs, a matching left parenthesis is popped off the stack. If the correct kind of left parenthesis is not on top of the stack, then the string is unbalanced. For example, when a curly right parenthesis '}' occurs in the string, the matching curly left parenthesis '{' should be on top of the stack.

All symbols other than parentheses are ignored. If all goes smoothly and the stack is empty at the end of the expression, then the parentheses match. On the other hand three things might go wrong: (1) The stack is empty when the algorithm needs to pop a symbol; or (2) The wrong kind of parenthesis appears at some point; or (3) Symbols are still in the stack after all the input has been read. In each of these cases, the parentheses are not balanced.

Let us look at some examples. Since no symbols other than parentheses can affect the results, we will use expressions of just parentheses symbols. All of the following are balanced (shading and arrows help find matching parentheses):

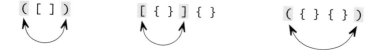

If you think about these examples, you can begin to understand the algorithm. In the first example, the parentheses match because they have the same number of left and right parentheses, but the algorithm does more than just count parentheses. The algorithm actually matches parentheses. Every time it encounters a ')', the symbol it pops off the stack is the matching '('. When it encounters a

']', the symbol it pops off the stack is the matching '['. When it encounters a '}', the symbol it pops off the stack is the matching '{'.

The complete sequences of stack configurations from two executions of the algorithm are shown in Figure 6.3. The stacks shown in the figure show the configuration after processing each character of the expression.

In general the stack works by keeping a stack of the unmatched left parentheses. Every time the algorithm encounters a right parenthesis, the corresponding left parenthesis is deleted (popped) from the stack. If the parentheses in the input match correctly, things work out perfectly, and the stack is empty at the end of the input line.

The balancing algorithm is implemented by the isBalanced method of Figure 6.4. One technique in the implementation may be new to you: acting on the string's next character via a *switch* statement. We'll discuss this technique after you've looked through the program.

FIGURE 6.3   Stack Configurations for the Parentheses Balancing Algorithm

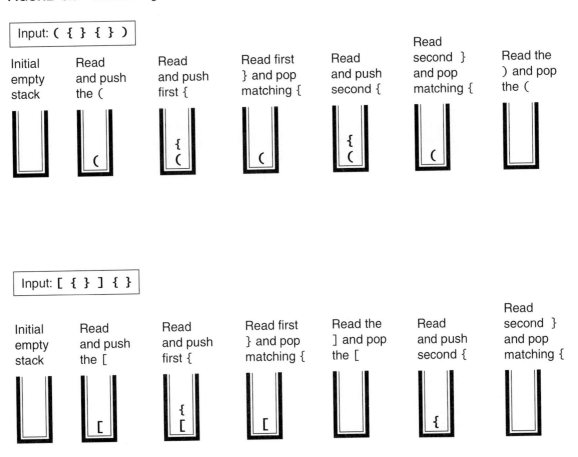

FIGURE 6.4	A Method to Check for Balanced Parentheses

A Method Implementation

```
public static boolean isBalanced(String expression)
// Postcondition: A true return value indicates that the parentheses in the
// given expression are balanced. Otherwise the return value is false.
// Note that characters other than ( ), { }, and [ ] are ignored.
{
    // Meaningful names for characters
    final char LEFT_NORMAL  = '(';
    final char RIGHT_NORMAL = ')';
    final char LEFT_CURLY   = '{';
    final char RIGHT_CURLY  = '}';
    final char LEFT_SQUARE  = '[';
    final char RIGHT_SQUARE = ']';

    CharStack store = new CharStack( ); // Stack to store left parentheses
    int i;                              // An index into the string
    boolean failed = false;             // Change to true for a mismatch

    for (i = 0; !failed && (i < expression.length( )); i++)
    {
        switch (expression.charAt(i))
        {
            case LEFT_NORMAL:
            case LEFT_CURLY:
            case LEFT_SQUARE:
                store.push(expression.charAt(i));
                break;
            case RIGHT_NORMAL:
                if (store.isEmpty( ) || (store.pop( ) != LEFT_NORMAL))
                    failed = true;
                break;
            case RIGHT_CURLY:
                if (store.isEmpty( ) || (store.pop( ) != LEFT_CURLY))
                    failed = true;
                break;
            case RIGHT_SQUARE:
                if (store.isEmpty( ) || (store.pop( ) != LEFT_SQUARE))
                    failed = true;
                break;
        }
    }

    return (store.isEmpty( ) && !failed);
}
```

TIP

Programming Tip: **The Switch Statement**

The for-loop in Figure 6.4 processes character number i of the expression during each iteration. There are several possible actions, depending on what kind of character appears at `expression.charAt(i)`. An effective statement to select among many possible actions is the *switch* statement, with the general form:

```
switch (<Control value>)
{
    <Body of the switch statement>
}
```

When the switch statement is reached, the control value is evaluated. The program then looks through the body of the switch statement for a matching case label. For example, if the control value is the character 'A', then the program looks for a case label of the form `case 'A':`. If a matching case label is found, then the program goes to that label and begins executing statements. Statements are executed one after another—but if a **break** statement (of the form `break;`) occurs, then the program skips to the end of the body of the switch statement.

If the control value has no matching case label, then the program will look for a **default label** of the form `default:`. This label handles any control values that don't have their own case label.

If there is no matching case label and no default label, then the whole body of the switch statement is skipped.

For the `isBalanced` method of Figure 6.4, the switch statement has one case label for each of the six possible kinds of parentheses. The three kinds of left parentheses are all handled together, by putting their case statements one after another. Each of the right parentheses is handled with its own case statement. For example, one of the right parentheses is the character RIGHT_NORMAL, which is an ordinary right parenthesis ')'. The RIGHT_NORMAL character is handled as shown here:

```
switch (expression.charAt(i))
{
    ...
    case RIGHT_NORMAL:
        if (store.isEmpty( ) || (store.pop( ) != LEFT_NORMAL))
            failure = true;
        break;
    ...
}
```

Evaluating Arithmetic Expressions

In this programming example we will design and write a calculator program. This will be an example of a program that uses two stacks—one is a stack of characters, and the other is a stack of double numbers.

Evaluating Arithmetic Expressions—Specification

The program takes as input a fully parenthesized numeric expression such as the following:

```
((((12 + 9)/3) + 7.2)*((6 - 4)/8))
```

input to the calculator program

The expression consists of integers or double numbers, together with the operators +, -, *, and /. To focus on the use of the stack (rather than on input details), we require that each input number is non-negative (otherwise it is hard to distinguish the subtraction operator from a minus sign that is part of a negative number). We will assume that the expression is formed correctly so that each operation has two arguments. Finally, we will also assume that the expression is fully parenthesized with ordinary parentheses '(' and ')', meaning that each operation has a pair of matched parentheses surrounding its arguments. We can later enhance our program so that these assumptions are no longer needed.

The output will simply be the value of the arithmetic expression.

output of the calculator program

Evaluating Arithmetic Expressions—Design

Most of the program's work will be carried out by a method that reads one line of input and evaluates that line as an arithmetic expression. To get a feel for the problem, let's start by doing a simple example by hand.

Consider the following expression:

```
(((6 + 9)/3)*(6 - 4))
```

do an example by hand

If we were to evaluate this expression by hand, we might first evaluate the innermost expressions, (6 + 9) and (6 - 4), to produce the smaller expression:

```
((15/3)*2)
```

Next we would evaluate the expression (15/3) and replace this expression with its value of 5. That would leave us with the expression (5*2). Finally, we would evaluate this last operation to get the answer of 10.

To convert this intuitive approach into a fully specified algorithm that can be implemented, we need to do things in a more systematic way: We need a specific way to find the expression to be evaluated next and a way to remember the results of our intermediate calculations.

First let us find a systematic way of choosing the next expression to be evaluated. (After that, we can worry about how we will keep track of the intermediate results.) We know that the expression to be evaluated first must be one of the innermost expressions—which is a subexpression that has just one operation. Let's decide to evaluate the leftmost of these innermost expressions. For instance, consider our example of

```
(((6 + 9)/3)*(6 - 4))
```

The innermost expressions are (6 + 9) and (6 – 4), and the leftmost one of these is (6 + 9). If we evaluate this *leftmost of the innermost expressions*, we obtain

```
((15/3)*(6 - 4))
```

We could now go back and evaluate the other innermost expression (6 – 4), but why bother? There is a simpler approach that spares us the trouble of remembering any other expressions. After we evaluate the leftmost of the innermost expressions, we are left with another simpler arithmetic expression, namely ((15/3)*(6 – 4)), so we can simply repeat the process with this simpler expression: We again evaluate the leftmost of the innermost expressions of our new simpler expression. The entire process will look like the following:

1. Evaluate the leftmost of the innermost expressions in

   ```
   (((6 + 9)/3)*(6 - 4))
   ```

   to produce the simpler expression ((15/3)*(6 - 4)).

2. Evaluate the leftmost of the innermost expressions in

   ```
   ((15/3)*(6 - 4))
   ```

   to produce the simpler expression (5*(6 - 4)).

3. Evaluate the leftmost of the innermost expressions in

   ```
   (5*(6 - 4))
   ```

   to produce the simpler expression (5* 2).

4. Evaluate the leftmost of the innermost expressions in

   ```
   (5*2)
   ```

   to obtain the final answer of 10.

translating the hand method to an algorithm

This method works fine with pencil and paper, but the algorithm must read the input one character at a time from left to right. How does the algorithm find *the leftmost of the innermost expressions*? Look at the preceding example. The end of the expression to be evaluated is always a right parenthesis ')', and moreover, it is always the *first* right parenthesis. After evaluating one of these innermost expressions, there is no need to back up; to find the next right parenthesis we can just keep reading left to right from where we left off. The next right parenthesis will indicate the end of the next expression to be evaluated.

Now we know how to find the expression to be evaluated next, but how do we keep track of our intermediate values? For this we use two stacks. One stack will contain numbers; there will be numbers from the input as well as numbers that were computed when subexpressions were evaluated. The other stack will hold symbols for the operations that still need to be evaluated. Because a stack processes data in a Last-In/First-Out manner, it will turn out that the correct two numbers are on the top of the number stack at the same time that the appropriate operation is at the top of the stack of operations. To better understand how the process works, let's evaluate our sample expression one more time, this time using the two stacks.

We begin by reading up to the first right parenthesis; the numbers we encounter along the way are pushed onto the number stack, and the operations we encounter along the way are pushed onto the operation stack. When we reach the first right parenthesis, our two stacks look like this:

Characters read so far (shaded):

Whenever we reach a right parenthesis, we combine the top two numbers (on the number stack) using the topmost operation (on the character stack). In our example, we compute 6 + 9, yielding 15, and this number 15 is pushed back onto the number stack:

Characters read so far (shaded):
(((6 + 9) / 3) * (6 – 4))

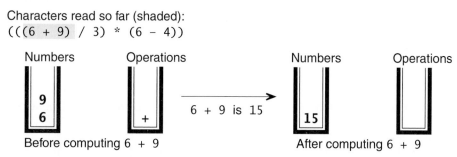

Notice that the leftmost operand (6 in this example) is the *second* number popped off the stack. For addition, this does not matter—who cares whether we have added 6 + 9 or 9 + 6? But the order of the operands does matter for subtraction and division.

Next we simply continue the process: by reading up to the next right parenthesis, pushing the numbers we encounter onto the number stack, and pushing the operations we encounter onto the operation stack. When we reach the next right parenthesis, we combine the top two numbers using the topmost operation. Here's what happens in our example when we reach the second right parenthesis:

Characters read so far (shaded):
(((6 + 9) / 3) * (6 - 4))

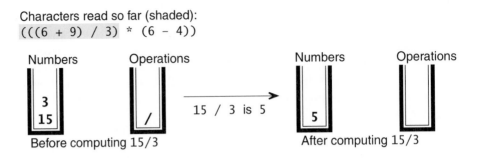

Again, the leftmost operand (15) is the second number popped off the stack, so the correct evaluation is 15/3, not 3/15. Continuing the process, we obtain:

Characters read so far (shaded):
(((6 + 9) / 3) * (6 - 4))

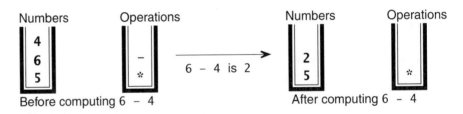

Finally, continuing the process one more time does not add anything to the stacks, but it does read the last right parenthesis and does combine two numbers from the numbers stack with an operation from the operation stack:

Characters read so far (shaded):
(((6 + 9) / 3) * (6 - 4))

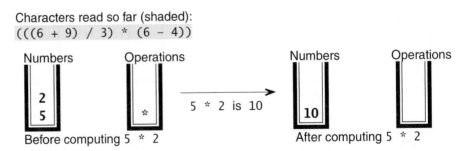

At this point there is no more input, and there is exactly one number in the number stack, namely 10. That number is the answer. Notice that when we used the two stacks we performed the exact same evaluations as we did when we first evaluated this expression in a simple pencil-and-paper fashion.

To evaluate our expression we only need to repeatedly handle the input items according to the following cases:

cases for evaluating an arithmetic expression

Numbers. When a number is encountered in the input, the number is read and pushed onto the numbers stack.

Operation characters. When one of the four operation characters is encountered in the input, the character is read and pushed onto the operations stack.

Right parenthesis. When a right parenthesis is read from the input, an "evaluation step" takes place. The step pops the top two numbers from the number stack and pops the top operation from the operation stack. The two numbers are combined using the operation (with the second number popped as the left operand). The result of the operation is pushed back onto the numbers stack.

Left parenthesis or blank. The only other characters that appear in the input are left parentheses and blanks. These are read and thrown away, not affecting the computation. A more complete algorithm would need to process the left parentheses in some way to ensure that each left parenthesis is balanced by a right parenthesis, but for now we are assuming that the input is completely parenthesized in a proper manner.

The processing of input items halts when the end of the input line occurs, indicated by '\n' in the input. At this point, the answer is the single number that remains in the number stack.

We now have our algorithm, which we plan to implement as a method meeting this specification:

- **readAndEvaluate**
    ```
    public static double readAndEvaluate(EasyReader input)
    ```
    Read and evaluate a fully parenthesized arithmetic expression.
    Parameters:
    `input` – an `EasyReader` from Appendix B, which may be connected to keyboard input (`System.in`) or to a file
    Precondition:
    The next line of characters in the `EasyReader` is a fully parenthesized arithmetic expression formed from non-negative numbers, parentheses, and the four operations +, -, *, and /.
    Postcondition:
    A line has been read from the `EasyReader` including the newline character. This line has been evaluated and the value returned.
    Throws: `IllegalArgumentException`
    Indicates an illegal input expression, such as unbalanced parentheses or a division by zero.

Using the `readAndEvaluate` Method

Using `readAndEvaluate` requires some understanding of the `EasyReader` class from Appendix B. This class is intended to be attached to keyboard input or to a file, and then the `readAndEvaluate` method can access the input using various simple input methods. For example, if a program wants `readAndEvaluate` to work from the keyboard, then it can set up an `EasyReader` that's attached to `System.in`, as shown here:

```
EasyReader stdin = new EasyReader(System.in);
double answer;

System.out.println
    ("Type a fully parenthesized arithmetic expression:");
answer = readAndEvaluate(stdin);
System.out.println("That evaluates to " + answer);
```

Implementation of `readAndEvaluate`

The `readAndEvaluate` method has an `EasyReader` parameter called `input`. The implementation will use these methods of `input`:

- The method `input.isEOLN( )` returns `true` if the next character of the input is the end of the line.

- The method `input.peek( )` returns the next character of the input, without actually reading it. This is useful to peek ahead and see what's coming next.

- The method `input.ignore( )` reads and discards the next character from the input. For example, this is useful when we see that the next input character is a space or some other character that's not part of the expression.

- The method `input.charInput( )` reads and returns the next character of the input. This is used to read any of the operation symbols +, −, *, or /. This method has a feature that we don't use—it skips any whitespace characters (spaces, tabs, and so on) before reading the character.

- The method `input.doubleInput( )` reads and returns a double number from the input. We use this when we notice that the next input character is a digit or a decimal point. This will handle all non-negative numbers (even one that begins with a decimal point such as .42).

- The method `input.skipLine( )` reads and throws away the rest of the input line, including the newline character that appears at the end of the line. We use this once we have read all the expression.

Our implementation also uses three other methods, two of which are part of the Java Class Libraries. These methods are listed on the top of the next page.

- The `isDigit` method (from Java's `Character` class) has this heading:

  ```
  public static boolean isDigit(char c)
  ```

  The method returns `true` if its argument is one of the digits 0 through 9. Otherwise it returns `false`. We'll use `isDigit` to test whether the next character of the input is a digit, as shown here:

  ```
  if (Character.isDigit(input.peek( ))) ...
  ```

- The `indexOf` method of Java's `String` class has this heading:

  ```
  public int indexOf(char c)
  ```

  The method is activated by a string and scans the string `s` for an occurrence of the character `c`. If the character `c` is found, then the method returns the index of that character. Otherwise, the −1 is returned. We'll create a string called SYMBOLS, defined as `"+-*/"`. Then we can test whether the next input character is one of the operation symbols by:

  ```
  if (SYMBOLS.indexof(input.peek( )) >= 0) ...
  ```

- We'll write and use a method, `evaluateStackTops`. The method pops two numbers off the number stack, combines them with an operation from the operations stack, and pushes the result back on the numbers stack.

The basic calculator program appears in Figure 6.5, including the implementations of both `readAndEvaluate` and `evaluateStackTops`.

FIGURE 6.5 | Basic Calculator Program

Java Application Program

```java
// FILE: BasicCalc.java
// This program reads and evaluates a fully parenthesized arithmetic expression.
// The purpose is to illustrate a fundamental use of stacks.

import edu.colorado.collections.CharStack;
import edu.colorado.collections.DoubleStack;
import edu.colorado.io.EasyReader;   // From Appendix B

public class BasicCalc
{
    public static void main(String[ ] args)
    {
        EasyReader stdin = new EasyReader(System.in);
        double answer;

        System.out.println("Type a fully parenthesized arithmetic expression:");
        answer = readAndEvaluate(stdin);
        System.out.println("That evaluates to " + answer);
    }
```

(continued)

(FIGURE 6.5 continued)

```
public static double readAndEvaluate(EasyReader input)
// Precondition: The next line of characters in the EasyReader is a fully
// parenthesized arithmetic expression formed from non-negative numbers,
// parentheses, and the four operations +, -, *, and /.
// Postcondition: A line has been read from the EasyReader, including the
// newline character. This line has been evaluated and the value returned.
// Exceptions: Can throw an IllegalArgumentException if the input line is an
// illegal expression, such as unbalanced parentheses or a division by zero.
// However, some illegal expressions are not caught by this implementation.
{
    final char DECIMAL            = '.';
    final char RIGHT_PARENTHESIS = ')';
    final String SYMBOLS          = "+-*/";

    DoubleStack numbers = new DoubleStack( );
    CharStack operations = new CharStack( );

    while (!input.isEOLN( ))
    {
        if (Character.isDigit(input.peek( )) || (input.peek( ) == DECIMAL))
        {   // Read a number and push it on the numbers stack.
            numbers.push(input.doubleInput( ));
        }
        else if (SYMBOLS.indexOf(input.peek( )) >= 0)
        {   // Read the + - * or / symbol and push it on the operations stack.
            operations.push(input.charInput( ));
        }
        else if (input.peek( ) == RIGHT_PARENTHESIS)
        {   // Evaluate the stuff on top of the stacks.
            input.ignore( );
            evaluateStackTops(numbers, operations);
        }
        else
        {   // Just read and ignore all other characters.
            input.ignore( );
        }
    }
    input.skipLine( ); // Read and ignore the newline character.

    if (numbers.size( ) != 1)
        throw new IllegalArgumentException("Illegal input expression.");
    return numbers.pop( );
}
```

(continued)

(FIGURE 6.5 continued)

```
public static void evaluateStackTops
(DoubleStack numbers, CharStack operations)
```
// *Precondition: The top of the operations stack contains +, -, *, or /, and*
// *the numbers stack contains at least two numbers.*
// *Postcondition: The top two numbers have been popped from the numbers stack, and the*
// *top operation has been popped from the operations stack. The two numbers have been*
// *combined using the operation (with the second number popped as the left operand).*
// *The result of the operation has then been pushed back onto the numbers stack.*
// *Exceptions: Throws an IllegalArgumentException if the stacks are illegal or if the*
// *operation results in a division by zero.*
```
{
    double operand1, operand2;

    // Check that the stacks have enough items, and get the two operands.
    if ((numbers.size( ) < 2) || (operations.isEmpty( )))
        throw new IllegalArgumentException("Illegal expression.");
    operand2 = numbers.pop( );
    operand1 = numbers.pop( );

    // Carry out an action based on the operation on the top of the stack.
    switch (operations.pop( ))
    {
        case '+': numbers.push(operand1 + operand2);
                break;
        case '-': numbers.push(operand1 - operand2);
                break;
        case '*': numbers.push(operand1 * operand2);
                break;
        case '/': if (operand2 == 0)
                    throw new IllegalArgumentException("Division by zero.");
                numbers.push(operand1 / operand2);
                break;
        default:  throw new IllegalArgumentException("Illegal operation.");
    }
}
}
```

A Sample Dialogue

```
Type a fully parenthesized arithmetic expression:
( ( (60 + 40)/50) * (16 - 4) )
That evaluates to 24.0
```

Evaluating Arithmetic Expressions—Testing and Analysis

testing

As usual, you should test your program on boundary values that are most likely to cause problems. For this program, one kind of boundary value consists of the simplest kind of expressions: those that combine only two numbers. To test that operations are performed correctly, you should test simple expressions for each of the operations +, -, *, and /. These simple expressions should have only one operation. Be sure to test the division and subtraction operations carefully to ensure that the operations are performed in the correct order. After all, 3/15 is not the same as 15/3, and 3 - 15 is not the same as 15 - 3. These are perhaps the only boundary values. But it is important also to test some cases with nested parentheses. And you can test an illegal division such as 15/0. What does the program do? It throws an `IllegalArgumentException` in the `evaluateStackTops` method.

time analysis

Let's estimate the number of operations that our program will use on an expression of length n. We will count each of the following as one program operation: reading or peeking at a symbol, performing one of the arithmetic operations (+, -, *, or /), pushing an item onto one of the stacks, and popping an item off of one of the stacks. We consider each kind of operation separately.

Time Spent Reading Characters. There are only n symbols in the input, so the program can read at most n symbols. No character is "peeked" at more than once either, so this aspect of the program has no more than $2n$ operations.

Time Spent Evaluating Arithmetic Operations. Each arithmetic operation performed by the program is the evaluation of an operation symbol in the input. Because there are no more than n arithmetic operations in the input, there are at most n arithmetic operations performed. In actual fact, there are far fewer than n operations, since many of the input symbols are digits or parentheses. But there are certainly no more than n arithmetic operation symbols, so it is safe to say that there are no more than n arithmetic operations performed.

Number of Push Operations. Since there are no more than n arithmetic operation symbols, we know that there are at most n operation symbols pushed onto the operation stack. The number stack may contain input numbers and numbers obtained from evaluating arithmetic expressions. Again, an upper bound will suffice: There are at most n input numbers and at most n arithmetic operations evaluated. Thus, at most, $2n$ numbers are pushed onto the number stack. This gives an upper bound of $3n$ total push operations onto the stacks.

Number of Pop Operations. Once we know the total number of items that are pushed onto the two stacks, we have a bound on how many things can be popped off of the two stacks. After all, you cannot pop off an item unless it was first pushed onto the stack. Thus, there is an upper bound of $3n$ pop operations from any of the stacks.

Total Number of Operations. Now, let's total things up. The total number of operations is no more than $2n$ reads/peeks, plus n arithmetic operations performed, plus $3n$ items pushed onto a stack, plus $3n$ items popped off of a stack—for a grand total of $9n$. The actual number of operations will be less than this because we have used generous upper bounds in several estimates, but $9n$ is enough to conclude that the algorithm for this program is $O(n)$; this is a linear algorithm.

Evaluating Arithmetic Expressions—Enhancements

The program in Figure 6.5 on page 295 is a fine example of how to use stacks. As a computer scientist, you will find yourself using stacks in this manner in many different situations. However, the program is not a fine example of a finished program. Before we can consider it to be a finished product, we need to add a number of enhancements to make the program more robust and friendly.

Some enhancements are easy. It is useful (and easy) to add a loop to the main program that will let the user evaluate more expressions until there is an indication that the user is finished with the calculator. Other enhancements are a bit harder, such as detecting all possible illegal expressions. Another nice enhancement would be to permit expressions that are not fully parenthesized, and to use the Java precedence rules to decide the order of operations when parentheses are missing. We will discuss topics related to this enhancement in Section 6.4, where (surprise!) we'll see that a stack is useful for this purpose too.

Self-Test Exercises

3. How would you modify the calculator program in Figure 6.5 on page 295 to allow the symbol ∧ to be used for exponentiation? Describe the changes; do not write out the code.

4. How would you modify the calculator program in Figure 6.5 on page 295 to allow for comments in the calculator input? Comments appear at the end of the expression, starting with a double slash // and continuing to the end of the line. Describe the changes; do not write out the code.

5. Write some illegal expressions that are caught by the calculator program in Figure 6.5 on page 295, resulting in an `IllegalArgumentException`.

6. Write some illegal expressions that are not caught by the calculator program in Figure 6.5 on page 295.

7. Carry out the operations of `readAndEvaluate` by hand on the input expression `( ( (60 + 40)/50) * (16 - 4) )`. Draw the two stacks after each push or pop.

6.3   IMPLEMENTATIONS OF THE STACK ADT

We will give two implementations of our stack ADT: an implementation using an array, and an implementation using a linked list. Each implementation will be for an Object Stack, but as we discussed earlier, we could change Object to any of the Java primitive types. For example, by changing Object to int we obtain an Int Stack.

Array Implementation of a Stack

Figure 6.6 gives the specification and implementation of a stack class that includes all the earlier methods that we mentioned (from Figure 6.1 on page 281). The class stores its items in an array, so the class also has extra methods for explicitly dealing with capacity. The class implementation uses two instance variables described here:

Invariant of the Stack ADT (Array Version)

1. The number of items in the stack is stored in the instance variable manyItems.

2. The items in the stack are stored in a partially filled array called data, with the bottom of the stack at data[0], the next item at data[1], and so on to the top of the stack at data[manyItems-1].

---

the stack items are stored in a partially filled array

In other words, our stack implementation is simply a partially filled array implemented in the usual way: an array and a variable to indicate how much of the array is being used. The stack bottom is at data[0] and the top position is the last array position used. Each method (except the constructor) may assume that the stack is represented in this way when the operation is activated. Each method has the responsibility of ensuring that the stack is still represented in this manner when the method finishes.

implementing the stack operations

The methods that operate on our stack are now straightforward. To initialize the stack, set the instance variable manyItems to zero, indicating an empty array and hence an empty stack. To add an item to the stack (in the push method), we store the new item in data[manyItems], and then we increment manyItems by one. To look at the top item in the stack (method peek), we simply look at the item in array position data[manyItems-1]. To remove an item from the stack (in the pop method), we decrement manyItems and then return the value of data[manyItems] (which is the value that was on top prior to the pop operation). The methods to test for emptiness and to return the size work by examining the value of manyItems.

FIGURE 6.6	Specification and Implementation of the Array Version of the Stack Class

Class ObjectStack

❖ **public class** ObjectⓈtack **from the package edu.colorado.collections**

An ObjectⓈtack is a stack of references to objects.

Limitations:

(1) The capacity of one of these stacks can change after it's created, but the maximum capacity is limited by the amount of free memory on the machine. The constructors, `clone`, `ensureCapacity`, `push`, and `trimToSize`, will result in an `OutOfMemoryError` when free memory is exhausted.

(2) A stack's capacity cannot exceed the largest integer 2,147,483,647 (`Integer.MAX_VALUE`). Any attempt to create a larger capacity results in failure due to an arithmetic overflow.

Specification

• **Constructor for the** ObjectⓈtack

`public ` ObjectⓈtack`( )`

Initialize an empty stack with an initial capacity of 10. Note that the `push` method works efficiently (without needing more memory) until this capacity is reached.

Postcondition:

This stack is empty and has an initial capacity of 10.

Throws: `OutOfMemoryError`

Indicates insufficient memory for: `new Object[10]`.

• **Second Constructor for the** ObjectⓈtack

`public ` ObjectⓈtack`(int initialCapacity)`

Initialize an empty stack with a specified initial capacity. Note that the `push` method works efficiently (without needing more memory) until this capacity is reached.

Parameters:

`initialCapacity` – the initial capacity of this stack

Precondition:

`initialCapacity` is non-negative.

Postcondition:

This stack is empty and has the given initial capacity.

Throws: `IllegalArgumentException`

Indicates that `initialCapacity` is negative.

Throws: `OutOfMemoryError`

Indicates insufficient memory for: `new Object[initialCapacity]`.

(continued)

(FIGURE 6.6 continued)

- **clone**

    `public Object clone( )`

    Generate a copy of this stack.

    Returns:

    The return value is a copy of this stack. Subsequent changes to the copy will not affect the original, nor vice versa. The return value must be typecast to an `Object`Stack before it is used.

    Throws: `OutOfMemoryError`

    Indicates insufficient memory for creating the clone.

- **ensureCapacity**

    `public void ensureCapacity(int minimumCapacity)`

    Change the current capacity of this stack.

    Parameters:

    `minimumCapacity` – the new capacity for this stack

    Postcondition:

    This stack's capacity has been changed to at least `minimumCapacity`. If the capacity was already at or greater than `minimumCapacity`, then the capacity is left unchanged.

    Throws: `OutOfMemoryError`

    Indicates insufficient memory for: `new Object[minimumCapacity]`.

- **getCapacity**

    `public int getCapacity( )`

    Accessor method to determine the current capacity of this stack. The `push` method works efficiently (without needing more memory) until this capacity is reached.

    Returns:

    the current capacity of this stack

- **isEmpty—peek—pop—push—size**

    `public boolean isEmpty( )`
    `public Object peek( )`
    `public Object pop( )`
    `public void push(Object item)`
    `public int size( )`

    These are the standard stack specifications from Figure 6.1 on page 282.

- **trimToSize**

    `public void trimToSize( )`

    Reduce the current capacity of this stack to its actual size (i.e., the number of items it contains).

    Postcondition:

    This stack's capacity has been changed to its current size.

    Throws: `OutOfMemoryError`

    Indicates insufficient memory for altering the capacity.

(continued)

(FIGURE 6.6 continued)

Implementation

```
// File: ObjectStack.java from the package edu.colorado.collections
// Complete documentation is available on pages 301-302 or from the ObjectStack link in
//    http://www.cs.colorado.edu/~main/docs/

package edu.colorado.collections;
import java.util.EmptyStackException;

public class ObjectStack implements Cloneable
{
    // Invariant of the ObjectStack class:
    //    1. The number of items in the stack is in the instance variable manyItems.
    //    2. For an empty stack, we do not care what is stored in any of data; for a
    //       nonempty stack, the items in the stack are stored in a partially filled array called
    //       data, with the bottom of the stack at data[0], the next item at data[1], and so on
    //       to the top of the stack at data[manyItems-1].
    private Object[ ] data;
    private int manyItems;

    public ObjectStack( )
    {
        final int INITIAL_CAPACITY = 10;
        manyItems = 0;
        data = new Object[INITIAL_CAPACITY];
    }


    public ObjectStack(int initialCapacity)
    {
        if (initialCapacity < 0)
            throw new IllegalArgumentException
            ("initialCapacity too small " + initialCapacity);
        manyItems = 0;
        data = new Object[initialCapacity];
    }
```

(continued)

(FIGURE 6.6 continued)

```
public Object clone( )
{   // Clone an ObjectStack.
    ObjectStack answer;

    try
    {
        answer = (ObjectStack) super.clone( );
    }
    catch (CloneNotSupportedException e)
    {
        // This exception should not occur. But if it does, it would probably indicate a
        // programming error that made super.clone unavailable.
        // The most common error would be forgetting the "Implements Cloneable"
        // clause at the start of this class.
        throw new RuntimeException
        ("This class does not implement Cloneable.");
    }

    answer.data = (Object[ ]) data.clone( );

    return answer;
}

public void ensureCapacity(int minimumCapacity)
{
    Object biggerArray[ ];

    if (data.length < minimumCapacity)
    {
        biggerArray = new Object[minimumCapacity];
        System.arraycopy(data, 0, biggerArray, 0, manyItems);
        data = biggerArray;
    }
}

public int getCapacity( )
{
    return data.length;
}

public boolean isEmpty( )
{
    return (manyItems == 0);
}
```

(continued)

(FIGURE 6.6 continued)

```java
public Object peek( )
{
    if (manyItems == 0)
        // EmptyStackException is from java.util and its constructor has no argument.
        throw new EmptyStackException( );
    return data[manyItems-1];
}

public Object pop( )
{
    if (manyItems == 0)
        // EmptyStackException is from java.util and its constructor has no argument.
        throw new EmptyStackException( );
    return data[--manyItems];
}

public void push(Object item)
{
    if (manyItems == data.length)
    {
        // Double the capacity and add 1; this works even if manyItems is 0. However, in
        // case that manyItems*2 + 1 is beyond Integer.MAX_VALUE, there will be an
        // arithmetic overflow and the bag will fail.
        ensureCapacity(manyItems * 2 + 1);
    }
    data[manyItems] = item;
    manyItems++;
}

public int size( )
{
    return manyItems;
}

public void trimToSize( )
{
    Object trimmedArray[ ];

    if (data.length != manyItems)
    {
        trimmedArray = new Object[manyItems];
        System.arraycopy(data, 0, trimmedArray, 0, manyItems);
        data = trimmedArray;
    }
}
}
```

Linked List Implementation of a Stack

A linked list is a natural way to implement a stack as a dynamic structure whose size can grow and shrink one item at a time. The head of the linked list serves as the top of the stack. Figure 6.7 contains the specification and implementation for a stack class that is implemented with a linked list. The class is called `ObjectLinkedStack` to distinguish it from our earlier `ObjectStack`. Here is a precise statement of the invariant of this version of the new stack ADT:

Invariant of the Stack ADT (Linked List Version)

1. The items in the stack are stored in a linked list, with the top of the stack stored at the head node, down to the bottom of the stack at the final node.

2. The instance variable `top` is the head reference of the linked list of items.

As usual, all methods (except the constructors) assume that the stack is represented in this way when the method is activated, and all methods ensure that the stack continues to be represented in this way when the method finishes.

Because we are using a linked list, there are no capacity worries. Thus, there are no methods that deal with capacity. A program could build a stack with more than `Integer.MAX_VALUE` items, limited only by its amount of memory. However, beyond `Integer.MAX_VALUE`, the return value of the `size` method will be wrong because of arithmetic overflow.

As a further consequence of using a linked list, it makes sense to utilize the `Node` class from Appendix E. Thus, in Figure 6.7 you will find this import statement:

```
import edu.colorado.nodes.Node;
```

By using the `Node` class, many of the stack methods can be implemented with just a line or two of code.

Discussion of the Linked List Implementation of the Stack

The constructor, `size`, and `isEmpty` each require just one line of code. The `size` method actually uses `Node.listLength` to do its work, since we are not maintaining an instance variable that keeps track of the number of nodes. Since the head node of the list is the top of the stack, the implementation of `peek` is easy: `peek` just returns the data from the head node. The operations `push` and `pop` work by adding and removing nodes, always working at the head of the linked list. Adding and removing nodes at the head of the linked list is straightforward using the techniques of Section 4.2. The `clone` method makes use of `Node.listCopy` to copy the original stack to the clone.

FIGURE 6.7	Specification and Implementation for the Linked List Version of the Stack Class

Class ObjectLinkedStack

❖ **public class Object LinkedStack from the package edu.colorado.collections**
An Object LinkedStack is a stack of references to objects.
Limitations:
Beyond Int.MAX_VALUE items, size is wrong.

Specification

- **Constructor for the Object LinkedStack**
  public Object LinkedStack( )
  Initialize an empty stack.
  Postcondition:
  This stack is empty.

- **clone**
  public Object clone( )
  Generate a copy of this stack.
  Returns:
  The return value is a copy of this stack. Subsequent changes to the copy will not affect the original, nor vice versa. The return value must be typecast to an Object LinkedStack before it is used.
  Throws: OutOfMemoryError
  Indicates insufficient memory for creating the clone.

- **isEmpty—peek—pop—push—size**
  public boolean isEmpty( )
  public Object peek( )
  public Object pop( )
  public void push(Object item)
  public int size( )
  These are the standard stack specifications from Figure 6.1 on page 282.

Implementation

```
// File: ObjectLinkedStatck.java from the package edu.colorado.collections
// Complete documentation is available above or from the ObjectLinkedStack link in
//    http://www.cs.colorado.edu/~main/docs/

package edu.colorado.collections;
import java.util.EmptyStackException;
import edu.colorado.nodes.Node;
```

(continued)

(FIGURE 6.7 continued)

```
public class ObjectLinkedStack implements Cloneable
{
    // Invariant of the ObjectLinkedStack class:
    //    1. The items in the stack are stored in a linked list, with the top of the stack stored
    //       at the head node, down to the bottom of the stack at the final node.
    //    2. The instance variable top is the head reference of the linked list of items.
    private Node top;

    public ObjectLinkedStack( )
    {
        top = null;
    }

    public Object clone( )
    {   // Clone an ObjectLinkedStack.
        ObjectLinkedStack answer;

        try
        {
            answer = (ObjectLinkedStack) super.clone( );
        }
        catch (CloneNotSupportedException e)
        {
            // This exception should not occur. But if it does, it would probably indicate a
            // programming error that made super.clone unavailable. The most common error
            // be forgetting the "Implements Cloneable" clause at the start of this class.
            throw new RuntimeException
            ("This class does not implement Cloneable.");
        }

        answer.top = Node.listCopy(top);
        return answer;
    }

    public boolean isEmpty( )
    {
        return (top == null);
    }

    public Object peek( )
    {
        if (top == null)
            // EmptyStackException is from java.util and its constructor has no argument.
            throw new EmptyStackException( );
        return top.getData( );
    }
```

(continued)

(FIGURE 6.7 continued)

```java
public Object pop( )
{
    Object answer;

    if (top == null)
        // EmptyStackException is from java.util and its constructor has no argument.
        throw new EmptyStackException( );

    answer = top.getData( );
    top = top.getLink( );
    return answer;
}

public void push(Object item)
{
    top = new Node(item, top);
}

public int size( )
{
    return Node.listLength(top);
}
}
```

Self-Test Exercises

8. For the array version of the stack, which element of the array contains the top of the stack? In the linked list version, where is the stack's top?

9. Give the full implementation of an accessor method that returns the second item from the top of the stack without actually changing the stack. Write separate solutions for the two different stack versions.

10. For the linked list version of the stack, do we maintain references to both the head and the tail?

11. Is the constructor really needed for the linked list version of the stack? What would happen if we omitted the constructor?

12. Do a time analysis of the size method for the linked list version of the stack. If the method is not constant time, then can you think of a different approach that is constant time?

13. What kind of exception is thrown if you try to pop an empty stack? Which Java Class Library defines this exception?

6.4 MORE COMPLEX STACK APPLICATIONS

Evaluating Postfix Expressions

infix versus prefix notation

We normally write an arithmetic operation between its two arguments, for example, the + operation occurs between the 2 and the 3 in the arithmetic expression 2 + 3. This is called *infix notation*. There is another way of writing arithmetic operations that places the operation in front of the two arguments, for example + 2 3 evaluates to 5. This is called **Polish prefix notation** or simply **prefix notation**.

the origin of the notation

A **prefix** is something attached to the front of an expression. You may have heard about similar prefixes for words, such as the prefix *un* in *unbelievable*. Thus, it makes sense to call this notation *prefix notation*. But why *Polish*? It is called Polish because it was devised by the Polish mathematician Jan Łukasiewicz. It would be more proper to call it *Łukasiewicz notation*, but apparently non-Polish-speaking people have trouble pronouncing *Łukasiewicz* (lü-kä-**sha**-vēch).

Using prefix notation, parentheses are completely avoided. For example, the expression (2 + 3) * 7 when written in this Polish prefix notation is:

The curved lines under the expression indicate groupings of subexpressions (but the lines are not actually part of the prefix notation).

postfix notation

If we prefer, we can write the operations after the two numbers being combined. This is called **Polish postfix notation**, or more simply **postfix notation** (or sometimes **reverse Polish notation**). For example, the expression (2 + 3) * 7 when written in Polish postfix notation is:

Once again, the curves merely clarify the groupings of subexpressions, and these curves are not actually part of the postfix notation.

Here's a longer example. The postfix expression 7 3 5 * + 4 − is equivalent to the infix expression (7 + (3*5)) − 4. Notice that an operation is applied to the two numbers that are immediately before it, so the multiplication is 3*5. Sometimes, one or both numbers for an operation are computed from a subexpression; for example, the + operation in the example is applied to the "number" 3*5 and the number before that (the 7), resulting in 7 + (3*5).

Do not intermix prefix and postfix notation. You should consistently use one or the other and not mix them together in a single expression.

Postfix notation is handy because it does not require parentheses and because it is particularly easy to evaluate (once you learn to use the notation). In fact, postfix notation often is used internally for computers because of the ease of evaluation. We will describe an algorithm to evaluate a postfix expression. When converted to a Java program, the postfix evaluation is similar to the calculator program (Figure 6.5 on page 295)—although, from our comments you might guess that the postfix evaluation is actually simpler than the infix evaluation required in the calculator program.

our goal: evaluation of postfix expressions

There are two input format issues that we must handle. When entering postfix notation we will require a space between two consecutive numbers so that you can tell where one number ends and another begins. For example, the input

35 6

consists of two numbers, 35 and 6, with a space in between. This is different from the input

356

which is just a single number, 356. A second input issue: You probably want to restrict the input to non-negative numbers in order to avoid the complication of distinguishing the negative sign of a number from a binary subtraction operation.

Our algorithm for evaluating a postfix expression uses only one stack, which is a stack of numbers. There is no need for a second stack of operation symbols, because *each operation is used as soon as it is read*. In fact, the reason why postfix evaluation is easy is precisely because each operation symbol is immediately used as soon as it is read. In the algorithm we assume that each input entry is either a number or an operation. For simplicity, we will assume that all the operations take two arguments. The complete evaluation algorithm is given in Figure 6.8, along with an example computation.

postfix evaluation algorithm

Let's study the example to see how the algorithm works. Each time an operation appears in the input, the operands for the operation are the two most recently seen numbers. For example, in Figure 6.8(c), we are about to read the * symbol. Since we have just pushed 3 and 2 onto the stack, the * causes a multiplication of 3*2, resulting in 6. The result of 6 is then pushed onto the stack, as shown in Figure 6.8(d).

Sometimes the "most recently seen number" is not actually an input number, but instead it is a number that we computed and pushed back onto the stack. For example, in Figure 6.8(d), we are about to read the first +. At this point, 6 is on top of the stack (as a result of multiplying 3*2). Below the 6 is the number 5. So, the "two most recently seen numbers" are the 6 (that we computed) and the 5 (underneath the 6). We add these two numbers, resulting in 11 (which we push onto the stack, as shown in 6.8(e)).

And so the process continues: Each time we encounter an operation, the operation is immediately applied to the two most recently seen numbers, which always reside in the top two positions of the stack. When the input is exhausted, the number remaining in the stack is the value of the entire expression.

FIGURE 6.8	Evaluating a Postfix Expression

Pseudocode

1. Initialize a stack of double numbers.
2. do
      `if` (the next input is a number)
          Read the next input and push it onto the stack.
      `else`
      {
          Read the next character, which is an operation symbol.
          Pop two numbers off the stack.
          Combine the two numbers with the operation (using the *second* number popped as the *left* operand), and push the result onto the stack.
      }
   `while` (there is more of the expression to read);

3. At this point, the stack contains one number, which is the value of the expression.

Example

Evaluate the postfix expression
   5   3   2   *   +   4   –   5   +

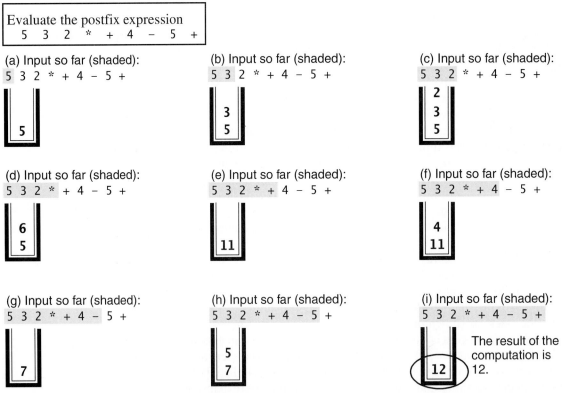

Translating Infix to Postfix Notation

infix expression

postfix expression

Because it is so easy to evaluate a postfix expression, one strategy for evaluating an ordinary infix expression is to first convert it to postfix notation and then evaluate the postfix expression. This is what compilers often do. In this section, we will present an algorithm to translate an infix expression to a postfix expression. The algorithm's input is an expression in infix notation, and the output is an equivalent expression in postfix notation. We will develop the algorithm as pseudocode and will not specify any precise form of input or output.

Until now we have assumed that the operands in our arithmetic expressions were all numbers. That need not be true. For example, an arithmetic expression may also contain variables. In this example, we will assume that the arithmetic expression can also contain variables. In fact, the operands may be anything at all, so long as we have a way of recognizing an operand when our algorithm encounters one. However, in our examples we will assume that the operands are either numbers or variables. We will also assume that all the operations are **binary operations** (which have two operands), such as addition and subtraction. There will be no **unary operations** (which have only one operand), such as sqrt for the square root function. We will present two algorithms, one for fully parenthesized expressions and one for more realistic expressions that omit some parentheses. Our algorithms apply to any sort of operations working on any sort of operands; so, in particular, our algorithms will work on boolean expressions as well as arithmetic expressions. However, in order to keep matters uncluttered, we will consider only arithmetic expressions in our examples.

algorithm for fully parenthesized expressions

If the infix expression is fully parenthesized, the algorithm is simple. All that's needed to convert from infix to postfix notation is to move each operation symbol to the location of the right parenthesis corresponding to that operation and then remove all parentheses. For example, the following infix expression will have its operation symbols moved to the location indicated by the arrows:

The result is the postfix expression:

```
A 7 + B C / * 2 D * -
```

This process of moving each operation to the location of its corresponding right parenthesis is more of an idea than a complete algorithm. A complete algorithm should read the expression from left to right and must somehow remember the operations and then determine when the corresponding right parenthesis has been found. We have some work to do before this idea becomes an algorithm.

First, observe that the operands (that is, the numbers and variables) in the equivalent postfix expression are in the same order as the operands in the corresponding infix expression that we start out with. So our algorithm can simply copy the infix expression operands, omitting parentheses, and inserting the operations, such as +, *, and so forth, at the correct locations. The problem is finding the location for inserting the operations in the postfix expression. How do we save the operations, and how do we know when to insert them? Look back at our example. If we push the operations onto a stack, then the operations we need will always be on top of the stack. When do we insert an operation? We insert an operation into the output whenever we encounter a right parenthesis in the input. Hence, the heart of the algorithm is to push the operations onto a stack and to pop an operation every time we encounter a right parenthesis. The algorithm is given in Figure 6.9. The algorithm does some checking to ensure that the input expression is fully parenthesized with balanced parentheses, although there is no checking to ensure that each operation appears between its operands (rather than before or after its operands).

FIGURE 6.9	Converting a Fully Parenthesized Infix Expression to a Postfix Expression

Pseudocode

1. Initialize a stack of characters to hold the operation symbols and parentheses.

2. `do`
       `if` (the next input is a left parenthesis)
           Read the left parenthesis and push it onto the stack.
       `else if` (the next input is a number or other operand)
           Read the operand and write it to the output.
       `else if` (the next input is one of the operation symbols)
           Read the operation symbol and push it onto the stack.
       `else`
       `{`
           Read and discard the next input symbol (which should be a right parenthesis).
           There should be an operation symbol on top of the stack, so pop this symbol and
           write it to the output. (If there is no such symbol, then print an error message
           indicating that there were too few operations in the infix expression, and halt.)
           After popping the operation symbol, there should be a left parenthesis on the
           top of the stack, so pop and discard this left parenthesis.
           (If there was no left parenthesis, then the input did not have balanced
           parentheses, so print an error message and halt.)
       `}`
     `while` (there is more of the expression to read);

3. At this point, the stack should be empty. Otherwise print an error message indicating that the expression was not fully parenthesized.

Using Precedence Rules in the Infix Expression

So far we have been assuming that our infix expression is fully parenthesized. However, in practice, infix expressions are usually not fully parenthesized, and the computer must rely on precedence rules to determine the order of operations for the missing parentheses. This adds a significant complication.

Let's start with an example. We will use the usual Java precedence rules in our example. Consider the following expression:

```
2 * (A - B) + 3 + C
```

In this case the subtraction is performed first, then the multiplication, and finally the two additions are performed from left to right. The subtraction is first because the parentheses indicate that (A - B) must be evaluated before combining the result with any other operands. The multiplication is performed next—before the additions—because multiplication has *higher precedence* than addition. The two additions are of equal precedence, and there are no parentheses to tell us which addition to perform first. Operations of equal precedence are performed in left to right order (when parentheses do not indicate some other order). Thus, the left-hand addition occurs before the right-hand addition. This order of evaluation means the expression is the same as this fully parenthesized expression:

```
(((2 * (A - B)) + 3) + C)
```

To help determine the order of evaluation for arithmetic expressions, we have been referring to the *precedence* of operations, such as +, −, and *. A **precedence** is just an ordering from high to low for the operations. Operations with a higher precedence are evaluated before operations with a lower precedence. Sometimes, two different operations, such as + and − have equal precedence, in which case we must specify whether the operations are to be evaluated left to right or right to left. We need to know only when one operation has higher precedence than another, and the direction of evaluation (left to right or right to left) for operations with equal precedence. For example, in Java, * and / have equal precedence; + and − also have equal precedence, but * and / have higher precedence than + and −. That is why we perform multiplication before addition (when there are no parentheses indicating otherwise).

Just to make sure they are fresh in our minds, let us review the Java rules for evaluating arithmetic expressions that are not fully parenthesized:

rules for using precedence

1. Parentheses, when they are present, determine the order of operations. Everything inside a pair of matching parentheses is evaluated, and that value is then combined with things outside the parentheses.

2. If the order is not indicated by parentheses, operations of higher precedence are performed before operations of lower precedence.

3. Arithmetic operations of equal precedence are performed in left-to-right order, unless parentheses indicate otherwise.

In Figure 6.9 we gave an algorithm to convert a fully parenthesized infix expression to an equivalent postfix expression. Now we can make our algorithm more general. The new version (Figure 6.10) does not require full parentheses for the input; the algorithm uses precedence to decide which operation to perform first. In other words, the expressions can be written as we normally write them with parentheses omitted in some cases. Figure 6.11 contains an example computation of our algorithm as it translates an infix expression into the corresponding postfix expression. Study the example now, then turn to page 318 to read the details of the algorithm.

FIGURE 6.10 Converting an Infix Expression to a Postfix Expression (General Case)

Pseudocode

1. Initialize a stack of characters to hold the operation symbols and parentheses.

2. `do`
    `if` (the next input is a left parenthesis)
        Read the left parenthesis and push it onto the stack.
    `else if` (the next input is a number or other operand)
        Read the operand and write it to the output.
    `else if` (the next input is one of the operation symbols)
    {
        Pop and print operations off the stack until one of three things occurs: (1) The stack becomes empty, or (2) The next symbol on the stack is a left parenthesis, or (3) The next symbol on the stack is an operation with lower precedence than the next input symbol. When one of these situations occurs, stop popping, read the next input symbol, and push this symbol onto the stack.
    }
    `else`
    {
        Read and discard the next input symbol (which should be a right parenthesis). Pop and print operations off the stack until the next symbol on the stack is a left parenthesis. (If no left parenthesis is encountered, then print an error message indicating unbalanced parentheses, and halt.) Finally, pop and discard the left parenthesis.
    }
    `while` (there is more of the expression to read);

3. Pop and print any remaining operations on the stack. (There should be no remaining left parentheses, otherwise the input expression did not have balanced parentheses.)

FIGURE 6.11	Example Computation for the Algorithm of Figure 6.10

Example

Convert the infix expression:
3 * X + (Y - 12) - Z

(a) Input so far (shaded):
3 * X + (Y - 12) - Z
The operand 3 is printed.

Output so far:
3

(b) Input so far (shaded):
3 * X + (Y - 12) - Z
The * is pushed.

Output so far:
3

(c) Input so far (shaded):
3 * X + (Y - 12) - Z
The operand X is printed.

Output so far:
3 X

(d) Input so far (shaded):
3 * X + (Y - 12) - Z
Pop and print the * since it has higher precedence than the +; then push the +.

Output so far:
3 X *

(e) Input so far (shaded):
3 * X + (Y - 12) - Z
Push the parenthesis.

Output so far:
3 X *

(f) Input so far (shaded):
3 * X + (Y - 12) - Z
The operand Y is printed.

Output so far:
3 X * Y

(g) Input so far (shaded):
3 * X + (Y - 12) - Z
The - is pushed.

Output so far:
3 X * Y

(h) Input so far (shaded):
3 * X + (Y - 12) - Z
The operand 12 is printed.

Output so far:
3 X * Y 12

(i) Input so far (shaded):
3 * X + (Y - 12) - Z
Pop until left parenthesis.

Output so far:
3 X * Y 12 -

(j) Input so far (shaded):
3 * X + (Y - 12) - Z
Pop and print the + since it has precedence equal to the -; then push the -.

Output so far:
3 X * Y 12 - +

(k) Input so far (shaded):
3 * X + (Y - 12) - Z
The operand Z is printed.

Output so far:
3 X * Y 12 - + Z

(l) Input so far (shaded):
3 * X + (Y - 12) - Z
Pop any remaining operations.

Output so far:
3 X * Y 12 - + Z -

Correctness of the Conversion from Infix to Postfix

In order for the conversion algorithm to be correct, we need to check these items:

1. The postfix expression contains the correct operands in the correct order.

2. The postfix expression evaluates subexpressions in the way indicated by the parentheses in the infix expression.

3. The postfix expression handles operations of differing precedence according to the precedence rules.

4. A sequence of operations of equal precedence in the infix expression is handled correctly when translated into the postfix expression.

1. the operands are in the right order

Let's consider each of these four issues. First we need to know that the operands (the numbers and variables) in the postfix expression are in the same order as they were in the input infix expression, but this is easy to see. Because operands are written out as soon as they are read in, they are clearly in the same order as in the input infix expression.

2. the parentheses are done correctly

Parentheses are a way of grouping subexpressions. Everything inside a pair of matching parentheses is treated as a single unit by anything outside the parentheses. The parentheses give the following message to the operations outside of the parentheses: *Don't look inside these parentheses. We will work things out among ourselves and deliver a single value for you to combine with other operands.* This means that all operations between a set of matching parentheses in the infix expression should form a subexpression of the postfix expression, and with this algorithm they do just that. To see that they do form a subexpression, we will show the following:

How the Infix to Postfix Algorithm Translates Subexpressions

Claim: All of the operations between a pair of matching parentheses (and no other operations) are output in the time between reading the opening parenthesis and the time that the algorithm reads the closing parenthesis.

Once we show that this claim is true, we will know that all the operations between a pair of matching parentheses in the infix expression will be together in a group within the output postfix notation, and so they will form a subexpression of the postfix expression. So, let's see exactly why the claim is valid.

The algorithm keeps track of expressions within matching parentheses by using the stack. When the algorithm encounters an opening parenthesis, that is, a '(', it pushes this parenthesis onto the stack. Now consider what happens between pushing the opening parenthesis and encountering the matching closing parenthesis, that is, the matching ')'. The algorithm will never output an operation from the stack that is below the opening parenthesis, '('. Thus, it outputs only operations that are within the pair of matching parentheses in the input (infix) expression. Moreover, it outputs all of these operations. When it encounters the matching closing parenthesis, it outputs all the remaining operations on the stack all the way down to that matching opening parenthesis.

When the infix expression contains an operation with low precedence followed by an operation with a higher precedence, then the algorithm should output these operations in reverse order. In other words, the higher precedence operation must be written first. A check of the algorithm will show that the operations are indeed output in reverse order.

3. the precedence is handled correctly

When the infix expression contains a sequence of operations of equal precedence, they represent an evaluation that goes from left to right. That means the operations should be output from left to right. If you check the algorithm, you will see that this is true. Operations are pushed onto the stack, but when the next operation of equal precedence is encountered, the operation in the stack is output and the new operation is pushed onto the stack. To confirm this, first check the algorithm in the case where the stack is empty at the time that the operations are encountered. That is the easiest case to see. After that, the other cases will be clearer, because they are similar.

4. operations of equal precedence are handled correctly

Self-Test Exercises

14. Evaluate the postfix expression 2 3 - 43 +.

15. Trace the algorithm from Figure 6.8 on page 312 to evaluate the postfix expression 15 9 6 * + 12 - 15 +. Draw the stack after each push or pop.

16. Trace the algorithm from Figure 6.10 on page 316 to create a postfix expression from 3 / A + (B + 12) - C.

CHAPTER SUMMARY

- A stack is a Last-In/First-Out data structure.
- Adding an item to a stack is called a *push* operation. Removing an item from a stack is called a *pop* operation.
- Attempting to pop an item off an empty stack is an error known as a *stack underflow*. A method can throw `java.util.EmptyStackException` to indicate this error.
- A stack can be implemented as a partially filled array or as a linked list. The Java Class Libraries also provide a stack class: `java.util.Stack`.
- Each of our stack implementations was a stack of objects. But the `Object` type can be changed to any other type without trouble to obtain a new implementation such as a stack of `int`.
- Stacks have many uses in computer science. The evaluation and translation of arithmetic expressions are two common uses.

? Solutions to Self-Test Exercises

1. Push a D; push an A; push an H; push an L; pop an L; pop an H; pop an A; pop a D; the output is LHAD.

2. Pop one item, storing it in a local variable called top. Then peek at the next item, storing it in another local variable called result. Push the top back on the stack, and return the result.

3. Within readAndEvaluate, there is a string called SYMBOLS that lists the legal operators. Add the symbol '^' to this string of operators. Also, add a new case to the switch statement within the method evaluateStackTops. The new case is for the exponentiation operator. This calculates operand1 raised to the power of operand2 and pushes the result back onto the numbers stack.

4. The modification is most easily accomplished in the method readAndEvaluate. Within this method, you can add a bit of code within the section that reads an operator symbol. The new code should read the symbol into a local variable, check whether the symbol is a slash ('/'), and peek ahead to see whether the next symbol is also a slash. If so, then read and discard the rest of the line (instead of pushing the operator onto the stack).

5. Here are some illegal expressions that are caught: a division by zero (3/0), too many right parentheses (3+4)), a missing operand (3 4), a missing right parenthesis (3+4.

6. Here are some illegal expressions that are not caught: illegal characters (3 +! 4), too many left parentheses ((3+4), missing left parentheses 3+4).

7. The solution is the same as the example that starts on page 291, but the numbers are changed. The final value is 24.

8. The array version: data[manyItems-1]. The linked list version has the top at the head of the list.

9. Here is one of the two solutions (for the linked list):

```
public Object second( )
{
    if (top == null)
        throw
        new EmptyStackException( );
    if (top.link == null)
        throw
        new NoSuchElementException( );

    return top.link.data;
}
```

10. We maintain only a head reference.

11. The constructor isn't needed because any instance variable that is a reference is automatically initialized to null.

12. Our size implementation uses listSize, which is linear time. For a constant time implementation, you could maintain another private instance variable to continually keep track of the list length.

13. An EmptyStackException, which is defined in java.util.EmptyStackException.

14. 42.

15. The trace is the same as the computation at the bottom of Figure 6.7 on page 307, except that the numbers are three times as large.

16. The trace is much the same as the computation in Figure 6.8 on page 312, except that the operations are different.

PROGRAMMING PROJECTS

1 Write an applet that is a simple stack-based calculator. The calculator should have a text field where you can enter a double number, and a text area that displays a stack of numbers. There should be an `enter` button that reads the number from the text field and pushes this number onto the stack. There are also several buttons for operations such as +, −, *, and /. When an operation button is pressed, the top two numbers are popped off the stack and the operation is applied. The first number popped is always the second operand.

2 Choose one of the stack implementations and implement a method with this specification:

```
Object itemAt(int n)
// Precondition: 0 <= n and n < size( ).
// Postcondition: The return value is the
// item that is n from the top (with the top at
// n = 0, the next at n = 1, and so on). The
// stack is not changed.
```

Throw a `NoSuchElementException` if the precondition is violated (from `java.util.NoSuchElementException`).

3 In this exercise you will need the `itemAt` method from the previous programming project. Write a program that prints all strings with at most *n* letters, where the letters are chosen from a range `first...last` of characters. Below is an outline for an algorithm to do this using a stack. Your program should use a stack to implement this algorithm:

```
// Writing all strings of 1 to n letters:
Push first onto the stack.
while  (the stack is not empty)
{
    Print all of the stack (using itemAt).
    if  (the stack contains fewer than n letters)
        Push first onto the stack.
```

```
    else
    {
```
Pop characters off the stack, until the stack is empty, or there is a character other than `last` on the top. (Note: if the top character is not `last`, then nothing is popped off the stack.)
```
        if  (the stack is not empty)
```
Pop a character c off the stack, and push c+1 (i.e., the next letter) onto the stack.
```
    }
}
```

4 Enhance the calculator program given in Figure 6.5 on page 295 so that it has all of the following features: After one expression is evaluated, the user is asked if he or she wants to evaluate another expression and is allowed to choose between evaluating another expression and quitting the program. Expressions need not be fully parenthesized, and when parentheses are missing, the usual Java precedence rules are followed. If the arithmetic expression entered is not well formed, then the user is told it is not well formed and asked to reenter the expression.

5 In Figure 6.5 on page 295 we presented a program to evaluate arithmetic expressions. In this exercise you will write a similar program to evaluate boolean expressions. Rather than arithmetic operations, the input expressions for this program will use the operations && (the "and" operation), ||(the "or" operation), and !(the "not" operation). Rather than combining numbers, the input expression will combine simple boolean comparisons of numbers such as (1 < 2) and (6 < 3). Assume all the numbers in these simple comparisons are integers. Allow the following comparison operations: <, >, <=, >=, ==, and !=. At first assume that all boolean expressions are fully parenthesized and well formed. Be sure to note that "not" is a unary operation. You can assume that the argument to "not" (which follows the !) is enclosed in parentheses. Your program should allow the user to evaluate additional expressions until the user says he/she wishes to end the program.

For a more difficult assignment, enhance your program by adding any or all of the following features: (a) The numbers need not be integers; (b) The expression need not be fully parenthesized and if parentheses are missing, then the Java precedence rules apply. (Note that innermost expressions such as (1 < 2) are still assumed to be in parentheses.) (c) The expression need not be well formed and if it is not well formed, then the user is asked to reenter the expression.

6 Write a program that evaluates an arithmetic expression in postfix notation. The basic algorithm is contained in "Evaluating Postfix Expressions" on page 310. Assume the input contains numbers (but no variables) as well as the arithmetic operations +, −, *, and /. Your program should allow the user to evaluate additional expressions until the user wants to end the program. You might also enhance your program so that the expression need not be well formed, and if it is not well formed, then the user must reenter the expression.

7 Write a program that takes as input an infix expression and outputs the equivalent postfix expression. The basic algorithm is contained in "Translating Infix to Postfix Notation" on page 313. Assume that the input may contain numbers, variables, arithmetic operations +, −, *, and /, as well as parentheses. However, the expression need not be fully parenthesized, and when parentheses are missing, the usual Java precedence rules are used to determine the order of evaluation. Your program should allow the user to enter additional expressions until the user says he/she wishes to end the program. For a more difficult assignment, enhance your program so that the expression need not be well formed and if it is not well formed, then the user is asked to reenter the expression.

8 Redo the calculator program given in Figure 6.5 on page 295, but this time implement it in a different way. To evaluate the arithmetic expression, your program will first convert the expression to postfix notation. After that, it will evaluate the postfix expression. Pseudocode for both of these subtasks is given in this chapter. For this exercise, you should not assume that expressions are fully parenthesized. When parentheses are missing, the usual Java precedence rules are used to determine the order of evaluation. Your program should allow the user to evaluate additional expressions until the user wants to end the program.

9 Write a program that evaluates an arithmetic expression in infix notation, without full parentheses. Use the following algorithm: There are two stacks: a numbers stack and an operators stack. When a number appears, push it on the numbers stack. Any parenthesis or operator should be treated as described in Step 2 of Figure 6.10 on page 316—with one change. Whenever you pop an operation off the stack, you should immediately use that operation by popping two numbers, applying the operation, and pushing the answer back on the numbers stack.

10 Suppose that you have *n* queens from a chess game, and that you also have an *n* by *n* chess board. Is it possible to place all *n* queens on the board so that no two queens are in the same row, no two queens are in the same column, and no two queens are on the same diagonal? For example, a solution with *n*=5 is shown here:

Solution to the
5-queens problem

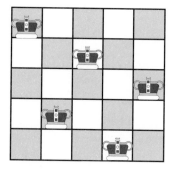

   This problem is called the *n*-queens problem. For this project, you are to write a method that has one integer parameter, *n*, and determines whether there is a solution to the *n*-queens problem. If a solution is found then the procedure prints the row and column of each queen (or displays the result graphically in an applet). Your program should solve the problem by making a sequence of choices, such as "Try placing the row 1 queen in column 1," or "Try placing the row 7 queen in column 3." Each time a choice is made, the choice is pushed onto a stack that already contains all the previously made choices. The purpose of the stack is to make it easy to fix incorrect choices, following the pseudocode, using a stack, `s`, and a boolean variable, `success`:

Push information onto the stack indicating the first choice is a queen in row 1, column 1.

```
success = false;

while (!success && !s.isEmpty( ))
{
```

   Check whether the most recent choice (on top of the stack) is in the same row, same column, or same diagonal as any other choices (below the top). If so, then we say there is a conflict; otherwise there is no conflict.

   `if` (there is a conflict)
      Pop items off the stack until the stack becomes empty, or the top of the stack is a choice that is not in column *n*. If the stack is now not empty, then increase the column number of the top choice by 1.
   `else if` (no conflict, and the stack size is *n*)
      Set `success` to `true` because we have found a solution to the *n*-queens problem.
   `else`
      Push information onto the stack indicating that the next choice is to place a queen at row number `s.size( )+1`, and column number `1`.

```
}
```

This technique is called **backtracking** since we keep our choices on a stack and *back up* to correct any mistakes that are made. Notice that when you check for a conflict, you will need access to the entire stack (not just the top), so that you should use the `itemAt` method from Programming Project 2 on page 321.

Queues

He who comes first, eats first.

EIKE VON REPKOW
Sachsenspiegel

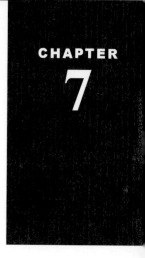

CHAPTER

7

A *queue* is a First-In/First-Out data structure similar to a line of people at a ticket window. It can be used whenever you need a data structure that allows items to "wait their turn." In this chapter we discuss applications of the queue data structure, give two implementations of a queue ADT, and discuss the differences between queues and stacks. We also discuss and implement a more flexible kind of queue called a *priority queue*.

7.1   INTRODUCTION TO QUEUES

The word *queue* is pronounced as if you were saying the letter Q; the word *queue* means the same thing as the word *line* when used in phrases like "waiting in a line." Every time you get in line at a supermarket or in a bank or at a ticket window, you are adding yourself to a queue. If everybody is polite, then people add themselves to the rear of the queue (the rear of the line), and the person at the front of the queue is always the person who is served first. The queue data structure works in exactly the same way, and the abstract definition of a queue reflects this intuition.

Queue Definition

A **queue** is a data structure of ordered items such that items can be inserted only at one end (called the **rear**) and removed at the other end (called the **front**). The item at the front end of the queue is called the **first item**.

When we say that the items in a queue are *ordered,* we refer to the items' position in the queue. There is a first one (the front one), a second one, a third one, and so forth. We do *not* require that the items can be compared using the < operator. The items may be of any type. In this regard, the situation is the same as it was for a stack.

stacks versus queues

Because items must be removed in exactly the same order that they were added to the queue, a queue is called a "First-In/First-Out" data structure (abbreviated **FIFO**). This differs from a stack, which is a Last-In/First-Out data structure, but apart from this difference, a stack and a queue are similar data structures. They differ only in the rule that determines which item is removed first. The contrast between stacks and queues is illustrated in Figure 7.1. In either structure the items depicted are entered in the order A, B, C, and D. With a queue, they are removed in the same order: A, B, C, D. With a stack, they are removed in the reverse order: D, C, B, A.

FIFO

A queue is a First-In/First-Out data structure. Items are taken out of the queue in the same order that they were put into the queue.

FIGURE 7.1 Contrasting a Stack and a Queue

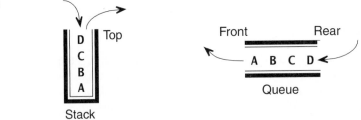

The Queue ADT

In Figure 7.2 we specify the key methods of a queue. The specification for the queue follows the same general pattern as the generic stack of Chapter 6. As with our stack, the queue is a queue of objects, using the Java `Object` type. But this underlying type can be changed to any other data type without problems. Later we will implement the queue as a Java class. By now you should be able to guess that we'll have two implementations. The first will store the items in an array, whereas the second uses a linked list.

The queue's methods include operations to remove the item from the front of the queue, to add an item to the rear of the queue, and so on. The method for adding an item to the queue is often called an **enqueue** operation (pronounced *en-q*), which is a shortening of "*en*tering the *queue*." But for adding an item, we will use the simpler name `insert`. The method for removing an item from the queue is often called a **dequeue** operation (pronounced *de-q*), which means "*de*leting from the *queue*," but we will use the simpler name `getFront`.

If a program attempts to remove an item from an empty queue, that is a kind of error called **queue underflow**. This is similar to a stack underflow (popping an empty stack), though there is one difference. Java provides a specific exception, `EmptyStackException`, to indicate a stack underflow. There is no specific exception for a queue underflow, so our `getFront` method will throw `NoSuchElementException` to indicate an underflow. (`NoSuchElementException` is part of `java.util`, and many collection classes use it to indicate some kind of underflow.) Anyway, to help you avoid these errors, the queue class provides a boolean method to test for an empty queue and a second method to return the current number of items in the queue. (The `isEmpty` method is redundant, since the `size` method can be used to test for an empty queue. However, using `isEmpty` can make the meaning of your code clearer.)

We could add other operations, such as a method to look at the front item of the queue without removing it from the queue, but this minimal set of operations will be enough for our purposes.

Uses for Queues

Uses for queues are easy to find—we often use queues in our everyday affairs, such as when we wait in line at a bank. To get a feel for using a queue in an algorithm we will first consider a simple example.

Suppose you want a program to read a word and then write the word. This is so simple that you may wonder why we bother to consider this task, but it is best to start with a simple example. One way to accomplish this task is to read the input one letter at a time and place each letter in a queue. After the word is read, the letters in the queue are written out. Because a queue is a First-In/First-Out data structure, the letters are written in the same order in which they were read. The pseudocode for this approach to copying a word appears after Figure 7.2.

copying a word

FIGURE 7.2	Specification of the Key Methods of a Queue Class

Specification

These are the key methods of a queue class, which we will implement in several different ways. The first part of the class name, [Object]Queue, is drawn in a box throughout the specification to indicate that the underlying type of items in the queue can be implemented as Java's `Object` type or as any of the primitive data types. For example, we can implement an [Int]Queue, [Double]Queue, etc.

- **Constructor for the [Object]Queue**
    ```
    public [Object]Queue( )
    ```
    Initialize an empty queue.
    Postcondition:
        This queue is empty.

- **getFront**
    ```
    public [Object] getFront( )
    ```
    Get the front item, removing it from this queue.
    Precondition:
        This queue is not empty.
    Postcondition:
        The return value is the front item of this queue, and the item has been removed.
    Throws: `NoSuchElementException`
        Indicates that this queue is empty.

- **insert**
    ```
    public void insert([Object] item)
    ```
    Add a new item to the rear of this queue. The new item may be the null reference.
    Parameters:
        `item` – the item to be added to this queue
    Postcondition:
        The item has been added to the rear of this queue.
    Throws: `OutOfMemoryError`
        Indicates insufficient memory for adding a new item to this queue.

- **isEmpty**
    ```
    public boolean isEmpty( )
    ```
    Determine whether this queue is empty.
    Returns:
        `true` if this queue is empty; otherwise `false`

- **size**
    ```
    public int size( )
    ```
    Accessor method to determine the number of items in this queue.
    Returns:
        the number of items in this queue

```
// Echoing a word
```
1. Declare a queue of characters.
2. `while` (there are more characters of the word to read)
   ```
   {
   ```
   Read a character.
   Insert the character into the queue.
   ```
   }
   ```
3. `while` (the queue is not empty)
   ```
   {
   ```
   Get the front character from the queue.
   Write the character to the screen.
   ```
   }
   ```

Because queues occur in real life situations, they are frequently used in simulation programs. For example, a program to simulate the traffic at an intersection might use a software queue to simulate the real-life situation of a growing line of automobiles waiting for a traffic light to change from red to green.

simulation programs

Queues also appear in computer system software, such as the operating system that runs on your PC. For example, consider a program that reads input from the keyboard. We think of a program as directly reading its input from the keyboard. However, if you think of what actually happens when you give a line of input to a program, you will realize that the program does not necessarily read a character when the corresponding keyboard key is pressed. This allows you to type input to the program, and that input is saved in a queue by software that is part of the operating system. When the program asks for input, the operating system provides characters from the front of its queue. This is called **buffering** the input, and is controlled by the PC's operating system software. In reality, a more sophisticated data structure is used rather than a queue, allowing you to back up and retype part of the line. Also, this form of buffering data in a queue is often used when one computer component is receiving data from another faster computer component. For example, if your fast CPU (central processor unit) is sending data to your printer, which is slow by comparison, then the data is buffered in a queue. By using the queue in this way, the CPU need not wait for the printer to finish printing the first character before the CPU sends the next character.

input/output buffering

Self-Test Exercises

1. Suppose a program uses a queue of characters to read a word and echo it to the screen. For the input word `LINE`, trace the algorithm, giving all the activations of the operations `insert` and `getFront`.

2. Name some common situations where a PC's operating system uses some kind of a queue.

3. Write pseudocode for an algorithm that reads an even number of characters. The algorithm then prints the first character, third character, fifth character, and so on. On a second output line, the algorithm prints the other characters. Use two queues to store the characters.

7.2   QUEUE APPLICATIONS

Before we actually implement the queue class, we'll show two applications that use the queue specified in Figure 7.2 on page 328. We'll assume that we have many different queues available—an ObjectQueue, CharQueue, IntQueue, and so on. These queues will be in the package edu.colorado.collections. The first application uses a queue of characters, and the second uses a queue of integers.

> In an implementation of
> ObjectQueue, we can
> change Object to any of
> the primitive types, so
> we're really doing these
> nine implementations at
> once:
>
>   ObjectQueue
>   BooleanQueue
>   ByteQueue
>   CharQueue
>   DoubleQueue
>   FloatQueue
>   IntQueue
>   LongQueue
>   ShortQueue

PROGRAMMING EXAMPLE: **Palindromes**

A **palindrome** is a string that reads the same forward and backward; that is, the letters are the same whether you read them from right to left or from left to right. For example, the one-word string "radar" is a palindrome. A more complicated example of a palindrome is the following sentence:

       Able was I ere I saw Elba

Palindromes are fun to make up, and they even have applications in at least one area—the analysis of genetic material.

Suppose we want a program to read a line of text and tell us if the line is a palindrome. We can do this by using both a stack and a queue. We will read the line of text into both a stack and a queue, and then write out the contents of the stack and the contents of the queue. The line that is written using the queue is written forward, and the line that is written using the stack is written backward. Now, if those two output lines are the same, then the input string must be a palindrome. Of course, the program need not actually write out the contents of the stack and the queue. The program can simply compare the contents of the stack and the queue character-by-character to see if they would produce the same string of characters.

A program that checks for palindromes in the way we just outlined is given in Figure 7.3. This program uses the stack class defined in Figure 6.1 on page 281 as well as the queue class from Figure 7.2 on page 328. In this program we treat both the uppercase and lowercase versions of a letter as being the same character. This is because we want to consider a sentence as reading the same forward and backward even though it might start with an uppercase letter and end with a lowercase letter. For example, the string "Able was I ere I saw Elba" when written backwards reads "ablE was I ere I saw elbA". The two strings match, provided we agree to consider upper- and lowercase versions of a letter as being equal. The treatment of the letters' cases is accomplished with a useful Java

---

FIGURE 7.3 | A Program to Recognize Palindromes

Java Application Program

```java
// FILE: Palindrome.java
// This program determines whether an input line is a palindrome. The program ignores
// everything except alphabetic letters, and it ignores the difference between
// upper- and lowercase letters.

import edu.colorado.collections.CharQueue;
import edu.colorado.collections.CharStack;
import edu.colorado.io.EasyReader;   // From Appendix B

public class Palindrome
{
    public static void main(String[ ] args)
    {
        EasyReader stdin = new EasyReader(System.in);
        CharQueue q = new CharQueue( );
        CharStack s = new CharStack( );
        char letter;
        int mismatches = 0;

        System.out.println("Enter a line and I will see if it's a palindrome:");

        while (!stdin.isEOLN( ))
        {
            letter = Character.toUpperCase(stdin.charInput( ));
            if (Character.isLetter(letter))
            {
                q.insert(letter);
                s.push(letter);
            }
        }

        while (!q.isEmpty( ))
        {
            if (q.getFront( ) != s.pop( ))
                mismatches++;
        }

        if (mismatches == 0)
            System.out.println("That is a palindrome.");
        else
            System.out.println("That is not a palindrome.");
    }
}
```

*the
toUpperCase
method
converts
lowercase
letters to
uppercase
letters*

method `Character.toUpperCase`. This method has one character as an argument. If this character is a lowercase letter, then the method converts it to the corresponding uppercase letter and returns this value. Otherwise, the method returns the character unchanged.

Our program also ignores many characters, requiring only that the *alphabetic letters* on the line read the same forward and backward. This way we can find more palindromes. If we look only at alphabetic letters, discarding spaces and punctuation, then there are many more palindromes. However, they are not always easy to spot. For example, you might not immediately recognize the following as a palindrome:

```
Straw? No, too stupid a fad. I put soot on warts.
```

*the isLetter
method
determines
which characters
are letters*

Depending on your current frame of mind, you may think that discovering such sentences is also a stupid fad, but nevertheless, our program ignores blanks and punctuation. Therefore, according to our program, the above is a palindrome. The determination of whether a character is a letter is accomplished with another Java method. The method, called `Character.isLetter`, returns `true` if its single argument is one of the alphabetic characters.

Two sample dialogues from the palindrome program are shown in Figure 7.4. As we often do, we have presented a minimal program to concentrate on the new material being presented. Before the program is released to users, it should be enhanced in a number of ways to make it more robust (such as better handling of a possible stack or queue overflow) and more friendly (such as allowing more than one sentence to be entered).

Self-Test Exercises

4. How would you modify the palindromes program so that it indicates the first position in the input string that violates the palindrome property? For example, consider the input "Able were you ere you saw Elba." This looks like a palindrome until you see the first "e" in "were," so a suitable output would be

```
That is not a palindrome.
Mismatch discovered at: Able we
```

5. How would you modify the palindromes program so that uppercase and lowercase versions of letters are considered different? In the modified program the string "able was I ere I saw elba" would still be considered a palindrome, but the string "Able was I ere I saw Elba" would no longer be considered a palindrome, since, among other things, the first and last letters, "A" and "a," are not the same under these changed rules.

FIGURE 7.4	Sample Dialogues from the Palindrome Program

First Sample Dialogue

```
Enter a line and I will see if it's a palindrome:
Straw? No, too stupid a fad. I put soot on warts.
That is a palindrome.
```

Second Sample Dialogue

```
Enter a line and I will see if it's a palindrome:
Able were you ere you saw Elba.
That is not a palindrome.
```

PROGRAMMING EXAMPLE: Car Wash Simulation

The *Handy-Dandy Hand Car Wash Company* has decided to modernize and change its image. It has installed a fast, fully automated car-washing mechanism that can wash a car in one to ten minutes. It will soon reopen under its new name *The Automatic Auto Wash Emporium*. The company wants to know the most efficient way to use its new car-washing mechanism. If the mechanism is used on the fast setting, it can wash a car in one minute, but because of the high pressure required to operate at such speed, the mechanism uses a great deal of water and soap at this setting. At slower settings, it takes longer to wash a car but uses less soap and water. The company wants to know how many customers will be served and how long customers will have to wait in line when the washing mechanism is used at one of the slower speeds. The company also wants to know whether its new motto, "You Ought to Autowash your Auto," will be effective. We respectfully refuse comment on the motto, but we agree to write a program that will simulate automobiles waiting in line for a car wash. This way the manager of the car wash can see how the speed of the car wash, the length of the line, and various other factors interact.

Car Wash Simulation—Specification

Input. The program has three input items: (1) the amount of time needed to wash one car (in total seconds); (2) the probability that a new customer arrives during any given second (we assume that, at most, one customer arrives in a second); and (3) the total length of time to be simulated (in seconds).

Output. The program produces two pieces of output information: (1) the number of customers serviced in the simulated time; and (2) the average time that a customer spent in line during the simulation (in seconds).

Car Wash Simulation—Design

We will carry out a design of the program in a way that is common for many simulation tasks. The approach is to propose a collection of related object types that correspond to real-world objects in the situation that we are simulating. There are many possibilities—our particular approach focuses on the use of our queue class, which will be used to simulate a line of customers waiting to have their cars washed. We first discuss the queue and then go on to propose the other objects needed for the simulation.

the queue

We need to simulate a queue of customers, but we do not have real live customers, so we must decide how we will represent them. There are many ways to represent customers: We could use their names and place them in a queue of names; we could assign an arbitrary number to each customer and store that number in a queue of numbers; we could represent each customer by the make and year of the customer's automobile, or even by how dirty the automobile is. However, none of those representations has any relevance to the specified simulation. For this simulation, all we need to know about a customer is how long the customer waits in the queue. Hence, a good way to represent a customer is to use a number that represents the time that the customer entered the queue. Thus, our queue will be a queue of numbers. In a more complex simulation, it would be appropriate to implement the customers as objects, and one of the customer's methods would return the customer's arrival time.

> **Key Design Concept**
>
> *Determine which properties of a real-world object are relevant to the problem at hand.*

The numbers that record the times that customers entered the queue are called **time stamps**. Our simulation works in seconds, so a time stamp is just the number of simulated seconds that have passed since the start of the simulation. When the customer (represented by the time stamp) is removed from the queue, we can easily calculate the time the customer spent waiting: The time spent waiting is the total number of seconds simulated so far minus the time stamp.

propose a list of related object types

Now let's discuss other objects that will be useful in the simulation program. In addition to the queue, we propose three other object types, listed here:

Washer. A washer is an object that simulates the automatic car washing mechanism.

BooleanSource. An object of this class provides a sequence of boolean values. Some of the values in the sequence are `true`, and some are `false`. During the simulation, we will have one `BooleanSource` object that we query once per simulated second. If the query returns `true` as its response, this indicates that a new customer has arrived during the simulated second; a `false` return value indicates that no customer has arrived during the simulated second.

Averager. An averager computes the average of a group of numbers. For example, we might send the following four numbers into an averager: 10, 20, 2, and 12. The averager could then tell us that the average of these numbers is 11.0. The averager can also tell us how many numbers it has processed—in our example the averager processed four numbers. We'll use an averager to keep track of the average waiting time and the total number of cars washed.

A good way to design a simulation program is to first write pseudocode illustrating how the proposed objects will be used. From this pseudocode, we then extract the necessary methods for each object. The simulation program that we have in mind will carry out the simulation using one-second intervals, and to make the simulation simpler, we assume that at most one customer arrives during any particular second. The simulation contains a loop that is iterated once for each simulated second. In each loop iteration, all the activities that take place in one second, such as the possible arrival of a new customer or the removal of a customer from the queue, will be simulated. When the loop terminates, the simulation is over and the needed output values are obtained from the averager. The basic pseudocode for the simulation is shown in Figure 7.5.

write pseudocode indicating how the objects are used

FIGURE 7.5 | The Car Wash Simulation

Pseudocode

1. Declare a queue of integers, which will be used to keep track of arrival times of customers who are waiting to wash their cars. We also declare the following objects:

   (a) A `Washer`: The washer's constructor has an argument indicating the amount of time (in seconds) needed by the washer to wash one car.

   (b) A `BooleanSource`: The constructor has an argument that specifies how frequently the `BooleanSource` returns `true` (indicating how often customers arrive).

   (c) An `Averager`.

2. `for (currentSecond = 0; currentSecond <` the simulation length`; currentSecond++)`
   `{`
   > Each iteration of this loop simulates the passage of one second of time, as follows:
   > Ask the `BooleanSource` whether a new customer arrives during this second, and if so, enter the `currentSecond` into the queue.
   > `if` (the `Washer` is not busy and the queue is not empty)
   > `{`
   >> Remove the next integer from the queue, and call this integer `next`.
   >> This integer is the arrival time of the customer whose car we will now wash.
   >> So, compute how long the customer had to wait (`currentSecond - next`), and send this value to the `Averager`. Also, tell the `Washer` that it should start washing another car.
   > `}`
   > Indicate to the `Washer` that another simulated second has passed. This allows the `Washer` to correctly determine whether it is still busy.
   `}`

3. At this point, the simulation is completed. So we can get and print two items of information from the `Averager`: (1) how many numbers the `Averager` was given (i.e., the number of customers whose cars were washed); and (2) the average of all the numbers that it was given (i.e., the average waiting time for the customers, expressed in seconds).

determine the actions of each object

From an examination of the pseudocode, we can catalog the various actions of the objects one at a time. From this catalog we can later determine the list of methods for each class.

BooleanSource. During each simulated second, the `BooleanSource` provides us with a single boolean value indicating whether a new customer has arrived during that second. A `true` value indicates that a customer has arrived; a `false` indicates that no customer arrived. With this in mind, we propose two methods: a constructor and a method called `query`.

The constructor for the `BooleanSource` has one argument, which is the probability that the `BooleanSource` returns `true` to a query. The probability is expressed as a decimal value between 0 and 1. For example, suppose that our program uses the name `arrival` for its `BooleanSource`, and we want to simulate the situation where a new customer arrives during 1% of the simulated seconds. Then our program would have the declaration:

```
BooleanSource arrival = new BooleanSource(0.01);
```

The second method of the `BooleanSource` can be called to obtain the next value in the `BooleanSource`'s sequence of values. Here is the specification:

- **query (method of the BooleanSource)**
  ```
  public boolean query( )
  ```
  Get the next value from this `BooleanSource`.

  Returns:
  The return value is either `true` or `false`, with the probability of a `true` value being determined by the argument that was given to the constructor.

There are several ways of generating random boolean values, but at this specification stage we don't need to worry about such implementation details.

Averager. The averager has a constructor that initializes the averager so that it is ready to accept numbers. The numbers will be given to the averager one at a time through a method called `addNumber`. For example, suppose that our averager is named `waitTimes`, and the next number in the sequence is 10. Then we will activate `waitTimes.addNumber(10)`; the averager also has two methods to retrieve its results: One method returns the average of all the numbers that have been given to the averager, and the other method returns the count of how many numbers the averager has been given. Here are short versions of the four specifications:

- **Constructor for the Averager**
  ```
  public Averager( )
  ```
  Initialize an `Averager` so that it is ready to accept numbers.

- **addNumber**
  ```
  public void addNumber(double value)
  ```
  Give another number to this `Averager`.

◆ **average**

    public double average( )

The return value is the average of all numbers given to this `Averager`.

◆ **howManyNumbers**

    public int howManyNumbers( )

Provide a count of how many numbers have been given to this `Averager`.

Notice that the argument to `addNumber` is actually a double number rather than an integer. This will allow us to use the averager in situations where the sequence is more than just whole numbers. Also, the class will have some limitations (for example, the total count of numbers given to an averager cannot exceed `Integer.MAX_VALUE`). But we'll deal with those limitations during the implementation stage.

Washer. The simulation program requires one washer object. This washer is initialized with its constructor, and each time another second passes, the simulation program indicates the passage of a second to the washer. This suggests the following constructor and method:

◆ **Constructor for the Washer**

    public Washer(int s)

Initialize a `Washer`.

Postcondition:

This `Washer` has been initialized so that it takes s seconds to complete one wash cycle.

◆ **reduceRemainingTime**

    public void reduceRemainingTime( )

Reduce the remaining time in the current wash cycle by one second.

Postcondition:

If a car is being washed, then the remaining time in the current wash cycle has been reduced by one second.

The other two responsibilities of a washer are to tell the simulation program whether the washing mechanism is currently available and to begin the washing of a new car. These responsibilities are accomplished with two methods:

◆ **startWashing**

    public void startWashing( )

Start a wash cycle for this `Washer`.

Precondition:

`isBusy( )` is `false`.

Postcondition:

This `Washer` has started simulating one wash cycle.

Throws: `IllegalStateException`

Indicates that this `Washer` is busy.

- **isBusy**
    ```
    public boolean isBusy( )
    ```
    Determine whether this `Washer` is currently busy.

    Returns:
    `true` if this `Washer` is busy (in a wash cycle); otherwise `false`.

Car Wash Simulation—Implementing the Car Wash Classes

We have completed a specification for the three new classes that will be used in the car wash simulation. We'll implement these three classes in separate files: `BooleanSource.java` (Figure 7.6 on page 340), `Averager.java` (Figure 7.7 on page 341) and `Washer.java` (Figure 7.8 on page 343). All three are part of the package `edu.colorado.simulations`. The implementations are straightforward, but we'll provide a little discussion.

Implementation of the BooleanSource. The `BooleanSource` class has one instance variable, `probability`, which stores the probability that an activation of `query` will return `true`. The implementation of the `query` method first uses the `Math.random` method to generate a random number between 0 and 1 (including 0, but not 1). Hence, if the instance variable `probability` is the desired probability of returning `true`, then `query` should return `true` provided the following relationship holds: `Math.random( ) < probability`.

For example, suppose we want a 10% chance that `query` returns `true`, so that `probability` is 0.1. If `random` returns a value less than 0.1, then `query` will return `true`. The chance that `rand` returns a value less than 0.1 is 10%, since 0.1 marks a point that is 10% of the way through `random`'s output range. Therefore, there is about a 10% chance that `Math.random( ) < probability` will be `true`. It is this boolean expression that is used in the return statement of `query`.

Implementation of the Averager. The implementation of the averager is a direct implementation of the definition of "average" and some straightforward details. The class has two instance variables: one to keep track of how many numbers the averager has been given, and another to keep track of the sum of all those numbers. When the `average` method is activated, the method returns the average calculated as the sum of all the numbers divided by the count of how many numbers the averager was given.

Notice that the averager does *not* need to keep track of all the numbers individually. It is sufficient to keep track of the sum of the numbers and the count of how many numbers there were. However, the specification does indicate some limitations connected with possible arithmetic overflows.

Implementation of the Washer. The `Washer` class has two instance variables. The first instance variable, `secondsForWash`, is the number of seconds needed for one complete wash cycle. This variable is set by the constructor and remains constant thereafter. The second instance variable, `washTimeLeft`, keeps track of how many seconds until the current wash is completed. This value can be zero if the washer is not currently busy.

The washer's `reduceRemainingTime` method is activated to subtract one second from the remaining washing time. So, the `reduceRemainingTime` method checks whether a car is currently being washed. And if there is a car being washed, then the method subtracts one from `washTimeLeft`.

The washer's `isBusy` method simply checks whether `washTimeLeft` is greater than zero. If so, then there is a car in the washing mechanism. Otherwise, the washing mechanism is ready for another car.

When the car-washing mechanism is not busy, the `startWashing` method may be activated to start another car through the washer. The method starts the wash by setting `washTimeLeft` equal to `secondsForWash`.

Car Wash Simulation—Implementing the Simulation Method

We can now implement the simulation pseudocode from Figure 7.5 on page 335. The implementation is shown as a method in Figure 7.9 on page 345. This method could be activated from a main program that interacts with a user. There are three parameters for the method: (1) an integer, `washTime`, which is the amount of time needed to wash one car; (2) a double number, `arrivalProb`, which is the probability that a customer arrives during any particular second; and (3) another integer, `totalTime`, which is the total number of seconds to be simulated. The method writes a copy of its parameters to the screen and then runs the simulation.

Most of the simulation work is carried out in the large for-loop, where the local variable `currentSecond` runs from 1 to `totalTime`. This loop parallels the large loop from the original pseudocode (Step 2 in Figure 7.5 on page 335).

After the loop finishes, the simulation method obtains two pieces of information from the averager and writes these items to `System.out`.

Self-Test Exercises

6. Can a single program use both a stack and a queue?

7. Describe at least one assumption we made about the real-world car wash in order to make the simulation more manageable.

8. Use short sentences to describe the three main actions that occur during each second of simulated time in the car wash simulation.

9. When the car wash simulation finishes, there could still be some numbers in the queue. What do these numbers represent from the real world? (For a method of handling these leftover numbers, see Programming Project 8 on page 370.)

10. Our method in Figure 7.9 on page 345 uses an averager, and the method does not check that we don't give the averager more than `Integer` `MAX_VALUE` numbers. Is this a potential problem for a long simulation?

| **FIGURE 7.6** | Specification and Implementation of the BooleanSource Class |

Class BooleanSource

❖ **public class BooleanSource from the package edu.colorado.simulations**
    A `BooleanSource` provides a random sequence of `boolean` values.

Specification

• **Constructor for the BooleanSource**
    `public BooleanSource(double p)`
    Initialize a `BooleanSource`.
    Precondition: $0 <= p$ and $p <= 1$.
    Postcondition:
        This `BooleanSource` has been initialized so that p is the approximate probability of returning `true` in any subsequent activation of the `query` method.
    Throws: `IllegalArgumentException`
        Indicates that p is outside of its legal range.

• **query (method of the BooleanSource)**
    `public boolean query( )`
    Get the next value from this `BooleanSource`.
    Returns:
        The return value is either `true` or `false`, with the probability of a `true` value being determined by the argument that was given to the constructor.

Implementation

```
//  File: BooleanSource.java from the package edu.colorado.simulations
//  Complete documentation is listed above, or available from the BooleanSource link at
//     http://www.cs.colorado.edu/~main/docs/

package edu.colorado.simulations;
public class BooleanSource
{
    private double probability; // The probability of query( ) returning true.

    public BooleanSource(double p)
    {
        if ((p < 0) || (1 < p))
            throw new IllegalArgumentException("Illegal p: " + p);
        probability = p;
    }

    public boolean query( )
    {
        return (Math.random( ) < probability);
    }
}
```

FIGURE 7.7	Specification and Implementation for the Averager Class

Class Averager

❖ **public class Averager from the package edu.colorado.simulations**

An Averager computes an average of a sequence of numbers.

Specification

◆ **Constructor for the Averager**

```
public Average( )
```

Initialize an Averager.

Postcondition:

This Averager has been initialized and is ready to accept a sequence of numbers.

◆ **addNumber**

```
public void addNumber(double value)
```

Give another number to this Averager.

Parameters:

value – the next number to give to this Averager

Precondition:

howManyNumbers( ) < Integer.MAX_VALUE.

Postcondition:

This Averager has accepted value as the next number in the sequence of numbers.

Throws: IllegalStateException

Indicates that howManyNumbers( ) is Integer.MAX_VALUE.

◆ **average**

```
public double average( )
```

Provide an average of all numbers given to this Averager.

Returns:

the average of all the numbers that have been given to this Averager

Note:

If howManyNumbers( ) is zero, then the answer is Double.NaN ("not a number") because the average of an empty set of numbers is not defined. The answer may also be Double.POSITIVE_INFINITY or Double.NEGATIVE_INFINITY if there has been an arithmetic overflow during the summing of all the numbers.

◆ **howManyNumbers**

```
public int howManyNumbers( )
```

Provide a count of how many numbers have been given to this Averager.

Returns:

the count of how many numbers have been given to this Averager

(continued)

(FIGURE 7.7 continued)

Implementation

```
// File: Averager.java from the package edu.colorado.simulations
// Complete documentation is available on page 341 or from the Averager link in
//    http://www.cs.colorado.edu/~main/docs/

package edu.colorado.simulations;

public class Averager
{
    private int count;   // How many numbers have been given to this averager
    private double sum;  // Sum of all the numbers given to this averager

    public Averager( )
    {
        count = 0;
        sum = 0;
    }

    public void addNumber(double value)
    {
        if (count == Integer.MAX_VALUE)
            throw new IllegalStateException("Too many numbers.");
        count++;
        sum += value;
    }

    public double average( )
    {
        if (count == 0)
            return Double.NaN;
        else
            return sum/count;
    }

    public int howManyNumbers( )
    {
        return count;
    }
}
```

FIGURE 7.8	Specification and Implementation for the Washer Class

Class Washer

❖ **public class Washer from the package edu.colorado.simulations**
   A Washer simulates a simple washing machine.

Specification

◆ **Constructor for the Washer**
   public Washer(int s)
   Initialize a Washer.

   Parameter:
   s – the number of seconds required for one wash cycle of this Washer

   Postcondition:
   This Washer has been initialized so that it takes s seconds to complete one wash cycle.

◆ **isBusy**
   public boolean isBusy( )
   Determine whether this Washer is currently busy.

   Returns:
   true if this Washer is busy (in a wash cycle); otherwise false

◆ **reduceRemainingTime**
   public void reduceRemainingTime( )
   Reduce the remaining time in the current wash cycle by one second.

   Postcondition:
   If a car is being washed, then the remaining time in the current wash cycle has been reduced by one second.

◆ **startWashing**
   public void startWashing( )
   Start a wash cycle for this Washer.

   Precondition:
   isBusy( ) is false.

   Postcondition:
   This Washer has started simulating one wash cycle. Therefore, isBusy( ) will return true until the required number of simulated seconds has passed.

   Throws: IllegalStateException
   Indicates that this Washer is busy.

(continued)

(FIGURE 7.8 continued)

Implementation

```
// File: Washer.java from the package edu.colorado.simulations
// Complete documentation is available on page 343 or from the Washer link in
//   http://www.cs.colorado.edu/~main/docs/

package edu.colorado.simulations;

public class Washer
{
    private int secondsForWash;  // Seconds for a single wash
    private int washTimeLeft;     // Seconds until this washer is no longer busy

    public Washer(int s)
    {
        secondsForWash = s;
        washTimeLeft = 0;
    }

    public boolean isBusy( )
    {
        return (washTimeLeft > 0);
    }

    public void reduceRemainingTime( )
    {
        if (washTimeLeft > 0)
            washTimeLeft--;
    }

    public void startWashing( )
    {
        if (washTimeLeft > 0)
            throw new IllegalStateException("Washer is already busy.");
        washTimeLeft = secondsForWash;
    }

}
```

FIGURE 7.9	Specification and Implementation of the Car Wash Method

Specification

- **carWashSimulate**

  ```
  public static void carWashSimulate
  (int washTime, double arrivalProb, int TotalTime)
  ```
  Simulate the running of a car washer for a specified amount of time.

  Parameters:
  washTime – the number of seconds required to wash one car
  arrivalProb – the probability of a customer arriving in any second, for example 0.1 is 10%
  totalTime – the total number of seconds for the simulation

  Precondition:
  washTime and totalTime are positive; arrivalProb lies in the range 0 to 1.

  Postcondition:
  The method has simulated a car wash where washTime is the number of seconds needed to wash one car, arrivalProb is the probability of a customer arriving in any second, and totalTime is the total number of seconds for the simulation. Before the simulation, the method has written its three parameters to System.out. After the simulation, the method has written two pieces of information to System.out: (1) the number of cars washed, and (2) the average waiting time for customers that had their cars washed. (Customers that are still in the queue are not included in this average.)

  Throws: IllegalArgumentException
  Indicates that one of the arguments violates the precondition.

Sample Output

The carWashSimulate method could be part of an interactive or noninteractive Java program. For example, a noninteractive program might activate

```
carWashSimulate(240, 0.0025, 6000);
```

which can produce this output:

```
Seconds to wash one car: 240
Probability of customer arrival during a second: 0.0025
Total simulation seconds: 6000
Customers served: 13
Average wait: 111.07692307682308 sec
```

The actual output may be different because of variations in the random number generator that is used in the BooleanSource.

(continued)

(FIGURE 7.9 continued)

Implementation

```
public static void carWashSimulate
(int washTime, double arrivalProb, int totalTime)
{
   IntQueue arrivalTimes = new IntQueue( );
   int next;
   BooleanSource arrival = new BooleanSource(arrivalProb);
   Washer machine = new Washer(washTime);
   Averager waitTimes = new Averager( );
   int currentSecond;

   // Write the parameters to System.out.
   System.out.println("Seconds to wash one car: " + washTime);
   System.out.print("Probability of customer arrival during a second: ");
   System.out.println(arrivalProb);
   System.out.println("Total simulation seconds: " + totalTime);

   // Check the precondition:
   if (washTime <= 0 || arrivalProb < 0 || arrivalProb > 1 || totalTime < 0)
      throw new IllegalArgumentException("Values out of range.");

   for (currentSecond = 0; currentSecond < totalTime; currentSecond++)
   {   // Simulate the passage of one second of time.

      // Check whether a new customer has arrived.
      if (arrival.query( ))
         arrivalTimes.insert(currentSecond);

      // Check whether we can start washing another car.
      if ((!machine.isBusy( ))  &&  (!arrivalTimes.isEmpty( )))
      {
         next = arrivalTimes.getFront( );
         waitTimes.addNumber(currentSecond - next);
         machine.startWashing( );
      }

      // Subtract one second from the remaining time in the current wash cycle.
      machine.reduceRemainingTime( );
   }

   // Write the summary information about the simulation.
   System.out.println("Customers served: " + waitTimes.howManyNumbers( ));
   if (waitTimes.howManyNumbers( ) > 0)
      System.out.println("Average wait: " + waitTimes.average( ) + " sec");
}
```

7.3   IMPLEMENTATIONS OF THE QUEUE ADT

A queue seems conceptually simpler than a stack because we notice queues in our everyday lives. However, the implementation of a queue, while similar to that of a stack, is more complicated than the implementation of a stack. As was the case with the stack class, we will give two implementations of our queue class: an implementation that stores the items in an array, and an implementation using a linked list. Each implementation will be an `ObjectQueue`, but as we discussed earlier, we could change `Object` to any of the Java primitive types to obtain other queues, such as an `IntQueue`.

Array Implementation of a Queue

As we did with the stack class, we will implement the queue class as a partially filled array. With a queue, we add items at one end of the array and remove them from the other end. Hence, we will be accessing the used portion of the array at both ends, increasing the size of the used portion at one end and decreasing the size of the used portion at the other end. This differs from our use of a partially filled array for a stack, in that the stack accessed just one end of the array.

Because we now need to keep track of both ends of the used portion of the array, we will have *two* variables to keep track of how much of the array is used: One variable, called `front`, indicates the first index currently in use, and one variable, called `rear`, indicates the last index currently in use. If `data` is the array name, then the queue items will be in the array components:

keeping track of both ends of the partially filled array

    data[front], data[front + 1], ... data[rear].

To add an item we increment `rear` by one, and then store the new item in the component `data[rear]`, where `rear` is now one larger than it was before. To get the next item from the queue, we retrieve `data[front]` and then increment `front` by one, so that `data[front]` is then the item that used to be second.

There is one problem with this plan. The variable `rear` is incremented but never decremented. Hence, it will quickly reach the end of the array. At that point, it seems as if adding more items requires the array to increase capacity. Yet, there is likely to be room in the array. In a normal application, the variable `front` would also be incremented from time to time (when items are removed from the queue). This will free up the array locations with index values less than `front`. There are several ways to reuse these freed locations.

One straightforward approach for using the freed array locations is to maintain all the queue items so that `front` is always equal to 0 (the first index of the array). When `data[0]` is removed, we move all the items in the array down one location so the value of `data[1]` is moved to `data[0]`, and then all other items are also moved down one. This approach will work, but it is inefficient. Every time we remove an item from the queue, we must move every item in the queue. Fortunately, there is a better approach.

circular array

We do not need to move all the array elements. When the `rear` index reaches the end of the array, we can simply start using the available locations at the front of the array. One way to think of this arrangement is to think of the array as being bent into a circle so that the first component of the array is immediately after the last component of the array. In this way, the successor of the last array index is the first array index. In this circular arrangement, the free index positions are always "right after" `data[rear]`.

For example, suppose that we have a queue of characters with a capacity of 5, and the queue currently contains three items `'A'`, `'B'`, and `'C'`. Perhaps these values are stored with `front` equal to 0 and `rear` equal to 2, as shown here:

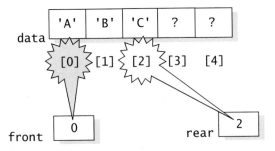

The question marks indicate unused spots in the array.

Let's remove two items (the `'A'` and `'B'`), and add two more items to the rear of this queue, perhaps the characters `'D'` and `'E'`. The result is shown here:

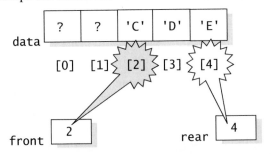

At this point, `front` is 2, `rear` is 4, and the queue items range from `data[2]` to `data[4]`. Suppose that now we add another character, `'F'`, to the queue. The new item cannot go after `rear`, since we have hit the end of the array. Instead, we go to the front of the array, adding the new `'F'` at location `data[0]`, as shown here:

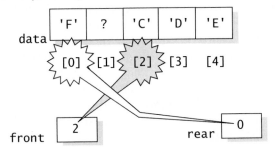

This may look peculiar, with the `rear` index of 0 being *before* the `front` index of 2. But keep in mind the *circular* view of the array. With this view, the queue's items start at `data[front]` and continue forward. If you reach the end of the array, then come back to `data[0]`, and keep going until you find the rear. It may help to actually view the array as bent into a circle, with the final array element attached back to the front, as shown here:

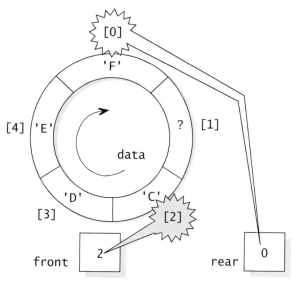

An array used in this way is called a **circular array**.

We now turn to a detailed presentation of our queue using the idea of a circular array. The specification and implementation for our queue are given in Figure 7.10 on page 351. The queue's items are held in an array, `data`, which is a private instance variable. The private instance variables `front` and `rear` hold the indexes for the front and the rear of the queue, as we have discussed. Whenever the queue is nonempty, the items begin at the location `data[front]`, continuing forward in the array. If the items reach the end of the array, then they continue at the first location, `data[0]`. In any case, `data[rear]` is the last item in the queue. One other private instance variable, `manyItems`, records the number of items that are in the queue. We will use `manyItems` to check whether the queue is empty, and also to produce the value returned by the `size` method.

The `Queue` class implementation also has a new feature: a *private* method called `nextIndex`. This is a method that we think will be useful for the implementation, but it is not part of the public specification. We don't want other programmers to use this method; it is just for our own use in implementing a specific kind of queue. A private method such as this is called a **helper method.**

the nextIndex helper method

The `nextIndex` helper method allows us to step easily through the array one index after another with wraparound at the end. The activation of `nextIndex(i)` usually returns `i+1`, with one exception. When `i` is equal to the last index of the array, `nextIndex(i)` returns zero (the first index of the array).

△   **TIP**

Programming Tip: Use Helper Methods to Improve Clarity

When a class requires some small computation that is likely to be used several times, consider implementing the computation with a helper method (that is, a private method). This will improve the clarity of your other code. Because a helper method is private, it does not need to be included in the documentation that's intended for other programmers, but you may write a precondition/postcondition contract for your own use.

The remaining implementation details are a straightforward implementation of a circular array, following this invariant:

Invariant of the Queue ADT (Array Version)

1. The number of items in the queue is stored in the instance variable `manyItems`.

2. For a nonempty queue, the items are stored in a circular array beginning at `data[front]` and continuing through `data[rear]`.

3. For an empty queue, `manyItems` is zero and `data` is a reference to an array, but we are not using any of the array and we don't care about `front` and `rear`.

---

ensureCapacity implementation

The `ensureCapacity` method requires a bit of thought. The implementation starts by checking whether the current length of the `data` array is at least as big as the requested capacity. If so, then the array is already big enough, and we return with no work. Otherwise, we must allocate a new larger array, and copy the elements from the original array to the new array. The allocation and copying are handled with three cases:

- If `manyItems` is zero, then we just allocate the new, larger array. There are no items to copy.

- If `manyItems` is nonzero, and `front` ≤ `rear`, then we allocate the new array and copy `data[front]` ... `data[rear]` into the new array. This is not difficult because all the items are contiguous. We copy them into the new array with a single activation of `System.arraycopy`.

- If `manyItems` is nonzero, and `front` > `rear`, then we allocate the new array, but it takes more care to copy the items into the new array. The items at the front of the queue are located at `data[front]` to the end of `data`. These items are followed by the items from `data[0]` to `data[rear]`. These two segments of items are copied into the new array by two separate activations of `System.arraycopy`, as shown at the top of the next page.

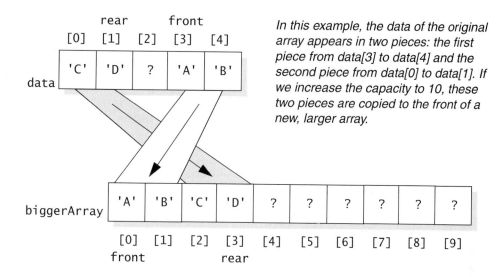

In this example, the data of the original array appears in two pieces: the first piece from data[3] to data[4] and the second piece from data[0] to data[1]. If we increase the capacity to 10, these two pieces are copied to the front of a new, larger array.

The `trimToSize` method has three similar cases that are similar to the `ensureCapacity` method.

All the methods and their specifications are given in Figure 7.10.

FIGURE 7.10 | Specification and Implementation of the Array Version of the Queue Class

Class ObjectQueue

❖ **public class** Object**Queue from the package edu.colorado.collections**

An ObjectQueue is a queue of references to objects.

Limitations:

(1) The capacity of one of these queues can change after it's created, but the maximum capacity is limited by the amount of free memory on the machine. The constructors, `clone`, `ensureCapacity`, `insert`, and `trimToSize`, will result in an `OutOfMemoryError` when free memory is exhausted.

(2) A queue's capacity cannot exceed the largest integer 2,147,483,647 (`Integer.MAX_VALUE`). Any attempt to create a larger capacity results in failure due to an arithmetic overflow.

(continued)

(FIGURE 7.10 continued)

Specification

- **Constructor for the ⟨Object⟩Queue**
  ```
  public ObjectQueue( )
  ```
  Initialize an empty queue with an initial capacity of 10. Note that the `insert` method works efficiently (without needing more memory) until this capacity is reached.

  Postcondition:
  This queue is empty and has an initial capacity of 10.

  Throws: `OutOfMemoryError`
  Indicates insufficient memory for: `new Object[10]`.

- **Second Constructor for the ⟨Object⟩Queue**
  ```
  public ObjectQueue(int initialCapacity)
  ```
  Initialize an empty queue with a specified initial capacity. Note that the `insert` method works efficiently (without needing more memory) until this capacity is reached.

  Parameters:
  `initialCapacity` – the initial capacity of this queue

  Precondition:
  `initialCapacity` is non-negative.

  Postcondition:
  This queue is empty and has the given initial capacity.

  Throws: `IllegalArgumentException`
  Indicates that `initialCapacity` is negative.

  Throws: `OutOfMemoryError`
  Indicates insufficient memory for: `new Object[initialCapacity]`.

- **clone**
  ```
  public Object clone( )
  ```
  Generate a copy of this queue.

  Returns:
  The return value is a copy of this queue. Subsequent changes to the copy will not affect the original, nor vice versa. The return value must be typecast to an ⟨Object⟩Queue before it is used.

  Throws: `OutOfMemoryError`
  Indicates insufficient memory for creating the clone.

- **ensureCapacity**
  ```
  public void ensureCapacity(int minimumCapacity)
  ```
  Change the current capacity of this queue.

  Parameters:
  `minimumCapacity` – the new capacity for this queue

  Postcondition:
  This queue's capacity has been changed to at least `minimumCapacity`. If the capacity was already at or greater than `minimumCapacity`, then the capacity is left unchanged.

  Throws: `OutOfMemoryError`
  Indicates insufficient memory for: `new Object[minimumCapacity]`.　　　　　*(continued)*

(FIGURE 7.10 continued)

◆ **getCapacity**
```
public int getCapacity( )
```
Accessor method to determine the current capacity of this queue. The `insert` method works efficiently (without needing more memory) until this capacity is reached.

Returns:
the current capacity of this queue

◆ **getFront—insert—isEmpty—size**
```
public Object getFront( )
public void insert(Object )
public boolean isEmpty( )
public int size( )
```
These are the standard queue specifications from Figure 7.2 on page 328.

◆ **trimToSize**
```
public void trimToSize( )
```
Reduce the current capacity of this queue to its actual size (i.e., the number of items it contains).

Postcondition:
This queue's capacity has been changed to its current size.

Throws: `OutOfMemoryError`
Indicates insufficient memory for altering the capacity.

Implementation

```
// File: ObjectQueue.java from the package edu.colorado.collections
// Complete documentation is available on pages 351-353 or from the ObjectQueue link in
//    http://www.cs.colorado.edu/~main/docs/

package edu.colorado.collections;
import java.util.NoSuchElementException;

public class ObjectQueue implements Cloneable
{
    // Invariant of the ObjectQueue class:
    //    1. The number of items in the queue is in the instance variable manyItems.
    //    2. For a nonempty queue, the items are stored in a circular array beginning at
    //       data[front] and continuing through data[rear].
    //    3. For an empty queue, manyItems is zero and data is a reference to an array, but
    //       we don't care about front and rear.
    private Object[ ] data;
    private int manyItems;
    private int front;
    private int rear;
```

(continued)

(FIGURE 7.10 continued)

```
public ObjectQueue( )
{
    final int INITIAL_CAPACITY = 10;
    manyItems = 0;
    data = new Object[INITIAL_CAPACITY];
    // We don't care about front and rear for an empty queue.
}

public ObjectQueue(int initialCapacity)
{
    if (initialCapacity < 0)
        throw new IllegalArgumentException
        ("initialCapacity is negative: " + initialCapacity);
    manyItems = 0;
    data = new Object[initialCapacity];
    // We don't care about front and rear for an empty queue.
}

public Object clone( )
{   // Clone an ObjectQueue.
    ObjectQueue answer;

    try
    {
        answer = (ObjectQueue) super.clone( );
    }
    catch (CloneNotSupportedException e)
    {
        // This exception should not occur. But if it does, it would probably indicate a
        // programming error that made super.clone unavailable.
        // The most common error would be forgetting the "Implements Cloneable"
        // clause at the start of this class.
        throw new RuntimeException
        ("This class does not implement Cloneable.");
    }

    answer.data = (Object[ ]) data.clone( );

    return answer;
}
```

(continued)

(FIGURE 7.10 continued)

```java
public void ensureCapacity(int minimumCapacity)
{
   Object biggerArray[ ];
   int n1, n2;

   if (data.length >= minimumCapacity)
      // No change needed.
      return;
   else if (manyItems == 0)
      // Just increase the size of the array because the queue is empty.
      data = new Object[minimumCapacity];
   else if (front <= rear)
   {  // Create larger array and copy data[front]...data[rear] into it.
      biggerArray = new Object[minimumCapacity];
      System.arraycopy(data, front, biggerArray, front, manyItems);
      data = biggerArray;
   }
   else
   {  // Create a bigger array, but be careful about copying items into it. The queue items
      //  occur in two segments. The first segment goes from data[front] to the end of the
      //  array, and the second segment goes from data[0] to data[rear]. The variables n1
      //  and n2 will be set to the number of items in these two segments. We will copy
      //  these segments to biggerArray[0...manyItems-1].
      biggerArray = new Object[minimumCapacity];
      n1 = data.length - front;
      n2 = rear + 1;
      System.arraycopy(data, front, biggerArray, 0, n1);
      System.arraycopy(data, 0, biggerArray, n1, n2);
      front = 0;
      rear = manyItems-1;
      data = biggerArray;
   }
}


public int getCapacity( )
{
   return data.length;
}
```

(continued)

(FIGURE 7.10 continued)

```java
public Object getFront( )
{
    Object answer;

    if (manyItems == 0)
        throw new NoSuchElementException("Queue underflow.");
    answer = data[front];
    front = nextIndex(front);
    manyItems--;
    return answer;
}

public void insert(Object item)
{
    if (manyItems == data.length)
    {
        // Double the capacity and add 1; this works even if manyItems is 0. However, in
        // case that manyItems*2 + 1 is beyond Integer.MAX_VALUE, there will be an
        // arithmetic overflow and the bag will fail.
        ensureCapacity(manyItems*2 + 1);
    }

    if (manyItems == 0)
    {
        front = 0;
        rear = 0;
    }
    else
        rear = nextIndex(rear);

    data[rear] = item;
    manyItems++;
}

public boolean isEmpty( )
{
    return (manyItems == 0);
}

private int nextIndex(int i)
{
    || See the answer to Self-Test Exercise 13.
}
```

(continued)

(FIGURE 7.10 continued)

```
public int size( )
{
    return manyItems;
}

public void trimToSize( )
{
    ‖  See the answer to Self-Test Exercise 14.
}
}
```

Linked List Implementation of a Queue

A queue can also be implemented as a linked list. One end of the linked list is the front, and the other end is the rear of the queue. The approach uses two references to nodes: One refers to the first node (`front`), and the other refers to the last node (`rear`), as diagrammed here for a queue with three items:

Figure 7.11 on page 359 shows the specification and implementation for a queue class that is implemented in this way. The class, called `ObjectLinked-Queue`, has no capacity problems, so it is considerably simpler than the array version. Here is the invariant that we use in the linked list implementation:

Invariant of the Queue ADT (Linked List Version)

1. The number of items in the queue is stored in the instance variable `manyNodes`.

2. The items in the queue are stored in a linked list, with the front of the queue stored at the head node, and the rear of the queue stored at the final node.

3. For a nonempty queue, the instance variable `front` is the head reference of the linked list of items, and the instance variable `rear` is the tail reference of the linked list. For an empty queue, both `front` and `rear` are the null reference.

Each of the queue methods (except the constructors) may assume that the invariant is valid when the method is activated, and each method must ensure that the invariant is valid when the method finishes its work. Notice that the invariant includes an instance variable called manyNodes to keep track of the total number of items in the queue. We could get by without manyNodes, but its presence makes the size method quicker.

Most of the methods' work will be accomplished by the methods of our Node class that we developed in Chapters 4 and 5 (with a complete implementation in Appendix E). We'll look at the implementations of two queue methods—insert and getFront—in some detail.

The insert method. The insert operation adds a node at the rear of the queue. For example, suppose we start with three items shown here:

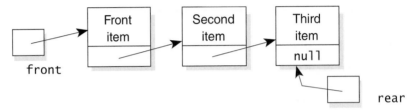

After adding a fourth item, the list would look like this:

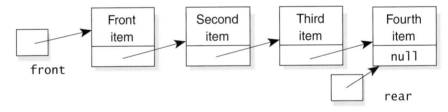

The new fourth item is placed in a newly created node at the end of the list. Normally, this is accomplished by two statements:

```
Node.addNodeAfter(rear, item);
rear = rear.getLink( );
```

To add the first item, we need a slightly different approach because the empty list has only null references for the front and rear. In this case we should add the new item at the front of the list, and then assign rear to also refer to the new node, as shown in this code:

```
if (isEmpty( ))
{   // Insert first item.
    front = new Node(item, null);
    rear = front;
}
else
{   // Insert an item that is not the first.
    rear.addNodeAfter(item);
    rear = rear.getLink( );
}
```

In fact, this code is most of the `insert` method. The only other work is to add one to the `manyNodes` instance variable.

The getFront method.   The `getFront` method removes a node from the front of the queue. For example, suppose we start with this queue:

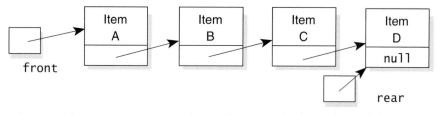

In this example, the `getFront` method will return the item that is labeled "Item A." This item will also be removed from the queue, so that when `getFront` returns, the list will have only three items shown here:

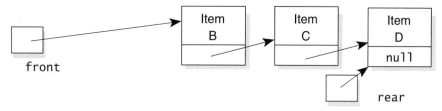

The implementation of `getFront` uses the technique from page 179 to remove a node from the head. Most of the work is carried out by these statements:

```
Object answer;
...
answer = front.getData( );
front = front.getLink( );
...
return answer;
```

The only other work in the complete implementation is to check the precondition (that the queue has some items), and if we remove the final item of the queue, then we must also set `rear` to null.

FIGURE 7.11	Specification and Implementation for the Linked List Version of the Queue Class

Class ObjectLinkedQueue

❖ **public class** Object**LinkedQueue from the package edu.colorado.collections**

An ObjectLinkedQueue is a queue of references to objects.

Limitations:

Beyond `Int.MAX_VALUE` items, `size` is wrong.

(continued)

(FIGURE 7.11 continued)

Specification

- **Constructor for the** $\boxed{\text{Object}}$**LinkedQueue**
    ```
    public Object LinkedQueue( )
    ```
    Initialize an empty queue.
    Postcondition:
    This queue is empty.

- **clone**
    ```
    public Object clone( )
    ```
    Generate a copy of this queue.
    Returns:
    The return value is a copy of this queue. Subsequent changes to the copy will not affect the original, nor vice versa. The return value must be typecast to an $\boxed{\text{Object}}$Queue before it is used.
    Throws: OutOfMemoryError
    Indicates insufficient memory for creating the clone.

- **getFront—insert—isEmpty—size**
    ```
    public Object getFront( )
    public void insert( )
    public boolean isEmpty( )
    public long size( )
    ```
    These are the standard queue specifications from Figure 7.2 on page 328.

Implementation

```
// File: ObjectLinkedQueue.java from the package edu.colorado.collections
// Complete documentation is written above or is available from the ObjectLinkedQueue link in
//    http://www.cs.colorado.edu/~main/docs/

package edu.colorado.collections;
import java.util.NoSuchElementException;
import edu.colorado.nodes.Node;

public class ObjectLinkedQueue implements Cloneable
{
   // Invariant of the ObjectLinkedQueue class:
   //    1. The number of items in the queue is stored in the instance variable manyNodes.
   //    2. The items in the queue are stored in a linked list, with the front of the queue
   //       stored at the head node, and the rear of the queue at the final node.
   //    3. For a nonempty queue, the instance variable front is the head reference of the
   //       linked list of items and the instance variable rear is the tail reference of the
   //       linked list. For an empty queue, both front and rear are the null reference.
   private int manyNodes;
   Node front;
   Node rear;

   public ObjectLinkedQueue( )
   {
      front = null;
      rear = null;
   }
```

(continued)

(FIGURE 7.11 continued)

```
public Object clone( )
|| See the answer to Self-Test Exercise 15.

public Object getFront( )
{
    Object answer;

    if (manyNodes == 0)
        // NoSuchElementException is from java.util and its constructor has no argument.
        throw new NoSuchElementException("Queue underflow.");
    answer = front.getData( );
    front = front.getLink( );
    manyNodes--;
    if (manyNodes == 0)
        rear = null;
    return answer;
}

public void insert(Object item)
{
    if (isEmpty( ))
    {   // Insert first item.
        front = new Node(item, null);
        rear = front;
    }
    else
    {   // Insert an item that is not the first.
        rear.addNodeAfter(item);
        rear = rear.getLink( );
    }
     manyNodes++;
}

public boolean isEmpty( )
{
    return (manyNodes == 0);
}

public int size( )
{
    return manyNodes;
}

}
```

Pitfall: Forgetting Which End Is Which

PITFALL

We implemented our queue with the front of the queue at the head of the list and the rear of the queue at the tail of the list. As it turns out, this was not an arbitrary choice. Can you see why? What would have happened if we had tried to do things the other way around, as shown in this wrong diagram?

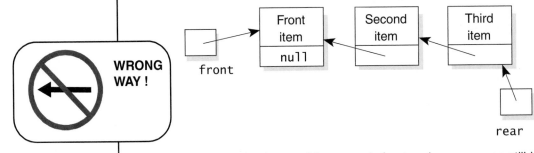

WRONG WAY !

With this wrong arrangement of the queue's front and rear, we can still implement the insert operation, adding a new node at the rear of the queue. We also have easy access to the front item. But it will be difficult to actually *remove* the front item. After the removal, the front must be positioned so that it refers to the next node in the queue, and there is no constant time algorithm to accomplish that (though a linear time algorithm could start at the rear and move through the whole list).

So, keep in mind that it's easy to insert and remove at the head of a linked list, but insertion is the only easy operation at the tail.

Self-Test Exercises

11. Write a new accessor method that returns a copy of the item at the front of the queue. Use the array version of the queue.

12. A programmer who sees our array implementation of a queue shown in Figure 7.10 on page 351 gives us the following suggestion: "Why not eliminate the manyItems instance variable, since the number of items in the queue can be determined from the values of front and rear?" Is there a problem with the suggestion?

13. Implement the nextIndex method for the array version of the queue.

14. Implement the trimToSize method for the array version of the queue.

15. Implement the clone method for the linked list version of the queue. You should use Node.listCopyWithTail.

16. Write a new accessor method that returns a copy of the item at the front of the queue. Use the linked list version of the queue.

17. Write another accessor method that returns a copy of the item at the *rear* of the queue. Use the linked list version of the queue.

18. What goes wrong if we try to put the front of the queue at the tail of the linked list?

7.4   PRIORITY QUEUES

Using a queue ensures that customers are served in the exact order in which they arrive. However, we often want to assign priorities to customers and serve the higher priority customers before those of lower priority. For example, a hospital emergency room will handle the most severely injured patients first, even if they are not "first in line." A computer operating system that keeps a queue of programs waiting to use some resource, such as a printer, may give interactive programs a higher priority than batch processing programs that will not be picked up by the user until the next day, or it might give higher priority to short programs and lower priority to longer programs. A **priority queue** is a data structure that stores items along with a priority for each item. Items are removed in order of priorities. The highest priority item is removed first. If several items have equally high priorities, then the one that was placed in the priority queue first is the one removed first.

For example, suppose the following customer names and priorities are entered into a priority queue in the order given:

higher numbers indicate a higher priority

Ginger Snap, priority 0
Natalie Attired, priority 3
Emanual Transmission, priority 2
Gene Pool, priority 3
Kay Sera, priority 2

The higher numbers indicate a higher priority. The names would be removed in the following order: first Natalie Attired (with the highest priority), then Gene Pool, then Emanual Transmission, then Kay Sera, and finally Ginger Snap (with the lowest priority). Note that both Natalie Attired and Gene Pool have priority 3, which is the highest priority, but Natalie Attired entered the priority queue before Gene Pool, so Natalie Attired is removed before Gene Pool.

Priority Queue ADT—Specification

Figure 7.12 gives the specification for some methods of a priority queue class. When an item is added to a priority queue it is entered with a specified priority, which is an integer in the range 0...highest, where highest is a parameter to the priority queue constructor. Items are removed from the queue in order of priority. For example, suppose highest is 2. In that case, items of priority 2 are removed first. When there are no items of priority 2 left, then items of priority 1 are removed. When there are no items of priority 1 left, then items of priority 0 are removed. Items with the same priority are removed in the order in which they were entered into the priority queue.

| FIGURE 7.12 | Specification of the Key Methods of a `PriorityQueue` Class |

Specification

These are the constructor, `getFront`, and `insert` methods of a priority queue class.

- **Constructor for the `Object`PriorityQueue**

  `public ObjectPriorityQueue(int highest)`

  Initialize an empty priority queue.

  Parameters:

    `highest` – the highest priority allowed in this priority queue

  Precondition:

    `highest >= 0`.

  Postcondition:

    This priority queue is empty.

  Throws: `IllegalArgumentException`

    Indicates that `highest` is negative.

- **getFront**

  `public Object getFront( )`

  Get the highest priority item, removing it from this priority queue.

  Precondition:

    This queue is not empty.

  Postcondition:

    The return value is the highest priority item of this queue, and the item has been removed. If several items have equal priority, then the one that entered first will come out first.

  Throws: `NoSuchElementException`

    Indicates that this queue is empty.

- **insert**

  `public void insert(Object item, int priority)`

  Add a new item to this priority queue.

  Parameters:

    `item` – the item to be added to this queue
    `priority` – the priority of the new item

  Precondition:

    `0 <= priority` and `priority` is no more than the highest priority.

  Postcondition:

    The item has been added to this priority queue.

  Throws: `IllegalArgumentException`

    Indicates an illegal priority.

  Throws: `IllegalArgumentException`

    Indicates insufficient memory for adding a new item to this priority queue.

Priority Queue ADT—An Implementation That Uses an Ordinary Queue

You may have noticed that the priority queue has a lot in common with the ordinary queue. We used the same names for the methods, and only `insert` has an extra parameter for the priority of the new item. This suggests that much of the priority queue work has already been accomplished in the queue implementation—but what is the best way to take advantage of this?

One possibility is to provide the priority queue with an array of ordinary queues. For example, suppose `highest` is 2. In this case, a priority queue can be implemented using three ordinary queues: one to hold the items with priority 0, another queue for the items of priority 1, and a third queue for the lofty items with priority 2. Using this idea, we could implement a priority queue by defining a private instance variable that is an array of ordinary queues, as shown in the highlighted line here:

```
// Import a class for an ordinary Queue:
import edu.colorado.collections.ObjectQueue;

public class ObjectPriorityQueue
{
    private ObjectQueue[ ] queues;
    ...
```

an array of ordinary queues

In this implementation, the constructor allocates the memory for the array of queues. The array has `highest+1` elements (from `queues[0]` through `queues[highest]`).

The items with priority 0 are stored in the ordinary queue called `queues[0]`. Items with priority 1 are stored in `queues[1]`. And so on, up to the ordinary queue called `queues[highest]`. To enter an item into the priority queue with a given priority, all we need to do is enter the item into the correct ordinary queue. For example, suppose that `highest` is 3 and that items are put into the priority queue in the following order:

Ginger Snap, priority 0
Natalie Attired, priority 3
Emanual Transmission, priority 2
Gene Pool, priority 3
Kay Sera, priority 2

each item of the priority queue is placed in one of the ordinary queues

After these items, the array of ordinary queues looks like this:

`queues[3]`: Natalie Attired (at the front), followed by Gene Pool;
`queues[2]`: Emanual Transmission (at the front), followed by Kay Sera;
`queues[1]`: empty;
`queues[0]`: Ginger Snap.

When an item needs to be removed, we move down through the ordinary queues, starting with the highest priority, until we find a nonempty queue. We then remove the front item from this nonempty queue.

With this approach, we can implement a priority queue as an array of ordinary queues and do not need to duplicate a lot of the previous work. In fact, it is possible to implement the priority queue with no instance variables other than the `queues` array. However, some efficiency is gained by adding two other instance variables.

The first is a number, `totalSize`, which keeps track of the total number of items in all of the queues. With this instance variable, a `size` method for the priority queue can operate in constant time.

The second extra instance variable is an integer, which keeps track of the highest priority that is currently in the priority queue. This makes `getFront` more efficient, since without the extra instance variable, we must always search from `highest` downward until we find a nonempty queue. With the extra private instance variable, `getFront` can go straight to the correct queue and remove an item. (Of course, this extra instance variable also must be maintained correctly so that its value is always the priority of the highest item.) We leave the remainder of the details of writing this array-based implementation for Programming Project 4 on page 369.

Priority Queue ADT—A Direct Implementation

If the number of possible priorities is large, then an array of queues might be impractical. In this case, you might think of several alternatives. One possibility is to implement the priority queue as an ordinary linked list, where the data in each node contains two things: the item from the queue, and the priority of that item. This implementation works regardless of how large the priority range is. We will leave the details of the implementation as another exercise (Programming Project 5 on page 369).

Self-Test Exercises

19. Implement the `insert` method of the priority queue. Use the implementation that has an array called `queues` of ordinary queues.

20. Suppose you knew that the number of priorities that will be used in a priority queue application is small, but you do not know what the actual priorities will be. For example, suppose you know that the priorities can be any integer values in the range 0 to 1,000,000, but you also know that there will be at most 25 different numbers used. How might you implement the priority queue as an array of ordinary queues in such a way that the array size is much smaller than 1,000,000?

CHAPTER SUMMARY

- A queue is a First-In/First-Out data structure.
- A queue can be used to buffer data that is being sent from a fast computer component to a slower component. Queues also have many other applications: in simulation programs, operating systems, and elsewhere.
- A queue can be implemented as a partially filled circular array.
- A queue can be implemented as a linked list.
- When implementing a stack, you need keep track of only one end of the list of items, but when implementing a queue, you need to keep track of both ends of the list.
- A priority queue can be implemented as an array of ordinary queues or in various ways as a linked list.

Solutions to Self-Test Exercises ?

1. The operations are insert 'L', insert 'I', insert 'N', insert 'E', followed by four `getFront` operations that return 'L', then 'I', then 'N', then 'E'.

2. Reading input from a keyboard, and sending output to a printer.

3. Read the characters two at a time. Each pair of characters has the first character placed in queue number 1 and the second character placed in queue number 2. After all the reading is done, print all characters from queue number 1 on one line, and print all characters from queue number 2 on a second line.

4. A straightforward approach is to use a second queue, called `line`. As the input is being read, each character is placed in the `line` queue (as well as being placed in the original stack and queue). During the comparison phase, we also keep track of how many characters correctly matched. If a mismatch occurs, we can then print an appropriate amount of the `line` queue as part of the error message.

5. Do not apply the `toUpperCase` method.

6. Yes.

7. We assumed that no more than one customer arrives during any particular second.

8. (a) Sometimes add a new customer to the arrivals queue; (b) sometimes start a new car through the washer; (c) tell the washer that another second has passed.

9. These are cars that arrived during the simulation, but they are still waiting in line at the end of the simulation.

10. The total number of cars can never exceed `Integer.MAX_VALUE` because there is at most one car per second and the total number of seconds in the simulation is an integer.

11. The body of the method should check that `size( ) > 0`, and then return `data[front]`.

12. The main problem is that you cannot tell when the queue is empty because `front` and `rear` have no meaning for an empty queue.

13. Here's the private method with its precondition/postcondition contract:

```
private int NextIndex(int i)
// Precondition: 0 <= i and i < data.length
// Postcondition: If i+1 is data.length,
// then the return value is zero; otherwise
// the return value is i+1.
{
    if (++i == data.length)
        return 0;
    else
        return i;
}
```

14. The `trimToSize` method should handle these cases: (1) If the length of the array is already equal to the number of items, then do no work; (2) if the number of items is zero, then change data to an array of capacity zero, and return with no other work; (3) if (`front<=rear`) then allocate a new array of the correct size and activate `System.arraycopy` once to copy the items from the old array to the new array; (4) if (`front>rear`) then allocate a new array of the correct size and activate `System.arraycopy` twice to copy the two segments into the new array.

The fourth case is similar to the final case of `ensureCapacity`. If you copy the items into the front of the new array, then make sure that you also change `front` and `rear` to reflect the new positions of the items.

15. Here's the extra work after initially setting answer with `super.clone`:

```
Node[ ] cloneInfo;
cloneInfo =
    Node.listCopyWithTail(front);
answer.front = cloneInfo[0];
answer.rear = cloneInfo[1];
return answer;
```

16. The body of the method should check that `size( ) > 0`, and then return with:
```
return front.getData( );
```

17. The body of the method should check that `size( ) > 0`, and then return with:
```
return rear.getData( );
```

18. Removals will be hard to implement.

19. The implementation should check that the priority is valid. Then activate the method `queues[priority].insert[item]`. If you are keeping track of other items (such as the current highest priority and the total size), then those items should be updated, too.

20. Since you know that there are at most 25 different priorities, you could get by with an array of only 25 ordinary queues, plus a second array of integers called `value`. The number in `value[i]` would be the priority of all the items in `queues[i]`. It might also make sense to keep the arrays sorted according to priorities.

PROGRAMMING PROJECTS

1 In Figure 7.3 on page 331 we presented a program that checks a string to see if the letters in the string read the same forward and backward. These strings are called palindromes. Another kind of palindrome is one in which we look at words, rather than letters. A **word-by-word palindrome** is a string of words such that the words read the same forward and backward. For example, the quote "You can cage a swallow, can't you, but, you can't swallow a cage, can you?" is a word-by-word palindrome. Write a program to test an input string and tell whether or not it is a word-by-word palindrome. Consider upper- and lowercase letters to be the same letter. Define a word as any string consisting of only letters or an apostrophe, and bounded at each end with one of the following: a space, a punctuation mark, the beginning of the line, or the end of the line. Your program should have a friendly interface and allow the user to check more lines until the user wishes to quit the program.

In Figure 7.3 on page 331 we presented a program that checks a string to see if the letters in the string read the same forward and backward. The previous exercise performed a similar check using words in place of letters. In this exercise, you are to write a program that runs a similar check using lines rather than words or letters. Write a program that reads in several lines of text and decides if the passage reads the same whether you read the lines top to bottom or bottom to top; this is yet another kind of palindrome. For example, the following poem by J.A. Lindon, reads the same whether you read the lines from top to bottom or from bottom to top:

> *As I was passing near the jail*
> *I met a man, but hurried by.*
> *His face was ghastly, grimly pale.*
> *He had a gun. I wondered why.*
> *He had. A gun? I wondered...why,*
> *His face was ghastly! Grimly pale,*
> *I met a man but hurried by,*
> *As I was passing near the jail.*

Consider upper- and lowercase versions of a letter to be the same letter. Consider word boundaries to be significant, so for example, the words in the first line must read the same as the words in the last line in order to pass the test (as opposed to just the letters reading the same); however, consider all word delimiters as being equivalent; i.e., a punctuation mark, any number of spaces, the beginning or end of a line, or any combination of these are all considered to be equivalent. The end of the passage should be marked by a line containing only the word "end," spelled with any combination of upper- and lowercase letters, and possibly with blanks before and/or after it. Your program should have a friendly interface and allow the user to check more passages until the user wishes to quit the program. Note that to test your program, you need not use such well-constructed poems. Your program will check any passage, regardless of its literary merit.

3 Enhance the car wash simulation method in Figure 7.9 on page 345 so that it has the following additional property. There is an additional parameter, which is a maximum length for the queue. When the queue gets as long as this maximum, any customer who arrives will leave without entering the queue (because she or he does not want to wait that long). There should also be one additional simulation result that is printed. In addition to the output shown in Figure 7.9, the method also prints the number of simulated customers who left because the queue was too long. Embed the method in a program that allows the user to repeat simulations with different arguments until the user says she or he wishes to quit the program.

4 Give a complete implementation of a priority queue using an array of ordinary queues. For your ordinary queue, use the version from `edu.colorado.collections.ObjectQueue` in Figure 7.10 on page 351.

5 Give a complete implementation of a priority queue, using the idea from the direct implementation on page 366.

6 In this chapter we gave a linked list implementation of a queue. This implementation used two references, called `front` and `rear`, to refer to the front and the rear nodes of the queue (linked list). A **circular linked list** is similar to a regular linked list, except that the link field in the "last node" refers back to the "first node." (Of course, after this change it is no longer clear which node, if any, is intrinsically "first.") If we use a circular linked list, then we need only one reference to implement a queue, since the front node and the rear node are adjacent nodes, as shown here:

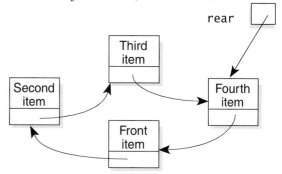

In the diagram we have called the single reference `rear`, because it refers to the last node in the queue. It turns out that this gives a more efficient implementation than having it refer to the first node in the queue. Redo the queue class using a circular linked list.

7 A **double-ended queue** is a list that allows the addition and removal of items from either end. One end is arbitrarily called the **front** and the other the **rear**, but the two ends behave identically. Specify, design, and implement a class for a double-ended queue. Include operations to check if it is empty, and to return the number of items in the list. For each end, include operations for adding and deleting items. Implement the double-ended queue as a doubly linked list. Call your class **Deque** (pronounced "deck").

8 Make improvements to the carwash simulation program from Section 7.2. One particular improvement that you should make is to handle the customers who are still in the queue at the end of the simulation. These customers should have their cars washed one after another, but no new customers should be allowed to join the queue during this time. The wait times of these leftover customers should be counted along with all the other customers.

9 Write a simulation program for a small airport that has only one runway. There will be a queue of planes waiting to land and a queue of planes waiting to take off. However, only one plane can use the runway at a time. So there can be only one takeoff or one landing in progress at any one time. Assume that all takeoffs take the same amount of time. Assume that all landings take the same amount of time, but this need not be the same as the takeoff time. Assume that planes arrive for landing at random times, but with a specified probability of a plane arriving during any given minute. Similarly, assume that planes arrive at the takeoff queue at random times, but with a (possibly different) specified probability of a departure. (Despite the fact that takeoffs and landings are scheduled, delays make this a reasonable assumption.) Since it is more expensive and more dangerous to keep a plane waiting to land than it is to keep a plane waiting to take off, landings will have priority over takeoffs. Thus, as long as some plane is waiting to land, no plane can take off. Use a clock that is an integer variable that counts the number of minutes simulated. Use a random number generator to simulate arrival and departure times of airplanes.

This simulation can be used, among other things, for deciding when the air traffic has become so heavy that a second runway must be built. Hence, the simulation will simulate conditions that would be a disaster in which planes crash because they run out of fuel while waiting too long in the landing queue. By examining the simulated situation, the airport authority hopes to avoid the real tragedy. Assume all planes can remain in the queue the same amount of time before they run out of fuel. If a plane runs out of fuel, your simulation will not discover this until the simulated plane is removed from the queue; at that point, the fact that the plane crashed is recorded, that plane is discarded, and the next plane is processed. A crashed plane is not considered in the calculation of waiting time. At the end of the simulated time, the landing queue is examined to see whether any of the planes in the simulated queue have crashed. You can disregard the planes left in the queue at the end of the simulation, other than those that crashed for lack of sufficient fuel. Use the following input and output specification:

Input: (1) The amount of time needed for one plane to land; (2) the amount of time needed for one plane to take off; (3) the average amount of time between arrival of planes to the landing queue; (4) the average amount of time between arrival of planes to the takeoff queue; (5) the maximum amount of time that a plane can stay in the landing queue without running out of fuel and crashing; (6) the total length of time to be simulated.

Output: (1) The number of planes that took off in the simulated time; (2) the number of planes that landed in the simulated time; (3) the number of planes that crashed because they ran out of fuel before they could land; (4) the average time that a plane spent in the takeoff queue; (5) the average time that a plane spent in the landing queue.

10 Do an airplane simulation that is more complex than the previous project. In this version, planes arrive for landing with a random amount of fuel, which determines how long they can remain in the air. A plane will crash unless it lands within the time assigned to it. Your simulation will keep planes in a priority queue, where the priority of a plane is equal to the number of minutes before midnight that the plane will crash.

Recursive Thinking

"Well," said Frog, "I don't suppose anyone ever is completely self-winding. That's what friends are for." He reached for the father's key to wind him up again.

RUSSELL HOBAN
The Mouse and His Child

Often, during top-down design, you'll meet a remarkable situation: One of the subtasks to be solved is nothing more than a simpler version of the same problem you are trying to solve in the first place. In fact, this situation occurs so frequently that experienced programmers start *expecting* to find simpler versions of a large problem during the design process. This expectation is called **recursive thinking**. Programming languages, such as Java, support recursive thinking by permitting a method implementation to actually activate itself. In such cases, the method is said to use **recursion**.

In this chapter, we start encouraging you to recognize situations where recursive thinking is appropriate. We also discuss recursion in Java, both how it is used to implement recursive designs and the mechanisms that occur during the execution of a recursive method.

one of the subtasks is a simpler version of the same problem you are trying to solve in the first place

8.1   RECURSIVE METHODS

A First Example of Recursive Thinking

We start with an example. Consider the task of writing a non-negative integer to the screen with its decimal digits stacked vertically. For example, the number 1234 should be written as:

```
1
2
3
4
```

a case with an easy solution . . .
and a case that needs more work

One version of this problem is quite easy: If the integer has only one digit, then we can just print that digit. But if the number has more than one digit, the solution is not immediately obvious, so we might break the problem into two subtasks: (1) Print all digits except the last digit, stacked vertically; (2) then print the last digit. For example, if the number is 1234, then the first step will write:

```
1
2
3
```

and the second step will output the last digit, 4.

Several factors influenced our selection of these two steps. One factor is the ease of providing the necessary data for these two steps. For example, with our input number 1234, the first step needs the digits of 123, which is easily expressed as 1234/10 (since dividing an integer by 10 results in the quotient, with any remainder discarded). In general, if the integer is called number, and number has more than one digit, then the first step prints the digits of number/10, stacked vertically. The second step is equally easy: It requires us to print the last digit of number, which is easily expressed as number % 10 (this is the remainder upon dividing number by 10). Simple expressions, such as number/10 and number % 10, are not so easy to find for other ways of breaking down the problem (such as printing only the first digit in the first step, then printing the rest of the digits in the second step).

The pseudocode for our solution is as follows:

```
// Printing the digits of a non-negative number, stacked vertically
if (the number has only one digit)
     Write that digit.
else
{
     Write the digits of number/10 stacked vertically.
     Write the single digit of number % 10.
}
```

At this point, your recursive thinking cap should be glowing: One of the steps— *write the digits of* number/10 *stacked vertically*—is a simpler instance of the same task of writing a number's digits vertically. It is simpler because number/10 has one fewer digit than number. This step can be implemented by activating writeVertical itself. This is an example of a method activating itself to solve a smaller problem, which is a **recursive call**. The implementation, with a recursive call, is shown in Figure 8.1. This implementation is a static method that could be part of any class. Within this class itself, the static method can be activated by the simple name writeVertical(...). From outside the class, the method can be activated by giving the class name followed by ".writeVertical(...)".

one of the steps is a simpler instance of the same task

FIGURE 8.1	The writeVertical Method

Specification

- **writeVertical**
  ```
  public static void writeVertical(int number)
  ```
  Print the digits of a non-negative integer vertically.
  Parameters:
  number – the number to be printed
  Precondition:
  number >= 0
  The method does not check the precondition, but the behavior is wrong for negative numbers.
  Postcondition:
  The digits of number have been written, stacked vertically.

Implementation

```
public static void writeVertical(int number)
{
   if (number < 10)
      System.out.println(number);           // Write the one digit.
   else
   {
      writeVertical(number/10);             // Write all but the last digit.
      System.out.println(number % 10);      // Write the last digit.
   }
}
```

Sample Results of writeVertical(1234)

```
1
2
3
4
```

In a moment we'll look at the exact mechanism that occurs during the activation of a method such as `writeVertical(1234)`, but first there are two notions to explain.

1. The Stopping Case. If the problem is simple enough, it is solved without recursive calls. In `writeVertical`, this occurs when `number` has only one digit. The case without any recursion is called the **stopping case** or **base case**. In Figure 8.1, the stopping case of `writeVertical` is implemented with the two lines

```
if (number < 10)
    System.out.println(number); // Write the one digit.
```

2. The Recursive Call. In Figure 8.1, the method `writeVertical` makes a recursive call. The recursive call is the highlighted statement here:

```
else
{
    writeVertical(number/10);    // Write all but the last digit.
    System.out.println(number % 10); // Write the last digit.
}
```

This is an instance of the `writeVertical` method activating itself to solve the simpler problem of writing all but the last digit.

Tracing Recursive Calls

During a computation such as `writeVertical(3)`, what actually occurs? The first step is that the argument 3 is copied to method's formal parameter, `number`. This is the way that all primitive types are handled as a parameter: The argument provides an initial value for the formal parameter.

Once the formal parameter has its initial value, the method's code is executed. Since 3 is less than 10, the boolean expression in the if-statement is `true`. So, in this case, it is easy to see that the method just prints 3 and does no more work.

Next, let's try an argument that causes us to enter the else-part, for example:

```
writeVertical(37);
```

When the method is activated, the value of `number` is set equal to 37, and the code is executed. Since 37 is not less than 10, the two statements of the else-part are executed. Here is the first statement:

```
writeVertical(number/10);    // Write all but the last digit.
```

example of a recursive call   In this statement, (number/10) is (37/10), which is 3. So, this is an activation of `writeVertical(3)`. We already know the action of `writeVertical(3)`: Print 3 on a single line of output. After this activation of `writeVertical` is completely finished, the second line in the else-part executes:

```
System.out.println(number % 10);
```

This just writes number % 10. In our example, number is 37, so the statement prints the digit 7. The total output of the two lines in the else-part is:

```
3
7
```

The method writeVertical uses recursion. Yet we did nothing new or different in carrying out the computation of writeVertical(37). We treated it just like any other method. We simply substituted the actual argument for number and then executed the code. When the computation reached the recursive call of writeVertical(3), we simply activated writeVertical with the argument 3.

PROGRAMMING EXAMPLE: An Extension of writeVertical

Suppose we want to extend writeVertical to a more powerful method, called superWriteVertical, which handles all integers including negative integers. With a negative input, the new method prints the negative sign on the first line of output, above any of the digits. For example,

```
superWriteVertical(-361)
```

produces this output with a minus sign on the first line:

```
-
3
6
1
```

How do we handle a negative number? The first step seems clear enough: Print the negative sign. After this, we must print the digits of number, which are the same as the digits of -1*number, which is *positive* (because number itself is negative). So, the pseudocode for superWriteVertical is an extension of our original pseudocode:

```
if (the number is negative)
{
      Write a negative sign.
      Write the digits of -1*number stacked vertically.
}
else if (the number has only one digit)
      Write that digit.
else
{
      Write the digits of number/10 stacked vertically.
      Write the single digit of number % 10.
}
```

If you think recursively, you will recognize that the step *write the digits of -1*number stacked vertically* is a simpler version of our original problem (simpler because the negative sign does not need to be written). This suggests the implementation in Figure 8.2, with two recursive calls: one for the new case that writes the digits of -1*number and a second call for the original case that writes the digits of number/10. The implementation has one simplification using "-number" instead of "-1*number". We also have added comments in the code, identifying two particular locations "Spot #1" and "Spot #2" to aid in taking a closer look at recursion.

FIGURE 8.2   The superWriteVertical Method

Specification

- **superWriteVertical**
    ```
    public static void superWriteVertical(int number)
    ```
    Print the digits of an integer vertically.

    Parameters:
    number – the number to be printed

    Postcondition:
    The digits of number have been written, stacked vertically. If number is negative, then a negative sign appears on top.

Implementation

```
public static void superWriteVertical(int number)
{
    if (number < 0)
    {
        System.out.println("-");              // Print a negative sign.
        superWriteVertical(-number);          // -1*number is positive.
        ‖  This is Spot #1 referred to in the text.
    }
    else if (number < 10)
        System.out.println(number);           // Write the one digit.
    else
    {
        superWriteVertical(number/10);        // Write all but the last digit.
        ‖  This is Spot #2 referred to in the text.
        System.out.println(number % 10);      // Write the last digit.
    }
}
```

Sample Results of superWriteVertical(-36)

```
-
3
6
```

A Closer Look at Recursion

The computer keeps track of method activations in the following way: When a method is activated, the computer temporarily stops the execution. Before actually executing the method, some information is saved that will allow the computation to return to the correct location after the method's work is completed. The computer also provides memory for the method's parameters and any local variables that the method uses. Next, the actual arguments are plugged in for the parameters, and the code of the activated method begins to execute.

If the execution should encounter an activation of *another* method—recursive or otherwise—then the first method's computation is temporarily stopped. This is because the second method must be executed before the first method can continue. Information is saved that indicates precisely where the first method should resume when the second method is completed. The second method is given memory for its own parameters and local variables. The execution then proceeds to the second method. When the method is completed, the execution returns to the correct location within the first method. And the first method resumes its computation.

how methods are executed

This mechanism is used for both recursive and nonrecursive methods. As an example of the mechanism in a recursive method, let's completely trace the work of `superWriteVertical(-36)`. Initially, we activate `superWriteVertical` with `number` set to –36. The actual argument, –36, is copied to the parameter, `number`, and we start executing the code. At the moment when the method's execution begins, all of the important information that the method needs to work is stored in a memory block called the method's **activation record.** The activation record contains information as to where the method should return when it is done with its computation, and it also contains the values of the method's local variables and parameters. For example, if our `superWriteVertical` method was called from a main program, then the activation record might contain this information:

> Activation record for first call to
> superWriteVertical
> _____
>
> number: –36
>
> When the method returns, the
> computation should continue at
> line 57 of the main program.

The return location specified in a real activation record does not actually refer to lines of code in the main program, but when you're imagining an activation record, you can think of a return location in this manner.

With the activation record in place, the method starts executing. Because the number is negative, the boolean test of the if-statement is true, and the negative sign is printed. At this point, the computation is about to make a recursive call, indicated here:

```
if (number < 0)
{
    System.out.println("-");
    superWriteVertical(-number);
    ‖ This is Spot #1 referred to in the text.
}
```

A recursive call is made in the superWriteVertical method.

This method generates its own activation record with its own value of number (which will be 36) and its own return location. The new activation record is placed on top of the other activation record, like this:

In fact, the collection of activation records is stored in a *stack* data structure called the **execution stack.** Each activation of a method pushes the next activation record on top of the execution stack.

In our example, the second call of superWriteVertical executes with its own value of number equal to 36. The method's code executes, taking the last branch of the if-else control structure, arriving at another recursive call shown here:

Another recursive call is made in the superWriteVertical method.

```
else
{
    superWriteVertical(number/10);
    ‖ This is Spot #2 referred to in the text.
    System.out.println(number % 10);
}
```

To execute this recursive call, another activation record is created (with number now set to 3), and this activation record is pushed onto the execution stack, as shown at the top of the next page.

The `superWriteVertical` method begins executing once more. With number set to 3, the method enters the section to handle a one-digit number. At this point, the digit 3 is printed, and no other work is done during this activation.

When the third method activation ends, its activation record is popped off the stack. But just before it is popped, the activation record provides one last piece of information—telling where the computation should continue. In our example, the third activation record is popped off the stack, and the computation continues at Spot #2 in Figure 8.2 on page 376. At this point we have the two remaining activation records shown here:

As we said, the computation is now at Spot #2 in Figure 8.2 on page 376. This is the highlighted location shown here:

```
else
{
    superWriteVertical(number/10);
    ‖  This is Spot #2 referred to in the text.
    System.out.println(number % 10);
}
```

The next statement is an output statement. What does it print? From the activation record on top of the stack, we see that `number` is 36, so the statement prints 6 (which is 36 % 10). The second method activation then finishes, returning to Spot #1 in Figure 8.2 on page 376. But there is no more work to do after Spot #1, so the first method also returns. The total effect of the original method activation was to print three characters: a minus sign, and then 3, and finally 6. The tracing was all accomplished with the usual mechanism for activating a method—no special treatment was needed to trace recursive calls. In the example there are two levels of recursive calls:

1. `superWriteVertical(-36)` made a recursive call to
   `superWriteVertical(36);`

2. `superWriteVertical(36)` made a recursive call to
   `superWriteVertical(3)`.

In general, recursive calls may be much deeper than this, but even at the deepest levels the activation mechanism remains the same as the example that we have traced.

General Form of a Successful Recursive Method

Java places no restrictions on how recursive calls are used within a method. However, in order for recursive methods to be useful, any sequence of recursive calls must ultimately terminate with some piece of code that does not depend on recursion—in other words, there must be a *stopping case*. The method may call itself, and that recursive call may call the method again. The process may be repeated any number of times. However, the process will not terminate unless eventually one of the recursive calls does not itself make a recursive call. The general outline of a recursive method definition is as follows.

Recursive Thinking

Suppose that a problem has one or more cases in which some of the subtasks are simpler versions of the same problem you are trying to solve in the first place. These subtasks are solved by recursive calls.

A method that makes recursive calls must also have one or more cases in which the entire computation is accomplished without recursion. These cases without recursion are called **stopping cases** or **base cases**.

Often a series of if-else statements determines which of the cases will be executed. A typical scenario is for the first method activation to execute a case that includes a recursive call. That recursive call may in turn execute a case that requires another recursive call. For some number of times each recursive call produces another recursive call, but eventually one of the stopping cases applies. Every call of the method must eventually lead to a stopping case or else the execution will never end because of an infinite sequence of recursive calls. In practice, infinite recursion will terminate with a Java exception called Stack-OverflowError, indicating that the execution stack has run out of memory for more activation records.

Self-Test Exercises

1. What is the output produced by f(3), for each of the following?

```
public static void f(int n)
{
    System.out.println(n);
    if (n > 1)
        f(n-1);
}
```

```
public static void f(int n)
{
    if (n > 1)
        f(n-1);
    System.out.println(n);
}
```

```
public static void f(int n)
{
    System.out.println(n);
    if (n > 1)
        f(n-1);
    System.out.println(n);
}
```

2. What is the output of the following method with an argument of 3?

```
public static void cheers(int n)
{
    if (n <= 1)
        System.out.println("Hurrah");
    else
    {
        System.out.println("Hip");
        cheers(n-1);
    }
}
```

3. Modify the cheers method from the previous exercise so that it first prints "Hurrah" followed by n-1 "Hip"s. Make a further modification so that n-1 "Hip"s occur both before and after the "Hurrah". Make another modification so that approximately half of the "Hip"s occur before the "Hurrah", and half appear after.

4. Write a recursive method with a parameter that is a non-negative integer. The method writes that number of asterisks to the screen, followed by that number of exclamation points. Use no loops or local variables.

8.2 STUDIES OF RECURSION: FRACTALS AND MAZES

Recursive thinking makes its biggest impact on problems in which one of the *subtasks* is a simpler version of the *same* problem that you are working on. For example, when we write the digits of a long number, our first step is to write the digits of the smaller number, number/10. This section provides additional examples of recursive thinking and the methods that recursion leads to.

FIGURE 8.3
The First Few Steps in Generating a Random Fractal

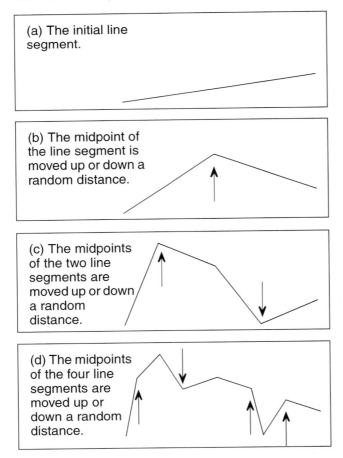

(a) The initial line segment.

(b) The midpoint of the line segment is moved up or down a random distance.

(c) The midpoints of the two line segments are moved up or down a random distance.

(d) The midpoints of the four line segments are moved up or down a random distance.

PROGRAMMING EXAMPLE:
Generating Random Fractals

Fractals are one of the techniques that graphics programmers use to artificially produce remarkably natural scenes of mountains, clouds, trees, and other objects. We'll explain fractals in a simple setting and develop a recursive method to produce a certain kind of fractal.

To understand fractals, think about a short line segment, as shown in Figure 8.3(a). Imagine grabbing the middle of the line and moving it vertically a random distance. The two endpoints of the line stay fixed, so the result might look like Figure 8.3(b). This movement has created two smaller line segments: the left half of the original segment and the right half. For each of these smaller line segments, we'll grab the midpoint and move it up or down a random distance. Once again, the endpoints of the line segments remain fixed, so the result of this second step might look like Figure 8.3(c). One more step might produce Figure 8.3(d). The process continues as long as you like, with each step creating a slightly more jagged line.

After several more steps, the line could appear as shown here:

Status of the line after several more steps

Perhaps you can imagine that this jagged line is the silhouette of a mountain skyline.

The line that we're generating has an interesting property. Suppose that we carry out thousands of steps to create our line and then magnify a small portion of the result, as shown here:

Magnifying a portion of the line

The magnified portion is not identical to the entire line, but there is a lot of similarity. **Fractal** is the term coined by the mathematician Benoit Mandelbrot to describe objects, such as our line, that exhibit some kind of similarity under magnification. In fact, the first fractals studied were mathematically defined sets that remain *completely unchanged* when magnified to certain powers. In nature, objects don't generally remain completely unchanged under magnification, but magnified views commonly exhibit similarities with the larger object (such as our line, or a cloud, or a fern). Also, in nature (and our line), the powers of magnification where the similarities occur are limited, so nature's fractals are really rough approximations to the more formal mathematical fractals. Even so, the term *fractal* is often applied to any object that exhibits similarities under some magnification. The jagged line that we have described is called a **random fractal** because of the randomness in its generation.

fractals, nature's fractals, and random fractals

A Method for Generating Random Fractals—Specification

We wish to write a method that can draw a random fractal in the way that we have described. The input to this method includes the locations of the two endpoints of the original line, measured from the top side and the left side of the drawing area. For example, consider the line segment shown here:

In computer graphics, these distances are measured in **pixels**, which are the individual dots on a computer screen. Today's typical screens have about 100 pixels per inch, so the endpoint just shown might have an x-coordinate of 100 (the distance from the left side) and a y-coordinate of 55 (the distance below the top side). These y-coordinates are probably different than what you're used to because positive coordinates occur below the top side, whereas normal mathematics coordinates have positive numbers going upward—but that's the way computer graphics are usually measured, from the top down.

The x- and y-coordinates of both endpoints will be four of the parameters to the fractal-generating method. The method also has a fifth parameter called drawingArea. The drawingArea is a Java Graphics object, which is a class from the java.awt package. A Graphics object allows a program to draw images based on pixels. For example, one of the Graphics methods is specified here:

- **drawLine** (from the Graphics class)
  ```
  public void writeVertical(int x1, int y1, int x2, int y2)
  ```
  Draws a line on this Graphics object.

  Parameters:
  x1 and y1 – the x and y pixel coordinates of one endpoint of the line
  x2 and y2 – the x and y pixel coordinates of the other endpoint of the line

  Postcondition:
  A line has been drawn on this Graphics object from (x1, y1) to (x2, y2).

Java programs have several ways to create Graphics objects, but we don't need to know about that yet. Instead, we'll provide the specification of the fractal method, without worrying about exactly how the program generates a Graphics object. Here is a listing of the method with its five parameters:

```
public static void randomFractal(
    int leftX,
    int leftY,
    int rightX,
    int rightY,
    Graphics drawingArea
)
```

Now we must consider the method's behavior. Let's look at an example using an initial line segment shown here with its x- and y-coordinates:

Notice that we're using pixel coordinates, so the higher point has the lower y-coordinate.

Normally, the first step of randomFractal is to find the approximate x- and y-coordinates of the segment's midpoint. We'll call these coordinates midX and midY, as shown here:

We are keeping track of the coordinates with integers, so the y-midpoint is a bit inaccurate—the real midpoint is $47\frac{1}{2}$. The statements to compute the approximate midpoints use integer division (throwing away any remainder), as shown here:

```
midX = (leftX + rightX) / 2;
midY = (leftY + rightY) / 2;
```

Next, the y-midpoint must be shifted up or down a random amount. To limit the rise and fall of the fractal, the complete shift will be no more than half of the distance from leftX to rightX. The amount of the shift is stored in a variable called delta, computed randomly with the statement:

```
delta = (int)((Math.random( ) - 0.5) * (rightX - leftX));
```

The random part of this expression, Math.random( ), provides a random double number from 0 up to but not including 1. So, (Math.random( ) - 0.5) is from -0.5 to 0.5 (not including 0.5). And the assignment to delta is this random number times the distance between the x-coordinates, and rounded to an integer.

Once we have delta, this value is added to midY with the statement:

```
midY += delta;
```

For example, suppose that `delta` is 25. Then the `midY` shifts down 25 pixels, as shown here:

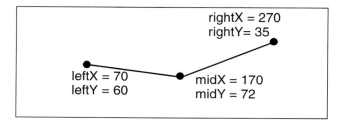

After computing the location of the displaced midpoint, we have two segments: (a) from the left endpoint of the original segment to the displaced midpoint, and (b) from the displaced midpoint to the right endpoint of the original segment. And what work do we have left to do? *We must generate a random fractal for each of these two smaller line segments.* This work can be accomplished with two recursive calls:

```
randomFractal(leftX,  leftY,  midX,   midY,   drawingArea);
randomFractal(midX,   midY,   rightX, rightY, drawingArea);
```

two recursive calls solve two smaller versions of the original problem

The first of these recursive calls generates a random fractal for the leftmost smaller line segment. Let's examine the arguments of the first recursive call: The first two arguments are the left coordinates of the leftmost segment (`leftX` and `leftY`); the next two arguments are the right coordinates of the leftmost segment (`midX` and `midY`); and the final argument is the `Graphics` object that we are drawing on. The second recursive call handles the rightmost line segment in a similar way.

To summarize, the `randomFractal` method normally carries out these six statements:

```
midX = (leftX + rightX) / 2;
midY = (leftY + rightY) / 2;
delta = (int)((Math.random( ) - 0.5) * (rightX - leftX));
midY += delta;
randomFractal(leftX,  leftY,  midX,   midY,   drawingArea);
randomFractal(midX,   midY,   rightX, rightY, drawingArea);
```

stopping case for the random fractal method

These six statements cannot be all of `randomFractal`. For one thing, no drawing takes place in these statements. For another, these statements on their own will lead to infinite recursion—there is no stopping case. The solution is a stopping case that's triggered when `leftX` and `rightX` get close to each other. In this case, the horizontal extent of the segment is small and further subdividing of the segment has little effect. So this will be our stopping case, and we will simply draw a line from the left endpoint to the right endpoint. This approach is taken in Figure 8.4, which we discuss further on the next page.

FIGURE 8.4   A Method to Generate a Random Fractal

Specification

- **randomFractal**

```
public static void randomFractal(
    int leftX,
    int leftY,
    int rightX,
    int rightY,
    Graphics drawingArea
)
```

Draws a random fractal on a `Graphics` object.

Parameters:

`leftX` and `leftY` – the x and y pixel coordinates of one endpoint of a line segment
`rightX` and `rightY` – the x and y pixel coordinates of the other endpoint of a line segment
`drawingArea` – a `Graphics` object on which to draw a random fractal

Postcondition:

A random fractal has been drawn on the `Graphics` object. The fractal extends from
(`leftX`, `leftY`) to (`rightX`, `rightY`).

Implementation

```
public static void randomFractal
(
    int leftX,
    int leftY,
    int rightX,
    int rightY,
    Graphics drawingArea
)
{
    final int STOP = 4;
    int midX, midY;
    int delta;

    if ((rightX - leftX) <= STOP)
        drawingArea.drawLine(leftX, leftY, rightX, rightY);
    else
    {
        midX = (leftX + rightX) / 2;
        midY = (leftY + rightY) / 2;
        delta = (int)((Math.random( ) - 0.5) * (rightX - leftX));
        midY += delta;
        randomFractal(leftX, leftY, midX, midY, drawingArea);
        randomFractal(midX, midY, rightX, rightY, drawingArea);
    }
}
```

The Stopping Case for Generating a Random Fractal

The `randomFractal` method from Figure 8.4 reaches a stopping case when the distance from `leftX` to `rightX` gets small enough, as shown here:

```
if ((rightX - leftX) <= STOP)
    drawingArea.drawLine(leftX, leftY, rightX, rightY);
```

The constant, `STOP`, is defined as 4 at the top of the `randomFractal` method. In the stopping case, we use the `Graphic drawLine` method to draw a line segment from the left endpoint to the right endpoint.

Putting the Random Fractal Method in an Applet

There's one item that you're probably still wondering about. How does a program get a `Graphics` object to draw on? One approach can be used by any applet that draws a single fixed image with no user interaction. This approach has five easy steps, though you must also be familiar with the general format of applets as described in Section 3.4.

The fixed-image approach for an applet follows these steps:

1. Import `java.awt.*`, which provides the `Graphics` class and another class called `Image`.

2. The applet declares two private instance variables, like this:

   ```
   private Image display;
   private Graphics drawingArea;
   ```

   An `Image` is an area that can store a drawing. Sometimes these drawings are obtained from external files, but the drawings can also be created by the applet itself by attaching a `Graphics` object to the `Image`. This is what we plan to do; the `drawingArea` (a `Graphics` object) will be attached to the `display` (an `Image`).

3. The applet's `init` method initializes the `Image` and sets the `Graphics` object to draw on that image. This takes four statements:

   ```
   int height = getSize( ).height;
   int width = getSize( ).width;
   display = createImage(width, height);
   drawingArea = display.getGraphics( );
   ```

   The `width` and `height` variables are initialized with `getSize( ).width` and `getSize( ).height`, which provide the current size of a running applet. The `createImage` method is also part of any applet, and it creates an `Image` with a given width and height in pixels. The fourth statement sets `drawingArea` to a `Graphics` object that can be used to draw on the `Image`.

4. The rest of the applet's `init` method draws any items that you want to appear in the image. These are drawn using the `drawingArea` Graphics object. For example, we want an applet that draws a random fractal, so our `init` method will have this complete implementation:

```
public void init( )
{
    int height = getSize( ).height;
    int width = getSize( ).width;
    display = createImage(width, height);
    drawingArea = display.getGraphics( );

    randomFractal(0, height/2, width, height/2, drawingArea);
}
```

The last line of the `init` method does the actual drawing by calling the `randomFractal` method. The fractal will be drawn in `drawingArea`, which is the Graphics object that we set to draw in the `display` Image.

As with any applet, the `init` method is automatically called when the applet starts. This will put the `randomFractal` image in the `display` Image.

5. To actually show the image, we need to provide one more applet method called `paint`. The `paint` method is called when the applet is started and whenever the applet's location or shape changes, such as moving from behind some other window. For the applet to draw a single fixed image, the paint method is simply this:

```
public void paint(Graphics g)
{
    g.drawImage(display, 0, 0, null);
}
```

The argument, g, is the underlying Graphics object where all applet drawing takes place. It is different than `drawingArea` (which is the Graphics object attached to the image that we drew). The one statement that we placed in the `paint` method will draw our `display` image in the applet's drawing area, aligned in the upper left corner. (The first argument is the image we are drawing; the second and third arguments indicate the coordinates to place the upper left corner of the image; the fourth argument is a Java object called an observer, but we can set it to `null` if we are not using this feature.)

As we said, any applet that draws a single fixed image can follow these five steps. A fractal-drawing applet following these steps is shown in Figure 8.5 on page 390, along with a picture of how the applet looks when it runs.

FIGURE 8.5 | Implementation of an Applet to Draw a Random Fractal

Java Applet Implementation

```
// File: Fractal.java
// This applet is a small example to illustrate the randomFractal method.

import java.applet.Applet;
import java.awt.*;              // Provides Graphics, Image

public class Fractal extends Applet
{
    private Image display;
    private Graphics drawingArea;

    public void init( )
    {
      int height = getSize( ).height;
      int width = getSize( ).width;
      display = createImage(width, height);
      drawingArea = display.getGraphics( );

      randomFractal(0, height/2, width, height/2, drawingArea);
    }

    public void paint(Graphics g)
    {
        g.drawImage(display, 0, 0, null);
    }

    public static void randomFractal
    (
        int leftX,
        int leftY,
        int rightX,
        int rightY,
        Graphics drawingArea
    )
    {
        ‖ See Figure 8.4 on page 387.
    }
}
```

Sample of the Applet Running

PROGRAMMING EXAMPLE: **Traversing a Maze**

Suppose that your friend Jervis has a maze in his backyard. One day, Jervis mentions two facts about the maze:

1. Somewhere in the maze is a magic tapestry that contains the secret of the universe.

2. You may keep this tapestry (and its secret) if you can enter the maze, find the tapestry, and return to the maze's entrance. (So far, many have entered, but none has returned.)

The maze is built on a rectangular grid. At each point of the grid, there are four directions to move: north, east, south, or west. Some directions, however, may be blocked by an impenetrable wall. You decide to accept Jervis's challenge and enter the maze—but only with the help of your portable computer and a method that we'll write to guide you into the maze *and back out.*

Traversing a Maze—Specification

We plan to write a method, `traverseMaze`, which you can execute on a portable computer that you will carry through the maze. The method will give you directions and ask you questions to take you to the magic tapestry and back out. Here's the complete specification:

- **traverseMaze**
  ```
  public static boolean traverseMaze( )
  ```
  Provides interactive help to guide a user through a maze and back out.

  Precondition:
  The user of the program is facing an unblocked spot in the maze, and this spot has not previously been visited by the user.

  Postcondition:
  The method has asked a series of queries, and provided various directions to the user. The queries and directions have led the user through the maze and back to the exact same position where the user started. If there was a magic tapestry that could be reached in the maze, then the user has picked up this tapestry and the method returns `true`; otherwise the method returns `false`.

Figure 8.6 shows a drawing of what the maze might look like, along with a sample dialogue. A sample dialog written at this point—before we've written the program—is called a **script**, and it can help clarify a loose specification. As you might suspect, Jervis's actual maze is rather more complex than this sample dialog might suggest, but simplicity often results in the best scripts.

FIGURE 8.6   Script for the Maze Traversal Method

A Sample Dialogue

```
Step forward & write your name on the ground.
Have you found the tapestry? [Y or N]
N
Please turn left 90 degrees.
Are you facing a wall? [Y or N]
N
Is your name written ahead of you? [Y or N]
N
Step forward & write your name on the ground.
Have you found the tapestry? [Y or N]
N
Please turn left 90 degrees.
Are you facing a wall? [Y or N]
Y
Please turn right 90 degrees.
Are you facing a wall? [Y or N]
N
Is your name written ahead of you? [Y or N]
N
Step forward & write your name on the ground.
Have you found the tapestry? [Y or N]
Y
Pick up the tapestry, and take a step backward.
Please turn right 90 degrees.
Please turn right 90 degrees.
Please step forward, then turn 180 degrees.
Please turn right 90 degrees.
Please turn right 90 degrees.
Please turn right 90 degrees.
Please step forward, then turn 180 degrees.
```

> This dialogue supposes that the user starts at the entrance to the maze drawn below. The starting point of the user is represented by the arrow in a circle, with the arrow pointing in the direction that the user is facing. The large X is the magic tapestry.

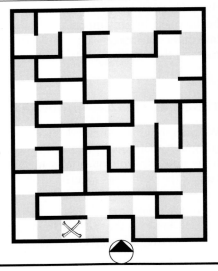

Traversing a Maze—Design

The traverseMaze method appears to perform a pretty complex task. When the method starts, all that's really known is that the user of the program is facing some spot in the maze, and that spot has not been previously visited. The method must take the user into the maze, eventually leading the user back to the exact starting spot. Hopefully, along the way the user will find the magic tapestry. Recursive thinking can make the task easier.

We'll call the method's user Judy. We'll always start by asking Judy to take a step forward onto the spot that she hasn't visited before. We'll also ask her to write her name on the ground so that later we can tell whether she's been to this spot before. After these two steps we will ask her whether she has found the tapestry at this new spot and place her true or false answer in a local variable named found.

Now there is one easy case: If the tapestry is at this spot, then we will have Judy pick up the tapestry and ask her to take a step backward to her starting spot. This is the stopping case, and the method returns `true` to indicate that the tapestry was found.

But what if Judy does not find the tapestry at this spot? In this case, there are three possible directions for Judy to explore: going forward, leftward, or rightward. We won't worry about exploring backward because that is the direction that Judy just came from. Also, sometimes we do not need to explore all three directions (forward, left, and right). A direction is a "dead end" if (a) there is a wall blocking that direction, or (b) Judy's name is written on the ground in that direction (indicating she has already been there)—and there is no need to explore dead ends. We also don't need to explore a direction if Judy already found the tapestry in one of the other directions.

This description suggests the following steps if the user has not found the tapestry at this spot:

1. Have the user face left (the first direction to explore).

2. `for` each of the three directions
   ```
   {
   ```
   > `if (!found &&` the direction that is now being faced isn't a dead end)
   > ```
   > {
   > ```
   >> Explore the direction that is now being faced, returning to this exact spot after the exploration and setting `found` to `true` if the tapestry was found.
   >
   > ```
   > }
   > ```
   > Have the user turn 90 degrees to the right (the next direction).
   ```
   }
   ```

3. The user is now facing the direction she came from, so ask her to step forward and turn around (so that she is facing the same spot that she was before this method was activated).

Are you thinking recursively? The highlighted step "Explore the direction that is now being faced. . ." is a simpler instance of the problem that we are trying to solve. The instance is simpler because one spot in the maze has been eliminated from consideration—namely, the spot that the user is at does not contain the tapestry. In our implementation, we'll solve this simpler problem with a recursive call.

Traversing a Maze—Implementation

Our implementation will benefit from two methods to carry out various subtasks. Figure 8.7 shows the methods we have in mind. The first method provides a simple way to ask a question and get a yes/no answer. The other method determines whether the user has reached a dead end.

A short discussion of these two methods appears after the figure.

FIGURE 8.7	Two Methods to Simplify the Maze Traversal

Specification

- **inquire**
  ```
  public static boolean inquire(String query)
  ```
  Asks a yes/no question and reads the answer.

  Parameters:
  query – a question to ask

  Postcondition:
  The query has been printed to System.out, and a one-character response read from System.in (skipping any whitespace characters). The method returns true if the user's response was 'Y' or 'y', and returns false if the user's response was 'N' or 'n'. (If the response is some other character, then the query is repeated and a new answer is read.)

- **deadend**
  ```
  public static boolean deadend( )
  ```
  Determines whether the person traversing the maze has reached a dead end.

  Postcondition:
  The return value is true if the direction directly in front of the user is a dead end (that is, a direction that cannot contain the tapestry).

Implementation

```
public static boolean inquire(String query)
{
    char answer = 'N';

    do
    {
        System.out.println(query + " [Y or N]");
        try
        {
            do
                answer = (char) System.in.read( );
            while (Character.isWhitespace(answer));
        }
        catch (IOException e)
        {
            System.err.println("Standard input error: " + e);
            System.exit(0);
        }
        answer = Character.toUpperCase(answer);
    } while ((answer != 'Y') && (answer != 'N'));

    return (answer == 'Y');
}
```

(continued)

(FIGURE 8.7 continued)

```
public static boolean deadend( )
{
    return inquire("Are you facing a wall?")
           ||
           inquire("Is your name written in front of you?");
}
```

The two methods in Figure 8.7 are:

- inquire: This method asks the user a yes/no question; it returns true if the user answers "Y" or "y", and returns false if the user answers "N" or "n".

- deadend: This method determines whether the direction in front of the user is a "dead end." Remember that dead ends are caused by a wall or by a direction that the user has already explored. The method returns true (for a dead end) or false (for no dead end).

The implementation of the deadend method is short, as shown here:

```
return inquire("Are you facing a wall?")
       ||
       inquire("Is your name written in front of you?");
```

This implementation of deadend makes two activations of the inquire method and returns the "or" of the results (using the || operation). When the "or" expression is evaluated, the inquire method is called to ask the user, "Are you facing a wall?" If the user answers "Y" or "y", then the inquire method returns true, and the rest of the "or" expression will not be executed. This follows the general rule of **short-circuit evaluation** that we have seen before—meaning that the evaluation of a logical expression stops when there is enough information to determine whether the expression is true or false. On the other hand, if the user answers "N" or "n" to the first query, then the inquire method returns false, and the rest of the "or" expression will be executed (asking the second question, "Is your name written in front of you?").

In all, the method returns true if the user indicates that he or she is facing a wall, or if the user says there is no wall and then answers "Y" or "y" to the second question (the user's name is written in front of him or her).

The actual traverseMaze method is given in Figure 8.8. It follows our pseudocode quite closely. You might enjoy knowing that the magic tapestry really does exist in a book called *Castle Roogna* (Ballantine Books) by Piers Anthony. The hero of the book actually becomes part of the tapestry, whereupon his quest leads him to a *smaller* version of the *same* tapestry.

FIGURE 8.8	A Method to Traverse a Maze

Specification

- **traverseMaze**
  ```
  public static boolean traverseMaze( )
  ```
  Provides interactive help to guide a user through a maze and back out.

  Precondition:
  The program's user is facing an unblocked spot that has not been previously visited.

  Postcondition:
  The method has asked a series of questions and provided various directions to the user. The questions and directions have led the user through the maze and back to the exact same position where the user started. If there was a magic tapestry that could be reached in the maze, then the user has picked up this tapestry and the method returns `true`; otherwise the method returns `false`.

Implementation

```
public static boolean traverseMaze( )
{
    int direction;   // Counts 1, 2, 3 for the three directions to explore
    boolean found;   // Will be set to true if we find the tapestry

    System.out.println("Step forward & write your name on the ground.");
    found = inquire("Have you found the tapestry?");

    if (found)
    {  // Pick up the tapestry and step back from whence you came.
        System.out.println("Pick up the tapestry and take a step backward.");
    }
    else
    {  // Explore the three directions (not counting the one that you just came from). Start
       // with the direction on your left, and then turn through each of the other directions.
        System.out.println("Please turn left 90 degrees.");
        for (direction = 1; direction <= 3; direction++)
        {
            if ( !found && !deadend( ) )
                found = traverseMaze( );
            System.out.println("Please turn right 90 degrees.");
        }
        // You're now facing the direction from whence you came, so step forward and turn
        // around. This will put you in the same spot when the method was activated.
        System.out.println("Please step forward, then turn 180 degrees.");
    }
    return found;
}
```

The Recursive Pattern of Exhaustive Search with Backtracking

The `traverseMaze` method of Figure 8.8 follows a recursive pattern that you may find useful elsewhere. The pattern is useful when a program is searching for a goal within a space of individual points that have connections between them. In the maze problem, the "points" are the individual squares of the maze and the "connections" are the possible steps that the explorer can take in the four compass directions. Later you'll run into many data structures that have the form of "points and connections"—in fact, our very next chapter introduces trees that are such a structure.

The task of searching such a structure can often follow this pattern:

- Start by marking the current point in some way. In the maze, the mark was obtained by asking the explorer to write her name on the ground. The purpose of the mark is to ensure that we don't mistakenly return to this point and end up going around in circles, continually returning to this same spot.

    This "marking" step is not always necessary; sometimes there are other mechanisms to prevent unbounded repetitions of searching the same direction.

- Check whether the current point satisfies the goal. If so, return some value that indicates the success of the search.

- On the other hand, if the current point does not satisfy the goal, then one by one examine the other points that are connected to the current point. For each such point, check to see whether the point is marked; if so, we can ignore the point because we have already been there. On the other hand, if a connected point is not marked, then make a recursive call to continue the search from the connected point onwards. If the recursive call finds the goal then we won't bother checking any other points, but if the recursive call fails then we will check each of the other unmarked connected points by further recursive calls.

This pattern is called **exhaustive search with backtracking**. The term *exhaustive search* means that all possibilities are tried. *Backtracking* is the process of a recursive call returning without finding the goal. When such a recursive call returns, we are "back where we started," and we can explore other directions with further recursive calls.

Exhaustive search with backtracking is most useful when the known search space doesn't get too large. But even with huge search spaces, programmers often use variants that try to cut down the search space in an intelligent manner. You'll find successful variants in programs that play games such as chess, which have an enormous number of possibilities to search. As one more recursive example, we'll write a method to play a game with a definite small search space, so we won't need to cut down this space at all.

PROGRAMMING EXAMPLE: **The Teddy Bear Game**

Here are the rules of the Teddy Bear game: Your friend is going to give you a certain number of bears. The number of bears is called `initial`, and your goal is to end up with a particular number of bears, called the `goal` number.

There are two other integer parameters to the game: `increment` and n. At any point in the game you have two choices: (a) You can ask for (and receive) `increment` more bears, or (b) if you have an even number of bears, then you may give half of them back to your friend. Each time you do (a) or (b), that is called a *step* in the game, and the goal must be reached in n steps or fewer. For example, if `initial` is 99, `increment` is 53, and n is at least 4, then the following sequence of steps will reach the goal of 91:

$$99 \quad \underset{\text{step a}}{\rightarrow} \quad 152 \quad \underset{\text{step b}}{\rightarrow} \quad 76 \quad \underset{\text{step b}}{\rightarrow} \quad 38 \quad \underset{\text{step a}}{\rightarrow} \quad 91$$

We want to write a recursive method, `bears`, which determines whether it is possible to reach a `goal` starting with some `initial` and `increment` numbers, and allowing no more than n steps. The implementation follows the pattern from the previous page—although the first marking step of the pattern is not needed since we can prevent going around in circles by stopping when the parameter n reaches zero. So the pattern has only these two steps:

- Check whether the `initial` value is equal to the `goal`. If so, return `true` to indicate that the goal can be reached.

- On the other hand, if the `initial` value does not equal the `goal`, then we'll check that n is positive (otherwise we have no more moves to make and must return `false` because the goal cannot be reached). When n is positive, we'll solve the problem by making one or two recursive calls. One call starts by taking an (a)-step and the other starts by taking a (b)-step—although this second call is made only if `initial` is an even number.

The implementation of the bear method appears in Figure 8.9. Notice the expression (`inital % 2 == 0`) to determine whether the initial number of bears is even.

Self-Test Exercises

5. Suppose you activate `randomFractal` with the distance between the x-coordinates equal to 24, and a stopping case when this distance is less than or equal to 4. Then `randomFractal` will make two recursive calls, and each of those will make two more calls, and so on until `width` is less than or equal to 4. How many total calls will be made of `random-Fractal`, including the original activation?

6. Draw a copy of the maze from Figure 8.6 on page 392, moving the magic tapestry to a more difficult location. Run the `traverseMaze` method, pretending that you are in this maze and following the method's directions. (Do not peek over the walls.)

7. Revise the `randomFractal` method so that the movements of the midpoints are no longer random. Instead, the first midpoint should be moved upward by half the distance between the x-coordinates, the midpoints at the next level of recursion should be moved down by half the distance between the x-coordinates, the next level will move up again, then down, and so on.

8. Suppose that you are exploring a rectangular maze containing ten rows and twenty columns. What is the maximum number of recursive calls that can be generated if you start at the entrance of the maze and activate `traverseMaze`? Include the initial activation as part of your count.

FIGURE 8.9	A Method to Play the Teddy Bear Game

Specification

- **bears**

  `public static boolean bears(int initial, int goal, int increment, int n)`
  Determines whether the goal can be reached in the Teddy Bear game.

  Precondition:
  All parameters should be non-negative.

  Postcondition:
  The method has determined whether it is possible to reach the goal in the following Teddy Bear game. In the game, your friend gives you a certain number of bears. The number of bears is called `initial`, and your goal is to end up with a particular number of bears, called the goal number. At any point in the game you have two choices: (a) You can ask for (and receive) `increment` more bears, or (b) if you have an even number of bears, then you may give half of them back to your friend. Each time you do (a) or (b), that is called a *step* in the game.
      The return value is `true` if and only if the goal can be reached in n steps or fewer.

Implementation

```
public static boolean bears(int initial, int goal, int increment, int n)
{
    if (initial == goal)
        return true;
    else if (n == 0)
        return false;
    else if (bears(initial+increment, goal, increment, n-1))
        return true;
    else if ((initial % 2 == 0) && bears(initial/2, goal, increment, n-1))
        return true;
    else
        return false;
}
```

8.3   REASONING ABOUT RECURSION

After a lecture on cosmology and the structure of the solar system, William James was accosted by a little old lady.

"Your theory that the sun is the center of the solar system, and the earth is a ball which rotates around it has a very convincing ring to it, Mr. James, but it's wrong. I've got a better theory," said the little old lady.

"And what is that, madam?" inquired James politely.

"That we live on a crust of earth which is on the back of a giant turtle."

Not wishing to demolish this absurd little theory by bringing to bear the masses of scientific evidence he had at his command, James decided to gently dissuade his opponent by making her see some of the inadequacies of her position.

"If your theory is correct, madam," he asked, "what does this turtle stand on?"

"You're a very clever man, Mr. James, and that's a very good question," replied the little old lady, "but I have an answer to it. And it is this: the first turtle stands on the back of a second, far larger, turtle, who stands directly under him."

"But what does this second turtle stand on?" persisted James patiently.

To this the little old lady crowed triumphantly. "It's no use, Mr. James—it's turtles all the way down."

J. R. ROSS
Constraints on Variables in Syntax

In all our examples of recursive thinking, the series of recursive calls eventually reaches a call that does not involve further recursion (that is, it reaches a *stopping case*). If, on the other hand, every recursive call produces another recursive call, then a recursive call will, in theory, run forever. This is called **infinite recursion**. In practice, such a method will run until the computer runs out of memory for the activation records and throws a `StackOverflowError` indicating that the execution stack has run out of memory for activation records. Phrased another way, a recursive declaration should not be "recursive all the way down." Otherwise, like the lady's explanation of the solar system, a recursive call will never end, except perhaps in frustration.

In this section, we will show you how to reason about recursion, both to show that there is no infinite recursion, and to show that a recursive method's results are correct. As an example, we'll start with a new recursive method called `power`, which computes powers of the form x^n, where x is any double number and n is an integer. So, `power(3.0, 2)` is 3.0^2 (which is 9.0), and `power(4.2, 3)` is 4.2^3 (which is 74.088). For any nonzero value of x, the value of x^0 is defined to be 1, so for example, `power(9.1, 0)` is 1. For a negative exponent, $-n$, the value returned is defined by:

$$x^{-n} = 1/x^n \quad \{ \ x \text{ is any real number, and } -n \text{ is a negative integer } \}$$

For example, `power(3.0, -2)` is $1/3.0^2$ (which is $\frac{1}{9}$). The only forbidden power is taking 0^n when n is not positive. The complete specification of the `power` method follows.

◆ **power**
  ```
  public static double power(double x, int n)
  ```
  Computes the value of x^n.

  Precondition:
    If x is zero, then n must be positive.

  Returns:
    x raised to the n power

  Throws: `IllegalArgumentException`
    Indicates that x is zero and n is not positive.

Our implementation begins by checking the precondition, and then deals with several cases. The first case, when n is non-negative, is easy. This case is computed by setting a local variable, `product`, to 1, and then repeatedly multiplying `product` by x. The repeated multiplication occurs n times, in this loop:

```
if (n >= 0)
{
    product = 1;
    for (count = 1, count <= n; count++)
        product = product * x;
    return product;
}
```

To understand what is needed for a negative exponent, let's consider a concrete case. Suppose that we are computing power(3.0, -2), which must return the value 3.0^{-2}. But this value is equal to $\frac{1}{3^2}$. Negative powers are the same as positive powers in the denominator. This means that if we know that the method returns the correct answer when n is positive, then we can calculate the correct value for power(3.0, -2) by the expression 1/power(3.0, 2). By thinking recursively, whenever n is negative, power can compute its answer with a recursive call, like this:

```
return 1/power(x, -n); // When n is negative (and so -n is positive)
```

Remember, in this statement, n is negative (such as -2), so that -n is positive, and therefore, the recursive call in the expression 1/power(x, -n) has a positive second argument. With a positive second argument, our power method makes no further recursive calls (i.e., a stopping case), and so the recursion ends.

This brings us to our first general technique for reasoning about recursion, which can be applied to the complete power method of Figure 8.10.

One Level Recursion

Suppose that every case is either a stopping case or it makes a recursive call that is a stopping case. Then the deepest recursive call is only one level deep, and therefore no infinite recursion occurs.

FIGURE 8.10   Implementation of the power Method with Only One Level of Recursion

---

Specification

- **power**

    ```
    public static double power(double x, int n)
    ```
    Computes the value of x^n.

    Precondition:
    If x is zero, then n must be positive.

    Returns:
    x raised to the n power

    Throws: IllegalArgumentException
    Indicates that x is zero and n is not positive.

Implementation

```
public static double power(double x, int n)
{
    double product; // The product of x with itself n times
    int count;

    if (x == 0 && n <= 0)
        throw new IllegalArgumentException("x is zero and n=" + n);

    if (n >= 0)
    {
        product = 1;
        for (count = 1; count <= n; count++)
            product = product * x;
        return product;
    }
    else
        return 1/power(x, -n);
}
```

Sample Results of the Method

Call with these arguments		Return value of the method
x	n	
3.0	2	9.0
2.0	-3	0.125
4.1	0	1.0
-2.0	3	-8.0

How to Ensure That There is No Infinite Recursion in the More General Case

In general, recursive calls don't stop just one level deep. A recursive call does not need to reach a stopping case immediately. Programmers have developed methods to reason about recursive calls that go beyond one level, based on the principles of *mathematical induction*. The reasoning can increase your confidence that a recursive method avoids infinite recursion. As an example to show that there is no infinite recursion, let's rewrite the method power so that it uses more recursion.

The revision is based on the observation that for any number x and any positive integer n, the following relation holds: $x^n = x(x^{n-1})$. This formula means that an alternative way to define x^n is as follows:

- The value of x^n is undefined when $n \leq 0$ and $x = 0$

- Otherwise the value is 0 when $x = 0$

- Otherwise the value is 1 when $n = 0$

- Otherwise the value is x times x^{n-1} when $n > 0$

- Otherwise the value is $1/x^{-n}$ when $n < 0$

The Java version of a recursive method that computes in this way is given in Figure 8.11. To avoid confusion, we have used a slightly different name, pow, for this version of the method.

an alternative algorithm for computing powers

FIGURE 8.11   Alternate Implementation of a Method to Compute Powers

Implementation

```java
public static double pow(double x, int n)
{
    if (x == 0 && n <= 0)
        throw new IllegalArgumentException("x is zero and n=" + n);
    else if (x == 0)
        return 0;
    else if (n == 0)
        return 1;
    else if (n > 0)
        return x * pow(x, n-1);
    else // x is nonzero, and n is negative.
        return 1/pow(x, -n);
}
```

Tracing a recursive method such as pow can quickly overwhelm you, but there are relatively simple ways of showing that there is no infinite recursion without actually tracing through the execution. The most common way to ensure that a stopping case is *eventually* reached is to define a numeric quantity called the *variant expression*. This quantity must associate each legal recursive call to a single number. In a moment we'll discuss the properties that the variant expression should have, but first let's look at the kind of quantity we have in mind for the variant expression of the pow method. The variant expression for pow is:

The Variant Expression for pow

The variant expression is abs(n) + 1 (when n is negative), and the variant expression is n (when n is non-negative).

With this definition we can examine a sequence of recursive pow calls, beginning with pow(2.0, -3), as follows.

A Sequence of Recursive Calls

pow(2.0, -3) has a variant expression abs(n) + 1, which is 4; it makes a recursive call of pow(2.0, 3).

pow(2.0, 3) has a variant expression n, which is 3; it makes a recursive call of pow(2.0, 2).

pow(2.0, 2) has a variant expression n, which is 2; it makes a recursive call of pow(2.0, 1).

pow(2.0, 1) has a variant expression n, which is 1; it makes a recursive call of pow(2.0, 0).

pow(2.0, 0) has a variant expression n, which is 0; this is the stopping case.

There are two important points to this example: (a) Each time a recursive call is made, the variant expression is reduced by at least one; and (b) when the variant expression reaches zero, there is a stopping case that terminates with no further recursive calls.

In general, a **variant expression** is a numeric quantity that is decreased by at least some fixed amount on each recursive call. And, once the variant expression reaches a small enough value, then a stopping case occurs. The "small enough value" that guarantees a stopping case is called the **threshold**. In the pow example, the threshold is zero, and each recursive call reduces the variant expression by one. A summary of the general technique for proving that a recursive call terminates is shown here:

variant expression and threshold

Ensuring That There Is No Infinite Recursion

To prove that a recursive call does not lead to infinite recursion, it is enough to find a *variant expression* and a *threshold* with the following properties:

1. Between one call of the method and any succeeding recursive call of that method, the value of the variant expression decreases by at least some fixed amount.

2. If the method is activated and the value of the variant expression is less than or equal to the threshold, then the method terminates without making any recursive calls.

It is important that the reduction is at least a fixed amount. Otherwise, the variant expression might start at 1, then decrease to one-half, then to one-quarter, then to one-eighth, and so on, decreasing by ever-smaller amounts and never reach the threshold. In the most common case, such as pow, the variant expression always decreases by at least one, and the threshold is zero.

To see that these two conditions guarantee no infinite recursion, reason as follows. Suppose the two conditions hold. Since Condition 1 is true, every recursive call will decrease the variant expression. This means that either the method will terminate, which is fine, or else the variant expression will decrease until it reaches the threshold. But if Condition 2 holds, then once the variant expression reaches the threshold, the method will terminate. That covers all the cases.

Inductive Reasoning about the Correctness of a Recursive Method

In addition to checking that a recursive method terminates, you should also check that it always behaves correctly—in other words that it meets its precondition/postcondition contract. The usual method for showing correctness of a recursive method is called **induction**. (And, in fact, the technique is the same as *mathematical induction,* which you may have used in math classes.) The

induction

induction approach requires a programmer to demonstrate the following facts about the method's behavior:

Induction Method to
Show That a Recursive Method Is Correct

To show that a recursive method meets its precondition/ postcondition contract, first show that there is no infinite recursion (by showing Conditions 1 and 2), and then show that the following two conditions are also valid:

3. Whenever the method makes no recursive calls, then it meets its precondition/postcondition contract. (This is called the **base step**.)

4. Whenever the method is activated *and* all the recursive calls it makes meet their precondition/postcondition contract, then the original call will also meet its precondition/ postcondition contract. (This is called the **induction step**.)

The conditions are numbered 3 and 4 to emphasize that they ensure correctness only if you know that there is no infinite recursion. You must also ensure that Conditions 1 and 2 hold for an appropriate variant expression and threshold.

Let's return to the method pow defined in Figure 8.11 on page 403. To complete our demonstration that it performs as desired, we must show that 3 and 4 hold.

It is easy to see that Condition 3 holds. The only way that the method can terminate without a recursive call is if the value of x is zero or n is zero. If x is zero the method returns 0, which is the correct answer; and if n is zero (and x is not zero) the method returns 1, which is also correct.

To see that Condition 4 holds we need only recall the algebraic identities:

$$x^n = x(x^{n-1}) \quad \text{and} \quad x^n = 1/x^{-n}$$

To summarize how to reason about recursion: First check that the method always terminates (no infinite recursion); next make sure that the stopping cases work correctly; finally, for each recursive case, pretend that you know the recursive calls will work correctly, and use this to show that each recursive case works correctly.

Recursion versus Loops

Programmers sometimes implement recursive methods and then worry about the extra cost of the recursive calls. After all, each recursive call requires the same resources as any other method activation. In particular, an activation record is created to store local variables and other information about the recursive call. This activation record is placed on the execution stack, on top of all the other activation records. If the sequence of recursive calls continues for a long time before the stopping case occurs, then we'll end up with a huge execution stack of activation records, possibly too large for the system resources, resulting in a StackOverflowError.

Because of this possibility, the programmer of a recursive method should have some idea of the maximum number of recursive calls before a stopping case is reached. This number is called the **depth of recursion**. When the depth of recursion is likely to cause a StackOverflowError, the programmer should rewrite the method using loops instead of recursion. Even without deep recursion, a programmer may want to rewrite a critical recursive method to avoid the overhead of making recursive calls.

One situation where recursion is easy to eliminate is called *tail recursion*. **Tail recursion** means that the recursive calls occur only at the end, just before the method is about to return. For example, here is a recursive method to calculate the length of a linked list, using the Node class from Appendix E:

```java
public static int listLength(Node head)
// Recursive version
{
    if (head == null)
        return 0;
    else
        return 1 + listLength(head.link);
}
```

This is a fine use of recursive thinking. The length of the whole list is one more than the length of the smaller list that contains everything except the head. But each node of the list causes the recursion depth to grow by one. For a list of 1000 nodes, the recursive listLength will create 1000 activation records, all piled one on another in the execution stack. Because of the large depth of recursion, the version with a loop (iterative version) is preferable, as shown here:

```java
public static int listLength(Node head)
{
    Node cursor;
    int answer;

    answer = 0;
    for (cursor = head; cursor != null; cursor = cursor.link)
        answer++;

    return answer;
}
```

Programming Tip: Avoid Tail Recursion

It's fine to think about a linked list recursively: A nonempty list has a head node followed by a smaller list that contains everything except the head. But avoid tail recursion in methods that manipulate linked lists because of the high depth of recursion that occurs.

By the way, some programming languages such as Lisp and Scheme have a heavy dependence on list manipulation. The compilers and other tools for those languages often have automatic mechanisms to convert tail recursion to a loop. In such a language, you can think recursively, program recursively, and have no worries about tail recursion causing a high depth of recursion.

Also, it is always possible to remove recursion, even if the recursion is not tail recursion. The general removal technique uses a stack to keep track of the unfinished work. You'll see an example of this technique when we remove recursion from a sorting algorithm in Programming Project 1 on page 614.

Self-Test Exercises

9. Write a recursive method that computes the number of digits in an integer n. (You might recall from page 22 that this is $\lfloor \log_{10} n \rfloor + 1$ for positive numbers.) Do not use any local variables in your method declaration. Find a variant expression and threshold to show that your method has no infinite recursion.

10. Use inductive reasoning to show that your method from the previous exercise is always correct.

11. Find variant expressions and thresholds to show that the methods `randomFractal` and `traverseMaze` (Section 8.2) never result in infinite recursion.

12. Use induction to show that `randomFractal` meets its precondition/postcondition contract.

13. Rewrite the pow method using these two facts for x^n:
    - If n is positive and even, then $x^n = x^{n/2} \times x^{n/2}$.
    - If n is positive and odd, then $x^n = x \times x^{n-1}$.

CHAPTER SUMMARY

- If a problem can be reduced to smaller instances of the same problem, then a recursive solution is likely to be easy to find and implement.
- A recursive algorithm for a method implementation contains two kinds of cases: one or more cases that include a *recursive call* and one or more *stopping cases* in which the problem is solved without the use of any recursive calls.
- When writing recursive methods, always check to see that the method will not produce infinite recursion. This can be done by finding an appropriate *variant expression* and *threshold*.
- *Inductive reasoning* can be used to show that a recursive method meets its precondition/postcondition contract.

Solutions to Self-Test Exercises

1. The top-left method prints 3, then 2, then 1. The top-right method prints 1, then 2, then 3. The bottom method prints 3, then 2, then 1, then 1 again, then 2 again, then 3 again.

2. The output is Hip, then Hip, then Hurrah, on three separate lines.

3. For the first modification, change the two lines in the else-block to:
```
cheers(n-1);
System.out.println("Hip");
```
For the second modification, change the lines to:
```
System.out.println("Hip");
cheers(n-1);
System.out.println("Hip");
```
For the third modification, change the lines to:
```
if (n % 2 == 0)
   System.out.println("Hip");
cheers(n-1);
if (n % 2 == 1)
   System.out.println("Hip");
```

4. The method's implementation is:
```
public static void exercise4(int n)
{
    if (n > 0)
    {
        System.out.print('*');
        exercise4(n-1);
        System.out.print('!');
    }
}
```

5. The original activation makes two calls with an x-distance of 12. Each of those calls makes two calls with an x-distance of 6, so there are four calls with an x-distance of 6. Each of those four calls makes two more calls, again cutting the width in half, so there are eight calls with an x-distance of 3. These eight calls do not make further calls since width has reached the stopping point. The total number of calls, including the original call, is 1 + 2 + 4 + 8, which is 15 calls.

6. Did you peek?

7. The easiest solution requires an extra parameter, called `level`, which indicates how deep the recursion has proceeded. When the revised method is called from a program, the value of `level` should be given as zero. Each recursive call increases the level by one. When the level is an even number, then the midpoint is moved upward; when the level is odd, then the midpoint is moved downward. The code to do the movement is as follows:

```
if (level % 2 == 0)
    midY += (rightX - leftX)/2;
else
    midY -= (rightX - leftX)/2;
```

8. Each recursive call steps forward into a location that has not previously been visited. Therefore, the number of calls can be no more than the number of locations in the maze, which is 200.

9. The method's implementation is:

```
int digits(int n)
{
    if (n < 10) && (n > -10))
        return 1;
    else
        return 1 + digits(n/10);
}
```

A good variant expression is "the number of digits in n," with the threshold of 1.

10. The stopping case includes numbers that are less than ten and more than negative ten. All these numbers have one digit, and the method correctly returns the answer 1. For the induction case, we have a number *n* with more than one digit. The number of digits will always be one more than *n*/10 (using integer division), so if we assume that the recursive call of `digits(n/10)` returns the right answer, then `1 + digits(n/10)` is the correct number of digits in *n*.

11. For `randomFractal`, a good variant expression is `(rightX-leftX)`. If we make a recursive call, then this expression is greater than 4 and the recursive call cuts the expression in half. Therefore, each recursive call subtracts at least 2 from the expression. When the expression reaches 4 (or less), the recursion stops. Therefore, 4 is the threshold.

The method `traverseMaze` has a variant expression that is expressed in English as "the number of locations in the maze that do not yet have your name written on the ground." This value is reduced by at least one during each recursive call, and when this value reaches zero, there can be no further recursive calls. Therefore, 0 is the threshold.

12. We have already found a variant expression and threshold for Conditions 1 and 2, showing that `randomFractal` does not result in infinite recursion. For Condition 3, we must show that the method has correct behavior for the stopping case. In this case, `(rightX-leftX)` is no more than `STOP`, and therefore the line segment does not need further dividing. We only need to draw the current line segment, which is what the method does. In Condition 4 of the inductive reasoning, we assume that the two recursive calls correctly generate a random fractal for the two smaller line segments that we have created. Putting these two smaller random fractals together correctly gives us the larger random fractal.

13. In Figure 8.11 on page 403, we change the `(n > 0)` block to this:

```
if ((n > 0) && (n % 2 == 1))
    return x * pow(x, n-1);
else if ((n > 0) && (n % 2 == 0))
{
    double partial = pow(x, n/2);
    return partial * partial;
}
```

PROGRAMMING PROJECTS

1 Write a method that produces the following output:

```
This was written by call number 1.
 This was written by call number 2.
  This was written by call number 3.
   This was written by call number 4.
   This ALSO written by call number 4.
  This ALSO written by call number 3.
 This ALSO written by call number 2.
This ALSO written by call number 1.
```

In this example, the recursion stopped when it reached four levels deep, but your method should be capable of continuing to any specified level.

2 Write a method with two parameters, `prefix` (a string) and `levels` (a nonnegative integer). The method prints the string `prefix` followed by "section numbers" of the form 1.1., 1.2., 1.3., and so on. The `levels` argument determines how many levels the section numbers have. For example, if `levels` is 2, then the section numbers have the form `x.y`. If `levels` is 3, then the section numbers have the form `x.y.z`. The digits permitted in each level are always `'1'` through `'9'`. As an example, if `prefix` is the string `"BOX:"` and `levels` is 2, then the method would start by printing

```
BOX:1.1.
BOX:1.2.
BOX:1.3.
```

and finish by printing

```
BOX:9.7.
BOX:9.8.
BOX:9.9.
```

The stopping case occurs when `levels` reaches zero. The primary string manipulation technique that you will need is the ability to create a new string that consists of `prefix` followed by a digit and a period. If s is the string you want to create and i is the digit (an integer in the range 1 to 9), then the following statement will perform this task:

```
s = prefix + '.' + i;
```

The last part of the expression puts the character that corresponds to the integer i onto the end of the string. This new string, s, can be passed as a parameter to recursive calls.

3 Write a recursive method that has two parameters, `first` and `second`, which are both strings. The method should print all rearrangements of the letters in `first`, followed by `second`. For example, if `first` is the string `"CAT"` and `second` is the string `"MAN"`, then the method would print the strings CATMAN, CTAMAN, ACTMAN, ATCMAN, TACMAN, and TCAMAN. The stopping case of the method occurs when the length of `first` has zero characters. We'll leave the recursive thinking up to you, but we should mention three string techniques that will make things go smoother. These techniques are:

(1) The following expression is a string consisting of all of `first` followed by character number i from `second`:

```
first + second.charAt(i)
```

(2) The following expression is a string consisting of all of `second` with character i removed. The value of i must be less than the last index of the string. The first part of the expression is everything

from location 0 to location i-1, and the second part of the expression is everything after location i.

```
second.substring(0, i)
+
second.substring(i+1);
```

(3) The following expression is a string consisting of all of second except the last character. In order for this to work, the string must be nonempty.

```
second.substring(0, s.length()-1)
```

The stopping case occurs when the length of the second string is zero (in which case you just print the first string). For the recursive case, make one recursive call for each character in the second string. During each recursive call, you take one character out of second and add it to the end of first.

4 Write an interactive program to help you count all of the boxes in a room. The program should begin by asking something like *How many unnumbered boxes can you see?* Then the program will have you number those boxes from 1 to *m*, where *m* is your answer. But, remember that each box might have smaller boxes inside, so once the program knows you can see *m* boxes, it should ask you to open box number 1 and take out any boxes you find, numbering those boxes 1.1, 1.2, and so on. It will also ask you to open box number 2 and take out any boxes you find there, numbering those boxes 2.1, 2.2, and so on. This continues for box 3, 4, up to *m*. And, of course, each time you number a box 1.1 or 3.8 or something similar, *that* box might have more boxes inside. Boxes that reside inside of 3.8 would be numbered 3.8.1, 3.8.2, and so on. At the end, the program should print a single number telling you the total number of boxes in the room.

5 Write a recursive method called sumover that has one argument *n,* which is a nonnegative integer. The method returns a double value, which is the sum of the reciprocals of the first *n* positive integers. (The reciprocal of *x* is the fraction 1/*x*.) For example, sumover(1) returns 1.0 (which is 1/1); sumover(2) returns 1.5 (which is 1/1 + 1/2); sumover(3) returns approximately 1.833 (which is 1/1 + 1/2 + 1/3). Define sumover(0) to be zero. Do not use any local variables in your method.

6 The formula for computing the number of ways of choosing *r* different things from a set of *n* things is the following:

$$C(n, r) = \frac{n!}{r!(n-r)!}$$

In this formula, the factorial function is represented by an exclamation point (!), and defined as the product:

$$n! = n \times (n-1) \times (n-2) \times \ldots \times 1$$

Discover a recursive version of the *C(n, r)* formula and write a recursive method that computes the value of the formula. Embed the method in a program and test it.

7 Write a recursive method that has as arguments an array of characters and two bounds on array indexes. The method should reverse the order of those entries in the array whose indexes are between the two bounds. For example, suppose that the array is:

```
a[0] = 'A'   a[1] = 'B'   a[2] = 'C'
a[3] = 'D'   a[4] = 'E'
```

and the bounds are 1 and 4. Then after the method is run the array elements should be:

```
a[0] = 'A'   a[1] = 'D'   a[2] = 'C'
a[3] = 'B'   a[4] = 'e'
```

Embed the method in a program and test it.

8 Write a recursive method to produce a pattern of *n* lines of asterisks. The first line contains one asterisk, the next line contains 2, and so on up to the *n*[th] line, which contains *n* asterisks. Line number *n*+1 again contains *n* asterisks, the next line has *n*-1 asterisks, and so on until line number 2*n*, which has just one asterisk.

9 Examine this pattern of asterisks and blanks, and write a recursive method that can generate exactly this pattern:

```
*
*   *
    *
*   *   *
    *
        *   *
        *
*   *   *   *   *   *   *   *
    *
        *   *
        *
            *   *   *
            *
                *   *
                *
```

With recursive thinking, the method needs only seven or eight lines of code (including two recursive calls). How is this pattern a fractal? Your method should also be capable of producing larger or smaller patterns of the same variety. Hint: Have two parameters. One parameter indicates the indentation of the leftmost line in the pattern; the other parameter indicates the number of stars in the longest line.

10 Write a program that asks the user to think of an integer between 1 and 1,000,000, and then guesses the number through a series of yes/no questions. To guess the number, the program calls a recursive method `guess` that has two parameters, `low` and `high`. The precondition for the method requires that the user's number lie in the range `low...high`, so that the program's initial call is to `guess(1, 1000000)`. What is a good stopping case for `guess`, when it can guess the user's number with little or no work? Answer: If (`low == high`) then there is only one possible number, and the method can guess that number. On the other hand, if (`low < high`) then the method should calculate a point near the middle of the range:

```
midpoint = (low + high) / 2;
```

Then the method asks the user whether the midpoint is the correct number. If so, then the method is finished. On the other hand, if the midpoint is not the user's number, then the method asks whether the correct number is larger than `midpoint`. If so, then the method knows that the user's number lies in the range `midpoint + 1` to `high`, and a recursive call can be made to solve the smaller problem of finding a user's number in the range `midpoint + 1` to `high`. On the other hand, if the user's number is not larger than `midpoint`, then a recursive call can be made to solve the smaller problem of finding a user's number in the range `low` to `midpoint - 1`. This method of searching is called **binary search**, which we will explore further in Chapter 11.

11 This project uses the `Towers` class from Chapter 3's Programming Project 12 on page 170. For the project, write a recursive method that computes and prints a solution to the Towers of Hanoi game. The method should meet this specification:

```
public static void Hanoi(
    Towers t,
    int n,
    int start,
    int target,
    int spare
);
// Precondition: start, target, and spare are
// three different peg numbers of the game,
// and n is non-negative.
// Also, the n smallest rings currently are on
// the top of the start peg.
// Postcondition: The method has activated
// a sequence of moves for the tower t, so
// that the total effect of these moves is to
// shift the top n rings from the start peg to
// the target peg, using spare as the extra
// peg. None of the other rings has been
// disturbed. Each time a move is made,
// a message describing the move is
// printed.
```

Your solution should have a simple stopping case: When *n* is zero, there is no work to do. When *n* is more than zero, use a recursive call to move *n*-1 rings from the start peg to the spare peg. Then call the move method to move one ring from the start peg to the target peg. Finally, make another recursive call to move $n-1$ rings from the spare peg to the target peg.

---

12 For this project, you are to write a recursive method that prints all of the objects in a bag. Use the bag specification from Figure 4.12 on page 211, which is a bag of integers. The integers are to be printed in a random order—without using any of the bag private instance variables. For an empty bag, the method has no work to do (that is, the stopping case). For a nonempty bag, the method carries out four steps: (a) grab a random integer from the bag, storing it in a local variable oneItem; (b) print oneItem; (c) print any items that remain in the bag; (d) put oneItem back in the bag. You'll need to identify which of these steps is the "simpler version of the same problem."

13 Let's think about your computer science class for a moment. You might know several students, perhaps Judy, Jervis, Walter, and Michael. Each of those students knows several other students, and each of those knows more students and so on. Now, there is one particular student named Dor that you would like to meet. One way to meet Dor would be if you had a mutual acquaintance. You know Judy, and Judy knows Dor, so Judy could introduce you to Dor. Or, there might be a longer path of acquaintances: For example, you know Judy, and Judy knows Harry, and Harry knows Cathy, and Cathy knows Dor. In this case, Judy can introduce you to Harry, Harry can introduce you to Cathy, and Cathy can introduce you to Dor.

Write an interactive program to help you figure out whether there is a path of acquaintances from you to Dor. The program should include a recursive method that has one argument, person, which is the name of a person in your class. The method determines whether there is a path of acquaintances from person to Dor. Hint: This problem is similar to the maze problem in Section 8.2, but beware of potential infinite recursion! One way to avoid infinite recursion is to include a bag of student names, which keeps track of the names of the students you have already visited on your search for a path to Dor.

14 A *pretty print* program takes a program, which may not be indented in any particular way, and produces a copy with the same program indented so that bracket pairs ({ and }) line up with inner pairs indented more than outer pairs, so that if-else statements are indented as we have been doing, and so that other indenting is as we have been doing. Write a program that reads a Java program from one text file and produces a pretty print version of the program in a second text file. To make it easier, simply do this for each method, ignoring the things outside of methods.

Trees

Some people call it the Tree of Heaven. No matter where its seed fell, it made a tree which struggles to reach the sky.

BETTY SMITH
A Tree Grows in Brooklyn

CHAPTER

9

This chapter presents a new data structure, a tree, which is our first example of a **nonlinear structure**. In a nonlinear structure the components do not form a simple sequence of first element, second element, third element, and so on. Instead, there is a more complex linking between the components; this is why they are called *non*linear. The nonlinear structure often allows dramatically improved efficiency for collection classes.

nonlinear structures

The chapter starts with definitions of various kinds of trees and their applications. We then show how to represent trees and implement a node class for building and manipulating trees. The node is useful for many ADTs such as the binary search tree used in the final section of this chapter.

415

9.1   INTRODUCTION TO TREES

Binary Trees

Before I left my bed in the morning, little Adèle came running in to tell me that the great horse-chestnut at the bottom of the orchard had been struck by lightning in the night, and half of it split away.

CHARLOTTE BRONTË
Jane Eyre

a real tree. . .

The first kind of tree that we'll look at is a *binary tree*, which is the most commonly used tree data structure. A binary tree is not too different from a real tree. The real tree starts at its root, growing upward. At some point, the trunk splits into two smaller branches. Each of the smaller branches continues, perhaps splitting into two still smaller branches, and so forth until each branch ends with some leaves.

If you take that tree, pull it out of the ground, and stick its root in the air, you will have a computer scientist's tree. You see, a computer scientist draws a tree with the root at the top, branches below that, and leaves at the very bottom. And, of course, a computer scientist's tree contains data of one kind or another. Let's be more specific, with a concrete example of a binary tree of integers, shown in Figure 9.1.

. . .and a computer scientist's tree

Each of the boxes in Figure 9.1 is called a **node** of the tree, and each node contains some data—in this case each piece of data is an integer, but we might also have trees of double numbers, trees of strings, even trees where each node's data is a complex type like a stack or a queue. The node at the top of the diagram, which has the number 14, is called the **root**. Each node in a binary tree may have up to two nodes below it, one linked on its left and one linked on its right. These are called the node's **left child** and **right child**. For example, the root's left child is the node containing 17, and its right child contains 11. Some nodes have only a left child, some have only a right child, and some have no children at all.

FIGURE 9.1   A Binary Tree of Integers

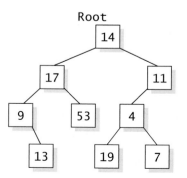

A node with no children is called a **leaf**. In more general kinds of trees, a node may have more than two children, but for the **binary** trees that we're discussing, each node is limited to at most two children. One other point: With the exception of the root, each node is the child of just one node; the root is not the child of any node.

Much of the terminology for trees comes from family relations, such as the word "child." Perhaps you can guess the meaning of some other terms: *parent, sibling, ancestor, descendant.* These definitions are given later, but first we'll provide a complete definition of a binary tree:

Binary Trees

A **binary tree** is a finite set of "nodes." The set might be empty (no nodes, which is called the **empty tree**). But if the set is not empty, it follows these rules:

1. There is one special node, called the **root**.

2. Each node may be associated with up to two other different nodes, called its **left child** and its **right child**. If a node *c* is the child of another node *p*, then we say that "*p* is *c*'s **parent**."

3. Each node, except the root, has exactly one parent; the root has no parent.

4. If you start at a node and move to the node's parent (provided there is one), then move again to that node's parent, and keep moving upward to each node's parent, you will eventually reach the root.

Here are some other terms used with trees, with examples selected from Figure 9.2 on page 418.

tree terminology

Parent. The **parent** of a node is the node linked above it. More precisely, if a node *c* is the child of another node *p*, then we say that "*p* is *c*'s **parent**." Except for the root, every node has just one parent, and the root has no parent. In Figure 9.2(a), the node containing 17 is the parent of the nodes containing 9 and 53.

Sibling. Two nodes are **siblings** if they have the same parent. In Figure 9.2(a), the nodes containing 9 and 53 are siblings.

Ancestor. A node's parent is its first ancestor. The parent of the parent is the next ancestor. The parent of the parent of the parent is the next ancestor . . . and so forth, until you reach the root. The root is an ancestor of each other node.

FIGURE 9.2 More Examples of Binary Trees

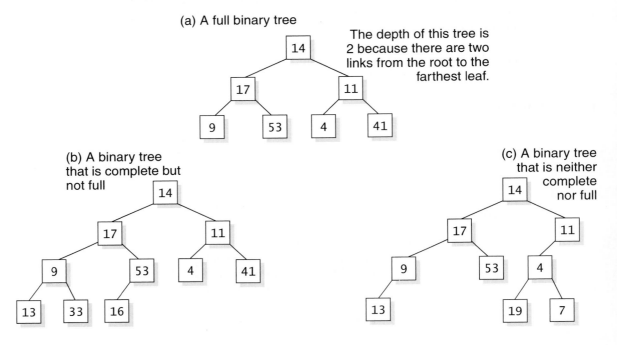

(a) A full binary tree

The depth of this tree is 2 because there are two links from the root to the farthest leaf.

(b) A binary tree that is complete but not full

(c) A binary tree that is neither complete nor full

Descendant. A node's children are its first descendants. The children's children are its next descendants. The children of the children of the children are... well, you get the idea.

Subtree. Any node in a tree also can be viewed as the root of a new, smaller tree. This smaller tree contains the node that we've picked as the new root and all of the new root's descendants. This is called a **subtree** of the original tree. In Figure 9.2(a), we may choose 17 as the root of a new subtree, and that subtree has three nodes: the nodes containing 17, 9, and 53.

Left and Right Subtrees of a Node. For a node in a binary tree, the nodes beginning with its left child and below are its **left subtree.** The nodes beginning with its right child and below are its **right subtree.**

Depth of a Node. Suppose you start at a node *n* and move upward to its parent. We'll call this "one step." Then move up to the parent of the parent—that's a second step. Eventually, you will reach the root, and the number of steps taken is called the **depth of the node** *n*. The depth of the root itself is zero; a child of the root has depth one. In Figure 9.2(b), the node containing 13 has depth three.

Depth of a Tree. The **depth of a tree** is the maximum depth of any of its leaves. In Figure 9.2(b), the leaf containing 13 has depth three, and there is no deeper leaf. So the depth of the example tree is three. If a tree has only one node, the root, then its depth is zero (since the depth of the root is zero). The empty tree doesn't have any leaves, so we use −1 for its depth. Just to confuse things, you'll often see the term *height* of a tree used instead of *depth*, but they both mean the same thing.

Full Binary Trees. In a **full binary tree**, every leaf has the same depth, and every nonleaf has two children. Figure 9.1 on page 416 is not a full tree because it has leaves at different depths—some with depth two and some with depth three. Also, some of the nonleaves have only one child. In Figure 9.2, part (a) is full, but parts (b) and (c) are not full.

Complete Binary Trees. Suppose you take a full binary tree and start adding new leaves at a new depth from left to right. All the new leaves have the same depth—one more than where we started—and we always add leftmost nodes first. For example, if you add three nodes to Figure 9.2(a), then one possible result is Figure 9.2(b). The tree is no longer a full tree because some leaves are a bit deeper than others. Instead, we call this a **complete binary tree**. In order to be a complete tree, every level except the deepest must contain as many nodes as possible; and at the deepest level, all the nodes are as far left as possible.

Binary Taxonomy Trees

Binary trees are useful in many situations. We'll look at one example, **binary taxonomy trees**, which can be used to store certain kinds of knowledge. The particular example we have in mind stores information about a collection of animals. Each leaf in a binary taxonomy tree contains the name of an animal, and each nonleaf node contains a question about animals.

binary taxonomy trees store knowledge about a collection of animals

For example, suppose that we want a taxonomy tree for four animals: a kangaroo, a mouse, a trout, and a robin. The tree might look like Figure 9.3. To use a binary taxonomy tree, you start at the root and ask the question that is written there. If the answer is "yes," you move to the left child, and if the answer is "no,"

FIGURE 9.3 A Small Binary Taxonomy Tree

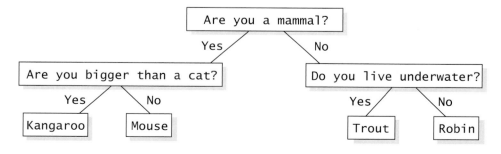

you move to the right child. Eventually, you will reach a leaf, and the name at the leaf tells you which animal you have been examining—or at least it does if the animal is one of the animals that the tree knows about.

General Trees

Each node in a binary tree has at most two children. In fact, that's why the word "binary'" is used. But in general, a node in a tree may have any number of children. Figure 9.4 shows an example where some nodes have one child, some have two, and some have three. A node in a general tree might even have more than three children (although three is the most in Figure 9.4). In Figure 9.4 we have not written any data at the nodes—but we could have written integers or strings or whatever data type we were interested in storing.

Trees

A **tree** is a finite set of "nodes." The set might be empty (no nodes, which is called the **empty tree**). But if the set is not empty, then it must follow these rules:

1. There is one special node, called the **root**.

2. Each node may be associated with one or more different nodes, called its **children**. If a node *c* is the child of another node *p*, then we say that "*p* is *c*'s **parent**."

3. Each node except the root has exactly one parent; the root has no parent.

4. If you start at any node and move to the node's parent (provided there is one), then move again to that node's parent (provided there is one), and keep moving upward to each node's parent, you will eventually reach the root.

FIGURE 9.4 A General Tree

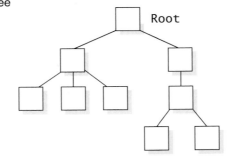

There are other special kinds of trees. For example, Section 10.2 uses B-trees, which are trees where the number of children of each node must lie between a certain minimum and a certain maximum.

Self-Test Exercises

1. Draw a binary tree with 12 nodes. Circle the root, and put asterisks at each leaf. Find two nodes that are siblings, and connect them with a wiggly line. Choose one of the leaves, and shade all of its ancestors.

2. Draw a tree that contains members of your family. The root should contain your mother's mother. Her children nodes contain her actual children, and those nodes contain her children's children, and so on.

3. What is the depth of the tree from Exercise 2? What is the depth of the node that contains *you*. Draw a circle around all nodes that are your ancestor nodes. Does each of these nodes contain one of your real-life ancestors? Draw a big square around all nodes that are descendants of your mother. Does each of these nodes contain one of her real-life descendants?

4. Create a binary taxonomy tree with 16 animals. Is your tree full? Is it complete?

9.2   TREE REPRESENTATIONS

This section discusses two kinds of trees and how they typically are represented in a data structure. For the most part, if you understand these two representations, you can also manage other kinds of trees.

Array Representation of Complete Binary Trees

Complete binary trees have a simple representation using arrays. The representation may use a fixed-sized array, so that the number of nodes in the tree is limited to the size of the array. Or the representation can use an array that grows according to the number of nodes (as in the collection classes of Chapter 3).

Remember that in a complete binary tree, all of the depths are full, except perhaps for the deepest. At the deepest depth, the nodes are as far left as possible. For example, here is a complete binary tree with ten nodes where the element contained in each node is a character. In this example, the first seven nodes completely fill the levels at depth zero (the root), depth one (the root's children), and depth two. There are three more nodes at depth three, and these nodes are as far left as possible.

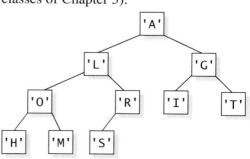

The ten characters that the tree contains can be stored in an array of characters, starting with the root's character in the [0] location of the array, as shown here:

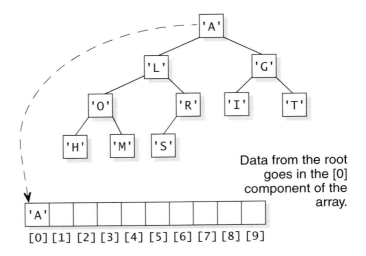

Data from the root goes in the [0] component of the array.

After the root, the two nodes with depth one are placed in the array, as shown here:

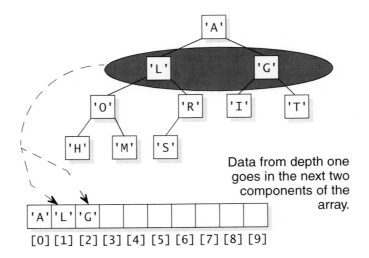

Data from depth one goes in the next two components of the array.

We continue in this way, placing the four nodes of depth two next and finishing off with the nodes of depth three. The entire representation of the tree by an array is shown at the top of the next page.

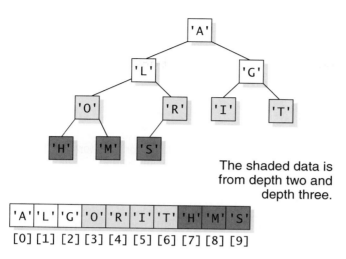

The shaded data is
from depth two and
depth three.

There are several reasons why the array representation is convenient:

1. The data from the root always appears in the [0] component of the array.

2. Suppose that the data for a nonroot node appears in component [i] of the array. Then the data for its parent is always at location [(i-1)/2] (using integer division).

3. Suppose that the data for a node appears in component [i] of the array. Then its children (if they exist) always have their data at these locations:

Left child at component [2i+1];

Right child at component [2i+2].

formulas for storing data from a complete binary tree in the components of an array

These formulas make it easy to implement algorithms that traverse the tree, moving from node to node in various ways, processing data along the way.

Before long you will implement some ADTs that store data in a tree. If the tree is a complete binary tree, then the ADT can store the complete binary tree in an array, using the formulas that we have written. Such a class will have at least two private instance variables: (1) The array itself is one instance variable, and (2) a second instance variable keeps track of how much of the array is used. The actual links between the nodes are not stored. Instead, these links exist only via the formulas that determine where an element is stored in the array based on the element's position in the tree.

As a complete binary tree grows, the array size can be increased as necessary to handle more and more nodes.

Noncomplete binary trees can also be implemented using an array, although a problem arises in determining which children of a node actually exist. We'll address this problem in Programming Project 3 on page 479. But for now, let's look at the other alternative: an implementation of binary trees that allocates and releases nodes as needed.

Representing a Binary Tree with a Class for Nodes

A binary tree can be represented by its individual nodes, where each node is an object of a new binary tree node class that we will define, similar to the way that we used a node class to build linked lists. Here is the basic idea:

> ### Node Representation of Binary Trees
>
> Each node of a binary tree can be stored as an object of a binary tree node class. The class contains private instance variables that are references to other nodes in the tree. An entire tree is represented as a reference to the root node.

For a binary tree, each node will contain references to its left child and right child. The node also has at least one instance variable to hold some data. The type of the data could be one of the eight primitive types, such as a char value, or each node could hold data that is a Java Object. Here are two definitions that we could use for binary tree nodes that contain different kinds of data:

This implementation has char data in each node:

```
class CharBTNode
{
    private char data;
    private CharBTNode left;
    private CharBTNode right;
    ...
```

This implementation has Object data in each node:

```
class BTNode
{
    private Object data;
    private BTNode left;
    private BTNode right;
    ...
```

When we get around to implementing the class, we'll use Java's Object type for the data, but keep in mind that we could use one of the primitive types instead. In any implementation, the data instance variable of a node holds some information that occurs in the node. Each binary tree node also contains two instance variables, left and right, which refer to the left and right children of the node. When a reference to a child is null, it indicates that the particular child does not exist. We could include other references in a binary tree node: perhaps a reference to the node's parent, or to the root of the entire tree, or even to siblings. But many applications need only references to the children.

We can draw a boxes-and-arrows representation of a small tree, as in Figure 9.5. This is a tree of characters, so each node is stored in a CharBTNode, and the entire tree is accessed through a reference to the root node of the tree. Within the diagram, a null reference is drawn as a slash. The reference to the root node is similar to the head of a linked list, providing a starting point to access all the nodes in the tree. If the tree was empty (with no nodes), then the root reference would be null.

FIGURE 9.5   A Binary Tree Represented with the CharBTNode Class

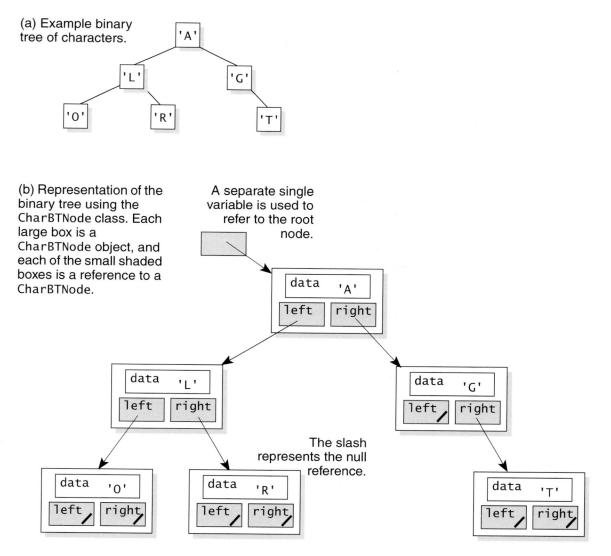

(a) Example binary tree of characters.

(b) Representation of the binary tree using the CharBTNode class. Each large box is a CharBTNode object, and each of the small shaded boxes is a reference to a CharBTNode.

A separate single variable is used to refer to the root node.

The slash represents the null reference.

Self-Test Exercises

5. Consider a complete binary tree with exactly 10,000 nodes, implemented with an array. Suppose that a node has its value stored in location 4999. Where is the value stored for this node's parent? Where is the value stored for its left child? What can you say about its right child?

6. Draw a boxes-and-arrows representation of a small binary tree with three nodes containing integers. Put 10 in the root, 20 in the left child of the root, and 30 in the right child of the root.

7. Define the instance variables for a new node implementation that could be used for a tree where each node has up to four children, and each node also has a reference to its parent. Store the references to the children in an array of four references to nodes. The node data is a Java `Object`.

9.3   A CLASS FOR BINARY TREE NODES

We now have an understanding of the instance variables for a binary tree node. With this in hand, we're ready to write methods for the BTNode class, which begins like this:

```
public class BTNode
{
    private Object data;     // The data stored in this node
    private BTNode left;     // Reference to the left child
    private BTNode right;    // Reference to the right child
    ...
```

We begin with a constructor that's responsible for initializing the three instance variables of a new binary tree node.

Constructor for the BTNode class. The node's constructor has three arguments, which are the initial values for the node's data and link variables, as specified here:

◆ **Constructor for the BTNode**
```
public BTNode
    (Object initialData, BTNode initialLeft, BTNode initialRight)
```
Initialize a node with a specified initial data and links to children. Note that a reference to a child may be null, which indicates that there is no child.

Parameters:
    `initialData` – the initial data of this new node
    `initialLeft` and `initialRight` – references to the children

Postcondition:
    This new node contains the specified data and links to its children.

This constructor creates a new node with specified data. When the node is created, the programmer also specifies references to the left and right children. These references may be null to indicate that a child doesn't exist. The implementation merely fills in the three instance variables from the values of the three parameters, as shown here:

```
public BTNode(
    Object initialData,
    BTNode initialLeft,
    BTNode initialRight
)
{
    data = initialData;
    left = initialLeft;
    right = initialRight;
}
```

Getting and setting data and links.   There are three methods for setting the data and links of a node. Three other methods get the data and links. The headings of the get and set methods are given here:

```
public Object getData( )  // Gets the data from this node
public BTNode getLeft( )  // Gets reference to left child of this node
public BTNode getRight( ) // Gets reference to right child of this node

public void setData(Object newData)    // Set data of this node
public void setLeft(BTNode newLeft)    // Set left child
public void setRight(BTNode newRight)  // Set right child
```

getData
getLeft
getRight
setData
setLeft
setRight

The six implementations are straightforward. Keep in mind that a node might not have children; for example, if there is no left child, then this implementation of getLeft will return the null reference:

```
public BTNode getLeft( )
{
    return left;
}
```

Testing whether a node is a leaf.   Our next method tests whether a node is a leaf. You can write the specification yourself. Here is our implementation:

```
public boolean isLeaf( )
{
    return (left == null) && (right == null);
}
```

isLeaf

Getting data from the leftmost or rightmost node.   Some applications need to retrieve the data from the leftmost or rightmost node of a tree. The leftmost node is obtained by starting at the root and following only left links. For example, consider this tree of strings:

In this example, the leftmost node contains the string "Chicago" (not "Denver," since getting to "Denver" uses one right link). Here's the method to find the data from the leftmost node:

getLeftmostData
getRightmostData

- **getLeftmostData**

     public Object getLeftmostData( )
     Accessor method to get the data from the leftmost node of the tree starting with this node.

     Returns:
       the data from the deepest node that can be reached from this node following left links

```
public Object getLeftmostData( )
{
    if (left == null)
        return data;
    else
        return left.getLeftmostData( );
}
```

This is a recursive implementation. In the base case, there are no more left links to follow, so the method returns the data from the node that activated the method. On the other hand, if there is a left link, then we get the leftmost data by making the recursive call `left.getLeftmostData( )`, which gets the leftmost data from the left subtree.

   You can write a similar method to get the data from the rightmost node.

Removing the leftmost or rightmost node.   Some programs remove the leftmost or rightmost node of a tree, resulting in a new, smaller tree. For example, if we remove the rightmost node from the tree of strings shown above, we end up with this smaller tree (without "Wichita"):

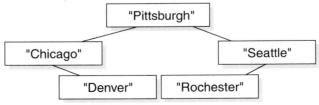

The specification of a method to remove the leftmost node is given here:

removeLeftmost
removeRightmost

+ **removeLeftmost**
    `public BTNode removeLeftmost( )`
    Remove the leftmost node of the tree with this node as its root.
    Postcondition:
    The tree starting at this node has had its leftmost node removed (i.e., the deepest node that can be reached by following left links). The return value is a reference to the root of the new (smaller) tree. This return value could be null if the original tree had only one node (since that one node has now been removed).
    Example:
    If n is a reference to a node in a tree, and n has a right child, then we can remove the leftmost node of n's right subtree with the statement:
        `n.setRight(n.getRight( ).removeLeftmost( ));`

Let's look at the example from the specification. For this example, suppose that n refers to the root node of this tree:

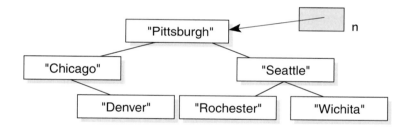

We would like to remove the leftmost node in n's right subtree, which is the node containing "Rochester." Now, `n.getRight( )` is a reference to the "Seattle" node, so `n.getRight( ).removeLeftmost( )` will remove "Rochester" and have a return value that is the reference to the root of the new smaller subtree. We need to set n's right link to the new smaller tree, so the complete statement to remove the leftmost node in n's right subtree is:

```
n.setRight(n.getRight( ).removeLeftmost( ));
```

The resulting tree will look like this:

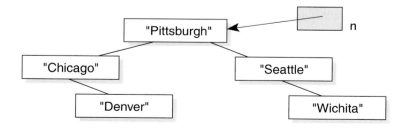

Notice that our statement for the removal actually sets n's right link to the root of the new smaller subtree. This is important because in some cases the root of the subtree might now be null or it could be a different node. For example, suppose we want to remove the leftmost node of n's right subtree a second time. We start from this situation:

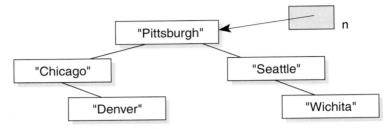

From this situation we activate:

```
n.setRight(n.getRight( ).removeLeftmost( ));
```

The leftmost node of the right subtree now contains "Seattle" itself, so the activation of n.getRight( ).removeLeftmost( ) will remove the "Seattle" node and return a reference to the new smaller subtree (which contains only "Wichita"). The right link of n is set to refer to the new smaller tree, so we end up with this situation:

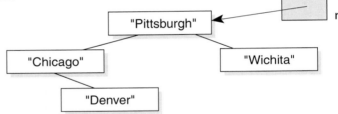

The implementation of removeLeftmost has a simple case when the node that activates removeLeftmost has no left child. This is the situation that we just saw, where the "Seattle" node had no left child. In this case, the node that activates removeLeftmost is itself the leftmost node of the tree (or subtree). So, we simply return a reference to the rest of the tree, which is on the right side. Thus, the implementation begins like this:

```
public BTNode removeLeftmost( )
{
    if (left == null)
        return right;
    . . .
```

For the preceding example, this code returns a reference to the node that contains "Wichita."

And what if there is a left child? In this case we want to remove the leftmost node from the left subtree. For example, suppose that the root of this tree activates `removeLeftmost`:

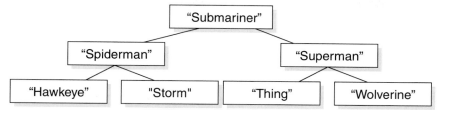

We must remove the leftmost node from the tree. Since the root has a left child, we can accomplish our task by removing the leftmost node from the left subtree (remove the leftmost node from the subtree that has its root at "Spiderman"). This is a smaller version of the very problem that we are trying to solve, and we can solve this smaller problem by a recursive call of `left.removeLeftmost( )`. The recursive call will remove the leftmost node from the left subtree (removing "Hawkeye"), and return a reference to the new smaller left subtree. This new smaller left subtree may have a different root than the original left subtree, so we need to set our left link to refer to the new smaller subtree. The complete statement to remove the leftmost node from the left subtree and set the left link to this new smaller tree is:

```
left = left.removeLeftmost( );
```

This is a recursive call because we are using `removeLeftmost` to solve a smaller version of the `removeLeftmost` problem. After the recursive call, the tree looks like this:

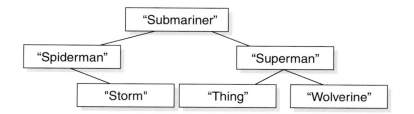

In this recursive solution, there is one last task. We must return a reference to the entire tree. This entire tree is now smaller than the tree that we began with ("Hawkeye" has been lost). The root to this smaller tree is the very node that activated `removeLeftmost` in the first place—so how do we refer to that node so that we can use it in the method's return statement? The answer is Java's keyword "`this`." Within any method, the keyword "`this`" is always a reference to the object that activated the method. So, `removeLeftmost` uses "`this`" as shown in the following complete implementation.

```
public BTNode removeLeftmost( )
{
    if (left == null)
    {   // The leftmost node is at the root because there is no left child.
        return right;
    }
    else
    {   // A recursive call removes the leftmost node from my left subtree.
        left = left.removeLeftmost( );
        return this;
    }
}
```

Notice the final line in the recursive case—`return this`—which returns a reference to the original node that activated the method. In the example at the bottom of the previous page, this would return a reference to the "Submariner" node.

You can implement `removeRightmost` yourself, using a similar recursive pattern.

Copying a tree. Our last method is a static method that may be used at any time to copy an entire tree. The parameter to this method is a reference to the root node of a tree that we are copying, as shown here:

treeCopy

♦ **treeCopy**
  `public static BTNode treeCopy(BTNode source)`
  Copy a binary tree.

  Parameters:
  `source` – a reference to the root node of a binary tree that will be copied
  (which may be an empty tree where `source` is null)

  Returns:
  The method has made a copy of the binary tree starting at `source`. The
  return value is a reference to the root of the copy.

  Throws: `OutOfMemoryError`
  Indicates that there is insufficient memory for the new tree.

Notice that the parameter, `source`, may be null. This would indicate that the tree that we are copying is empty (has no nodes), and in this case the `treeCopy` method returns the null reference. On the other hand, if the root reference is not null, then the tree has at least one node. The tree can be copied with these three steps (using local variables `leftCopy` and `rightCopy`, which are both references to nodes):

1. Make `leftCopy` refer to a copy of the left subtree (which might be empty).
2. Make `rightCopy` refer to a copy of the right subtree (which might be empty).
3. `return new BTNode(source.data, leftCopy, rightCopy);`

The first two steps of the pseudocode are "smaller versions of the problem we are solving in the first place." Therefore these two steps can be solved with recursive calls. The complete implementation of `treeCopy` is given here:

```
public static BTNode treeCopy(BTNode source)
{
    BTNode leftCopy, rightCopy;

    if (source == null)
        return null;
    else
    {
        leftCopy = treeCopy(source.left);
        rightCopy = treeCopy(source.right);
        return new BTNode(source.data, leftCopy, rightCopy);
    }
}
```

By the way, do you see why `treeCopy` is a static method? The reason is that we may copy an empty tree. If it was an ordinary method, activated by the tree that we are copying, then we could not activate `null.treeCopy( )`. But with a static method there is no problem activating `BTNode.treeCopy(null)`.

The specifications for the constructor, `isLeaf`, and `treeCopy` appear in Figure 9.6. We'll postpone the complete implementation for now because there will be a few more methods that we haven't mentioned yet. But even with these few methods we can look at a programming example beginning on page 435.

FIGURE 9.6	Specification of the Key Methods of a Class for Binary Tree Nodes

Specification

These are the key methods of a class for binary tree nodes, which we will implement later. In this specification, each node contains data which is a Java `Object`. Our final implementation will contain additional methods that are discussed in Section 9.4.

- **Constructor for the BTNode**
    `public BTNode(Object initialData, BTNode initialLeft, BTNode initialRight)`
    Initialize a node with a specified initial data and links to children. Note that a reference to a child may be null, which indicates that there is no child.
    Parameters:
        `initialData` – the initial data of this new node
        `initialLeft` and `initialRight` – references to the children of this new node
    Postcondition:
        This new node contains the specified data and links to its children.

(continued)

(FIGURE 9.6 continued)

- **getData—getLeft—getRight**
  ```
  public Object getData( )
  public BTNode getLeft( )
  public BTNode getRight( )
  ```
  These are accessor methods to obtain this node's data or a reference to one of the children. Any of these objects may be null. A null reference to a child indicates that the child does not exist.

- **getLeftmostData**
  ```
  public Object getLeftmostData( )
  ```
  Accessor method to get the data from the leftmost node of the tree below this node.

  Returns:
  The data from the deepest node that can be reached from this node following left links.

- **getRightmostData**
  ```
  public Object getRightmostData( )
  ```
  Accessor method to get the data from the rightmost node of the tree below this node.

  Returns:
  The data from the deepest node that can be reached from this node following right links.

- **isLeaf**
  ```
  public boolean isLeaf( )
  ```
  Accessor method to determine whether a node is a leaf.

  Returns:
  true (if this node is a leaf); false otherwise.

- **setData—setLeft—setRight**
  ```
  public void setData(Object newData)
  public void setLeft(BTNode newLeft)
  public void setRight(BTNode newRight)
  ```
  These are modification methods to set this node's data or a reference to one of the children. Any of these objects may be null. Setting a child to null indicates that the child does not exist.

- **removeLeftmost**
  ```
  public BTNode removeLeftmost( )
  ```
  Remove the leftmost node of the tree with this node as its root.

  Postcondition:
  The tree starting at this node has had its leftmost node removed (i.e., the deepest node that can be reached by following left links). The return value is a reference to the root of the new (smaller) tree. This return value could be null if the original tree had only one node (since that one node has now been removed).

  Example:
  If n is a reference to a node in a tree, and n has a right child, then we can remove the leftmost node of n's right subtree with the statement:
  ```
  n.setRight(n.getRight( ).removeLeftmost( ));
  ```
  (continued)

(FIGURE 9.6 continued)

◆ removeRightmost

```
public BTNode removeRightmost( )
```
Remove the rightmost node of the tree with this node as its root.

Postcondition:

The tree starting at this node has had its rightmost node removed (i.e., the deepest node that can be reached by following right links). The return value is a reference to the root of the new (smaller) tree. This return value could be null if the original tree had only one node (since that one node has now been removed).

Example:

If n is a reference to a node in a tree, and n has a left child, then we can remove the rightmost node of n's left subtree with the statement:
```
n.setLeft(n.getLeft( ).removeRightmost( ));
```

◆ treeCopy

```
public static BTNode treeCopy(BTNode source)
```
Copy a binary tree.

Parameters:

source – a reference to the root node of a binary tree that will be copied (which may be an empty tree where source is null)

Returns:

The method has made a copy of the binary tree starting at source. The return value is a reference to the root of the copy.

Throws: OutOfMemoryError

Indicates that there is insufficient memory for the new tree.

PROGRAMMING EXAMPLE: **Animal Guessing**

Now we'll write a small program that uses a binary tree. The program is a simple guessing game: You pretend that you are an animal, and the program asks questions to try to guess what animal you are. If the program guesses correctly, another round of the game is started. And if the program can't figure out what you are, you provide some more knowledge to the program so that the next time the game is played, the program is a bit smarter.

As an example, suppose you are pretending to be a raccoon. The program might start by asking "*Are you a mammal?*" and you answer, "Yes." Next, the program wants to know "*Are you bigger than a cat?*" and again you answer, "Yes." Finally, the program guesses: "*Are you a kangaroo?*" and with a smug smile you reply, "No, don't be ridiculous."

At this point, the program says, "*I give up. What are you?*" You explain that you are a raccoon. You then provide the program with a question that the

an animal guessing program that gets smarter and smarter

program can use in the future to distinguish a kangaroo from a raccoon—perhaps *"Are you a marsupial?"*—and you tell the program that the answer to this question is "yes" for a kangaroo but "no" for a raccoon. The next time that you are a raccoon, the program will have enough information to guess correctly. Here's a sample dialogue with the program:

```
Are you a mammal? [Y or N] Y
Are you bigger than a cat? [Y or N] Y
My guess is Kangaroo. Am I right? [Y or N] N
I give up. What are you? Raccoon
Please type a yes/no question that will distinguish a Raccoon
from a Kangaroo.
Your question: Are you a marsupial?
As a Raccoon, Are you a marsupial? Please answer [Y or N] N
Shall we play again? [Y or N] N
Thank you for teaching me a thing or two.
```

As you might guess, the data used by the program is stored in a binary taxonomy tree, as described on page 419, with each nonleaf node containing a question. When the program begins, it will know only four animals, and the taxonomy tree will look like this:

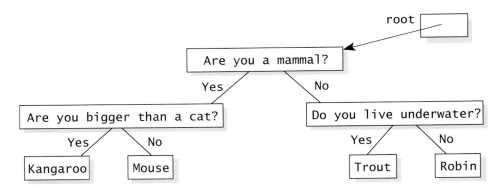

The program maintains a reference to a node called root, which is root of the binary taxonomy tree. As the game is being played, the program also maintains a second reference called current. The current reference starts at the root and travels down the tree according to the answers that the user provides.

For example, suppose that the user answers "yes" to the first question *"Are you a mammal?"* Then the program will move its current to the left subtree, as shown at the top of the next page.

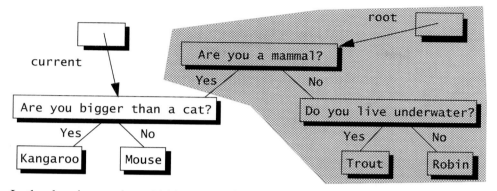

In the drawing we have hidden part of the tree to indicate that only the left sub-tree is now relevant to the game. The rest of the tree and the reference to the root are still present, but they are not needed at this point in the game.

The program continues asking questions. Each time the user answers "yes" to a question, the `current` reference is moved left. Each "no" answer moves `current` right. This continues until the program reaches a leaf. When a leaf is reached, the program guesses that you are the animal whose name is stored at the leaf. If the leaf contains the correct animal, then all is well. But if the guess is wrong, then the program elicits information from the user, and that information is used to improve the taxonomy tree.

In the sample dialogue, where you were a raccoon, the program would use the information to modify the taxonomy tree, resulting in the larger taxonomy tree of Figure 9.7(a). After playing several rounds of the game, the taxonomy tree might contain quite a few animals. Figure 9.7(b) shows what the tree could look like with seven animals. As an exercise, pretend you are a squid, and follow the route that would be taken from the root to the squid leaf in this tree.

Animal Guessing Program—Design and Implementation

Now that we have a general idea of how the program works, let's carry out a top-down design. The main method has three steps, shown in this pseudocode:

1. Print the instructions for the user.
2. Create a small initial taxonomy tree with four animals. The reference variable `root` refers to the root of this initial tree; each node contains a `String` as its data.

   the data at each node is a string

3. Repeat the following steps as often as the user wants:

   a. Activate a method called `play` that plays one round of the game, perhaps adding information to the bottom of the tree.

   b. Ask the user, "Shall we play again?" and read the answer.

FIGURE 9.7 Two Possible Taxonomy Trees

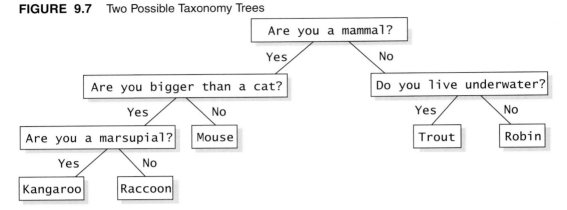

(a) Taxonomy tree after adding a raccoon

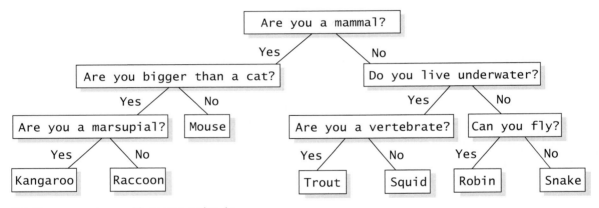

(b) Taxonomy tree with seven animals

The first two steps from our outline will be accomplished by methods that we call `instruct` and `beginningTree`. For Step 3, the user's input will be read through an `EasyReader` object; we have used `EasyReader` objects to simplify input before, and they are fully described in Appendix B. In this program, the `EasyReader` object will be a static instance variable, attached to `System.in`. It can be used by any method of the program that needs input from the user.

One of the methods that needs input is called `play`, which we'll design for Step 3a. Step 3b can be accomplished with the `query` method of our `Easy-Reader`, which asks a yes/no question, returning `true` if the user replies "Y" or "y" and returning `false` if the user replies "N" or "n." Putting the steps together, we can declare the `EasyReader` and write the main method as shown next.

```
private static EasyReader stdin = new EasyReader(System.in);

public static void main(String[ ] args)
{
    BTNode root;

    instruct( );
    root = beginningTree( );
    do
        play(root);
    while (stdin.query("Shall we play again?"));

    System.out.println
        ("Thanks for teaching me a thing or two.");
}
```

We discuss all the methods that are used in the `main` method next.

The `instruct` method. This method prints instructions explaining the game. You can write it yourself with the heading: `public static void instruct( )`.

The `query` and `stringQuery` methods. These are EasyReader methods. The `stdin.query` method asks a yes/no question and reads the answer. The `stdin.stringQuery` method asks a question and reads an entire string for the answer.

The `beginningTree` method. This method creates the initial binary taxonomy tree and returns a reference to the root of this tree, as shown in this outline:

```
public static BTNode beginningTree( )
{
    BTNode root;
    BTNode child;
```

1. Make `root` refer to a new node with the data "Are you a mammal?" Both children are initially null.
2. Make `child` refer to a new node with the data "Are you bigger than a cat?" Give it two leaves as children with the data "Kangaroo" on the left and "Mouse" on the right. Then activate `root.setLeft(child);`
3. Make `child` refer to a new node with the data "Do you live underwater?" Give it two leaves as children with the data "Trout" on the left and "Robin" on the right. Then activate `root.setRight(child);`
4. `return root;`

```
}
```

The complete implementation will be shown as part of a program in a moment. For now, you should notice that the operations of `beginningTree` can be accomplished with the node's constructor, `setLeft` and `setRight`. When `beginningTree` finishes, the `root` in the main program will refer to the root node of our initial taxonomy tree.

The `play` method. The `play` method has one parameter, which initially is a reference to the root of the binary taxonomy tree, as shown in this specification:

> ◆ **play (for the Animal Guessing Program)**
>   `public static void play(BTNode current)`
>   Plays one round of the animal-guessing game.
>
>   **Parameters:**
>   `current` – a reference to the root node of a binary taxonomy tree that will be used to play the game
>
>   **Postcondition:**
>   The method has played one round of the game, and possibly added new information about a new animal.
>
>   **Throws:** `OutOfMemoryError`
>   Indicates that there is insufficient memory to add information to the tree.

The method causes the `current` reference to move down the tree in response to the user's replies. (The `root` reference, back in the main program, will stay put at the root.) When the current reference reaches a leaf, an animal is guessed.

We'll use one other method to carry out some of `play`'s work. The method, called `learn`, is used after the game reaches a leaf and the animal at the leaf is wrong. The method elicits information from the user and thereby improves the tree, as specified here:

> ◆ **learn (for the Animal Guessing Program)**
>   `public static void learn(BTNode current)`
>   Elicits information from the user to improve the binary taxonomy tree.
>
>   **Parameters:**
>   `current` – a reference to a leaf node of a binary taxonomy tree
>
>   **Precondition:**
>   `current` is a reference to a leaf in a binary taxonomy tree
>
>   **Postcondition:**
>   Information has been elicited from the user, and the tree has been improved.
>
>   **Throws:** `OutOfMemoryError`
>   Indicates that there is insufficient memory to add information to the tree.

Using the methods we have described, the implementation of `play` is relatively short, as shown here:

```
public static void play(BTNode current)
{
    while (!current.isLeaf( ))
    {
        if (stdin.query((String) current.getData( )))
            current = current.getLeft( );
        else
            current = current.getRight( );
    }

    System.out.print("My guess is " + current.getData( ) + ". ");
    if (!stdin.query("Am I right?"))
        learn(current);
    else
        System.out.println("I knew it all along!");
}
```

Within this implementation we used the query method to ask the questions, for example:

```
if (stdin.query((String) current.getData( )))...
```

Notice that the if-statement includes a typecast "(String)" to tell the compiler that the return value from current.getData( ) is a string. This is necessary because the actual return type from getData is a Java Object, and the argument to stdin.query is required to be a String.

We use current.getData( ) in a second place without a typecast:

```
System.out.print("My guess is " + current.getData( ) + ". ");
```

This use of current.getData( ) does not require a typecast because the "+" operation of strings will automatically convert any object to a string, by activating the object's toString method. (Even without the "+" operation, any object can be printed by the print method; the object's toString will always be used.)

So what's left to do? Implement the learn method, which we'll do now.

The learn method. This method is activated when the game reaches a leaf and makes a wrong guess. The method takes several steps to improve the taxonomy tree. The method's argument is a reference to the node that contains the incorrect guess, as shown in this heading:

```
public static void learn(BTNode current)
```

For example, suppose we just made an incorrect guess of a kangaroo from this tree:

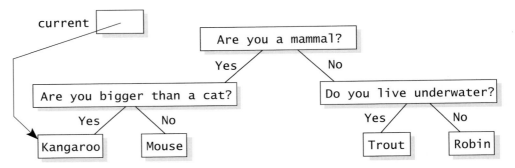

The `learn` method first sets three local `String` variables:

1. What animal was guessed? This is obtained from `current.getData( )` and stored in a local variable called `guessAnimal`. For this example, the `guessAnimal` is "Kangaroo."

2. What is the correct animal? The user's answer to this question is read into a local `String` variable called `correctAnimal`. To read the answer, we use the `stdin.readLine` method. This method reads an entire line of input, including blanks, and returns this line as a `String` value. For this example, suppose that the user's answer is "Raccoon," which is assigned to the local variable, `correctAnimal`.

3. What is a yes/no question that can distinguish the right animal from the animal that was guessed? In our example, we need a question that can distinguish a kangaroo from a raccoon. The user might provide the question "Are you a marsupial?" We'll read this question (with the `readLine` method) and store it in another local `String` variable, `newQuestion`.

With the three strings set, we need one more piece of information. In particular, we need to know whether the correct animal answers "yes" or "no" to the question that the user has just provided. In our example, we need to know whether a raccoon answers "yes" or "no" to the question "Are you a marsupial?" Of course, a raccoon is not a marsupial, so based on this "no" answer, we can proceed with the these three steps:

- Copy the new question into `current.data`.
- Copy the *guessed* animal into a new leaf, which is created to be the left child of the current node.
- Copy the *correct* animal into a new leaf, which is created to be the right child of the current node.

In our example, these steps improve the taxonomy tree as shown here:

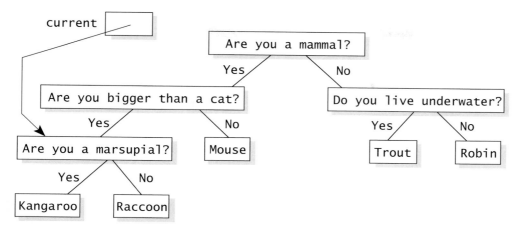

The other possibility is that the new animal has a "Yes" answer to the new question. For example, the question to distinguish a raccoon from a kangaroo could be "Do you have a ringed tail?" In this case, the new animal (raccoon) would be added as the left child of the new question, and the old animal (kangaroo) added on the right.

As an exercise, you should implement the `learn` method and add it to the complete program from Figure 9.8 on page 444. This program uses a BTNode class with the operations from Figure 9.6 on page 433. We'll actually implement the BTNode in the next section of this chapter.

Animal Guessing Program—Improvements

Our animal program suffers from one problem: Each time the program is executed, it starts out by knowing only four animals. An improvement will allow it to store the current taxonomy tree in a file and read that file whenever the program starts. This way it remembers all the animals that you have taught it.

Self-Test Exercises

8. Implement the `learn` method from the animal guessing program.
9. Write a new BTNode method that computes the number of children that a node has.
10. Write a new BTNode method that computes the number of nodes in a binary tree. Add another method to compute the depth of a binary tree. Both methods should be static and work correctly for an empty tree.

FIGURE 9.8 | The Animal Guessing Program

Java Application Program

```java
// FILE: Animal.java
// This animal-guessing program illustrates the use of the binary tree node class.

import edu.colorado.nodes.BTNode;
import edu.colorado.io.EasyReader;

public class Animal
{
    private static EasyReader stdin = new EasyReader(System.in);

    public static void main(String[ ] args)
    {
        BTNode root;

        instruct( );
        root = beginningTree( );
        do
            play(root);
        while (stdin.query("Shall we play again?"));

        System.out.println("Thanks for teaching me a thing or two.");
    }

    public static void instruct( )
    │ The implementation of this method is omitted—write it yourself!

    public static void play(BTNode current)
    {
        while (!current.isLeaf( ))
        {
            if (stdin.query((String) current.getData( )))
                current = current.getLeft( );
            else
                current = current.getRight( );
        }

        System.out.print("My guess is " + current.getData( ) + ". ");
        if (!stdin.query("Am I right?"))
            learn(current);
        else
            System.out.println("I knew it all along!");
    }
```

(continued)

(FIGURE 9.8 continued)

```
public static BTNode beginningTree( )
{
    BTNode root;
    BTNode child;

    final String ROOT_QUESTION = "Are you a mammal?";
    final String LEFT_QUESTION = "Are you bigger than a cat?";
    final String RIGHT_QUESTION = "Do you live underwater?";
    final String ANIMAL1 = "Kangaroo";
    final String ANIMAL2 = "Mouse";
    final String ANIMAL3 = "Trout";
    final String ANIMAL4 = "Robin";

    // Create the root node with the question "Are you a mammal?"
    root = new BTNode(ROOT_QUESTION, null, null);

    // Create and attach the left subtree.
    child = new BTNode(LEFT_QUESTION, null, null);
    child.setLeft(new BTNode(ANIMAL1, null, null));
    child.setRight(new BTNode(ANIMAL2, null, null));
    root.setLeft(child);

    // Create and attach the right subtree.
    child = new BTNode(RIGHT_QUESTION, null, null);
    child.setLeft(new BTNode(ANIMAL3, null, null));
    child.setRight(new BTNode(ANIMAL4, null, null));
    root.setRight(child);

    return root;
}


public static void learn(BTNode current)
```
The implementation of this method is Self-Test Exercise 8.

9.4   TREE TRAVERSALS

And then he got up, and said: "And the only reason for making honey is so as I can eat it." So he began to climb the tree.

He climbed and he climbed and he climbed, and as he climbed he sang a little song to himself.

A. A. MILNE
Winnie-the-Pooh

We're almost ready to implement the BTNode, but first we'll look at one more action that can be taken on a binary tree—a tree traversal.

Traversals of Binary Trees

Programs that use tree structures often need to process all of the nodes in a tree, applying the same operation to each node. This processing is called a **tree traversal**. For example, suppose we have a tree where each node contains an integer, and we need to print a list of all the integers in the tree. For a binary tree, there are three common ways of doing this kind of processing: **pre-order traversal, in-order traversal,** and **post-order traversal.** This section defines and implements the three traversal methods for binary trees. We also implement a modified pre-order traversal that uses indentation in a meaningful way for printing a tree. We start with a description of each method.

Pre-order traversal. The word "pre-order" refers to when the root is processed; it is processed *pre*vious to its two subtrees. So, a pre-order traversal has these three steps for a nonempty tree:

pre-order: the root is processed prior to its two subtrees

1. Process the root.
2. Process the nodes in the left subtree with a recursive call.
3. Process the nodes in the right subtree with a recursive call.

Let's look at the case where we just want to be able to print the contents of each node. In this case we could add this method to the BTNode of Section 9.3:

+ **preorderPrint (for the BTNode)**
    ```
    public void preorderPrint( )
    ```
    Uses a pre-order traversal to print the data from each node at or below this node of the binary tree.

    Postcondition:
    The data of this node and all its descendants have been written by System.out.println using a pre-order traversal.

Using recursion, the method's implementation is short, as shown next.

```
public void preorderPrint( )
{
    System.out.println(data);
    if (left != null)
        left.preorderPrint( );
    if (right != null)
        right.preorderPrint( );
}
```

Notice how the processing of the two subtrees is accomplished by activating `left.preorderPrint( )` and `right.preorderPrint( )`. These are recursive calls of the `preorderPrint` method, with each recursive call responsible for solving a smaller version of the original problem.

Let's look at an execution of the pre-order traversal in more detail. We'll trace `preorderPrint`, applied to the binary tree shown below. This example tree consists of `Integer` objects, using Java's `Integer` wrapper class described on page 245. Each `Integer` object contains a primitive `int` value, but it is also a full-blown Java `Object`, so it can be used as the data of a `BTNode`.

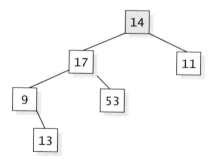

Suppose that we activate `preorderPrint` for the shaded root in the diagram. The method's first step is to print the number at the root, so after this step, the only number printed is 14 (from the root).

The method's second step makes the recursive call, `left.preorderPrint( )`. In effect, the recursive call says "do a pre-order traversal of the left subtree." To illustrate that we are now doing a traversal of a subtree, we will temporarily hide everything except the left subtree, as shown here:

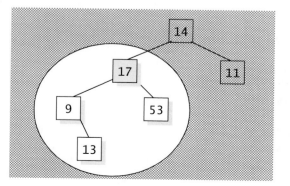

In this recursive call, the shaded node containing 17 has activated `preorder-Print`. The first step of the recursive call is to print the number at the root of the subtree, so after that step the total output contains two numbers:

```
14
17
```

The second step of the recursive call is to make yet another recursive call, for its own left subtree. In other words, this second recursive call will begin at the shaded node containing 9 in this drawing:

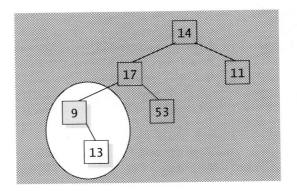

We now have three calls that are active: the original method activation by the root of the whole tree (containing 14), the first recursive call by the left child of the root (containing 17), and the second recursive call by the shaded node shown above (containing 9). This second recursive call carries out its appointed task by first printing a 9. After this, the total output consists of these three lines:

```
14
17
9
```

This time the method does not make a recursive call to the left because there is no left child. So, the call continues executing the code at the spot marked here with an arrow:

```
System.out.println(data);
if (left != null)
    left.preorderPrint( );
if (right != null)
    right.preorderPrint( );
```

At this point in the recursive call, we have already printed the 9 and dealt with the empty left subtree. So the next step will make another recursive call to process the right subtree. The node that activates this recursive call contains 13, as shown in this drawing:

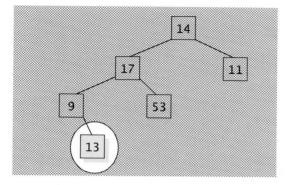

This recursive call prints the number 13, so that the entire output now has four numbers:

    14
    17
    9
    13

Both the left and right subtrees are empty for the node containing 13. So there are no further calls for those two empty subtrees. The recursive call, which printed 13, returns. Where do matters go from there? Can you finish tracing the pre-order traversal? By the time the last recursive call has returned, we've "visited" every node in the tree, and the numbers have been printed out, in this order:

    14
    17
    9
    13
    53
    11

In-order traversal. The only change for an in-order traversal is that the root is processed *in* between the processing of its two subtrees. Here are the three steps for a nonempty tree:

in-order: the root is processed in between its two subtrees

1. Process the nodes in the left subtree with a recursive call.
2. Process the root.
3. Process the nodes in the right subtree with a recursive call.

The implementation of an in-order print method is a rearrangement of the pre-order print, as shown next.

```
public void inorderPrint( )
{
   if (left != null)
      left.inorderPrint( );
   System.out.println(data);
   if (right != null)
      right.inorderPrint( );
}
```

*post-order:
the root is
processed
after its two
subtrees*

Post-order traversal. In a post-order traversal, the processing of the root is *post*poned until last in a nonempty tree:

1. Process the nodes in the left subtree with a recursive call.
2. Process the nodes in the right subtree with a recursive call.
3. Process the root.

We'll leave the implementation as an exercise in rearrangement.

Can you work out the order of the output numbers for the in-order and post-order traversals on an example such as Figure 9.5 on page 425? You'll be asked to work that out in Self-Test Exercise 11 at the end of this section.

Printing a Tree with an Indentation to Show the Depths

In early 1998, Sun Microsystems introduced the Java Foundation Classes (JFC), also known as the "Swing" components. Among other things, the JFC allows the building and graphical display of general trees. Significant programming projects can use the JFC trees and their displays, but there are still times where you would like a quick display of a binary tree, in Java or some other programming language. In this case, you should consider implementing a pre-order traversal that prints each node with an indentation that is equal to four times its depth. For example, consider the small tree shown here, along with the output from the traversal with indentation:

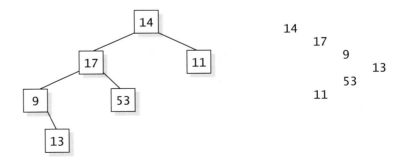

There's a small trick that will make the output more useful. The trick is to print a dash at any place where there is a child that has no sibling. For example, if a right child has no sibling to its left, then we print "--" to indicate the missing left child, as shown here:

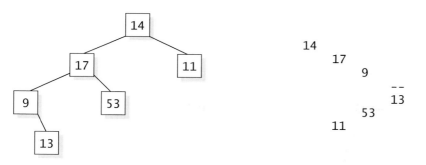

Why is this output useful? It's easy to interpret the tree structure: The root is the first number printed, with no indentation. Each node's children appear somewhere below it with an extra four spaces of indentation. A node with a single child has the dash "--" in place of the missing child. If necessary, you can easily draw lines by hand to connect a node to its children, as shown here:

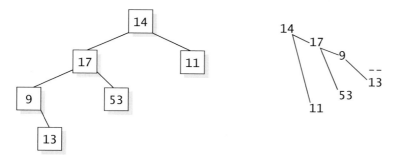

The specification and implementation of the print method are part of the complete BTNode given in Figure 9.9 on page 453.

BTNode, IntBTNode, and Other Classes

Figure 9.9 on page 453 shows the complete specification and implementation for the BTNode class. The class has one extra method, treeSize, which computes the number of nodes in a binary tree. We could add other methods; for example, Programming Project 6 on page 480 asks you to write traversals to create a Java Vector that contains all the elements from a binary tree.

The data in each BTNode is a Java Object, but we could have used other kinds of data. For example, if we change each Object variable to an int, then we have a new class of binary tree nodes in which each node contains int data. We'll use the name IntBTNode for the version that uses int data. This IntBTNode will be used in the next section of this chapter for an application that needs a binary tree of int values.

> *In the implementation of BTNode, we can change the Object to any of the primitive types, so we're really doing nine implementations at once:*
> BTNode
> BooleanBTNode
> ByteBTNode
> CharBTNode
> DoubleBTNode
> FloatBTNode
> IntBTNode
> LongBTNode
> ShortBTNode

In all, there are nine implementations of binary tree nodes, with the names shown in the box to the right. The basic node, with a Java Object as the data, is called BTNode and shown completely in Figure 9.9. You can modify the BTNode to obtain any of the other eight nodes, or you can find the complete implementations in the directory:

http://www.cs.colorado.edu/~main/edu/colorado/nodes/

Self-Test Exercises

11. Look at the tree in Figure 9.5 on page 425. In what order are the letters printed for an in-order traversal? What about a post-order traversal?

12. Rewrite the pre-order traversal from page 446 so that it is a static method with one parameter (a reference to the root node of the tree). In what way is the static method more general than the nonstatic method?

13. Suppose we do a traversal of the tree in Figure 9.1 on page 416, printing out the numbers in the order 13, 9, 53, 17, 19, 7, 4, 11, 14. What kind of traversal did we do? In what order are the numbers printed for the other kinds of traversals?

14. Suppose that you have a tree where the left subtree contains 3000 nodes, and the right subtree contains 100 nodes. For each of the different kinds of traversals, how many nodes are processed before the root node?

15. Here is an output from the tree-printing method for a tree of characters:

```
45
     9
          17
               20
               --

          3
     54
          53
          54
```

For this exercise, draw pencil lines to show the links between the nodes in this tree.

16. Which of the traversal methods make sense for general trees where there is no limit to the number of children that a node may have?

FIGURE 9.9	Specification and Implementation of the Binary Tree Node Class

Class BTNode

❖ **public class BTNode from the package edu.colorado.nodes**

> A BTNode provides a node for a binary tree with a reference to an object as the data in each node.

> **Limitations:**

> Beyond Int.MAX_VALUE elements, treeSize is wrong.

Specification

• **Constructor for the BTNode**

> public BTNode(Object initialData, BTNode initialLeft, BTNode initialRight)
>
> Initialize a node with a specified initial data and links to children. Note that a reference to a child may be null, which indicates that there is no child.

> **Parameters:**

> initialData – the initial data of this new node
>
> initialLeft and initialRight – references to the children of this new node

> **Postcondition:**

> This new node contains the specified data and links to its children.

• **getData—getLeft—getRight**

> public Object getData( )
>
> public BTNode getLeft( )
>
> public BTNode getRight( )
>
> These are accessor methods to obtain this node's data or a reference to one of the children. Any of these objects may be null. A null reference to a child indicates that the child does not exist.

• **getLeftmostData**

> public Object getLeftmostData( )
>
> Accessor method to get the data from the leftmost node of the tree below this node.

> **Returns:**

> The data from the deepest node that can be reached from this node following left links.

• **getRightmostData**

> public Object getRightmostData( )
>
> Accessor method to get the data from the rightmost node of the tree below this node.

> **Returns:**

> The data from the deepest node that can be reached from this node following right links.

(continued)

(FIGURE 9.9 continued)

◆ **inorderPrint—postorderPrint—preorderPrint**

```
public void inorderPrint( )
public void postorderPrint( )
public void preorderPrint( )
```

Uses a traversal to print the data from each node at or below this node of the binary tree.

Postcondition:
The data of this node and all its descendants have been written by `System.out.println` using one of three traversal techniques.

◆ **isLeaf**

```
public boolean isLeaf( )
```

Accessor method to determine whether a node is a leaf.

Returns:
`true` (if this node is a leaf); `false` otherwise.

◆ **print**

```
public void print(int depth)
```

Uses an in-order traversal to print the data from each node at or below this node of the binary tree, with indentation to indicate the depth of each node.

Parameters:
`depth` – the depth of this node (with 0 for the root, 1 for the root's children, and so on)

Precondition:
`depth` is the depth of this node.

Postcondition:
The data of this node and all its descendants have been written by `System.out.println` using an in-order traversal. The indentation of each line of data is four times its depth in the tree. A dash "--" is printed at any place where a child has no sibling.

◆ **removeLeftmost**

```
public BTNode removeLeftmost( )
```

Remove the leftmost node of the tree with this node as its root.

Postcondition:
The tree starting at this node has had its leftmost node removed (i.e., the deepest node that can be reached by following left links). The return value is a reference to the root of the new (smaller) tree. This return value could be null if the original tree had only one node (since that one node has now been removed).

Example:
If n is a reference to a node in a tree, and n has a right child, then we can remove the leftmost node of n's right subtree with the assignment:

```
n.setRight(n.getRight( ).removeLeftmost( ));
```

(continued)

(FIGURE 9.9 continued)

- **removeRightmost**
    ```
    public BTNode removeRightmost( )
    ```
    Remove the rightmost node of the tree with this node as its root.

    Postcondition:
    The tree starting at this node has had its rightmost node removed (i.e., the deepest node that can be reached by following right links). The return value is a reference to the root of the new (smaller) tree. This return value could be null if the original tree had only one node (since that one node has now been removed).

    Example:
    If n is a reference to a node in a tree, and n has a left child, then we can remove the rightmost node of n's left subtree with the assignment:
    ```
    n.setLeft(n.getLeft( ).removeRightmost( ));
    ```

- **setData—setLeft—setRight**
    ```
    public void setData(Object newData)
    public void setLeft(BTNode newLeft)
    public void setRight(BTNode newRight)
    ```
    These are modification methods to set this node's data or a reference to one of the children. Any of these objects may be null. Setting a child to null indicates that the child does not exist.

- **treeCopy**
    ```
    public static BTNode treeCopy(BTNode source)
    ```
    Copy a binary tree.

    Parameters:
    source – a reference to the root node of a binary tree that will be copied (which may be an empty tree where source is null)

    Returns:
    The method has made a copy of the binary tree starting at source. The return value is a reference to the root of the copy.

    Throws: OutOfMemoryError
    Indicates that there is insufficient memory for the new tree.

- **treeSize**
    ```
    public static int treeSize(BTNode root)
    ```
    Compute the number of nodes in a binary tree.

    Parameters:
    root – the reference to the root of a binary tree (which may be an empty tree with a null root)

    Returns:
    the number of nodes in the tree with the given root

    Note:
    A wrong answer occurs for trees larger than Int.MAX_VALUE.

(continued)

(FIGURE 9.9 continued)

Implementation

```java
// File: BTNode.java from the package edu.colorado.nodes
// Complete documentation is available from the BTNode link in
//     http://www.cs.colorado.edu/~main/docs/

package edu.colorado.nodes;

public class BTNode
{
    // Invariant of the BTNode class:
    //     1. Each node has one reference to an Object, stored in data.
    //     2. The instance variables left and right are references to the node's children.
    private Object data;
    private BTNode left, right;

    public BTNode(Object initialData, BTNode initialLeft, BTNode initialRight)
    {
        data = initialData;
        left = initialLeft;
        right = initialRight;
    }

    public Object getData( )
    {
        return data;
    }

    public BTNode getLeft( )
    {
        return left;
    }

    public BTNode getRight( )
    {
        return right;
    }

    public Object getLeftmostData( )
    {
        if (left == null)
            return data;
        else
            return left.getLeftmostData( );
    }
```

(continued)

(FIGURE 9.9 continued)

```java
public Object getRightmostData( )
{
    if (right == null)
        return data;
    else
        return right.getRightmostData( );
}

public void inorderPrint( )
{
    if (left != null)
        left.inorderPrint( );
    System.out.println(data);
    if (right != null)
        right.inorderPrint( );
}

public boolean isLeaf( )
{
  return (left == null) && (right == null);
}

public void postorderPrint( )
{
    if (left != null)
        left.postorderPrint( );
    if (right != null)
        right.postorderPrint( );
    System.out.println(data);
}

public void preorderPrint( )
{
    System.out.println(data);
    if (left != null)
        left.preorderPrint( );
    if (right != null)
        right.preorderPrint( );
}
```

(continued)

(FIGURE 9.9 continued)

```java
public void print(int depth)
{
    int i;

    // Print the indentation and the data from the current node:
    for (i = 1; i <= depth; i++)
       System.out.print("   ");
    System.out.println(data);

    // Print the left subtree (or a dash if there is a right child and no left child)
    if (left != null)
       left.print(depth+1);
    else if (right != null)
    {
       for (i = 1; i <= depth+1; i++)
          System.out.print("   ");
       System.out.println("--");
    }

    // Print the left subtree (or a dash if there is a left child and no left child)
    if (right != null)
       right.print(depth+1);
    else if (left != null)
    {
       for (i = 1; i <= depth+1; i++)
          System.out.print("   ");
       System.out.println("--");
    }
}


public BTNode removeLeftmost( )
{
    if (left == null)
    {  // The leftmost node is at the root because there is no left child.
       return right;
    }
    else
    {  // A recursive call removes the leftmost node from my own left child
       left = left.removeLeftmost( );
       return this;
    }
}
```

(continued)

(FIGURE 9.9 continued)

```java
public BTNode removeRightmost( )
{
    if (right == null)
    {   // The rightmost node is at the root because there is no right child.
        return left;
    }
    else
    {   // A recursive call removes the rightmost node from my own right child
        right = right.removeRightmost( );
        return this;
    }
}

public void setData(Object newData)
{
    data = newData;
}

public void setLeft(BTNode newLeft)
{
    left = newLeft;
}

public void setRight(BTNode newRight)
{
    right = newRight;
}

public static BTNode treeCopy(BTNode source)
{
    BTNode leftCopy, rightCopy;

    if (source == null)
        return null;
    else
    {
        leftCopy = treeCopy(source.left);
        rightCopy = treeCopy(source.right);
        return new BTNode(source.data, leftCopy, rightCopy);
    }
}

public static int treeSize(BTNode root)
{
    if (root == null)
        return 0;
    else
        return 1 + treeSize(root.left) + treeSize(root.right);
}
}
```

9.5 BINARY SEARCH TREES

*Lucy looked very hard between the trees and could just see
in the distance a patch of light that looked like daylight.
"Yes," she said, "I can see the wardrobe door."*

C.S. LEWIS
The Lion, the Witch and the Wardrobe

Perhaps you thought that you would never see another bag after Chapter 3 (storing the bag's elements in an array), Chapter 4 (the linked list bag), and Chapter 5 (extending the bags so that the elements are Java objects). But binary trees offer yet another way to improve our bag ADT, so we will have one last look at bags.

The Binary Search Tree Storage Rules

Binary trees offer an improved way of implementing the bag ADT. The improvement generally performs faster than our previous bags. Or at least *sometimes* the improved approach may be taken. The improved implementation requires that the bag's elements can be compared to each other using operations such as the usual integer comparisons <, >, ==, <=, >=, and !=. These comparisons must form a *total order semantics*. Intuitively, a total order semantics requires that the different values of a class can all be placed on a single line, proceeding from smaller to larger along the line. This intuition is sufficient for most programming tasks, although you may sometimes need to know the more formal definition of a total order semantics shown in Figure 9.10.

FIGURE 9.10 Total Order Semantics

A **total order semantics** for a class requires the six comparison operators (==, !=, >=, <=, >, <) to be defined, forming a total order that meets these requirements:

1. **Equality:** (x == y) is true if and only if the two values, x and y, are identical.
2. **Totality:** For any two values x and y, exactly one of these three comparisons is true:
    (x < y), (x == y), or (x > y).
3. **Consistency:** For any two values x and y:
    (x > y) is the same as (y < x)
    (x >= y) is the same as ((x > y) || (x == y))
    (x <= y) is the same as ((x < y) || (x == y))
    (x != y) is the same as !(x == y)
4. **Transitivity:** Whenever there are three values (x, y, and z) with (x < y) and (y < z), then
    (x < z) is also true.

We'll develop our bag as a bag of integers, but keep in mind that any data type could be used, so long as there is some way to compare the elements using some total order semantics. The comparisons might be carried out with the usual operations ($<$, $>$ ==, and so on)—or the comparisons might be incorporated within the methods of a class. For example, Java's string type has a method with this specification:

- **compareTo (method for the String class)**
  ```
  public boolean compareTo(String str)
  ```
  Compares this string to another string.

  Returns:
  The return value is zero if this string is equal to `str`;
  The return value is negative if this string is lexicographically before `str`;
  The return value is positive if this string is lexicographically after `str`.

As you can see, `compareTo` returns zero if `str` is equal to the string that activates the method. If the strings are not equal, then they are compared in the **lexicographic order**, which is the normal alphabetical order for ordinary words of all lowercase letters. For example, if `s` is the string `"chaos"`, then `s.compareTo("order")` will return some negative number, since `"chaos"` is alphabetically before `"order"`. On the other hand, `s.compareTo("action")` will return some positive integer. Therefore, our new bag could contain strings, which are compared to each other with the `compareTo` method.

Apart from requiring a total order semantics, the new bag ADT has a specification that is identical to our earlier bags. Therefore, a programmer who is using the bag ADT may switch to the new, improved bag without difficulty.

So, what good do we obtain from the total order semantics? We'll take advantage of the order to store the elements in the nodes of a binary tree, using a strategy that will make it easy to find elements. The strategy is to follow a collection of rules called the **binary search tree storage rules,** defined here:

Binary Search Tree Storage Rules

In a **binary search tree,** the elements of the nodes can be compared with a total order semantics. These two rules are followed for every node *n*:

1. Every element in *n*'s left subtree is less than or equal to the element in node *n*.

2. Every element in *n*'s right subtree is greater than the element in node *n*.

FIGURE 9.11 Using a Binary Search Tree

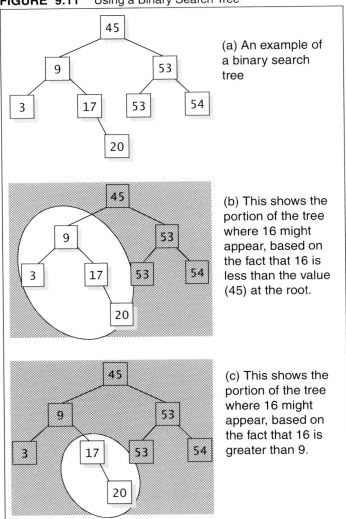

(a) An example of a binary search tree

(b) This shows the portion of the tree where 16 might appear, based on the fact that 16 is less than the value (45) at the root.

(c) This shows the portion of the tree where 16 might appear, based on the fact that 16 is greater than 9.

For example, suppose we want to store the numbers {3, 9, 17, 20, 45, 53, 53, 54} in a binary search tree. Figure 9.11(a) shows a binary search tree with these numbers. You can check that each node follows the Binary Search Tree Storage Rules. Binary search trees also can store a collection of strings, or real numbers, or *anything* that can be compared using some sort of total order semantics.

Can you see an advantage to storing a bag in a binary search tree rather than in an array or a linked list? The previous implementations of the bag ADT, using an array or a linked list, have a striking inefficiency: When we count the number of occurrences of an element in the bag, it is necessary to examine *every* element of the bag. Even if we are interested only in whether or not an element appears in the bag, we will often look at many elements before we stumble across the one we seek.

With a binary search tree, searching for an element is often much quicker. For example, suppose we're looking for the number 16 in the tree of Figure 9.11(a). We'll start at the root and compare 16 to the root's number. Since 16 is less than the root's number (45), we immediately know that 16 can appear only in the left subtree—if it appears at all. In Figure 9.11(b), we show the area where 16 might appear, based on knowing that 16 is less than the value at the root. Next we'll compare 16 with the root of the left subtree. Since 16 is greater than 9, this eliminates another portion of the tree, as shown in 9.11(c).

The number 16 is smaller than the next point on the tree (17), so we should continue to the left . . . but we've run out of tree. At this point, we can stop and conclude that 16 is nowhere in the binary search tree, even though we only looked at the three numbers 45, 9, and 17. In fact, the most we'll ever have to look at is the depth of the tree plus one—four entries in this case.

This efficiency is the motivation for representing bags with a binary search tree. In order for the idea to work, the comparisons between entries must form a total order according to the rules of Figure 9.10 on page 460. In the remainder of this section, we'll use binary search trees to implement a bag of integers, as specified in Figure 9.12. This class is called an `IntTreeBag` and it has the same methods as our earlier bags.

FIGURE 9.12 Specification of the `IntTreeBag` Class

Class *IntTreeBag*

❖ **public class IntTreeBag from the package edu.colorado.collections**
   An `IntTreeBag` is a collection of `int` numbers.
   Limitations:
      Beyond `Integer.MAX_VALUE` elements, `countOccurrences` and `size` are wrong.

Specification

♦ **Constructor for the IntTreeBag**
   `public IntTreeBag( )`
   Initialize an empty bag.
   Postcondition:
      This bag is empty.

♦ **add**
   `public void add(int element)`
   Add a new element to this bag.

   Parameters:
      `element` – the new element that is being added
   Postcondition:
      A new copy of the element has been added to this bag.
   Throws: `OutOfMemoryError`
      Indicates insufficient memory for adding a new element.

(continued)

(FIGURE 9.12 continued)

- **addAll**
    ```
    public void addAll(IntTreeBag addend)
    ```
    Add the contents of another bag to this bag.

    Parameters:
    addend – a bag whose contents will be added to this bag

    Precondition:
    The parameter, addend, is not null.

    Postcondition:
    The elements from addend have been added to this bag.

    Throws: `IllegalArgumentException`
    Indicates that addend is null.

    Throws: `OutOfMemoryError`
    Indicates insufficient memory to increase the size of this bag.

- **clone**
    ```
    public Object clone( )
    ```
    Generate a copy of this bag.

    Returns:
    The return value is a copy of this bag. Subsequent changes to the copy will not affect the original, nor vice versa. The return value must be type cast to an `IntTreeBag` before it is used.

    Throws: `OutOfMemoryError`
    Indicates insufficient memory for creating the clone.

- **countOccurrences**
    ```
    public int countOccurrences(int target)
    ```
    Accessor method to count the number of occurrences of a particular element in this bag.

    Parameters:
    target – the element that needs to be counted

    Returns:
    the number of times that target occurs in this bag

- **remove**
    ```
    public boolean remove(int target)
    ```
    Remove one copy of a specified element from this bag.

    Parameters:
    target – the element to remove from the bag

    Postcondition:
    If target was found in the bag, then one copy of target has been removed and the method returns `true`. Otherwise the bag remains unchanged and the method returns `false`.

(continued)

(FIGURE 9.12 continued)

- **size**

  ```
  public int size( )
  ```
  Accessor method to determine the number of elements in this bag.

  Returns:
  the number of elements in this bag

- **union**

  ```
  public static IntTreeBag union(IntTreeBag b1, IntTreeBag b2)
  ```
  Create a new bag that contains all the elements from two other bags.

  Parameters:
  b1 – the first of two bags
  b2 – the second of two bags

  Precondition:
  Neither b1 nor b2 is null.

  Returns:
  a new bag that is the union of b1 and b2

  Throws: IllegalArgumentException
  Indicates that one of the arguments is null.

  Throws: OutOfMemoryError
  Indicates insufficient memory for the new bag.

The Binary Search Tree Bag—Implementation of Some Simple Methods

Our new bag will have only one instance variable, which is a reference to the root of a binary search tree that contains the integers. If the bag is empty, then the root reference will be null. We could add other instance variables, such as a count of the number of nodes. But limiting ourselves to only the root will allow us to clearly focus on the necessary tree algorithms. Here's the start of the new class implementation:

```
public class IntTreeBag implements Cloneable
{
    // Invariant of the IntTreeBag class:
    //    1. The elements in the bag are stored in a binary search tree.
    //    2. The instance variable root is a reference to the root of the
    //       binary search tree (or null for an empty tree).
    private IntBTNode root;
    ...
```

Notice that we are using the IntBTNode class, which is the same as the BTNode from Figure 9.9 on page 453, except that IntBTNode uses int elements instead of Java objects.

Now we're ready to dive into the implementations of the bag methods. For the most part, we will provide only pseudocode that you can implement yourself. Keep in mind that you should use the methods of the `IntBTNode` as much as possible.

Constructor. The constructor sets `root` to null. This isn't absolutely needed since a reference variable that is an instance variable is automatically initialized to null. So another alternative is not to bother implementing the constructor at all.

The clone method. Since our bag uses dynamic memory, we must implement a `clone` method. The method can be implemented by following the three-step outline on page 78. Which method of the `IntBTNode` will you use to carry out the actual copying of the tree? (Use the `treeCopy` method.)

The `size` method. The `size` method simply returns the answer from `IntBT-Node.treeSize(root)`, using the `treeSize` method from the `IntBTNode`.

Counting the Occurrences of an Element in a Binary Search Tree

The `countOccurrences` method counts the number of occurrences of an element called `target`. We'll keep track of these occurrences in a local variable called `count` (which is initialized to zero). The important point is that we will not look at every element in the binary search tree. Instead, we'll have a local variable called `cursor`, which is initialized to the root. We'll use a loop to move the cursor down through the tree, always moving along the path where the target might occur. At each point in the tree we have four possibilities:

1. The cursor can become `null`, indicating that we've moved off the bottom of the tree. In this case, we have counted all the occurrences of the target. So the loop can end, and we should return the current count.

2. The target might be smaller than the data at the cursor node. In this case, the target can appear only in the left subtree. For example, suppose we are counting occurrences of the integer 4 in the following binary search tree. The cursor's data might be 16, and the situation looks like this:

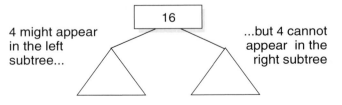

4 might appear in the left subtree...   16   ...but 4 cannot appear in the right subtree

In this situation, we'll continue our search by assigning:

```
cursor = cursor.getLeft( );
```

3. The target might be larger than the data at the cursor node. This is similar to the previous case, except that we must continue our search to the right instead of the left, using the assignment:

```
cursor = cursor.getRight( );
```

4. The target might equal the data at the cursor node. In this case we add one to the count and continue the search to the left (since elements to the left are less than *or equal to* the element at the cursor node).

The implementation of these steps is straightforward using a while-loop.

Adding a New Element to a Binary Search Tree

The add method puts a new element into a binary search tree, using this method header:

```
public void add(int element)
```

We suggest that you handle one special case first: When the first element is added, simply activate `root = new IntBTNode(element, null, null)`.

The other case is when there are already some other elements in the tree. In this case, we'll set a `cursor` to refer to the current root, then we will pretend to search for the exact element that we are trying to add. But the search runs a bit differently than a real search. The main difference is that we stop the search just before the cursor falls off the bottom of the tree, and we add the new element at the spot where the cursor was about to fall off. For example, consider the task of adding 16 to this binary search tree:

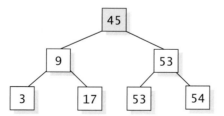

The cursor starts at the shaded node (with 45). If we were searching for the 16, we would continue the search to the left. So, we move our cursor to the left, resulting in the cursor referring to the node that contains 9:

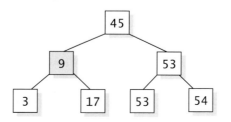

Again pretend that you are searching for the 16 instead of adding it, so that now the cursor moves right to the node containing 17:

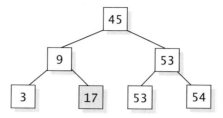

At this point, an ordinary search would continue to the left, stepping off the bottom of the tree. But instead, we add the new element at this position, resulting in this tree:

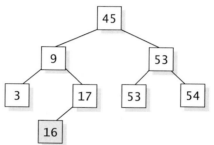

To implement the scheme, we suggest a boolean variable called done, which is initialized to false. We then have a loop that continues until done becomes true. Each iteration of the loop handles these two cases:

1. Suppose the new element is less than or equal to the data at the cursor node. In this case, check the left child. If cursor.getLeft( ) is null, then create a new node containing the new element (setting the cursor's left child to this new node), and set done to true. On the other hand, if the left child is not null, then continue the search by moving the cursor to the left with the assignment statement:

   ```
   cursor = cursor.getLeft( );
   ```

2. Suppose the new element is greater than the data at the cursor node. In this case, follow the same procedure as Case 1, but use the right child instead of the left.

After the loop ends, the method has no more work.

Removing an Element from a Binary Search Tree

The remove method allows us to remove a specified element from a binary search tree, with this header:

```
public boolean remove(int target)
```

The method returns `true` if it finds and removes one copy of the target. Otherwise it returns `false` without changing the tree.

The implementation has two parts. In the first part, we move a cursor down the tree to find the element that we are removing. To make the removal easier, we'll also maintain a variable called `parentOfCursor`, which usually refers to the parent of the cursor node. Once we find the target, there are several different cases for carrying out the actual removal. Here's the complete pseudocode:

`public boolean remove(int target)`

Start by setting up the `cursor` and `parentOfCursor`, which are both local `IntBTNode` variables. Initialize `cursor` to the root and initialize `parentOfCursor` to null. Then move `cursor` down the tree until it reaches the target, or it becomes null (meaning that the target is not in the tree). Also, whenever we are about to move the cursor downward, we will assign `parentOfCursor = cursor`. After moving the cursor, there are four possibilities:

1. The `cursor` could be null, indicating that the target was not in the tree. In this case, the method returns `false` with no further work.

2. The `cursor` could be at the root of the tree, but it has no left child. For example, we might be removing 45 from this tree:

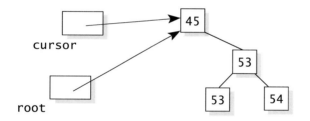

In this case, the 45 can be removed from the tree by moving the root rightward with the assignment `root = root.getRight( )`. The result is:

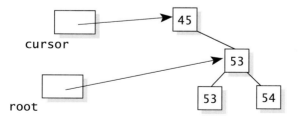

The node containing 45 still exists, but it is no longer part of the tree because it is not below the root. The method can return the value `true` to indicate that it found and removed the target. When the method does return, the local variable `cursor` will no longer be available, and Java's automatic garbage collection will eventually reuse the node that contains 45. The final tree without the 45 is shown here:

3. The cursor could be further down the tree, but still without a left child of its own. For example, we could be removing the 9 from this tree:

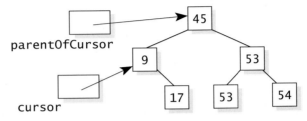

In this situation, we'll take one of the parent's links and shift it to the right child of the cursor. To be more specific, the link that connects the parent to the cursor node will be changed by this code:

```
if (cursor == parentOfCursor.getLeft( ))
{   // The cursor is on the left side of the parent,
    //  so change parent's left link.
    parentOfCursor.setLeft( cursor.getRight( ) );
}
else
{   // The cursor is on the right side of the parent,
    //  so change parent's right link.
    parentOfCursor.setRight( cursor.getRight( ) );
}
```

In our example, the cursor is the left child of its parent, so we will move the parent's left link down to the cursor's right child, resulting in this:

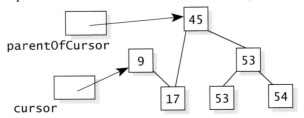

The method can now return `true`, indicating that it found and removed the target. When the method returns, the cursor is no longer available and the node containing 9 will be garbage-collected, resulting in the final tree at the top of the next page.

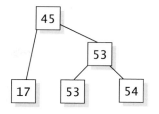

4. The cursor could be non-null and it does have a left child, so we can't simply ignore the left subtree of the cursor (as we did in cases 2 and 3). We could check whether there is a right child, and if not, we could have a plan that ignores the right subtree of the cursor—but we have a more general plan in mind. The plan is to find some element in the nonempty left subtree, and move this element up to the cursor. But which element? Here's an example to help you figure out which element should be taken from the left subtree to replace the cursor's element. In this example, we are deleting 45 from this tree:

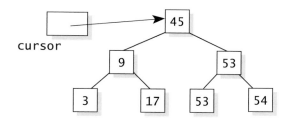

The plan is to replace the cursor's data with one of the three elements in the left subtree. Which of these elements can safely be moved to the cursor node? Not the 3 or 9, because a remaining element in the left subtree (the 17) would be larger than the new cursor (violating the binary search tree storage rules). So, we must select the 17 to move to the cursor node. The reason for this selection is that 17 is the largest element in the cursor's left subtree.

We'll actually carry out the movement in two steps. The first step is the statement:

```
cursor.setData(cursor.getLeft( ).getRightmostData( ));
```

This step sets the data in the cursor node to the rightmost element in the cursor's left subtree. The rightmost element in the cursor's left subtree is always the largest element in this subtree, so for our example we now have the tree at the top of the next page.

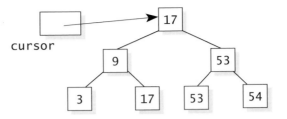

We have eliminated the 45, but we now have an extra copy of the 17. We must eliminate one of these extra 17s. We can do so with the statement:

```
cursor.setLeft(cursor.getLeft( ).removeRightmost( ));
```

This statement removes the rightmost node from the cursor's left subtree, and it sets the left link of the cursor to this new smaller subtree. The end result is this tree:

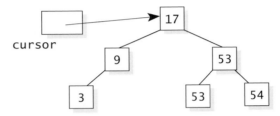

We're done with the pseudocode for the remove method. Case 4 was the most interesting step in the pseudocode. In this case, we had a node that was difficult to remove, so instead we found an easier node to remove (the rightmost node in the cursor's left subtree). We took the value from the "easy" node and copied this value on top of the element that we wanted to remove. Then we removed the extra copy of the value that we copied (by removing the easy node).

By the way, you should check that cases 2 and 3 also work correctly if the cursor happens to be a leaf. In Case 2, the pseudocode sets the root to null, indicating that we have just removed the final node from the tree. In Case 3, the pseudocode sets the parent's link to null, indicating that the parent no longer has a child on that side.

The addAll and union Methods

The last two operations for the bag are the addAll and union methods. The addAll method has this heading:

addAll

```
public void addAll(IntTreeBag addend)
```

When b.addAll(c) is activated, all the elements from the bag c are added to the bag b. This is an example of a method that will benefit from a private helper method. Private helper methods were described on page 350, and they may be used whenever there is a job to carry out, but you don't want other programmers to have access to the method that carries out the job. The helper method that we propose has this specification:

```
private void addTree(IntBTNode addroot)
// Precondition: addroot is a reference to the root of a binary search tree
//   that is separate from the binary search tree of the bag that activated
//   this method.
// Postcondition: All the elements from the addroot's binary search tree
//   have been added to the binary search tree of the bag that activated this
//   method.
```

Our intention is that this method is a new *private* method of the bag. Since the method is private, it won't be published for other programmers to use, and the specification can use private information, such as the fact that the bag is implemented with a binary search tree.

As a private method, the implementation of addTree must be placed with the other methods in the bag's implementation. The approach is to traverse the tree that we are adding, putting a copy of each traversed element into the bag that activated the operator. For example, if we use a pre-order traversal, then the pseudocode for addTree is:

pseudocode for the private method addTree

```
if (addroot != null)
{

    add(addroot.getData( ));
    Make a recursive call to add all of addroot's left subtree.
    Make a recursive call to add all of addroot's right subtree.

}
```

Our pseudocode explicitly uses a pre-order traversal of the nodes. If you wish, you may use a post-order traversal instead. But avoid an in-order traversal. The problem with an in-order traversal is that the nodes of the addend tree will be processed in order from smallest to largest. Therefore, these nodes will be added to the other bag from smallest to largest. This is a bad way to build a binary search tree. The resulting tree ends up with a single long narrow path, with only right children. Sometimes such long narrow trees are hard to avoid. But do avoid such trees when you can, because searching and other algorithms are inefficient when the trees lose their branching structure. In the next chapter we will examine some specific ways to ensure that long narrow trees are not created.

Pitfall: Violating the addTree Precondition

PITFALL

The specification of the addTree method indicates that the binary tree that is being added must be separate from the binary tree of the bag that activates the method. What goes wrong if we violate the precondition? An example can show the problem. For the example, suppose that the binary search tree of a bag contains one element, the number 42, as shown next.

root

Now, suppose that we activate addTree with the parameter, addroot, being the same as root, as shown here:

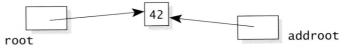

root   addroot

In this case, the first step of addTree will add a second copy of 42 to the tree, like this:

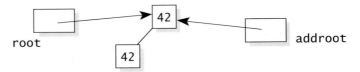

root   addroot

Now, the second step of addTree makes a recursive call to add a copy of addroot's left subtree—but that left subtree has now changed from its original form (an empty tree) to a new small subtree that contains 42. The consequence is that the recursive call adds another 42, and makes another recursive call, and so on—an unbounded stream of 42s.

So, when we do use the private addTree method, we'll be careful to make sure that the parameter's tree is not the same as the bag's tree.

Here's the implementation of the public addAll method, using the private addTree:

```
public void addAll(IntTreeBag addend)
{
   BTNode addroot;

   if (root == addend.root)
   {  // Addend is the same as the bag that activated this method.
      addroot = treeCopy(addend.root);
      addTree(addroot);
   }
   else
      addTree(addend.root);
}
```

Notice that we do have a bit of complication when the addend is the same bag as the bag that activated the addAll method (as in the statement b.addAll(b)).

In this case we must make a second copy of the addend's tree and activate addTree, using the second copy rather than using the addend's tree directly. The reason for this complication is the restriction of addTree's precondition, which requires that the tree that's being added "is separate from the binary search tree of the bag that activated this method."

Finally, let's look at the union method, which is a static method with this heading:

the union method

```
public static IntTreeBag union(IntTreeBag b1, IntTreeBag b2)
```

The method is easy to implement by using the addTree method. The answer bag should be initially empty. Then use answer.addTree to add the elements from b1, and use answer.addTree a second time to add the elements from b2.

Time Analysis and an Internal Iterator

With the descriptions that we've given, you can put together the implementation file for the new bag. We'll carry out a time analysis of the operations after we've seen a few more trees (see Section 10.3).

You might also want to add methods that provide an internal or external iterator as described in Section 5.4. An iterator allows a programmer to step through the elements of the bag one at a time. One method for implementing an iterator utilizes a stack and is described in Programming Project 9 on page 481.

Self-Test Exercises

17. Add a new method to the bag. The method should print all elements in the bag from smallest to largest. (Hint: Use a traversal.)

18. Write a static bag method called join with this heading:

```
public static void join(
    IntTreeBag top,
    IntTreeBag left,
    IntTreeBag right
)
```

The precondition of the method requires that top has just one element, that everything in left is less than or equal to the element in top, and that everything in right is greater than the element in top. The postcondition requires that top now contains its original element plus everything from left and right, and that left and right are now both empty. Your method should take constant time.

CHAPTER SUMMARY

- *Trees* are a nonlinear structure, with many applications including organizing information (such as taxonomy trees) and implementing an efficient version of the bag ADT (using binary search trees). The Programming Projects and the next chapter provide more examples of tree applications.

- Trees may be implemented with either arrays or dynamic data structures with nodes that contain references to other nodes. An array is particularly appropriate for *complete binary trees* because of the conditions that require the nodes of a complete tree to occur in specific locations.

- A *tree traversal* consists of processing a tree by applying some action to each node. Three common traversal methods—pre-order traversal, in-order traversal, and post-order traversal—differ only in the order in which the nodes are processed. A pre-order traversal with indentations is a quick and convenient way to print the data from a tree in a readable format.

- Binary search trees are one common application of trees, which permit us to store a bag of ordered elements in a manner where adding, removing, and searching for elements is potentially much faster than with a linear structure.

- Operations on trees are good candidates for recursive thinking. This is because many tree operations include a step to process one or more subtrees, and this step is "a smaller version of the same problem."

? Solutions to Self-Test Exercises

1. Here is one possible solution:

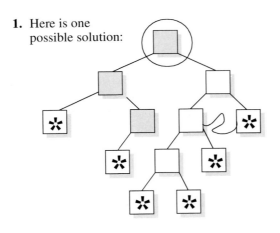

2. and 3. Here is a solution. The depth of this tree is 3. The node containing me has a depth of 2. My ancestors are circled, and my mother's descendants have a big square around them.

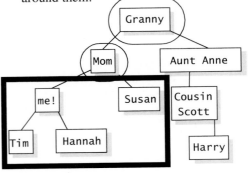

4. This solution is both full and complete. "Yes" answers move left and "No" answers move right.

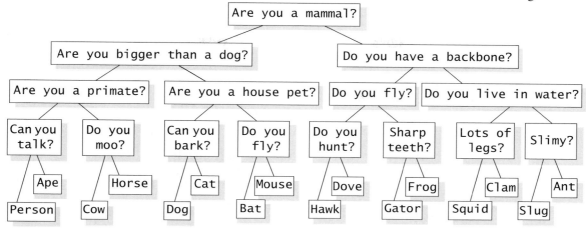

5. We use the formulas from page 423. The parent is stored at index 2499, which is (4999–1)/2. The left child is stored at index 9999, which is (2*4999)+1. If there was a right child, it would be stored at index 10,000 (which is (2*4999)+2). But since the last index is 9999, there is no right child.

6. A separate single reference variable is used to refer to the root node.

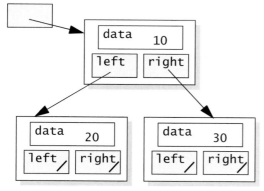

7.
```
public class TreeNode
{
    private Object data;
    private TreeNode parent;
    private TreeNode links[4];
    ...
```

8. See Figure 9.13 on page 478.

9. Here is one solution:
```
public int kids( )
// Postcondition: The return value is
//   the number of children of this node.
{
    int answer = 0;
    if (left != null) answer++;
    if (right != null) answer++;
    return answer;
}
```

10. The node counting method is `treeSize` from the bottom of Figure 9.9 on page 459. The depth method has a similar recursive implementation.

11. The in-order traversal prints O, L, R, A, G, T. The post-order traversal prints O, R, L, T, G, A.

12. This static method works correctly even if the parameter is the null reference (indicating an empty tree):
```
public static void pre(BTNode root)
{
    if (root != null)
    {
        System.out.println(root.data);
        pre(root.left);
        pre(root.right);
    }
}
```

FIGURE 9.13   The `learn` Method for the Solution to Self-Test Exercise 8

Implementation

```
public static void learn (BTNode current)
// Precondition: current is a reference to a leaf in a taxonomy tree. This
// leaf contains a wrong guess that was just made.
// Postcondition: Information has been elicited from the user, and the tree
// has been improved.
{
    String guessAnimal;    // The animal that was just guessed
    String correctAnimal;  // The animal that the user was thinking of
    String newQuestion;    // A question to distinguish the two animals

    // Set Strings for the guessed animal, correct animal, and a new question.
    guessAnimal = (String) current.getData( );
    correctAnimal = stdin.stringQuery("I give up. What are you? ");
    System.out.println("Please type a yes/no question that will distinguish a ");
    System.out.println(correctAnimal + " from a " + guessAnimal + ".");
    newQuestion = stdin.stringQuery("Your question: ");

    // Put the new question in the current node, and add two new children.
    current.setData(newQuestion);
    System.out.println("As a " + correctAnimal + ", " + newQuestion);
    if (stdin.query("Please answer"))
    {
        current.setLeft(new BTNode(correctAnimal, null, null));
        current.setRight(new BTNode(guessAnimal, null, null));
    }
    else
    {
        current.setRight(new BTNode(guessAnimal, null, null));
        current.setLeft(new BTNode(correctAnimal, null, null));
    }
}
```

13. This would be a post-order traversal. For in-order: 9, 13, 17, 53, 14, 19, 4, 7, 11. For pre-order: 14, 17, 9, 13, 53, 11, 4, 19, 7.

14. Pre-order: zero. Post-order: 3100. In-order: 3000.

15.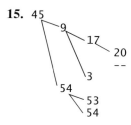

16. Pre-order would process a node before any of its children are processed. Post-order would process a node after all of its children are processed. In-order doesn't really make sense for a general tree.

17. For a nonempty bag, the body of your method should activate:
```
root.inorderPrint( );
```

18. The method needs four statements, as shown here:
```
top.root.setLeft(left.root);
left.root = null;
top.root.setRight(right.root);
right.root = null;
```

PROGRAMMING PROJECTS

1 This project deals with a simple kind of *expression tree*, where there are two kinds of nodes:

(a) Leaf nodes, which contain a real number as their element;

(b) Nonleaf nodes, which contain either the character '+' or the character '*' as their element, and have exactly two children.

For this project, implement a class for expression trees, including operations for building expression trees. Also include a recursive function to "evaluate" a nonempty expression tree using these rules:

(a) If the tree has only one node (which must be a leaf), then the evaluation of the tree returns the real number which is the node's element;

(b) If the tree has more than one node, and the root contains '+', then first evaluate the left subtree, then evaluate the right subtree, and add the results. If the root contains '*', then evaluate the two subtrees and multiply the results.

For example, consider the small expression tree shown to the right. The left subtree evaluates to 3+7, which is 10. The right subtree evaluates to 14. So the entire tree evaluates to 10*14, which is 140.

2 Specify, design, and implement an ADT for *complete* binary trees using the array representation from Section 9.2. You should have only one method that adds a new node (since there is only one place where a node may be added), and one method that removes the last node of the tree.

3 Specify, design, and implement an ADT for binary trees where the node's elements are stored in an array, similar to the way that a complete binary tree is usually stored. However, these binary trees do not need to be complete. Instead, you should have a second private instance variable that is an array of boolean values called `isPresent`. The `isPresent` array indicates which nodes actually exist in the tree. For example, if the tree has a root node, then `isPresent[0]` is `true`. If the root has a left child, then `isPresent[1]` is `true`. If the root has a right child, then `isPresent[2]` is `true`, and so on.

The class should have methods to create the first node and to move a cursor around the tree. After the first node, new nodes may be added only as children of the cursor.

4 Revise the animal guessing program from Figure 9.8 on page 444 so that the initial knowledge tree is obtained by reading information from a file. Also, when the program ends, the knowledge tree at that point is written to the same file. You must carefully specify the format of the data in this file. The format should make it easy to do two things: (a) read the file and set the initial tree, and (b) write the knowledge tree to the file, using some kind of traversal.

5 This project requires that you know how to determine the actual time taken for a method to execute. Write a test program for the bag ADT from Section 9.5. The program should allow the user to specify an integer, *n*. The program then adds *n* randomly selected integers to a bag and then counts the number of occurrences of each integer between 1 and *n*, keeping track of the amount of time needed for the entirety of these operations. Also use the test program to test one of the earlier bag implementations. Graph the results of your tests on a plot that has elapsed time on the y-axis and *n* on

the x-axis. (In the next chapter, we will do an analysis to explain these times.)

6 Implement a new method for the BTNode from Figure 9.9 on page 453. The new method creates a Java Vector that contains the data from all nodes in a tree, as specified in Figure 9.14. Details about the Java Vector class are provided in Appendix D, although the only Vector method that you'll use is addElement.

Also specify and implement similar methods that use in-order and post-order traversals instead of a pre-order traversal. Which of your three new methods creates a Vector with the entries sorted from smallest to largest?

7 Binary search trees have their best performance when they are *balanced*, which means that at each node, *n*, the size of the left subtree of *n* is within one of the size of the right subtree of *n*. Write a static method that takes a sorted array of integers and produces a balanced binary

---

FIGURE 9.14	Method to Copy Data from the Nodes of a Binary Tree to a Java Vector

Specification

- **preorderVector (for the BTNode)**

  `public void preorderVector(Vector v)`

  The method does a pre-order traversal of all nodes at or below this node, appending the data from each node to a Vector.

  Parameters:
  v – the Vector that will have data appended to it

  Precondition:
  v is not null.

  Postcondition:
  The node and all its descendants have been traversed with a pre-order traversal, and all data has been appended to v using v.addElement.

  Throws: NullPointerException
  Indicates that v is null.

  Throws: OutOfMemoryError
  Indicates that there is insufficient memory for the Vector's append method to add a new element to the Vector.

search tree. (The array is sorted with smallest integers at front to largest at the end.)

If useful, you may add extra parameters to the method, such as the total number of entries in the list. Hint: First build the left subtree of the root, then the right subtree of the root, then put the pieces together with the `join` method from Self-Test Exercise 18 on page 475.

As an alternative, you may have the integer data come from a Java `Vector` rather than an array.

---

9 An *internal iterator* for a bag is a collection of methods that allows a programmer to step through the elements of a bag one at a time. For example, we might have an internal iterator consisting of four methods: `start`, `advance`, `isCurrent`, and `getCurrent`. The `start` method initializes the internal iterator; the `isCurrent` method is a boolean method that tells whether the iterator has a specified current element that can be retrieved with the `getCurrent` method; the `advance` method moves the iterator to its next element.

For this project, add an internal iterator to the bag from Section 9.5. The implementation technique is to use a private instance variable called `s`. The instance variable `s` is a stack of references to nodes.

Each of the elements in the stack refers to a node whose element has not yet been processed by the internal iterator. The current element of the internal iterator is always in the node at the top of the stack. The pseudocode for the internal iterator methods is given here:

The `start` method: Clear the stack. For an empty tree, there is no more work. For a nonempty tree, do an in-order traversal of the tree's nodes, pushing a reference to each node onto the stack.

The `isCurrent` method: Return `true` if the stack is nonempty.

The `getCurrent` method: Check the precondition (the stack must be nonempty). Then peek at the top node on the stack (without removing it). Return the data element from this node.

The `advance` method: Check the precondition (the stack must be nonempty). Then pop the top node off the stack.

Changing the bag by adding or removing elements should invalidate the internal iterator (by clearing the stack).

When the internal iterator is started, we used an in-order traversal to push node references onto the stack. As we pop the stack, these references come off in reverse order so that the iterator will advance through the elements from largest to smallest. If you prefer a smallest-to-largest order, you could use a queue instead of a stack.

---

10 Write a class for a bag of strings, where the strings are stored in a binary search tree. In creating the binary search tree, you should use the string's `compareTo` method, which is described on page 461. The tree itself should use the `BTNode` class from Figure 9.9 on page 453.

---

11 Java 1.2 introduced a new interface called `Comparable`. A class that implements the `Comparable` interface must have a method with this specification:

* **compareTo**
  `public boolean compareTo(Object obj)`
  Compares this object to another object of the same type.

  Returns:
  The return value is zero if this object is equal to `obj`; the return value is negative if this object is smaller than `obj`; The return value is positive if this object is larger than `obj`.

  Throws: `ClassCastException`
  Indicates that `obj` is the wrong type of object to be compared with this object.

Write a class for a bag of `Comparable` objects, where the objects are stored in a binary search tree. The tree itself should use the `BTNode` class from Figure 9.9 on page 453.

---

12 Expand the class from Project 10 or 11 so that there is an extra method that produces a Java `Iterator` for the bag. (The Java `Iterator` interface is discussed in Section 5.4.)

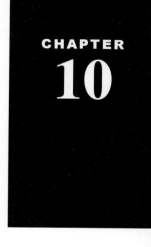

Tree Projects

The great, dark trees of the Big Woods stood all around the house, and beyond them were other trees and beyond them were more trees.

LAURA INGALLS WILDER
The Little House in the Big Woods

This chapter outlines two programming projects involving trees. The projects are improvements of ADTs that we've seen before: the priority queue ADT (Section 7.4) and the set ADT (which is like a bag, but does not allow more than one copy of an element). Both projects take advantage of *balanced* trees, in which the different subtrees below a node are guaranteed to have nearly the same height. We also analyze the time performance of tree algorithms, concentrating on a connection between trees and logarithms, and explaining the advantages obtained from balanced trees.

10.1 HEAPS

The Heap Storage Rules

A **heap** is a binary tree where the elements can be compared with each other using *total order semantics.* As we've seen before (Figure 9.10 on page 460), a total order semantics means that all the elements in the class can be placed in a single line, proceeding from smaller to larger along the line. In this way, a heap is similar to a *binary search tree*, but the arrangement of the elements in a heap follows some new rules that are different from a binary search tree:

Heap Storage Rules

If the elements of a set can be compared with a total order semantics, then these elements can be stored in a *heap*. A **heap** is a binary tree in which these two rules are followed:

1. The element contained by each node is greater than or equal to the elements of that node's children.

2. The tree is a complete binary tree, so that every level except the deepest must contain as many nodes as possible; and at the deepest level, all the nodes are as far left as possible (see "Complete Binary Trees" on page 419).

As an example, suppose that elements are integers. Here are three trees with six elements. Only one is a heap—which one?

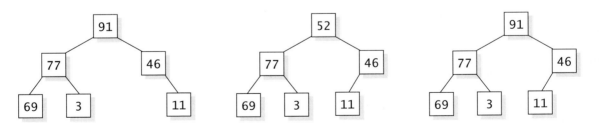

The tree on the left is not a heap because it is not complete—a complete tree must have the nodes on the bottom level as far left as possible. The middle tree is not a heap because one of the nodes (containing 52) has a value that is smaller than its child (which contains 77). The tree on the right *is* a heap.

A heap could be implemented with the binary tree nodes from the classes of Chapter 9. But wait! A heap is a *complete* binary tree, and a complete binary tree is more easily implemented with an array than with the node class (see "Array Representation of Complete Binary Trees" on page 421). If we know the maximum size of a heap in advance, then the array implementation can use an array with a single fixed size. If we are uncertain about the heap's maximum size, then the array can grow and shrink as needed.

In Self-Test Exercise 2 on page 490, you'll be asked to write definitions that would support the array implementation of a heap. The rest of this section will show how heaps can be used to implement an efficient priority queue—and we won't worry much about the exact implementation.

implement heaps with a fixed array or with an array that grows and shrinks

The Priority Queue ADT with Heaps

Priority queues were introduced in Section 7.4. A priority queue behaves much like an ordinary queue: Elements are placed in the queue and later taken out. But unlike an ordinary queue, each element in a priority queue has an associated number called its priority. When elements leave a priority queue, the highest priority elements always leave first. We have already seen one implementation of a priority queue using the specification from Figure 7.12 on page 364. Now we'll give an alternative implementation that uses the same specification of methods, but uses a heap as the underlying data structure to store the queue's elements.

In the heap implementation of a priority queue, each node of the heap contains one element along with the element's priority, and the tree is maintained so that it follows the heap storage rules using the elements' priorities to compare nodes. Therefore:

an alternative way to implement priority queues

1. The element contained by each node has a priority that is greater than or equal to the priorities of the elements of that node's children.
2. The tree is a complete binary tree.

We'll focus on two priority queue operations: adding a new element (along with its priority), and removing the element with the highest priority. In both operations, we must ensure that the structure remains a heap when the operation concludes. Also, both operations can be described without worrying about precisely how we've implemented the underlying heap.

Adding an Element to a Heap

Let's start with the operation that adds a new element. As an example, suppose that we already have nine elements that are arranged in a heap with the following priorities:

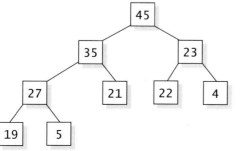

In this diagram, we have shown only the elements' priorities. In an actual priority queue, each element would also have some additional data in each node.

Suppose that we are adding a new element with a priority of 42. The first step is to add this element in a way that keeps the binary tree complete. In this case the new element will be the left child of the node with priority 21:

add the new element in a way that keeps the binary tree complete

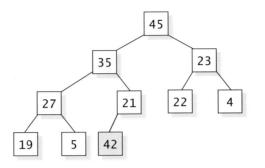

But now the structure is no longer a heap, since the node with priority 21 has a child with a higher priority. The algorithm fixes this problem by causing the new element (with priority 42) to rise upward until it reaches an acceptable location. This is accomplished by swapping the new element with its parent:

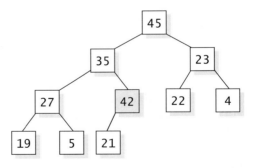

The new element is *still* bigger than its parent, so a second swap is done:

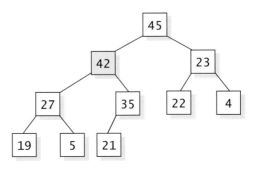

FIGURE 10.1   Adding an Element to a Priority Queue

Pseudocode for Adding an Element

The priority queue has been implemented as a heap.

1. Place the new element in the heap in the first available location. This keeps the structure as a complete binary tree, but it might no longer be a heap since the new element might have a higher priority than its parent.

2. `while` (the new element has a priority that is higher than its parent)
      Swap the new element with its parent.

Notice that the process in Step 2 will stop when the new element reaches the root, or when the new element's parent has a priority that is at least as high as the new element's priority.

Now the new element stops rising, because its parent (with priority 45) has a higher priority than the new element. In general, the "new element rising" stops when the new element has a parent with a higher or equal priority, or when the new element reaches the root. The rising process is called **reheapification upward**.

reheapification upward

The steps for adding an element are outlined in Figure 10.1. Some of the details depend on how the underlying heap is implemented. For example, if the heap is implemented with a nongrowing array, then the first step must check that there is room for a new element. With an array that grows, the first step might need to increase the size of the array.

Removing an Element from a Heap

When an element is removed from a priority queue, we must always remove the element with the highest priority—the element that stands "on top of the heap." For example, suppose the priority queue contains the ten priorities drawn below. The element at the root, with priority 45, will be removed, and this is the element that is returned by the operation:

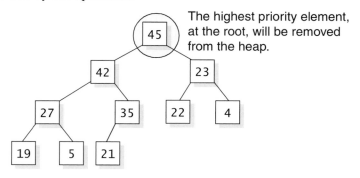

The highest priority element, at the root, will be removed from the heap.

But here we are ignoring a potential problem: There might be several elements with the highest priority. As described in Section 7.4, when several elements have equal priority, the elements should exit the priority queue as in first-in/first-out (FIFO) order. Our adding and deleting mechanisms do not provide a way to determine which of several elements arrived first. So, in this discussion we will suspend the requirement that elements with equal priority be treated in FIFO order. We will address this problem in Programming Project 1 on page 523.

The problem of removing the root from a heap remains. During the removal, we must ensure that the resulting structure remains a heap. If the root is the only element in the heap, then there is really no more work to do except to decrement the instance variable that is keeping track of the size of the heap. But if there are other elements in the tree, then the tree must be rearranged because a heap is not allowed to run around without a root. The rearrangement begins by moving the last element in the last level up to the root, like this:

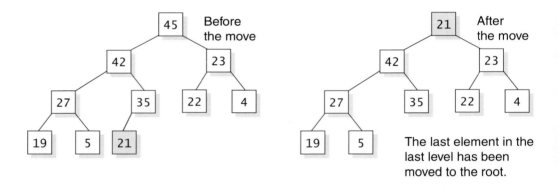

The structure is now a complete tree, but it is not a heap because the root is smaller than its children. To fix this, we can swap the root with its larger child, as shown here:

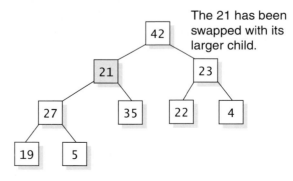

The structure is not yet a heap, so again we swap the out-of-place node with its larger child, giving this tree:

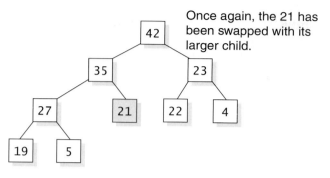

Once again, the 21 has been swapped with its larger child.

At this point, the node that has been sinking has reached a leaf, so we can stop and the structure is a heap. The process would also stop when the sinking node no longer has a child with a higher priority. This process, called **reheapification downward**, is summarized in Figure 10.2.

reheapification downward

Heaps have several other applications, including a sorting algorithm that is discussed in Chapter 12.

FIGURE 10.2 | Removing an Element from a Priority Queue

Pseudocode for Removing an Element

The priority queue has been implemented as a heap.

1. Copy the element at the root of the heap to the variable that is used to return a value.
2. Copy the last element in the deepest level to the root, and then take this last node out of the tree. This element is called the "out-of-place" element.
3. `while` (the out-of-place element has a priority that is lower than one of its children)
   Swap the out-of-place element with its highest-priority child.
4. Return the answer that was saved in Step 1.

Notice that the process in Step 3 will stop when the out-of-place element reaches a leaf or when the out-of-place element has a priority that is at least as high as its children.

Self-Test Exercises

1. The most appropriate way to implement a heap is with an array rather than a linked structure. Why?

2. Define the instance variables for a Java class that would be appropriate for a priority queue that is implemented as a heap. Each node should have an integer priority and a piece of data that is a Java `Object`.

3. In the description of reheapification downward, we specified that the out-of-place element must be swapped with the larger of its two children. What goes wrong if we swap with the smaller child instead?

4. Start with an empty heap, and enter ten elements with priorities 1 through 10. Draw the resulting heap.

5. Remove three elements from the heap that you created in the previous exercise. Draw the resulting heap.

10.2 B-TREES

Binary search trees were used in Section 9.5 to implement a bag ADT. But the efficiency of binary search trees can go awry. This section explains the potential problem and shows one way to fix it. Most of the presentation is not tied to any particular programming language.

FIGURE 10.3 Two Troublesome Search Trees

The Problem of Unbalanced Trees

Let's create a troublesome binary search tree of integers. The first number is 1, then we add 2, then 3, 4, and 5, in that order. The result appears in Figure 10.3(a). Perhaps you've spotted the problem. Suppose next we add 6, 7, 8, 9, and 10, in that order, ending up with Figure 10.3(b). The problem is that the levels of the tree are only sparsely filled, resulting in long, deep paths and defeating the purpose of binary trees in the first place. For example, if we are searching Figure 10.3(b) for the number 12, then we'll end up looking at every node in the tree. In effect, we are no better off than the linked list implementation. Similar problems arise for adding and deleting elements.

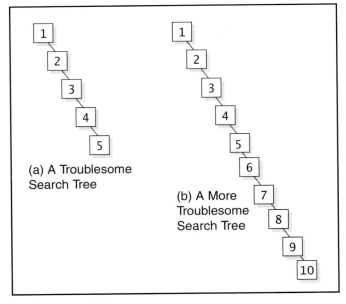

(a) A Troublesome Search Tree

(b) A More Troublesome Search Tree

The problem has several possible solutions, all of which involve trees where the depth of the leaves remains small. For example, one solution is to balance the search trees periodically, as described in Programming Project 7 in Chapter 9 (page 480). Another solution uses a particular kind of tree called a B-tree, where leaves cannot become too deep (relative to the number of nodes). These trees were proposed by R. Bayer and E. M. McCreight in 1972 (see "Organization and Maintenance of Large Ordered Indexes" in *Acta Informatica,* Volume 1, Number 3 [1972], pages 173–189). The rest of this section discusses a B-tree implementation.

The B-Tree Rules

A B-tree is a special kind of tree, similar to a binary search tree, where each node holds elements of some type. As with binary search trees, the implementation requires the ability to compare two elements via a total order semantics. But a B-tree is not a binary search tree—in fact, a B-tree is not even a *binary* tree because *B-tree nodes have many more than two children.* Another important property of B-trees is that *each node contains more than just a single element.* The rules for a B-tree make it easy to search for a specified element, and the rules also ensure that leaves do not become too deep.

B-trees are not binary trees

The precise B-tree rules may be formulated so that the B-tree stores a bag of elements similar to the bag implementations that we have seen before. Alternatively, a B-tree may be formulated to store a *set* of elements. The difference between a set and a bag is that a given element can occur many times in a bag but only once in a set. We'll look at the set formulation of the B-tree rules, but keep in mind that a bag formulation is also possible.

B-tree rules may be formulated for either a bag or a set

The elements in a B-tree node. Every B-tree depends on a positive constant integer called MINIMUM. The purpose of the constant is to determine how many elements are held in a single node, as shown in the first two B-tree rules:

> **B-tree Rule 1:** The root may have as few as one element (or even no elements if it also has no children); every other node has at least MINIMUM elements.

> **B-tree Rule 2:** The maximum number of elements in a node is twice the value of MINIMUM.

Although MINIMUM may be as small as 1, in practice much larger values are used—perhaps several hundred, or even a couple thousand.

The many elements of a B-tree node are stored in an array, so that we can talk about "the element at index 0," or "the element at index 1," and so on. Within the array, the elements must be sorted from smallest to largest. This provides our third B-tree rule:

> **B-tree Rule 3:** The elements of each B-tree node are stored in a partially filled array, sorted from the smallest element (at index 0) to the largest element (at the final used position of the array).

The subtrees below a B-tree node. The number of subtrees below a node depends on how many elements are in the node. Here is the rule:

> **B-tree Rule 4:** The number of subtrees below a nonleaf node is always one more than the number of elements in the node.

For example, suppose a node has 42 elements. Then this node will have 43 children. We will refer to the many subtrees of a node from left to right as "subtree number 0, subtree number 1, . . ." and so on up to the last subtree.

The elements in each subtree are organized in a way that makes it easy to search the B-tree for any given element. Here is the rule for that organization:

> **B-tree Rule 5:** For any nonleaf node: (a) An element at index i is greater than all the elements in subtree number i of the node, and (b) an element at index i is less than all the elements in subtree number $i + 1$ of the node.

Let's look at an example to illustrate Rules 4 and 5. Suppose that a nonleaf node contains two integer elements, the numbers 93 and 107. This node must have three subtrees, organized as follows:

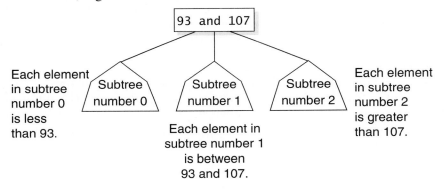

A B-tree is balanced. The final B-tree rule ensures that a B-tree avoids the problem of an unbalanced tree:

> **B-tree Rule 6:** Every leaf in a B-tree has the same depth.

An Example B-Tree

As another example, here is a complete B-tree of ten integers (with `MINIMUM` set to 1). Can you verify that all six B-tree rules are satisfied?

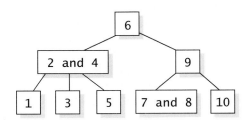

The Set ADT with B-Trees

The rest of this section discusses the algorithms for implementing a set class using B-trees. For concreteness, the elements in our set are integers, but we could use any data type that can be ordered from smallest to largest. The class, called `IntBalancedSet`, has public methods for adding and removing elements, and also for checking whether a given element is in the set. As you can see in our complete specification (Figure 10.4), the class also implements the `Cloneable` interface so that a programmer can make a clone of a set.

Figure 10.4 also provides an outline of the implementation. Let's examine the private instance variables that are used in this outline. The set class has two constants, shown here with a selection of 200 for `MINIMUM`:

```
private static final MINIMUM = 200;
private static final MAXIMUM = 2 * MINIMUM;
```

two private constants of the set

These constants are *private* because a programmer who *uses* the set class does not need to know about their existence. Access to these private values is needed only by the programmer who *implements* the set class. When you are actually implementing and testing the class, it's better to use smaller constants, perhaps `MINIMUM=1`. After debugging, you can increase `MINIMUM` and recompile.

After the declaration of the private constants, the set class has four private instance variables. The purpose of these four instance variables is to store all the information about the root node of the B-tree. Here are the first three instance variables from the set class in Figure 10.4 on page 494:

```
int dataCount;
int[ ] data = new int[MAXIMUM + 1];
int childCount;
```

instance variables store information about the root of the B-tree

Keep in mind that the instance variables store information about the *root* node. For example, `dataCount` stores the number of elements in the B-tree's root (not in the entire B-tree). The root's elements are stored in the partially filled array called `data`, ranging from `data[0]` through `data[dataCount-1]`. The complete size of the data array is `MAXIMUM + 1`, which allows space for one extra element beyond the usual maximum number. You'll see the benefit of this extra space when we discuss the implementations of the set's methods.

The number of children of the root node is stored in the instance variable `childCount`. The children of the root have an important property that will allow us to use *recursive thinking* in our implementations. Here is the property that you should burn into your memory:

> Every child of the root node is also the root of a smaller B-tree.

(text continues on page 496)

FIGURE 10.4 | The Set of Integers

Class *IntBalancedSet*

❖ **public class IntBalancedSet from the package edu.colorado.collections**
   An `IntBalancedSet` is a set of `int` numbers, stored in a B-tree.

Specification

♦ **Constructor for the IntBalancedSet**
   `public IntBalancedSet( )`
   Initialize an empty set.

Postcondition:
   This set is empty.

Throws: `OutOfMemoryError`
   Indicates insufficient memory for creating the set.

♦ **add**
   `public void add(int element)`
   Add a new element to this set.

Parameters:
   `element` – the new element that is being added

Postcondition:
   If the element was already in this set, then there is no change. Otherwise, the element has been added to this set.

Throws: `OutOfMemoryError`
   Indicates insufficient memory for adding a new element.

♦ **clone**
   `public Object clone( )`
   Generate a copy of this set.

Returns:
   The return value is a copy of this set. Subsequent changes to the copy will not affect the original, nor vice versa. The return value must be type cast to an `IntBalancedSet` before it is used.

Throws: `OutOfMemoryError`
   Indicates insufficient memory for creating the clone.

(continued)

(FIGURE 10.4 continued)

- **contains**

  ```
  public boolean contains(int target)
  ```
  Accessor method to determine whether a particular element is in this set.

  Parameters:

  target – an element that may or may not be in this set

  Postcondition:

  true (if target is in this set) or false (if target is not in this set).

- **remove**

  ```
  public boolean remove(int target)
  ```
  Remove a specified element from this set.

  Parameters:

  target – the element to remove from this set

  Postcondition:

  If target was found in this set, then it has been removed and the method returns true. Otherwise this set remains unchanged and the method returns false.

Implementation (outline)

```
//  FILE: IntBalancedSet.java from the package edu.colorado.collections
//  Documentation is available at the top of this figure or from the IntBalancedSet link in
//     http://www.cs.colorado.edu/~main/docs/

package edu.colorado.collections;

public class IntBalancedSet implements Cloneable
{
    //  INVARIANT for the IntBalancedSet ADT:
    //     1. The elements of the Set are stored in a B-tree, satisfying the six B-tree rules.
    //     2. The number of elements in the tree's root is in the instance variable dataCount, and
    //        the number of subtrees of the root is stored in the instance variable childCount.
    //     3. The root's elements are stored in data[0] through data[dataCount-1].
    //     4. If the root has subtrees, then subtree[0] through subtree[childCount-1] are
    //        references to these subtrees.
    private static final int MINIMUM = 200;
    private static final int MAXIMUM = 2*MINIMUM;
    int dataCount;
    int[ ] data = new int[MAXIMUM + 1];
    int childCount;
    IntBalancedSet[ ] subset = new IntBalancedSet[MAXIMUM + 2];
```

> The public methods are implemented here. The programmer who implements the class may wish to add further private methods, which are discussed in the text.

```
}
```

Let's look at an example to illustrate the rule "Every child of the root node is also the root of a smaller B-tree." For the example, consider the following B-tree (with MINIMUM equal to 1):

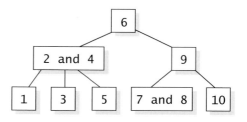

The root of this B-tree has two children, and each of these children is also the root of a smaller B-tree. These two smaller B-trees are clearly shown here:

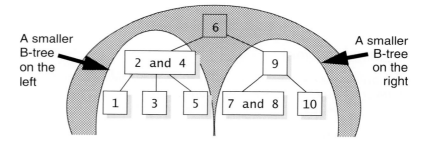

Each of the smaller B-trees also contains a set of elements. We will call these two smaller sets "subset number 0" and "subset number 1." If there were more children, we would continue with "subset number 2," and so on. The last subset is "subset number childCount-1."

Now consider how to store the subsets. The best solution is to store each subset as *an actual IntBalancedSet object*. In the root node itself, we will store *references* to these smaller IntBalancedSet objects. These references are stored in the fourth instance variable of the set class, declared here:

```
IntBalancedSet[ ] subset = new IntBalancedSet[MAXIMUM+2];
```

The instance variable subset is a partially filled array of references to smaller subsets. It is able to hold up to MAXIMUM + 2 such references—which is one more than the maximum number of children that a B-tree node may have. As with the elements, the benefit of this "space for one extra" will become evident shortly.

As an example, suppose a B-tree root has two children. Then subset[0] is a reference to "subset number 0," and subset[1] is a reference to "subset number 1." With this in mind, let's again consider the B-tree shown at the top of the next page.

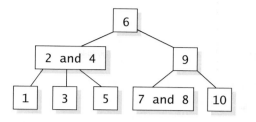

The root contains one element and two children, so the instance variables of the set object for this B-tree will look like this:

The important idea is that each `subset[i]` is a reference to another Int-BalancedSet object. We will be able to use all of the `IntBalancedSet` methods with these objects in various recursive calls. Here is the complete invariant for our `IntBalancedSet` class:

Invariant for the Set ADT Implemented with a B-Tree

1. The elements of the set are stored in a B-tree, satisfying the six B-tree rules.

2. The number of elements in the tree's root is stored in the instance variable `dataCount`, and the number of subtrees of the root is stored in the instance variable `childCount`.

3. The root's elements are stored in `data[0]` through `data[dataCount-1]`.

4. If the root has subtrees, then `subset[0]` through `subset[childCount-1]` are references to these subtrees.

Searching for an Element in a B-Tree

The set class has a method, `contains`, that determines whether an element called `target` appears in the set. Searching for an element in a B-tree follows the same idea as searching a binary search tree, although there's more work needed to handle nodes that contain many elements instead of just one. The basic idea: Start with the entire B-tree, checking to see whether the target is in the root. If the target does appear in the root, the search is done—the method can return `true` to indicate that it found the target. A second possibility is that the target is not in the root, and the root has no children. In this case, the search is also done—the method can return `false` to indicate that the target is not in the set. The final possibility is that the target is not in the root, but there are sub-trees below. In this case, there is only one possible subtree where the target can appear, so the method makes a recursive call to search that one subtree for the target.

The entire method can benefit from one preliminary step, shown as the first step of this pseudocode:

```
// Searching for a target in a set
```

1. Make a local variable, `i`, equal to the first index such that `data[i] >= target`. If there is no such index, then set `i` equal to `dataCount`, indicating that none of the elements is greater than or equal to the target.

2. ```
   if (we found the target at data[i])
           return true;
   else if (the root has no children)
           return false;
   else
           return subset[i].contains(target);
   ```

Be careful how you test the condition at the start of Step 2. In order to "find the target at `data[i]`," you must ensure that `i < dataCount` and also that the target is actually equal to `data[i]`.

The recursive call in the pseudocode is highlighted. The recursive call works well in this situation because the subset is *smaller* than the entire set. Thus, the recursive call is solving a *smaller* version of the original problem.

As an example of executing the pseudocode, suppose we are searching for 10 in the following B-tree:
   ```

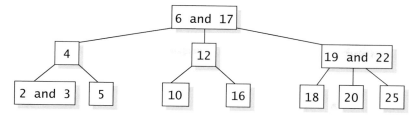

The search begins by finding the first element in the root that is greater than or equal to the target 10. This is the element 17, which occurs at `data[1]` in the root, so Step 1 sets i to the index 1. In Step 2 we notice that we have not found the target at `data[1]`, but the root does have children. So, we make a recursive call, searching subtree number 1 for the target 10. You can visualize the recursive call `subtree[1].contains(10)` as searching for a 10 in this part of the tree:

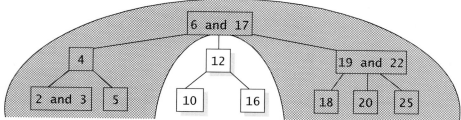

The recursive call of the `contains` method has its own copy of the local variable i. This variable i is set to 0 in Step 1 of the recursive call (since `data[0]` of the subtree is greater than or equal to the target 10). Again, we have not found the target, so the recursion continues, activating the `contains` method for the still smaller subtree shown here:

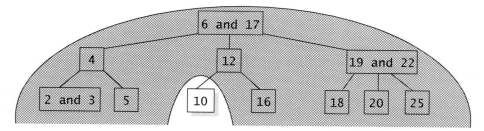

The recursive call finds the target, returning `true` to the previous recursive call. That previous recursive call then returns `true` to the original call, and the original call can also return `true`, indicating that the target was found somewhere in the set.

There are several parts of the pseudocode for you to clarify in your implementation. How do you determine whether the target was found at `data[i]`? How do you determine whether the root has children? The implementation of the first step of the pseudocode is smoother if you first implement a private method along these lines:

```
private int firstGE(int target)
// Postcondition: The return value x is the first location in the root such
// that data[x] >= target. if there is no such location, then the return value
// is dataCount.
```

Programming Tip: Private Methods to Simplify Implementations

Carefully selected private methods can simplify the implementations of other methods. You should write a specification for each private method, but these specifications do not need to be published for other programmers to see. Also, since the method is private, its specification can use information that only you know, such as the way that private instance variables are used.

Adding an Element to a B-Tree

The add method of the set class adds a new element to the B-tree. It is easier to add a new element to a B-tree if we relax one of the B-tree rules. In particular, we will allow a somewhat "loose addition" method to complete its work with the possibility that there is one element too many in the root node of the B-tree. In other words, a loose addition might result in MAXIMUM + 1 elements in the root. For example, consider this B-tree where MAXIMUM is 2:

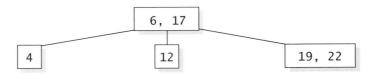

Suppose that we want to add 18 to the tree. The end result of a loose addition could be the following illegal B-tree:

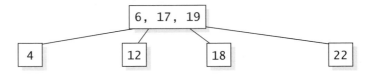

The B-tree is illegal because the root node has three elements, which is one more than the value of MAXIMUM. Notice that *only the root* may have an extra element after the "loose addition." Our plan is for the add method to begin by activating a private method that carries out a loose addition. After the loose addition, the usual add method will examine the root node. If the root node has too many elements, then the add method will fix that problem in a way that we'll describe later. For now, though, we'll turn our attention to the design of the loose addition method.

The Loose Addition Operation for a B-Tree

From our previous discussion, you can design a specification for a loose addition. The method will be a private method called looseAdd. The specification is given here:

```
private void looseAdd(int element)
// Precondition: The entire B-tree is valid.
// Postcondition: If the element was already in this set, then this set is
// unchanged. Otherwise, the element has been added to this set, and the
// entire B-tree is still valid EXCEPT that the number of elements in the root
// of this set might be one more than the allowed maximum.
```

Since this is a *private* method, it may violate the usual invariant for the set ADT. As you can see, the precondition does satisfy the usual invariant, but the post-condition allows for a violation of the invariant. This precondition/postcondition contract will not appear in the set's documentation. It is present only in the implementation file, as an aid to the programmer who implements the class.

The first step of our approach for the loose addition is identical to the first step of the searching method. This step finds the first location in the root's data that is greater than or equal to the new element. Once we have this location, there are three possibilities listed in Step 2 of the pseudocode:

```
// Pseudocode for the looseAdd method
```

1. Make a local variable, i, equal to the first index such that data[i] >= element. If there is no such index, then set i equal to dataCount, indicating that none of the elements is greater than or equal to the target.

2. if (we found the new element at data[i])
>2a. Return with no further work (since the new element is already in the set, and we may not have two copies of the same element).
>
>else if (the root has no children)
>2b. Add the new element to the root at data[i]. (The original elements at data[i] and afterwards must be shifted right to make room for the new element.)
>
>else
>{   2c.
>subset[i].looseAdd(element);
>If the root of subset[i] now has an excess element, then fix that problem before returning.
>}

pseudocode for the looseAdd method

Looking through the pseudocode, Steps 2a and 2b are fairly easy. You already have a private method for Step 2a (firstGE on page 500), and you can write another private method for Step 2b. The more interesting work occurs in Step 2c, where we have not found the new element, nor are we ready to add the new element. In this case, we make a recursive call to do a loose addition of the new element in the appropriate subset. Since the recursive call is a *loose* addition, we may end up with one excess element in the root of our subset. This excess element must be dealt with before returning because the postcondition does not allow subsets to have nodes with extra elements.

As an example of executing the pseudocode, suppose we are making a loose addition of 18 into this B-tree (with MAXIMUM set to 2):

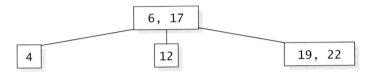

Step 1 of the pseudocode finds the first element in the root that is greater than or equal to the new element 18. As you see, none of the root elements is greater than or equal to 18, so what does Step 1 do instead? From the pseudocode, you see that the index i will be set to 2 (the number of elements in the root node).

In Step 2 we notice that we have not found the new element in the root, nor are we at a leaf. So we proceed to Step 2c, making a recursive call to add 18 to subtree number 2, as shown here:

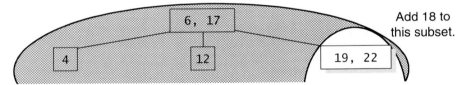

Add 18 to this subset.

The recursive call finds a small subtree with just a root. Following Step 2b, the recursive call adds the number 18 into the root of the subtree and then returns. After the recursive call returns, the entire tree looks like this:

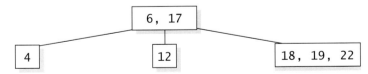

When the recursive call returns, we carry out the rest of Step 2c, checking whether the root of the subtree now has too many elements. Indeed, the root of subset[2] now has three elements, which is one more than the allowed maximum. We must fix this problem child, but how? It seems that fixing the child may take quite a bit of work, so we will propose another private method to carry out this work.

A Private Method to Fix an Excess in a Child

Here's the specification for the private method that we have in mind:

```
private void fixExcess(int i)
// Precondition: (i < childCount) and the entire B-tree is valid EXCEPT that
// subset[i] has MAXIMUM + 1 elements.
// Postcondition: The tree has been rearranged so that the entire B-tree is
// valid EXCEPT that the number of elements in the root of this set might be
// one more than the allowed maximum.
```

Looking at the specification, you can see that the method starts with a problem child. When the method finishes, the child no longer has a problem, although the *root* may now have a problem. The approach of the fixExcess method can be simply stated:

Fixing a Child with an Excess Element

To fix a child with MAXIMUM + 1 elements, the child node is split into two nodes that each contain MINIMUM elements. This leaves one extra element, which is passed up to the parent.

Let's examine an example of this approach. In the example, suppose that MINIMUM is 2, so that the maximum number of elements in a node is 4 (which is 2*MINIMUM). We want to fix subtree number 1 (the shaded subtree) in this example tree:

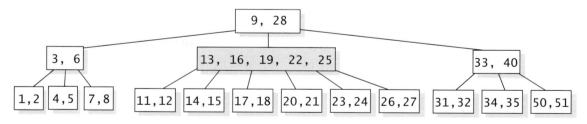

The approach taken by fixExcess is to split the problem node (with 2*MINIMUM + 1 elements) into two smaller nodes (with MINIMUM elements each). This leaves one element unaccounted for, and that one extra element will be passed upward to the parent of the split node. Therefore, the parent of the split node gains one additional child (from splitting the full node) and also gains one additional element (the extra element that is passed upward). In the example shown above, the result of the splitting is shown on the next page.

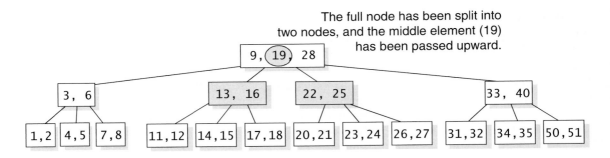

The full node has been split into two nodes, and the middle element (19) has been passed upward.

It is always the *middle* element of the split node that moves upward. Also, notice that the children of the split node have been equally distributed between the two smaller nodes.

As another example of `fixExcess` in action, suppose that MAXIMUM is 2, and we have the problem child shown here:

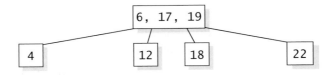

subset[2] has an excess element.

After `fixExcess(2)` returns, the problem child will be split into two nodes, with the middle element passed upward, as shown here:

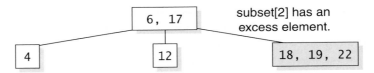

As you can see in this example, fixing the problem child can create a root with an excess element—but that is all right because the postcondition of `fixExcess` permits the root to have an extra element.

In your implementation of `fixExcess`, you will find it helpful to use the `System.arraycopy` method (see page 120), and you may also want to write more private methods to help with the work.

Back to the add Method

We need to finish the discussion of the original add method. By using the `looseAdd` method, the public add method has just two steps:

pseudocode for add

```
// Pseudocode for the public add method
looseAdd(element);
if (dataCount > MAXIMUM)
    Fix the root of the entire tree so that it no longer has too many elements.
```

In this pseudocode, how do we "fix the root of the entire tree so that it no longer has too many elements"? The step can be accomplished in two parts. The first part copies all instance variables from the root to a newly allocated node and clears out the root, giving it new arrays with only one child (which is the newly allocated node) and no elements. For example, suppose that we do a loose addition, and then the B-tree looks like this (with MAXIMUM set to 2):

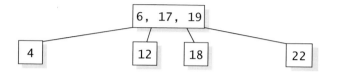

We will copy everything from the root to a new node and clear out the root. In the resulting tree, the root will have no elements, and everything else has moved down one level, as shown here:

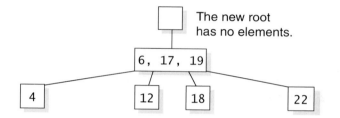

Once we have shifted things in this way, the problem is now with the child of the root. We can fix this problem by splitting the subset[0] of the root into two nodes and passing the middle element upward. In fact, if you are careful in writing fixExcess, this splitting can be carried out by activating fixExcess(0). Care must be taken because this root has no elements, so fixExcess must be prepared to deal with such a situation. (If you take this approach, you should document the extended ability of fixExcess in its precondition.)

In this example, after splitting subset[0] we have the completely valid B-tree shown here:

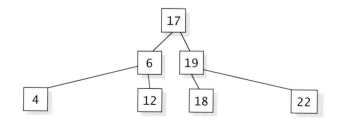

B-trees gain height only at the root

By the way, this growth at the root (within the add method) is the only point where a B-tree gains height.

FIGURE 10.5 Top-down Design

The add method activates:
- `looseAdd`
- `fixExcess`

The `looseAdd` method is recursive and also activates:
- `firstGE`
- `fixExcess`

The `fixExcess` method activates:
- `System.arraycopy`
- Other private methods that you may write

Employing Top-Down Design

As you work on the project, keep in mind the top-down design that we have employed. As shown in Figure 10.5, the original add method activates the private method `looseAdd`. Both the ordinary add and the `looseAdd` methods activate `fixExcess`. The `fixExcess` method uses `System.arraycopy`, and you may have written other private methods to help with the `fixExcess` work.

Removing an Element from a B-Tree

The `remove` method of the set removes an element from the B-tree. Most of the removal work will be accomplished with a private method, `looseRemove`, which performs a *loose removal* that is analogous to the loose addition. The looseness in `looseRemove` occurs because it is allowed to leave a root that has one element too few. In other words, it might leave the root of the whole tree with zero elements (which is not permitted unless there are also no children), or it might leave the root of an internal subtree with fewer than MINIMUM elements. The specification of `looseRemove` is given here:

```
private boolean looseRemove(int target)
// Precondition: The entire B-tree is valid.
// Postcondition: If target was in this set, then it has been removed from
//   this set and the method returns true; otherwise this set is unchanged
//   and the method returns false. The entire B-tree is still valid
//   EXCEPT that the number of elements in the root of this set might be one
//   less than the allowed minimum.
```

Our complete `remove` method will first activate `looseRemove`. Afterwards, if necessary, we can fix a root that may have been left with zero elements and one child. Thus, the remove pseudocode has just these steps:

pseudocode for remove

```
// Pseudocode for the public remove method
answer = looseRemove(target);
if ((dataCount == 0) && (childCount == 1))
      Fix the root of the entire tree so that it no longer has zero elements.
return answer;
```

In this pseudocode, how do we "fix the root of the entire tree so that it no longer has zero elements"? For example, we might have the tree that is shown at the top of the next page.

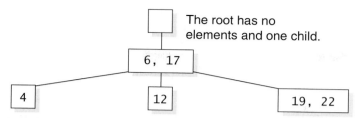

The root has no elements and one child.

Our solution for this problem is to reassign each of our four instance variables to equal the four instance variables from our only child. For example, the first assignment is `dataCount = subset[0].dataCount`. Make sure that the last of the four assignments is `subset = subset[0].subset` . (If you do this assignment too early, then you lose contact with `subset[0]`.) After this rearrangement, our tree will be one level shorter, as shown here:

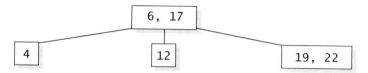

This shrinking at the root (within the `remove` method) is the only point where a B-tree loses height.

B-trees lose height only at the root

Now we are left with the task of designing the loose removal.

The Loose Removal from a B-Tree

The private `looseRemove` method starts in the same way as the search and add methods, by finding the first index i such that `data[i]` is greater than or equal to the target. Once we have found this index, there are four possibilities, shown here:

// *Removing a target from a set*
1. Make a local variable, i, equal to the first index such that `data[i] >= target`. If there is no such index, then set i equal to `dataCount`, indicating that none of the elements is greater than or equal to the target.

pseudocode for loose remove

2. Deal with one of these four possibilities:

    2a. The root has no children, and we did not find the target: In this case, there is no work to do, and the method returns `false`.

    2b. The root has no children, and we found the target: In this case, remove the target from the data array, and return `true`.

    2c. The root has children, and we did not find the target (see below).

    2d. The root has children, and we found the target (see below).

Cases 2c and 2d require further development.

Case 2c.   In this case, we did not find the target in the root, but the target still might appear in `subset[i]`. We will make a recursive call:

```
answer = subset[i].looseRemove(target);
```

The local variable `answer` is a boolean variable to keep track of whether the recursive call actually removed the target. If `looseRemove` did remove the target from `subset[i]`, then we are left with the problem that the root of `subset[i]` might have only MINIMUM − 1 elements. If so, then we'll fix the problem by activating another private method with the specification shown here:

```
private void fixShortage(int i)
// Precondition: (i < childCount) and the entire B-tree is valid EXCEPT that
// subset[i] has MINIMUM - 1 elements.
// Postcondition: The tree has been rearranged so that the entire B-tree is
// valid EXCEPT that the number of elements in the root of this set might be
// one less than the allowed minimum.
```

After we fix any possible shortage, we should return `answer` to indicate whether `target` was removed from the set. We'll look at the design of `fixShortage` later.

Case 2d.   In this case, we have found the target in the root, but we cannot simply remove it from the data array because there are children below (and removing an element would thereby violate B-tree Rule 4 on page 492). Instead, we will go into `subset[i]` and remove the *largest* element in this subset. We will take a copy of this largest element and place it into `data[i]` (which contains the target). The total effect is the same as removing the target.

For example, suppose we have found the target 28 at `data[1]` in the root of this B-tree:

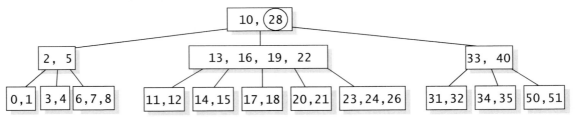

Our plan is to go into `subset[1]`, remove the largest element (the 26), and place a copy of this 26 on top of the target. After these steps, the B-tree no longer has the 28:

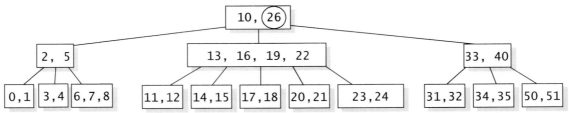

The combination of removing the largest element from `subset[i]` and placing a copy of the largest element into `data[i]` can be accomplished by activating another new private method, `removeBiggest`, with a specification shown here:

```
private int removeBiggest( )
// Precondition: (dataCount > 0) and this entire B-tree is valid.
// Postcondition: The largest element in this set has been removed, and the
// return value is this removed element. The entire B-tree is still valid,
// EXCEPT that the number of elements in the root of this
// set might be one less than the allowed minimum.
```

By using `removeBiggest`, most of Step 2d is done with one statement:

```
data[i] = subset[i].removeBiggest( );
```

After this statement finishes, we have deleted the largest element from `subset[i]` and placed a copy of this element into `data[i]` (replacing the target). The work that remains is to fix the possible shortage that may occur in the root of `subset[i]` (since the postcondition of `subset[i].removeBiggest` allows for the possibility that the root of `subset[i]` ends up with MINIMUM – 1 elements). How do we fix such a shortage? We can use the same `fixShortage` method that we used at the end of Step 2c. Thus, the entire code for Step 2d is the following:

```
data[i] = subset[i].removeBiggest( );
if (subset[i].dataCount < MINIMUM)
    fixShortage(i);
return true;  // To indicate that we removed the target.
```

We have two more issues to deal with: the designs of `fixShortage` and `removeBiggest`.

A Private Method to Fix a Shortage in a Child

When `fixShortage(i)` is activated, we know that `subset[i]` has MINIMUM – 1 elements. How can we correct this problem? There are four situations that you can consider:

four situations for the fixShortage pseudocode

Case 1 of `fixShortage`: Transfer an extra element from `subset[i-1]`.
Suppose that `subset[i-1]` has more than the minimum number of elements. Then we can carry out these transfers:

a. Transfer `data[i-1]` down to the front of `subset[i].data`. Remember to shift over the existing elements to make room, and add one to `subset[i].dataCount`.

b. Transfer the final element of `subset[i-1].data` up to replace `data[i-1]`, and subtract one from `subset[i-1].dataCount`.

c.   If `subset[i-1]` has children, transfer the final child of `subset[i-1]` over to the front of `subset[i]`. This involves shifting over the existing array `subset[i].subset` to make room for the new child at `subset[i].subset[0]`. Also add one to `subset[i].childCount`, and subtract one from `subset[i-1].childCount`.

For example, let's activate `fixShortage(2)` for this tree (with MINIMUM set to 2):

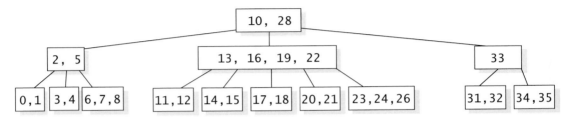

In this example, we need to fix `subset[2]`, which has only one element. Following the steps outlined earlier, we can transfer an element from `subset[1]`. This transferred element is the 22, which gets passed up to `data[1]`, and the 28 (from `data[1]`) comes down to be the new first element of the problem node. One child is also transferred from the end of `subset[1]` to the front of `subset[2]`, as shown here:

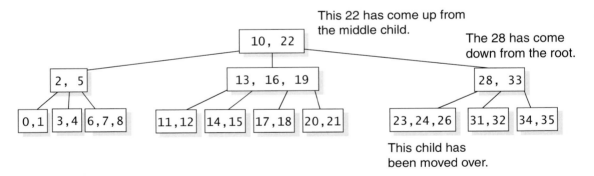

Case 2 for `fixShortage`: Transfer an extra element from `subset[i+1]`.
Another possibility is to transfer an extra element from `subset[i+1]`. The work is similar to what you have just seen for transferring an element from `subset[i-1]`.

Case 3 for `fixShortage`: Combine `subset[i]` with `subset[i-1]`.
Suppose that `subset[i-1]` is present (in other words, `i > 0`), but it has only MINIMUM elements. In this case, we cannot transfer an element from `subset[i-1]`, but we can combine `subset[i]` with `subset[i-1]`. The combining occurs in three steps, listed at the top of the next page.

a. Transfer `data[i-1]` down to the end of `subset[i-1].data`. This actually removes the element from the root, so shift `data[i]`, `data[i+1]`, and so on, leftward to fill in the gap. Also remember to subtract one from `dataCount`, and add one to `subset[i-1].dataCount`.

b. Transfer all the elements and children from `subset[i]` to the end of `subset[i-1]`. Remember to update the values of `subset[i-1].dataCount` and `subset[i-1].childCount`.

c. Disconnect the node `subset[i]` from the B-tree by shifting `subset[i+1]`, `subset[i+2]`, and so on leftward. Also reduce `child-Count` by one. (Once `subset[i]` is no longer part of the tree, Java's automatic garbage collector will reclaim its memory.)

For example, let's activate `fixShortage(2)` for this tree (with `MINIMUM` set to 2):

In this example, `subset[2]` is merged with its sibling to the left. During the merge, the 28 also is passed down from the root to become a new element of the merged nodes. The result is the following tree:

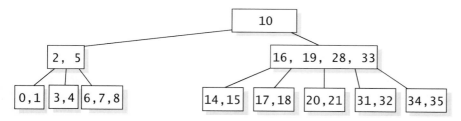

As you can see, this tree has too few elements in its own root, but that is okay because the postcondition of `fixShortage` allows the root of the resulting tree to have one less than the required number of elements.

Case 4 for `fixShortage`: Combine `subset[i]` with `subset[i+1]`.
Our fourth case is to combine the problem subset with `subset[i+1]`. The work is similar to what you have just seen for combining with `subset[i-1]`.

You now have enough information to write the `fixShortage` method. You should emphasize a clear logical structure to determine which of the four approaches is appropriate. Your implementation will be cleaner if you provide four new private methods to do the actual work in each of the four cases.

Removing the Biggest Element from a B-Tree

Our last method has this specification:

```
private int removeBiggest( )
// Precondition: (dataCount > 0) and the entire B-tree is valid.
// Postcondition: The largest element in the set has been removed, and the
// value of this element is the return value. The entire B-tree is still valid,
// EXCEPT that the number of elements in the root of this
// set might be one less than the allowed minimum.
```

The work of `removeBiggest` is easy if the root has no children. In this case, we remove and return the last element of the partially filled data array with the single statement: `return data[--dataCount]`. That's all! We might be left with a node that has one less than the allowed minimum number of elements, but according to the postcondition, that is okay.

What if the root has children? In this case, we make a recursive call to remove the largest element from the rightmost child. The recursive call is:

```
answer = subset[childCount-1].removeBiggest( );
```

The result of the recursive call is stored in a local variable, `answer`, so that the method can later return this value. But before returning, there is one remaining problem. The recursive call might leave the root of `subset[childCount-1]` with one element too few. How can we fix a child that has a shortage of elements? The `fixShortage` method can fix such a node. So, after the recursive call, you should check the number of elements in the root of `subset[child-Count-1]`. If the number of elements is less than MINIMUM, then activate `fixShortage(childCount-1)`.

Programming Tip: Write and Test Small Pieces

TIP

If you are implementing the entire set ADT, don't try to do the whole thing at once. Instead, write and test methods one at a time. In this project, you should also carry out a major testing after you have completed the add and `contains` methods, and before you have started on any of the removal machinery.

When you start on the removal, draw a diagram of the top-down design that you are implementing.

Test pieces as soon as you can. Early testing can be aided by initially implementing all of your planned methods with a single line that simply prints the name of the method, indicating that the method has been activated. A single line such as this is called a **stub**. With stubs in place, you can test any method as soon as you have written the complete version. For example, as soon as you implement the remove method, you can test it. You know that it should activate the `looseRemove` method, so you expect the `looseRemove` stub to print a message indicating that `looseRemove` has been activated.

Throughout your implementation work, it will be useful if you can print some representation of a B-tree. We suggest that you temporarily add a public print method, similar to the method shown in Figure 10.6.

In order for the output of the print method to be understandable, keep the value of MINIMUM small during testing—perhaps 1 or 2.

External B-Trees

Programmers may use B-trees to ensure quick behavior from the fact that the trees are always balanced (all the leaves are at the same depth). If a balanced tree is your only objective, then the choice of the MINIMUM constant is not critical. Sometimes MINIMUM is simply 1, meaning that each node has one or two elements, and nonleaf nodes have *two or three* children. This situation is called a **2-3 tree,** which was proposed by John E. Hopcroft several years before B-trees were devised.

FIGURE 10.6	Implementing a Temporary Method That Prints a Set's B-Tree

Implementation

```
public void print(int indent)
// This is a temporary public method for use by the programmer who implements the
// class. The method prints a representation of the set's B-tree. The elements of the root node
// are printed with an indentation given by the parameter, and each subtree has an extra
// four spaces of indentation.
{
    final int EXTRA_INDENTATION = 4;
    int i;
    int space;

    // Print the indentation and the data from this node.
    for (space = 0; space < indent; space++)
        System.out.print(" ");
    for (i = 0; i < dataCount; i++)
        System.out.print(data[i] + " ");
    System.out.println( );

    // Print the subtrees.
    for (i = 0; i < childCount; i++)
        subset[i].print(indent + EXTRA_INDENTATION);
}
```

most of the nodes reside in slower secondary memory

Sometimes B-trees become large—so large that the entire tree cannot reside in the computer's main memory at one time. For example, a residential phone book of the United States contains about 100 million entries. The set of elements can still be organized as a B-tree, but most of the nodes must be stored in slower secondary memory such as a hard drive or a CD-ROM. Typically, the root node is loaded into main memory, where it stays for the life of the program. But, non-root nodes must be loaded from the secondary memory whenever they are needed. This situation is called an **external B-tree.**

A primary consideration with external B-trees is to reduce the total number of accesses to the secondary memory device. Therefore, the `MINIMUM` constant will be set quite large. With `MINIMUM` set to 1000, we can store more than one billion (10^9) elements with just the root and two levels below it. Because the root is always kept in memory, no search will ever require more than two nodes from the secondary memory device.

Another factor concerns the retrieval mechanism used by the secondary storage device. When a request is made to read from a hard disk or CD-ROM, there is a relatively long initial *access time* to position the disk's read head over the requested section of the disk. Once the head has been positioned, contiguous data can be read fairly quickly. This data is transferred in fixed-sized blocks, using a relatively high *sustained transfer rate.* Today's 24X CD-ROM drives have an access time around $\frac{1}{10}$ of a second. Once the head is positioned, the drive transfers about 4 million bytes per second. With this in mind, you need to ensure that each node is stored in a contiguous area of the disk—for if the node is spread out in several different areas, each area will require $^1/_{10}$ of a second access time to reposition the head.

Self-Test Exercises

6. Suppose `MINIMUM` is 200 for a B-tree. What is the maximum number of elements that a node may contain? What is the minimum number of elements that a nonroot node may have? What is the maximum number of children that a node may have? What is the minimum number of children that a nonleaf, nonroot node may have?

7. Suppose `MINIMUM` is 1000 for a B-tree. The tree has a root and one level of 1000 nodes below that. What is the minimum number of elements that this tree might have? What is the maximum?

8. Start with an empty B-tree, with `MINIMUM` set to 1. Enter the integers 1 through 10. Draw the resulting tree.

9. Remove the numbers 8, 3, and 6 from the tree that you created in the previous exercise. Draw the resulting tree after each removal.

10.3 TREES, LOGS, AND TIME ANALYSIS

The implementations in this chapter—heaps and B-trees—are efficient for a simple reason: The depth of the trees is kept small so that following a path from the root to a leaf does not examine too many nodes. In fact, we can make a strong statement relating the depth of a tree, and the worst-case time required for the operations we have implemented:

Worst-Case Times for Tree Operations

The worst-case time performance for the following operations are all $O(d)$, where d is the depth of the tree:

1. Adding an element to a binary search tree, a heap, or a B-tree.

2. Removing an element from a binary search tree, a heap, or a B-tree.

3. Searching for a specified element in a binary search tree or a B-tree.

For example, consider adding an element to a heap. The new element is placed at the next available location of the heap at the deepest level, d. The priority of the new element is then compared with its parent's priority, and the new element might be swapped with its parent. In the worst case, this process continues, comparing the new element with its parent and swapping, until the new element reaches the root. In this worst case, the new element had to be compared with its parent and swapped d times, where d is the depth at which the new element began its life. Since one comparison and swap requires a fixed number of operations, the total number of operations in the algorithm is a fixed number times d, which is $O(d)$. You can carry out a similar analysis for each of the other operations listed above.

This could be the end of our story, except that time analyses for these operations are more useful if they are given in terms of the number of elements in the tree, rather than in terms of the tree's depth. To express the time analyses in these terms, we must first answer a secondary question: *What is the maximum depth for a tree with n elements?* We'll answer this question for binary search trees and heaps, leaving the case of B-trees for your exercises. Once this question is answered, we can provide worst-case time analyses in terms of the number of elements in a tree.

Time Analysis for Binary Search Trees

Suppose a binary search tree has n elements. What is the maximum depth the tree could have? A binary tree must have at least one node at each level. For example, a binary tree with depth 2 must have a root (at level 0), at least one child of the root (at level 1), and at least one child of the child (at level 2). If a tree has n nodes, then the first node may appear at the root level, the second node at level 1, the third node at level 2, and so on until the nth node, which appears at depth $n-1$. So, a binary tree with n elements could have a depth as big as $n-1$.

What does this say about the worst-case time analysis of the binary search tree operations in terms of the number of elements in a tree? Here's the analysis:

Worst-Case Times for Binary Search Trees

Adding an element, removing an element, or searching for an element in a binary search tree with n elements is $O(d)$, where d is the depth of the tree. Since d is no more than $n-1$, the operations are $O(n-1)$, which is $O(n)$ (since we can ignore constants in big-O notation).

Time Analysis for Heaps

In a heap, we can examine the relationship between depth and number of elements by first computing the smallest number of elements required for a heap to reach a given depth d. Remember that a heap is a complete binary tree so that each level must be full before proceeding to the next level. The first element goes at level 0 (the root level). The next two elements must go at level 1, the next four elements at level 2, the next 8 elements at level 3, and so on. Let's present this information in a table.

Level	Number of nodes to fill the level
0	1 node
1	2 nodes
2	4 nodes
3	8 nodes
4	16 nodes
...	
d	2^d nodes

The values in the table are the maximum number of nodes that may occur at each level. Using the table, we can obtain the total number of nodes needed to reach level d:

> *Number of nodes needed for a heap to reach depth d is*
> $$(1 + 2 + 4 + \ldots + 2^{d-1}) + 1$$

The first part of the formula, up to 2^{d-1}, is the number of elements required to completely fill the first $d-1$ levels, and the extra "+ 1" at the end is required because there must be at least one element in level d.

This formula can be simplified by shifting the +1 to the front:

> *Number of nodes needed for a heap to reach depth d is*
> $$1 + 1 + 2 + 4 + \ldots + 2^{d-1}$$

Why is this a simplification? Look at the start of the formula, which begins $1 + 1\ldots$. Then combine the two 1's, like this:

$$1 + 1 + 2 + 4 + \ldots + 2^{d-1} \quad = \quad 2 + 2 + 4 + \ldots + 2^{d-1}$$

Now we have a formula that begins with two 2s, which can also be combined:

$$2 + 2 + 4 + \ldots + 2^{d-1} \quad = \quad 4 + 4 + \ldots + 2^{d-1}$$

Now we have a formula that begins with two 4s, and if we combine the 4s we get two 8s, and so on until we eventually end up with just $2^{d-1} + 2^{d-1}$. So:

> *Number of nodes needed for a heap to reach depth d is*
> $$= (1 + 2 + 4 + \ldots + 2^{d-1}) + 1$$
> $$= 2^{d-1} + 2^{d-1}$$

This last formula, $2^{d-1} + 2^{d-1}$, is the same as 2^d, so we have the following result:

> The number of nodes needed for a heap
> to reach depth d is 2^d.

Expressed another way: The number of nodes in a heap is at least 2^d, where d is the depth of the heap.

This is certainly a simple formula, but in order to use it, we need to explain a bit about **base 2 logarithms**. For any positive number, x, the base 2 logarithm of x is an exponent r such that:

$$2^r = x$$

The number r in this equation is usually written $\log_2 x$. For example:

$$2^0 = 1, \text{ so that } \log_2 1 = 0$$
$$2^1 = 2, \text{ so that } \log_2 2 = 1$$
$$2^2 = 4, \text{ so that } \log_2 4 = 2$$
$$2^3 = 8, \text{ so that } \log_2 8 = 3$$
$$2^4 = 16, \text{ so that } \log_2 16 = 4$$
$$2^d = 2^d, \text{ so that } \log_2 2^d = d$$

The last line of this table is the key to our heap analysis. We know that in a heap the number of elements, n, is at least 2^d, where d is the depth of the heap. Therefore:

$$\log_2 n \geq \log_2 2^d \text{ (since } n \geq 2^d)$$

Since $\log_2 2^d = d$, this implies that:

$$\log_2 n \geq d.$$

This is the relationship that we need between the number of elements, n, and the depth of a heap. Here's the analysis:

Worst-Case Times for Heap Operations

Adding or removing an element in a heap with n elements is $O(d)$, where d is the depth of the tree. Because d is no more than $\log_2 n$, the operations are $O(\log_2 n)$, which is $O(\log n)$ (since we can ignore log bases in big-O notation).

The time analysis for B-trees will also result in $O(\log n)$ time, as you'll be asked to show in Self-Test Exercise 11.

Omitting the subscript, 2, from $O(\log_2 n)$ may be a bit confusing, but to explain why the omission is valid, we need to look at logarithms in more depth. This look at logarithms will also give us a good understanding of the behavior that is expected from logarithmic algorithms, such as adding and deleting from a heap.

Logarithms

The definition of $\log_2 x$ is a number r such that $2^r = x$. The number 2 is called the **base of the logarithm,** and the definition extends to other bases. For example, $\log_{10} x$ is the number r such that $10^r = x$. Or consider base 16, where $\log_{16} x$ is the number r such that $16^r = x$.

Here are some specific examples for base 10:

$$10^0 = 1, \qquad \text{so that } \log_{10} 1 = 0$$
$$10^1 = 10, \qquad \text{so that } \log_{10} 10 = 1$$
$$10^{1.5} = \text{about } 32, \quad \text{so that } \log_{10} 32 = \text{about } 1.5$$
$$10^3 = 1000, \qquad \text{so that } \log_{10} 1000 = 3$$

From these examples, you can see why we said in Chapter 1 that the number of digits in a positive integer n is approximately $\log_{10} n$. You can work out a little table:

For n in the range 1 to 9, $0 \leq \log_{10} n < 1$

For n in the range 10 to 99, $1 \leq \log_{10} n < 2$

For n in the range 100 to 999, $2 \leq \log_{10} n < 3$

For n in the range 1000 to 9999, $3 \leq \log_{10} n < 4$

Extrapolating from this table, you can find a precise relationship between the number of digits in a positive integer and base 10 logarithms (using $\lfloor \log_{10} n \rfloor$ to indicate rounding down the logarithm to an integer):

> The number of digits in a positive integer n is $\lfloor \log_{10} n \rfloor + 1$.

There is also a relationship between logarithms in one base and logarithms in another base:

> For any two bases, a and b, and a positive number x:
> $$(\log_b a) \times (\log_a x) = \log_b x$$

This equation is the reason why bases generally are omitted from big-O notation. For example, if an algorithm requires $\log_2 n$ operations, then that is the same as $4 \times \log_{16} n$ operations, since $\log_2 16$ is 4. In big-O notation, the multiplication by a constant (such as 4) is ignored, and this is why we write simply $O(\log n)$ rather than $O(\log_2 n)$.

Logarithmic Algorithms

Logarithmic algorithms are algorithms with worst-case time $O(\log n)$, such as adding and deleting from a heap. These algorithms have a characteristic time behavior:

Time Behavior of Logarithmic Algorithms

For a logarithmic algorithm, doubling the input size will make the time increase by a fixed number of new operations.

For example, consider adding a new element to a heap with n elements. The algorithm may look at as many as $\log_2 n$ nodes. If we double the number of nodes to $2n$, then the algorithm may look at as many as $\log_2 2n$ nodes—but $\log_2 2n$ is just one more than $\log_2 n$. (For example, $\log_2 1024 = 10$, and $\log_2 2048 = 11$.) So we can double the number of elements in a heap, and the process of adding a new element requires us to examine only one extra node.

Self-Test Exercises

10. Evaluate the following logarithms:

$$\log_2 32 \qquad \log_5 125 \qquad \log_{16} 256$$
$$\log_{10} 100 \qquad \log_{37} 1 \qquad \log_9 81$$

11. Show that adding, removing, and searching in a B-tree have worst-case time $O(\log n)$.

12. Use the definition of logarithms to show that $\log_2 2n$ is always just one more than $\log_2 n$.

CHAPTER SUMMARY

- A *heap* is a complete binary tree that follows the rule that the element at any node is never less than any of its children's elements. Heaps provide an efficient implementation of priority queues.

- A *B-tree* is a tree for storing elements in a manner that follows six rules. The first two rules specify the minimum and maximum number of elements for each node. The third rule requires each node's elements to be sorted from smallest to largest. Rules 4 and 5 indicate how many subtrees a nonleaf node must have and provide an order on the elements of the subtrees. The last rule requires each leaf to be at the same depth.

- The tree algorithms that we have seen for binary search trees, heaps, and B-trees all have worst-case time performance of $O(d)$, where d is the depth of the tree.

- The depth of a heap or B-tree is never more than $O(\log n)$, where n is the number of nodes. Hence, the operations on these structures are also $O(\log n)$.

Solutions to Self-Test Exercises ?

1. Because a heap is a complete binary tree.

2. One approach is to store the complete binary tree of the heap in two separate arrays. One array, called `priority`, contains the priorities of the nodes. Another array, called `data`, contains the data of the nodes. For example, `priority[0]` and `data[0]` contain the priority and data of the root of the heap.

    With this idea, we can write a priority queue implementation as shown here:

```
public class PriorityQueue
{
    private int[ ] priority;
    private Object[ ] data;
    int size;
    ...
```

The `size` instance variable indicates how much of the arrays are currently being used. The constructor is responsible for allocating the initial arrays. The method that adds a new element to the priority queue may need to increase the size of these arrays.

3. If we swap with the smaller child, then the larger child will still have a priority that exceeds its parent's priority.

4. With our addition algorithm, you end up with this heap:

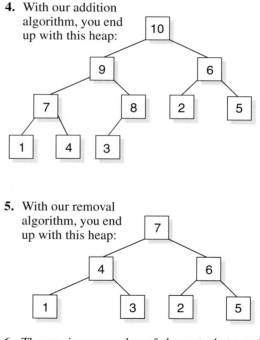

5. With our removal algorithm, you end up with this heap:

6. The maximum number of elements that a node may contain is 400, although during an addition we may temporarily have a node with 401 elements. The minimum number of elements that a nonroot node may have is 200, although

during a removal we may temporarily have a node with 199 elements. The maximum number of children that a node may have is 401, although during an addition, we may temporarily have a node with 402 children. The minimum number of children that a non-leaf, non-root node may have is 201, although during a removal we may temporarily have a node with 200 children.

7. The root has 999 elements, and each of the 1000 nodes at the next level has between 1000 and 2000 elements. Therefore, the total number of elements in the tree is between 1,000,999 elements and 2,000,999.

8. With our addition algorithm, you end up with this B-tree:

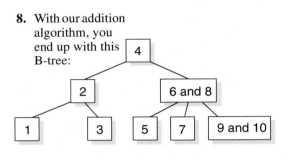

9. After removing the 8:

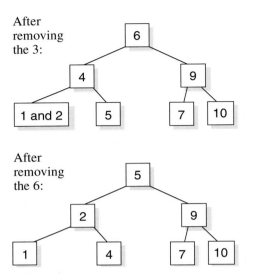

10. The logarithms are:

$$\log_2 32 = 5 \qquad \log_5 125 = 3 \qquad \log_{16} 256 = 2$$
$$\log_{10} 100 = 2 \qquad \log_{37} 1 = 0 \qquad \log_9 81 = 2$$

11. In all three algorithms, the number of total steps is a constant times the height of the B-tree. This height is no more than $\log_M n$, where M is the MINIMUM constant and n is the number of elements in the tree. Thus, the algorithms all require no more than $O(\log n)$ operations.

12. All logarithms in this solution are base 2:

$$2^{1 + \log n} = 2 \times 2^{\log n} = 2n = 2^{\log 2n}$$

Therefore, $1 + \log n = \log 2n$.

PROGRAMMING PROJECTS

1 Using a heap, implement the priority queue ADT from Section 7.4. You may store the heap in arrays, similar to the solution to Self-Test Exercise 1. In order to have FIFO behavior for elements with equal priority, you should have a third array called `entered`. The value of `entered[i]` tells when the data in node number i entered the priority queue. For example, the first element added has an entered value of 1, the second element has an entered value of 2, and so on. When you are comparing two elements with equal priority, use the entered value to "break the tie," (so that if two elements have the same priority number, then the one with the earlier entered value will come out of the priority queue first).

Make sure that you keep track of how many elements are in the heap, so that if the size of the heap reaches the size of the arrays, you can increase the size of the arrays.

2 Use a B-tree to implement the `Set` class from Figure 10.4 on page 494. Be sure to write and test small pieces.

3 The `java.lang.Math` class provides a static method `log(x)`, which returns the logarithm of x with a base that is approximately 2.71828. This base is written e, and the logarithms with this base are called **natural logarithms** or **Napierian logarithms,** after the Scottish mathematician John Napier (1550–1617) who invented these logarithms. The number e may seem like a strange choice for the base of a logarithm, but the choice is motivated by the fact that natural logarithms are easy to approximate as the sum of a series. Anyway, in this project, you are to write a method:

```
double log10(double x)
```

The method returns the base 10 logarithm of x. Make use of the `java.lang.Math.log` method and the formulas in Section 10.3. You can also use the fact that $\log_{10} e$ is about 0.4342944819032.

By the way, Napier also invented a calculator called "Napier's bones." The device performed multiplication and division through a series of connected rods with tables marked on them.

Searching

As long as Bruce was busy rooting around under boulders and logs searching for a feast of beetles and grubs there was no need to worry.

BILL PEET
Big Bad Bruce

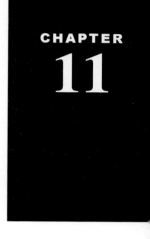

CHAPTER

11

Searching a list of values is a common computational task. An application program might retrieve a student record, bank account record, credit record, or any other type of record using a search algorithm. In this chapter, we present and analyze some of the most common (and some of the most efficient) methods of searching for a particular element. The algorithms include serial search, binary search, and search by hashing.

We also use the search algorithms to develop additional techniques for analyzing the running times of algorithms, particularly average-time analyses and the analysis of recursive algorithms.

11.1 SERIAL SEARCH AND BINARY SEARCH

Serial Search

Our starting point is the searching algorithm, shown in Figure 11.1. This algorithm, called a **serial search,** steps through part of an array one element at a time looking for a "desired element." The search stops when the element is found or when the search has examined each element without success. In the pseudocode we did not specify the precise return value of the algorithm—it might return the actual index where the item is found (returning –1 if the element is not found), or it might return a boolean value to indicate whether the element was found, or perhaps there is some other action that the algorithm takes when it finds the element. In any case, the algorithm is easy to write and applicable to many situations.

Serial Search—Analysis

The running time of the serial search is easy to analyze, but some care is needed to specify the precise kind of analysis. As always, we will count the number of "operations" required by the algorithm rather than measuring actual elapsed time. For searching an array, a common approach is to count one operation each time that the algorithm accesses an element of the array. With the serial search, the size of the array is one important factor in determining the number of array accesses—but even if we use a particular fixed array, the number of array

---

FIGURE 11.1   Serial Search Algorithm

Pseudocode

```
// Searches for a desired element in the n array elements starting at a[first]
Set an int variable i to 0  (to use as an index), and set a boolean variable found to false.
while ((i < n) && !found)
{
    if (a[first+i] is the desired element)
        found = true;
    else
        i++;
}

if (found)
    The desired element is in a[first+i].
else
    The desired element does not appear in the n items starting at a[first].
```

accesses will still vary depending on precisely which target we are looking for. If the target is the first element in the array, then there will be only one array access. If the target is near the middle of the array, then the serial search accesses about half of the array elements.

Usually when we discuss running times, we consider the "hardest" inputs, for example, a target that requires the algorithm to access the largest number of array elements. This is called the **worst-case** running time. For the serial search, the worst-case running time occurs when the target is not in the array. In this case, the algorithm accesses every element, and we have the following formula:

worst case

Worst-Case Time for Serial Search

For an array of n elements, the worst-case time for serial search requires n array accesses.

Most of the time, a serial search of an n-element array requires fewer than n array accesses. Thus, the worst-case expression "n array accesses" makes serial search sound worse than it often is. An alternative is the **average-case** running time, which is obtained by averaging the different running times for all different inputs of a particular kind. For example, we can develop an expression for the average-case running time of serial search based on all the targets that are actually in the array. To be concrete in this first example, suppose that the array has ten elements, so that there are ten possible targets. If we are searching for the target that occurs at the first location, then there is just one array access. If we are searching for the target that occurs at the second location, then there are two array accesses, and so on, through the final target, which requires ten array accesses. In all, there are ten possible targets, which require 1, 2, 3, 4, 5, 6, 7, 8, 9, or 10 array accesses. The average of all these searches is:

average case

$$\frac{1 + 2 + 3 + 4 + 5 + 6 + 7 + 8 + 9 + 10}{10} = 5.5$$

We can generalize this example so that the average-case running time of the serial search is written as an expression with part of the expression being the size of the array. Using n as the size of the array, this expression for the average-case running time is:

$$\frac{1 + 2 + \ldots + n}{n} = \frac{n(n + 1)/2}{n} = (n + 1)/2$$

The first equality in this formula is obtained from the formula that we developed on page 21. We can summarize the average-case running time for serial search:

Average-Case Time for Serial Search

For an array of *n* elements, the average-case time for serial search to find an element that is in the array requires (*n* + 1)/2 array accesses.

You may have noticed that both the worst-case time and the average-case time are $O(n)$ expressions, but nevertheless, the average case is about half the time of the worst case.

best case
A third way to measure running times is called **best-case** running time, and as the name suggests, it takes the most optimistic view possible. The best-case running time is defined as the smallest of all the running times on inputs of a particular size. For serial search, the best case occurs when the target is found at the front of the array, requiring only one array access:.

Best-Case Time for Serial Search

For an array of *n* elements, the best-case time for serial search is just one array access.

Unless the best-case behavior occurs with high probability, the best-case running time generally is not used during an analysis.

Binary Search

Serial search is easy to implement, easy to analyze, and fine to use if you are searching a small array only a few times. However, if a search algorithm will be used over and over, it is worthwhile to find a faster algorithm. A dramatically faster search algorithm is sometimes available. The algorithm, called *binary search,* may be used only if the array is sorted. Here are three examples for which binary search is applicable:

- Searching an array of integers, where the array is sorted from the smallest integer (at the front) to the largest integer (at the end of the array)
- Searching an array of strings, where the strings are sorted alphabetically
- Searching an array where each component is an `Object` containing information about some item such as an auto part, and the array is sorted by "part numbers" from the smallest to the largest

For concreteness, we'll develop the algorithm for the first of these three cases (searching a sorted array of integers), but keep in mind that the same algorithm applies to any other kind of sorted search space.

Our integer version of the binary search will be implemented with a static method called `search`. The parameter list for `search` has four parameters. The first three parameters provide the array itself, the starting index of the portion of the array that we are searching, and the number of elements to search. The fourth parameter is the target that we are searching for. For example, consider

```
search(b, 17, 10, 42);
```

This example shows the four arguments needed to search for the number 42 occurring somewhere in the ten elements from `b[17]` through `b[26]`.

The search method usually returns an index of the array—the index where the target was found. But if the target does not appear in the specified portion of the array, then the method returns −1 instead of an index. Here is the specification:

- **search**
    ```
    public static int search(int[ ] a, int first, int size, int target)
    ```
    Search part of a sorted array for a specified target.

    Parameters:
    a – the array to search
    first – the first index of the part of the array to search
    size – the number of elements to search, starting at a[first]
    target – the element to search for

    Precondition:
    If size > 0, then first through first+size-1 must be valid indexes for the array a. Also, starting at a[first], the next size elements are sorted in increasing order from small to large.

    Returns:
    If target appears in the array segment starting at a[first] and containing size elements, then the return value is the index of a location that contains target; otherwise the return value is −1.

    Throws: ArrayIndexOutOfBoundsException
    Indicates that some index in the range first through first+size-1 is outside the range of valid indexes for the array a.

Binary Search—Design

Let's produce an algorithm to perform this search task. It will help to visualize the problem in concrete terms. Suppose that the array of numbers is a list of invalid credit card numbers, and it is so long that it takes a book to list them. If you are a clerk and are handed a credit card, you must check to see if it is on the list and hence invalid. How would you proceed? Open the book to the middle and see if it is there. If not and it is smaller than the middle number, then work toward the beginning of the book. If it is larger than the middle number, work toward the back of the book. This idea produces our first draft of an algorithm, shown in the following pseudocode.

```
if (size <= 0)
    return -1;
else
{
```
        `middle` = index of the approximate midpoint of the array segment;
        `if (target == a[middle])`
           the target has been found at `a[middle]` so return `middle`;
        `else if (target < a[middle])`
           search for the target in the area before the midpoint;
        `else if (target > a[middle])`
           search for the target in the area after the midpoint;
```
}
```

It is natural to use recursive calls for the two substeps that "search smaller areas," and that is what our implementation will do. As with any recursive method, we must ensure that the method terminates rather than producing infinite recursion. This insurance is provided by noting that each recursive call searches a shorter area, and when the size reaches zero there can be no further recursive calls. This reasoning can be formalized as in Chapter 8 (see "How to Ensure That There Is No Infinite Recursion in the More General Case" on page 403). Using the Chapter 8 technique, we see that the parameter `size` is a valid *variant expression*, with a *threshold* of zero. In other words, the `size` parameter is always reduced by at least one on each recursive call, and when `size` reaches zero, there is no further recursion.

Our complete implementation of the pseudocode is shown in Figure 11.2. As an example of the binary search in action, suppose that we activate `search(a, 0, 10, 42)` to search the following array for the number 42:

The binary search is searching the ten elements of this array (`first` is 0 and `size` is 10). The algorithm sets the variable `middle` to `first + size/2`, which is 5 in this example. Now `a[5]` is 52, which is greater than the target 42, so the algorithm makes a recursive call, `search(a, 0, 5, 42)`, to search for the number 42 in the first five elements of the array. The part of the array that will be searched by the recursive call is shown in the unshaded part of this drawing:

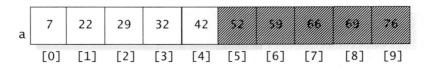

In the recursive call, the new local variable `middle` is assigned the value 2. Since a[2] is 29, which is smaller than 42, the next recursive call throws away everything at or before a[2]. This recursive call, `search(a, 3, 2, 42)`, searches the two elements starting at a[3], as shown here:

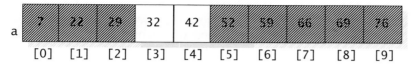

The important property of binary search is that each recursive call throws away at least half of the remaining elements.

In this example, the second recursive call sets its local variable `middle` to 4, and the search finds the target 42 at a[4]. Therefore, this recursive call returns the index 4 to the previous call, which returns 4 to the original call—and the final answer is 4.

FIGURE 11.2 The Binary Search Method

Implementation

```
public static int search(int[ ] a, int first, int size, int target)
{
    int middle;

    if (size <= 0)
        return -1;
    else
    {
        middle = first + size/2;
        if (target == a[middle])
            return middle;
        else if (target < a[middle])
            // The target is less than a[middle], so search before the middle.
            return search(a, first, size/2, target);
        else
            // The target must be greater than a[middle], so search after the middle.
            return search(a, middle+1, (size-1)/2, target);
    }
}
```

Sample Results of `search(b, 2, 5, 42)` **when b contains**

-7	3	8	39	42	63	70
[0]	[1]	[2]	[3]	[4]	[5]	[6]

The method returns the index 4 since b[4] is the target 42.

PITFALL

Pitfall: Common Indexing Errors in Binary Search Implementations

Binary search and similar array-based algorithms are notorious for having errors involving the array indexes. A common place for an error is the calculation of the size of the array for the recursive call. The implementation in Figure 11.2 has two recursive calls, and it's important to double-check the expression for the size of the array segment that is being searched in these recursive calls. For example, one of our recursive calls searches the segment that occurs before a[middle]. This segment begins at a[first] going up to (but not including) a[middle]. How many components are there in this segment? The answer is middle-first, which is the same as size/2, according to this calculation:

middle - first = (first + size/2) - first = size/2

In our recursive call, we use the expression size/2 for the argument that expresses the size of the array, since this expression conveys the idea that the recursive call searches about half of the original array.

You should carry out a similar calculation to verify that the number of elements after a[middle] is (size-1)/2. Hence, the size argument in our second recursive call is the expression (size-1)/2.

Binary Search—Analysis

We want to estimate the running time for the binary search algorithm given in Figure 11.2. The algorithm tests to see if the middle element of the array has the target that we are looking for. If it does, the algorithm stops, returning the index of this middle element. If our sought-after target is not in the middle of the array, the algorithm searches either the half above or the half below this midpoint. This narrows the search to about half of the array elements, then another recursive call can take it to half of that, then half of that, and so forth. The algorithm runs longest if the target is not in the array. If the target is not in the array, then eventually the algorithm will make a recursive call to search an array with zero elements. Of course, the target cannot occur in an empty array, so at that point the algorithm returns and tells us that the target could not be found. We want to analyze this algorithm for worst-case running time.

The binary search algorithm is a recursive algorithm so we need to compute the amount of time taken by all recursive calls, and recursive calls of recursive calls, etc. As in other cases, we will simply count the number of operations performed. The only operations mentioned in the algorithm are addition, subtraction, division, assignment, tests for equality or "less than," and the array access operation.

Let *n* be the number of elements in the array segment being searched (i.e., the value of size). We want to know how many operations the algorithm will perform in the worst case. As it turns out, the worst case is when the target is not in the array so we will assume that target is not in the array.

When the algorithm starts out, it tests to see if the array segment is empty (size <= 0). This is a stopping case for the recursion. We'll charge one operation for this test for emptiness.

one operation

After that, the algorithm computes the midpoint index as follows:

three more operations

```
middle = first + size/2;
```

This adds an additional three operations, one each of division, addition, and assignment.

Next the algorithm tests to see whether the target equals a[middle]. This requires one array access, and one application of ==, and so counts as two more operations.

two more operations

We are assuming that the target is not in the array. So the algorithm then goes on to do the comparison:

another two operations

```
(target < a[middle])
```

This also requires two operations—one for the array access and one for the comparison.

The algorithm then makes a recursive call, which requires a few operations to provide the arguments. The exact number of operations depends on the way that the methods are activated and the return value provided. Rather than selecting a particular number, let's just use the symbol c for the number of operations for passing the arguments and obtaining the return value. In addition, there will be the operations carried out by the recursive call, but we have not begun to worry about that yet.

If we total up all the operations used, we've estimated that the algorithm performs no more than $8+c$ operations, not counting the work of the recursive call. The recursive call can produce another recursive call, which in turn produces another recursive call, until the procedure gets to a stopping case. Each of these recursive calls is preceded by $8+c$ (or fewer) operations. The total number of operations is thus no more than $8+c$ times the length of this chain of recursive calls, plus the number of operations performed in the stopping case. Using the symbol $T(n)$ for the worst-case running time to search an array of n elements, we therefore have:

$T(n) = \quad (8 + c) \times$ (the length of the longest chain of recursive calls)

$\quad\quad +$

the number of operations performed in the stopping case

There are two possible stopping cases—when the size becomes zero, or when the target is found. Since the worst case is when the target is not in the array, we assume that the target is not found. The stopping case when the target is not found requires two operations (a test of size <= 0 and an operation to return the answer -1).

Thus, the running time of the method can be expressed by

$$T(n) = (8 + c) \times \text{(the length of the longest chain of recursive calls)} + 2$$

There is a standard term for the long phrase in parentheses, namely **the depth of recursive calls**.

Depth of Recursive Calls

The length of the longest chain of recursive calls in the execution of an algorithm is called the **depth of recursive calls** for that algorithm.

This definition allows us to replace the long phrase in our formula with this standard term and so obtain the slightly more compact formula:

$$T(n) = (8 + c) \times \text{(the depth of recursive calls)} + 2$$

Rather than compute the exact value for the depth of recursive calls, we will determine an upper bound approximation to the number of recursive calls. The figure we obtain may be slightly larger than the actual number of calls but will be a close approximation. This is common practice when analyzing running times. It is often easier to calculate an upper bound than it is to calculate the exact running time. As long as we use an upper bound so that we are estimating higher than the true value, then we will always be safe. This way our algorithm might turn out to be a bit faster than we thought, but never slower. Now let us calculate this upper bound on the length of the longest string of recursive calls.

The array contains n elements to be searched. Each recursive call is made on an array segment that contains, at most, half of the elements. Hence, to approximate the depth of recursive calls, all we need to do is determine how many times we can divide n in half, and then divide that half in half again, then divide that result in half yet again, and so on until the array is "all gone." The array is "all gone" when there are no elements to divide in half (that is, when size is zero).

Depth of Recursive Calls for Binary Search of an *n*-Element Array

The depth of recursive calls is, at most, the number of times that n can be divided by two, stopping when the result is less than one.

We can now estimate the number of operations performed by the binary search algorithm on an array with n elements. We know that the number of operations is at most $T(n) = (8 + c) \times$ (the depth of recursive calls) $+ 2$, which is:

$$= (8 + c) \times \text{(the number of times that } n \text{ can be divided by two, stopping when the result is less than one)} + 2$$

Let us denote the second expression in parentheses by $H(n)$ and call it the **halving function.**

The Halving Function

The **halving function** $H(n)$ is defined by $H(n) =$ (the number of times that n can be divided by two, stopping when the result is less than one).

With this new definition, we can express our estimate of the running time for the binary search algorithm compactly. The worst-case running time is closely approximated by:

$$T(n) = (8 + c) \times H(n) + 2$$

To get a feel for how fast this running time is, we must know a little about the function $H(n)$. As it turns out $H(n)$ is nearly equal to the base 2 logarithm of n, which is written $\log_2 n$. To be even more precise, for any positive integer n:

Value of the Halving Function

$H(n) =$ (the number of times that n can be divided by two, stopping when the result is less than one) has the value:
$$H(n) = \lfloor \log_2 n \rfloor + 1$$

The symbols $\lfloor \ \rfloor$ mean that we round fractional numbers down to the next lowest whole number. For example, $\lfloor 3.7 \rfloor$ is 3. The notation $\lfloor \ \rfloor$ is called the **floor function**, and we used it before in Chapter 1 when we noted that the number of digits in a positive integer n is $\lfloor \log_{10} n \rfloor + 1$. Since $H(n)$ is a whole number and $\log_2 n$ might include a fractional part, they cannot always be exactly equal, but the above equality means that $H(n)$ and $\log_2 n$ will never differ by more than one. Let's explore what this equality tells us about the running time of binary search.

For an array with n elements ($n > 0$), we have seen that the worst-case running time of the binary search algorithm is:

$$T(n) = (8 + c) \times H(n) + 2 = (8 + c) \times (\lfloor \log_2 n \rfloor + 1) + 2$$

If we throw out the constants, the result says that the worst-case running time is *logarithmic* (that is, $O(\log n)$).

Worst-Case Time for Binary Search

For an array of *n* elements, the worst-case time for binary search is logarithmic.

An algorithm with logarithmic running time is fast because the logarithm of *n* is much smaller than *n*. Moreover, the larger that *n* is, the more dramatic this difference becomes. For example, the base two logarithm of 2 is 1, the base two logarithm of 8 is 3, the base two logarithm of 64 is 6, the base two logarithm of a thousand is less than 10, and the base two logarithm of a million is less than 20.

binary search is an O(log n) algorithm

This means that the binary search algorithm is very efficient. For example, suppose the constant c is 10. Then an array with a thousand elements has a running time of $18(\lfloor \log_2 n \rfloor + 1) + 2$, which is less than 182 operations. Even with a million elements, the worst-case time is fewer than 400 operations.

average time is also O(log n)

We won't give a rigorous analysis of the average running time for binary search, but we can tell you that the average running time for actually finding a number is $O(\log n)$. It is not hard to see why this is true. We have already seen that when a target is not found, the depth of recursion is $\lfloor \log_2 n \rfloor + 1$. In the worst case, even a found target requires a recursion depth of $\lfloor \log_2 n \rfloor$ (just one less than not finding a target). In some cases, the algorithm will not need that many recursive calls. If the sought-after target is found, the algorithm can terminate without additional recursive calls. Thus, on some inputs the depth of recursive calls will be 0, on others it will be 1, on others 2, and so forth up to $\lfloor \log_2 n \rfloor$. However, a more complete analysis would show that nearly half the keys in the array end up taking a recursion depth of $\lfloor \log_2 n \rfloor$. Even if the other half of the keys had no recursion at all, this would still result in an *average* recursion depth of one half of $\lfloor \log_2 n \rfloor$. Thus, the average number of recursive calls for finding a key is at least one half of $\lfloor \log_2 n \rfloor$. So, the average case can save us only a factor of $\frac{1}{2}$ or less over the worst case. But constants like $\frac{1}{2}$ do not matter in big-*O* expressions; therefore the average-case running time is $O(\log n)$, the same as the worst-case running time.

Self-Test Exercises

1. Reimplement the search method from Figure 11.2 on page 531 as a serial search. Use the pseudocode from Figure 11.1 on page 526, and make appropriate adjustments to the precondition/postcondition contract.

2. This exercise requires familiarity with Java's `Comparable` interface (Programming Project 11 on page 481). Rewrite the search method from Figure 11.2 on page 531 so that it searches an array of `Comparable` objects.

3. Consider the search method from Figure 11.2 on page 531. Rewrite the method so that there is no `size` parameter. Instead, there is a parameter called `last`, which is the last index of the array segment that is being searched. Your precondition may require `first <= last`.

4. Compute the following values (*H* is the halving function): $H(1)$, $H(2)$, $H(4)$, $H(7)$, $H(8)$, $H(9)$.

11.2   OPEN-ADDRESS HASHING

In this section we will present another approach to storing and searching for values. The technique, called *hashing,* has a worst-case behavior that is linear for finding a target, but with some care, hashing can be dramatically fast in the average case. Hashing also makes it easy to add and remove elements from the collection that is being searched, providing an advantage over binary search (since binary search must ensure that the entire list stays sorted when elements are added or removed).

As a bonus, Java has a standard hash table class, `java.util.Hashtable`, which can generally be used instead of implementing your own hash table. We'll look at the standard hash table after we've examined some of the issues involved in designing and implementing a hash table.

Introduction to Hashing

The Sixth Column Tractor Company sells all kinds of tractors with various stock numbers, prices, and other details. They want us to store information about each tractor in an inventory so that they can later retrieve information about any particular tractor simply by entering its stock number. To be specific, suppose the information about each tractor is an object in a class called `Tractor`. The `Tractor` class might have methods to return or change information about various tractor properties such as the tractor's cost, horsepower, stock number, and so on.

If the stock numbers have values ranging from 0 to 49, we could store the tractors in the following array, placing stock number i in location `data[i]`:

```
Tractor[ ] data = new Tractor[50]; // Array of 50 tractors
```

The tractor for stock number i can be retrieved immediately since we know it is in `data[i]`.

But what if the stock numbers do not form a neat range like 0...49. Suppose that we know there will be 50 or fewer different stock numbers, but that they will be distributed in the range 0 through 4999. We could use an array with 5000 components, but that seems wasteful since only a small fraction of the array would be used. It appears that we have no alternative but to store the objects in an array with 50 elements and to use a serial search through the array whenever we wish to find a particular stock number. Things are not that bad. If we are clever, we can store the objects in a relatively small array and yet retrieve particular stock numbers much faster than we would by serial search.

To illustrate the trick involved, suppose that an inside informer at the Sixth Column Tractor Company tells us that the stock numbers will be these:

0, 100, 200, 300, ... 4800, 4900

In this case, we can store the objects in an array called `data` with only 50 components. The tractor with stock number i can be stored at `data[i/100]`. With this storage plan, we can make do with the indexes 0 through 49, even though the numbers become as large as 4900. If we want stock number 700, we compute 700/100 and obtain the index 7. The tractor for stock number 700 is stored in array component `data[7]`.

hash function

This general technique is called **hashing.** Each element added to the table requires a unique identifying value called its **key.** In our example, the key was the tractor's stock number, but other, more complex keys are sometimes used. A computation, called the **hash function,** maps key values to array indexes. Suppose we implement our hash function as a method called `hash`. If an element has a key value of i, then we will try to store that element at location `data[hash(i)]`. Using the hash function to compute the correct array index is called **hashing the key to an array index.** The hash function must be chosen so that its return value is always a valid index for the array. The hash function may be either a Java method or a simple arithmetic expression. In our example, `hash(i)` was this expression:

i/100

collisions

In our example, every key produced a different index value when it was hashed. That is a perfect hash function, but unfortunately a perfect hash function cannot always be found. Suppose we change the example so that we no longer have stock number 400, but we have 399 instead. Then the object with stock number 300 will be placed in `data[3]` as before, but where will stock number 399 be placed? Stock number 399 is supposed to be placed in `data[399/100]`. In other words, the object for stock number 399 is supposed to be placed in `data[3]`. There are now two different objects that belong in `data[3]`. This situation is known as a **collision.** In this case we could redefine the hash function to avoid the collision. But in practice, you do not know the exact numbers that will occur as keys, and therefore you cannot design a hash function that is guaranteed to be free of collisions (unless, perhaps, your insider at the tractor company has a lot of pull). Something must be done to cope with the tractor collisions.

Typically you do not know what numbers will be used as the key values, but you do know an upper bound on how many there will be. The usual approach is to use an array size that is larger than needed—later we will see formulas that indicate how many extra positions are needed. The extra array positions make collisions less likely. A good hash function will distribute the key values uniformly through the index range of the array. If the array indexes range from 0 to 99, then you might use the following hash function to produce an array index for an object with a given `key`:

```
Math.abs(key) % 100
```

This hash function always produces a value in the range 0 to 99 (that is, the remainder when the absolute value of `key` is divided by 100).

Here's one way of dealing with collisions:

dealing with collisions

// *Basic storage by hashing algorithm*

1. For an object with key value given by `key`, compute the index `hash(key)`.
2. If `data[hash(key)]` does not already contain an object, then store the object in `data[hash(key)]` and end the storage algorithm.
3. If the location `data[hash(key)]` already contains an object, then try `data[hash(key)+1]`. If that location already contains an object, try `data[hash(key)+2]`, and so forth until a vacant position is found. When the highest numbered array position is reached, simply go to the start of the array. For example, if the array indexes are 0...99, and 98 is the key, then try 98, 99, 0, 1, and so on, in that order.

This storage algorithm is called **open-address hashing,** or more simply **open addressing.** In open addressing, collisions are resolved by placing the object in the next *open* spot of the array.

Non-Integer Keys and Java's `hashCode` Method

Many applications require collections of objects with non-integer keys. For example, our tractors might have names, such as "Big Bad Bruce," instead of stock numbers. In this case, we want to be able to retrieve a tractor by its name rather than a number. A clerk can ask for all the information about "Big Bad Bruce," and we're expected to use the string "Big Bad Bruce" as the key to retrieve information about a particular tractor.

String keys or other non-integer keys are usually handled by having an **encoding function** that converts the key into an integer value. This integer value is then hashed to an array index and used in the same manner that we've seen before. In fact, all Java classes include a method called `hashCode`, which is designed to convert an object to an integer value that can be used for hashing. For example, suppose we have

- A `String` called `key` that we want to use as a key for an object, and
- A hash function called `hash` that converts integers to array indexes in our hash table

In this example, we would try to store the object at the location:

```
data[hash(key.hashCode( ))]
```

So, the hashCode method allows us to use any Java Object as a key for adding something to a hash table. As you might guess, strings are the most common kind of object to use for such keys. In the case of strings, the hashCode method returns an integer that is an arithmetic computation based on the values of the string's characters. You don't need to know how the computation works to be able to use the hashCode method—all you need to know is that s.hashCode( ) is an integer value. (By the way, "Big Bad Bruce" is actually a bear from a Bill Peet story, rather than a tractor. Java's hashCode for "Big Bad Bruce" is 2,136,477,814.)

The Table ADT—Specification

Storage by hashing forms the basis to implement a new collection class called a table. A **table** is a collection of objects with operations for adding, removing, and locating objects. This sounds a lot like a bag, but the difference is that each table operation is controlled by a single key rather than being controlled by the entire object's value.

The Table class that we implement will actually be a reduced version of the standard java.util.Hashtable. The purpose of this implementation is to illustrate the ideas behind the implementation—but when you find yourself actually needing a hash table, you can use java.util.Hashtable instead.

The next few paragraphs specify the six operations for our Table class.

The constructor. The Table class has a constructor that creates a hash table with a specified fixed capacity. Our table cannot grow beyond this capacity. There are several ways that we could allow for growing tables, but we will postpone that in order to focus on the table mechanism itself. So, a typical Table declaration would be as follows:

```
Table catalog = new Table(811); // Can hold up to 811 objects
```

The size and capacity methods. The size method returns the number of elements currently in the table. The capacity method returns the table's capacity, as determined by the argument to the constructor.

The put method. The Table class has a method to put a new object into the table. There are two possible outcomes from a put operation:

- There might already be an object with the same key as the new object. In this case, the old object is replaced by the new object with the same key.
- If the new object has a key that is not already in the table, then the new object is added to the table.

The complete specification of the `put` method is:

- **put**
    ```
    public Object put(Object key, Object element)
    ```
    Add a new element to this table, using the specified key.

    Parameters:
    key – the non-null key to use for the new element
    element – the new element that's being added to this table

    Precondition:
    If there is not already an element with the specified key, then this table's
    size must be less than its capacity (i.e., `size( )` < `capacity( )`).
    Also, neither key nor element may be null.

    Postcondition:
    If this table already has an object with the specified key, then that object
    is replaced by element, and the return value is a reference to the
    replaced object. Otherwise, the new element is added with the specified
    key and the return value is null.

    Throws: `IllegalStateException`
    Indicates that there is no room for a new object in this table.

    Throws: `NullPointerException`
    Indicates that key or element is null.

If the key is a new key (not already in the table), then the precondition of the
`put` method requires that the table is not already full (otherwise there won't
be room for the new object). This is different from the standard
`java.util.Hashtable`, which automatically grows as needed.

The `containsKey` and `get` methods. There are two accessor methods called
`containsKey` and `get`. These methods search the table for an object with a particular key. Here are the specifications of the methods:

- **containsKey**
    ```
    public boolean containsKey(Object key)
    ```
    Determines whether a specified key is in this table.

    Parameters:
    key – the non-null key to look for

    Precondition:
    key cannot be null.

    Returns:
    true (if this table contains an object with the specified key);
    false otherwise. Note that `key.equals( )` is used to compare the key to
    the keys that are in the table.

    Throws: `NullPointerException`
    Indicates that key is null.

• **get**
```
public Object get(Object key)
```
Retrieves an object for a specified key.

Parameters:
key – the non-null key to look for

Precondition:
key cannot be null.

Returns:
A reference to the object with the specified key (if this table contains such an object); `null` otherwise. Note that `key.equals( )` is used to compare the key to the keys that are in the table.

Throws: `NullPointerException`
Indicates that key is null.

The `remove` method. This method removes an object with a specified key, as specified here:

• **remove**
```
public Object remove(Object key)
```
Removes an object for a specified key.

Parameters:
key – the non-null key to look for

Precondition:
key cannot be null.

Postcondition:
If an object was found with the specified key, then that object has been removed from this table and a copy of the removed object is returned; otherwise, this table is unchanged and the null reference is returned. Note that `key.equals( )` is used to compare the key to the keys that are in this table.

Throws: `NullPointerException`
Indicates that key is null.

The Table ADT—Design

Now we'll move on to the design and implementation of our `Table` class. The class will have four private instance variables, shown here:

```
public class Table
{
    private int manyItems;
    private Object[ ] keys;
    private Object[ ] data;
    private boolean[ ] hasBeenUsed;
    ...
```

The variable `manyItems` indicates how many elements are currently in the table. The elements themselves are stored in the `data` array, and the keys to the objects are stored in the `keys` array. For example, if an element is placed at `data[i]`, then the key for that element will reside at `keys[i]`. The fourth instance variable, `hasBeenUsed`, is a boolean array. The value of `hasBeenUsed[i]` is `true` if `data[i]` and `key[i]` have been used at some point, either now or in the past. Later, you will see that the `hasBeenUsed` information provides some efficiency to the `containsKey`, `get`, and `remove` methods. All three arrays will be allocated in the table's constructor, with a length that is determined by the constructor's parameter.

Three Private Methods. During the process of adding a new element to the hash table, the first step will be to hash the key to an array index. This array index will be the preferred location for the new element, though if there is a collision we will use open addressing to move forward to find an available position. The keys are objects, so we will hash the keys by first computing their hash code, then converting the hash code to a valid array index. In fact, the table will have a short private method to carry out this computation, as shown here:

the hash function for this hash table

```
private int hash(Object key)
// The return value is a valid index of the table's arrays. The index is
// calculated as the remainder when the absolute value of the key's
// hash code is divided by the size of the table's arrays.
{
    return Math.abs(key.hashCode( )) % data.length;
}
```

A second private method will help us search the array for an open address. This method, called `nextIndex`, is used to step through the array one index after another, with wraparound at the end. The value of `nextIndex(i)` is usually `i + 1`, with one exception. When `i` is equal to the last index of the array, `nextIndex(i)` returns the first index of the array (zero).

nextIndex

The third private method, called `findIndex`, is intended to find the array index of an object with a particular key. The value of `findIndex(key)` searches for the specified key. If the key is found, the method returns the index of the key in the `keys` array. Otherwise the method returns –1 to indicate that the key is not in the `keys` array. This private method is similar to the public `get` method. The difference is that `get` returns a copy of the object with the specified key, whereas `findIndex` returns the array index of the specified key. The `findIndex` method will be useful for the implementor of the ADT because the implementor often needs to know where a particular key is located in the table. On the other hand, the programmer who uses the ADT doesn't need to know where a key is stored—in fact, that programmer doesn't even know that the elements happen to be stored in arrays.

findindex

Invariant for the Table ADT. With an understanding of the table's instance variables and the workings of the private methods, we can now state the complete invariant of the table ADT.

Invariant for the Table ADT

1. The number of elements in the table is in the instance variable manyItems.

2. The preferred location for an element with a given key is at index hash(key). If a collision occurs, then next-Index is used to search forward to find the next open address. When an open address is found at an index i, then the element itself is placed in data[i] and the element's key is placed at keys[i].

3. An index i that is not currently used has data[i] and key[i] set to null.

4. If an index i has been used at some point (now or in the past), then hasBeenUsed[i] is true; otherwise it is false.

The Table ADT—Implementation

The instance variables and three private methods have been defined for the Table class, and we know the ADT's invariant. The actual implementation is fairly straightforward. We'll discuss the methods one at a time.

The constructor. Most of the table constructor's work involves allocating the three arrays, as shown here:

```
public Table(int capacity)
{
    // The manyItems variable is automatically set to zero, which is the
    // correct initial value. The three arrays are allocated to the specified
    // capacity. The boolean array is automatically initialized to falses,
    // and the other two arrays are automatically initialized to all null.
    if (capacity <= 0)
        throw new IllegalArgumentException
            ("Capacity is negative.");
    keys = new Object[capacity];
    data = new Object[capacity];
    hasBeenUsed = new boolean[capacity];
}
```

Notice that the three arrays are allocated, but we don't need to put any initial values in the array components. The components of boolean arrays are automatically initialized to false, and the components of Object arrays are automatically initialized to null.

The put method. The put method has this heading:

```
public Object put(Object key, Object element)
```

The method puts the new element in the table with the specified key. If that key was already present in the table, then put returns a reference to the old element (which has been replaced); otherwise the put method returns null. Our implementation starts by searching the table to determine whether the key is already in the table. The search is done with the statement index = findIndex(key). The private findIndex method was described on page 543, and it returns a −1 if it can't find the index of the specified key. After setting index, there are three cases shown in this pseudocode:

1. if (index != -1)
    The key is already in the table, so replace the data at the index.

2. else if (manyItems < data.length)
    // There is room for a new element to be added
    2a. Use a loop to set index so that data[index] is the first vacant location at or after data[hash(key)]. If the loop reaches the end of the array, then it should continue searching at data[0].
    2b. Set keys[index], data[index] and hasBeenUsed[index].
    2c. manyItems++;

3. else
    There's no room for another element, so throw an exception.

In Case 1, we will return a reference to the replaced data; in Case 2 we will return the null reference. This pseudocode is implemented in the top of Figure 11.3 on page 546. Notice that the loop in Step 2a uses the private method nextIndex in this assignment statement:

```
index = nextIndex(index);
```

This assignment moves index to the next available array index, wrapping back to the start of the array when index reaches the last valid array index. Also notice how the put method works if there is already an element with the same key as the new element. In this case, the new element replaces the old element (and the private instance variable manyItems remains unchanged).

The remove method. In our put method, we made use of the private method, findIndex. The use of findIndex also simplifies the remove method, which has only three steps in its pseudocode (using local variables index and answer):

1. int index = findIndex(key);

2. Object answer = null;

3. if (index != -1)
    An element has been found with the specified key. Set answer to data[index]; then set data[index] and key[index] to null.

The remove implementation appears in the bottom of Figure 11.3.

FIGURE 11.3	Implementation of the put and remove Methods for the Open-Address Hash Table

Implementation

```java
public Object put(Object key, Object element)
{
    int index = findIndex(key);
    Object answer;

    if (index != -1)
    {  // The key is already in the table.
        answer = data[index];
        data[index] = element;
        return answer;
    }
    else if (manyItems < data.length)
    {  // The key is not yet in this table.
        index = hash(key);
        while (keys[index] != null)
            index = nextIndex(index);
        keys[index] = key;
        data[index] = element;
        hasBeenUsed[index] = true;
        manyItems++;
        return null;
    }
    else
    {  // The table is full.
        throw new IllegalStateException("Table is full.");
    }
}

public void Object remove(key)
{
    int index = findIndex(key);
    Object answer = null;

    if (index != -1)
    {
        answer = data[index];
        keys[index] = null;
        data[index] = null;
    }

    return answer;
}
```

The findIndex method. We have pushed a substantial amount of work into the findIndex method, which we will now implement. The method is responsible for finding the location in the array that contains a particular key value. Here is the specification of the private method:

```
private int findIndex(Object key)
// Postcondition: If the specified key is found in the table, then the return
// value is the index of the specified key. Otherwise, the return value is -1.
```

The method begins by hashing the key value to an array index and assigning this index to a local variable, i. The method then uses a loop to advance i through the possible indexes. Within the loop, we check whether we have found the index of the specified key. If so, we immediately return the value of i. On the other hand, if the loop determines that the key is not in the table, then the loop stops and the method returns −1.

In our description of this work, just what does it mean to "determine that the key is not in the table"? One possibility is that we have examined every location in the table without finding the key. But sometimes it is possible to determine that the key is not in the table even though some locations have not been examined. Recall that if there is an element with its key equal to the parameter key, then this element should be at position hash(key) or in the first available position after that. Our method starts searching at array index hash(key). Should it ever encounter a position that has *never* held an element, then we have an interesting fact: If the key were ever put in the array, then it would have occurred at or before this vacant spot. Hence, the method knows that it has looked at every place that the key could possibly occur. Therefore, in the findIndex implementation, the loop terminates if it reaches a position that has never been used, as shown in this implementation of the loop (count is a local variable that keeps track of how many elements we have examined):

```
int count = 0;
int i = hash(key);
while ((count < data.length) && (hasBeenUsed[i]))
{
    if (key.equals(keys[i]))
        return i;
    count++;
    i = nextIndex(i);
}
return -1;
```

Notice that this technique for terminating the search cannot simply stop when it encounters a position that is *currently* vacant, but the loop must continue until it encounters a position that has *never* held an element. We'll look at an example to illustrate this after you've examined the findIndex and other implementations in Figure 11.4.

FIGURE 11.4   Implementation of the Table Class

Implementation

```
// FILE: Table.java from the package edu.colorado.collections
// Documentation is available starting on page 540 or from the Table link in
//    http://www.cs.colorado.edu/~main/docs/

package edu.colorado.collections;

public class Table
{
    private int manyItems;
    private Object[ ] keys;
    private Object[ ] data;
    private boolean[ ] hasBeenUsed;

    public Table(int capacity)
    {
        if (capacity <= 0)
            throw new IllegalArgumentException("Capacity is negative.");
        keys = new Object[capacity];
        data = new Object[capacity];
        hasBeenUsed = new boolean[capacity];
    }


    public boolean containsKey(Object key)
    || See the answer to Self-Test Exercise 5.

    private int findIndex(Object key)
    // Postcondition: If the specified key is found in the table, then the return
    // value is the index of the specified key. Otherwise, the return value is -1.
    {
        int count = 0;
        int i = hash(key);

        while ((count < data.length) && (hasBeenUsed[i]))
        {
            if (key.equals(keys[i]))
                return i;
            count++;
            i = nextIndex(i);
        }

        return -1;
    }
```

(continued)

(FIGURE 11.4 continued)

```java
public Object get(Object key)
{
    int index = findIndex(key);

    if (index == -1)
        return null;
    else
        return data[index];
}
```

```java
private int hash(Object key)
// The return value is a valid index of the table's arrays. The index is
// calculated as the remainder when the absolute value of the key's
// hash code is divided by the size of the table's arrays.
{
    return Math.abs(key.hashCode( )) % data.length;
}
```

```java
private int nextIndex(int i)
// The return value is normally i+1. But if i+1 is data.length, then the return value is zero
// instead.
{
    if (i == data.length)
        return 0;
    else
        return i+1;
}
```

```java
private Object put(Object key, Object element)
|| See the implementation in Figure 11.3 on page 546
```

```java
private Object remove(Object key)
|| See the implementation in Figure 11.3 on page 546
}
```

A Practical Illustration of Open-Address Hashing

As an example of open addressing in action, I went to the undergraduate computing lab at the University of Colorado in Boulder. There were 1000 registered users of the lab. (I didn't make that up—round numbers do occur sometimes!) Each person has a user record with information such as his or her full name and telephone number. I took the information from each user record and stored it in a Java `Object`. These objects were then placed in an open-address hash table, using the user's login name as the key. The table's capacity was 1231, a number that I chose using guidelines that you'll see shortly.

Looking at parts of the resulting table can give you a good grasp of how open addressing works to solve collisions. For example, my own login name is `main`, and my entry occurs in this part of the hash table:

Index 402	Record for `landspar`, with a hash value of 402.
Index 403	Record for `harrisjm`, with a hash value of 403.
Index 404	Record for `lcheng`, with a hash value of 402.
Index 405	Record for `lindr`, with a hash value of 404.
Index 406	Record for `main`, with a hash value of 405.
Index 407	This spot has never been used to hold a record.

Let's go through this part of the hash table. The records at indexes 402 and 403 were placed in their correct spots with no collisions. For example, the hash value for `landspar` is 402 and that spot was free when `landspar` entered the table.

What about `lcheng` with a hash value of 402? When `lcheng` entered the table, location 402 was already occupied by `landspar`, so the open addressing algorithm moved to the next open location (403), which was also occupied. Finally, at 404 there was an open location where `lcheng` was placed.

When `lindr` entered the table, there was one collision (at 404), but 405 was open and `lindr` was placed there.

When my own record, `main`, was placed in the table, the hash value was 405, but that location already contained `lindr`. However, 406 was open and `main` was placed there.

Finally, location 407 is a spot in the hash table that was not used.

If we search the table for the `main` record, the search will begin at `main`'s hash value of 405. Since that record does not contain `main`, the search continues forward and finds `main` in the next spot.

Let's also examine what happens when a record is removed from the table. Suppose that the student lindr graduates. She will no doubt be happy, but she will have to leave the undergraduate lab and her record will be removed from the hash table, as shown in the revised hash table shown here. The drawing shows that location 405 used to have a record, but it's now empty. In our hash table implementation, this would be indicated by setting hasBeenUsed[405] to true.

In this situation, what happens if we again search for main? The search starts at location 405, which is now unoccupied. But the search cannot stop; it must continue because main might be later in the table (caused by a collision with the element that used to be at location 405). In this case, the search continues and finds main at 406. (By the way, some

Index 402	Record for landspar, with a hash value of 402.
Index 403	Record for harrisjm, with a hash value of 403.
Index 404	Record for lcheng, with a hash value of 402.
Index 405	This spot used to have a record, but it's now empty.
Index 406	Record for main, with a hash value of 405.
Index 407	This spot has never been used to hold a record.

search implementations will actually move main back to the earlier unoccupied spot when it has the chance, but our implementation does not do that.)

As a final example, suppose that we are searching for the name rickhall with a hash value of 405. The search does not find rickhall at location 405 or 406. When the search examines location 407, it sees that the spot has never been used (our implementation will have hasBeenUsed[407] set to false). Therefore, the search can conclude that rickhall is not in the table (since it would have been placed at or before location 407).

Out of interest, you might want to know that the undergraduate hash table has pretty good average behavior. There were 1000 used locations and 231 unused locations in the table. The average number of collisions during an insertion was 1.8, which means that a search examines only 2.8 elements on average. On the other hand, the worst entry, a user named zhuj, had a hash value of 863 and had 52 collisions ending up at location 915. The problem was caused partly by the fact that the table was getting full (zhuj was one of the last entries placed in the table). It's interesting to look at the big group of 52 entries that zhuj collided with—most of them have fewer than two collisions—but the fact that there is a long sequence with no remaining openings is a real problem. Let's look at this problem, called *clustering*, along with techniques to reduce the overall number of collisions.

Choosing a Hash Function to Reduce Collisions

We have used a simple hash function that hashes a given key to the array index:

```
Math.abs(key.hashCode( )) % data.length
```

This kind of hash function depends on the remainder upon division, and is therefore called a **division hash function.**

With a division hash function, certain table sizes are better than others at avoiding collisions that arise in data taken from real examples. C. E. Radke's 1970 study suggests that a good choice is a table size that is a prime number of the form $4k+3$. For example, 1231 is a prime number equal to $(4 \times 307) + 3$.

Although division hash functions are the most common, you may sometimes encounter data that produces many collisions regardless of the table size. In this case, you can try two other common kinds of hash functions:

- **Mid-square hash function:** The key is converted to an integer and multiplied by itself. The hash function returns some middle digits of the result.
- **Multiplicative hash function:** The key is converted to an integer and multiplied by a constant less than one. The hash function returns the first few digits of the fractional part of the result.

Double Hashing to Reduce Clustering

Consider what happens when you put a new element in a hash table and a collision occurs. The put moves forward from the original index until a vacant spot is found. For example, suppose that a new key hashes to location 330, but this location is full. Then we will try location 331, then 332, then 333, and so on. Searching for a vacant spot in this manner is called **linear probing.**

There is a problem with linear probing. When several different keys are hashed to the same array location, the result is a small cluster of elements, one after another. As the table approaches its capacity, these clusters tend to merge into larger and larger clusters. This is the problem of **clustering.** If the key values happen to be consecutive numbers (such as a run of consecutive stock numbers in an inventory), then a "division hash function" makes clustering even worse. As clustering gets worse, adding a new element takes longer because the put method must step all the way through a cluster to find a vacant location. Elements are placed farther and farther from their correct hashed index, and searches require more time.

The most common technique to avoid clustering is called **double hashing.** The technique uses a second hash function to determine how we move through an array to resolve a collision. To see how this works, let's call the original hash function hash1, and call the second hash function hash2. When an element is added, double hashing begins by hashing the key to an array index using hash1. If there is a collision, then we calculate hash2(key) using the result to tell us how far forward to move through the array in looking for a vacant spot. For example, suppose that a new key hashes to location 330, and that hash2(key) is 7. If location 330 is occupied, then we move forward 7 spots and try location 337.

If 337 is also occupied, then we move forward another 7 spots to location 344, and so on.

As we are stepping through the array, adding `hash2(key)` to the index at each step, there are two considerations:

- The array index must not leave the valid range of 0 to `data.length - 1`. We can keep the index in this range with the "%" operation. In particular, suppose that `i` is the index that we have just examined (with a collision). Then the next index to examine is:

    `(i + hash2(key)) % data.length`

    For example, suppose that `data.length` is 1231, and `hash2(key)` is 14. If a new key hashes to spot 1207, and there is a collision, then the next few spots that we will try are 1221, then 4, then 18, then 32. Notice that the 4 is calculated as (1221 + 14) % `data.length`.

- As we step through the array, we must ensure that every array position is examined. With double hashing, this is a potential problem. We could come back to our starting position before we have examined every available location. There is an easy way to avoid this problem: Make sure that the array's capacity is *relatively prime* with respect to the value returned by `hash2` (in other words, these two numbers must not have any common factors, apart from 1). One way to accomplish this is to choose `data.length` as a prime number, and have `hash2` return values in the range 1 through `data.length - 1`. With this in mind, the preeminent computer scientist Donald Knuth suggests the following possibility:

    1. Both `data.length` and `data.length - 2` should be prime numbers. For example, 1231 is prime and so is 1229. (Two such primes, separated by 2, are called **twin primes**.)
    2. `hash1(key) =`
       `Math.abs(key.hashCode( )) % data.length.`
    3. `hash2(key) =`
       `1 + (Math.abs(key.hashCode( )) % (data.length-2)).`

With our `Table` class from Figure 11.4 on page 548, double hashing can be incorporated in several ways. The easiest approach is to add another private method to compute `hash2`, and change `nextIndex` to return:

`(i + hash2(key)) % data.length`

This `nextIndex` method needs `key` as a second parameter.

At this point, you know enough to implement open-address hashing with linear probing or with double hashing. We'll delay the analysis of hashing until after the presentation of *chaining*, which is another way to resolve collisions. However, you might be interested in the results of double hashing for the undergraduate lab example. With double hashing, the average collisions drops from 1.8 to 1.0, and the maximum number of collisions drops from 52 to 21.

Self-Test Exercises

5. Write the table's `containsKey` method.

6. Describe an idea for rewriting the `Table` class without the boolean array `hasBeenUsed`. Your idea should still be able to keep track of which locations have previously been used, but it should do so without having an explicit boolean array.

7. Suppose that a hash table is full and you try to add a new element. What happens if the new element's key is already in the table? What happens if the new element's key is not already in the table?

8. In the implementation of the table's `findIndex` method, the method may sometimes find a key with a value of null. Why does the method need to continue to search?

9. An empty hash table has a capacity of 100, and you add six elements with hash codes 100, 0, 1199, 1299, 1399, and 2. Using linear probing and a division hash function, where will these elements be placed in the table? Where will they be placed with double hashing (with `hash2(key)` returning the value `1 + (Math.abs(key.hashCode( )) % 98)`).

10. Write a quick program to determine whether there is a pair of twin primes between 800 and 850, with the upper prime having the form $4k+3$ for some k. With this information, can you suggest a good size for a hash table that uses double hashing and has a capacity around 825?

11.3 USING JAVA'S HASHTABLE CLASS

Java has a standard hash table class called `java.util.Hashtable`. It has the same methods that you have seen in the example `Table` class from the previous section, but the `HashTable` class also grows automatically when it approaches full capacity. It also has a few additional methods that were not part of our `Table` class.

For example, the following statements create a hash table that stores phone numbers, using names as the keys. Both the phone numbers and the names are strings, and the sample statements put a few elements in the hash table:

```
import java.util.Hashtable;
...

Hashtable phonebook = new Hashtable(811); // Initial capacity 811
phonebook.put("Jean Luc", "622-1701");
phonebook.put("Katherine", "627-4656");
phonebook.put("Benjamin", "622-1764");
```

The statements have created a hash table with an initial capacity of 811. Java's hashtable is normally set to grow automatically when it becomes 75% full. After these statements, we could retrieve Katherine's phone number to store in a string variable with the statement:

```
String s = (String) phonebook.get("Katherine");
```

Notice that the return value of the get method is a Java Object. It must be type-cast to a String before assigning it to the String variable s.

A summary of the Hashtable constructors and other methods is given in Appendix D. The summary includes information about how to change the point at which the table grows. For guidelines on setting the growth point, you can refer to "Time Analysis of Hashing" on page 558.

11.4 CHAINED HASHING

In open-address hashing, a collision is handled by probing the array for an unused position. Each array component can hold just one element. When the array is full, no more items can be added to the table. We could handle this problem by resizing the array and rehashing all the elements, placing each element in a new larger array. But this would require a careful choice of the new size and probably require each element to have a new hash value computed. An alternate approach is to use a different collision resolution method called chained hashing.

In **chained hashing,** also called **chaining,** the hash table contains an array in which each component can hold more than one element of the hash table. As with all hashing, we still hash the key of each element to obtain an array index. But if there is a collision, we don't worry too much. We simply place the new element in its proper array component along with other elements that happened to hash to the same array index.

How does chaining place more than one element in each component of the array? The answer is that each array component must have some underlying structure. The most common structure is to have each array component be a head reference for a linked list. Each node of the linked list is an object of the class shown here:

```
class ChainedHashNode
{
    Object element;
    Object key;
    ChainedHashNode link;
}
```

Each object of this class has three instance variables, which are accessed directly rather than through methods. An implementation of a chained hash table can build an array of references to the heads of linked lists, where the nodes on the linked lists are objects of the `ChainedHashNode` class. For example, if the size of the chained hash table is 811, then the class declaration for the chained hash table can begin like this:

```
public class ChainedTable
{
    private ChainedHashNode[ ] table =
        new ChainedHashNode[811];
    ...
```

This implementation has an array called `table` with 811 components. In effect, the implementation has 811 separate linked lists, organized like this:

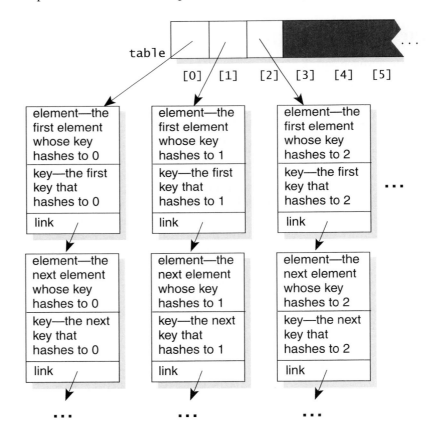

All the elements that hash to location i are placed on the linked list, which has its head reference stored in `table[i]`. An outline of the `Table` class declaration is shown in Figure 11.5, using this scheme. In this outline, the table's size is determined by the constructor. The separate class, `ChainedHashNode`, can be placed in the same file as the `ChainedTable` class.

FIGURE 11.5 Outline of the `ChainedTable` Class

Implementation

```
public class ChainedTable
{
    private ChainedHashNode[ ] table;

    public ChainedHashNode(int tableSize)
    {
        if (tableSize <= 0)
            throw new IllegalArgumentException("Table size must be positive.");
        // Allocate the table which is initially all null head references.
        table = new ChainedHashNode[tableSize];
    }

    public Object put(Object key, Object element)
    {
        ChainedHashNode cursor;
        Object answer = null;
```

> This code sets cursor to refer to the node that already contains the specified key.
> If there is no such node, then cursor is set to null.

```
        if (cursor == null)
        {   // Add a new node at the front of the list of table[hash(key)].
            int i = hash(key);
            cursor = new ChainedHashNode( );
            cursor.element = element;
            cursor.key = key;
            cursor.link = table[i];
            table[i] = cursor;
        }
        else
        {   // The new element replaces an old node.
            answer = cursor.element;
            cursor.element = element;
        }
        return answer;
    }
    ...other methods such as hash and get are implemented...
}

class ChainedHashNode
{
    Object element;
    Object key;
    ChainedHashNode link;
}
```

Each component of the array is a head reference for a linked list.

Self-Test Exercises

11. Consider the chaining version of the table that we have described. What value will be in each component of `table` after the constructor finishes?

12. Write a private method that can be used to carry out the two shaded lines in the outline of Figure 11.5 on page 557.

13. Use your `put` method to place six items in a hash table with a table size of 811. Use the keys 811, 0, 1623, 2435, 3247, and 2.

14. In our new `ChainedTable` class, the array is still a fixed size. It never grows after the constructor allocates it. So, is there a limit to the number of elements in the chained hash table?

15. Suppose that the keys can be compared using a `compareTo` method (such as in Programming Project 11 on page 481). Can you think of some advantage to keeping each linked list of the table sorted from smallest key to largest key?

11.5 TIME ANALYSIS OF HASHING

The worst-case for hashing occurs when every key gets hashed to the same array index. In this case, we may end up searching through all the items to find the one we are after—a linear operation, just like serial search. However, with some reasonable assumptions, the average time for a search of a hash table is dramatically fast, requiring us to examine just a handful of elements. This section provides the information needed for an average-time analysis of our three hashing methods.

The Load Factor of a Hash Table

Analyzing the average-time performance of hashing is complex, particularly if removals are allowed. However, Knuth's *The Art of Programming*, Volume 3, provides formulas that can guide our choice of hash-table algorithms. Knuth's most useful formulas provide the average number of table elements that must be examined during a successful search for a key. There are three different formulas for the three versions of hashing: open addressing with linear probing, open addressing with double hashing, and chained hashing.

These three formulas depend on how many items are in the table. When the table has many items, there are many collisions and the average time for a search is longer. With this in mind, we first define a fraction called the **load factor,** which is written α and defined by the formula given here:

$$\alpha = \frac{\text{Number of elements in the table}}{\text{The size of the table's array}}$$

definition of the load factor, α

For open-address hashing, each array component holds at most one element, so the load factor can never exceed 1. But with chaining, each array component can hold many elements, and the load factor might be higher than 1.

Average search time for open addressing (linear probing). Open-address hash tables with linear probing have just one hash function. Collisions are resolved by stepping forward, probing consecutive array components. With linear probing, and no removals, Knuth's formula for the average time of a successful search is:

Searching with Linear Probing

In open-address hashing with linear probing, a nonfull hash table, and no removals, the average number of table elements examined in a successful search is approximately:

$$\frac{1}{2}\left(1 + \frac{1}{1-\alpha}\right)$$

This formula is not exact, but it is a good approximation when the load factor (α) is below 1. You might notice that the formula completely fails when α is 1, since there is then a division by zero. But, that situation would indicate a full hash table, and you should avoid getting close to full anyway. If you insist on a full hash table of n elements, Knuth shows that the average time for a successful search is approximately $\sqrt{n(\pi/8)}$ —but better yet, steer clear of full tables, and you can use the formula in the box above. In addition to a nonfull table, the formula's derivation also assumes that we have not removed any elements, and that the hash function does a good job of uniformly distributing all possible keys throughout the array (which is called **uniform hashing**).

As an example of how to use the formula, suppose that we plan to put 649 elements in a table with a capacity of 811. This provides a load average of 649/811, or about 80%. On average, we expect successful searches to examine three table elements, as shown here:

$$\frac{1}{2}\left(1 + \frac{1}{1-\alpha}\right) = \frac{1}{2}\left(1 + \frac{1}{1-0.8}\right) = 3.0$$

Average search time for open addressing (double hashing). You have seen that open-address hash tables with double hashing provide some relief from clustering. The result is a smaller average time, given by the following formula (which uses "ln" to denote the natural logarithm of a number).

Searching with Double Hashing

In open-address hashing with double hashing, a nonfull hash table, and no removals, the average number of table elements examined in a successful search is approximately:

$$\frac{-\ln(1-\alpha)}{\alpha}$$

As with the previous formula, this estimate is approximate. It depends on a non-full hash table, no removals, and using a hash function with uniform hashing.

You don't need to memorize the formula, but you should know how to use it along with the ln key on your calculator. For example, ln(0.2) is about -1.6, so with a load factor of 0.8 we expect to examine an average of two elements in a successful search, as shown here:

$$\frac{-\ln(1-\alpha)}{\alpha} = \frac{-\ln(0.2)}{0.8} = \frac{1.6}{0.8} = 2$$

This is an improvement over the linear probing with the same load factor.

Average search time for chained hashing. With chaining, each component of the table's array is a reference to the head of a linked list, and each of these linked lists may have several table elements. Therefore, the load factor may be higher than one in this formula:

Searching with Chained Hashing

In open-address hashing with chained hashing, the average number of table elements examined in a successful search is approximately:

$$1 + \frac{\alpha}{2}$$

Once again, this estimate is approximate, and it depends on using uniform hashing. Unlike the other two formulas, the chaining formula remains valid even with removals.

With a load factor of 0.8, chained hashing expects to examine only 1.4 items during a successful search. Some other possible load factors are shown in Figure 11.6, where you can compare the average numbers for the three different hashing methods.

FIGURE 11.6 Average Number of Table Elements Examined during a Successful Search

Load factor (α)	Open addressing with linear probing $\frac{1}{2}\left(1 + \frac{1}{1-\alpha}\right)$	Open addressing with double hashing $\frac{-\ln(1-\alpha)}{\alpha}$	Chained hashing $1 + \frac{\alpha}{2}$
0.5	1.50	1.39	1.25
0.6	1.75	1.53	1.30
0.7	2.17	1.72	1.35
0.8	3.00	2.01	1.40
0.9	5.50	2.56	1.45
1.0			1.50
2.0	Not applicable		2.00
4.0			3.00

Self-Test Exercises

16. Suppose that you place 180 elements in a hash table with an array size of 200. What is the load factor? For each of the three hash methods, what is the average number of table elements that you expect to have examined during a successful search?

17. You want to place 1000 elements in a hash table, and you'd like an average search to examine just two table elements. How big does the table's array need to be? Give separate answers for the three hash methods.

CHAPTER SUMMARY

- Serial search is quick to program but requires linear time to find an element in both the worst case and the average case.

- Binary search works well on a sorted array, requiring $O(\log n)$ time in both the worst case and the average case. But as elements are added or removed, keeping the array in order may take considerable time (linear time for each addition or removal in the worst case).

- Hash tables are a good strategy for storing and retrieving elements with a key. In fact, it would be perfect if there were no collisions.

- One way to deal with collisions is **open addressing.** This scheme handles collisions by placing each new element in the first open location that is at or after the spot where the key hashes to. Two methods of searching for an open location are **linear probing** (which examines the array locations in consecutive order) and **double hashing** (which uses a second hash function to determine the size of the steps that are taken through the array). Double hashing is the better method, because it avoids clustering.

- Another way to deal with collisions is **chaining.** In the chaining approach, each location of the hash table's array is able to hold multiple elements. A common way to implement chaining is for each array location to be a reference to the head of a linked list of elements.

- The worst-case search time for a hash table is linear. But the average-case time is quite fast. Depending on the load factor and the precise method of hashing, the average case requires about two to five table elements to be examined during a successful search (see Figure 11.6 on page 561).

? Solutions to Self-Test Exercises

1. The precondition is modified so that the array no longer needs to be sorted. Here's the code:

```
public static int search(
    int a[ ],
    int first, int size,
    int target
)
{
    int i = 0;
    boolean found = false;

    while ((i < size) && !found)
    {
        if (a[first+i] == target)
            found = true;
        else
            i++;
    }
    if (found)
        return first+i;
    else
        return -1;
}
```

2. See Figure 11.7 on page 563.

3. The function is not difficult to write, but pay attention to the potential pitfalls from page 532.

4. $H(1)=1$, $H(2)=2$, $H(4)=3$, $H(7)=3$, $H(8)=4$, $H(9)=4$.

5. Here's one way to implement the method:

```
public boolean
containsKey(Object key)
{
    return (findIndex(key) != -1);
}
```

6. One idea is to set the keys[i] to null when the element at location i is removed, but keep data[i] so that it still refers to the removed data. Then we could tell when a spot has previously been used because data[i] would be non-null. The problem with this approach is that it can interfere with Java's garbage collection (the garbage collector would not collect the old data because the program still has a reference to it). So, a better approach is to have some object declared as an instance variable in the Table class. The object can be

called previouslyUsed, and when the element at location i is removed we can set keys[i] to null and set data[i] to refer to previouslyUsed.

7. If the key was already present, then the data with that key is overwritten. If the key was not already present, then the method tests whether there is room for a new element. When this test fails, the method throws an exception.

8. Suppose we start looking in the keys array at some index, say 34, and we move forward until we find a null key. Perhaps this first null key is at index 36. If hasBeenUsed[36] is

false, then that indicates that the location has never been used, and therefore no element with the given key appears in the table (since it would have been placed in this unused location, or perhaps in location 34 or 35 that we have already examined).

On the other hand, if hasBeenUsed[36] is true, then this location has previously been used and since removed. In this case, it is possible that there is an element with the given key in the table at a location after 36. It might be after this location, because at the time it was added, location 36 might have been in use.

FIGURE 11.7   The Binary Search Method for Comparable Objects

Implementation

```
// The method uses Java's Comparable interface from Programming Project 11 on page 481.
// Neither the target nor the array elements may be null references.
public static int search(Comparable[ ] a, int first, int size, Comparable target)
{
   int middle;
   int comparison;

   if (size <= 0)
      return -1;
   else
   {
      middle = first + size/2;
      comparison = target.compareTo(a[middle]);
      if (comparison == 0)
         return middle;
      else if (comparison < 0)
         // The target is less than a[middle], so search before the middle.
         return search(a, first, size/2, target);
      else
         // The target must be greater than a[middle], so search after the middle.
         return search(a, middle+1, (size-1)/2, target);
   }
}
```

9. For linear probing, the key/index pairs are: 100 at [0], 0 at [1], 1199 at [99], 1299 at [2], 1399 at [3], and 2 at [4]. For double hashing the key/index pairs are: 100 at [0], 0 at [1], 1199 at [99], 1299 at [25], 1399 at [27], and 2 at [2].

10. There is a twin prime pair at 809 and 811, which suggests that 811 is a good table capacity.

11. An array of objects is automatically initialized with null at every component.

12. We call our new method findNode:

```
public ChainedHashNode
findNode(Object key)
{
   ChainedHashNode cursor;

   cursor = table[hash(key)];
   while (cursor != null)
   {
      if (key.equals(cursor.key)
         return cursor;
      cursor = cursor.link;
   }
   return null;
}
```

13. The table[0] list will have the keys 0 and 811. The table[1] list will have the key 1623. The table[2] list will have the keys 2 and 2435. The table[3] list will have the key 3247. All other lists are empty.

14. There is no limit because each component of table is the head of a linked list that may contain many elements.

15. If the lists are kept in order, then a search can stop as soon as it reaches a key that is greater than the target.

16. The load factor is 0.9 (i.e., 180/200). With linear probing, the expected average is 5.50; with double hashing, the expected average is 2.56; with chained hashing, the expected average is 1.45.

17. For linear probing, we need a load factor of 2/3, which requires a table capacity of 1500. For double hashing, we need a load factor of just less than 0.8, requiring a table capacity of about 1250. For chaining, we need a load factor of 2, requiring an array size of 500.

▓ PROGRAMMING PROJECTS

1 Reimplement the binary search using a loop and no recursion. If you are familiar with Java's Comparable interface, then your implementation should search an array of Comparable objects rather than an array of int.

2 Use a binary search technique to write a game program that asks the user to think of an integer in a particular range and then tries to guess the number. The program may ask questions such as "Is your number bigger than 42?" Your result should have worst-case time of $O(\log n)$, where *n* is the size of the range of numbers.

3 For this project, you must first implement the Polynomial class from the Chapter 3 Programming Project 8 on page 169. Add a new method to the class, with four parameters: a polynomial f and three double numbers x, z, and epsilon. The precondition requires that epsilon is positive and f(x) <= 0 <= f(z).

The method searches for a number y between x and z, where f(y) is zero. Such a number is called a **root** of the polynomial. The method's return value might not be an exact root, but the difference between the return value and a real root should be no more than epsilon. The algorithm is a binary search of the numbers between x and z.

4 Use **double hashing** to reimplement the hash table from Figure 11.4 on page 548.

5 In our open-address hash tables, we have used linear probing or double hashing. Another probing method, which avoids some clustering, is called **quadratic probing.** The simplest version of quadratic probing works like this: Start by hashing the key to an array index. If there is a collision, then move to the next array index. If there is a *second* collision, then move forward *two* more spots through the array. After a *third* collision, we move forward *three* more spots, and so on. For example, suppose that a new key hashes to location 327, and this location is full. The next location that we try is 328. If 328 is a second collision, then we move two spots forward to location 330. If 330 is a third collision, then we move three spots forward to location 333. If our calculation of the next spot takes us beyond the end of the array, then we "wrap around" to the front of the array (similar to double hashing). In general, if location i has just caused a collision, and we have

already examined `count` elements, then we increase `i` according to the assignment:

$$i = (i + count) \% data.length;$$

In this formula, the "`% data.length`" causes the "wrap around" to the front of the array. In order for this approach to work correctly, the capacity must be a power of 2, such as $2^{10} = 1024$. Otherwise, the sequence of probes does not correctly examine all array items.

For this project, use quadratic hashing to reimplement the hash table from Figure 11.4 on page 548.

6 Rewrite one of your hash tables so that it has additional methods to provide statistics. You should include methods to calculate the load factor, the average number of items examined during a successful search, and the maximum number of items examined during a successful search.

Find a large collection of information to put in your hash table, perhaps the list of users at your computing site. Test how the statistics vary based on the capacity of the hash table.

Sorting

A place for everything and everything in its place.

ISABELLA MARY BEETON
The Book of Household Management

CHAPTER

12

One commonly encountered programming task is sorting a list of values. By way of examples, the list might consist of exam scores, and we may want to see them sorted from lowest to highest, or from highest to lowest; the list might be a list of words that we have misspelled, and we may want to see them in alphabetical order; the list might be a list of student records, and we may want them sorted by student number or alphabetically by student name. In this chapter we present and analyze a number of different sorting algorithms.

To maintain a sharp focus on the sorting algorithms, we will consider only arrays of integers and design algorithms to sort the integers into the order smallest to largest. However, if you are familiar with Java's `Comparable` interface (from Programming Project 11 on page 481), then you may easily adapt the algorithms to sort arrays of values of other types, or to sort values according to other ordering relations. Other adaptations are also possible. For example, one common way of ordering objects is to choose one special instance variable, which is then called the **key field**, and to sort the objects according to that key field. Using

sorting by key value

567

a key field, we could sort a list of student records by student number (with the student number serving as the key field). We could sort the same records alphabetically by student name (with the student name serving as the key field).

12.1 QUADRATIC SORTING ALGORITHMS

In this section we develop and implement two algorithms to sort a list of numbers into increasing order.

Selectionsort—Specification

We have an array of integers that we wish to sort into order from smallest to largest. To be concrete, we'll use this heading and specification:

```
public static void selectionsort(int[ ] data, int first, int n)
// Precondition: data has at least n components starting at data[first].
// Postcondition: The elements of data have been rearranged so
//   that data[first] <= data[first+1] <= ... <= data[first+n-1].
```

The method is a static method that could be part of a class that needs to do some sorting, or it could be part of a class that provides static sorting methods for other classes to use.

Selectionsort—Design

One way to design an algorithm is to rely on the definition of the problem. Our problem is to sort part of an array from smallest to largest. In particular, we must rearrange the n values starting at data[first] so that data[first] is the smallest, data[first+1] the next smallest, and so forth to data[first+n-1], which is the largest. That definition yields an outline for a straightforward algorithm (i is a local variable):

```
for (i = 0; i < n; i++)
    Move the smallest element of the segment
    data[first+i]...data[first+n-1] to location data[first+i].
```

This approach finds the smallest element, then the next smallest, and so on, placing the elements in data[first+0], data[first+1], ... as they are found. We can also work the approach the other way, finding the largest element, then the second largest, and so on:

```
for (i = n-1; i >= 0; i--)
    Move the largest element of the segment
    data[first]...data[first+i]  to location data[first+i].
```

There are many ways to realize either of these general approaches. The details could be developed using two arrays and copying the elements from one array to the other in sorted order. However, one array is both adequate and economical, and so we decide to develop the algorithm using only one array. To help in exploring the problem, we will use the concrete example shown here:

data

10	8	6	2	16	4	18	11	14	12
[0]	[1]	[2]	[3]	[4]	[5]	[6]	[7]	[8]	[9]

Consider sorting this entire array with a pencil and eraser according to the second version of the pseudocode that we have outlined (finding and placing the largest element, then the next largest, and so on). Because we are sorting the entire array, the parameters for our selectionsort will have first equal to 0 and n equal to 10.

We begin by searching the array for the largest element, and we find this largest element at data[6], which is the 18. We next want to set the final element of the array equal to this value of 18. In doing so, we must be careful not to lose the original value of 12 that was stored in array location data[9]. A simple assignment statement like the following would destroy the 12:

```
data[9] = data[6]; // No good: destroys the original data[9].
```

The algorithm must not simply destroy the original value 12 that was in the final spot of the array. Fortunately we have an array location in which to store it. We can place it in the location that used to have the largest element. In other words, we actually want to "swap" the largest element with the final element of the array. After the swap, the array looks like this:

The largest value has been swapped with the final value in the array.

The values of data[6] and data[9] have simply been swapped. A similar thing is done with the second-largest value of the array. We find this second largest value (the 16 at data[4]) and swap it with the next-to-last element of the array (data[8]), resulting in the array shown at the top of the next page.

The second-largest value has been swapped with the next-to-last value in the array.

The entire array can be sorted by a series of swaps such as these. Any sorting algorithm that is based on swapping elements is called an **interchange sort**.

The simplest interchange sorting algorithm, which we have been describing, is called **selectionsort**. The algorithm is a refinement of our previous pseudocode, as shown here:

```
for (i = n-1; i > 0; i--)
{
    Calculate big as the index of the largest value in
            data[first] through data[first+i];
    swap data[first+i] with data[big];
}
```

The control of the for-loop has one refinement from the original pseudocode: The loop executes only n-1 times, stopping as soon as i drops to zero. There is no need to execute the loop with i equal to zero because when i reaches zero, all the larger elements are already in their correct spots. Therefore, data[0] must already have the smallest element.

How do we calculate the index of the largest value in data[first] through data[first+i]? We can start by assuming that the biggest value is at the front of the segment, data[first]. Then we can use a loop to search through the rest of the segment, up to data[first+i]. Each time we find a bigger element, we'll place the index of this bigger element in a variable called big, as shown in the following refinement. In this refinement, big and j are local int variables:

```
for (i = n-1; i > 0; i--)
{
    // Calculate big as the index of the largest value in
    // data[first]...data[first+i]:
    big = first;
    for (j = first+1; j <= first+i; j++)
        if (data[big] < data[j])
            big = j;

    swap data[first+i] with data[big];
}
```

When the inner for-loop finishes, big is the index of the largest value in data[first] through data[first+i]. At this point, we need to swap data[first+i] with data[big]. Such a swap can always be done with three assignment statements and one extra local variable (usually called temp, because it is needed for a short *temp*orary time). The necessary assignment statements are shown at the bottom of the complete implementation in Figure 12.1.

Figure 12.1 also contains a small main method to test selectionsort. The main method declares an array of ten integers with the declaration:

```
int[ ] data = { 80, 10, 50, 70, 60, 90, 20, 30, 40, 0 };
```

A list like this, given after the declaration of an array variable, has two effects: First, a new array of the correct size (ten elements in this case) is allocated, and then the new array is initialized with the provided list of values.   *array initialization*

FIGURE 12.1   Selectionsort

Java Application Program

```java
// FILE: Select.java
// A demonstration program for the selectionsort method
public class Select
{
    public static void selectionsort(int[ ] data, int first, int n)
    // Precondition: data has at least n components starting at data[first].
    // Postcondition: The elements of data have been rearranged so
    // that data[first] <= data[first+1] <= ... <= data[first+n-1].
    {
        int i, j; // Loop control variables
        int big;  // Index of largest value in data[first]...data[first+i]
        int temp; // Used during the swapping of two array values

        for (i = n-1; i > 0; i--)
        {
            // Calculate big as the index of the largest value in data[first]...data[first+i]:
            big = first;
            for (j = first+1; j <= first+i; j++)
                if (data[big] < data[j])
                    big = j;

            // swap data[first+i] with data[big]:
            temp = data[first+i];
            data[first+i] = data[big];
            data[big]  = temp;
        }
    }
}
```

(continued)

(FIGURE 12.1 continued)

```
public static void main(String[ ] args)
{
    final String BLANKS = "  ";  // A String of two blanks
    int i;                        // Array index

    int[ ] data = { 80, 10, 50, 70, 60, 90, 20, 30, 40, 0 };

    // Print the array before sorting:
    System.out.println("Here is the original array:");
    for (i = 0; i < data.length; i++)
        System.out.print(data[i] + BLANKS);
    System.out.println( );

    // Sort the numbers, and print the result with two blanks after each number.
    selectionsort(data, 0, data.length);
    System.out.println("In sorted order, the numbers are:");
    for (i = 0; i < data.length; i++)
        System.out.print(data[i] + BLANKS);
    System.out.println( );
}

}
```

Sample Output

```
Here is the original array:
80  10  50  70  60  90  20  30  40  0
In sorted order, the numbers are:
10  20  30  40  50  60  70  80  90
```

Selectionsort—Testing

The main method in Figure 12.1 shows that selectionsort works correctly in one small situation. More testing should be carried out to improve confidence that we did not make a programming error. For sorting methods, it is important to test some random cases (such as the array in our main method), test the case where the array starts out already sorted (to make sure that the algorithm doesn't crash or mix up the order), test the case where the array starts out completely backwards, and test the boundary cases when the array size is one or zero. In the case of an array with zero elements, the method has no work to do (there are no elements to sort), and our selectionsort performs correctly (the loop begins with i set to −1, and therefore the body of the loop never executes).

Selectionsort—Analysis

We want to analyze the worst-case running time for the selectionsort algorithm that we implemented as the method `selectionsort` shown in Figure 12.1. Let's use n for the number of elements to be sorted. In outline form, the major work of the selectionsort algorithm is given here:

```
for (i = n-1; i > 0; i--)
    swap(data[first+i], data[suitable index]);
```

When i is equal to $n-1$, then `data[suitable index]` is the largest element in the portion of the array that we are sorting; when i is equal to $n-2$, then `data[suitable index]` is the second-largest element, and so forth.

How many operations are performed by the above for-loop? The answer is not easy. Many of the operations are hidden. The loop control variable, i, is compared to zero at the start of each loop iteration. The actual swapping uses three assignment operations, and the calculation of the "suitable index" requires some work. The value of i is decremented at the end of each loop iteration. We could determine the precise number of operations for each of these subtasks in the loop. However, that is more detail than we need. We are looking only for a big-O approximation, which means that we do not need the exact values for constants. This will simplify our analysis significantly.

During each iteration of the loop, there is some constant number of operations in managing the loop control variable, and there is some constant number of operations involved in the swapping of two array elements. So *the number of operations in each loop iteration* is the sum:

some constant + the cost of finding the suitable index

Since there are $n-1$ loop iterations, the total count of the number of operations performed is given by the product:

$(n-1) \times$ (some constant + the cost of finding the suitable index)

To change this into a nice formula expressed in terms of n, we need to determine the cost of finding the "suitable index."

As it turns out, when the algorithm is looking for the value to place in location `data[i]`, the "suitable index" is the index of the largest of the values:

`data[0], data[1], ..., data[i]`

The selectionsort algorithm uses a loop that determines the location of this largest element and thereby the value of the "suitable index." The loop has the following form.

```
big = first;
for (j = first+1; j <= first+i; j++)
    if (data[big] < data[j])
        big = j;
```

How much work is done each time these lines of code compute the "suitable index?" There are five operations to get things started: an assignment statement (big = first) before the loop, plus an addition/assignment (j = first+1), and an addition/boolean test (j <= first+i) to initialize the loop. Each time through the body of the loop, we perform some limited number of operations to examine one of the array elements. The body of the loop executes i times, so the number of operations of this code is no more than 5 plus a constant times i. We could ignore the 5 at this point, but let's leave it in and simplify in a different way by noticing that i is always less than n. With this simplification, our estimate of the number of operations to find this "suitable index" is *at most 5 plus a constant times n.*

Putting this information together, we see that the total count of the number of operations performed in the selectionsort is this:

$$\text{Total} = (n-1) \times (\text{some constant} + \text{the cost of finding the suitable index})$$
$$\leq (n-1) \times [\text{some constant} + 5 + (\text{some other constant}) \times n]$$

Now we need to estimate the quantity:

$$(n-1) \times [\text{some constant} + 5 + (\text{some other constant}) \times n]$$

If you multiply this out, there will be an n^2 term, an n term, and a constant term without any n. Thus, the number of operations performed is:

$n^2 \times (\text{some new constant})$
+
$n \times (\text{some other new constant})$
+
(yet another new constant)

This is our estimate of the worst-case run time for selectionsort. Because we are doing a big-O analysis, we can ignore the constants and consider only the highest exponent of n. Hence, we see that the worst-case running time for selectionsort is $O(n^2)$.

In arriving at the quadratic time analysis, we made one overestimate by replacing i with n. A more detailed time analysis would not make this simplification, but would still end up with a quadratic time. Our analysis of the running time for selectionsort did not depend on the initial values in the array. The selectionsort algorithm performs the same number of operations no matter what values are in the array that it sorts. Thus, the average-case running time (and even the best-case running time) is the same as the worst-case running time.

Selectionsort Running Time

The worst-case running time, the average-case running time, and the best-case running time for selectionsort are all quadratic.

Programming Tip: Rough Estimates Suffice for Big-*O*

TIP △

We have just computed big-*O* expressions for the worst-case running time of the selectionsort algorithm. Notice that when we performed the big-*O* analysis, we did not compute exact formulas for some running times. For example, when we estimated the number of operations in one iteration of the primary loop used in the algorithm, we decided that the algorithm performed the following number of operations in each loop iteration:

some constant + the cost of finding the suitable index

We never computed the exact value of "some constant." Because big-*O* expressions are accurate only to "within a constant multiple," the exact value of the constant does not matter. If we want only a big-*O* expression, there is no reason to spend time computing an exact value for this constant.

Insertionsort

Another simple and natural sorting algorithm is based on the following illustration of sorting an array that contains this list of ten integers:

(8, 2, 5, 3, 10, 7, 1, 4, 6, 9)

One way to proceed is to take the numbers one at a time and build up another sorted list of values. The first number is 8, so make a list that contains only the one number 8. That is certainly a sorted list. Next take the 2 and combine it with the 8 to obtain a longer sorted list, namely (2, 8). Next, add the 5 to obtain the list: (2, 5, 8).

If you keep adding numbers to the list, you will eventually obtain a sorted list containing all the numbers. The original list decreases by one on each iteration, and the list we are building increases by one on each iteration. The progress of this process is shown at the top of the next page for an example list.

( )   (8,   2,   5,   3,   10,   7,   1,   4,   6,   9)

(8)   (2,   5,   3,   10,   7,   1,   4,   6,   9)

(2,   8)   (5,   3,   10,   7,   1,   4,   6,   9)

(2,   5,   8)   (3,   10,   7,   1,   4,   6,   9)

(2,   3,   5,   8)   (10,   7,   1,   4,   6,   9)

(2,   3,   5,   8, 10)   (7,   1,   4,   6,   9)

(2,   3,   5,   7,   8, 10)   (1,   4,   6,   9)

(1,   2,   3,   5,   7,   8, 10)   (4,   6,   9)

(1,   2,   3,   4,   5,   7,   8, 10)   (6,   9)

(1,   2,   3,   4,   5,   6,   7,   8, 10)   (9)

(1,   2,   3,   4,   5,   6,   7,   8,   9, 10)   ( )

With the insertionsort, your first thought might be to use an additional array and copy values from one array to the other. The numbers in the left-hand lists in our drawings would be in one array, and the numbers in the right-hand lists would be in the other array. But, if you look carefully at the drawings, you will see that one list grows at exactly the same rate that the other list shrinks. So we need only one array. If we have ten numbers, we need only ten positions. One list can be kept at the front of the array and the other at the back of the array.

We can redraw the progress of the insertionsort in a way that makes it evident that one array is sufficient. At the start of the insertionsort, we have the same ten-element array that we have been working with:

data

8	2	5	3	10	7	1	4	6	9
[0]	[1]	[2]	[3]	[4]	[5]	[6]	[7]	[8]	[9]

We have called the array `data`. The first component, `data[0]`, is shaded to indicate that even at the start, the front part of the array—with only the one shaded element—can be viewed as a tiny sorted array on its own. The first actual work will be to insert the second element (`data[1]`, which is a 2) into the tiny sorted array, increasing the "sorted part" of the array to encompass two elements, as shown here:

data

2	8	5	3	10	7	1	4	6	9
[0]	[1]	[2]	[3]	[4]	[5]	[6]	[7]	[8]	[9]

So, at this point, the first two elements (2, 8) form a small sorted list, and we still need to insert the remaining elements (5, 3, 10, 7, 1, 4, 6, 9). After the insertion of the 5, we have the situation shown here:

data

2	5	8	3	10	7	1	4	6	9
[0]	[1]	[2]	[3]	[4]	[5]	[6]	[7]	[8]	[9]

The insertion process continues, taking the next element from the unsorted side of the array and inserting it into the sorted side of the array. Each insertion increases the size of the sorted side and decreases the unsorted side until the entire array is sorted.

All we need to do now is convert these ideas into a Java method with the heading and specification shown here:

```
public static void insertionsort(int[ ] data, int first, int n)
// Precondition: data has at least n components starting at data[first].
// Postcondition: The elements of data have been rearranged so
//   that data[first] <= data[first+1] <= ... <= data[first+n-1].
```

This specification should seem familiar. It's the same specification that we used for the selectionsort; only our algorithm will change.

The insertionsort can be accomplished with this pseudocode:

```
for (i = 1; i < n; i++)
    Insert the element from data[first+i] into the portion of the array
    from data[first] through data[first+i-1], so that all of
    data[first] through data[first+i] is now sorted.
```

Let's look at an example to help refine the pseudocode in the body of the loop. In the example, suppose first is 10 so that we are sorting a portion of the array beginning at data[10]. Also suppose that i is 4, so that we are entering the loop for the fourth time. In this situation, data[10] through data[13] are already sorted and we have the task of inserting data[14]. If the value of data[14] is 3, we might have this situation when the fourth iteration of the loop body begins:

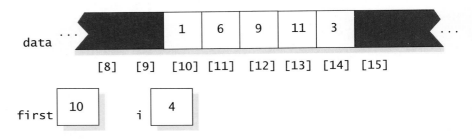

A useful initial step is to use a local variable to store a copy of the number that we are inserting. If we call the local variable entry, then this first step is accomplished with the assignment entry = data[first+i] After the assignment, we have this situation:

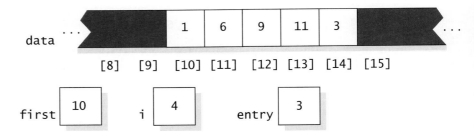

Once the extra copy of the new element has been made, we suggest that you shift elements at the end of the array rightward one position each until you find the correct position for the new entry. In our example, you would begin by shifting the 11 rightward from data[13] to data[14]; then move the 9 from data[12] to data[13]; then the 6 moves from data[11] to data[12]. At this point, the array contains the following values.

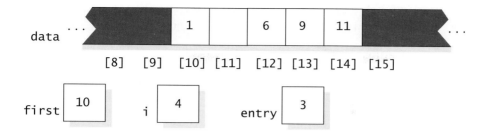

Of course, data[11] actually still contains a 6 since we just copied the 6 from data[11] to data[12]. But we have drawn data[11] as an empty box to indicate that data[11] is now available to hold the new entry (i.e., the 3 that we're inserting). At this point we can place the 3 in data[11], as shown here:

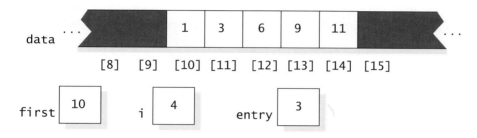

The pseudocode for shifting the elements rightward uses a for-loop. Each iteration of the loop shifts one element, as shown here:

```
for (j = first+i;  data[j] is the wrong spot for entry ; j--)
    data[j] = data[j-1];
```

The key to the loop is the test "data[j] is the wrong spot for entry." A position is wrong if (j > first) and the element at data[j-1] is greater than the new entry. We know that such a position must be wrong because placing the new entry at this position would end up with data[j-1] > data[j]. Can you now write the loop in Java and incorporate it into the actual insertionsort method? (See Self-Test Exercise 3 on page 582).

Insertionsort—Analysis

We'll analyze the insertionsort in a slightly different manner, determining how many times the algorithm must access an element of the array—either for a comparison, or for a swap of some sort. For many sorting algorithms, such as insertionsort, the count of array accesses is proportional to the total number of operations. Therefore, the final big-*O* analysis comes out the same.

We start by asking how many array accesses are required to insert just one new element, which occurs during each iteration of this pseudocode:

```
for (i = 1; i < n; i++)
    Insert the element from data[first+i] into the portion of the array
    from data[first] through data[first+i-1], so that all of
    data[first] through data[first+i] is now sorted.
```

Our implementation of the loop starts by comparing the new element to the final element from data[first] through data[first+i-1]. After this comparison, the algorithm works backward through the array until it finds the correct spot to insert a new element. In the worst case, the algorithm could compare and shift each element data[first] through data[first+i-1], and therefore the total number of array accesses is limited to a constant times n. In fact, an iteration of the loop may need significantly fewer than $O(n)$ accesses, since each iteration examines only i-1 elements of the array rather than all n. But $O(n)$ operations is a good overestimate because it is easy to express and easy to work with.

So, the insertion of one new element takes $O(n)$ time, and there are n elements to insert. Thus the total time for n separate insertions is no more than this:

$$\text{Total} = n \times (\text{the number of operations in an } O(n) \text{ algorithm})$$
$$= n \times (\text{some constant times } n)$$
$$= \text{some constant times } n^2$$
$$= O(n^2)$$

This analysis shows one important trick to remember:

Analysis for Quadratic Time

An $O(n)$ process that is performed n times results in a quadratic number of operations ($O(n^2)$).

In the case of insertionsort, we actually perform $n-1$ insertions rather than n, but the time for $n-1$ insertions is also quadratic.

Our analysis has used one major overestimation. We assumed that each insertion required the body of the loop to examine the full n elements of the array, but some insertions require the examination of far fewer elements. Will a more accurate estimate reduce the time analysis? The answer is no. A precise analysis of the worst-case running time still results in a quadratic formula. To see this, suppose that all the original elements are far from their correct places. In fact, these elements might be completely backwards, as shown at the top of the next page.

data

10	9	8	7	6	5	4	3	2	1
[0]	[1]	[2]	[3]	[4]	[5]	[6]	[7]	[8]	[9]

In this case, the first insertion must insert the 9 in front of the 10, resulting in this array:

data

9	10	8	7	6	5	4	3	2	1
[0]	[1]	[2]	[3]	[4]	[5]	[6]	[7]	[8]	[9]

The next insertion must insert the 8 in front of everything else. And then the 7 is inserted, again at the front. With the elements starting out backwards, each insertion must compare and shift all the elements in the currently sorted part of the array, placing the new element at the front. So, for an insertionsort to work on a completely backwards array requires these comparisons and shifts:

1 compare and shift to insert the 1st element
+
2 compares and shifts to insert the 2nd element
+
3 compares and shifts to insert the 3rd element
+
. . .
+
$n-1$ compares and shifts to insert the $(n-1)^{st}$ element

The total number of compare and shifts is thus $1 + 2 + 3 + \ldots + (n-1)$. You can use a technique similar to Figure 1.3 on page 21 to evaluate this sum. The result is $n(n-1)/2$, which is $O(n^2)$. So the worst case for insertionsort is indeed quadratic time, the same as for selectionsort.

The analysis of the average-case running time for insertionsort is essentially the same as that for the worst case. The only difference is that a single insertion will, on the average, stop after accessing half of the elements from the sorted side, rather than accessing them all. This means that the average-case running time is half that of the worst-case running time, but we know that a constant multiple, such as ½, does not affect a big-O expression. Thus, the average-case running time for insertionsort is quadratic, the same as the worst-case running time.

On the other hand, the best-case running time for insertionsort is much better than quadratic. In particular, suppose that the array is *already sorted* before we begin our work. This is certainly an advantage, though the advantage does not help all sorting algorithms. For example, starting with a sorted array does not help selectionsort, which still requires quadratic time. But starting with a sorted array does help insertionsort. In this case, each insertion of a new element will examine only a single element from the array. This single-element examination is carried out once to insert each new element, and the result is an $O(n)$ time.

You probably think that starting with an already sorted array does not happen too often, and perhaps you are right. But frequently an array is *nearly* sorted—perhaps a few new elements are out of place. Insertionsort is also quite quick for nearly sorted arrays.

Here is a summary of insertionsort times:

Insertionsort Running Time

Both the worst-case running time and the average-case running times are quadratic. But the best-case (when the starting array is already sorted) is linear, and the algorithm is also quick when the starting array is nearly sorted.

Self-Test Exercises

1. The `selectionsort` method in Figure 12.1 on page 571 sorts integers into increasing order. How would you change the method so that it sorts integers into decreasing order?

2. The `selectionsort` method in Figure 12.1 on page 571 sorts integers into increasing order. How would you change the function so that it sorts an array of strings into alphabetical order? All strings consist only of lowercase letters.

3. Give a complete implementation for insertionsort.

12.2 RECURSIVE SORTING ALGORITHMS

Divide-and-Conquer Using Recursion

Key Design Concept

Divide-and-conquer works best with two equally sized subproblems, each of which is solved with a recursive call.

Let's start with an explicit statement of a recursive design technique that we have used a few times in the past. The technique, called **divide-and-conquer,** is applicable to many problems. Here's the idea: When a problem is small, simply solve it. When the problem is large, divide the problem into two smaller subproblems, each of which is about half of the original problem. Solve each subproblem with a recursive call. After the recursive calls, extra work is sometimes needed to combine the solutions of the smaller problems, resulting in a solution to the larger problem.

Divide-and-conquer can work in slightly different ways, perhaps having more than two subproblems or having subproblems with unequal size, but the basic approach—two subproblems with roughly equal size—works best.

Applied to sorting, divide-and-conquer results in the following pattern:

The Divide-and-Conquer Sorting Paradigm

1. Divide the elements to be sorted into two groups of equal (or almost equal) size.
2. Sort each of these smaller groups of elements (by recursive calls).
3. Combine the two sorted groups into one large sorted list.

We will present two recursive sorting methods based on this divide-and-conquer paradigm.

Mergesort

The most straightforward implementation of the divide-and-conquer approach to sorting is the **mergesort** algorithm. Let's see how the mergesort works with a small array. The first step divides the array into two equally sized groups, as shown in this cut:

| 9 | 12 | 31 | 25 | 5 | 8 | 20 | 2 | 3 | 6 |

After the cut, we have two smaller arrays, with five elements each. These smaller arrays can separately be sorted with recursive calls, providing this result:

| 5 | 9 | 12 | 25 | 31 |

| 2 | 3 | 6 | 8 | 20 |

When the recursive calls return, the two half-arrays need somehow to be put together into one sorted array, as shown here:

| 2 | 3 | 5 | 6 | 8 | 9 | 12 | 20 | 25 | 31 |

As shown in this illustration, the mergesort algorithm divides the array near its midpoint, sorts the two half-arrays by recursive calls to the algorithm, and then merges the two halves to get a new sorted array of elements. The final "merging" step of the process will require some thought, so we'll postpone that part of the implementation by assuming that we have a separate method to carry out the merging. The specification for the separate merging method is shown here:

```
private static void merge
(int[ ] data, int first, int n1, int n2)
// Precondition: data has at least n1 + n2 components starting at
//   data[first]. The first n1 elements (from data[first] to
//   data[first + n1 - 1] are sorted from smallest to largest, and the
//   last n2 (from data[first + n1] to data[first + n1 + n2 - 1]) are also
//   sorted from smallest to largest.
// Postcondition: Starting at data[first], n1 + n2 elements of data
//   have been rearranged to be sorted from smallest to largest.
// Note: An OutOfMemoryError can be thrown if there is insufficient
//   memory for an array of n1+n2 ints.
```

This `merge` method will be used as the last step of our mergesort. Let's examine where the `merge` method is used, within the `mergesort` method of Figure 12.2.

The stopping case for mergesort's recursion is when the array to be sorted consists of only one element. In this stopping case, there is no work to do because a single element does not need to be "rearranged." On the other hand, if there is more than one element, then the mergesort carries out these steps:

1. Calculate the sizes of the two pieces of the array. The size of the first half, `n1`, is approximately half of the entire size (calculated by `n/2`, using integer division). The second size, `n2`, is whatever is left over (calculated by `n - n1`).

2. Use recursive calls to sort the two halves. Notice that the second recursive call, `mergesort(data, first+n1, n2)`, indicates that its work should begin at `data[first+n1]`, which is the starting point of the second half.

3. Finally, activate `merge` to combine the two sorted halves.

The operation of the `merge` method has some issues that we discuss next.

The Merge Function

The algorithm for the `merge` method uses a second temporary array that we will call `temp`. Elements will be copied from the array `data` to the array `temp` in such a way that the elements are completely sorted. After that, the values are simply copied back to the array `data`. The merging algorithm uses the precondition that the two halves of the array (`data[first]` through `data[first + n1 - 1]`, and `data[first + n1]` through `data[first + n1 + n2 - 1]`) are each sorted. Since they are both sorted, we know that `data[first]` contains the smallest element in the first half, and `data[first + n1]` contains the smallest element in the second half.

FIGURE 12.2 | Mergesort

Specification

- **mergesort**
    ```
    public static void mergesort(int data[ ], int first, int n)
    ```
    Sort an array of integers from smallest to largest.

    Parameters:
    data – the array to be sorted
    first – the start index for the portion of the array that will be sorted
    n – the number of elements to sort

    Precondition:
    data[first] through data[first+n-1] are valid parts of the array.

    Postcondition:
    If n is zero or negative then no work is done. Otherwise, the elements of data have been rearranged so that data[first] <= data[first+1] <= ... <= data[first+n-1].

    Throws: ArrayIndexOutOfBoundsException
    Indicates that first+n-1 is an index beyond the end of the array.

    Throws: OutOfMemoryError
    Indicates insufficient memory for creating a temporary array in the merge step.

Implementation

```
public static void mergesort(int data[ ], int first, int n)
{
    int n1; // Size of the first half of the array
    int n2; // Size of the second half of the array

    if (n > 1)
    {
        // Compute sizes of the two halves
        n1 = n / 2;                    The two subarrays are sorted
        n2 = n - n1;                   with recursive calls.

        mergesort(data, first, n1);        // Sort data[first] through data[first+n1-1]
        mergesort(data, first + n1, n2);   // Sort data[first+n1] to the end

        // Merge the two sorted halves.
        merge(data, first, n1, n2);
    }
}
```

Therefore, we know that the smallest element overall is either `data[first]` or `data[first + n1]`. The algorithm compares these two elements and copies the smallest one to the front of the temporary array (the location `temp[0]`). The algorithm then somehow marks the copied element as being "already copied." For example, suppose that `first` is 8 and both `n1` and `n2` are 5, so that the first half of the array goes from `data[8]` through `data[12]`, and the second half goes from `data[13]` to `data[17]`. After the first element is copied to `temp`, we might have this situation:

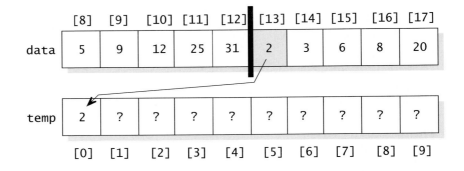

The drawing has a thick black line to separate the two halves of the `data` array. In this example, the 2 (at the front of the second half) is smaller than the 5 (at the front of the first half), so this 2 is copied to the first position of the temporary array. We marked the 2 as "already copied" by shading it in the diagram. In the actual algorithm, we'll keep track of which elements have been copied by maintaining three `int` variables:

```
int copied;    // Number of elements copied from data to temp
int copied1;   // Number copied from the first half of data
int copied2;   // Number copied from the second half of data
```

All three local variables are initialized to zero in the `merge` method. Each time that we copy an element from the first half of `data` to the temporary array, we add one to both `copied` and `copied1`. Each time that we copy an element from the second half of `data` to the temporary array, we add one to both `copied` and `copied2`. So, after copying the 2 in the above example, `copied` and `copied2` will both be 1, but `copied1` remains zero.

The merge algorithm proceeds by looking at the next uncopied elements from each half of the `data` array. The smaller of these two elements is copied to the next spot in the temporary array. In our example, we would next compare the 5 (from the first half) to the 3 (the next uncopied element from the second half).

Since the 3 is smaller, we copy the 3 to the next spot in the temp array, as shown here:

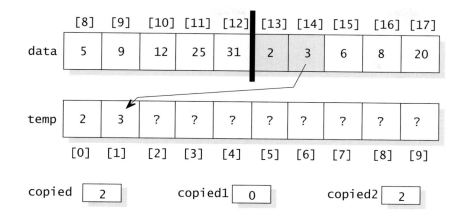

At this point we have copied a total of two elements (since copied is 2). Both of the copied elements came from the second half (since copied1 is 0 and copied2 is 2).

The next step of the algorithm will compare the 5 (from the first half) to the 6 (from the second half). The 5 is lower, so it gets copied to the temporary array, as shown here:

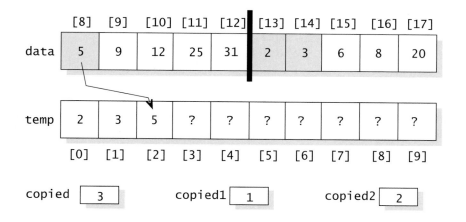

The loop proceeds in this way, moving through the two array halves. With this idea, we can write our first version of the pseudocode, shown next.

1. Allocate the `temp` array; and set `copied`, `copied1`, and `copied2` to zero.

2. `while` (both halves of the array have more elements to copy)
   `if` (the next element of 1st half is <= the next element of the 2nd half)
   {

   > Copy the next element of 1st half to the next spot in `temp`.
   > Add 1 to both `copied` and `copied1`.

   }
   `else`
   {

   > Copy the next element of 2nd half to the next spot in `temp`.
   > Add 1 to both `copied` and `copied2`.

   }

Using the local variables `copied`, `copied1`, and `copied2`, we can refine the pseudocode a bit. The "next spot in temp" is `temp[copied]`; the "next element in the 1st half" is `data[first + copied1]`. And the "next element in the 2nd half" is at `data[first + n1 + copied2]`, as shown in this refinement:

1. Allocate the `temp` array; and set `copied`, `copied1`, and `copied2` to zero.

2. `while` (both halves of the array have more elements to copy)
   `if` (`data[first + copied1]` <= `data[first + n1 + copied2]`)
   {

   > `temp[copied]` = `data[first + copied1]` ;
   > Add 1 to both `copied` and `copied1`.

   }
   `else`
   {

   > `temp[copied]` = `data[first + n1 + copied2]`;
   > Add 1 to both `copied` and `copied2`.

   }

In our actual implementation, the two assignment statements can be modified to also add 1 to `copied` and to the appropriate one of the other two local variables (`copied1` or `copied2`). The modified assignment statements make use of the ++ operator, as shown here:

1. Allocate the `temp` array; and set `copied`, `copied1`, and `copied2` to zero.

2. `while` (both halves of the array have more elements to copy)
   `if` (data[first + copied1] <= data[first + n1 + copied2])
      temp[`copied++`] = data[`first + (copied1++)`];
   `else`
      temp[`copied++`] = data[`first + n1 + (copied2++)`];

Using an index such as `copied++` has the effect of using the *current* value of the variable `copied` as the index and *afterwards* adding 1 to the variable. (If we wanted to add 1 before using the index, we would write `++copied` instead of `copied++`.)

This part of our algorithm works fine as long as neither half of the array runs out of elements. However, eventually one of the two halves will run out of elements. For our example, this will occur after we copy the last element (20) from the second half of the `data` array to the temporary array, as shown here:

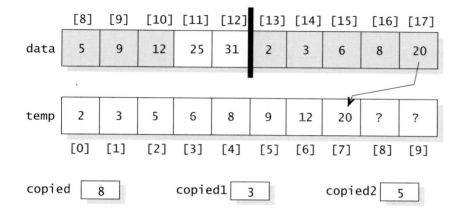

At a point like this, we want to copy the elements remaining in the uncompleted half into the temporary array. This yields the following final version of our pseudocode for the `merge` function:

1. Allocate the `temp` array; and set `copied`, `copied1`, and `copied2` to zero.

2. `while` (both halves of the array have more elements to copy)
   ```
   if (data[first + copied1] <= data[first + n1 + copied2])
       temp[copied++] = data[first + (copied++)];
   else
       temp[copied++] = data[first + n1 + (copied2++)];
   ```

3. Copy any remaining entries from the left or right subarray.

4. Copy the elements from `temp` back to `data`.

This pseudocode translates to the Java method shown in Figure 12.3.

FIGURE 12.3 | A Method to Merge Two Parts of an Array

Implementation

```
private static void merge
(int[ ] data, int first, int n1, int n2)
// Precondition: data has at least n1 + n2 components starting at data[first]. The first
// n1 elements (from data[first] to data[first + n1 - 1] are sorted from smallest
// to largest, and the last n2 (from data[first + n1] to data[first + n1 + n2 - 1]) are also
// sorted from smallest to largest.
// Postcondition: Starting at data[first], n1 + n2 elements of data
// have been rearranged to be sorted from smallest to largest.
// Note: An OutOfMemoryError can be thrown if there is insufficient
// memory for an array of n1+n2 ints.
{
    int[ ] temp = new int[n1+n2]; // Allocate the temporary array
    int copied  = 0; // Number of elements copied from data to temp
    int copied1 = 0; // Number copied from the first half of data
    int copied2 = 0; // Number copied from the second half of data
    int i;           // Array index to copy from temp back into data

    // Merge elements, copying from two halves of data to the temporary array.
    while ((copied1 < n1) && (copied2 < n2))
    {
        if (data[first + copied1] < data[first + n1 + copied2])
            temp[copied++] = data[first + (copied1++)];
        else
            temp[copied++] = data[first + n1 + (copied2++)];
    }

    // Copy any remaining entries in the left and right subarrays.
    while (copied1 < n1)
        temp[copied++] = data[first + (copied1++)];
    while (copied2 < n2)
        temp[copied++] = data[first + n1 + (copied2++)];

    // Copy from temp back to the data array.
    for (i = 0; i < n1+n2; i++)
        data[first + i] = temp[i];

}
```

Mergesort—Analysis

A complete analysis of mergesort's running time is beyond the scope of this book, but we can give the final result and hint at its derivation. First the result:

Mergesort Running Time

The worst-case running time, the average-case running time, and the best-case running time for mergesort are all $O(n \log n)$.

As usual, n is the number of elements to be sorted. Let us try to motivate this formula. In the case of the mergesort, the algorithm performs similarly on all inputs; so our motivation will apply to the worst-case, average-case, and best-case running times. Let's diagram the first few levels of recursive calls made by a typical mergesort:

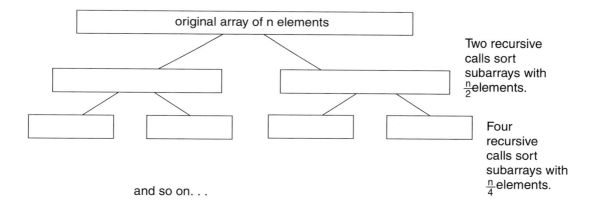

original array of n elements

Two recursive calls sort subarrays with $\frac{n}{2}$ elements.

Four recursive calls sort subarrays with $\frac{n}{4}$ elements.

and so on. . .

At the top level, we make two recursive calls to sort subarrays with $\frac{n}{2}$ elements each. At this level, we use `merge` once to merge those two $\frac{n}{2}$ pieces into a single n element array. At the second level, each $\frac{n}{2}$ piece is broken into two $\frac{n}{4}$ pieces. At this level there will be two `merge` activations, each of which merges a pair of $\frac{n}{4}$ pieces to create the two $\frac{n}{2}$ pieces. Continuing this pattern, you can determine the total number of activations of `merge`, as shown at the top of the next page.

At the top level, one activation of `merge` creates an array with *n* elements

+

At the next level, two activations of `merge` to create two $\frac{n}{2}$ pieces

+

At the next level, four activations of `merge` to create four $\frac{n}{4}$ pieces

+

At the next level, eight activations of `merge` to create eight $\frac{n}{8}$ pieces

+

. . .

The pattern continues until we cannot further subdivide the pieces (because we have only a single element).

At each level of the pattern, the *total* work done by merging is $O(n)$. For example, at the top level we have one `merge` activation to create an array with *n* elements, and the number of operations in this one activation is proportional to *n*. At the next level, there are two `merge` activations, but each of the activations does work that is proportional to $\frac{n}{2}$, so again the *total* work done at that level is $O(n)$. At the next level we have four `merge` activations; each does work that is proportional to $\frac{n}{4}$. And so on.

Each level does *total* work proportional to *n*. So the total cost of the mergesort is given by this formula:

(some constant) $\times n \times$ (the number of levels in the pattern)

The size of the array pieces is halved on each step down the pattern. So the number of levels in the pattern is approximately equal to the number of times that *n* can be divided by two, stopping when the result is less than or equal to one. That number of "halvings" is closely approximated by $\log_2 n$ (the base 2 logarithm of *n*). Therefore, mergesort appears to perform the following number of operations:

(some constant) $\times n \times \log_2 n$

As a big-*O* formula, we can throw out the multiplicative constant and also the constant 2 in the base of the logarithm. So the time is $O(n \times \log n)$. This time of *n* multiplied by a logarithm of *n* is usually written more simply as $O(n \log n)$, pronounced "big-*O* of *n* log *n*."

Our analysis has not been formal, but it is the correct answer, and a rigorous demonstration would follow the same outline as our intuitive explanation.

FIGURE 12.4

Value of $n \log_2 n$ versus n^2

n	$n \log_2 n$	n^2
2	2	4
8	24	64
32	160	1024
128	896	16,384
512	4608	262,144
2048	22,528	4,194,304

Mergesort has a worst-case running time of $O(n \log n)$ operations, which is faster than the quadratic running times for the selectionsort and insertionsort algorithms. But, how much faster is it? We can get a feel for the difference by comparing the function $n \log_2 n$ with n^2. The table in Figure 12.4 gives some representative values for comparison. As you can see by studying the table, an $n \log_2 n$ running time is substantially faster than an n^2 running time, particularly if the array to be sorted is large.

Mergesort for Files

The mergesort algorithm is actually a poor choice for sorting arrays. The quicksort and heapsort, which we will describe in a moment, are better because they don't require a temporary array for the merge step. However, mergesort can be modified to sort a file, even if the file is too large to fit in the largest possible array. In the mergesort of a file, the file is divided into several pieces, and each piece is sorted (perhaps with a recursive call of the mergesort method). The sorted pieces are then merged into a single sorted file, and the separate pieces can be removed.

With this use of mergesort, the separate file pieces get smaller and smaller with each recursive call. Eventually, a piece gets small enough to fit into an array. At this point, the piece should be read into an array and sorted using quicksort or heapsort.

Quicksort

We developed the mergesort algorithm as a special case of a general sorting technique that is called divide-and-conquer sorting. In this section we will develop another sorting algorithm based on this same basic divide-and-conquer approach. This sorting algorithm is called **quicksort**, first devised by the computer scientist C. A. R. Hoare. It is similar to mergesort in many ways. It divides the elements to be sorted into two roughly equal groups, sorts the two groups by recursive calls, and combines the two sorted groups into a single array of sorted values. However, the method for dividing the array in half is much more sophisticated than the simple method we used for mergesort. On the other hand, the method for combining these two groups of sorted elements is trivial compared to the method used in mergesort. In mergesort the division is trivial and the combining complicated. With quicksort the division is complicated and the combining is trivial.

pivot element

The basic idea of quicksort is simple: Suppose you know some particular value that belongs in the middle of the array, or at least the approximate middle of the array. We will call this value the **pivot element,** or simply, the **pivot.** Suppose we somehow put this pivot element into its correct location in the array, somehow put all the values less than or equal to the pivot in array positions before the pivot, and somehow put all the values greater than the pivot in array positions after the pivot element. At this point we have not sorted the values less than the pivot element, we simply placed them, in any order, in array positions before the pivot element. Similarly, we have not yet sorted the values greater than the pivot, but we simply placed them, in any order, in array positions after the pivot element.

After this initial moving of array elements, we have moved the array closer to being sorted. We know that the pivot element of the array is in the correct position. We also know that all other values are in the correct segment of the array, either the segment before the pivot element or the segment after the pivot element. However, although we know they are in the correct segment, those segments are still not sorted. One way to proceed is to sort the two segments separately. This works because we know that all values in the first segment are less than all values in the second segment, so no value ever needs to move from one segment to the other. How do we sort the two segments? These are smaller versions of the original sorting task, and so we can sort the two smaller array segments by recursive calls. If we continue to divide the array into smaller portions in the way we outlined, we will eventually get down to array segments of size one and we can use that as a stopping case (requiring no work).

This idea is sound except for one problem. How do we find a pivot element and its correct final position in the sorted array? There is no obvious way to quickly find the midpoint value until after the array is sorted. Our solution will be to take an arbitrary array value and use it as the pivot element. As a result, we may not be dividing the array exactly in half, but as long as we do divide it into smaller pieces, our algorithm will eventually sort the array. We perform the subtask of dividing the array elements with a private method called `partition`. The `partition` method chooses some arbitrary pivot element, places it at the correct index position, and divides the remaining array elements as we have described. The method will not necessarily do those three things in that order, but it will do them all. The method's specification is as follows:

```
private static int partition(int[ ] data, int first, int n)
// Precondition: n > 1, and data has at least n elements starting at
// data[first].
// Postcondition: The method has selected some "pivot value" that occurs
// in data[first]. . .data[first+n-1]. The elements of data have then been
// rearranged and the method returns a pivot index so that
//     -- data[pivot index] is equal to the pivot;
//     -- each element before data[pivot index] is <= the pivot;
//     -- each element after data[pivot index] is > the pivot.
```

We will formulate our sorting algorithm as a recursive method called `quicksort`, which uses the `partition` method. After the partitioning, the array and the pivot index look like this:

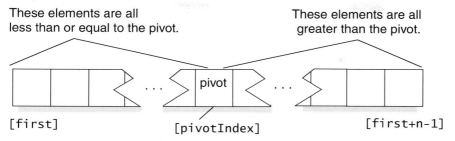

These elements are all less than or equal to the pivot.

These elements are all greater than the pivot.

[first]   [pivotIndex]   [first+n-1]

After the partition, our `quicksort` method makes two recursive calls. The first recursive call sorts the elements before the pivot element, from `data[first]` to `data[pivotIndex - 1]`. The second recursive call sorts the elements after the pivot element, from `data[pivotIndex + 1]` to `data[first + n - 1]`. The recursive calls are part of the `quicksort` implementation in Figure 12.5. We still need to derive the code for the `partition`.

FIGURE 12.5 | Quicksort

Implementation

```
public static void quicksort(int[ ] data, int first, int n)
// Precondition: data has at least n components starting at data[first].
// Postcondition: The elements of data have been rearranged so
//   that data[first] <= data[first+1] <= ... <= data[first+n-1].
{
    int pivotIndex; // Array index for the pivot element
    int n1;         // Number of elements before the pivot element
    int n2;         // Number of elements after the pivot element

    if (n > 1)
    {
        // Partition the array, and set the pivot index.
        pivotIndex = partition(data, first, n);

        // Compute the sizes of the two pieces.
        n1 = pivotIndex - first;
        n2 = n - n1 - 1;

        // Recursive calls will now sort the two pieces.
        quicksort(data, first, n1);
        quicksort(data, pivotIndex + 1, n2);
    }
}
```

The Partition Method

Since we have no information about the values in the array, all values have an equal probability of being the value that belongs in the middle of the array. Moreover, we know that the algorithm will work no matter what value we use for the pivot element. So, we arbitrarily choose the first array element to use as the pivot element. (On page 601 we discuss why this is not always the best choice and propose a method to fix the problem.)

The `partition` method will move all the values that are less than or equal to this pivot element toward the beginning of the array, that is, toward positions with lower numbered indexes. All values that are greater than this pivot element are moved the other way, toward the tail end of the array, with higher numbered indexes. Because the pivot element is not necessarily the value that belongs at the exact midpoint position of the array, we do not know where the dividing line between the two array portions belongs. Hence, we do not know how far forward we need to move elements less than or equal to the pivot element, nor do we know how far toward the end of the array we must move elements that are greater than the pivot element. We solve this dilemma by working inward from the two ends of the array. We move smaller elements to the beginning of the array, and we move larger elements to the tail end of the array. In this way we obtain two segments—one segment of smaller elements growing to the right from the beginning of the array, and one segment of larger elements growing to the left from the tail end of the array. When these two segments meet, we have correctly partitioned the array. The correct location for the pivot element is at the boundary of these two segments.

Starting at the `data[first]`, the algorithm passes over smaller elements at the beginning of the array until it encounters an element that is larger than the pivot element. This larger element is not in the correct segment and must somehow move to the tail end segment. Starting at the other end of the array, the algorithm passes over larger elements at that end of the array until it encounters an element that is smaller than (or equal to) the pivot element. This smaller element is not in the correct segment and must somehow move to the beginning segment. At that point we know that the elements in the two segments, up to but not including these out-of-place elements, are in the correct segment of the array. If we switch these two out-of-place elements, we will know that they also are in the correct portion of the array. Using this technique of locating and switching incorrectly placed elements at the ends of the array, our algorithm proceeds to continually expand the segment at the beginning of the array and the segment at the tail end of the array, until these two segments meet.

For example, suppose the following represents our array (with `first` equal to zero and `n` equal to 11):

40	20	10	80	60	50	7	30	100	90	70
[0]	[1]	[2]	[3]	[4]	[5]	[6]	[7]	[8]	[9]	[10]

We choose the first value, 40, as our pivot element. Starting at the beginning of the array, we look for the first element that is greater than the pivot. That is the 80. Starting from the other end we look for the first value that is less than or equal to the pivot. That is the 30. We use two variables called tooBigIndex and tooSmallIndex to hold the indexes of these two array elements. After finding the two out-of-place elements, the array can be represented as follows:

40	20	10	80	60	50	7	30	100	90	70
[0]	[1]	[2]	[3]	[4]	[5]	[6]	[7]	[8]	[9]	[10]

tooBigIndex | 3 | tooSmallIndex | 7 |

The two shaded elements are in incorrect segments of the array. If we interchange them, the array will be closer to being divided correctly. After the exchange the array will contain these elements:

40	20	10	30	60	50	7	80	100	90	70
[0]	[1]	[2]	[3]	[4]	[5]	[6]	[7]	[8]	[9]	[10]

tooBigIndex | 3 | tooSmallIndex | 7 |

We now repeat the process. Continuing from the places we left off, we increment tooBigIndex until we find another element larger than the pivot; we decrement tooSmallIndex until we find another element less than or equal to the pivot element. This changes the values of the two index variables as shown here:

40	20	10	30	60	50	7	80	100	90	70
[0]	[1]	[2]	[3]	[4]	[5]	[6]	[7]	[8]	[9]	[10]

tooBigIndex | 4 | tooSmallIndex | 6 |

Exchanging these two elements places them in the correct array portions and yields the following array value:

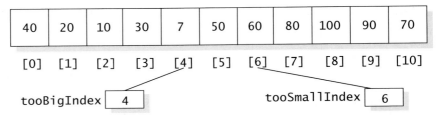

If we continue to look for elements to exchange, we will increment the too-BigIndex until it reaches the element that contains 50, and we will decrement the tooSmallIndex past the element 50 to the index of the element 7. At this point the two indexes have crossed each other, as shown here:

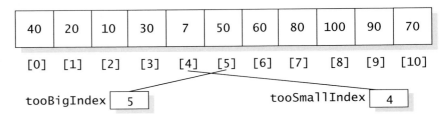

Once the indexes cross each other, we have partitioned the array. All elements less than or equal to the pivot element of 40 are in the first five positions. All elements greater than the pivot element of 40 are in the last six positions. However, the pivot is not yet at the dividing point between the two parts of the array. At this point, the correct spot for the pivot will always be at the location given by the variable tooSmallIndex. The reason is because the tooSmall-Index has just hit the tail end of the first of the two array segments.

So, we exchange the values of data[first] and data[tooSmallIndex]. After moving the pivot element, the array configuration is as follows:

7	20	10	30	40	50	60	80	100	90	70
[0]	[1]	[2]	[3]	[4]	[5]	[6]	[7]	[8]	[9]	[10]

tooBigIndex | 5   tooSmallIndex | 4

In addition to the local variables tooSmallIndex and tooBigIndex, our pseudocode for the complete partition method will also have a local variable called pivot to hold a copy of the pivot element. The array itself is called data, and the first element of the segment we are partitioning is data[first]. The total number of elements is n, and the precondition guarantees that n is at least 2. Here is the pseudocode:

```
private static int partition(int[ ] data, int first, int n)
// Precondition: n > 1, and data has at least n elements starting at
//   data[first].
// Postcondition: The method has selected some "pivot value" that occurs
//   in data[first]. . .data[first+n-1]. The elements of data have then been
//   rearranged and the method returns a pivot index so that
//      -- data[pivot index] is equal to the pivot;
//      -- each element before data[pivot index] is <= the pivot;
//      -- each element after data[pivot index] is > the pivot.
```

1. Initialize values:
   ```
   pivot = data[first];
   tooBigIndex = first + 1;        // Index of element after pivot
   tooSmallIndex = first + n - 1;  // Index of last element
   ```

2. Repeat the following until the two indexes cross each other (in other words, keep going while `tooBigIndex < tooSmallIndex`):

   2a. `while tooBigIndex` has not yet reached n, and `data[tooBigIndex]` is less than or equal to the pivot, move `tooBigIndex` up to the next index.

   2b. `while data[tooSmallIndex]` is greater than the pivot, move `tooSmallIndex` down to the previous index.

   2c. `if (tooBigIndex < tooSmallIndex)`, then there is still room for both end portions to grow toward each other, so swap the values of `data[tooBigIndex]` and `data[tooSmallIndex]`.

3. Move the pivot element to its correct position at `data[tooSmallIndex]`:

   3a. Move `data[tooSmallIndex]` (which still contains a value that is less than or equal to the pivot) to `data[first]` (which still contains the pivot).

   3b. `data[tooSmallIndex] = pivot;`

   3c. `return tooSmallIndex;` (i.e., the index where the pivot is).

Quicksort—Analysis

We want to estimate the running time of quicksort from Figure 12.5 on page 595. As always, *n* will be the number of elements to be sorted, and we will express our running times in terms of *n*. In the best situation, the analysis of quicksort is much like our mergesort analysis from page 591. In this situation, each partition places the pivot element in the precise middle so that each recursive call sorts about half of the current elements, as shown here:

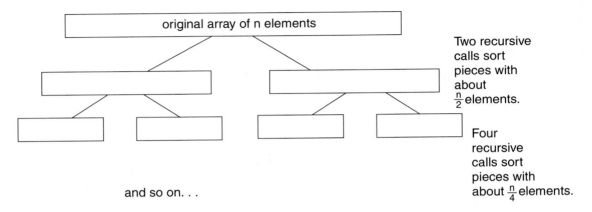

The total work carried out by the partitions on each level is $O(n)$, so that the total time for quicksort is

(some constant) $\times n \times$ (the number of levels in the pattern)

In the ideal case, with the pivot element near the middle of each piece, the number of levels is about $\log_2 n$ (just like the mergesort analysis). This results in a running time of $O(n \log n)$, which is the *best* that quicksort can manage.

But sometimes quicksort is significantly worse than $O(n \log n)$. In fact, the worst time behavior occurs when the array is already sorted before activating quicksort. In this case, the first element is smaller than everything else. Because we have been using the first element for the pivot, the pivot element is smaller than everything else. This causes a miserable partition, with everything to the right of the pivot, as shown here:

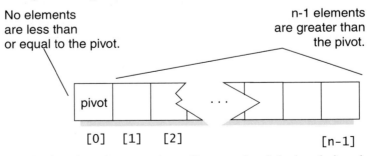

In this situation, the recursive call to sort the right-hand piece has a lot of work to do. It must sort $n-1$ elements. Even worse, when the recursive call does its own partitioning, its pivot element will be the smallest of its $n-1$ elements, and again a bad partitioning occurs. The recursive call at the next level will have to sort $n-2$ elements. This pattern of bad partitions continues with recursive calls to sort *n*–3, *n*–4, and so on right down to 1. The total work done by all these recursive calls is proportional to the familiar sum: $n + (n–1) + (n–2) + (n–3) + \ldots + 1$. What's the big-*O* analysis for this sum? It is $O(n^2)$ (see Figure 1.3 on page 21). So the *worst*-case running time for quicksort is quadratic.

Despite a poor worst-case time, quicksort generally is quite good. In fact, the average time (which we won't develop) turns out to be $O(n \log n)$. This is the same as mergesort, and we have the bonus of not needing to allocate an extra array for the merging process.

Quicksort Running Time

The worst-case running time of quicksort is $O(n^2)$. But the average-case running time and the best-case running time for quicksort are both $O(n \log n)$. Obtaining a good running time requires the choice of a good pivot element.

Quicksort—Choosing a Good Pivot Element

Our analysis of running times points out that the choice of a good pivot element is critical to the efficiency of the quicksort algorithm. If we can ensure that the pivot element is near the median of the array values, then quicksort is very efficient. One technique that is often used to increase the likelihood of choosing a good pivot element is to choose three values from the array and then use the middle of these three values as the pivot element. For example, if the three values chosen from the array are 10, 107, and 53—then 53 would be used as the pivot element. One possibility for the three values is to use the first array value, the last array value, and the value in the array position nearest to the midpoint of the array. However, with our particular partitioning pseudocode, using these three values actually has poor performance when the array starts in reverse order. A better choice is to use three randomly selected values from the array.

Several other common techniques to speed up quicksort are discussed in the Self-Test Exercises and Programming Projects.

Self-Test Exercises

4. Suppose that `data` is an array of 1000 integers. Write a line of code to activate the `quicksort` or `mergesort` method to sort the 100 elements `data[222]` through `data[321]`.

5. Which recursive sorting technique always makes recursive calls to sort pieces that are about half the size of the original array?

6. In quicksort, what time performance is obtained when good "splitting" of arrays continues for all recursive calls? What time performance occurs if there is bad splitting, so that many recursive calls reduce the array size by only one?

7. The `quicksort` method in Figure 12.5 on page 595 produces its worst-case running time when the array is already sorted. Suppose you know that the array might already be sorted or almost sorted. How should you modify the algorithm for quicksort?

8. One problem with both of our recursive sorting algorithms is that the recursion continues all the way down until we are sorting a piece with only one element. The one-element piece is our stopping case. This works fine, but once the size of a piece becomes fairly small, a lot of time is wasted making more and more recursive calls. To fix this problem, actual implementations usually stop making recursive calls when the size of an array segment becomes small. The definition of "small" can vary, but experiments have shown that somewhere around 15 elements is a good choice for small arrays. For this exercise, modify the recursive quicksort algorithm so that any small segment is sorted using insertion sort, and the process of partitioning and making recursive calls is done only for larger array segments.

stopping recursion before the pieces get too small

12.3 AN *O*(*N* LOG *N*) ALGORITHM USING A HEAP

Heapsort

Both mergesort and quicksort have an average-case running time that is $O(n \log n)$. Mergesort also has a worst-case running time that is $O(n \log n)$, whereas the worst-case running time for quicksort is $O(n^2)$. That makes mergesort sound preferable to quicksort. However, mergesort requires more storage since it requires an extra array. In this section we present a sorting algorithm, called *heapsort*, that combines the time efficiency of mergesort and the storage efficiency of quicksort. Like mergesort, heapsort has a worst-case running time that is $O(n \log n)$, and like quicksort it does not require an additional array.

heapsort is an interchange sorting algorithm

Like selectionsort, heapsort is an interchange sorting algorithm that works by repeatedly interchanging pairs of array elements. Thus, heapsort needs only some small constant amount of storage in addition to the array that holds the elements to be sorted. Heapsort is similar to selectionsort in another way as well. Selectionsort locates the largest value and places it in the final array position. Then it locates the next largest value and places it in the next-to-last array position, and so forth. Heapsort uses a similar strategy, locating the largest value, then the next largest, and so on. However, heapsort uses a much more efficient algorithm to locate the array values to be moved.

the array is made into a heap

Heapsort works by first transforming the array to be sorted into a *heap*. This notion of a heap is the same data structure that was used in Section 10.1 to implement a priority queue. As a quick review, here is the definition of a heap:

Heap Review
(from Section 10.1)

A **heap** is a binary tree where the elements of the nodes can be compared with a total order semantics. In addition, these two rules are followed:

1. The element contained by a node is greater than or equal to the elements of the node's children.

2. The tree is a complete binary tree, so that every depth except the deepest must contain as many nodes as possible; and at the deepest level, all the nodes are as far left as possible (see "Complete Binary Trees" on page 419).

A heap is a *complete* binary tree, and we have an efficient method for representing a complete binary tree in an array. This representation was first shown in Section 9.2, following these rules:

- Data from the root of the complete binary tree goes in the [0] component of the array.

- The data from the children of the root is placed in the next two components of the array.

- We continue in this way, placing the four nodes of depth two in the next four components of the array, and so forth. For example, a heap with ten nodes can be stored in a ten-element array, as shown here:

Location of the data for a complete binary tree, as stored in an array

To be more precise about the location of data in the array, we have these rules:

1. The data from the root always appears in the [0] component of the array.

2. Suppose that the data for a nonroot node appears in component [i] of the array. Then the data for its parent is always at location [(i-1)/2] (using integer division).

3. Suppose that the data for a node appears in component [i] of the array. Then its children (if they exist) always have their data at these locations:

   Left child at component [2i+1]

   Right child at component [2i+2]

With these facts in mind, we can easily state the general idea that underlies a heapsort algorithm with this specification:

- **heapsort**

   ```
   public static void heapsort(int data[ ], int n)
   ```
   Sort an array of integers from smallest to largest.

   Parameters:
   data – the array to be sorted
   n – the number of elements to sort (from data[0] through data[n-1])

   Precondition:
   data has at least n elements.

   Postcondition:
   If n is zero or negative then no work is done. Otherwise, the elements of data have been rearranged so that data[0] <= data[1] <= ... <= data[n-1].

   Throws: ArrayIndexOutOfBoundsException
   Indicates that data has fewer than n elements.

Notice that the heapsort sorts an array beginning at index [0]. This differs from our earlier sorting algorithms (which have a specified first index for the portion of the array that was being sorted). We could write the heapsort so that it dealt with a specified first index, but the algorithm will be clearer with the requirement of starting at index [0]. So, the heapsort starts with an array of values to be sorted. The algorithm treats the array values as if they were values in a complete binary tree using the three rules just listed. That much is easy since any array of *n* values represents some complete binary tree with *n* nodes.

first, the array is made into a heap

The first step of the heapsort algorithm is to rearrange the values in the array so that the corresponding complete binary tree is a heap. In other words, we rearrange the array so that the corresponding complete binary tree follows the heap storage rule: *The value contained in a node is never less than a value from one of the node's children.* For example, suppose that the array begins with the ten values at the top of the next page.

21	35	22	27	23	45	42	19	4	5
[0]	[1]	[2]	[3]	[4]	[5]	[6]	[7]	[8]	[9]

This array can be interpreted as representing the complete binary tree shown here:

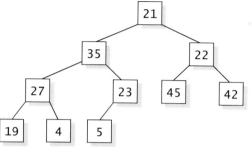

Of course, this complete binary tree is *not* a heap—for example, the data in the root's left child (35) is larger than the data in the root (21). So, the first step of the heapsort is to rearrange the array elements so that the corresponding complete binary tree is a heap.

For the ten-element example that we have just seen, the first step of the heapsort might rearrange the array so that the elements are in the following order:

45	27	42	21	23	22	35	19	4	5
[0]	[1]	[2]	[3]	[4]	[5]	[6]	[7]	[8]	[9]

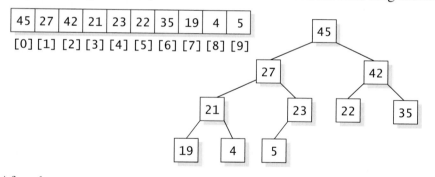

After the rearrangement of the array elements, the corresponding complete binary tree is a heap, and to aid your visualization, we have drawn the tree beside the array. But keep in mind that the only place that the numbers are stored is in the array. The tree is just our visualization of how those elements are structured. In a moment, we'll provide the details of how the rearrangement into a heap occurs, but first let's look at the rest of the heapsort algorithm.

Recall that the largest value in a heap is stored in the root, and that in our array representation of a complete binary tree, the root node is stored in the first array position. Thus, since the array represents a heap, we know that the largest array element is in the first array position. To get the largest value into the correct array position, we simply interchange the first and the final array elements. After interchanging these two array elements, we know that the largest array element

find the largest element, and move it to the end of the array is in the final array position, as shown here:

5	27	42	21	23	22	35	19	4	45
[0]	[1]	[2]	[3]	[4]	[5]	[6]	[7]	[8]	[9]

The dark vertical line in the array separates the sorted side of the array (on the right) from the unsorted side. Moreover, the unsorted side (on the left) still represents a complete binary tree, which is *almost* a heap, as shown here:

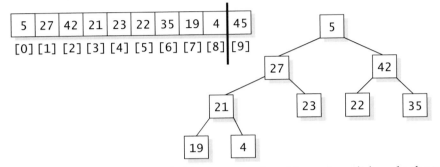

fix the heap   When we consider the *unsorted* side as a complete binary tree, it is only the root that violates the heap storage rule. This root is smaller than its children. So, the next step of the heapsort is to reposition this one out-of-place value in order to restore the heap. In Section 10.1 we discussed this process of restoring the heap by repositioning the out-of-place root. The process, called *reheapification downward*, begins by comparing the value in the root with the value of each of its children. If one or both children are larger than the root, then the root's value is exchanged with the larger of the two children. This moves the troublesome value down one level in the tree. For our example, the out-of-place value (5) is exchanged with its larger child (42), as shown here:

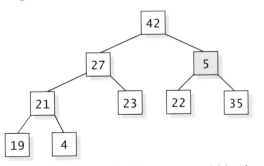

Of course, this exchange of values actually occurs within the array that represents the heap, so that the array now looks like this:

42	27	5	21	23	22	35	19	4	45
[0]	[1]	[2]	[3]	[4]	[5]	[6]	[7]	[8]	[9]

In this example, the 5 is still out of place, so we will once again exchange it with its largest child, resulting in the array (and heap) shown here:

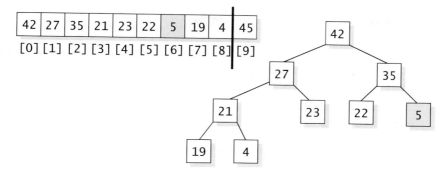

Keep in mind that only the unsorted side of the array must be maintained as a heap. In general, the reheapification continues until the troublesome value reaches a leaf or it reaches a spot where it is no larger than its children.

When the unsorted side of the array is once again a heap, the heapsort continues by exchanging the largest element in the unsorted side with the rightmost element of the unsorted side. For our example, the 42 is exchanged with the 4, as shown here:

4	27	35	21	23	22	5	19	42	45
[0]	[1]	[2]	[3]	[4]	[5]	[6]	[7]	[8]	[9]

As you can see, the sorted side has grown by one element—it now has the two largest elements, and the unsorted side is once again *almost* a heap, as shown here:

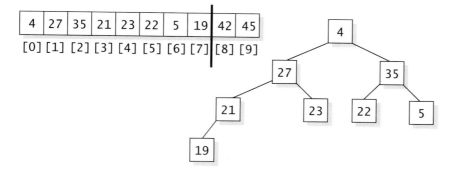

Only the root (4) is out of place, and that may be fixed by another reheapification downward. After the reheapification downward, the largest value of the unsorted side will once again reside at location [0], and we can continue to pull out the *next* largest value.

Here is the pseudocode for the heapsort algorithm that we have been describing:

// Heapsort for the array called data with n elements

1. Convert the array of *n* elements into a heap.
2. `unsorted = n;` *// The number of elements in the unsorted side*
3. `while (unsorted > 1)`
   ```
   {
       // Reduce the unsorted side by one.
       unsorted--;
       Swap data[0] with data[unsorted].
   ```
   The unsorted side of the array is now a heap with the root out of place.
   Do a reheapification downward to turn the unsorted side back into
   a heap.
   ```
   }
   ```

The implementation of this pseudocode is shown in Figure 12.6. In the implementation we use two methods, `makeHeap` and `reheapifyDown`, which we discuss next.

FIGURE 12.6   Heapsort

Implementation

```
public static void heapsort(int[ ] data, int n)
{
    int unsorted; // Size of the unsorted part of the array
    int temp;     // Used during the swapping of two array locations

    makeHeap(data, n);

    unsorted = n;

    while (unsorted > 1)
    {
        unsorted--;

        // Swap the largest element (data[0]) with the final element of unsorted part
        temp = data[0];
        data[0] = data[unsorted];
        data[unsorted] = temp;

        reheapifyDown(data, unsorted);
    }
}
```

Making the Heap

At the start of the heapsort algorithm, we must rearrange the array elements so that they form a heap. This rearrangement is accomplished by using a private method with the following specification:

```
private static void makeHeap(int[ ] data, int n);
// Precondition: data is an array with at least n elements.
// Postcondition: The elements of data have been rearranged so that the
// complete binary tree represented by this array is a heap.
```

There are two common ways to build an initial heap from the array. One method is relatively easy to program, and we will show that method here. A second, more efficient method requires more difficult programming that we will outline in Programming Project 5 on page 615.

The simple approach to makeHeap builds the heap one element at a time, starting at the front of the array. Initially we start with just one element, and this one element forms a small heap of one node. For example, we might start with the array shown here:

21	35	22	27	23	45	42	19	4	5
[0]	[1]	[2]	[3]	[4]	[5]	[6]	[7]	[8]	[9]

In this array, the area to the left of the vertical bar can be viewed as a heap with just one node, and the area to the right is still a jumble of random values.

21

the first array element forms a heap with one node

The makeHeap algorithm adds the array elements to the heap one at a time. In our example, we will next add the 35 to the heap, resulting in the following configuration. In this illustration, we have drawn both the array and the state of the heap that is formed from the elements to the left of the vertical bar.

As you can see, just adding the node in this way does not actually create a heap because the newly added node (35) has a value that is larger than its parent. However, we can fix this problem by pushing the out-of-place node upward until it reaches the root or it reaches a place with a larger parent. This process of pushing a new node upward is called *reheapification upward*. We have seen reheapification upward before, in Section 10.1. In that section, reheapification upward was used whenever a new element was added to the priority queue (which was represented as a heap).

The pseudocode for `makeHeap` uses reheapification upward, as shown here (with two local `int` variables called i and k):

```
//  Making a heap from an array called data with n elements
for (i = 1; i < n; i++)
{
    k = i;  //  The index of the new element
    while (data[k] is not yet the root, and data[k] is bigger than its parent)
        Swap data[k] with its parent, and reset k to be the index of its parent.
}
```

The complete implementation of this pseudocode as the method `makeHeap` is left up to you. The readability of your implementation can be improved if you also implement another method called `parent`, as shown here:

```
private static int parent(int k)
//  Precondition: k > 0.
//  Postcondition: The method assumes that k is the index of an array
//  element, where the array represents a complete binary tree. The return
//  value is the index of the parent of node k, using the formula from
//  Rule 3 on page 604.
{
    return (k-1)/2;
}
```

Whenever k is an index of an element in the array and k is not zero, the value of `parent(k)` is the array index of the parent of `data[k]`. You can use this method whenever you need to calculate the index of the parent of a node.

Reheapification Downward

We have one more method to implement, the reheapification downward, with this specification:

```
private static void reheapifyDown(int[ ] data, int n)
//  Precondition: n > 0, and data is an array with at least n elements. These
//  elements form a heap, except that data[0] may be in an incorrect
//  location.
//  Postcondition: The data values have been rearranged so that the first
//  n elements of data now form a heap.
```

The method works by continually swapping the out-of-place element with its largest child, as shown in the pseudocode at the top of the next page.

```
// Reheapification downward (for a heap where the root is out of place)
int current;           // Index of the node that's moving down
int bigChildIndex;     // Index of current's larger child
boolean heapOkay;      // Will become true when heap is correct

current = 0;
heapOkay = false;
```

```
while ((!heapOkay) && (the current node is not a leaf))
{
```
Set `bigChildIndex` to be the index of the larger child of the `current` node. (If there is only one child, then `bigChildIndex` will be set to the index of this one child.)

```
    if (data[current] < data[bigChildIndex])
    {
```
Swap `data[current]` with `data[bigChildIndex]`.
```
        current = bigChildIndex;
    }
    else
        heapOkay = true;
}
```

The swapping stops when the out-of-place element reaches a leaf, or when the out-of-place element is larger than both of its children.

Heapsort—Analysis

Let's count operations for the worst-case running time for the heapsort algorithm. As usual, we take the problem size *n* to be the number of elements to be sorted. If you look back at the implementation from Figure 12.6 on page 608, you will see that the total number of operations can be given as this sum:

(The operations to build the initial heap)
+
(The operations to pull the elements out of the heap one at a time)
+
(Some fixed number of operations for a few other assignments)

To refine this formula, we must calculate the number of operations to build the initial heap and the number of operations required when an element is pulled out of the heap.

Building the initial heap. To build the heap we add the elements one at a time, using reheapification upward to push the new element upward until it reaches the root or it reaches an acceptable spot (where the parent has a larger value). Since we actually add $n-1$ elements (rather than n), the total time is this:

$$(n - 1) \times \text{(number of operations for one reheapification upward)}$$

The maximum number of operations for one reheapification upward is a constant times the depth of the heap. In Section 10.3, we showed that the depth of a heap is no more than $\log_2 n$. Therefore, the worst-case time for building the heap is the following:

$$(n - 1) \times \text{a constant} \times (\log_2 n)$$

Removing the constants from this formula results in an $O(n \log n)$ running time to build the initial heap.

Pulling the elements out of the heap. Once the initial heap is built, we pull the elements out of the heap one at a time. After each element is removed, we perform a reheapification downward. We pull out a total of $n-1$ elements, and the number of operations in each reheapification downward is never more than a constant times the depth of the tree. Therefore, pulling all the elements out of the tree also requires $(n - 1) \times \text{a constant} \times (\log_2 n)$ operations, which is an $O(n \log n)$ running time.

worst case for heapsort

Total time for heap sort. We can now give a final estimate for the worst-case running time for the entire heapsort algorithm. Building the initial heap requires $O(n \log n)$ operations, and then pulling the elements out of the heap requires another $O(n \log n)$ operations. You might be tempted to write that the sum of all this work is $O(2n \log n)$, and you would be right. But remember that multiplication by a constant (such as 2) can be ignored in big-O notation, so in fact the entire algorithm from start to finish requires $O(n \log n)$ operations.

average case for heapsort

Although we won't give a derivation, it turns out that the average-case running time for heapsort is also $O(n \log n)$, the same as the worst-case running time.

Heapsort Running Time

The worst-case running time and the average-case running time for heapsort are both $O(n \log n)$.

Self-Test Exercise

9. How would you modify the heapsort algorithm so that it sorts integers into decreasing order rather than increasing order?

CHAPTER SUMMARY

- All the sorting algorithms presented in this chapter apply to any type of values sorted according to any reasonable ordering relation. The array values do not need to be integers.

- In the divide-and-conquer sorting method, the values to be sorted are divided into two approximately equal groups, the groups are sorted by a recursive call, and then the two sorted groups are combined into the final sorted list. Mergesort and quicksort are two examples of divide-and-conquer sorting algorithms.

- Selectionsort and insertionsort have quadratic running times in both the worst case and the average case. This is comparatively slow. However, if the arrays to be sorted are short, or if the sorting program will be used only a few times, then they are reasonable algorithms to use. Insertionsort is particularly good if the array is nearly sorted beforehand.

- Mergesort and quicksort are much more efficient than selectionsort and insertionsort. They each have an average-case running time that is $O(n \log n)$. If you need to sort a large number of long lists, it would be worth the extra effort of coding and debugging one of these more complicated algorithms.

- Mergesort has the advantage that its worst-case running time is $O(n \log n)$, but it has the disadvantage of needing to allocate a second array to use in the merging process.

- Quicksort has the disadvantage of a quadratic worst-case time. However, with some care in the pivot selection process, we usually can avoid this bad time. Quicksort can be further improved by stopping the recursive calls when the subarrays become small (around 15 elements). These small subarrays can be sorted with an insertionsort.

- Heapsort works by creating a heap from all the array elements and then pulling the largest element out of the heap, then the next largest, and so on. The worst-case and average-case running times for heapsort are both $O(n \log n)$.

Solutions to Self-Test Exercises ?

1. Instead of finding the index of the biggest element, find the index of the smallest element.

2. To sort strings, change each declaration of the array to an array of strings rather than an array of integers. The temp variable must also be changed to a string. Also, the comparison (`data[big]<data[j]`) is changed to compare strings:

   (`data[big].compareTo(data[j]) < 0`).

3. Here is one solution:
```
public static void insertionsort
(int[ ] data, int first, int n)
{
    int i, j;
    int entry;

    for (i = 1; i < n; i++)
    {
        entry = data[first+i];
        for (j = first+i; test ; j--)
            data[j] = data[j-1];
        data[j] = entry;
    }
}
```
The critical test in the implementation is
(j>first) && (data[j-1] > entry).

4. quicksort(data, 222, 100);

5. Mergesort always makes recursive calls to sort
subarrays that are about half the size of the
original array, resulting in $O(n \log n)$ time.

6. When there is good splitting in quicksort, the
resulting time is $O(n \log n)$. When there is bad
splitting in quicksort, the result can be quadratic time.

7. See "Quicksort—Choosing a Good Pivot Element" on page 601.

8. Your new quicksort method should have an if
statement that tests whether (n <= 15). If so,
then activate insertionsort; otherwise, proceed as in the original quicksort.

9. Change the heap rule so that the value in every
node is less than or equal to its children. Modify makeHeap to build this new kind of heap
by changing the test in the while-loop to this:
```
(k>0 && data[k] < data[parent(k)])
```
In reheapifyDown, change the series of if-
statements so that they find the index of the
smaller child. If this smaller child is less than
the current node, then swap the current node
with the smaller child and continue. Otherwise, the heap is okay.

PROGRAMMING PROJECTS

1 If you are familiar with Java's Comparable
interface (Programming Project 11 on page
481), then rewrite one of the sorting methods
so that it sorts an array of Comparable objects.
You may choose selectionsort, insertionsort,
mergesort, quicksort, or heapsort. For example,
with selectionsort you would have the specification shown here:

```
public static void selectionsort
(Comparable[ ] data, int first, int n)
// Precondition: data has at least n non-null
// components starting at data[first], and
// may all be compared with one another
// using their compareTo method.
// Postcondition: The elements of data
// have been rearranged so that
// data[first] <= data[first+1] <= ... <=
// data[first+n-1].
```

2 Redo the insertion sort algorithm so that the
values are inserted into a linked list rather
than an array. This eliminates the need to
move other values when a new value is inserted,
since your algorithm can simply insert a new node
where the new value should go. Analyze your algorithm to obtain a big-O expression of the worst-case
running time. Code your algorithm to produce a
complete Java program that reads in a list of ten integers, sorts the integers, and then writes out the
sorted list. Your program should allow the user to
repeat the process and sort another list until the user
says he or she wants to exit the program.

3 One of the advantages of mergesort is that it
can easily be adapted to sort a linked list of
values. This is because the algorithm retrieves
the values from the two lists being merged in the order that they occur in the lists. If the lists are linked

lists, then that algorithm can simply move down the list node after node. With heapsort or quicksort the algorithm needs to move values from random locations in the array so they do not adapt as well to sorting a linked list. Write a program that sorts a linked list of integers using mergesort. The program will read the integers into a linked list and then sort the linked list using mergesort. This will require additional linked lists, but you should use linked lists, not arrays, for all your list storage.

 Rewrite quicksort so that there are no recursive calls. The technique is to use a stack to keep track of which portions of the array still need to be sorted. Whenever we identify a portion of the array that still needs to be sorted, we will push two items onto the stack: (1) the starting index of the array segment, and (2) the length of the array segment. The entire quicksort can now work as follows (with no recursion):

1. Push `first` and n onto the stack (indicating that we must sort the n-element array segment starting at `data[first]`).
2. `while` (the stack is not empty)
   2a. Pop a size n and a starting index i off the stack. We must now sort the n-element array segment starting at `data[i]`. To do this sort, first use the assignment:
   `pivotIndex = partition(data,i,n);`
   2b. If the area before the pivot index has more than one element, then we must sort this area. This area begins at `data[i]` and has `pivotIndex-i` elements, so push i and `pivotIndex-i` onto the stack.
   2c. If the area after the pivot index has more than one element, then we must sort this area. Compute the starting point and length of this area in two local variables, and push their values onto the stack.

With this approach, in the worst case, the stack must be as big as the array that's being sorted. This worst case occurs when we keep pushing two-element array segments onto the stack. However, there is a modification that reduces the maximum stack size. When you do steps 2b and 2c, make sure that the *larger* array segment gets pushed onto the stack

first. With this modification, the maximum necessary stack size is just $2 \log_2 n$. With this in mind, you can use a stack with a fixed size—for example, a 100-element stack is enough to sort an array with 2^{50} elements.

5 The discussion on page 609 shows our algorithm for building the initial heap in the heapsort algorithm. The algorithm is reasonably efficient, but we can be even more efficient. The more efficient algorithm uses a method that creates a heap from a subtree of the complete binary tree. This method has the following specification:

```
private static void heapifySubtree(
    int[ ] data,
    int rootOfSubtree,
    int n
)
// Precondition: data is an array with at least
// n elements, and rootOfSubtree < n. We will
// consider data to represent a complete
// binary tree, and in this representation the
// node at data[rootOfSubtree] is the root of
// a subtree called s. This subtree s is already
// a heap, except that its root might be out of
// place.
// Postcondition: The subtree s has been
// rearranged so that it is now a valid heap.
```

You can write the `heapifySubtree` method yourself. Using this method, you can make an entire n-element array into a heap with the algorithm:

```
for (i = (n/2); i > 0; i--)
    heapifySubtree(data, i-1, n);
```

For example, with n=10, we will end up making the following sequence of activations:

```
heapifySubtree(data, 4, 10);
heapifySubtree(data, 3, 10);
heapifySubtree(data, 2, 10);
heapifySubtree(data, 1, 10);
heapifySubtree(data, 0, 10);
```

It turns out that this method is actually $O(n)$ rather than $O(n \log n)$.

For this project, reimplement `makeHeap`, as outlined above.

Software Reuse with Extended Classes

It is indeed a desirable thing to be well descended, but the glory belongs to our ancestors.

PLUTARCH
Morals

CHAPTER

13

Often you will find yourself with a class that is *nearly* what you require, but not quite. Perhaps the class that you require needs alterations to one or two of the methods of an existing class, or maybe an existing class just needs a few extra methods. Object-oriented languages provide support for this situation by allowing programmers to easily create new classes that acquire most of their properties from an existing class. The original class is called the **superclass** (or *parent* class, or *ancestor* class, or *base class*—the lingo isn't entirely stabilized), and the new, slightly different class is the **extended class** (or *derived* class, or *child* class, or *descendant* class, or *subclass*).

The first section of this chapter provides an introduction to extended classes. The next two sections show two detailed programming examples, including an illustration of how many of our previous ADTs might have benefited from using an extended class.

617

13.1 EXTENDED CLASSES

One of the exercises in Chapter 2 was a Clock class to keep track of one instance of a time value such as 9:48 P.M. (see Self-Test Exercise 5 on page 48). One possible specification for this class is shown in Figure 13.1—we're not concerned about the Clock implementation right now. Suppose you're writing a program with various kinds of clocks: 12-hour clocks, 24-hour clocks, alarm clocks, grandfather clocks, cuckoo clocks, maybe even a computer clock. Each of these things is a Clock, but each of these also has additional properties that don't apply to clocks in general. For example, a CuckooClock might have an extra method, isCuckooing, that returns true if its cuckoo bird is currently making noise. How would you implement a CuckooClock, which is a Clock with one extra isCuckooing method?

One possible solution uses no new ideas: Make a copy of the original Clock.java file, change the name of the class to CuckooClock, and add an extra method, isCuckooing. Can you think of some potential problems with this solution? We'll end up writing a separate class declaration for each different type of clock. Even though all of these clocks have similar or identical constructors and methods, we'll still end up repeating the method implementations for each different kind of clock.

FIGURE 13.1 | Specification for the Clock Class

Class Clock

❖ **public class Clock from the package edu.colorado.simulations**

A Clock object holds one instance of a time value such as 9:48 P.M.

Specification

◆ **Constructor for the Clock**
   public Clock( )
   Construct a Clock that is initially set to midnight.
   Postcondition:
   This Clock has been initialized with an initial time of midnight.

(continued)

(FIGURE 13.1 continued)

- **advance**

    ```
    public void advance(int minutes)
    ```
    Move this `Clock`'s time by a given number of minutes.

    Parameters:
    `minutes` – the amount to move this `Clock`'s time

    Postcondition:
    This `Clock`'s time has been moved forward by the indicated number of minutes. Note: A negative argument moves this `Clock` backward.

- **getHour**

    ```
    public int getHour( )
    ```
    Get the current hour of this `Clock`.

    Returns:
    the current hour (always in the range 1...12)

- **getMinute**

    ```
    public int getMinute( )
    ```
    Get the current minute of this `Clock`.

    Returns:
    the current minute (always in the range 0...59)

- **isMorning**

    ```
    public boolean isMorning( )
    ```
    Check whether this `Clock`'s time is before noon.

    Returns:
    If this `Clock`'s time lies from 12:00 midnight to 11:59 A.M. (inclusive), then the return value is `true`; otherwise the return value is `false`.

- **setTime**

    ```
    public void setTime(int hour, int minute, boolean morning)
    ```
    Set the current time of this `Clock`.

    Parameters:
    `hour` – the hour at which to set this `Clock`
    `minute` – the minute at which to set this `Clock`
    `morning` – indication of whether the new time is before noon

    Precondition:
    1 <= `hour` <= 12, and 0 <= `minute` <= 59.

    Postcondition:
    This `Clock`'s time has been set to the given hour and minute (using the usual 12-hour time notation). If the third parameter, `morning`, is `true`, then this time is from 12:00 midnight to 11:59 A.M. Otherwise this time is from 12:00 noon to 11:59 P.M.

    Throws: `IllegalArgumentException`
    Indicates that the `hour` or `minute` is illegal.

The solution to the clock problem is a new concept, called **extended classes**, described here:

Extended Classes

Extended classes use a concept called **inheritance**. In particular, once we have a class, we can then declare new classes that contain all of the methods and instance variables of the original class—plus any extras that you want to throw in. This new class is called an extended **class** of the original class. The original class is called the **superclass**. And the methods that the extended class receives from its superclass are called **inherited** methods.

How to Declare an Extended Class

In the declaration of an extended class, the name of the extended class is followed by the keyword `extends`, and then the name of the superclass. For example, suppose that we want to declare an extended class `CuckooClock` using the existing `Clock` class as the superclass. The beginning of the `CuckooClock` class declaration would then look like this:

```
public class CuckooClock extends Clock
{
    ...
```

This declaration indicates that every `CuckooClock` is also an ordinary `Clock`. The primary consequence is that all of the public methods and instance variables of an ordinary `Clock` are immediately available as public members of a `CuckooClock`. These members are said to be **inherited** from the `Clock`. Notice that it is the *public* members of the `Clock` that are accessible to the `Cuckoo-Clock`. In some sense, the private members of the `Clock` are also present in a `CuckooClock`—they must be present because some of the public methods access other private members. But, these private members cannot be accessed directly in a `CuckooClock`, not even by the programmer who implements a `CuckooClock`.

For future reference, you should know that there is another kind of access that can be provided to a method or instance variable. The access is called **protected**. In most respects, a protected member is just like a private member, but the programmer of an extended class has direct access to protected members. None of our examples will use protected members.

Now, let's finish our `CuckooClock` declaration and see how it can be used in a program. Our complete `CuckooClock` is shown in Figure 13.2. As you can see, a `CuckooClock` has one extra public method: a boolean method called `isCuck-ooing`, which returns `true` when the clock's cuckoo is making noise. In the implementation of `isCuckooing`, our cuckoos make noise whenever the current minute of the time is zero. In this implementation, we use the ordinary clock method, getMinute, to determine whether the current minute is zero.

Once the CuckooClock declaration is available, a program may declare CuckooClock objects using all the public Clock methods and also using the new isCuckooing method. In this usage, there are some special considerations for the constructors. We'll discuss these considerations next.

FIGURE 13.2	The CuckooClock Is an Extension of the Ordinary Clock

Class CuckooClock

- ❖ **public class CuckooClock from the package edu.colorado.simulations**
- ➤ **extends Clock**

A CuckooClock is a Clock that cuckoos when the minute is zero. The primary purpose of this class is to demonstrate how an extended class is implemented.

Specification

In addition to the Clock methods, a CuckooClock has:

- **isCuckooing**

     public boolean isCuckooing( )

     Check whether this CuckooClock is currently cuckooing.

     Returns:

     If this CuckooClock's current minute is zero, then the return value is true; otherwise the return value is false.

Implementation

```
//  File: CuckooClock.java from the package edu.colorado.simulations
//  Documentation is available at the top of this diagram or from the CuckooClock link in
//     http://www.cs.colorado.edu/~main/docs/

package edu.colorado.simulations;

public class CuckooClock extends Clock
{

    public boolean isCuckooing( )
    {
        return (getMinute( ) == 0);
    }

}
```

The Constructors of an Extended Class

An extended class may declare its own constructors, or it may use a no-arguments constructor that is inherited from the superclass. Other superclass constructors, with arguments, are not inherited by the extended class. For the cuckoo clock, the inherited no-arguments constructor, from the ordinary clock, is sufficient. For example, a program can allocate a new CuckooClock object with the statement:

```
CuckooClock noisy = new CuckooClock( );
```

This activates the inherited no-arguments constructor from the Clock to create a new CuckooClock.

Several important aspects of constructors for an extended class are:

1. If an extended class has new instance variables that are not part of the superclass, then an inherited no-arguments constructor will set these new values to their default values (such as zero for an int), and then do the work of the superclass's constructor.

2. Other superclass constructors, with arguments, are not inherited by the extended class.

3. If an extended class declares any constructors of its own, then none of the superclass constructors are inherited, not even the no-arguments constructor. Later we will examine the special format that should be used to write an extended class with its own declared constructors.

Using an Extended Class

We now know enough to write a bit of code that uses an extended class. For example, here is a bit of code that declares a cuckoo clock, advances the cuckoo clock some number of minutes, and then prints a message about whether the cuckoo clock is currently cuckooing:

```
CuckooClock noisy = new CuckooClock( );

noisy.advance(42);

System.out.print("The noisy clock's time is now ");
System.out.println
    (noisy.getHour( ) + ":" + noisy.getMinute( ));

if (noisy.isCuckooing( ))
    System.out.println("Cuckoo cuckoo cuckoo.");
else
    System.out.println("All's quiet on the cuckoo front.");
```

The key feature is that a cuckoo clock may use ordinary clock methods (such as `advance`), and it may also use the new `isCuckooing` method. The inheritance is accomplished with little work on our part. We only need to write the body of `isCuckooing`; none of the ordinary clock methods needs to be rewritten for the cuckoo clock.

There's another advantage to extended classes: An object of the extended class may be used at any location where the superclass is expected. For example, suppose you write a method to compare the times on two clocks, as shown in Figure 13.3. This method could be part of the `Clock` class or it could be

---

FIGURE 13.3   A Method to Compare the Time of Two Clocks

Implementation

```
public static boolean earlier (Clock c1, Clock c2)
// Postcondition: Returns true if the time on c1 is earlier than the time on c2
// over a usual day (starting at midnight and continuing to 11:59 P.M.); otherwise returns false.
{
    // Check whether one is morning and the other is not.
    if (c1.isMorning( ) && !c2.isMorning( ))
        return true;
    else if (c2.isMorning( ) && !c1.isMorning( ))
        return false;

    // Check whether one is 12 o'clock and the other is not.
    else if ((c1.getHour( ) == 12) && (c2.getHour( ) != 12))
        return true;
    else if ((c2.getHour( ) == 12) && (c1.getHour( ) != 12))
        return false;

    // Check whether the hours are different from each other.
    else if (c1.getHour( ) < c2.getHour( ))
        return true;
    else if (c2.getHour( ) < c1.getHour( ))
        return false;

    // The hours are the same, so check the minutes.
    else if (c1.getMinute( ) < c2.getMinute( ))
        return true;
    else
        return false;
}
```

implemented elsewhere. We can use this method to compare two ordinary clocks, but we can also compare objects of the clock's extended classes. For example, consider the code shown here:

```
CuckooClock sunrise = new CuckooClock( );
CuckooClock yourTime = new CuckooClock( );

...code that sets the clocks to some time...

if (earlier(sunrise, yourTime))
    System.out.println("That's before sunrise!");
else
    System.out.println("That's not before sunrise.");
```

In fact, we can even use the `earlier` method to compare an ordinary `Clock` with a `CuckooClock`, or to compare two objects from different extended classes.

Any methods that you write to manipulate a clock will also be able to manipulate all of the clock's extended classes. Without extended classes, we would need to write a separate method for each kind of clock that we want to manipulate.

Overriding Inherited Methods

Frequently, an extended class needs to perform some method differently from the way the superclass does. For example, the original clock provides the current hour via `getHour`, using a 12-hour clock. Suppose we want to implement an extended class that provides its hour on a 24-hour basis, ranging from 0 to 23. The new clock can be defined as an extended class called `Clock24`. The `Clock24` class inherits everything from the ordinary clock, but it provides a new `getHour` method. This is called **overriding** an inherited method.

To override an inherited method, the extended class redefines the method within its own class declaration. For example, the `Clock24` class in Figure 13.4 overrides the original `getHour` method of the original `Clock`. Within this implementation, we can use the name `super.getHour` to refer to the original `getHour` method of the superclass.

Programming Tip: Make the Overriding Method Activate the Original

In the example of the `Clock24` `getHour` method, the first action of the overriding method is to activate the original method. Generally, the overriding method will activate the original method to do some of its work. The reason is that the original method does work to correctly maintain the superclass. Frequently the activation of the original method will be the *first* action of an overriding method.

FIGURE 13.4	The Clock24 Class Overrides the Clock's getHour Method

Class Clock24

❖ **public class Clock24 from the package edu.colorado.simulations**
➤ **extends Clock**

A Clock24 object is a Clock with its hour in 24-hour format (0 to 23) instead of 12-hour format. The purpose is to show how an extended class may override a method of the superclass.

Specification

In addition to the Clock methods, a Clock24 object has:

• **getHour (overriden from the superclass Clock)**

```
public int getHour( )
```

Get the current hour of this Clock24, in 24-hour format.

Returns:

the current hour (always in the range 0...23)

Implementation

```
// File: Clock24.java from the package edu.colorado.simulations
// Documentation is available at the top of this diagram or from the Clock24 link in
//    http://www.cs.colorado.edu/~main/docs/

package edu.colorado.simulations;

public class Clock24 extends Clock
{
    public int getHour( )
    {
        int ordinaryHour = super.getHour( );

        if (isMorning( ))
        {
            if (ordinaryHour == 12)
                return 0;
            else
                return ordinaryHour;
        }
        else
        {
            if (ordinaryHour == 12)
                return 12;
            else
                return ordinaryHour + 12;
        }
    }
}
```

Widening Conversions for Extended Classes

In Java, assignments are allowed from an extended class to the superclass, for example:

```
Clock ordinary;
Clock24 scientific = new Clock24( );

scientific.advance(780);
ordinary = scientific;
```

Advance the scientific clock to 1 P.M. and assign the ordinary clock to equal the scientific clock.

The assignment `ordinary = scientific` is an example of a *widening conversion*, which we first saw in Chapter 5 on page 243. It is a widening conversion because the variable `ordinary` is capable of referring to many different kinds of clocks (an ordinary `Clock`, or a `CuckooClock`, or a `Clock24`), thus the `ordinary` variable has a wider variety of possibilities than the `scientific` variable (which may refer to a `Clock24` object only). Assigning an object of the extended class to a variable of the superclass is always permitted, and the assignment acts like any other Java assignment. After the above statements, both `ordinary` and `scientific` refer to the same clock, and this clock is the `Clock24` object that was allocated and advanced 780 minutes.

During the execution of a Java program, the Java runtime system keeps track of the class of each object. In the above code, the Java runtime system knows that the one clock object is really a `Clock24` object, so we might diagram the above situation like this (after the assignment statement):

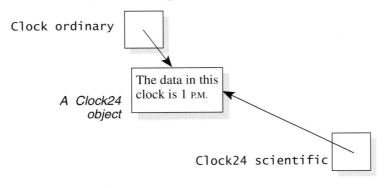

```
Clock ordinary
```

The data in this clock is 1 P.M.

A Clock24 object

```
Clock24 scientific
```

What happens if we activate `scientific.getHour( )`? The `Clock24` `getHour` method is activated (from Figure 13.4 on page 625), and the answer 13 is returned (which is the hour corresponding to 1 P.M.). That's not surprising since `scientific` was declared as a `Clock24` variable.

But what happens when we activate `ordinary.getHour( )`? In this situation, the answer is still 13, even though `ordinary` is declared as a `Clock` variable rather than a `Clock24` variable. Here's the reason:

How Java Methods Are Activated

When a program is running and a method is activated, the Java Runtime System checks the data type of the actual object, and uses the method from that type (rather than the method from the type of the reference variable).

This technique of method activation is called **dynamic method activation** because the actual method to activate is not determined until the program is running. A method that behaves like this is called a **virtual method**. Some programming languages, such as C++, allow both virtual methods (where the method to activate is determined by the actual object when the program is running) and nonvirtual methods (where the method to activate is determined by the type of the variable during the compilation). But Java has virtual methods only.

Narrowing Conversions for Extended Classes

Assignments are also permitted from a superclass to one of its extended types, but the compiler needs a bit of extra reassurance to permit the assignment. For example, suppose that `c` is a `Clock` variable and `fancy` is a `CuckooClock` variable. To make an assignment from `c` to `fancy` we must write

```
fancy = (CuckooClock) c;
```

The typecast `(CuckooClock) c` tells the compiler that the reference variable `c` is really referring to a `CuckooClock` object, even though it was declared as a `Clock`. With the typecast in place, the assignment always compiles correctly, though during the execution there is an extra check. When the assignment is executed, the Java Runtime System checks that `c` really does refer to a `Cuckoo-Clock`, and if it doesn't then a `ClassCastException` is thrown.

The assignment `fancy = (CuckooClock) c` is an example of a *narrowing conversion*, which we first saw in Chapter 5 on page 244. In Java, a narrowing conversion always requires a typecast to reassure the compiler that you really did mean to make that assignment. Even with the typecast, a programming error can cause a `ClassCastException` at runtime if the object is the wrong type.

Several features of extended classes remain to be seen, such as extended classes that require new private instance variables. These considerations will arise in the examples from the rest of this chapter.

Self-Test Exercises

1. Design and implement an extended class called `DaylightClock`. A daylight clock is like a clock except that it has one extra boolean method to determine whether it is currently daylight. Assume that daylight stretches from 7 A.M. through 6:59 P.M.

2. Using your `DayLightClock` from the previous exercise, write an example of a widening conversion and a narrowing conversion.

3. Suppose an extended class does not declare any constructors of its own. What constructors is it given automatically?

4. Design and implement an extended class called `NoonAlarm`. A noon alarm object is just like a clock, except that whenever the `advance` method is called to advance the clock forward through 12 o'clock noon, an alarm message is printed (by the `advance` method).

13.2 SIMULATION OF AN ECOSYSTEM

A is-a B means that A is a particular kind of B

There are many potential uses for extended classes, but one of the most frequent uses comes from the is-a relationship. "A is-a B" means that each A object is a particular kind of B object. For example, a cuckoo clock is a particular kind of clock. Some other examples of is-a relationships for living organisms are shown in Figure 13.5. The relationships are drawn in a tree called an **object hierarchy** tree. In this tree, each superclass is placed as the parent of its extended classes.

FIGURE 13.5 An Object Hierarchy

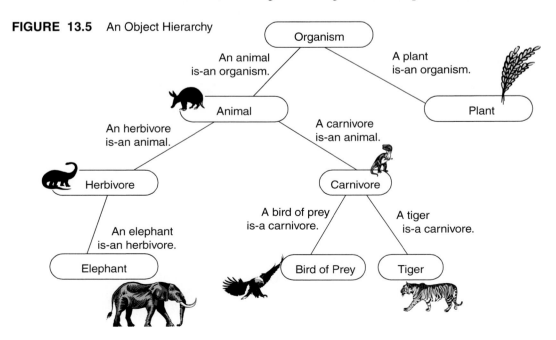

Programming Tip: When to Use an Extended Class

Look at each line in the object hierarchy tree (Figure 13.5). For each child and its parent, does it make sense to say "A is a B"? Whenever it makes sense to say "A is a B," consider implementing the class for A as an extended class of B. This lets the new A class benefit from inheriting all of B's public members.

Implementing Part of the Organism Object Hierarchy

We will implement four classes from the object hierarchy tree of living organisms, and use these four classes in a program that simulates a small ecosystem. The four classes that we will implement are:

- A general class, called Organism, that can be used by a program to simulate the simplest properties of organisms, such as being born, growing, and eventually dying.

- Two classes that are extended from an Organism. The classes, called Animal and Plant, can do everything that an ordinary organism can do—but they also have extra abilities associated with animals and plants.

- The final class, called Herbivore, is extended from the animal class. It is a special kind of animal that eats plants.

Keep in mind that the extended classes might have new instance variables as well as new methods.

The Organism Class

At the top of our object hierarchy tree is a class called Organism. Within a program, every organism is given an initial size, measured in ounces. Each organism is also given a growth rate, measured in ounces per week. A program that wants to simulate the growth of an organism will start by specifying an initial size and growth rate as arguments to the organism's constructor. Throughout the computation, the program may activate a method called simulateWeek, which causes the organism to simulate the passage of one week in its life—in other words, activating simulateWeek makes the organism grow by its current growth rate. The Organism class has a few other methods specified in Figure 13.6 on page 630, and a usage of the Organism class is shown in Figure 13.7 on page 632.

| **FIGURE 13.6** | Specification for the Organism Class |

Class Organism

❖ **public class Organism from the package edu.colorado.simulations**
   An Organism object simulates a growing organism such as a plant or animal.

Specification

• **Constructor for the Organism**
   ```
   public Organism(double initSize, double initRate)
   ```
   Construct an Organism with a specified size and growth rate.

   Parameters:
   initSize – the initial size of this Organism, in ounces
   initRate – the initial growth rate of this Organism, in ounces per week

   Precondition:
   initSize >= 0. Also, if initSize is zero, then initRate must also be zero.

   Postcondition:
   This Organism has been initialized. The value returned from getSize( ) is now initSize,
   and the value returned from getRate( ) is now initRate.

   Throws: IllegalArgumentException
   Indicates that initSize or initRate violates the precondition.

• **alterSize**
   ```
   public void alterSize(double amount)
   ```
   Change the current size of this Organism by a given amount.

   Parameters:
   amount – the amount to increase or decrease the size of this Organism (in ounces)

   Postcondition:
   The given amount (in ounces) has been added to the size of this Organism. If this new size
   is less than or equal to zero, then expire is also activated.

• **expire**
   ```
   public void expire( )
   ```
   Set this Organism's size and growth rate to zero.

   Postcondition:
   The size and growth rate of this Organism have been set to zero.

(continued)

(FIGURE 13.6 continued)

- **getRate**
  ```
  public double getRate( )
  ```
  Get the growth rate of this Organism.
  Returns:
  > the growth rate of this Organism (in ounces per week)

- **getSize**
  ```
  public double getSize( )
  ```
  Get the current size of this Organism.
  Returns:
  > the current size of this Organism (in ounces)

- **isAlive**
  ```
  public boolean isAlive( )
  ```
  Determine whether this Organism is currently alive.
  Returns:
  > If this Organism's current current size is greater than zero, then the return value is true; otherwise the return value is false.

- **setRate**
  ```
  public void setRate(double newRate)
  ```
  Set the current growth rate of this Organism.
  Parameters:
  > newRate – the new growth rate for this Organism (in ounces per week)

  Precondition:
  > If the size is currently zero, then newRate must also be zero.

  Postcondition:
  > The growth rate for this Organism has been set to newRate.

  Throws: IllegalArgumentException
  > Indicates that the size is currently zero, but the newRate is nonzero.

- **simulateWeek**
  ```
  public void simulateWeek( )
  ```
  Simulate the passage of one week in the life of this Organism.
  Postcondition:
  > The size of this Organism has been changed by its current growth rate. If the new size is less than or equal to zero, then expire is activated to set both size and growth rate to zero.

FIGURE 13.7	Sample Program from the Movie, *The Blob*

Java Application Program

```java
// FILE: Blob.java
// This small demonstration shows how the Organism class is used.
import edu.colorado.simulations.Organism

public class Blob
{
    public static void main(String[ ] args)
    {
        Organism blob = new Organism(20.0, 100000.0);
        int week;

        // Untroubled by conscience or intellect, the Blob grows for three weeks.
        for (week = 1; week <= 3; week++)
        {
            blob.simulateWeek( );
            System.out.print("Week " + week + ":" + " the Blob is ");
            System.out.println(blob.getSize( ) + " ounces.");
        }

        // Steve McQueen reverses the growth rate to -80000 ounces per week.
        blob.setRate(-80000.0);
        while (blob.isAlive( ))
        {
            blob.simulateWeek( );
            System.out.print("Week " + week + ":" + " The Blob is ");
            System.out.println(blob.getSize( ) + " ounces.");
            week++;
        }
        System.out.println("The Blob (or its son) shall return.");
    }

}
```

Sample Dialogue

```
Week 1: The Blob is 100020.0 ounces.
Week 2: The Blob is 200020.0 ounces.
Week 3: The Blob is 300020.0 ounces.
Week 4: The Blob is 220020.0 ounces.
Week 5: The Blob is 140020.0 ounces.
Week 6: The Blob is 60020.0 ounces.
Week 7: The Blob is 0.0 ounces.
The Blob (or its son) shall return.
```

Can anyone stop the Blob?!

Steve McQueen comes to the rescue at the end of week 3!

The `Organism` class has methods to set a new growth rate, a method to alter the organism's current size, and methods to return information about the organism's current size and growth rate.

The organism class is not hard to implement, and we'll leave its implementation up to you. But we will give one example of using the organism class. Movie buffs may recall the 1958 film, *The Blob*. The Blob came to Earth from outer space at a mere 20 ounces, but "untroubled by conscience or intellect," it absorbs anything and anyone in its path. Without giving away the whole plot, let's suppose that the Blob grows at the astonishing rate of 100,000 ounces per week for three weeks. Then our hero (Steve McQueen) manages to reverse its growth to a rate of negative 80,000 ounces per week. A program to simulate the movie plot is shown in Figure 13.7.

The Animal Class: An Extended Class with New Private Instance Variables

Now we want to implement a class that can be used to simulate an animal. Since an animal *is-an* organism, it makes sense to declare the `Animal` class as an extended class of the `Organism`. In our design, an animal is an organism that must consume a given amount of food each week to survive. If a week has passed and the animal has consumed less than its required amount of food, then death occurs. With this in mind, the `Animal` class will have two new private instance variables, which are not part of the `Organism` class, as shown at the front of this partial declaration:

```
public class Animal extends Organism
{
    private double needEachWeek;
    private double eatenThisWeek;

    We discuss the animal's public methods in a moment.
    ...
```

the extended class has two new private instance variables

The first new instance variable, `needEachWeek`, keeps track of how many ounces of food the animal must eat each week in order to survive. The second new instance variable, `eatenThisWeek`, keeps track of how many ounces of food the animal has eaten so far this week.

When an extended class has some new instance variables, it will usually need a new constructor to initialize those instance variables. This is the first example that we have seen where an extended class has a new constructor rather than using the inherited constructors that were described on page 622.

How to Provide a New Constructor for an Extended Class

When an extended class has a new constructor, the implementation of the new constructor appears in the class declaration, just like any other constructor. The inherited no-arguments constructor can no longer be used to create an object of the extended class.

In the case of the animal, the new constructor will have three arguments. The first two arguments are the same as the arguments for any organism, providing the initial size and the initial growth rate. The third argument will indicate how much food the animal needs, in ounces per week. Thus, the start of the animal's declaration is given here:

```
public class Animal extends Organism
{
    public double needEachWeek;
    public double eatenThisWeek;

    public Animal
    (double initSize, double initRate, double initNeed)
    ...
```

The constructor has no argument for `eatenThisWeek`, since we plan to have that instance variable initialized to zero, indicating that a newly constructed animal has not yet eaten.

The work of the animal's constructor is easy enough to describe: The first two arguments must somehow initialize the size and growth rate of the animal; the last argument initializes `needEachWeek`; the value of `eatenThisWeek` is initialized to zero. But how do we manage to use `initSize` and `initRate` to initialize the size and growth rate of the animal? Most likely the size and growth rate are stored as private instance variables of the `Organism` class, but the animal has no direct access to the organism's private instance variables.

Java provides a solution to this problem, called a **super constructor.** A super constructor is any constructor of the superclass. Usually, a constructor for an extended class will activate the super constructor in its first line of code. This is done with the keyword `super`, followed by the argument list for the super constructor.

Here is the implementation of our animal constructor, with the activation of the super constructor highlighted:

```
public Animal
(double initSize, double initRate, double initNeed)
{
    super(initSize, initRate);
    if (initNeed < 0)
        throw new IllegalArgumentException("negative need");
    needEachWeek = initNeed;
    // eatenThisWeek will be given its default value of zero.
}
```

If a constructor for an extended class does not activate the super constructor, then Java arranges for the superclass's no-arguments constructor to be automatically activated at the start of the extended class's constructor.

The Other Animal Methods

The animal has four new methods that deal with eating, and the `simulateWeek` method must also be overridden. The four new methods are called `assign-Need`, `eat`, `stillNeed`, and `getNeed`. We'll discuss each of these methods now.

The `assignNeed` method. This method has this heading:

```
void assignNeed(double newNeed)
```

The method is activated when a simulation needs to specify how much food an animal must eat to survive a week. For example, if `spot` is an animal that needs 30 ounces of food to survive a week, then `spot.assignNeed(30)` is activated. During a simulation, the food requirements may change, so that `assignNeed` can be activated several times with different arguments.

The eat method. Whenever the animal, `spot`, eats `m` ounces of food, the method `spot.eat(m)` records this event. Here's the heading of the method:

```
void eat(double amount)
```

The amount of food that has been eaten during the current week is stored in a private instance variable, `eatenThisWeek`. So, activating `eat(m)` will simply add `m` to `eatenThisWeek`.

Two accessor methods. There are two animal methods that are accessor methods called `getNeed` and `stillNeed`. The `getNeed` method returns the total amount of food that the animal needs in a week, and the `stillNeed` method returns the amount of food that the animal still needs in the current week (which is the total need minus the amount already eaten).

Overriding the `simulateWeek` method. The animal must do some extra work in its `simulateWeek` method. Therefore, it will override the organism's `simulateWeek` method. The animal's `simulateWeek` will first activate `super.simulateWeek` to carry out whatever work an ordinary organism does to simulate one week. Next, the animal's `simulateWeek` determines whether the animal has had enough food to eat this week. If `eatenThisWeek` is less than `needEachWeek`, then `expire` is activated. Also, `eatenThisWeek` is reset to zero to restart the recording of food eaten for the animal's next week.

At the top of the next page, we show some example code to illustrate the coordination of the new methods. It begins by declaring a 160-ounce animal, `spot` (perhaps a cat). Spot is not currently growing (since `initRate` is zero in the constructor), but she does require 30 ounces of food per week.

```
Animal spot = new Animal(160, 0, 30);

spot.eat(10);                              Spot catches a 10-ounce fish
spot.eat(25);                              and steals 25 ounces of
spot.simulateWeek( );                      chicken from the kitchen.
if (spot.isAlive( ))
    System.out.println("Spot lives!");     Spot still lives at the
else                                       end of her first week.
    System.out.println("Spot has died.");


spot.eat(10);                              Spot catches another 10-ounce
spot.eat(15);                              fish, but gets only 15 ounces
spot.simulateWeek( );                      of chicken this week.
if (spot.isAlive( ))
    System.out.println("Spot lives!");     Sadly, Spot dies at the
else                                       end of her second week.
    System.out.println("Spot has died.");
```

The specification and implementation for the animal appears in Figure 13.8. Since the animal is in the same package as the organism (edu.colorado.simulations), there is no need to import the Organism class.

The next class that we'll build is a class to simulate a plant. The Plant class is extended from an organism, and it has one extra method—but the work is left up to you in the next few exercises.

Self-Test Exercises

5. Draw an object hierarchy diagram for various kinds of people.

6. Declare a new class called Plant, extended from Organism with one extra method:

    > void NibbledOn(double amount)
    > // *Precondition: 0 <= amount <= getSize( ).*
    > // *Postcondition: The size of this Plant has been decreased by*
    > // *amount. If this reduces the size to zero, then expire is activated.*

Suppose fern is a plant. Activating fern.NibbledOn(m) corresponds to some beast eating m ounces of fern. Notice that NibbledOn differs from the existing alterSize method, since in the NibbledOn method, the amount is removed from the size (rather than adding to the size), and there is also a strict precondition on the amount eaten. The nibbledOn implementation should activate alterSize to do some of its work.

Your Plant class should have one constructor with the same parameters as the Organism constructor. The plant's constructor merely activates the super constructor with these same parameters.

7. Write a static method with one argument, which is a Java `Vector`, as shown in this header:

```
public static double totalMass(Vector organisms)
```

The method's precondition requires that every object in the `Vector` is a non-null `Organism`. The return value is the total mass of all these organisms. You may need to read more about the `Vector` class in Appendix D.

FIGURE 13.8 The Animal Class

Class Animal

❖ **public class Animal from the package edu.colorado.simulations**
➤ **extends Organism**

An `Animal` is an `Organism` with extra methods that deal with eating.

Specification

In addition to the `Organism` methods, an `Animal` has a new constructor and these new methods:

- **Constructor for the Animal**
  ```
  public Animal(double initSize, double initRate, double initNeed)
  ```
  Construct an `Animal` with a specified size, growth rate, and weekly eating need.

  Parameters:
  `initSize` – the initial size for this `Animal`, in ounces
  `initRate` – the initial growth rate for this `Organism`, in ounces per week
  `initNeed` – the initial weekly eating requirement for this `Animal`, in ounces per week

  Precondition:
  `initSize >= 0` and `initNeed >= 0`. Also, if `initSize` is zero, then `initRate` must also be zero.

  Postcondition:
  This `Animal` has been initialized. The value returned from `getSize( )` is now `initSize`, the value returned from `getRate( )` is now `initRate`, and this `Animal` must eat at least `initNeed` ounces of food each week to survive.

  Throws: `IllegalArgumentException`
  Indicates that `initSize`, `initRate`, or `initNeed` violates the precondition.

(continued)

(FIGURE 13.8 continued)

◆ **eat**

    `public void eat(double amount)`

    Have this `Animal` eat a given amount of food.

    Parameters:

      amount – the amount of food for this `Animal` to eat (in ounces)

    Precondition:

      amount >= 0.

    Postcondition:

      The amount (in ounces) has been added to the food that this `Animal` has eaten this week.

    Throws: `IllegalArgumentException`

      Indicates that amount is negative.

◆ **getNeed**

    `public double getNeed( )`

    Determine the amount of food that this `Animal` needs each week.

    Returns:

      the total amount of food that this `Animal` needs to survive one week (measured in ounces)

◆ **setNeed**

    `public void setNeed(double newNeed)`

    Set the current growth weekly food requirement of this `Animal`.

    Parameters:

      newNeed – the new weekly food requirement for this `Animal` (in ounces)

    Precondition:

      newNeed >= 0.

    Postcondition:

      The weekly food requirement for this `Animal` has been set to newNeed.

    Throws: `IllegalArgumentException`

      Indicates that newNeed is negative.

◆ **simulateWeek (overriden from the superclass Organism)**

    `public void simulateWeek( )`

    Simulate the passage of one week in the life of this `Animal`.

    Postcondition:

      The size of this `Animal` has been changed by its current growth rate. If the new size is less than or equal to zero, then `expire` is activated to set both size and growth rate to zero. Also, if this `Animal` has eaten less than its need over the past week, then `expire` has been activated.

◆ **stillNeed**

    `public double stillNeed( )`

    Determine the amount of food that this `Animal` still needs to survive this week.

    Returns:

      the ounces of food that this `Animal` still needs to survive this week
      (which is the total need minus the amount eaten so far)   *(continued)*

(FIGURE 13.8 continued)

Implementation

```java
// File: Animal.java from the package edu.colorado.simulations
// Documentation is available on pages 637-638 or from the Animal link in
//    http://www.cs.colorado.edu/~main/docs/

package edu.colorado.simulations;

public class Animal extends Organism
{
    private double needEachWeek;    // Amount of food needed (in ounces per week)
    private double eatenThisWeek;   // Ounces of food eaten so far this week

    public Animal(double initSize, double initRate, double initNeed)
    {
        super(initSize, initRate);
        if (initNeed < 0)
            throw new IllegalArgumentException("negative need");
        needEachWeek = initNeed;
        // eatenThisWeek will be given its default value of zero.
    }

    public void eat(double amount)
    {
        if (amount < 0)
            throw new IllegalArgumentException("amount is negative");
        eatenThisWeek += amount;
    }

    public double getNeed( )
    {
        return needEachWeek;
    }

    public void setNeed(double newNeed)
    {
        if (newNeed < 0)
            throw new IllegalArgumentException("newNeed is negative");
        needEachWeek = newNeed;
    }
```

(continued)

(FIGURE 13.8 continued)

```
public void simulateWeek( )
{
    super.simulateWeek( );
    if (eatenThisWeek < needEachWeek)
        expire( );
    eatenThisWeek = 0;
}

public double stillNeed( )
{
    if (eatenThisWeek >= needEachWeek)
        return 0;
    else
        return needEachWeek - eatenThisWeek;
}
}
```

The Herbivore Class

We're almost ready to start designing a simulation program for a small ecosystem. The ecosystem will be a small pond containing weeds and weed-eating fish. The weeds will be modeled by the `Plant` class from Self-Test Exercise 6 on page 636, and the fish will be a new class that is extended from the animal class that we have just completed.

The new class for the fish, called `Herbivore`, is an animal that eats plants. This suggests that an herbivore should have one new method, which we call `nibble`. The method will interact with a plant that the herbivore is nibbling, and this plant is a parameter to the new method. Here is the specification:

- **nibble (from the Herbivore class)**
  ```
  public void nibble(Plant meal)
  ```
  Have this `Herbivore` eat part of a `Plant`.

  Parameters:
  `meal` - the `Plant` that will be partly eaten

  Postcondition:
  Part of the `Plant` has been eaten by this `Herbivore`, by activating both `eat(amount)` and `meal.nibbledOn(amount)`. The amount is usually half of the `Plant`, but it will not be more than 10% of this `Herbivore`'s weekly need nor more than the amount that this `Herbivore` still needs to eat to survive this week.

For example, suppose that `carp` is an `Herbivore`, and `bushroot` is a `Plant`. If we activate `carp.nibble(bushroot)`, then `carp` will eat some of `bushroot`, by activating two other methods: (1) its own `eat` method, and (2) the `bushroot.nibbledOn( )` method.

The `nibble` method follows a few rules about how much of the plant is eaten. The rules state that `carp.nibble(bushroot)` will usually cause `carp` to eat half of `bushroot`, but a single nibble will not eat more than 10% of the herbivore's weekly need nor more than the amount that the herbivore still needs to eat in order to survive the rest of the week. In an actual model, these rules would be determined from behavior studies of real herbivores.

The complete herbivore documentation is shown in Figure 13.9, along with the implementation of the herbivore's methods.

FIGURE 13.9 | The Herbivore Class

Class Herbivore

❖ **public class Herbivore from the package edu.colorado.simulations**
➤ **extends Animal**

    An `Herbivore` is an `Animal` with an extra method for eating a `Plant`.

Specification

In addition to the `Animal` methods, an `Organism` has a new constructor and the following new methods:

* **Constructor for the Herbivore**
  `public Herbivore(double initSize, double initRate, double initNeed)`
  This is the same as the `Animal` constructor.

* **nibble (from the Herbivore class)**
  `public void nibble(Plant meal)`
  Have this `Herbivore` eat part of a `Plant`.
  Parameters:
  `meal` - the `Plant` that will be partly eaten
  Postcondition:
  Part of the `Plant` has been eaten by this `Herbivore`, by activating both `eat(amount)` and `meal.nibbledOn(amount)`. The amount is usually half of the `Plant`, but it will not be more than 10% of this `Herbivore`'s weekly need nor more than the amount that this `Herbivore` still needs to eat to survive this week.

(continued)

(FIGURE 13.9 continued)

Implementation

```
// File: Herbivore.java from the package edu.colorado.simulations
// Documentation is available on the preceding page or from the Herbivore link in
//    http://www.cs.colorado.edu/~main/docs/

package edu.colorado.simulations;

public class Herbivore extends Animal
{
    public Herbivore(double initSize, double initRate, double initNeed)
    {
        super(initSize, initRate, initNeed);
    }

    public void nibble(Plant meal)
    {
        final double PORTION = 0.5;        // Eat no more than this portion of
                                           // the plant
        final double MAX_FRACTION = 0.1;   // Eat no more than this fraction of
                                           // the weekly need

        double amount;                     // How many ounces of the plant will
                                           // be eaten

        // Set amount to some portion of the Plant, but no more than a given maximim fraction
        // of the total weekly need, and no more than what this Herbivore still needs to eat this
        // week.
        amount = PORTION * meal.getSize( );
        if (amount > MAX_FRACTION * getNeed( ))
            amount = MAX_FRACTION * getNeed( );
        if (amount > stillNeed( ))
            amount = stillNeed( );

        // Eat the Plant.
        eat(amount);
        meal.nibbledOn(amount);
    }
}
```

The Pond Life Simulation Program

A simulation program can use objects such as our herbivores to predict the effects of changes to an ecosystem. We'll write a program along these lines to model the weeds and fish in a small pond. The program stores the pond weeds in a collection of plants. To be more precise, we have Java `Vector` that will contain all the `Plant` objects of the simulation program. Check Appendix D if you need information on the `Vector` collection class.

For example, suppose the pond has 2000 weeds with an initial size of 15 ounces each and a growth rate of 2.5 ounces per week. Then we will create a `Vector` of 2000 plants, as shown here:

```
public static final int    MANY_WEEDS = 2000;
public static final double WEED_SIZE  =   15;
public static final double WEED_RATE  =  2.5;
...
Vector weeds = new Vector(MANY_WEEDS);

int i; // Loop control variable

for (i = 0; i < MANY_WEEDS; i++)
   weeds.addElement( new Plant(WEED_SIZE, WEED_RATE) );
```

Let's start our explanation of this code with the highlighted expression `new Plant(WEED_SIZE, WEED_RATE)`. This expression uses the `new` operator to allocate a new `Plant` object. After the type name, `Plant`, we have an argument list (WEED_SIZE, WEED_RATE). This is the form of `new` that allocates a new plant using a constructor with two arguments WEED_SIZE and WEED_RATE. The statement `weeds.addElement(new Plant(WEED_SIZE, WEED_RATE) )` is executed 2000 times in the code. Each of the 2000 allocations results in a new plant, and references to these 2000 plants are placed in the `weeds` `Vector`.

Our simulation has a second `Vector`, called `fish`, which is a `Vector` of `Herbivore` objects. Initially, we'll stock the fish `Vector` with 300 full-grown fish.

With the weeds and fish in place, our simulation may proceed. Throughout the simulation, various fish nibble on various weeds. Each week, every weed increases by its growth rate (stated as 2.5 ounces/week in the code). Some weeds will also be nibbled by fish, but during our simulation no weed will ever be completely eaten, so the weeds never die, nor do we ever create new weeds beyond the initial 2000. On the other hand, the number of fish in the pond may vary throughout the simulation. When a fish dies (because of insufficient nibbling), the reference to that fish is removed from the fish `Vector`. New fish are also born each week at a rate that we'll explain in a moment. For now, though, you should be getting a good idea of the overall simulation. Let's lay out these ideas precisely with some pseudocode.

// Pseudocode for the pond life simulation

1. Create a bunch of new plants, and put the references to these new plants in a `Vector` called `weeds`. The exact number of weeds, their initial size, and their growth rate are determined by static constants called `MANY_WEEDS`, `WEED_SIZE`, and `WEED_RATE`.

2. Create a bunch of new herbivores, and put the references to these new herbivores in a `Vector` called `fish`. The number of fish and their initial size are determined by static constants `INIT_FISH` and `FISH_SIZE`. In this simple simulation, the fish will not grow (their growth rate is zero), and their weekly need will be their initial size times a static constant called `FRACTION`.

3. For each week of the simulation, we will first cause some randomly selected fish to nibble on randomly selected weeds. On average, each fish will nibble on `AVERAGE_NIBBLES` weeds (where `AVERAGE_NIBBLES` is yet another constant in our program). After all these nibbles, we will activate `simulateWeek` for each fish and each weed. Dead fish will be removed from the fish `Vector`. At the end of the week, we will give birth to some new fish. The total number of newly spawned fish is the current number of fish times a constant called `BIRTH_RATE`. To simplify the simulation, we will have the new fish born fully grown with a growth rate of zero.

At the end of each week (simulated in Step 3), our program prints a few statistics. These statistics show the number of fish that are currently alive and the total mass of the weeds.

Our program implementing the pseudocode is given in Figure 13.10. The top of the program lists the various constants that we have mentioned, from `MANY_WEEDS` to `BIRTH_RATE`. Within the program, we use two static methods to carry out some subtasks. One of the methods, called `pondWeek`, carries out the simulation of one week in the pond, as described in Step 3 of the pseudocode. The other method, `totalMass`, computes the total mass of all the plants in the pond.

We discuss some implementation details starting on page 648.

FIGURE 13.10	The Pond Life Simulation

Java Application Program

```
// FILE: PondLife.java
// A simple simulation program to model the fish and weeds in a pond

import edu.colorado.simulations.*; // Provides Organism, Plant, Herbivore classes
import java.util.Vector;

public class PondLife
{
    // Number of weeds in the pond
    public static final int MANY_WEEDS = 2000;

    // Initial size of each weed, in ounces
    public static final double WEED_SIZE = 15;

    // Growth rate of weeds, in ounces/week
    public static final double WEED_RATE = 2.5;

    // Initial number of fish in the pond
    public static final int INIT_FISH = 300;

    // Fish size, in ounces
    public static final double FISH_SIZE = 50;

    // A fish must eat FRACTION times its size during one week, or it will die.
    public static final double FRACTION = 0.5;

    // Average number of weeds nibbled by a fish over a week
    public static final int AVERAGE_NIBBLES = 30;

    // At the end of each week, some fish have babies. The total number of new fish born is the
    // current number of fish times the BIRTH_RATE (rounded down to an integer).
    public static final double BIRTH_RATE = 0.05;

    // Number of weeks to simulate
    public static final int MANY_WEEKS  = 38;
```

(continued)

(FIGURE 13.10 continued)

```java
public static void main(String[ ] args)
{
    Vector fish = new Vector(INIT_FISH);     // A Vector of our fish
    Vector weeds = new Vector(MANY_WEEDS);   // A Vector of our weeds
    int i;                                   // Loop control variable

    // Initialize the Vectors of fish and weeds
    for (i = 0; i < INIT_FISH; i++)
        fish.addElement(new Herbivore(FISH_SIZE, 0, FISH_SIZE * FRACTION));
    for (i = 0; i < MANY_WEEDS; i++)
        weeds.addElement(new Plant(WEED_SIZE, WEED_RATE));

    // Print headings for the output, using tabs (\t) to separate columns of data
    System.out.println("Week \tNumber \tPlant Mass");
    System.out.println("     \tof     \t(in ounces)");
    System.out.println("     \tFish");

    // Simulate the weeks
    for (i = 1; i <= MANY_WEEKS; i++)
    {
        pondWeek(fish, weeds);
        System.out.print(i + "\t");
        System.out.print(fish.size( ) + "\t");
        System.out.print((int) totalMass(weeds) + "\n");
    }
}

public static double totalMass(Vector organisms)
{
    int i;
    double answer = 0;
    Organism next;

    for (i = 0; i < organisms.size( ); i++)
    {
        next = (Organism) organisms.elementAt(i);
        if (next != null)
            answer += next.getSize( );
    }
    return answer;
}
```

(continued)

(FIGURE 13.10 continued)

```java
public static void pondWeek(Vector fish, Vector weeds)
{
       int i;
       int manyIterations;
       int index;
       Herbivore nextFish;
       Plant nextWeed;

       // Have randomly selected fish nibble on randomly selected plants
       manyIterations = AVERAGE_NIBBLES * fish.size( );
       for (i = 0; i < manyIterations; i++)
       {
          index = (int) (Math.random( ) * fish.size( ));
          nextFish = (Herbivore) fish.elementAt(index);
          index = (int) (Math.random( ) * weeds.size( ));
          nextWeed = (Plant) weeds.elementAt(index);
          nextFish.nibble(nextWeed);
       }

       // Simulate the weeks for the fish
       i = 0;
       while (i < fish.size( ))
       {
          nextFish = (Herbivore) fish.elementAt(i);
          nextFish.simulateWeek( );
          if (nextFish.isAlive( ))
              i++;
          else
              fish.removeElementAt(i);
       }

       // Simulate the weeks for the weeds
       for (i = 0; i < weeds.size( ); i++)
       {
          nextWeed = (Plant) weeds.elementAt(i);
          nextWeed.simulateWeek( );
       }

       // Create some new fish, according to the BIRTH_RATE constant
       manyIterations = (int) (BIRTH_RATE * fish.size( ));
       for (i = 0; i < manyIterations; i++)
          fish.addElement(new Herbivore(FISH_SIZE, 0, FISH_SIZE * FRACTION));
    }
}
```

Pondlife—Implementation Details

The implementations of `totalMass` and `pondWeek` are part of Figure 13.10. The `pondWeek` implementation requires the ability to grab a random element out of a `Vector`, and this is accomplished by generating a random integer via the `Math.random` method.

Both `totalMass` and `pondWeek` require the ability to step through the items of a `Vector` one at a time. This could be accomplished by using an `Iterator` (as discussed in Section 5.4), but we just stepped through the elements one at a time in a for-loop, using the `elementAt` method. For example, within the `pondWeek` method, we activate `simulateWeek` for each plant by using the for-loop, as shown here:

```
// Simulate the weeks for the weeds.
for (i = 0; i < weeds.size( ); i++)
{
    nextWeed = (Plant) weeds.elementAt(i);
    nextWeed.simulateWeek( );
}
```

Notice that the return value from `elementAt` is a Java `Object`, so we need the typecast to assure the compiler that this is an acceptable narrowing conversion to a `Plant`. A similar loop steps through the fish, simulating one week for each fish and removing dead fish.

Using the Pond Model

No doubt you have noticed that our pond model is not entirely rooted in reality. For example, each fish is born full grown and does not continue to grow. Some extensions to make the model more realistic are given in the Programming Projects of this chapter. Nevertheless, even our simple program illustrates the principles of simulation programs. Let's look at one way that a simulation program such as ours could be used.

Suppose that your friend Judy owns a pond with 2000 weeds, about 15 ounces each. And perhaps the pond is too choked with weeds for Judy's taste. One way to control the weeds is to introduce a weed-eating species of fish, and the pond life program can help us predict what will happen when a certain number of fish are put in the pond. For example, suppose we have a species of fish where the program's constants (Figure 13.10 on page 645) are accurate. When we run the program with these constants, we get the output in Figure 13.11 on page 649.

Actually, if you run the program, you may get slightly different output because of the use of the random factor in the selection of which fish nibble which weeds. What does the program predict will happen in the pond if we introduce 300 of this kind of fish? Each output line gives the fish population and the plant mass at the end of one more week. The model predicts that the mass of the weeds will decrease fairly rapidly. This is followed by a period of some oscillation in both the fish and plant populations, including a rather catastrophic week for the fish when their population drops from 359 to 144. Sudden declines such as this are observed in real ecosystems when a species is allowed to expand, limited only by its food supply.

This kind of model can provide predictions and test theories of interactions in an ecosystem. It's also important to remember that any predictions are only as accurate as the underlying model.

Self-Test Exercises

8. Write code to declare a Vector. Put ten new organisms in the Vector, with an initial size of 16 ounces and a growth rate of 1 ounce per week. Grab five random organisms, and alter their growth rates to 2 ounces per week. Finally, calculate the total of all the organisms' growth rates, and print the result.

9. In the previous exercise, you started with ten organisms growing at 1 ounce per week. Five random organisms had their growth rates changed to 2 ounces per week, so you might think that the total of all the organisms' rates would be 5*1 + 5*2, which is 15. But when I ran the program, the total was only 14. Why?

10. What advantages did we get by storing the fish and weeds in vectors rather than in a partially filled array?

FIGURE 13.11	Pond Life Results

Sample Output

Week	Number of Fish	Plant Mass (in ounces)
1	315	27500
2	330	24625
3	346	21375
4	363	17725
5	379	13654
6	359	9286
7	144	6462
8	109	7960
9	112	10245
10	117	12445
11	122	14520
12	128	16470
13	134	18270
14	140	19920
15	147	21420
16	154	22745
17	161	23895
18	169	24870
19	177	25645
20	185	26220
21	194	26595
22	203	26745
23	213	26670
24	223	26345
25	234	25770
26	245	24920
27	257	23795
28	268	22374
29	281	20674
30	292	18656
31	306	16356
32	313	13720
33	301	10984
34	244	8689
35	189	7812
36	163	8225
37	161	9176
38	164	10159

11. Design and implement a new class extended from the `Animal` class. The new class, called `Carnivore`, has one new method with the heading shown here:

```
public void chase(Animal prey, double chance)
```

When `chase(prey, chance)` is activated for some carnivore, the carnivore chases the prey. The probability of actually catching the prey is given by the parameter `chance` (which should lie between 0 and 1—for example 0.75 for a 75% chance). If the prey is actually caught, then this will also activate the carnivore's `eat` method and (sadly) activate the prey's `expire` method.

Note: You can use the `Math.random` method to determine whether the animal is caught, as shown here:

```
if (Math.random( ) < chance)
{
    || Code for catching and eating the prey
}
```

13.3   USING EXTENDED CLASSES FOR ADTS

Many ADTs from previous chapters can be implemented as extended classes, resulting in less programming and less debugging—an all around good way to reuse previous work. For example, consider the stack ADT from Section 6.1. Many of the stack operations are similar to the sequence ADT that you first implemented in Section 3.3, and later revised in Section 4.5.

Now suppose that you have implemented a sequence class with documentation shown in Figure 13.12. This version of the sequence class is implemented with a linked list, and it stores a collection of Java objects. We don't really care about the details of the implementation—in fact, perhaps some other programmer implemented this sequence, and we don't have access to the implementation details.

Our question is this: *Is there some way that the sequence class can be used to quickly implement a new stack class?* Yes. A new stack class can be implemented as an extended class, using the `LinkedSequence` class as the superclass. The plan is for the stack to push and pop items from only one end of the list, ignoring many of the other features of a sequence.

| FIGURE 13.12 | Documentation for a Sequence Class |

Class LinkedSeq

❖ **public class LinkedSeq from the package edu.colorado.collections**

A LinkedSeq is a sequence of references to Objects. The sequence can have a special "current element," which is specified and accessed through four methods that are not available in the bag classes (start, getCurrent, advance and isCurrent).

Limitations:

Beyond Int.MAX_VALUE elements, the size method does not work.

Specification

♦ **Constructor for the LinkedSeq**

```
public LinkedSeq( )
```

Initialize an empty sequence.

Postcondition:

This sequence is empty.

♦ **addAfter and addBefore**

```
public void addAfter(Object element)
public void addBefore(Object element)
```

Adds a new element to this sequence, either before or after the current element.

Parameters:

element – a reference to the new element that is being added

Postcondition:

A reference to the element has been added to this sequence. If there was a current element, then addAfter places the new element after the current element and addBefore places the new element before the current element. If there was no current element, then addAfter places the new element at the end of the sequence and addBefore places the new element at the front of the sequence. In all cases, the new element becomes the new current element of the sequence. Note that the newly added element may be a null reference.

Throws: OutOfMemoryError

Indicates insufficient memory to increase the size of this sequence.

(continued)

(FIGURE 13.12 continued)

♦ addAll

```
public void addAll(LinkedSeq addend)
```
Place the contents of another sequence at the end of this sequence.

Parameters:
addend – a sequence whose contents will be placed at the end of this sequence

Precondition:
The parameter, addend, is not null.

Postcondition:
The elements from addend have been placed at the end of this sequence. The current element of this sequence remains where it was, and the addend is also unchanged.

Throws: `NullPointerException`
Indicates that addend is null.

Throws: `OutOfMemoryError`
Indicates insufficient memory to increase the size of this sequence.

♦ advance

```
public void advance( )
```
Move forward, so that the current element is now the next element in the sequence.

Precondition:
`isCurrent( )` returns `true`.

Postcondition:
If the current element was already the end element of the sequence (with nothing after it), then there is no longer any current element. Otherwise, the new element is the element immediately after the original current element.

Throws: `IllegalStateException`
Indicates that there is no current element, so advance may not be activated.

♦ clone

```
public Object clone( )
```
Generate a copy of this sequence.

Returns:
The return value is a copy of this sequence. Subsequent changes to the copy will not affect the original, nor vice versa. The return value must be type cast to a `LinkedSeq` before it is used.

Throws: `OutOfMemoryError`
Indicates insufficient memory for creating the clone.

(continued)

(FIGURE 13.12 continued)

◆ **concatenation**

```
public static LinkedSeq concatenation(LinkedSeq s1, LinkedSeq s2)
```
Create a new sequence that contains all the elements from one sequence followed by another.

Parameters:

s1 and s2 – two sequences

Precondition:

Neither s1 nor s2 is null.

Returns:

a new sequence that has the elements of s1 followed by s2 (with no current element)

Throws: NullPointerException

Indicates that one of the arguments is null.

Throws: OutOfMemoryError

Indicates insufficient memory for the new sequence.

◆ **getCurrent**

```
public Object getCurrent( )
```
Accessor method to determine the current element of the sequence.

Precondition:

isCurrent( ) returns true.

Returns:

the current element of the sequence

Throws: IllegalStateException

Indicates that there is no current element.

◆ **isCurrent**

```
public boolean isCurrent( )
```
Accessor method to determine whether this sequence has a specified current element that can be retrieved with the getCurrent method.

Returns:

true (there is a current element) or false (there is no current element at the moment)

◆ **removeCurrent**

```
public boolean removeCurrent( )
```
Remove the current element from this sequence.

Precondition:

isCurrent( ) returns true.

Postcondition:

The current element has been removed from the sequence, and the following element (if there is one) is now the new current element. If there was no following element, then there is now no current element.

Throws: IllegalStateException

Indicates that there is no current element, so removeCurrent may not be activated.

(continued)

(FIGURE 13.12 continued)

- **size**

  ```
  public long size( )
  ```
  Accessor method to determine the number of elements in this sequence.

  Returns:
    the number of elements in this sequence

- **start**

  ```
  public void start( )
  ```
  Set the current element at the front of the sequence.

  Postcondition:
    The front element of this sequence is now the current element (but if the sequence has no elements at all, then there is no current element).

Pushing and Popping for the Extended Stack Class

Our new stack class will extend the `LinkedSeq` class from Figure 13.12. The extension will add new methods so that a programmer can use the extended class as if it were a stack. A programmer can also use our new stack as if it were an object of the superclass, `LinkedSeq`.

Our plan is to have the extended class act like a stack by "pushing" and "popping" elements from the head of the sequence that is maintained by the superclass. Also, each time a push or pop occurs, the "current element" of the sequence will be set to the front of the sequence. With this plan, the push and pop of the extended can be implemented as shown here:

```
public void push(Object element)
{
   start( );
   addBefore(element);
}

public Object pop( )
{
   Object answer;

   if (size( ) < 0)
       throw new EmptyStackException( );
   start( );
   answer = getCurrent( );
   removeCurrent( );
   return answer;
}
```

Notice that within the implementations, the methods of the superclass can be activated just like any other method.

The documentation and implementation for the new stack class are shown in Figure 13.13. We have also included the stack's isEmpty and peek methods, so that the resulting stack has all the important stack methods from Figure 6.1 on page 281. The approach we have taken is similar to Java's own stack (java.util.Stack), which is extended from java.util.Vector. There are two other points that you should notice about the new stack, involving the constructor and the clone method.

The constructor.   Notice that the new stack does not declare its own constructor. Therefore, it can automatically use the no-arguments constructor of its superclass. For example, a program can make the declaration

```
DerivedStack s = new DerivedStack( );
```

Cloning a DerivedStack.   We did not implement a clone method for the DerivedStack. However, the superclass, LinkedSeq, implements the Cloneable interface, and it has a clone method. Therefore, the extended class also inherits the clone method, and we can clone a DerivedStack object. With this example in mind, we can now explain the pattern that must be used for every clone method that you implement. The pattern, introduced in Chapter 2 on page 78, looks like this:

```
public Object clone( )
{
    Location answer;

    try
    {
        answer = (Location) super.clone( );
    }
    catch (CloneNotSupportedException e)
    {
        throw new InternalError(e.toString( ));
    }
    ...other work that needs to modify the answer...
```

When we write all of our clone methods with this pattern, each clone activation will eventually activate the clone method from Java's Object class. And this clone method always creates an object of the correct type (of the same type as the object that activated clone in the first place). Therefore, if s is a DerivedStack, then s.clone( ) will return an object that is really a DerivedStack (and not just a LinkedSeq object).

FIGURE 13.13	The Stack Class Derived from LinkedSeq

Class DerivedStack

❖ **public class DerivedStack from the package edu.colorado.collections**
➤ **extends LinkedSeq**

A DerivedStack is a LinkedSeq that can easily be used as if it were a stack of Objects.

Specification

In addition to the LinkedSeq methods, a DerivedStack object has:

◆ **isEmpty**
```
public boolean isEmpty( )
```
Determine whether this stack is empty.
Returns:
true if this stack is empty; otherwise false.

◆ **peek**
```
public Object peek( )
```
Get the top item of this stack, without removing the item.
Precondition:
This stack is not empty.
Returns:
the top element of the stack (and sets the current element to the head of the sequence)
Throws: EmptyStackException
Indicates that this stack is empty.

◆ **pop**
```
public Object pop( )
```
Get the top element, removing it from this stack.
Precondition:
This stack is not empty.
Postcondition:
The return value is the top item of this stack, and the element has been removed. The new current element of the sequence is the element that used to be second.
Throws: EmptyStackException
Indicates that this stack is empty.

◆ **push**
```
public void push(Object element)
```
Push a new item onto this stack.
Parameters:
item – the item to be pushed onto this stack
Postcondition:
The item has been pushed onto this stack (and it is now the current element of the sequence)
Throws: OutOfMemoryException
Indicates insufficient memory for pushing a new item onto this stack.   *(continued)*

(FIGURE 13.13 continued)

Implementation

```
// FILE: DerivedStack.java from the package edu.colorado.geometry
// Documentation is available on the previous page or from the DerivedStack link in
//    http://www.cs.colorado.edu/~main/docs/

package edu.colorado.collections;
import java.util.EmptyStackException;

public class DerivedStack extends LinkedSeq
{
    public boolean isEmpty( )
    {
        return (size( ) == 0);
    }

    public Object peek( )
    {
        if (size( ) < 0)
            throw new EmptyStackException( );
        start( );
        return getCurrent( );
    }

    public Object pop( )
    {
        Object answer;

        if (size( ) < 0)
            throw new EmptyStackException( );
        start( );
        answer = getCurrent( );
        removeCurrent( );
        return answer;
    }

    public void push(Object element)
    {
        start( );
        addBefore(element);
    }

}
```

Self-Test Exercises

12. Our original stack from Chapter 6 has a `size` method. Does a `Derived-Stack` have a `size` method?

13. Suppose that you are implementing an extended class called `Tribble`. The superclass, called `Willis`, implements the `Cloneable` interface and `Tribble` does not override the `clone` method. If `t` is a `Tribble`, then what is the actual data type of the `Object` returned by `t.clone( )`? (To read more about Willis, you'll have to track down *Red Planet* by Robert A. Heinlein.)

14. Implement a new method of the stack class. The method has one parameter, `i`, and the precondition requires the stack to contain at least `i` elements. The method returns the element that is `i` positions from the top of the stack, and it sets the current element of the sequence to this element. For example, an argument of 1 will return the top element, an argument of 2 returns the element under the top, and so on.

15. Which would be easier: to implement a bag as an extended class of the sequence, or to implement the sequence as an extended class of the bag?

CHAPTER SUMMARY

- Object-oriented programming supports the use of *reusable components* by permitting new *extended classes* to be declared that automatically *inherit* all members of an existing superclass.

- All members of a superclass are inherited by the extended class, but only the nonprivate members of the superclass can be accessed by the programmer who implements the extended class. This is why most of our examples of superclasses do not specify the precise form of the private members of the superclass.

- The connection between an extended class and its superclass can often be characterized by the *is-a* relationship. For example, an herbivore *is-a* particular kind of animal, so it makes sense to implement `Herbivore` as an extended class of the `Animal` superclass.

- When you implement a new class, ask yourself whether the new class is an example of an existing class with slightly different capabilities or extra capabilities. In these cases, the new class can be implemented as an extended class of the existing class.

FURTHER READING

This chapter has introduced the concept of extended classes and inheritance, which is a central concept for OOP programming. In your future programming, further inheritance is likely to be important. You can consult a comprehensive Java language guide such as *Just Java and Beyond* by Peter van der Linden.

1. The declaration for the extended class is shown here, along with the implementation of the new method:

```
public class DaylightClock
extends Clock
{
    public boolean isDay( )
    {
        if (isMorning( ))
            return (getHour( ) >= 7);
        else
            return (getHour( ) < 7);
    }
}
```

2. Suppose d is a DayLightClock and c is a Clock. The assignment c = d is a widening conversion. An example of a narrowing conversion is d = (DayLightClock) c.

3. It inherits the no-arguments constructor of the superclass.

4. The NoonAlarm overrides the advance method of the ordinary clock. Here is one solution:

```
public class NoonAlarm extends Clock
{
    public void advance(int minutes)
    {
        int untilNoon;

        // Calculate number of minutes until
        // noon.
        if (isMorning( ))
            untilNoon =
                60 * (12-getHour( ))
                - getMinute( );
        else if (getHour( ) != 12)
            untilNoon =
                60 * (24 - getHour( ))
                - getMinute( );
        else
            untilNoon =
                60 * 24
                - getMinute( );
```

```
        // Maybe print an alarm message.
        if (minutes >= untilNoon)
            System.out.print("!!");

        // Activate the superclass method.
        super.advance(minutes);
    }
}
```

5.

6. The Plant declaration is:

```
public class Plant extends Organism
{
    public Plant
    (double initSize, double initRate)
    {
        super(initSize, initRate);
    }

    public void
    NibbledOn(double amount)
    {
        if (amount < 0)
            throw new
            IllegalArgumentException
            ("amount is negative");
        if (amount > getSize( ))
            throw new
            IllegalArgumentException
            ("amount is too big");
        alterSize(-amount);
    }
}
```

7. See the solution in Figure 13.10 on page 646. Another approach would be to use the vector's iterator.

8. Here is one solution:
```
Vector blob = new Vector(10);
int i;
double answer;
Organism thing;

for (i = 1; i <= 10; i++)
  blobs.addElement
  (new Organism(16, 1));

for (i = 1; i <= 5; i++)
{
  thing = (Organism)
    blobs.elementAt
    ((int) Math.random( ) * 10);
  thing.setRate(2);
}

answer = 0;
for (i = 0; i <= 10; i++)
{
  thing =
    (Organism) blobs.elementAt(i);
  answer += things.getRate( );
}

System.out.println
(answer + " total of rates");
```

9. The random method must have selected one organism twice (and three other organisms were selected once each).

10. We didn't have to worry about the number of elements going beyond the size of the array. We also get to use various methods such as `removeElementAt`.

11. We'll leave some of this to you, but here is most of the new method:
```
public void chase
(Animal prey, double chance)
{
    ...check that chance is in 0...1
    if (Math.random() < chance)
    {
        eat(prey.getRate( ));
        prey.expire( );
    }
}
```

12. Yes. The `size` method is inherited.

13. `Tribble`

14. Here is one implementation:
```
public Object get(int i)
{
    int count;
    Item answer;

    start( );
    for (count=1; count<i; count++)
        advance( );

    answer = current( );

    return answer;
}
```

15. The easy task is to implement a bag as an extended class, with the sequence as the superclass.

PROGRAMMING PROJECTS

1 A *set* is like a *bag*, except that a set does not allow multiple copies of any element. If you try to insert a new copy of an item that is already present in a set, then the set simply remains unchanged. For this project, implement a set as a new class that is extended from one of your bags.

2 Rewrite the pond life program from Figure 13.10 on page 645 so that the values declared at the start of the program are no longer constant. The program's user should be able to enter values for all of these constants. Also, improve the program so that the fish are more realistic. In particular, the fish should be born at a small size and grow to some maximum size. Each fish should also have a weekly food requirement that is proportional to its current size.

3 Rewrite the pond life program from Figure 13.10 on page 645 so that the output is presented as a graph in an applet window.

The applet can use most of the same graphing techniques as the fractal applet from page 388 in Chapter 8. You should use different colors for graphing the populations of the weeds and the fish.

4 Extend the `Organism` object hierarchy from Section 13.2 so that there is a new class `Carnivore` as described in Self-Test Exercise 11 on page 650. Use the hierarchy in a model of life on a small island that contains shrubs, geese that eat the shrubs, and foxes that eat the geese. The program should allow the user to vary the initial conditions on the island (such as number of foxes, the amount of food needed to sustain a fox, and so on).

5 Implement a bag class as an extended class of a seqeunce. Use the sequence from Figure 13.12 on page 651.

Graphs

So many gods, so many creeds,
So many paths that wind and wind,
When just the art of being kind
Is all this sad world needs.

ELLA WHEELER WILCOX
The World's Need

CHAPTER
14

Graphs are the most general data structure in this text. In fact, it's fair to say that graphs are the ultimate commonly used data structure. Many of the data structures that you will study in the future can be expressed in terms of graphs. This chapter provides an introduction to graphs and their algorithms, including the implementation of a graph class in Java.

14.1 GRAPH DEFINITIONS

A graph, like a tree, is a nonlinear data structure consisting of nodes and links between the nodes. In the trees that we have already seen, the nodes are somewhat orderly: The root is linked to its children, which are linked to their children, and so on to the leaves. But in a graph, even this modicum of order is gone. Graph nodes may be linked in any pattern—or lack of pattern—dependent only upon the needs of an application.

graphs occur in several varieties, the simplest of which is an undirected graph

Graphs occur in several varieties. We'll start with the simplest form: *undirected graphs.*

Undirected Graphs

An undirected graph is a set of nodes and a set of links between the nodes. Each node is called a **vertex**, each link is called an **edge**, and each edge connects two vertices. Undirected graphs are drawn by putting a circle for each vertex and a line for each edge. For example, here is a drawing of an undirected graph with five vertices and six edges:

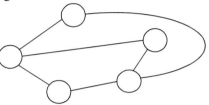

Often we'll need to refer to the vertices and edges of a graph, and we can do this by writing names next to each vertex and edge. For example, the following graph has vertices named v_0, v_1, v_2, v_3, and v_4, whereas its edges are named e_0, e_1, e_2, e_3, e_4, and e_5:

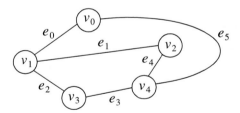

in a drawing, the placement of the vertices and edges is unimportant

In a drawing such as this, the actual placement of the vertices and edges is unimportant. The only important points are which vertices are connected and which edges are used to connect them. So, when you are feeling like a contortionist, you might draw the graph differently:

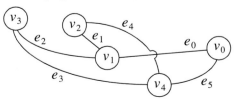

This is the same as the previous graph—we have just drawn it differently.

Here's a formal definition of these graphs:

Undirected Graphs

An **undirected graph** is a finite set of "vertices" together with a finite set of "edges." Both sets might be empty (no vertices and no edges), which is called the **empty graph**.

Each edge is associated with two vertices. We sometimes say that the edge **connects** its two vertices. The order of the two connected vertices is unimportant, so it does not matter whether we say "This edge connects vertices u and v," or "This edge connects vertices v and u."

An edge is even allowed to connect a single vertex to itself—we'll see examples of this later, and we'll also see several different variants of graphs. Many applications will require additional data to be attached to each vertex or to each edge, but even without these extras, we can give the flavor of a graph application with an example.

PROGRAMMING EXAMPLE: Undirected State Graphs

As an example of a problem where graphs are useful, we'll look at a little game. To start the game, you place three coins on the table in a line, as shown here:

     The start of the game

At the start of the game, the middle coin is "tails" and the other two are "heads." The goal is to change the configuration of the coins so that the middle coin is heads and the other two are tails, like this:

    The goal of the game

Now, this wouldn't be much of a game without a few good rules. Here are the rules:

1. You may flip the middle coin (from heads to tails or vice versa) whenever you want to.

2. You may flip one of the end coins (from heads to tails or vice versa) only if the other two coins are the same as each other (both heads or both tails).

You are not allowed to change the coins in any other way, such as shuffling them around. But within these rules you may flip coins. For example, if you start with the position *head-tail-head*, then the first rule allows you to flip the middle coin resulting in three heads:

From the start position,
flip the middle coin.

*a graph may
represent the
legal moves in
a game*

If you play the game for a while, you'll soon figure out how to get from the starting position (*head-tail-head*) to the goal position (*tail-head-tail*) within the limits of the rules. But our *real* goal is to figure out how a graph can aid in solving this kind of problem—even if the rules were beyond human manageability. The graph we'll use is called an undirected state graph, which is a graph where each of the vertices represents one of the possible configurations of the game. These configurations are called "states," and the coin game has eight states ranging from head-head-head to tail-tail-tail. Therefore, these eight states are the vertices of the state graph for the coin game. Figure 14.1 shows each vertex as a large oval so that we have room inside the oval to draw the state of the coins. Two vertices of the undirected state graph are connected by an edge whenever it is possible to move back and forth between the two states using one of the rules. For example, Rule 1 allows us to move between head-head-head and head-tail-head, so one of the edges in the graph goes from the topmost state in Figure 14.1 (head-head-head) to the state directly below it (head-tail-head). Figure 14.1 shows a total of eight edges: The four vertical edges come from Rule 1, and the four diagonal edges come from Rule 2. You may have noticed a curious fact about our rules: Whenever it is possible to move from one state to another (such as moving head-head-head to head-tail-head), it is also possible to move in the other direction (such as head-tail-head to head-head-head). If you

FIGURE 14.1   Undirected State Graph for the Coin Game

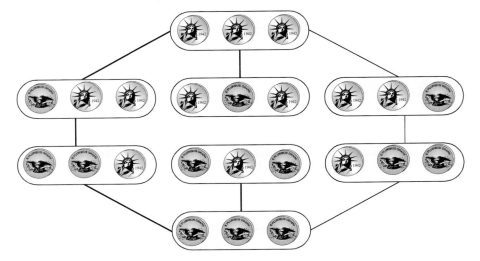

study the rules, you will see that this is true. The way we have drawn the edges reflects this symmetry. The edges are drawn as line segments connecting two vertices, with no indication as to which direction a movement must proceed. In this game, if an edge connects two vertices v_0 and v_1, then a movement is permitted in both directions, from v_0 to v_1, or from v_1 to v_0. This property of the coin game is the reason why we may use an undirected state graph. Later, we will see more complex games where movements might be permitted in only one direction, and hence we will need more complex graphs.

Once we know the undirected state graph, the game becomes a problem of finding a path from one vertex to another, where the path is allowed only to follow edges. According to our rules, we need to find a path from the vertex *head-tail-head* to the vertex *tail-head-tail*, and one such path consists of edges 1 through 5, highlighted here:

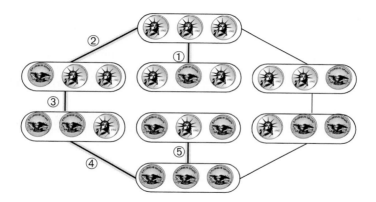

The coin game is a small problem, and the state graph isn't vital to the solution. But the important idea of the example goes beyond this small game.

Graphs in Problem Solving

Often, a problem can be represented as a graph, and the solution to the problem is obtained by solving a problem on the corresponding graph.

Because of this wide applicability of graphs, we will study many different kinds of graphs, exploring how to implement the graphs and how to solve problems such as "Is there a path from here to there?" The rest of this section shows the kinds of graphs we'll study and some of the problems that we'll solve.

Directed Graphs

The graphs we have seen so far are all *undirected*, which means that each edge connects two vertices with no particular orientation or direction. An edge just connects two vertices—there is no "first vertex" or "second vertex." But there is another kind of graph called a *directed graph*, where each edge has an orientation connecting its first vertex (called the edge's **source**) to its second vertex (the edge's **target**). Here is the formal definition of a directed graph:

Directed Graphs

A **directed graph** is a finite set of "vertices" together with a finite set of "edges." Both sets might be empty (no vertices and no edges), which is called the **empty graph**.

Each edge is associated with two vertices, called its **source** and **target** vertices. We sometimes say that the edge **connects** its source to its target. The order of the two connected vertices *is* important, so it *does* matter whether we say "This edge connects vertex *u* to vertex *v*," or "This edge connects vertex *v* to vertex *u*."

Directed graphs are drawn as diagrams with circles representing the vertices and *arrows* representing the edges. Each arrow starts at an edge's source and has the arrowhead at the edge's target, for example:

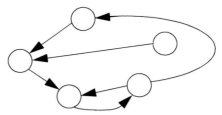

One application of directed graphs is a state graph for a game where reversing a move is sometimes forbidden. For such a game, the state graph might have an edge from a source v_1 to a target v_2 but *not* include the reverse edge from v_2 to v_1. This would indicate that the game's rules permit a move from state v_1 to state v_2, but not the other way around. For example, we could use a large state graph to represent the different states in a game of tic-tac-toe. Two of the many possible states are shown next, with a directed edge between them.

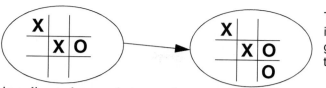

Two states
in the state
graph for
tic-tac-toe

There is a directed arrow between these two states, since it is possible to move
from the first state to the second state (by placing an O), but it is not possible to
move the other direction (since once an O is placed, it may not be removed).

More Graph Terminology

Loop. A **loop** is an edge that connects a vertex to itself. In the diagrams that
we've been using, this is drawn as a line (or arrow) with both ends at the same
location. The highlighted edges at the left of these two graphs are both loops:

Path. A **path** in a graph is a sequence of vertices, $p_0, p_1, \ldots p_m$, such that each
adjacent pair of vertices p_i and p_{i+1} are connected by an edge. In a directed
graph, the connection must go from the source p_i to the target p_{i+1}.

Multiple edges. In principle, a graph may have two or more edges connecting
the same two vertices in the same direction. These are called **multiple edges**. In
a diagram, each edge is drawn separately, for example:

Multiple edges in
an undirected
graph

Multiple
edges in a
directed
graph

Note that the two edges at the bottom of the directed graph are not multiple
edges because they connect the two vertices in different directions. Many applications do not require multiple edges. In fact, many implementations of graphs
do not permit multiple edges. Throughout the graph implementations of this
chapter, we will specify which implementations permit multiple edges and
which implementations forbid them.

Simple Graphs. The simplest of graphs have no loops and no multiple edges.
Appropriately enough, these graphs are called **simple** graphs. Many applications
require only simple directed graphs, or even simple undirected graphs.

Airline Routes Example

airline routes form a directed graph

Let's examine a directed graph that represents the flights of a small airline called Crocodile Airlines. Each vertex in the graph is a city, and each edge represents a regularly scheduled flight from one city to another. Crocodile's complete collection of flights is shown in Figure 14.2. Notice that the graph is directed; for example, it's possible to fly from Darwin to Canberra on a nonstop flight but not the other way around.

The point of expressing the flights as a graph is that questions about the airline can be answered by carrying out common algorithms on the graph. For example, a sheep farmer might wonder what is the fewest number of flights required to fly from Black Stump to Melbourne. This is an example of a *shortest path* problem that we will solve in Section 14.4. With a small graph such as Figure 14.2, you can probably see that the shortest path from Black Stump to Melbourne consists of four edges, but a manual examination might not suffice for a larger graph.

FIGURE 14.2   Crocodile Airlines Routes

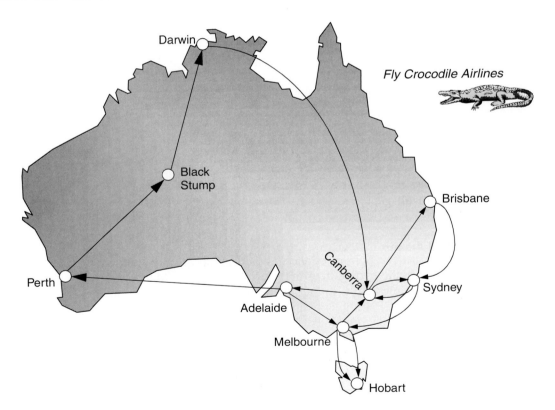

Self-Test Exercises

1. How many vertices and edges does the graph in Figure 14.2 have? How many loops? How would you interpret a loop in this graph?

2. Is Figure 14.2 a simple graph? Why or why not?

3. Suppose we have four coins in the coin game instead of just three. At the start of the game, the coins are in a line, with the two end coins heads and the other two coins tails. The goal is to change the configuration so that the two end coins are tails, and the other two coins are heads. There are three rules for this game: (1) Either of the end coins may be flipped whenever you want to; (2) A middle coin may be flipped from heads to tails only if the coin to its immediate right is already heads; (3) A middle coin may be flipped from tails to heads only if the coin to its immediate left is already tails. Your mission: Draw the directed state graph for this game, and determine whether it is possible to go from the start configuration to the goal. Why does the graph need to be directed?

14.2 GRAPH IMPLEMENTATIONS

"I could spin a web if I tried," said Wilbur, boasting. "I've just never tried."

E. B. WHITE
Charlotte's Web

Different kinds of graphs require different kinds of implementations, but the fundamental concepts of all graph implementations are similar. We'll look at several representations for one particular kind of graph: directed graphs in which loops are allowed. Some of the representations allow multiple edges, and some do not. In each of the representations, the vertices of the graph are named with numbers 0, 1, 2,..., so that we may refer to each vertex individually by saying "vertex 0," "vertex 1," and so on.

Representing Graphs with an Adjacency Matrix

Let's start with a directed graph with no multiple edges. The graph's edges may be represented in a square grid of boolean (`true`/`false`) values, called the graph's *adjacency matrix*. The top of the next page shows an example of a graph with four vertices and its adjacency matrix.

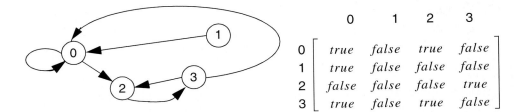

	0	1	2	3
0	*true*	*false*	*true*	*false*
1	*true*	*false*	*false*	*false*
2	*false*	*false*	*false*	*true*
3	*true*	*false*	*true*	*false*

a true component at row i and column j indicates an edge from vertex i to vertex j

Each component of the adjacency matrix indicates whether a certain edge is present. For example, is there an edge from vertex 0 to vertex 2? Yes, because `true` appears at row 0 of column 2. But is there also an edge from vertex 2 to vertex 0? No, because `false` appears at row 2 of column 0. The general rule for using an adjacency matrix is given here:

Adjacency Matrix

An **adjacency matrix** is a square grid of `true`/`false` values that represent the edges of a graph. If the graph contains *n* vertices, then the grid contains *n* rows and *n* columns. For two vertex numbers *i* and *j*, the component at row *i* and column *j* is `true` if there is an edge from vertex *i* to vertex *j*; otherwise the component is `false`.

Using a Two-Dimensional Array to Store an Adjacency Matrix

in a two-dimensional array, every component has two indexes

In Java, an adjacency matrix can be stored in a **two-dimensional array** in which every component has two indexes rather than the usual one index. Programmers usually view a two-dimensional array as a grid of elements, where the first index provides the row number of a component, and the second index provides the column number of a component. In a declaration of a two-dimensional array, the data type of the components is followed by two pairs of brackets, as shown here:

```
double[ ][ ] budget;
```

As with any array, the declaration just provides a reference variable that is capable of refering to a two-dimensional array. The actual array must be allocated with the new operator. For example, this allocates a two-dimensional array of double numbers with 12 rows and 8 columns, as declared here:

```
budget = new double [12][8];
```
Allocating a two-dimensional array with 12 rows and 8 columns.

Within the program, the individual components of a two-dimensional array can be accessed by providing both indexes. For example, we can assign the value 3.14 to row number 2 and column number 6 with this assignment statement:

```
budget[2][6] = 3.14;
```

As with an ordinary array, the index numbers begin with zero, so our `budget` has rows numbered from 0 to 11, and columns numbered from 0 to 7.

For an adjacency matrix, we use a two-dimensional array with one row and one column for each vertex of the graph. The components of the array are boolean `true`/`false` values. For example, the adjacency matrix for a graph with four vertices can be stored using this declaration of a two-dimensional array:

```
boolean[ ][ ] adjacent = new boolean[4][4];
```

The location `adjacent[i][j]` contains `true` if there is an edge from vertex *i* to vertex *j*. A `false` value indicates no edge. Edges of a graph can be added (by placing `true` in a location of the matrix) or removed (by placing `false`). Once the adjacency matrix has been set, an application can examine locations of the matrix to determine which edges are present and which are missing.

Representing Graphs with Edge Lists

Again, suppose we have a directed graph with no multiple edges. Such a graph can be represented by creating a linked list for each vertex. Here's an example:

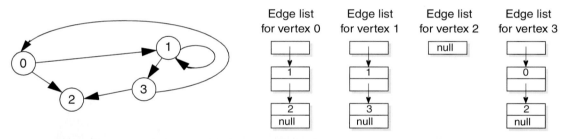

To understand the example, look at the linked list for vertex number 0. This list contains 1 and 2, which means that there is an edge from vertex 0 to vertex 1, and a second edge from vertex 0 to vertex 2. In general, the linked list for vertex number *i* is a list of vertex numbers following this rule:

Linked List Representation of Graphs

A directed graph with *n* vertices can be represented by *n* different linked lists. List number *i* provides the connections for vertex *i*. To be specific: For each entry *j* in list number *i*, there is an edge from *i* to *j*.

Loops are allowed in this representation; for example, look at the list for vertex 1 in the edge lists given above. Number 1 appears on this list itself, so there is an edge from vertex 1 to vertex 1 in the graph. We may also have vertices that are not the source of any edge—for example, vertex 2 in the graph above. Since vertex 2 is not the source of any edge, the edge list for vertex 2 is empty. If we allow the same element to appear more than once on the list, then multiple edges could also be allowed. But often, multiple edges are not allowed.

In a graph with n vertices, there are n edge lists. References to the heads of the n edge lists can be stored in an array of n node variables. When we need to determine whether an edge exists from vertex i to vertex j, we check to see whether j appears on list number i.

Representing Graphs with Edge Sets

Another implementation of graphs requires a previously programmed implementation of a set ADT. For example, suppose that we have declared `IntSet` as a class capable of holding a set of integers. Presumably, the set class has operations to add an integer, check whether an integer is in the set, remove an integer, and so forth. To represent a graph with 10 vertices, we can declare an array of 10 sets of integers, as shown here:

```
IntSet[ ] connections = new IntSet[10];
```

Using this representation, a set such as `connections[i]` contains the vertex numbers of all of the vertices to which vertex i is connected. For example, suppose that `connections[3]` contains the numbers 1 and 2. In this case, there is an edge from vertex 3 to vertex 1, and another edge from vertex 3 to vertex 2.

Which Representation Is Best?

If the space is available, then an adjacency matrix is easier to implement and generally easier to use than edge lists or edge sets. But sometimes there are other considerations. For example, how often will you be doing each of the following operations?

1. Adding or removing edges.
2. Checking whether a particular edge is present.
3. Iterating a loop that executes one time for each edge with a particular source vertex.

The first two operations require only a small constant amount of time with the adjacency matrices. But in the worst case, both (1) and (2) require $O(n)$ operations with the edge list representation (where n is the number of vertices). This worst case occurs when the operation must traverse an entire edge list, and that edge list might contain as many as n edges. With edge sets, both (1) and (2) might also require $O(n)$ operations—but this time could be cut to $O(\log n)$ by using a fast set representation such as B-trees from Section 10.2.

On the other hand, the edge lists are efficient for the third operation. With an edge list, the third operation can be carried out by simply stepping through the list one element at a time. The time required is $O(e)$, where e is the number of edges that have vertex i as their source. A good set ADT should also provide the operations to step through the elements of the set one at a time. In this way, both edge lists and edge sets are likely to require just $O(e)$ operations to step through the edges with a particular source vertex. But with an adjacency matrix, the act of stepping through the edges with source vertex i requires each component of row i to be examined. This traversal of the entire row is necessary just to see whether each entry is `true` or `false`. This always requires $O(n)$ time, where n is the number of vertices.

In general, your choice of representations should be based on your expectations as to which operations are most frequent. The availability of a previously programmed set ADT may also affect your choice. One last consideration is the average number of edges originating at a vertex. If each vertex has only a few edges (a so-called **sparse** graph), then an adjacency matrix is mostly wasted space filled with the value `false`.

PROGRAMMING EXAMPLE: **Labeled Graph ADT**

Now we'll implement a class called `Graph` for directed graphs with no multiple edges. This first ADT has only a few methods; for example, the number of vertices is set by the constructor and there is no way to add or remove vertices later. An n-vertex graph always has its vertices numbered from zero to $n-1$. This simple form of the first `Graph` class provides a sharp focus on graphs and their algorithms.

With our `Graph` class, there are methods to add or remove edges between the vertices. The edges are stored in an adjacency matrix, which is implemented as the two-dimensional boolean array called `edges`. The `edges` array is allocated within the constructor, based on the number of vertices that are required for the graph.

Even though we're implementing our graph using an adjacency matrix, the class will also have a method, called `neighbors`, that computes an edge list for a specified vertex. This edge list will be provided as an array of integers that contains all of the vertex numbers for the targets of edges that start at a specified source. Here's an example to show the integer array that's computed and returned by `g.neighbors(3)` for a particular graph:

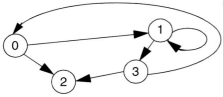

If g is the graph shown here,
then `g.neighbors(3)` returns the array:

0	2
[0]	[1]

This means that vertex 3 is the source of two edges, going to vertices 0 and 2.

The `neighbors` method may take $O(n)$ time to compute one of its arrays, but once an array is available, it can be used to quickly traverse all the neighbors of a vertex. Notice that the length of the array computed by `g.neighbors(i)` is equal to the number of edges that have vertex i as the source, and this could even be zero (resulting in the unusual occurrence of an array with zero components).

Our `Graph` class will have one extra feature: The vertices will have information attached to them in the same way that we attached information to tree nodes. For example, in the airline route graph of Figure 14.2 on page 670, each vertex is associated with a city name. The addition of information at each vertex makes the graph a **labeled graph**, and the information itself is called a vertex's **label**. Of course, the information might be any data type—integers, doubles, strings, you-name-it—which suggests that we should use Java's `Object` type for the labels. This does not allow us to use the eight primitive types for labels, though if we do want something like an integer label we could use the `Integer` wrapper class described on page 245.

The labels of the vertices will be stored in a private instance variable named `labels`, which is an ordinary one-dimensional array. The label for vertex number i will be stored in `labels[i]`. Thus, our graph implementation has a total of two instance variables, as shown here:

```
public class Graph
{
    private boolean[ ][ ] edges;
    private Object[ ] labels;

    We'll discuss the methods in a moment.

}
```

The Graph Constructor and `size` Method

When a graph is initialized with the constructor, it has a given number of vertices and no edges, as shown in this specification of the constructor:

♦ **Constructor for the Graph**
   `public Graph(int n)`
   Initialize a `Graph` with n vertices, no edges, and null labels.

   Parameters:
   n – the number of vertices for this `Graph`

   Precondition:
   n >= 0.

   Postcondition:
   This `Graph` has n vertices, numbered from 0 to n-1. It has no edges and all vertex labels are null.

   Throws: `OutOfMemoryError`
   Indicates insufficient memory to create this `Graph`.

   Throws: `NegativeArraySizeException`
   Indicates that n is negative.

The only work in the implementation is the allocation of the two instance variables, which are both arrays, as shown here:

```
public Graph(int n)
{
    edges = new boolean[n][n];   // All values initially false
    labels = new Object[n];      // All values initially null
}
```

After construction, the current number of vertices can be obtained from an accessor method named size.

Methods for Manipulating Edges

Two methods, addEdge and removeEdge, allow us to add and remove edges. One other method, called isEdge, determines whether a specified edge is present. The methods have these specifications:

- **addEdge —and— isEdge —and— removeEdge**
    ```
    public void addEdge(int source, int target)
    public boolean isEdge(int source, int target)
    public void removeEdge(int source, int target)
    ```
    Add an edge, test whether an edge exists, or remove an edge of this Graph.

    Parameters:
    source – the vertex number of the source of the edge
    target – the vertex number of the target of the edge

    Precondition:
    Both source and target are non-negative and less than size( ).

    Postcondition:
    For addEdge, the specified edge is added to this Graph (unless it was already present); for isEdge, the return value is true if the specified edge exists and false otherwise; for removeEdge, the specified edge is removed from this Graph (unless it was already not present).

    Throws: ArrayIndexOutOfBoundsException
    Indicates that the source or target was not a valid vertex number.

The implementations of these methods will be short. The addEdge method sets edges[source][target] to true, and the removeEdge method sets it to false. The isEdge method just returns the current value of edges[source][target]. In all cases, an illegal parameter will try accessing edges[source][target] and result in an ArrayIndexOutOfBoundsException.

As we have already discussed, there is also a method called neighbors to generate an array that contains an edge list for a specified vertex.

Methods for Manipulating Vertex Labels

There are two methods for setting and retrieving the label of a vertex:

- **getLabel**
  ```
  public Object getLabel(int vertex)
  ```
  Accessor method to get the label of a vertex of this Graph.
  Parameters:
  vertex – a vertex number
  Precondition:
  vertex is non-negative and less than size( ).
  Returns:
  The label of the specified vertex in this Graph.
  Throws: ArrayIndexOutOfBoundsException
  Indicates that the vertex was not a valid vertex number.

- **setLabel**
  ```
  public void setLabel(int vertex, Object newLabel)
  ```
  Change the label of a vertex of this Graph.
  Parameters:
  vertex – a vertex number
  newLabel – a vertex number
  Precondition:
  vertex is non-negative and less than size( ).
  Postcondition:
  The label of the specified vertex in this Graph has been changed to
  newLabel.
  Throws: ArrayIndexOutOfBoundsException
  Indicates that the vertex was not a valid vertex number.

For example, the following statements create the two-vertex graph shown in the picture. In this graph, vertex number zero (v_0) has the string "bar" as its label, and vertex number one (v_1) has the string "goo" as its label:

```
Graph t = new Graph(2);
```

```
t.setLabel(0, "bar"); // Provides vertex number 0 with label of "bar"
t.setLabel(1, "goo"); // Provides vertex number 1 with label of "goo"
t.addEdge(1, 0);       // Adds an edge from vertex 1 to vertex 0
```

Labeled Graph ADT—Implementation

The complete specification and implementation for the graph ADT are given in Figure 14.3. In addition to the methods that we have already mentioned, the Graph class also implements the Cloneable interface.

FIGURE 14.3 | Specification and Implementation of the Graph Class

Class Graph

❖ **public class Graph from the package edu.colorado.graphs**
   A Graph is a labeled graph with a fixed number of vertices.

Specification

- **Constructor for the Graph**
   ```
   public Graph(int n)
   ```
   Initialize a Graph with n vertices, no edges, and null labels.

   Parameters:
   n – the number of vertices for this Graph

   Precondition:
   n >= 0.

   Postcondition:
   This Graph has n vertices, numbered from 0 to n-1. It has no edges and all vertex labels are null.

   Throws: OutOfMemoryError
   Indicates insufficient memory to create this Graph.

   Throws: NegativeArraySizeException
   Indicates that n is negative.

- **addEdge —and— isEdge —and— removeEdge**
   ```
   public void addEdge(int source, int target)
   public boolean isEdge(int source, int target)
   public void removeEdge(int source, int target)
   ```
   Add an edge, test whether an edge exists, or remove an edge of this Graph.

   Parameters:
   source – the vertex number of the source of the edge
   target – the vertex number of the target of the edge

   Precondition:
   Both source and target are non-negative and less than size( ).

   Postcondition:
   For addEdge, the specified edge is added to this Graph (unless it was already present); for isEdge, the return value is true if the specified edge exists and false otherwise; for removeEdge, the specified edge is removed from this Graph (unless it was already not present).

   Throws: ArrayIndexOutOfBoundsException
   Indicates that the source or target was not a valid vertex number.

(continued)

(FIGURE 14.3 continued)

- **clone**

    ```
    public Object clone( )
    ```
    Generate a copy of this Graph.

    Returns:
    The return value is a copy of this Graph. Subsequent changes to the copy will not affect the original, nor vice versa. The return value must be type cast to a Graph before it is used.

    Throws: OutOfMemoryError
    Indicates insufficient memory for creating the clone.

- **getLabel**

    ```
    public Object getLabel(int vertex)
    ```
    Accessor method to get the label of a vertex of this Graph.

    Parameters:
    vertex – a vertex number

    Precondition:
    vertex is non-negative and less than size( ).

    Returns:
    The label of the specified vertex in this Graph.

    Throws: ArrayIndexOutOfBoundsException
    Indicates that the vertex was not a valid vertex number.

- **neighbors**

    ```
    public int[ ] neighbors(int vertex)
    ```
    Accessor method to obtain a list of neighbors of a specified vertex of this Graph.

    Parameters:
    vertex – a vertex number

    Precondition:
    vertex is non-negative and less than size( ).

    Returns:
    The return value is an array that contains all the vertex numbers of vertices that are targets of edges with a source at the specified vertex.

    Throws: ArrayIndexOutOfBoundsException
    Indicates that the vertex was not a valid vertex number.

(continued)

(FIGURE 14.3 continued)

◆ **setLabel**

```
public void setLabel(int vertex, Object newLabel)
```
Change the label of a vertex of this Graph.

Parameters:
vertex – a vertex number
newLabel – a vertex number

Precondition:
vertex is non-negative and less than size( ).

Postcondition:
The label of the specified vertex in this Graph has been changed to newLabel.

Throws: ArrayIndexOutOfBoundsException
Indicates that the vertex was not a valid vertex number.

◆ **size**

```
public int size( )
```
Accessor method to determine the number of vertices in this Graph.

Returns:
the number of vertices in this Graph

Implementation

```
// File: Graph.java from the package edu.colorado.graphs
// Complete documentation is on pages 679—680 or from the Graph link in
//    http://www.cs.colorado.edu/~main/docs/

package edu.colorado.graphs;

public class Graph implements Cloneable
{
    // Invariant of the Graph class:
    //    1. The vertex numbers range from 0 to labels.length-1.
    //    2. For each vertex number i, labels[i] contains the label for vertex i.
    //    3. For any two vertices i and j, edges[i][j] is true if there is a vertex from i to j;
    //       otherwise edges[i][j] is false.
    private boolean[ ][ ] edges;
    private Object[ ] labels;

    public Graph(int n)
    {
        edges = new boolean[n][n];   // All values initially false
        labels = new Object[n];      // All values initially null
    }
```

(continued)

(FIGURE 14.3 continued)

```java
public void addEdge(int source, int target)
{
    edges[source][target] = true;
}


public Object clone( )
{   // Clone a Graph object.
    Graph answer;

    try
    {
        answer = (Graph) super.clone( );
    }
    catch (CloneNotSupportedException e)
    {
        // This exception should not occur. But if it does, it would probably indicate a
        // programming error that made super.clone unavailable. The most common
        // error would be forgetting the "Implements Cloneable"
        // clause at the start of this class.
        throw new RuntimeException
        ("This class does not implement Cloneable");
    }

    answer.edges = (boolean [ ][ ]) edges.clone( );
    answer.labels = (Object [ ]) labels.clone( );

    return answer;
}


public Object getLabel(int vertex)
{
    return labels[vertex];
}


public boolean isEdge(int source, int target)
{
    return edges[source][target];
}
```

(continued)

(FIGURE 14.3 continued)

```java
public int[ ] neighbors(int vartex)
{
    int i;
    int count;
    int[ ] answer;

    // First count how many edges have the vertex as their source
    count = 0;
    for (i = 0; i < labels.length; i++)
    {
        if (edges[vertex][i])
            count++;
    }

    // Allocate the array for the answer
    answer = new int[count];

    // Fill the array for the answer
    count = 0;
    for (i = 0; i < labels.length; i++)
    {
        if (edges[vertex][i])
            answer[count++] = i;
    }

    return answer;
}

public void removeEdge(int source, int target)
{
    edges[source][target] = false;
}

public void setLabel(int vertex, Object newLabel)
{
    labels[vertex] = newLabel;
}

public int size( )
{
    return labels.length;
}
}
```

Self-Test Exercises

4. Write a new `Graph` method to remove a specified number of vertices from a graph. The removed vertices should be the k vertices with the highest numbers. Write another method to add a specified number of new vertices.

5. Write a new `Graph` method that interchanges two specified vertices. For example, after interchanging vertices i and j, the original neighbors of vertex i will now be neighbors of vertex j and vice versa.

6. We have assumed that there are no multiple edges in a graph, and therefore we could store simple `true/false` in the adjacency matrix. Describe how adjacency matrixes might be used even if the graphs do have multiple edges.

7. Compare and contrast adjacency lists and edge lists.

8. Write a static method with one `Graph` parameter g. The precondition requires that g has at least one vertex. The method's return value is the number of the vertex that is the source of the most edges. If there are several vertices with an equally high number of edges, then you may return whichever vertex number you prefer.

14.3 GRAPH TRAVERSALS

In the chapter on trees, we saw three different binary tree traversals. Each traversal visits all of a binary tree's nodes and does some processing at each node. The three traversals had similar recursive implementations, with the distinguishing factor being whether a node was visited before, after, or in between its two children. A graph vertex doesn't have children like a tree node, so the tree traversal algorithms are not immediately applicable to graphs. But there are two common ways of traversing a graph. One of the methods (breadth-first search) uses a queue to keep track of vertices that still need to be visited, and the other method (depth-first search) uses a stack. The depth-first search can also be implemented recursively in a way that does not explicitly use a stack of vertices.

when the traversal finishes, all of the vertices that can be reached from the start vertex have been processed

This section discusses the two traversal algorithms in a general way and then provides implementations of the algorithms to traverse a `Graph` object (using the `Graph` class (Figure 14.3 on page 679). Both of the traversal algorithms have the same underlying purpose: to start at one vertex of a graph (the "start" vertex), process the information contained at that vertex, and then move along an edge to process a neighbor. When the traversal finishes, all of the vertices that can be reached from the start vertex (via some directed path) have been processed.

A traversal algorithm must be careful that it doesn't enter a repetitive cycle—for example, moving from the start vertex to a neighbor, from there to the neighbor's neighbor, and possibly from there back to the starting point and back to the same neighbor, and back to the same neighbor's neighbor, and so on. To prevent this potential "spinning your wheels," we will include an ability to *mark* each vertex as it is processed. If a traversal ever returns to a vertex that is already marked, then reprocessing is not done. If we are drawing the graphs, then we might indicate a marked vertex by shading it. For example, suppose a traversal starts at vertex 0 of this graph:

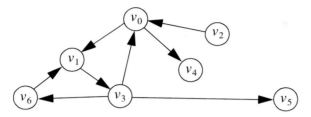

The traversal begins by processing vertex number 0. We don't really care what kind of processing occurs—maybe the labels are printed out, or perhaps there is more complicated processing. In any case, there will be some processing of vertex number 0, and then we will mark it as processed, looking like this:

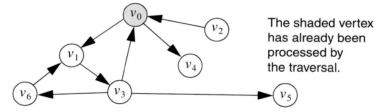

The shaded vertex
has already been
processed by
the traversal.

The progress of a traversal after the start vertex depends on the traversal method being used. We'll start by looking at how a depth-first search proceeds.

Depth-First Search

After processing vertex 0, a depth-first search moves along a directed edge to one of vertex 0's neighbors. In our example, there are two possibilities: moving to vertex 1 (along the edge from 0 to 1) or to vertex 4 (along the edge from 0 to 4). In our example, it is not possible to move from vertex 0 to 3, or from vertex 0 to 2, because the edges go in the wrong direction. So the traversal has a choice: Move to vertex 1 or move to vertex 4. Right now we won't worry about exactly how the choice is made—let's just assume that the next vertex processed is vertex 1. After processing vertex 1, the picture looks like this:

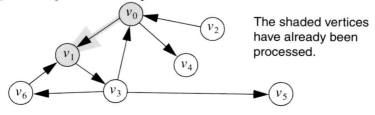

The shaded vertices
have already been
processed.

In the drawing we have highlighted the edge from vertex 0 to vertex 1 to indicate the intuitive notion of "moving from one vertex to another."

From here, the traversal moves to one of vertex 1's neighbors. You may think of vertex 1 as being at the "leading edge" of the depth-first traversal. It is the vertex that has most recently been processed, and so we will continue pushing forward from vertex 1, moving to one of vertex 1's unprocessed neighbors. In this example, there is only one unprocessed neighbor to consider, vertex 3. So we will move to vertex 3 and process it. At this point, we have processed three of the vertices, as shown here:

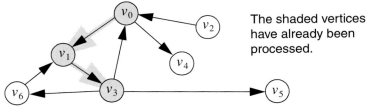

The shaded vertices have already been processed.

to prevent going around in circles, never move forward to a marked vertex

One of vertex 3's neighbors is vertex 0—but vertex 0 has already been marked as previously processed. So, to prevent the traversal from going around in circles, we will not move from 3 back to 0. In general, *we will never move forward to a marked vertex (since it has already been processed)*. But we will move to vertex 3's other neighbors (vertices 5 and 6). Suppose we move to vertex 5 first. After processing vertex 5, the picture looks like this:

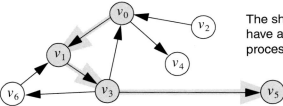

The shaded vertices have already been processed.

Since vertex 5 has no neighbors, the depth-first traversal cannot proceed forward any farther. Instead, the traversal comes back to see if the previous vertex—vertex 3—has any more unmarked neighbors:

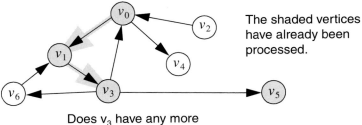

The shaded vertices have already been processed.

Does v_3 have any more unmarked neighbors?

In this drawing, you can see that four vertices have been processed. And the "leading edge" of the search has pulled back to vertex v_3. Does v_3 have any more unmarked neighbors where the search can proceed? Yes—v_6 is an unmarked neighbor of v_3, so again the search plunges forward, along the edge from v_3 to v_6. Vertex 6 is processed, giving the following picture:

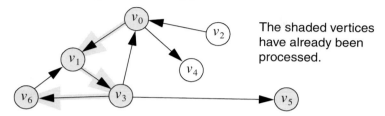

The shaded vertices have already been processed.

What now? Vertex 6 does have a neighbor—vertex 1—but v_1 has already been marked. So, since vertex 6 has no *unmarked* neighbors, the traversal again backs up to see if v_3 has any more unmarked neighbors. After the backup, we have this situation:

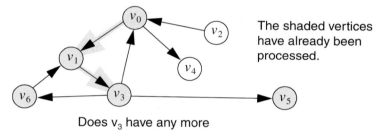

The shaded vertices have already been processed.

Does v_3 have any more unmarked neighbors?

Vertex 3 has no more unmarked neighbors (thank goodness!). So back we go to the previous vertex—vertex 1—to check whether it has any unmarked neighbors:

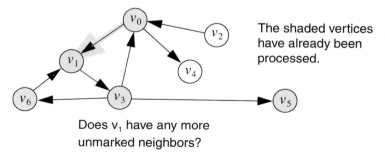

The shaded vertices have already been processed.

Does v_1 have any more unmarked neighbors?

You can see that the leading edge of the search is now at v_1, and that v_1 has no more unmarked neighbors, so back we go to vertex 0, to see if it has any unfinished business. This situation is drawn at the top of the next page.

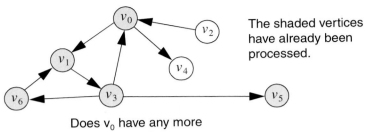

The shaded vertices
have already been
processed.

Does v_0 have any more
unmarked neighbors?

From vertex 0 we can still travel to the unmarked vertex 4 and process it, as shown here:

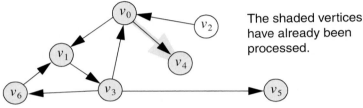

The shaded vertices
have already been
processed.

Vertex 4 has no neighbors, so we back up once more to vertex 0:

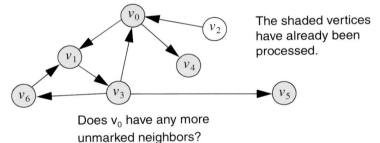

The shaded vertices
have already been
processed.

Does v_0 have any more
unmarked neighbors?

Vertex 0 has no more unmarked neighbors—and since this was the starting point there is no place left to back up to. That's the end of the traversal.

some vertices are not processed because they can't be reached from the start vertex

In this example, vertex 2 was never processed because there was no path from the start vertex (vertex 0) to vertex 2. A traversal processes only those vertices that can be reached from the start vertex.

There's one other important point about a *depth-first* search: From the start vertex, the traversal proceeds to a neighbor and from there to another neighbor and so on—always going as far as possible before it ever backs up. In describing this behavior, it seems as if there's a lot to keep track of: where we start, where we go from there, and where we go from there. But the actual implementation can use recursion to keep track of most of these details in a simple way. We'll tackle that recursive implementation after looking at an alternative method: breadth-first search.

Breadth-First Search

A breadth-first search uses a queue to keep track of which vertices might still have unprocessed neighbors. The search begins with a starting vertex, which is processed, marked, and placed in the queue. For example, suppose we are processing this graph with vertex 0 as our starting point, so that vertex 0 is the first vertex to be processed, marked, and placed into the queue:

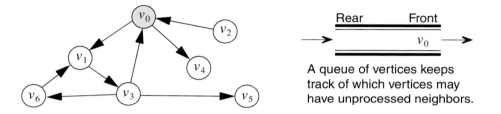

A queue of vertices keeps track of which vertices may have unprocessed neighbors.

Once the starting vertex has been processed, marked, and placed in the queue, the main part of the breadth-first search begins. This consists of repeatedly carrying out the following steps:

1. Remove a vertex, v, from the front of the queue.

2. For each unmarked neighbor, u of v: Process u, mark u, and then place u in the queue (since u may have further unprocessed neighbors).

These two steps are repeated until the queue becomes empty. Let's look at our example to see how these two steps are carried out when vertex 0 is at the head of the queue. The vertex 0 is removed from the queue, and we note that it has two unprocessed neighbors: vertices 1 and 4. Vertices 1 and 4 will each be processed, marked, and placed in the queue. Let's assume that vertex 1 is placed in the queue first, and then vertex 4. (The queuing could also occur the other way, with vertex 4 placed first; the algorithm is correct either way.) After 1 and 4 are in the queue, the situation looks like this:

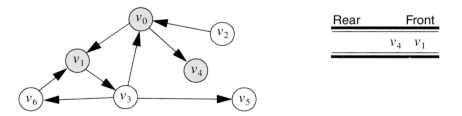

Since the queue still has entries, we repeat the two steps again: Remove the front entry (vertex 1), process and mark any unmarked neighbors of vertex 1, and enter these neighbors into the queue. The only unmarked neighbor of vertex

1 is vertex 3, so after processing, marking, and entering vertex 3, the situation looks like this:

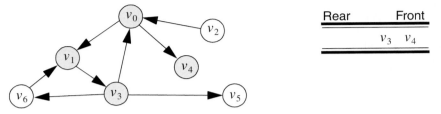

Next we remove vertex 4 from the front of the queue. Since vertex 4 has no neighbors, no new entries are processed or placed in the queue. The situation is now:

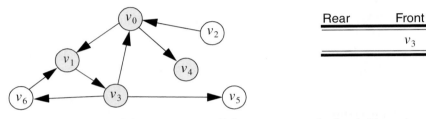

Vertex 3 comes out of the queue next. It has two unmarked neighbors (vertices 5 and 6) that are processed, marked, and placed in the queue, like this:

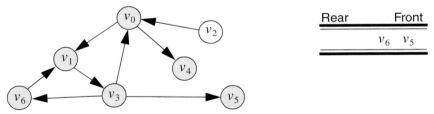

Notice that vertex 0 (which is also a neighbor of vertex 3) does not get reprocessed because it is already marked.

the effects of breadth-first and depth-first search are similar—only the order of processing vertices differs

At this point, we remove vertex 5 from the front of the queue, but it has no unmarked neighbors to worry about. We then remove vertex 6 from the queue. It also has no unmarked neighbors. The queue is finally empty, which ends the breadth-first search.

The effect of the breadth-first search is similar to the depth-first search: Vertices 0, 1, 3, 4, 5, and 6 have all been processed since they could all be reached from the starting point (vertex 0). Vertex 2 was not processed since there is no directed path from vertex 0 to vertex 2. However, the breadth-first search processes the vertices in a different order than the depth-first search. The breadth-first search first processed vertex 0, then processed the neighbors of the start point (1 and 4), then processed *their* neighbors (vertex 3), and so on. This contrasts with a depth-first search that processed the vertices 0, 1, 3, and 5 to start with (in that order).

You should now be able to carry out depth-first and breadth-first searches by hand on a directed graph. Next we will specify and implement the two searches as static methods that can print the labels of the vertices of a `Graph`.

Depth-First Search—Implementation

One way to print the labels of graph is with a depth-first search as specified in this static method:

- **depthFirstPrint**
  `public static void depthFirstPrint(Graph g, int start)`
  Static method to print the labels of a graph with a depth-first search.

  Parameters:
  `g` – a non-null `Graph`
  `start` – a vertex number from the `Graph` `g`

  Precondition:
  `start` is non-negative and less than `g.size( )`.

  Postcondition:
  A depth-first search of `g` has been conducted, starting at the specified `start` vertex. Each vertex visited has its label printed using `System.out.println`. Note that vertices that are not connected to the start will not be visited.

  Throws: `NullPointerException`
  Indicates that `g` is null.

  Throws: `ArrayIndexOutOfBoundsException`
  Indicates that the `start` was not a valid vertex number.

  Throws: `OutOfMemoryError`
  Indicates that there is insufficient memory for an array of boolean values used by this method.

In this specification, the parameter g may be any `Graph` with labels that can be printed by `System.out.println`. During a search, each time a vertex v is reached, that vertex is "processed" by activating `System.out.println` with the label of v as the argument.

The implementation of `depthFirstPrint` uses an array of boolean values declared as a local variable of the method, shown here:

```
boolean[ ] marked = new boolean[g.size( )];
```

This array has one component for each possible vertex of the graph g, and its purpose is to keep track of which vertices have been marked as visited by the search. In general, for a vertex number v, the component `marked[v]` is `true` if v has already been visited by the search, and `false` otherwise. The complete pseudocode for `depthFirstPrint` is short, as shown next.

pseudocode for depth-first search

1. Allocate the marked array (which automatically has all of its components set to `false`).
2. Activate a separate static method to actually carry out the search.

You may be wondering, "Why use a separate method in Step 2? Why can't we just carry out the search in the body of the `depthFirstPrint` method itself?" Good question. The answer is that we plan to use recursion: The start vertex is processed and then recursive calls are made to process each of the start vertex's neighbors. Further recursive calls are made to process the neighbors' neighbors, and so on. So, if the work were carried out in the body of the `depthFirstPrint` method, each time a recursive call is made, we would do Step 1—clearing the marked array—and . . . oops! Clearing the marked array at every recursive call will definitely lead to trouble.

The new method, executed in Step 2, will be called `depthFirstRecurse` with this specification:

> ♦ **depthFirstRecurse**
>
> ```
> public static void depthFirstRecurse
>     (Graph g, int v, boolean[ ] marked)
> ```
> Recursive method to carry out the work of `depthFirstPrint`.
>
> **Parameters:**
> g – a non-null Graph
> v – a vertex number from the Graph g
> marked – an array to indicate which vertices of g have already been visited
>
> **Precondition:**
> v is non-negative and less than g.size( ).
> marked.length is equal to g.size( ); for each vertex x of g, marked[x] is true if x has already been visited by this search; otherwise marked[x] is false. The vertex v is an unmarked vertex at which the search has just arrived.
>
> **Postcondition:**
> The depth-first search of g has been continued through vertex v and beyond to all vertices that can be reached from v via a path of unmarked vertices. Each vertex visited has its label printed using `System.out.println`.
>
> **Throws:** `NullPointerException`
> Indicates that g is null.
>
> **Throws:** `ArrayIndexOutOfBoundsException`
> Indicates that v was not valid, or marked was the wrong size.

Now let's examine the implementation of the `depthFirstRecurse` method. The first task is to mark and process the vertex v. After this we will examine each of v's neighbors. Each time we find an unmarked neighbor we will make a recursive call to continue the search through that neighbor and beyond. The phrase "and beyond" is important because if a neighbor has another unmarked neighbor, then there will be another recursive call at that level, and so on until we reach a vertex with no unmarked neighbors. This description of depthFirstRecurse is implemented at the top of Figure 14.4, and the actual depthFirstPrint method is implemented at the bottom of the figure.

Breadth-First Search—Implementation

The breadth-first search is implemented with a queue of vertex numbers. The start vertex is processed, marked, and placed in the queue. Then the following steps are repeated until the queue is empty: (1) remove a vertex, *v*, from the front of the queue, and (2) for each unmarked neighbor *u* of *v*: process *u*, mark *u*, and then place *u* in the queue (since *u* may have further unprocessed neighbors).

The implementation of this breadth-first search is Programming Project 1.

FIGURE 14.4   Depth-First Search

Implementations

```
public static void depthFirstRecurse(Graph g, int v, boolean[ ] marked)
{
    int[ ] connections = g.neighbors(v);
    int i;
    int nextNeighbor;

    marked[v] = true;
    System.out.println(g.getLabel(v));

    // Traverse all the neighbors, looking for unmarked vertices:
    for (i = 0; i < connections.length; i++)
    {
        nextNeighbor = connections[i];
        if (!marked[nextNeighbor])
            depthFirstRecurse(g, nextNeighbor, marked);
    }
}

public static void depthFirstPrint(Graph g, int start)
{
    boolean[ ] marked = new boolean[g.size( )];

    depthFirstRecurse(g, start, marked);
}
```

Self-Test Exercises

9. Do a depth-first search of the Australia graph (Figure 14.2 on page 670), starting at Sydney. List the order in which the cities are processed. Do the same for a breadth-first search.

10. Suppose you are doing a breadth-first search of a graph with n vertices. How large can the queue get?

11. What kind of search occurs if you replace breadth-first search's queue with a stack?

14.4 PATH ALGORITHMS

Determining Whether a Path Exists

Frequently, a problem is represented by a graph, and the answer to the problem can be found by answering some question about paths in the graph. For example, a network of computers can be represented by a graph, with each vertex representing one of the machines in the network, and each edge representing a communication wire between two machines. The question of whether one machine can send a message to another machine boils down to whether the corresponding vertices are connected by a path.

Either breadth-first search or depth-first search may be used to determine whether a path exists between two vertices u and v. The idea is to use u as the start vertex of the search and proceed with a breadth-first or depth-first search. If the vertex v is ever visited, then the search may stop and announce that there is a path from u to v. On the other hand, if v is never visited, then there is no path from u to v.

Graphs with Weighted Edges

Often we need to know more than just *"Does a path exist?"* In the network example, each edge represents a communication wire between machines. Such a wire might have a "cost" associated with using the wire. The cost could be the amount of energy required to use the path, or perhaps the amount of time required for the wire to transmit a message, or even a dollars-and-cents cost required to use the wire to send one message. In any case, there could be many paths from one vertex to another, and we might want to find the path with the lowest total cost (that is, the path with the lowest possible sum of its edge costs).

This kind of question can be solved by using a graph where each edge has a non-negative integer value attached to it, called the **weight** or **cost** of the edge.

Here's an example of a graph with edge weights:

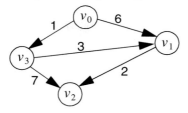

In this example, there are several paths from vertex v_0 to vertex v_2. The path with the lowest total cost traverses the edge from v_0 to v_3 (with a cost of 1), then from v_3 to v_1 (with a cost of 3), and finally from v_1 to v_2 (with a cost of 2). The total cost of this path is $1 + 3 + 2$, which is 6. There is a path with fewer edges (such as the path from v_0 to v_1 to v_2), but no other path has a lower total cost. The path with the lowest total cost is called the **shortest path**. (If you think of the weights as distances, then the term *shortest path* will sound like a sensible term.) The problem of finding the shortest path between two vertices of a graph occurs often in computer science (such as the network example) and in applications (such as finding the shortest driving distance between two points on a road map).

the shortest path between two vertices is the path with lowest total cost

Here is a summary of the concepts we have introduced:

Weighted Edges and Shortest Paths

A **weighted edge** is an edge together with a non-negative integer called the edge's **weight.**

The **weight of a path** is the total sum of the weights of all edges in the path. (Note: The weight of the empty path, with no edges, is always zero.)

If two vertices are connected by at least one path, then we can define the **shortest path** between two vertices. This is the path that has the smallest weight. (There may be several paths with equally small weights, in which case each of the paths is called "smallest.")

Shortest Distance Algorithm

In this section we will present an efficient algorithm called *Dijkstra's algorithm* (named for computer scientist Edsgar Dijkstra, who proposed the algorithm) for finding the shortest path between two vertices. Throughout the section we will use graphs with weighted edges where each weight is a non-negative integer. We will use pseudocode rather than a particular language such as Java.

We start with a problem that's simpler than actually finding the shortest path from one vertex to another. We'll concentrate on simply finding the *weight* of the shortest path—in other words the smallest possible sum of edge weights along a path from one vertex to another. This weight is called the *shortest distance*.

we'll actually find shortest distances rather than shortest paths

Dijkstra's algorithm actually provides more information than just the shortest distance from one vertex to another. In fact, the algorithm provides the shortest distance from a starting vertex (which we call `start`) to *every* vertex in the graph. The algorithm uses an integer array called `distance`, with one component for each vertex in the graph. Here is the algorithm's goal:

Goal of the Shortest Distance Algorithm

The goal is to completely fill the distance array so that for each vertex v, the value of `distance[v]` is the weight of the shortest path from `start` to v.

We'll illustrate how the algorithm works with this small graph:

The starting vertex is v_0.

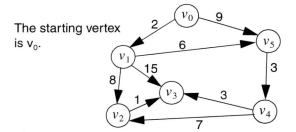

The algorithm begins by filling in one value in the distance array. We fill in zero for the component that is indexed by the `start` vertex itself, indicating that the weight of the shortest path from the `start` vertex to the `start` vertex itself is zero. This is correct since the empty path exists from the `start` vertex to itself. At this point, the distance array has one known value:

`distance`
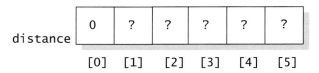

| [0] | [1] | [2] | [3] | [4] | [5] |

At this point we have one correct value, `distance[0]`. In the other locations we will write a value based on what we know so far. Because we don't know too much, our initial values won't be too accurate, but that's okay. In fact, the values that we fill in will all be *infinity*, represented by the symbol ∞. The distance array, with mostly ∞, is shown at the top of the next page.

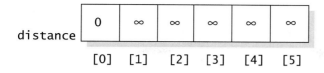

In an actual implementation, we would use some special integer value for ∞. For example, we could use –1 and make sure that all the rest of our programming always treats an occurrence of –1 as if it were infinity.

Now we are ready to do some processing that will steadily improve the values in the distance array. We begin with an observation about the initial values that we've placed in the distance array: These initial values are actually correct, *if we are permitting only the empty path and ignoring all other paths*. In other words, if the empty path is the only path that we are permitting, then there is a path from the start vertex to itself (namely the empty path with weight zero). But there is no way to get from the start vertex to any other vertex, and the fact that there is no path is represented by ∞ in the distance array.

Of course, permitting *only* the empty path is an overwhelming restriction. The key to the algorithm is in gradually relaxing this restriction, allowing more vertices to appear in permitted paths. As more and more vertices are allowed, we will continually revise the distance array so that its values are correct, *for paths that pass through only allowed vertices*. By the end of the algorithm, all vertices are allowed, and the distance array has values that are entirely correct.

the algorithm gradually improves the values in the distance array

The idea we have described needs some refinement. How are newly allowed vertices selected? How do we keep track of which vertices are currently allowed? How is the distance array revised to permit the newly allowed vertices to appear in a path? These questions are addressed in the following list of three steps for the complete algorithm.

Step 1. Fill in the distance array with ∞ at every location with the exception of distance[Start], which is assigned the value zero.

Step 2. Initialize a *set* of vertices, called allowedVertices, to be the empty set. Throughout the algorithm a *permitted path* is a path that starts at the start vertex, and where each vertex on the path (except perhaps the final vertex) is in the set of allowed vertices. The final vertex on a permitted path does not need to be in the allowedVertices set. At this point, allowedVertices is the empty set, so the only permitted path is the empty path without any edges. (This empty path does contain one vertex, the start vertex. But since this vertex is the *final* vertex on the path, the vertex is not required to be in the allowed vertices set.)

Step 3. The third step is a loop. Each time through the loop we will add one more vertex to allowedVertices and then update the distance array so that all the allowed vertices may appear on paths. Here's a brief summary of the loop:

```
//  Loop in Step 3 of the shortest distance algorithm:
//  n is the number of vertices in the graph

for (allowedSize = 1; allowedSize <= n; allowedSize++)
{
    //  At this point, allowedVertices contains allowedSize - 1 vertices,
    //  which are the allowedSize  - 1 closest vertices to the start vertex.
    //  Also, for each vertex v, distance[v] is the shortest distance from
    //  the start vertex to vertex v, provided that we are
    //  considering only permitted paths  (i.e., paths where
    //  each vertex except the final vertex must be in
    //  allowedVertices).
```

Step 3a. Let `next` be the closest vertex to the start vertex that is not yet in the set of allowed vertices (if several vertices are equally close, then you may choose `next` to be any of them).

Step 3b. Add the vertex `next` to the set `allowedVertices`.

Step 3c. Revise the distance array so that the new vertex (`next`) may appear on permitted paths.

```
}
```

The loop's computation hinges on the condition written just before Step 3a. The condition indicates that the `allowedVertices` set actually contains the `allowedSize-1` vertices that are *closest* to the start vertex. The condition also indicates that `distance[v]` is always the shortest distance from the start vertex to vertex v, provided that we are considering only permitted paths (that is, paths where all vertices except the final vertex must be in the set of allowed vertices). This condition is `true` the first time the loop is entered, and it is also `true` at the start of each subsequent iteration. The responsibility of the three steps—3a, 3b, and 3c—is to ensure that the condition remains valid at the start of each iteration. Let's examine the three steps in some detail.

Step 3a. This step must determine which of the *unallowed* vertices is closest to the start vertex. There is a simple rule for choosing this vertex:

How to Choose the Next Vertex in Step 3a

In Step 3a, we will always choose the unallowed vertex that has the *smallest* current value in the distance array. (If several vertices have equally small distances, then we may choose any of them.)

For example, suppose we reach Step 3a, and we have this situation:

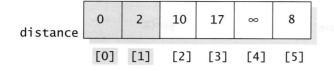

In this example, the two shaded vertices, 0 and 1,
are already in the set of allowed vertices.

Since vertices 0 and 1 are already in the allowed set, we may not choose them as
the next vertex. Among the other vertices, vertex 5 has the smallest current
value in the distance array (the value is 8). So, we would choose vertex 5 as the
next vertex. In the answer to Self-Test Exercise 12, we will explain precisely
why this rule works, but for now it is sufficient to know that this is the correct
way to select the next vertex.

Step 3b. In this step we "add the vertex `next` to the set `allowedVertices`."
The implementation of this step depends on how the set of allowed vertices is
represented. One possibility is to implement `allowedVertices` as a set of vertex
numbers, using an ADT for a set of integers. In this case, Step 3b merely inserts
`next` into the set.

Step 3c. Finally, we must revise the distance array so that the newly allowed
vertex, `next`, is permitted on a path from the start vertex to another vertex. An
example will explain the necessary revisions. Suppose that vertices 0, 1, and 5
are already in the `allowedVertices` set, and that we have just added vertex 2 as
our next vertex, as shown here:

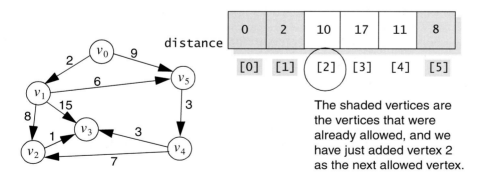

The shaded vertices are
the vertices that were
already allowed, and we
have just added vertex 2
as the next allowed vertex.

Since we have just added vertex 2 as a newly allowed vertex, we must now
update the distance array to reflect the fact that vertex 2 may now appear on
paths.

For example, `distance[3]` is currently 17. This means that there is a path from the start vertex to vertex 3 that uses only vertices 0, 1, and 5, and that has a length of 17. Here's the key question: *If we also allow vertex 2 to appear on a path from the start vertex to vertex 3, can we obtain a distance that is smaller than 17?* A smaller distance might be possible by taking a two-part path, shown here:

The first part of the path goes from the start vertex v_0 to the newly allowed vertex v_2 . . .

. . . and the second part of the path consists of one more edge from the newly allowed vertex v_2 to vertex v_3.

This path has two parts: the part from the start vertex to vertex 2, followed by the part that has the single edge from vertex 2 to vertex 3. The total weight of this path is:

`distance[2]` + (weight of the edge from vertex 2 to vertex 3)

In our example, this sum is 11, which is smaller than the current "best distance to vertex 3." Therefore we should replace `distance[3]` with this smaller sum. We must also create similar two-part paths for each of the other unallowed vertices, and if the two-part path is smaller than the current distance, then we modify the distance array. This provides the following refined pseudocode for Step 3c:

Step 3c. Revise the distance array so that the new vertex (`next`) may appear on permitted paths. The integer n is the number of vertices; v and sum are local integer variables, as shown in this code:

```
for (v = 0; v < n; v++)
    if ((v is not an allowed vertex) and (there is an edge from next to v))
    {
        sum = distance[next] + (weight of the edge from next to v);
        if (sum < distance[v])
            distance[v] = sum;
    }
```

Notice that we do not consider a possible new smaller distance to vertices that are already allowed vertices. That is because these vertices are all closer to the start vertex than `next` is, so that `distance[next]` is going to be larger than the shortest distance to any of these vertices.

Also, when we are creating the new two-part paths, we consider only the case where the second part of the path is a *single edge* from `next` to the end vertex. The reason for this is that a longer path from `next` to the end vertex would have to pass through other allowed vertices, meaning that we have a path that goes from the start vertex, through `next`, through *another* allowed vertex, and finally to the end vertex. But such a path will always be shorter by avoiding the `next` vertex altogether—just go from the start vertex to that other allowed vertex (using the shortest path) and then to the end vertex. Such a path, which does not go through the `next` vertex, is already permitted. We don't need to consider such a path again—we need only consider new paths that pass through the `next` newly allowed vertex.

The complete pseudocode for the algorithm is shown in Figure 14.5. The main loop actually stops at the number of vertices minus 1 because at that point there is only one unallowed vertex, and this must be the farthest vertex from the start vertex so that no shortest paths can go through this farthest vertex.

We'll execute the algorithm on our example graph. Here's the situation after initializing the distance array:

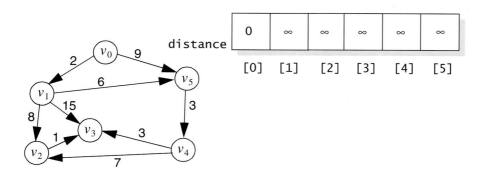

At this point, the set of allowed vertices is empty, and we will enter the main loop for the first time. In Step 3a, the value of `next` is set to vertex 0 (since `distance[0]` is the smallest value in the distance array). We then look at each unallowed vertex v with an edge from vertex 0 to vertex v. These are vertices 1 and 5, so we check to see whether we need to revise `distance[1]` and `distance[5]`:

- `distance[0]` + (the weight of the edge from 0 to 1) is 2. Since this is smaller than the current value of `distance[1]`, we replace `distance[1]` with 2.

- `distance[0]` + (the weight of the edge from 0 to 5) is 9. Since this is smaller than the current value of `distance[5]`, we replace `distance[5]` with 9.

FIGURE 14.5 Dijkstra's Shortest Distance Algorithm

Pseudocode

Input. A directed graph with positive, integer edge weights and n vertices. One of the vertices, called `start`, is specified as the start vertex.

Output. A list of the shortest distances from the start vertex to every other vertex in the graph.

The algorithm uses an array of n integers (called `distance`) and a set of vertices (called `allowedVertices`). The variables v, `allowedSize`, and sum are local integer variables. There is some special value (∞) that we can place in the distance array to indicate an infinite distance (which means there is no path).

Step 1. Initialize the distance array to contain all ∞, except `distance[start]`, which is set to zero.

Step 2. Initialize the set of allowed vertices to be the empty set.

Step 3. Compute the complete distance array:

```
for (allowedSize = 1; allowedSize < n; allowedSize++)
{
```
```
    //  At this point, allowedVertices contains allowedSize – 1 vertices, which are the
    //  allowedSize – 1 closest vertices to the start vertex. Also, for each vertex v, distance[v]
    //  is the shortest distance from the start vertex to vertex v, provided that we are
    //  considering only permitted paths (i.e., paths where each vertex except the final vertex
    //  must be in allowedVertices).
```

Step 3a. Let `next` be the closest vertex to the start vertex, which is not yet in the set of allowed vertices (if several vertices are equally close, then you may choose `next` to be any of them).

Step 3b. Add the vertex `next` to the set `allowedVertices`.

Step 3c. Revise the distance array so that the new vertex (`next`) may appear on permitted paths:

```
for (v = 0; v < n; v++)
    if ((v is not an allowed vertex)  and (there is an edge from next to v))
    {
        sum = distance[next] + (weight of the edge from next to v);
        if (sum < distance[v])
            distance[v] = sum;
    }
}
```

Step 4. Output the values in the distance array. (Each `distance[v]` is the shortest distance from the start vertex to vertex v.)

At this point, the distance array is as shown below (with the allowed vertices shaded):

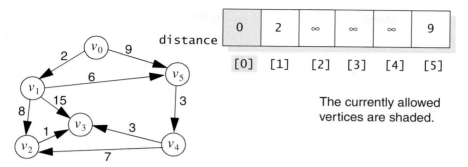

0	2	∞	∞	∞	9
[0]	[1]	[2]	[3]	[4]	[5]

distance

The currently allowed vertices are shaded.

The second time we enter the main loop, the value of next is set to vertex 1 (since distance[1] is the smallest value of the unallowed vertices). We then look at each unallowed vertex v with an edge from vertex 1 to vertex v. These are vertices 2, 3, and 5, so we check to see whether we need to revise distance[2], distance[3], and distance[5]:

- distance[1] + (the weight of the edge from 1 to 2) is 10. Since this is smaller than the current value of distance[2], we replace distance[2] with 10.

- distance[1] + (the weight of the edge from 1 to 3) is 17. Since this is smaller than the current value of distance[3], we replace distance[3] with 17.

- distance[1] + (the weight of the edge from 0 to 5) is 8. Since this is smaller than the current value of distance[5], we replace distance[5] with 8.

At this point, the distance array is:

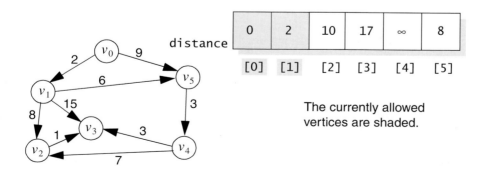

0	2	10	17	∞	8
[0]	[1]	[2]	[3]	[4]	[5]

distance

The currently allowed vertices are shaded.

The third time we enter the main loop, the value of next will be set to vertex 5 (since distance[5] is the smallest value of the unallowed vertices). We then look at each unallowed vertex v with an edge from vertex 5 to vertex v. Vertex 4 is the only vertex that is the target of an edge from vertex 5, so we check to see whether we need to revise distance[4]:

- distance[5] + (the weight of the edge from 5 to 4) is 11. Since this is smaller than the current value of distance[4], we replace distance[4] with 11.

At this point, we have this situation:

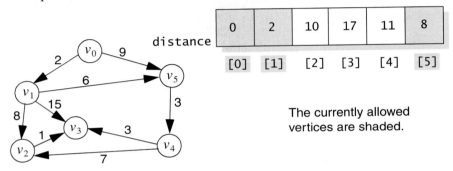

The currently allowed vertices are shaded.

The fourth time we enter the main loop, the value of next will be set to vertex 2 (since distance[2] is the smallest value of the unallowed vertices). We then look at each unallowed vertex v with an edge from vertex 2 to vertex v. Vertex 3 is the only such vertex, so we check to see whether we need to revise distance[3]:

- distance[2] + (the weight of the edge from 2 to 3) is 11. Since this is smaller than the current value of distance[3], we replace distance[3] with 11.

At this point, the situation is:

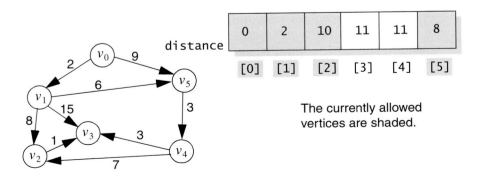

The currently allowed vertices are shaded.

The fifth time we enter the main loop, the value of next will be set to either vertex 3 or vertex 4 (since both distance[3] and distance[4] are 11). It doesn't matter which one we choose, so let's choose vertex 4. We then look at each unallowed vertex v with an edge from vertex 4 to vertex v. This is only vertex 3, so we check to see whether we need to revise distance[4]:

- distance[4] + (the weight of the edge from 4 to 3) is 14. Since this is *larger* than the current value of distance[3], we do not replace distance[3].

At this point, we are nearly done:

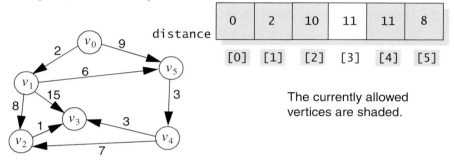

	0	2	10	11	11	8

distance

[0] [1] [2] [3] [4] [5]

The currently allowed vertices are shaded.

The main loop of the algorithm now stops. We don't need to process that last unallowed vertex (3), since it is the farthest vertex from the start vertex. For each vertex v, the value of distance[v] is the shortest distance from the start vertex (vertex 0) to v.

Shortest Path Algorithm

We have shown how to compute the *weight* of the shortest path from a start vertex to each other vertex in a graph. But how can we compute the actual sequence of vertices that occurs along the shortest path? It turns out that Dijkstra's shortest distance algorithm contains enough information to actually print the shortest path from the start vertex to any other vertex, provided that we keep track of one extra piece of information:

Predecessor Information for Shortest Paths

For each vertex v, we will keep track of which vertex was the next vertex when distance[v] was given a new smaller value. We will keep track of these values in an array called predecessor, so that for each vertex v, predecessor[v] is the value of next at the time when distance[v] was given a new smaller value. (Note: predecessor[start] does not need to have a value, since distance[start] is never updated.)

The predecessor information is easy to keep track of. Each time that we update distance[v] with the assignment distance[v] = sum , we must also update predecessor[v] with this assignment:

```
predecessor[v] = next;
```

When the algorithm finishes, the value of distance[v] is the weight of the shortest path from the start vertex to vertex v. Or distance[v] might be infinity, indicating that there is no path from the start vertex to vertex v. But when distance[v] is not infinity, we can actually print out the vertices on the shortest path from the start vertex to vertex v, using the following code:

```
// Printing the vertices on the shortest path from the start vertex to v:
// Vertices are printed in reverse order, starting at v, and going to start.

vertexOnPath = v; // The last vertex on the path.
System.out.println(vertexOnPath); // Print the final vertex.
while (vertexOnPath != start)
{
    vertexOnPath = predecessor[vertexOnPath];
    System.out.println(vertexOnPath);
}
```

In other words, the last vertex on the path to v is vertex v itself. The next-to-last vertex is predecessor[v]. And the vertex before that is obtained by applying predecessor to the next-to-last vertex—and so on, right back to the start vertex. As indicated, this algorithm manages to print the vertices in reverse order, from vertex v back to the start vertex.

Self-Test Exercises

12. When we select the next vertex in the shortest distance algorithm, we need to select the unallowed vertex that is closest to the start vertex. How is this selection done?

13. Consider the graph that we have been using throughout this section, except change the weight of the edge that goes from 0 to 5. Its new weight is 4. Go through the entire algorithm to compute the new distance array.

14. Compute the complete predecessor array for the previous exercise, and use it to find the actual shortest path from vertex 0 to vertex 3.

CHAPTER SUMMARY

- Graphs are a flexible data structure with many occurrences in computer science and in applications. Many problems can be solved by asking an appropriate question about paths in a graph.
- There are several different kinds of graphs: undirected graphs (where edges have no particular orientation), directed graphs (where each edge goes from a source vertex to a target vertex), graphs with loops (i.e., an edge connecting a vertex to itself), graphs with multiple edges (i.e., more than one edge may connect the same pair of vertices), labeled graphs (where each vertex has an associated label), and graphs with weighted edges (where each edge has an associated number, called its weight).
- There are two common ways to implement a graph: an adjacency matrix or edge lists. The different implementations have different time performance for common operations such as determining whether two vertices are connected.
- There are two common ways to traverse a graph: depth-first search and breadth-first search
- Dijkstra's algorithm provides an efficient way to determine the shortest path from a given start vertex to every other vertex in a graph with weighted edges.

Solutions to Self-Test Exercises   **?**

1. The airline route graph has nine vertices, 14 edges, and no loops. A loop would be an excursion flight that takes off and lands at the same city.

2. It is simple (no loops, no multiple edges).

3. Your state graph should have 16 vertices and 48 directed edges. (There are 32 edges from Rule 1, and eight edges each from Rules 2 and 3.) It is possible to go from the start state to the goal state in four moves.

4. For the removal method, suppose that k is the number of vertices that are being removed, and that this will leave m vertices in the new, smaller graph. The method should allocate new smaller arrays for the edges and labels (and these new arrays can be referred to by local variables of the method). Then copy the information for the first m vertices into these smaller arrays.

   The method that adds new vertices must allocate new, larger arrays and copy all the information from the old arrays to the new arrays.

   In both methods, the final step is to make the instance variables (edges and labels) refer to the new arrays.

5. Suppose that the vertex numbers of the two vertices are i and j. The method must interchange their labels and also interchange the

rows and columns of the edges matrix. If you aren't careful, you might accidently interchange edges[i][i] with edges[j][j] two times (once when you are interchanging the rows and once when you are interchanging the columns.)

6. The adjacency matrix, a, could be a two-dimensional array of integers with a[i][j] storing the number of edges from vertex i to vertex j.

7. This is an open-ended question, but your answer should consider space requirements for each representation, and time requirements for common operations.

8. Here is one solution:

```
public static int maxEdges(Graph g)
{
    int i;
    int answer;
    int manyEdges;
    int maxEdges = 0;
    int[ ] ni;

    if (g.size( ) == 0)
        throw new
        IllegalArgumentException
        ("Graph is empty");

    for (i = 0; i < g.size( ); i++)
    {
        ni = g.neighbors(i);
        manyEdges = ni.length;
        if (manyEdges >= maxEdges)
        {
            answer = i;
            maxEdges = manyEdges;
        }
    }

    return answer;
}
```

9. Traversals sometimes make choices about which vertex to visit next. When we have such a choice, we will visit the vertex that is alphabetically first, giving these two orders: *Depth-first:* Sydney, Canberra, Adelaide, Melbourne, Hobart, Perth, Black Stump, Darwin, Brisbane. *Breadth-first:* Sydney, Canberra, Melbourne, Adelaide, Brisbane, Hobart, Perth, Black Stump, Darwin.

10. If n is 1, then the queue needs room for only one vertex. If n is more than 1, then the queue will never have more than $n-1$ entries. Here is why: The start vertex is only in the queue once (by itself), and then we remove the start vertex from the queue. Each other vertex is placed in the queue at most once, so the largest queue needed would occur if all $n-1$ vertices are neighbors of the start vertex.

11. A depth-first search.

12. From among the unallowed vertices, we select the vertex with the smallest current value in the distance array. This works because the current distance array contains the correct distance values if we are only permitting allowed vertices, and the currently allowed vertices are the n-1 closest vertices. Therefore, the shortest path to the nth closest vertex must pass through only currently allowed vertices, and therefore the distance array contains the correct value for that n^{th} closest vertex.

13. The new final distance array: (0, 2, 10, 10, 7, 4).

14. The new shortest path to vertex 3: vertex 0 to vertex 5, vertex 5 to vertex 4, vertex 4 to vertex 3.

PROGRAMMING PROJECTS

 1 Rewrite the depthFirstPrint method from Figure 14.4 on page 693, so that it carries out a breadth-first search instead.

 2 Use edge lists to reimplement the Graph class from Figure 14.3 on page 679. There should be no limit to the number of vertices. Also provide a new method that returns the edge list of a specified vertex.

 3 Use edge sets to reimplement the Graph class from Figure 14.3 on page 679. There should be no limit to the number of vertices. Also provide a new method that returns the edge set of a specified vertex.

 4 Implement a new class that is derived from the Graph. The new class should permit both edges and vertices to have labels.

5 Implement a method with three arguments: a graph, a starting vertex number, and an ending vertex number. The method determines whether there is a directed path from the starting vertex to the ending vertex.

6 Implement a new class for graphs with weighted edges. Use the ordinary Graph class as a superclass for your implementation. After implementing the new class, provide two extra methods to implement Dijkstra's shortest distance and shortest path algorithms.

7 Write a program to help a traveler plan the shortest traveling path from one city to another. The program should read a file of data containing a list of cities and a list of roads connecting the cities. Each road has a distance attached to it. Allow the user to enter queries of the form "City1, City2" and have the program print the shortest sequence of roads to travel from City1 to City2.

8 Write a program to help you make better social connections. The program should read a file of data containing a list of people in your community and a list of who-knows-whom. Allow the user to enter various queries about which people know each other, such as "How many people does Harry know?" or "Is there anyone that both Harry and Cathy know?"

Appendix A
Java's Primitive Types and Arithmetic Overflow

Java has eight primitive data types for storing numerical and other basic values. This appendix lists the eight types and some of their properties such as the arithmetic overflow that can occur with the integer types.

```
byte
char
short
int
long
```

- These are Java's five integer types. Notice that the `char` type is included as one of the "integer" types, though it does have some special properties discussed below. Any value of these types is a whole number in the following limited ranges:

	Storage requirement	Minimum value	Maximum value
`byte`	1 byte	−128	127
`char`	2 bytes	0	65,535
`short`	2 bytes	−32,768	32,767
`int`	4 bytes	−2,147,483,648	2,147,483,647
`long`	8 bytes	−9,223,372,036,854,775,808	9,223,372,036,854,775,807

- Constant integer values are written as a sequence of digits with no commas and sometimes a negative sign at the front; for example, 4200 or −3942. Fixed long values include the letter L after the digits such as 923672159321877L.

- When an integer expression is evaluated, the operands are examined to see if there is any `long` data. If so, then all the operands are converted to the `long` type, and the answer is also `long`. If there is no `long` data, then any `byte`, `char`, or `short` operands are converted to `int` and the answer is also `int`.

  The fact that `byte`, `char`, and `short` operands are converted to `int` has consequences in the arithmetic of these values. For example, suppose that s, s1, and s2 are short variables with s1 containing 1 and s2 containing 2. Then the assignment s = s1+s2 causes a compilation error because s1 and s2 are converted to `int` values, and even though s1+s2 is only 3, it is considered an `int` value. Java's compiler does not permit an assignment of one integer data type to a variable of a shorter type. The solution is a typecast that informs the compiler that the computed value is intended to be the `short` data type. In this example, we can correctly write the assignment:

      s = (short)(s1 + s2);

- When an integer value is too large for its data type, the result is called **arithmetic overflow**. In Java, an integer arithmetic overflow results in a wrong answer. For example, adding 1 to the largest `int` gives the smallest negative number as the answer. Arithmetic overflow can occur during an assignment to a variable, or it can occur in an intermediate value that is part of a larger arithmetic expression. Some examples are shown here:

```
// Compute an addition that causes arithmetic overflow because the answer is
// larger than the largest int value.
int i;
int i1 = 1000000000;
int i2 = 2000000000;
i = i1 + i2;
System.out.println(i); // Prints wrong answer of -1294967296

// Compute approximately 2/3 of an integer value in a way that can cause overflow.
// The overflow occurs because the intermediate value k*2 could be more than
// the largest int, therefore the final result is wrong.
int j;
int k = 2000000000;
j = k * 2 / 3;
System.out.println(j); // Prints wrong answer of -98322432

// Compute 2/3 of an integer value in a better way. By doing the division first
// there is no possibility of an overflow.
j = 2 * (k / 3);
System.out.println(j); // Prints right answer of 1333333332
```

Special Properties of the char Type:

- Char values are non-negative integers used to represent printable characters. Each printable character is assigned one of these numbers, called the Unicode value of the character. For example, the Unicode value of 'A' is 65. The values from 0 to 127 match the ASCII character code that you may have used in other programming languages. The complete list of Unicode characters is available at `http://charts.unicode.org/`.

- When a `char` value is printed, the printable character is displayed rather than the integer value.

- A `char` constant can be written in four ways:
  — A single character within quote marks such as 'A'.
  — One of the special character escape sequences, which are: '\n' (newline), '\r' (carriage return), '\b' (backspace), '\f' (form feed), '\t' (tab), '\'' (single quote), '\"' (double quote), and '\\' (backslash).
  — A sequence of up to three octal digits of the form '\nnn'. The number nnn is a base-8 (octal) number from 0 to 377 (which corresponds to a base 10 number from 0 to 255). For example, an alternate representation of 'A' is '\101' since 101 (base 8) is the same as 65 (base 10).
  — A Unicode escape sequence of the form '\unnnn', where nnnn is a base 16 (hexadecimal) number with exactly four hex digits. For example, '\u0041' is 'A' since 41 (base 16) is the same as 65 (base 10).

float
double

These are Java's two data types for numbers that have decimal places. Double values follow an 8-byte format called the IEEE 754 standard for 64-bit floating point numbers. This standard has these properties:

- Double values range from about -1.7×10^{308} to 1.7×10^{308}. Numbers can be defined close to zero, down to about 4.9×10^{-324} on the positive side of zero, or to about -4.9×10^{-324} on the negative size of zero.

- Double constant values with base 10 exponents can be written by placing the letter 'e' or 'E' before the exponent. For example: 4.2E19 is 4.2×10^{19}.

- Double values have about 14 to 15 significant digits. This means that the actual number stored in the computer can have inaccuracies beginning around the 15th digit. Because of these inaccuracies, you should avoid testing double numbers for exact equality (using the == operator).

- Special values: Computations that result in a value greater than about 1.7×10^{308} will result in a constant called `Double.POSITIVE_INFINITY`. Values smaller than about -1.7×10^{308} will result in `Double.NEGATIVE_INFINITY`. Values that are too close to zero will result in 0.0 (on the positive side) or −0.0 (on the negative side). Any undefined computation (such as division by zero) results in a constant called `Double.NaN`. Because of these special constants, computations with double numbers never cause an exception or crash. Instead, arithmetic overflow or illegal computations simply provide the appropriate constant value as a result.

The `float` type is similar to `double`, but with only 4 bytes of storage (the IEEE 754 standard for 32-bit floating point numbers). Therefore, float values have a smaller range (about -3.4×10^{38} to 3.4×10^{38}), the values cannot get so close to zero, and the accuracy is only six or seven digits.

If an arithmetic computation involves `float` values but no `double` variables or constants, then the arithmetic is carried out using 4-byte `float` values with the corresponding limitations on ranges and accuracy. There are separate constants for `Float.NaN`, `Float.POSITIVE_INFINITY`, and `Float.NEGATIVE_INFINITY`.

boolean

A `boolean` value is one of two constants: `true` or `false`.

Appendix B
Java Input and Output

This appendix gives the specifications and implementations of two classes that simplify Java input and output.

The EasyReader Class

An EasyReader is designed to be attached to an input file or to the keyboard. Here are two examples:

```
// Create an EasyReader called stdin that is attached to the System.in keyboard:
EasyReader stdin = new EasyReader(System.in);

// Create a second EasyReader called datafile that is attached to a file "data.txt"
EasyReader datafile = new EasyReader("data.txt");
```

Once an EasyReader is set up, numbers strings and other items can be read with easy-to-use methods. For example, after stdin is set up, a string is read into a variable s with the statement:

```
String s = stdin.stringInput( );
```

The complete specification and implementation of the EasyReader class begins on page 715. The source code is also available at
```
http://www.cs.colorado.edu/~main/edu/colorado/io/EasyReader.java
```

The FormatWriter Class

The FormatWriter class provides several static methods for printing numbers and other objects in a specified format. All output goes to System.out. The complete specification and implementation of the FormatWriter class begins on page 729. The source code is also available at

```
http://www.cs.colorado.edu/~main/edu/colorado/io/FormatWriter.java
```

Class *EasyReader*

❖ **public class EasyReader from the package edu.colorado.io**
An `EasyReader` object has a small collection of methods for reading some primitive data values from an input stream or file.

Limitations:
If an `IOException` or `FileNotFoundException` occurs during any operation, the `EasyReader` prints an error message and halts the program. The exceptions are not passed back to the calling program, so the calling program does not need to catch any exceptions.

Example:
This example declares an `EasyReader` that is attached to keyboard input (`System.in`). It then uses `doubleQuery` to ask the user to enter a `double` number. The square of this `double` number is then printed to `System.out`:

```
import edu.colorado.io.EasyReader;
...
EasyReader stdin = new EasyReader(System.in); // Attaches to keyboard
double d;
d = stdin.doubleQuery("Please type a double value: ");
System.out.println("The square of that is: " + d*d);
```

Notes:
The `EasyReader` class includes:

(1) Three constructors to create an `EasyReader` object from a file name, from an `InputStream`, or from an `InputStreamReader`.

(2) `Query` methods: The names of these methods end with "Query", and they are intended for use with interactive input. Each method prints a prompt (which is a `String` parameter) and then reads one line of input, converting the line to some type (`char`, `double`, `int`, or `String`). All of the `Query` methods reject improperly formed input lines (such as 1.5 for an integer input). When an input is rejected, the method prompts the user for a correctly formatted input. This continues until an input line is typed in the correct format.

(3) `Peek` method: This method returns the next character of the input without actually reading it.

(4) `Input` methods: The names of these methods end with "Input" or "InputLine". The methods read input and convert it to some type (`char`, `double`, `int`, or `String`). The `Input` methods just read the data, whereas the `InputLine` methods read the data and then discard the rest of the line.

(5) Boolean methods: The names of these methods begin with "is". They return various information about the input status.

(6) The `skipLine` and `ignore` methods: These read and throw away various input.

Specification

- **Constructors for the EasyReader**
  ```
  public EasyReader(String name)
  public EasyReader(InputStream in)
  public EasyReader(InputStreamReader isr)
  ```
  Initialize this `EasyReader` to read from a file, an `InputStream`, or an `InputStreamReader`.

  Parameters:
    name – the name of a file from which this `EasyReader` will read
    in – the `InputStream` from which this `EasyReader` will read
    isr – the `InputStreamReader` from which this `EasyReader` will read

  Postcondition:
    This `EasyReader` has been initialized so that its subsequent input comes from the specified location. If the location is a file name and the file does not exist, then an error message is printed and the program exits.

  Examples:
  ```
  // Create an EasyReader called stdin that is attached to the System.in keyboard
  EasyReader stdin = new EasyReader(System.in);

  // Create a second EasyReader called datafile that is attached to a file "data.txt"
  EasyReader datafile = new EasyReader("data.txt");
  ```

- **charInput—charInputLine**
  ```
  public char charInput( )
  public char charInputLine( )
  ```
  Read a character from this `EasyReader`.

  Returns:
    a character that's been read

  Note:
    The method first reads and throws away any whitespace. Then it reads and returns the next character. If end-of-file has been reached, it returns ASCII value zero. The `charInputLine` version also activates `skipLine( )` after reading the character.

- **charQuery**
  ```
  public char charQuery(String prompt)
  ```
  Print a prompt, then read a character from this `EasyReader`.

  Parameters:
    prompt – a prompt to print

  Postcondition:
    The prompt has been printed to `System.out`. Then a character has been read and returned with `charInputLine( )`.

◆ doubleInput—doubleInputLine

```
public double doubleInput( )
public double doubleInputLine( )
```

Read a `double` number from this `EasyReader`.

Returns:

a `double` number that's been read

Input Method:

An attempt is made to read the following items into a `String`:

(1) Zero or more whitespace characters (which are discarded).

(2) An optional + or – sign.

(3) A sequence of digits that form the integer part of the number.

(4) If the next character is a decimal point, then it is read along with a sequence of digits that form the fractional part of the number.

(5) If the next character is 'e' or 'E', then it is read with an optional + or – sign and digits that form the exponent part of the number.

(6) After these items are read, the `doubleInputLine` version also activates `skipLine( )`.

These items are converted to a `double` number using `Double.valueOf`. If a `NumberFormatException` occurs, then the method returns `Double.NaN` and an immediate activation of `isFormatProblem` will return `true`.

◆ doubleQuery

```
public double doubleQuery(String prompt)
```

Print a prompt, then read a `double` number from this `EasyReader`.

Parameters:

prompt – a prompt to print

Postcondition:

The prompt has been printed to `System.out`. Then a `double` number has been read and returned with `doubleInputLine( )`.

Format Problems:

If `doubleInputLine` encounters a format problem, but the end of file is not yet reached, then the user is prompted to type a new input line until a correct `double` value is provided. If the end of file is reached, then the method returns `Double.NaN` and an immediate activation of `isFormatProblem` will return `true`.

◆ ignore

```
public void ignore( )
```

Read and discard one character from this `EasyReader`.

Postcondition:

One character has been read and discarded from this `EasyReader`.

+ **intInput—intInputLine**

    ```
    public int intInput( )
    public int intInputLine( )
    ```
    Read an `int` number from this `EasyReader`.

    Returns:

    an `int` number that's been read

    Input Method:

    An attempt is made to read the following items into a `String`:

    (1) Zero or more whitespace characters (which are discarded).

    (2) An optional + or – sign.

    (3) A sequence of digits that form the integer.

    (4) After these items are read, the `intInputLine` version also activates `skipLine( )`.

    These items are converted to an `int` number using `Integer.parseInt`. If a `NumberFormatException` occurs, then the method returns `Integer.MIN_VALUE` and an immediate activation of `isFormatProblem` will return `true`.

+ **intQuery**

    ```
    public int intQuery(String prompt)
    ```
    Print a prompt, then read an `int` number from this `EasyReader`.

    Parameters:

    prompt – a prompt to print

    Postcondition:

    The prompt has been printed to `System.out`. Then an `int` number has been read and returned with `intInputLine( )`.

    Format Problems:

    If `intInputLine` encounters a format problem, but the end of file is not yet reached, then the user is prompted to type a new input line until a correct `int` value is provided. If the end of file is reached, then the method returns `Integer.MIN_VALUE` and an immediate activation of `isFormatProblem` will return `true`.

+ **isEOF**

    ```
    public boolean isEOF( )
    ```
    Determine whether this `EasyReader` has reached the end of file.

    Returns:

    If this `EasyReader` has reached the end of file (reading all characters up to but not including EOF), then the return value is `true`; if an attempt to read causes an `IOException`, then the return value is also `true`. Otherwise the return value is `false`.

    Notes:

    A user at the keyboard indicates EOF by typing `ctrl-z` (MS Windows) or `ctrl-c` (Unix). For an interactive user, this method does pause until the user provides some input or indicates EOF by typing a control character.

- **isEOLN**
    ```
    public boolean isEOLN( )
    ```
    Determine whether this EasyReader has reached the end of a line.
    Returns:
    If the next input character is a newline ('\n') or carriage return ('\r'), then the return value is true; if isEOF( ), then the return value is also true. Otherwise the return value is false.

- **isFormatProblem**
    ```
    public boolean isFormatProblem( )
    ```
    Determine whether there was incorrectly formatted input to the most recent input operation.
    Returns:
    A true return value indicates that the most recent activation of an input method had an IOException or was given input of the wrong format (such as "abc" instead of an integer). Note that the return value is applicable to only the MOST RECENT activation of these input methods: doubleInput, doubleInputLine, doubleQuery, intInput, intInputLine, intQuery.

- **pause**
    ```
    public static void pause(long milliseconds)
    ```
    Make the computation pause for a specified number of milliseconds.
    Parameters:
    milliseconds – the number of milliseconds to pause
    Postcondition:
    The computation has paused for the specified time.

- **peek**
    ```
    public char peek( )
    ```
    Peek ahead at the next character from this EasyReader.
    Returns:
    The return value is the next character that will be read from this EasyReader. If there is no next character (because of the EOF marker), then the return value is ASCII zero.

- **query**
    ```
    public boolean query(String prompt)
    ```
    Print a prompt, then read a yes/no answer from this EasyReader.
    Parameters:
    prompt – a prompt to print
    Postcondition:
    stringQuery(prompt) has been called to ask a question and read the answer, which is considered true if it begins with 'Y' or 'y' and false if it begins with 'N' or 'n'. If the answer does not begin with one of these letters, then the process is repeated until a correct yes/no answer is provided. If EOF is encountered, then false is returned.

- **skipline**

  `public void skipline( )`

  Read and discard the rest of the current input line.

  Postcondition:

  Characters have been read and discarded, up to and including the end of the current input line (or to the end of file).

- **stringInput**

  `public String stringInput( )`

  Read a `String` (terminted by whitespace) from this `EasyReader`.

  Returns:

  a `String` that's been read

  Input Method:

  Whitespace is first skipped, and then a string is read up to but not including the next whitespace character.

- **stringInputLine**

  `public String stringInputLine( )`

  Read a `String` from a complete line of this `EasyReader`.

  Returns:

  a `String` that's been read

  Input Method:

  An entire line of characters has been read up to and including the end of the current line. All characters before the end are returned in a `String`.

- **stringQuery**

  `public String StringQuery(String prompt)`

  Print a prompt, then read a `String` from this `EasyReader`.

  Parameters:

  prompt – a prompt to print

  Postcondition:

  The prompt has been printed to `System.out`. Then a `String` has been read and returned with `StringInputLine( )`.

Implementation

```
//  File: EasyReader.java from the package edu.colorado.io
//  Complete documentation begins on page 716 or is available from the EasyReader link in
//    http://www.cs.colorado.edu/~main/docs/

package edu.colorado.io;

import java.io.FileNotFoundException;
import java.io.FileReader;
import java.io.InputStream;
import java.io.InputStreamReader;
import java.io.IOException;
import java.io.PushbackReader;

public class EasyReader extends PushbackReader
{
    final static int  EOF_VALUE = -1;        // Returned by read( ) at EOF
    final static char ZERO_CHAR = '\0';      // Unicode character zero

    private boolean formatProblem = false;

    public EasyReader(InputStream in)
    {
        super(new InputStreamReader(in));
    }

    public EasyReader(String name)
    {
        super(makeFileReader(name));
    }

    public EasyReader(InputStreamReader isr)
    {
        super(isr);
    }

    public char charInput( )
    {
        readSpaces( );
        return readChar( );
    }

    public char charInputLine( )
    {
        char answer = charInput( );
        skipLine( );
        return answer;
    }
```

```java
public char charQuery(String prompt)
{
   char answer;

   System.out.print(prompt);
   return charInputLine( );
}


public double doubleInput( )
{
   final char POINT = '.';
   StringBuffer input = new StringBuffer( );

   readSpaces( );
   input.append(readSign( ));
   input.append(readDigits( ));
   if (peek( ) == POINT)
   {  // Read the decimal point and fractional part.
      input.append(readChar( ));
      input.append(readDigits( ));
   }
   if (Character.toUpperCase(peek( )) == 'E')
   {  // Read the E and exponent.
      input.append(readChar( ));
      input.append(readSign( ));
      input.append(readDigits( ));
   }

   try
   {
      formatProblem = false;
      return Double.valueOf(input.toString( )).doubleValue( );
   }
   catch (NumberFormatException e)
   {
      formatProblem = true;
      return Double.NaN;
   }
}


public double doubleInputLine( )
{
   double answer = doubleInput( );
   skipLine( );
   return answer;
}
```

```java
public double doubleQuery(String prompt)
{
    double answer;

    System.out.print(prompt);
    answer = doubleInputLine( );
    while (formatProblem)
    {
        System.out.print("Invalid response. Please type a double value: ");
        if (isEOF( ))
            return Double.NaN;
        answer = doubleInputLine( );
    }

    return answer;
}

private static void handleException(Exception e)
// Print an error message and halt the program.
{
    System.err.println("Exception:" + e);
    System.err.println("EasyReader will cause program to halt.");
    System.exit(0);
}

public void ignore( )
{
    readChar( );
}

public int intInput( )
{
    String input = null;

    readSpaces( );
    input = readSign( ) + readDigits( );

    try
    {
        formatProblem = false;
        return Integer.parseInt(input);
    }
    catch (NumberFormatException e)
    {
        formatProblem = true;
        return Integer.MIN_VALUE;
    }
}
```

```java
public int intInputLine( )
{
    int answer = intInput( );
    skipLine( );
    return answer;
}

public int intQuery(String prompt)
{
    int answer;

    System.out.print(prompt);
    answer = intInputLine( );
    while (formatProblem)
    {
        System.out.print("Invalid response. Please type an integer value: ");
        if (isEOF( ))
            return Integer.MIN_VALUE;
        answer = intInputLine( );
    }

    return answer;
}

public boolean isEOF( )
{
    return (readAhead( ) == EOF_VALUE);
}

public boolean isEOLN( )
{
    int next = readAhead( );
    return (next == '\n') || (next == '\r') || (next == EOF_VALUE);
}

public boolean isFormatProblem( )
{
    return formatProblem;
}
```

```java
private static FileReader makeFileReader(String name)
// Create and return a FileReader to read from the named file. If the file doesn't exist then print
// an error message and halt the program.
{
    try
    {
        return new FileReader(name);
    }
    catch (FileNotFoundException e)
    {
        handleException(e);
        return null;
    }
}

public static void pause(long milliseconds)
{
    try
    {
        Thread.sleep(milliseconds);
    }
    catch (InterruptedException e)
    {
        // Resume execution
    }
}

public char peek( )
{
    int next = readAhead( );
    if (next == EOF_VALUE)
        return ZERO_CHAR;
    else
        return (char) next;
}

public boolean query(String prompt)
{
    String answer;

    System.out.print(prompt + " [Y or N] ");
    answer = stringInputLine( ).toUpperCase( );
    while (!answer.startsWith("Y") && !answer.startsWith("N"))
    {
        System.out.print("Invalid response. Please type Y or N: ");
        if (isEOF( ))
            return false;
        answer = stringInputLine( ).toUpperCase( );
    }

    return answer.startsWith("Y");
}
```

```
private int readAhead( )
// Peek ahead and return the next character (or –1 for EOF).
{
    int next = EOF_VALUE;

    try
    {
        next = read( );
        if (next == EOF_VALUE)
        {
            // End-of-file was encountered. We pause 1 second to allow the
            // ctrl-z from the keyboard to be processed since it blocks output
            // to the screen on some systems.
            pause(1000);
        }
        else
            unread(next);
    }
    catch (IOException e)
    {
        handleException(e);
    }

    return next;
}

private char readChar( )
// Read and return the next character (or –1 for EOF).
{
    int next = EOF_VALUE;

    try
    {
        next = read( );
        if (next == EOF_VALUE)
        {
            next = ZERO_CHAR;
            // End-of-file was encountered. We pause 1 second to allow the
            // ctrl-z from the keyboard to be processed since it blocks output
            // to the screen on some systems.
            pause(1000);
        }
    }
    catch (IOException e)
    {
        handleException(e);
    }

    return (char) next;
}
```

```java
private String readDigits( )
// Read a sequence of digits and return the sequence as a String.
{
    StringBuffer buffer = new StringBuffer( );

    while (Character.isDigit(peek( )))
        buffer.append(readChar( ));

    return buffer.toString( );
}
```

```java
private String readSign( )
// Read a + or - sign (if one is present) and return the read characters as a string.
{
    StringBuffer buffer = new StringBuffer(1);
    char possibleSign;

    possibleSign = peek( );
    if ((possibleSign == '-') || (possibleSign == '+'))
        buffer.append(readChar( ));

    return buffer.toString( );
}
```

```java
private String readSpaces( )
// Read a sequence of whitespace characters and return the sequence as a String.
{
    StringBuffer buffer = new StringBuffer( );

    while (Character.isWhitespace(peek( )))
        buffer.append(readChar( ));

    return buffer.toString( );
}
```

```java
public void skipLine( )
{
    while (!isEOLN( ))
        readChar( );
    if (peek( ) == '\r')
        readChar( );
    if (peek( ) == '\n')
        readChar( );
}
```

```java
public String stringInput( )
{
    StringBuffer buffer = new StringBuffer( );

    formatProblem = false;
    readSpaces( );
    while (!isEOF( ) && !Character.isWhitespace(peek( )))
        buffer.append(readChar( ));
    return buffer.toString( );
}


public String stringInputLine( )
{
    StringBuffer buffer = new StringBuffer( );

    while (!isEOLN( ) && !isEOF( ))
        buffer.append(readChar( ));
    skipLine( );
    return buffer.toString( );
}


public String stringQuery(String prompt)
{
    System.out.print(prompt);
    return stringInputLine( );
}



// DEMONSTRATION PROGRAM:
// To run the demonstration: java edu.colorado.io.EasyReader
public static void main(String[ ] args)
{
    EasyReader stdin = new EasyReader(System.in);

    double d = stdin.doubleQuery("Double: ");
    if (stdin.isFormatProblem( ))
        System.out.println("A format error resulted in " + d);
    else
        System.out.println(d + " is a fine double number.");

    int sum = 0;
    System.out.println("Type one int per line & press ctrl-z to end:");
    while (!stdin.isEOF( ))
        sum += stdin.intInputLine( );
    System.out.println("Total sum: " + sum);
}


} // END OF EasyReader CLASS
```

Class FormatWriter

❖ **public class FormatWriter from the package edu.colorado.io**
The `FormatWriter` class has a collection of static methods for writing formatted output to System.out.

Examples:
```
printNumber(12345.27, 8, 1); // Prints with 8 total spaces and 1 decimal digit.
printWhole(12345, 8);        // Prints with 3 leading spaces.
printLeft("Foo", 8);         // Prints left-justified (5 spaces on right).
printRight("Foo", 8);        // Prints right-justified (5 spaces on left).
```

Specification

♦ **printNumber**
```
public static void printNumber(double d, int minimumWidth, int fractionDigits)
```
Print a number to `System.out`, using a specified format.
Parameters:
d – the number to be printed
`minimumWidth` – the minimum number of characters in the entire output
`fractionDigits` – the number of digits to print on the right side of the decimal point
Precondition:
`fractionDigits` is not negative.
Postcondition:
The number d has been printed to `System.out`. This printed number is rounded to the specified number of digits on the right of the decimal. If `fractionDigits` is 0, then only the integer part of d is printed. If necessary, spaces appear at the front of the number to raise the total number of printed characters to the minimum. Additional formatting details are obtained from the current locale. For example, in the United States, a period is used for the decimal and commas are used to separate groups of integer digits.
Throws: `IllegalArgumentException`
Indicates that `fractionDigits` is negative.
Example:
```
printNumber(12345.27, 8, 1); // Prints 12,345.3 in the U.S.
```

♦ **printLeft—printRight**
```
public static void printLeft(Object output, int minimumWidth)
public static void printLeft(Object output, int minimumWidth)
```
Print an `Object` (such as a `String`) using a specified width and left or right justification.
Parameters:
output – the `Object` to be printed
`minimumWidth` – the minimum number of characters in the entire output
Postcondition:
The `Object` has been printed to `System.out`. If necessary, spaces appear at the end (for left justification) or front (for right justification) to raise the total number of printed characters to `minimumWidth`.

- **printWhole**

   ```
   public static void printWhole(long n, int minimumWidth)
   ```
   Print a whole number to System.out, using a specified format.

   Parameters:
   n – the number to be printed
   minimumWidth – the minimum number of characters in the entire output

   Postcondition:
   The number n has been printed to System.out. If necessary, spaces appear at the front of the number to raise the total number of printed characters to the minimum. Additional formatting details are obtained from the current locale. For example, in the United States, commas are used to separate groups of integer digits.

   Example:
   ```
   printWhole(12345, 8); // Prints   12,345 in the U.S. (with 2 spaces in front).
   ```

Implementation

```java
// File: FormatWriter.java from the package edu.colorado.io
// Complete documentation begins on page 729 or is available from the FormatWriter link in
//    http://www.cs.colorado.edu/~main/docs/

package edu.colorado.io;
import java.text.NumberFormat;

public class FormatWriter
{
    // Note: getNumberInstance( ) creates a NumberFormat object using local
    // information about the characters for a decimal point and separators.
    private static NumberFormat form = NumberFormat.getNumberInstance( );

    public static void printNumber(double d, int minimumWidth, int fractionDigits)
    {
        String output;
        int i;
        int length;

        // Set the number of digits to appear on the right of the decimal.
        if (fractionDigits < 0)
            throw new IllegalArgumentException("fractionDigits < 0:" + fractionDigits);
        form.setMinimumFractionDigits(fractionDigits);
        form.setMaximumFractionDigits(fractionDigits);

        // Round and format the number.
        output = form.format(d);
        length = output.length( );
        if (fractionDigits == 0 && length > 1 && output.charAt(length-2) == '.')
            output = "  " + output.substring(0,length-2);

        printRight(output, minimumWidth);
    }
```

```java
public static void printLeft(Object output, int minimumWidth)
{
   int i;
   String s = output.toString( );

   // Print any trailing spaces and the Object itself.
   System.out.print(s);
   for (i = s.length( ); i < minimumWidth; i++)
      System.out.print(' ');
}

public static void printRight(Object output, int minimumWidth)
{
   int i;
   String s = output.toString( );

   // Print any leading spaces and the Object itself.
   for (i = s.length( ); i < minimumWidth; i++)
      System.out.print(' ');
   System.out.print(s);
}

public static void printWhole(long n, int minimumWidth)
{
   String output;

   // Format the number.
   output = form.format(n);

   // Print any leading spaces and the number itself.
   printRight(output, minimumWidth);
}

// DEMONSTRATION PROGRAM:
// To run the demonstration: java edu.colorado.io.FormatWriter
public static void main(String[ ] args)
{
   System.out.print("Output of printNumber(12345.27, 8, 1) is: [");
   printNumber(12345.27, 8, 1);
   System.out.println(']');
   System.out.print("Output of printLeft(\"Foo\", 8) is:        [");
   printLeft("Foo", 8);
   System.out.println(']');
   System.out.print("Output of printRight(\"Foo\", 8) is:       [");
   printRight("Foo", 8);
   System.out.println(']');
   System.out.print("Output of printWhole(12345, 8) is:       [");
   printWhole(12345, 8);
   System.out.println(']');
}
} // END OF FormatWriter CLASS
```

Appendix C
Throwing and Catching Java Exceptions

An **exception** is a Java Object that is used to indicate abnormal conditions. When a method detects an abnormal condition, it can create an exception object, and pass this object upwards to the place where the method was activated—the whole process is called **throwing** an exception.

When an exception is thrown, the problem can sometimes be corrected—a technique called **catching the exception**. Other times, the problem is too serious to correct, and it will remain uncaught, eventually causing the Java runtime system to print an error message and halt the program.

How to Throw an Exception

Some Java statements automatically throw an exception when they are incorrectly used. For example, the evaluation of the expression (42/0) will throw an ArithmeticException because an integer division by zero is illegal. At other times, a method may detect a problem itself and throw an exception to indicate this problem. For example, Chapter 1 has a method with a specification that begins like this:

- **celsiusToFahrenheit**
    public static double celsiusToFahrenheit(double c)
    Convert a temperature from Celsius degrees to Fahrenheit degrees.
    Parameters:
        c – a temperature in Celsius degrees
    Precondition:
        c >= -273.16.

It is a programming error to call celsiusToFahrenheit with an argument that is below −273.16. In such a case, the celsiusToFahrenheit method will detect that the precondition has been violated and throw an IllegalArgumentException, with statements such as these:

```
if (c < -273.16)
    throw new IllegalArgumentException("Temperature too small.");
```

The general form for throwing an exception uses the keyword throw, following this pattern:

throw new _____ ("_____");

This is the type of the exception that we are throwing.

This is an error message that will be passed as part of the exception.

Figure C.1 shows a list of common exceptions that a programmer may use to indicate problems. In Java terminology, these are actually called Throwable objects, and the list also indicates a further classification for each kind of Throwable object. We'll look at the meaning of that further classification on page 734.

FIGURE C.1   Partial List of Java's `Throwable` Objects

Name of the Class	Typical Meaning	Examples or Discussion	Further Classification
`ClassCast Exception`	Attempting to use a reference as if it referred to an object of some class—but it doesn't.	Page 75	`Exception`
`CloneNotSupported Exception`	The `clone` method was activated in a class that forgot to implement Cloneable	Page 79	`Exception (not Runtime)`
`EmptyStack Exception*`	Tried to pop or peek from an empty `Stack`.	Page 281	`Runtime Exception`
`IllegalArgument Exception`	An argument to a method violates the precondition.	Page 8	`Runtime Exception`
`IllegalState Exception`	A method was activated when the object was in a state that violates the method's precondition.	Page 137	`Runtime Exception`

`IndexOutOfBounds Exception`	An array index was used beyond the array's capacity.	`int[ ] a;`
		`a = new int[40];`
		`a[42] = 0;`
			`Runtime Exception`

`IOException`	An input or output error.	Trying to read after the end of a file.	`Exception (not Runtime)`

`NegaviteArraySize Exception`	Allocating an array with a negative number of components.	`int[ ] a;`
		`int s = -1;`
		`a = new int[s];`
			`Runtime Exception`

`NoSuchElement Exception*`	Attempting to get another element out of an `Iterator` or other collection class when there are no more elements.	Page 269 or Page 327	`Runtime Exception`
`NullPointer Exception`	Attempting to access a method or instance variable of the null reference.	Page 51	`Runtime Exception`
`OutOfMemory Error`	The heap has no more memory.	Page 106	`Error`
`StackOverflow Error`	The execution stack has no more memory.	Page 381	`Error`
`UnsupportedOperation Exception`	A method of a class is not being provided by the class's programmer.	Page 268	`Runtime Exception`

*`EmptyStackException` and `NoSuchElementException` are part of `java.util`.
See http://www.cs.colorado.edu/~main/java.html for a listing of all Java `Throwable` objects.

The `RuntimeException` and `Error` Classes

Most of the exceptions listed in Figure C.1 have a "further classification" of `RuntimeException` or `Error`. These are two particular kinds of `Throwable` objects, with conventional meanings for programmers:

- `RuntimeException`: These tend to be exceptions that are caused by programming mistakes, such as the violation of a precondition.
- `Error`: These are problems with resources and the Java Virtual Machine. For example, running out of memory is a resource problem. Not having a needed class is an example of a problem with the Java Virtual Machine.

Catching an Exception

Sometimes an exception occurs, but the programmer has some way to handle the problem. In this situation, the programmer can use `try-catch` blocks of the following form:

```
try
{
    ‖  Statements that might cause an exception to be thrown.
}
catch ( Type of the possible exception  e)
{
        These are statements to handle the problem. Within these
        statements, the name e refers to the exception object. For example,
        e.toString( ) is a message that's attached to the exception.
}
```

In this example, the variable name e was used for the name of the exception, but you can choose whatever name you like. The "type of the possible exception" is one of the exception data types such as `CloneNotSupportedException`.

As a specific example, consider the following code that tries to fill an array with clones of a given object. However, if the object is not clonable, then the code fills the array with references to the actual object (rather than clones of the object):

```
// In this code, obj is a non-null reference to a Java Object and copies is an array of objects.
// The variable i is an int.
try
{
    for (i = 0; i < copies.length; i++)
        copies[i] = obj.clone( );
}
catch (CloneNotSupportedException e)
{   // Fill the array with references to the actual object instead of clones.
    for (i = 0; i < copies.length; i++)
        copies[i] = obj;
}
```

If a section of code has the possibility of throwing several different types of exceptions, then the try-block may be followed by several different `catch`-blocks. After the final catch-block, there can be one more block that starts with the keyword `finally`. The `finally`-block is executed at the end, whether or not the exception is caught. For example, the following format has two catch-blocks and a `finally`-block:

```
try
{
      ‖   Statements that might cause an exception to be thrown.
}
catch ( Type of the first possible exception   e1)
{
        These are statements to handle the problem. Within these
        statements, the name e1 refers to the exception object. For example,
        e1.toString( ) is a message that's attached to the exception.
}
catch ( Type of the second possible exception   e2)
{
        These are statements to handle the problem. Within these
        statements, the name e2 refers to the exception object.
}
finally
{
        These are statements that will always be executed after the above
        try- and catch-blocks. Note that this code is executed in all cases:
        when no exception occurs, when an exception is thrown and caught,
        or when an uncaught exception is thrown.
}
```

The throws Clause

Java has some exceptions that are neither a `RuntimeException` nor an `Error`. The examples in our list are `CloneNotSupportedException` and `IOException`, but there are several dozen more and programmers can even create new classes of exceptions. You must follow a special rule when you write a statement that might throw one of these exceptions:

> When a method includes a statement that might throw an exception that is neither `RuntimeException` nor an `Error`, then there are two possibilities: (1) Catch the exception, or (2) Include the name of the exception in a `throws` clause after the heading of the method.

The format of a `throws` clause is the keyword `throws` followed by the type of the possible exception. If there are several possible exceptions, then their types may be written separated by commas in a single `throws` clause. For example, the following `main` method has a `throws` clause indicating that it may throw a `CloneNotSupportedException` or an `IOException`:

```
public static main(String[ ] args)
throws CloneNotSupportedException, IOException
{
```

> These are statements that might throw an uncaught
> `CloneNotSupportedException` or an uncaught `IOException`.

```
}
```

Further Information

For a complete list of Java exceptions, follow the `Exceptions` link in the file
`http://www.cs.colorado.edu/~main/java.html`

Appendix D
Java's Vector and Hashtable Classes

The Java Class Libraries in Java Version 1.2 include many collection classes. This appendix summarizes two of those classes, the `Vector` and `Hashtable`. For complete documentation of the other JCL Collection Classes, please see the `Collections` link in
    `http://www.cs.colorado.edu/~main/java.html`

The java.util.Vector Class

A `Vector` is similar to an array of objects, except that when the specified capacity is exceeded, the `Vector` automatically grows by a specified increment amount. If the increment amount is zero, then the `Vector` size doubles whenever the capacity is exceeded. For efficiency, a programmer can also set an explicit capacity. In this case, the add operations will work efficiently (without allocating more memory) until the specified capacity is exceeded. The most important `Vector` methods are summarized here.

Constructor, `clone`, and `toString` Methods
`Vector( )`
    Create an empty `Vector` with an initial capacity of 10 and an increment amount of zero.
`Vector(int initialCapacity)`
    Create an empty `Vector` with the specified initial capacity and an increment amount of zero.
`Vector(int initialCapacity, int capacityIncrement)`
    Create an empty `Vector` with the specified initial capacity and specified increment amount.
`public Object clone( )`
    Returns a clone of this `Vector`. The elements within this `Vector` are not cloned.
`public String toString( )`
    Returns a printable `String` representation of this `Vector`.

Accessor Methods
`public int capacity( )`
    Returns the current capacity of this `Vector`. The add operations work efficiently (without allocating new memory) until this capacity is exceeded.
`public boolean contains(Object obj)`
    The `obj.equals` method is used to determine whether `obj` occurs anywhere in this `Vector`.
`public void copyInto(Object[ ] objArray)`
    All elements of this `Vector` are copied into the `objArray`.
`public Object elementAt(int index)`
    Returns a reference to the element at the given index of this `Vector`.
`public Object firstElement( )`
    Returns a reference to the first element of this `Vector` (at index [0]).

`public int indexOf(Object obj)`
> Searches for the first occurrence of `obj` in this `Vector`, using `obj.equals` to test for equality. Returns the index of this occurence (or −1 if `obj` does not occur).

`public int indexOf(Object obj, int index)`
> Searches for the first occurrence of `obj` in this `Vector`, at or after the given `index` and using `obj.equals` to test for equality. Returns the index of this occurence (or −1 if `obj` does not occur).

`public boolean isEmpty( )`
> Tests whether this `Vector` is empty.

`public Iterator iterator( )`
> This new method (added for Java 1.2) returns an `Iterator` for the elements of this `Vector`.

`public Object lastElement( )`
> Returns a reference to the final element of this `Vector` (at the highest index).

`public int lastIndexOf(Object obj)`
> Searches for the final occurrence of `obj` in this `Vector`, using `obj.equals` to test for equality. Returns the index of this occurence (or −1 if `obj` does not occur).

`public int lastIndexOf(Object obj, int index)`
> Searches for the last occurrence of `obj` in this `Vector`, at or before the given `index` and using `obj.equals` to test for equality. Returns the index of this occurence (or −1 if `obj` does not occur).

`public int size( )`
> Returns the number of elements currently in this `Vector`.

Modification Methods

`public void addElement(Object obj)`
> Adds the specified element to this `Vector` at the next available index.

`public void ensureCapacity(int minimumCapacity)`
> Resets the current capacity of this `Vector` to at least `minimumCapacity`. The add operations work efficiently (without allocating new memory) until this capacity is exceeded.

`public void insertElementAt(Object obj, int index)`
> Adds the specified element to this `Vector` at the given `index` (which may be no bigger than the current size). Other elements that were at or after this `index` have been shifted upward to make room for the new element.

`public void removeAllElements( )`
> Resets this `Vector` so that it is empty.

`public boolean removeElement(Object obj)`
> Removes the first occurence of the specified element from this `Vector`. The `obj.equals` method is used to find this occurrence, and the return value indicates whether or not such a value was found.

`public void removeElementAt(int index)`
> Removes the element of this `Vector` from the specified `index` (which must be less than the current size). Other elements that were after this `index` have been shifted downward one spot.

`public void setElementAt(Object obj, int index)`
> Changes an element of this `Vector` at the given index (which must be less than the current size). The new value for this element is `obj`, and the old value is no longer present at the `index`.

`public void setSize(int newSize)`
> Sets the size of this `Vector`. If the new size is greater than the current size, new null items are added to the end. If the new size is less than the current size, all components beyond the new size are removed.

`public void trimToSize( )`
> Set the current capacity of this `Vector` equal to the number of elements it contains.

The `java.util.Hashtable` Class

Java's `Hashtable` is an open-address hash table similar to the class in Section 11.2 of this book. It has a specified capacity and a maximum load factor. When the maximum load factor is exceeded, the `Hashtable` automatically grows and all entries are reentered into the larger table. The most important `Hashtable` methods are summarized here:

Constructor, `clone` and `toString` Methods

`Hashtable( )`
> Create an empty `Hashtable` with a default initial capacity and a maximum load factor of 0.75.

`Hashtable(int initialCapacity)`
> Create an empty `Hashtable` with a specified initial capacity and a maximum load factor of 0.75.

`Hashtable(int initialCapacity, float loadFactor)`
> Create an empty `Hashtable` with a default initial capacity and a specified maximum load factor.

`public Object clone( )`
> Returns a clone of this `Hashtable`. The elements within this `Hashtable` are not cloned.

`public String toString( )`
> Returns a printable `String` representation of this `Hashtable`.

Accessor methods:

`public boolean containsKey(Object key)`
> Determines whether key is the key of some object in this `Hashtable` (using `key.equals` to test for equality of a key).

```
public Object get(Object key)
```
Searches this `Hashtable` for an element that has the specified `key` (using `key.equals` to test for equality). If such an element is found, then the return value is a reference to that element; otherwise the return value is null.

```
public boolean isEmpty( )
```
Tests whether this `Hashtable` is empty.

```
public int size( )
```
Returns the number of key/element pairs currently in this `Hashtable`.

Modification Methods

```
public Object put(Object key, Object element)
```
Adds the specified `key/element` pair to this `Hashtable`. If there was already an element with the specified `key`, then the return value is a reference to that old element (which is no longer in the table); otherwise the return value is null.

```
public Object remove(Object key)
```
If the specified `key` appears in this `Hashtable`, then that key and its associated element are removed and the return value is a reference to the removed element; otherwise the return value is null.

Appendix E
A Class for Nodes in a Linked List

This appendix gives a class for nodes in a linked list, where each node contains data that is a Java `Object`. The class was originally developed in Chapter 4 using integer data; the modification to contain Java Object data was described in Chapter 5. The source code of this class is available at
    `http://www.cs.colorado.edu/~main/edu/colorado/nodes/Node.java`

Class Node

❖ **public class Node from the package edu.colorado.nodes**
> A `Node` provides a node for a linked list. Each node contains a piece of data (which is a reference to an object) and a link (which is a reference to the next node of the list). The reference stored in a node can be null. Lists can be of any length, limited only by the amount of free memory on the heap. But beyond `Integer.MAX_VALUE`, the answer from `listLength` is incorrect because of arithmetic overflow.

Specification

♦ **Constructor for the Node**
> `public Node(Object initialData, Node initialLink)`
> Initialize a node with a specified initial data and link to the next node. Note that the `initialLink` may be the null reference, which indicates that the new node has nothing after it.
> **Parameters:**
>> `initialData` – the initial data of this new node
>> `initialLink` – a reference to the node after this new node—this reference may be null to indicate that there is no node after this new node.
> **Postcondition:**
>> This new node contains the specified data and link to the next node.

♦ **addNodeAfter**
> `public void addNodeAfter(Object element)`
> Modification method to add a new node after this node.
> **Parameters:**
>> `element` – the data to be placed in the new node
> **Postcondition:**
>> A new node has been created and placed after this node. The data for the new node is `element`. Any other nodes that used to be after this node are now after the new node.
> **Throws:** `OutOfMemoryError`
>> Indicates that there is insufficient memory for a new `Node`.

♦ **getData**
> `public Object getData( )`
> Accessor method to get the data from this node.
> **Returns:**
>> the data from this node

- **getLink**

  `public Node getLink( )`

  Accessor method to get a reference to the next node after this node.

  Returns:
  a reference to the node after this node (or the null reference if there is nothing after this node)

- **listCopy**

  `public static Node listCopy(Node source)`

  Copy a list.

  Parameters:
  source – the head reference for a linked list that will be copied (which may be an empty list where source is null)

  Returns:
  The method has made a copy of the linked list starting at source. The return value is the head reference for the copy.

  Throws: `OutOfMemoryError`
  Indicates that there is insufficient memory for the new list.

- **listCopyWithTail**

  `public static Node[ ] listCopyWithTail(Node source)`

  Copy a list, returning both a head and tail reference for the copy.

  Parameters:
  source – the head reference for a linked list that will be copied (which may be an empty list where source is null)

  Returns:
  The method has made a copy of the linked list starting at source. The return value is an array where the [0] element is a head reference for the copy and the [1] element is a tail reference for the copy.

  Throws: `OutOfMemoryError`
  Indicates that there is insufficient memory for the new list.

- **listLength**

  `public static int listLength(Node head)`

  Compute the number of nodes in a linked list.

  Parameters:
  head – the head reference for a linked list (which may be an empty list with a null head)

  Returns:
  the number of nodes in the list with the given head

  Note:
  A wrong answer occurs for lists longer than `Int.MAX_VALUE`, because of arithmetic overflow.

◆ **listPart**

    `public static Node[ ] listPart(Node start, Node end)`

    Copy part of a list, providing a head and tail reference for the new copy.

    Parameters:

        `start` and `end` – references to two nodes of a linked list

    Precondition:

        `start` and `end` are non-null references to nodes on the same linked list, with the `start` node at or before the `end` node.

    Returns:

        The method has made a copy of part of a linked list, from the specified `start` node to the specified end node. The return value is an array where the `[0]` component is a head reference for the copy and the `[1]` component is a tail reference for the copy.

    Throws: `IllegalArgumentException`

    Indicates that `start` and end do not satisfy the precondition.

    Throws: `OutOfMemoryError`

    Indicates that there is insufficient memory for the new list.

◆ **listPosition**

    `public static Node listPosition(Node head, int position)`

    Find a node at a specified position in a linked list.

    Parameters:

        `head` – the head reference for a linked list (which may be an empty list with a null head)

        `position` – a node number

    Precondition:

        `position > 0`

    Returns:

        The return value is a reference to the node at the specified position in the list. (The head node is position 1, the next node is position 2, and so on.) If there is no such position (because the list is too short), then the null reference is returned.

    Throws: `IllegalArgumentException`

    Indicates that `position` is zero.

◆ **listSearch**

    `public static Node listSearch(Node head, Object target)`

    Search for a particular piece of data in a linked list.

    Parameters:

        `head` – the head reference for a linked list (which may be an empty list with a null head)

        `target` – a piece of data to search for

    Returns:

        The return value is a reference to the first node that contains the specified `target`. If the `target` is non-null, then the `target.equals` method is used to find such a node. The `target` may also be null, in which case the return value is a reference to the first node that contains a null reference for its data. If there is no node that contains the `target`, then the null reference is returned.

- **removeNodeAfter**
  ```
  public void removeNodeAfter( )
  ```
  Modification method to remove the new node after this node.

  Precondition:
    This node must not be the tail node of the list.

  Postcondition:
    The node after this node has been removed from the linked list. If there were further nodes after that one, they are still present on the list.

  Throws: `NullPointerException`
    Indicates that this was the tail node of the list, so there is nothing after it to remove.

- **setData**
  ```
  public void setData(Object newdata)
  ```
  Modification method to set the data in this node.

  Parameters:
    `newData` – the new data to place in this node

  Postcondition:
    The data of this node has been set to `newData`. This data is allowed to be null.

- **setLink**
  ```
  public void setLink(Node newLink)
  ```
  Modification method to set a reference to the next node after this node.

  Parameters:
    `newLink` – a reference to the node that should appear after this node in the linked list (or the null reference if there should be no node after this node)

  Postcondition:
    The link to the node after this node has been set to `newLink`. Any other node (that used to be in this link) is no longer connected to this node.

Implementation

```
// File: Node.java from the package edu.colorado.nodes
// Documentation is available from pages 741-744 or from the Node link in
//    http://www.cs.colorado.edu/~main/docs/

package edu.colorado.nodes;

public class Node
{
    // Invariant of the Node class:
    //   1. Each node has one reference to an Object, stored in the instance variable data.
    //   2. For the final node of a list, the link part is null. Otherwise, the link part is a
    //      reference to the next node of the list.
    private Object data;
    private Node link;
```

```java
public Node(int initialData, Node initialLink)
{
   data = initialData;
   link = initialLink;
}


public void addNodeAfter(Object element)
{
   link = new Node(element, link);
}


public Object getData( )
{
   return data;
}


public Node getLink( )
{
   return link;
}


public static Node listCopy(Node source)
{
   Node copyHead;
   Node copyTail;

   // Handle the speciai case of the empty list.
   if (source == null)
      return null;

   // Make the first node for the newly created list.
   copyHead = new Node(source.data, null);
   copyTail = copyHead;

   // Make the rest of the nodes for the newly created list.
   while (source.link != null)
   {
      source = source.link;
      copyTail.addNodeAfter(source.data);
      copyTail = copyTail.link;
   }

   // Return the head reference for the new list.
   return copyHead;
}
```

```java
public static Node[ ] listCopyWithTail(Node source)
{
   Node copyHead;
   Node copyTail;
   Node[ ] answer = new Node[2];

   // Handle the special case of the empty list.
   if (source == null)
      return answer; // The answer has two null references.

   // Make the first node for the newly created list.
   copyHead = new Node(source.data, null);
   copyTail = copyHead;

   // Make the rest of the nodes for the newly created list.
   while (source.link != null)
   {
      source = source.link;
      copyTail.addNodeAfter(source.data);
      copyTail = copyTail.link;
   }

   // Return the head and tail references.
   answer[0] = copyHead;
   answer[1] = copyTail;
   return answer;
}



public static int listLength(Node head)
{
   Node cursor;
   int answer;

   answer = 0;
   for (cursor = head; cursor != null; cursor = cursor.link)
      answer++;

   return answer;
}
```

```java
public static Node[ ] listPart(Node start, Node end)
{
   Node copyHead;
   Node copyTail;
   Node cursor;
   Node[ ] answer = new Node[2];

   // Check for illegal null at start or end.
   if (start == null)
      throw new IllegalArgumentException("start is null");
   if (end == null)
      throw new IllegalArgumentException("end is null");

   // Make the first node for the newly created list.
   copyHead = new Node(start.data, null);
   copyTail = copyHead;
   cursor = start;

   // Make the rest of the nodes for the newly created list.
   while (cursor != end)
   {
      cursor = start.link;
      if (cursor == null)
         throw new IllegalArgumentException
         ("end node was not found on the list");
      copyTail.addNodeAfter(cursor.data);
      copyTail = copyTail.link;
   }

   // Return the head and tail references.
   answer[0] = copyHead;
   answer[1] = copyTail;
   return answer;
}

public static Node listPosition(Node head, int position)
{
   Node cursor;
   int i;

   if (position == 0)
         throw new IllegalArgumentException("position is zero");

   cursor = head;
   for (i = 1; (i < position) && (cursor != null); i++)
      cursor = cursor.link;

   return cursor;
}
```

```java
public static Node listSearch(Node head, int target)
{
   Node cursor;

   if (target == null)
   {  // Search for a node in which the data is the null reference.
      for (cursor = head; cursor != null; cursor = cursor.link)
         if (cursor.data == null)
            return cursor;
   }
   else
   {  // Search for a node that contains the non-null target.
      for (cursor = head; cursor != null; cursor = cursor.link)
         if (target.equals(cursor.data))
            return cursor;
   }

   return null;
}

public void removeNodeAfter( )
{
   link = link.link;
}

public void setData(Object newData)
{
   data = newData;
}

public void setLink(Node newLink)
{
   link = newLink;
}

}  // END OF Node CLASS
```

Appendix F
A Class for a Bag of Objects

This appendix gives a class for nodes in a linked list, where each node contains data that is a Java `Object`. The class was originally developed in Chapter 4 using integer data; the modification to contain Java Object data was described in Chapter 5. The source code of this class is available at:

```
http://www.cs.colorado.edu/~main/edu/colorado/collections/LinkedBag.java
```

Class LinkedBag

❖ **public class LinkedBag from the package edu.colorado.collections**
  A `LinkedBag` is a collection of references to objects. The objects in the bag are allowed to be null.

  Limitations:
    (1) Beyond `Int.MAX_VALUE` elements, the methods `countOccurrences`, `size`, and `grab` are wrong.

    (2) Because of the slow linear algorithms of this class, large bags will have poor performance.

Specification

• **Constructor for the LinkedBag**
  `public LinkedBag( )`
  Initialize an empty bag.

  Postcondition:
    This bag is empty.

• **add**
  `public void add(Object element)`
  Put a reference to an object into this bag. The new element may be the null reference.

  Parameters:
    `element` – the element to be added to this bag

  Postcondition:
    A reference to the specified object has been added to this bag.

  Throws: `OutOfMemoryError`
    Indicates insufficient memory for a new node.

+ **addAll**
    ```
    public void addAll(LinkedBag addend)
    ```
    Add the contents of another bag to this bag.

    Parameters:
    addend – a bag whose contents will be added to this bag

    Precondition:
    The parameter, addend, is not null.

    Postcondition:
    The elements from addend have been added to this bag.

    Throws: NullPointerException
    Indicates that addend is null.

    Throws: OutOfMemoryError
    Indicates insufficient memory to increase the size of this bag.

+ **clone**
    ```
    public Object clone( )
    ```
    Generate a copy of this bag.

    Returns:
    The return value is a copy of this bag. Subsequent changes to the copy will not affect the original, nor vice versa. The return value must be type cast to a LinkedBag before it is used.

    Throws: OutOfMemoryError
    Indicates insufficient memory for creating the clone.

+ **countOccurrences**
    ```
    public int countOccurrences(Object target)
    ```
    Accessor method to count the number of occurrences of a particular element in this bag.

    Parameters:
    target – the reference to an Object to be counted

    Returns:
    The return value is the number of times that target occurs in this bag. If target is non-null, then the occurrences are found using the target.equals method.

+ **grab**
    ```
    public Object grab( )
    ```
    Accessor method to retrieve a random element from this bag.

    Precondition:
    This bag is not empty.

    Returns:
    a randomly selected element from this bag

    Throws: IllegalStateException
    Indicates that the bag is empty.

◆ **iterator**

```
public Lister iterator( )
```
Accessor method to generator and return a `Lister` that contains all the elements that are currently in this bag.

Returns:
a `Lister` containing the elements of this bag

Throws: `OutOfMemoryError`
Indicates insufficient memory for a new `Lister`.

Notes:
A `Lister` is a simple kind of `Iterator` implemented in `edu.colorado.nodes.Lister` (see Figure 5.3 on page 270). If changes are made to this bag before the `Lister` returns all of its elements, then the subsequent behavior of the `Lister` is unspecified.

◆ **remove**

```
public boolean remove(Object target)
```
Remove one copy of a specified element from this bag.

Parameters:
`target` – an element to remove from this bag

Postcondition:
If `target` was found in the bag, then one copy of `target` has been removed and the method returns `true`. Otherwise the bag remains unchanged and the method returns `false`. Note that if `target` is non-null, then `target.equals` is used to find `target` in the bag.

◆ **size**

```
public int size( )
```
Accessor method to determine the number of elements in this bag.

Returns:
the number of elements in this bag

◆ **union**

```
public static LinkedBag union(LinkedBag b1, LinkedBag b2)
```
Create a new bag that contains all the elements from two other bags.

Parameters:
b1 – the first of two bags
b2 – the second of two bags

Precondition:
Neither b1 nor b2 is null.

Returns:
a new bag that is the union of b1 and b2

Throws: `NullPointerException`
Indicates that one of the arguments is null.

Throws: `OutOfMemoryError`
Indicates insufficient memory for the new bag.

Implementation

```
// File: LinkedBag.java from the package edu.colorado.collections
// Complete documentation is on pages 749-751 or from the LinkedBag link in
//    http://www.cs.colorado.edu/~main/docs/

package edu.colorado.collections;

import edu.colorado.nodes.Node;
import edu.colorado.nodes.Lister;

public class LinkedBag implements Cloneable
{
    // Invariant of the LinkedBag class:
    //   1. The elements in the bag are stored on a linked list.
    //   2. The head reference of the list is in the instance variable head.
    //   3. The total number of elements in the list is in the instance variable manyNodes.
    private Node head;
    private int manyNodes;

    public Linkedbag( )
    {
        head = null;
        manyNodes = 0;
    }

    public void add(Object element)
    {
        head = new Node(element, head);
        manyNodes++;
    }

    public void addAll(LinkedBag addend)
    {
        Node[ ] copyInfo;

        // The precondition indicates that addend is not null. If it is null,
        // then a NullPointerException is thrown here.
        if (addend.manyNodes > 0)
        {
            copyInfo = Node.listCopyWithTail(addend.head);
            copyInfo[1].setLink(head);   // Link the tail of copy to my own head...
            head = copyInfo[0];          // and set my own head to the head of the copy.
            manyNodes += addend.manyNodes;
        }
    }
```

```java
public Object clone( )
{  // Clone a LinkedBag object.
   LinkedBag answer;

   try
   {
      answer = (LinkedBag) super.clone( );
   }
   catch (CloneNotSupportedException e)
   {  // This exception should not occur. But if it does, it would probably indicate a
      // programming error that made super.clone unavailable. The most common error
      // would be forgetting the "Implements Cloneable" clause at the start of this class.
      throw new RuntimeException
         ("This class does not implement Cloneable");
   }

   answer.head = Node.listCopy(head);
   return answer;
}


public int countOccurrences(Object target)
{
   int answer;
   Node cursor;

   // Implementation note: listSearch will use == when target is null.
   // listSearch will use target.equals(...) when target is not null.
   answer = 0;
   cursor = Node.listSearch(head, target);
   while (cursor != null)
   {  // Each time that cursor is not null, we have another occurrence of target, so we add one to
      // answer and then move cursor to the next occurrence of the target.
      answer++;
      cursor = cursor.getLink( );
      cursor = Node.listSearch(cursor, target);
   }
   return answer;
}


public Object grab( )
{
   int i;
   Node cursor;

   if (manyNodes == 0)
      throw new IllegalStateException("Bag size is zero");

   i = (int)(Math.random( ) * manyNodes) + 1;
   cursor = Node.listPosition(head, i);
   return cursor.getData( );
}
```

```java
public Lister iterator( )
{
    return new Lister(head);
}

public boolean remove(Object target)
{
    Node targetNode; // The node that contains the target

    // Implementation note: listSearch will use == when target is null.
    // listSearch will use target.equals(...) when target is not null.
    targetNode = Node.listSearch(head, target);
    if (targetNode == null)
        // The target was not found, so nothing is removed.
        return false;
    else
    { // The target was found at targetNode. So copy the head data to targetNode
      // and then remove the extra copy of the head data.
        targetNode.setData(head.getData( ));
        head = head.getLink( );
        manyNodes--;
        return true;
    }
}

public int size( )
{
    return manyNodes;
}

public static LinkedBag union(LinkedBag b1, LinkedBag b2)
{
    // The precondition requires that neither b1 nor b2 is null.
    // If one of them is null, then addAll will throw a NullPointerException.
    LinkedBag answer = new LinkedBag( );

    answer.addAll(b1);
    answer.addAll(b2);
    return answer;
}

} // END OF LinkedBag CLASS
```

Appendix G
Further Big-*O* Notation

Formal Definition of Big-*O*

Throughout the text, we analyze the running times of algorithms in terms of the size of an algorithm's input. For example, in Section 11.1 we developed a binary search algorithm to search an array of n elements, looking for a specified target. On page 535, we saw that the maximum number of operations for the binary search is given by the formula:

$$T(n) = \text{the maximum number of operations to search an } n\text{-element array}$$
$$= 18(\lfloor \log_2 n \rfloor + 1) + 2$$

Big-*O* notation is a way of analyzing a function such as $T(n)$. The analysis throws away some information about the function, but keeps other information that is most relevant to determining algorithm performance. In an informal way, you know enough to examine the function $T(n)$ for the binary search; you can "throw out the constants" and conclude that $T(n)$ is an $O(\log n)$ function.

In general, when we examine a function, such as $T(n)$, the big-*O* analysis results in some simpler expression, such as $\log n$. The simpler expression is also a function of n. If we call this $F(n)$, then a typical big-O analysis provides a result of the form "$T(n)$ is an $O(F(n))$ function." In mathematical terms, this kind of result has a precise definition, as follows:

Formal Definition of Big-*O*

When we say that "$T(n)$ is an $O(F(n))$ function," we mean that there is some fixed number that we call the *threshold*, and some constant multiplier that we call c, such that:

$$\text{Whenever } n \geq threshold, \text{ then } T(n) \leq cF(n).$$

For example, consider the function $T(n) = 3n^2 + 9n$. Some arithmetic shows that whenever $n \geq 5$, then $3n^2 + 9n \leq 4n^2$. Therefore, using a threshold of 5, and a constant multiplier of 4, we can see that

$$3n^2 + 9n \text{ is an } O(n^2) \text{ function.}$$

The graph at the top of the next page illustrates the meaning of a big-*O* expression. Notice that before the *threshold*, either of the two functions may be larger; anything can happen before this threshold value. But once n exceeds the threshold, the function $cF(n)$ is always greater than $T(n)$. Also notice that it is c multiplied by $F(n)$, and not simply $F(n)$, that we are comparing to $T(n)$.

So, the graph illustrates the fact that "$T(n)$ is an $O(F(n))$ function."

If not used with some care, big-*O* expressions can grossly misrepresent the true running time of an algorithm. For example, if an algorithm runs in $O(n)$ time, then we could also say that it runs in $O(n^2)$ time (since any function that is below a constant times *n* will also be below the same constant times n^2). But of course, it would be silly to say that an algorithm runs in $O(n^2)$ time, when we know that it runs in $O(n)$ time. When a programmer gives a big-*O* time, he or she usually means that it is a "good" big-*O* expression.

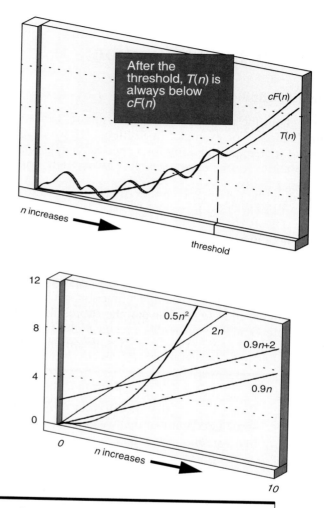

What Big-*O* Expressions Indicate

Big-*O* expressions are ad-mittedly crude, but they do contain some infor-mation. A big-*O* analysis will not distin-guish between a running time of $4n+3$ and a running time of $100n+50$, but it will let us distinguish between some running times and determine that some algorithms are faster than others. Look at the graphs of the four functions to the right. Notice that all three $O(n)$ functions eventually fall below the $O(n^2)$ func-tion. This leads us to the following important big-*O* principle:

Big-*O* Comparison of Algorithms

Suppose that two different algorithms perform the same task with different big-*O* times. With a sufficiently large input, the algorithm with the better big-*O* analysis will perform faster.

What exactly does it mean when we say "with a sufficiently large input"? Does this mean that an input size of *n*=100 will result in a faster time from the algorithm with the better big-*O*? Or does it require *n*=1000, or maybe even *n*=1,000,000? Unfortunately, a big-*O* analysis does not tell us *how big* the input needs to be in order for the better big-*O* time to result in a faster algorithm. All that's known is that larger and larger inputs will *eventually* result in a faster time for the algorithm with the better big-*O* time.

Appendix H
Javadoc

Throughout the book, we have used nicely formatted comments to provide the specifications for Java classes. For example, the following specification for `celciusToFahrenheit` appears just before its implementation in Figure 1.1 on page 10:

◆ **celsiusToFahrenheit**
   `public static double celsiusToFahrenheit(double c)`
   Convert a temperature from Celsius degrees to Fahrenheit degrees.
Parameters:
   c – a temperature in Celsius degrees
Precondition:
   `c >= -273.16.`
Returns:
   the temperature c converted to Fahrenheit degrees
Throws: `IllegalArgumentException`:
   Indicates that c is less than the smallest Celsius temperature (−273.16).

How are pretty comments such as this generated? The answer is a special documentation comment that appears in a `.java` file, such as this:

```
/**
* Convert a temperature from Celsius degrees to Fahrenheit.
* @param c
*    a temperature in Celsius degrees
* <dt><b>Precondition:</b><dd>
*    c >= -273.16.
* @return
*    the temperature c converted to Fahrenheit
* @exception IllegalArgumentException
*    Indicates that c is less than the smallest Celsius temperature (-273.16).
**/
```

This **documentation comment** is arranged to interact with a documentation tool called **javadoc**, which is freely distributed with Sun Microsystems' Java Development Kit. Javadoc reads the documentation comments from a `.java` file and produces a collection of documentation pages in a format called **html** (hyper-text markup language). As you may know, html pages are read and displayed by web browsers such as Netscape Navigator, Microsoft Internet Explorer, or Sun's Hot-Java Web Browser. For example, javadoc can be applied to the the `celsiusToFahrenheit` documentation comment shown above, and the resulting html page will contain the nicely formatted comment shown at the top of the page. The exact format may look different in your web browser, but the result will be roughly as shown. The html page created by Javadoc contains only documentation and no actual Java code. As you might guess, the motivation for this kind of documentation is *information hiding.* The documentation allows other programmers to use the items that you implement, without knowing how you implemented those items. Let's look at the precise steps that you carry out when you want to make your programming available to other programmers, but still retain information hiding.

How to Use Javadoc to Provide Your Work to Other Programmers

1. **Documentation comments appear in your .java files.** Write your .java files in the usual way, but include documentation comments such as the one shown earlier. We'll discuss the general format for these documentation comments in a moment.

2. **Other programmers need access to your .class files.** Compile each .java file in the usual way. Each .java file that you compile creates a corresponding .classes file. For example when you compile TemperatureConversion.java, you get TemperatureConversion.classes. You can move your .classes files to a location where other programmers can access them.

3. **Run the Javadoc tool on each of your .java files.** From the command line, Javadoc is executed by typing the command javadoc and the name of the .java file. In order to enable a special "author" option, you should also include the word -author after the javadoc command. For example, we can run javadoc on TemperatureConversion.java by typing the following on the command line:

   ```
   javadoc -author TemperatureConversion.java
   ```

   Javadoc creates an html file. In this example, you'll get one file called TemperatureConversion.html.

4. **Move all your Javadoc html files to a public place where a web browser can read them.** For example, I have moved all my Javadoc html files to the directory http://www.cs.colorado.edu/~main/docs/. If you point your web browser at this directory, you will see all of my public documentation. You may need to talk with your computer system administrator to find out how to create a public place for your own documentation to reside.

5. **Put the JDK graphics files in an images subdirectory.** Below your javadocs directory, you should create a subdirectory called images. The Java Development Kit provides a collection of graphics images and you can copy these to your own images subdirectory. Javadoc will use the graphics in the html pages that it creates. (The latest JDK release places these images in a subdirectory java\docs\api\images for Windows or java/docs/api/images for Unix.)

Now you need to know how to write those Javadoc documentation comments. (They're not as cryptic as they look.)

How to Write Javadoc Documentation Comments

We will put Javadoc comments in two places: before each class definition (such as public class TemperatureConversion), and before most public methods (such as public static void printNumber).

Documentation comments begin with /** (two stars rather than just one). A documentation comment ends with */, but for consistency you can use **/ instead. Many programmers place a single asterisk (*) at the start of each line in the comment. The single asterisk is not required, but it does make it easy to see the entire extent of the documentation comment (and Javadoc ignores the asterisks).

Javadoc Documentation for a Description of the Whole Class

The top of each documentation comment contains a description of the class or method. Javadoc uses the first sentence of the description as part of an index, so aim for a concise account of the most important behavior in the first sentence. If needed, subsequent sentences can provide details.

After the description, the rest of the documentation consists of a series of **Javadoc tags**. Each tag alerts the Javadoc tool about certain information. For example, one of my classes, called TemperatureConversion, has the Javadoc comment shown here, just before the class declaration:

```
/**
 * The TemperatureConversion Java application prints a table
 * converting Celsius to Fahrenheit degrees.
 * @author
 *   Michael Main (main@colorado.edu)
 **/
public class TemperatureConversion...
```

The Javadoc tag "@author" indicates that the name of the class's author will appear next (perhaps with extra information such as an e-mail address). In the html page produced by Javadoc, a large heading is provided for the whole class and each individual tag is made into a boldface heading, so within a web browser, the html page contains a section similar to this:

❖ **public class TemperatureConversion**
   The TemperatureConversion Java application prints a table converting Celsius to Fahrenheit degrees.
   Author:
   Michael Main (main@colorado.edu)

The documentation for a class will usually contain a description and an author tag.

Javadoc Documentation for Individual Public Methods

Each public method of a class may also have a Javadoc comment preceding its implementation. My documentation for a method generally includes these items:

1. **A Description of the Method.** For example, celsiusToFahrenheit has this description at the top of the documentation comment:

```
/**
 * Convert a temperature from Celsius degrees to Fahrenheit.
```

2. **Parameters.** Each parameter of the method is documented by using the tag @param, followed by the parameter name and a description of the parameter. For example, part of our first Javadoc comment is:

```
* @param c
*      a temperature in Celsius degrees
```

Warning: Some of the other tags shown below won't work unless you put at least one @param tag first. If there are no parameters, I suggest an @param tag that looks like this:

```
* @param - none
```

3. **Precondition.** The most recent Javadoc tool does not have a tag for preconditions. However, if you know a little bit about html pages, you can more or less create your own tags. For example, at the start of a precondition you can write this: `<dt><b>Precondition:</b><dd>`. The `<dt><b>` means that you are giving a boldface title, the `</b>` turns off the boldface, and the `<dd>` means that you are going to provide text to go under the title. So, our Javadoc comment lists the precondition as shown here:

```
* <dt><b>Precondition:</b><dd>
*    c >= -273.16.
```

4. **The Returns Condition or Postcondition.** You can list a return condition after the Javadoc tag @return. For example, we wrote:

```
* @return
*      the temperature c converted to Fahrenheit
```

A returns condition is appropriate when the method's behavior is entirely described by its return value. More complex methods need a complete postcondition instead of a returns condition. A complete postcondition describes other effects of the method, such as printing output. There is no Javadoc postcondition tag, but you can use this: `<dt><b>Postcondition:</b><dd>`. For example, suppose that our method converted the parameter c to Fahrenheit degrees and printed the result instead of returning the value. Then the documentation could look like this:

```
* <dt><b>Postcondition:</b><dd>
*    The Fahrenheit temperature equivalent to c has been
*    printed to System.out.
```

5. **Exceptions.** Each exception that a method can throw should be listed in the documentation comment. Start with the tag @exception, then write the name of the exception type (such as IllegalArgumentException) followed by a description of what the exception indicates. For example, our exception was documented like this:

```
* @exception IllegalArgumentException
*    Indicates that c is less than the smallest Celsius
*    temperature (-273.16).
```

6. **An Example.** For a complex method, you can include an example tag, like this:

```
* <dt><b>Example:</b><dd>
*    printNumber(12345,27, 8, 1); // Prints 12,345.3 in the U.S.
```

Controlling HTML Links and Fonts

The six Javadoc tags that have been described are sufficient to clearly document the code that you'll write throughout this text. There are two other features that you might want to add. Under the `@author` tag, you list your name and e-mail address. It would be nice if a reader could simply click on that address in a web browser to send e-mail to you. This is possible by using some simple `html` to revise the author section as shown in the shaded portion here:

```
/**
 * The <CODE>TemperatureConversion</CODE> Java application prints a table
 * converting Celsius to Fahrenheit degrees.
 * @author
 *   Michael Main
 *   <A HREF="mailto:main@colorado.edu"> (main@colorado.edu) </A>
 **/
```

The first part of the shaded line, `<A HREF="mailto:main@colorado.edu">`, is an `html` command that will put a **mailto link** on the documentation page. Within a web browser, the link appears as the text `(main@colorado.edu)`. To send e-mail to the address, a user clicks on the link. The characters `</A>` at the end of the line are an `html` command to indicate the end of the link. Within a browser, the new documenation appears like this:

❖ **public class TemperatureConversion**
> The `TemperatureConversion` Java application prints a table converting Celsius to Fahrenheit degrees.
> **Author:**
> Michael Main <u>(main@colorado.edu)</u>

The difference between this and the original version is that the link <u>(main@colorado.edu)</u> is underlined and probably in a bright color to indicate that it is a link.

You may have noticed a second difference: In this version, the name `TemperatureConversion` appears in a special "code" font that looks like code from a program. This font was controlled by putting the html tage `<CODE>` to turn on the special font, and the tag `</CODE>` to turn off the special font.

Running Javadoc

Once you have Javadoc comments in your code, you can run the Javadoc program to produce the html files. I usually run Javadoc from the command line, like this:

```
javadoc -author -public  Names of one or more .java files to process
```

The rest of this appendix lists the complete `TemperatureConversion` implementation, including all Javadoc comments that are printed in bold.

Java Application Program

```java
// File: TemperatureConversion.java
// A Java application to print a temperature conversion table.
// Additional Javadoc information is available in Figure 1.2 on page 14 or at
//    http://www.cs.colorado.edu/~main/docs/TemperatureConversion.html

import java.text.NumberFormat; // Used in the printNumber method.

/***********************************************************************************
 * The <CODE>TemperatureConversion</CODE> Java application prints a table
 * converting Celsius to Fahrenheit degrees.
 *
 * @author Michael Main
 *    <A HREF="mailto:main@colorado.edu"> (main@colorado.edu) </A>
 **********************************************************************************/
public class TemperatureConversion
{
    /**
     * The main method prints a Celsius to Fahrenheit conversion table.
     * The String arguments (args) are not used in this implementation.
     * The bounds of the table range from –50C to +50C in 10 degree increments.
     **/
    public static void main(String[ ] args)
    {
        // Declare values that control the table's bounds.
        final double TABLE_BEGIN = -50.0; // The table's first Celsius temperature
        final double TABLE_END   =  50.0; // The table's final Celsius temperature
        final double TABLE_STEP  =  10.0; // Increment between temperatures in table
        final int    WIDTH       =     6; // Number of characters in output numbers
        final int    ACCURACY    =     2; // Number of digits to right of decimal point

        double celsius;                   // A Celsius temperature
        double fahrenheit;                // The equivalent Fahrenheit temperature

        System.out.println("TEMPERATURE CONVERSION");
        System.out.println("----------------------");
        System.out.println("Celsius     Fahrenheit");
        for (celsius = TABLE_BEGIN; celsius <= TABLE_END; celsius += TABLE_STEP)
        {   // The for-loop has set celsius equal to the next Celsius temperature of the table.
            fahrenheit = celsiusToFahrenheit(celsius);
            printNumber(celsius, WIDTH, ACCURACY);
            System.out.print("C        ");
            printNumber(fahrenheit, WIDTH, ACCURACY);
            System.out.println("F");
        }
        System.out.println("----------------------");
    }
```

```
/**
 * Convert a temperature from Celsius degrees to Fahrenheit degrees.
 * @param c
 *   a temperature in Celsius degrees
 * <dt><b>Precondition:</b><dd>
 *   c >= -273.16.
 * @return
 *   the temperature c converted to Fahrenheit
 * @exception IllegalArgumentException
 *   Indicates that c is less than the smallest Celsius temperature (-273.16).
 **/
public static double celsiusToFahrenheit(double c)
{
   final double MINIMUM_CELSIUS = -273.16;
   if (c < MINIMUM_CELSIUS)
      throw new IllegalArgumentException("Argument " + c + " is too small.");
   return (9.0/5.0) * c + 32;
}


/**
 * Print a number to <CODE>System.out</CODE>, using a specified format.
 * @param d
 *   the number to be printed
 * @param minimumWidth
 *   the minimum number of characters in the entire output
 * @param fractionDigits
 *   the number of digits to print on the right side of the decimal point
 * <dt><b>Precondition:</b><dd>
 *   <CODE>fractionDigits</CODE> is not negative.
 * <dt><b>Postcondition:</b><dd>
 *   The number <CODE>d</CODE> has been printed to <CODE>System.out</CODE>.
 *   This printed number is rounded to the specified number of digits on the
 *   right of the decimal. If <CODE>fractionDigits</CODE> is 0,
 *   then only the integer part of <CODE>d</CODE> is printed.
 *   If necessary, spaces appear at the front of the number to raise
 *   the total number of printed characters to the minimum. Additional
 *   formatting details are obtained from the current locale. For example,
 *   in the United States, a period is used for the decimal and commas are
 *   used to separate groups of integer digits.
 * @exception IllegalArgumentException
 *   Indicates that <CODE>fractionDigits</CODE> is negative.
 * <dt><b>Example:</b><dd>
 *   <code>printNumber(12345.27, 8, 1); // Prints 12,345.3 in the U.S. </code>
 **/
public static void printNumber(double d, int minimumWidth, int fractionDigits)
{
   // Note: getNumberInstance( ) creates a NumberFormat object using local
   // information about the characters for a decimal point and separators.
   NumberFormat form = NumberFormat.getNumberInstance( );
   String output;
```

```
        int i;

        //  Set the number of digits to appear on the right of the decimal.
        if (fractionDigits < 0)
            throw new IllegalArgumentException("fractionDigits < 0:" + fractionDigits);
        form.setMinimumFractionDigits(fractionDigits);
        form.setMaximumFractionDigits(fractionDigits);

        //  Round and format the number.
        if (d >= 0)
            output = form.format(d + 0.5 * Math.pow(10, -fractionDigits));
        else
            output = form.format(d - 0.5 * Math.pow(10, -fractionDigits));

        //  Print any leading spaces and the number itself.
        for (i = output.length( ); i < minimumWidth; i++)
            System.out.print(' ');
        System.out.print(output);
    }

}
```

Index

Symbols

+= (add and assign) 43
⌊ ⌋ (floor function) 22, 535

A

abstract data type 36
access 47, 61
   package 61
   private 47, 61, 177
   protected 620
   public 47, 61, 177
accessor method 40, 72
action listener 153–160
activating a method 49
activation record 377
add method 152
adjacency matrix 672
ADT 36
   invariant of an ADT 114
algorithm 3
ancestor
   of a tree node 417
Animal class 633–636
animal guessing 435–443
Anthony, Piers 395
applet 146–164
   add method 152
   button 151
   drawing lines 153
   init method 152
   text area 152
   text button 151
appletviewer 164
argument 69
arithmetic expression
   evaluating with a stack 288–299,
      310–311
   precedence rules 315
arithmetic overflow 44, 711
array 96–101
   assignment 98
   circular 349
   clone 99

   length 97
   parameter 100
   partially filled 113
   return value of method 201
   two-dimensional 672
   versus linked list 234
Array Index Out Of Bounds
   Exception 97
assignment
   array 98
   reference variable 51
average-case time 27, 527
Averager class 334

B

backtracking 323, 397
Bag class
   array version 101–132
   grabbing random item 223
   linked list version 211–226
   of objects 247–262, 749–754
   summary of four versions 274
   tree version 463–475
   with iterator 272–273
balanced tree 483
base case
   of induction 406
   of recursion 374
bear game 398
best-case time 27, 528
big-*O* 23–27, 575, 755–756
binary search 528–536
binary search tree 460–475
   counting occurrences 466
   internal iterator 475
   removing a node 468
   union operation 472
binary tree 416–420
   complete 419, 421–423
   full 419
   node representation 424–425
   taxonomy 419
   See also tree.
black box testing 168
Blob 632
Boole, George 42
boolean 42
boolean values
   short-circuit evaluation 119
BooleanSource class 334
boundary values 28
breadth-first search 689–690, 693
BTNode class 426–435, 446–459

buffering 329
button 151
byte 711

C

car wash simulation 333–339
catching exceptions 734–735
chained hashing 555–557
   average search time 560
char 711, 712
child
   of a tree node 416
circular array 349
class 36–41
   calling a method 49
   collection 95
   instance variable 38
   invariant 114
   member 36, 38
   method 40
Class Cast Exception 75
Clock class 48, 618–619
clone 54, 76–80, 251, 267
   array 99
   class with linked list 218
Cloneable 78, 267
clustering 552
code reuse 4
coin game 665
collection class 95
   of objects 250
collision 539
complete binary tree 419
   array representation 421–423
constant time 131
constructor 38
   for extended class 633
   no-arguments 40
cursor
   traversing a linked list 193, 234
   two-way 234

D

Dahl, Roald 283
dateCheck 13
debugger 31
debugging 28–31
deep clone 251, 277
depth
   of a tree 419
   of a tree node 418
   of recursive calls 534